congratulations!

Thank you for purchasing a new copy of *Computer Science: A[...] textbook includes six months of prepaid access to the book's C[...] prepaid subscription provides you with full access to all student support a[...]s, including:

- Chapter-by-chapter activities that extend topics in the text and provide opportunities to explore related topics.
- Software simulators for the example machine used throughout Chapter 2.
- Laboratory manuals that teach the rudiments of either C++ or Java in a context compatible with the text.

To access the *Computer Science: An Overview* Companion Website for the first time:
You will need to register online using a computer with an Internet connection and a Web browser. The process takes just a couple of minutes and only needs to be completed once.

1. Go to **http://www.aw-bc.com/brookshear**.
2. Click **Student Resources**.
3. Click the **Register** button.
4. Use a coin to scratch off the gray coating below and reveal your student access code*. Do not use a knife or other sharp object, which can damage the code.

5. On the registration page, enter your student access code. Do not type the dashes. You can use lowercase or uppercase.
6. Follow the on-screen instructions. If you need help at any time during the online registration process, simply click the **Need Help?** icon.
7. Once your personal Login Name and Password are confirmed, you can begin using the *Computer Science: An Overview* Companion Website!

To log into this Web site after you've registered:
You only need to register for this Companion Website once. After that, you can access the site by going to http://www.aw-bc.com/brookshear, clicking "Student Resources," and providing your Login Name and Password when prompted.

*IMPORTANT: The Access Code on this page can only be used once to establish a subscription to the *Computer Science: An Overview*, Eighth Edition Companion Website. This subscription is valid for six months upon activation, and is not transferable. If this access code has already been scratched off, it may no longer be valid. If this is the case, you can purchase a subscription by going to http://www.aw-bc.com/brookshear and clicking "Student Resources."

Computer Science

an overview

EDITION 8

J. Glenn Brookshear

PEARSON

Addison
Wesley

Boston San Francisco New York
London Toronto Sydney Tokyo Singapore Madrid
Mexico City Munich Paris Cape Town Hong Kong Montreal

Senior Acquisitions Editor: Michael Hirsch
Project Editor: Katherine Harutunian
Senior Production Supervisor: Juliet Silveri
Project Management: Dartmouth Publishing, Inc.
Composition and Art: Dartmouth Publishing, Inc.
Text Design: Dartmouth Publishing, Inc.
Cover Design Supervisor: Joyce Cosentino Wells
Marketing Manager: Nathan Schultz
Marketing Coordinator: Lesly Hershman
Cover Designer: Night & Day Design
Copyeditor: Barbara Passero
Proofreaders: Mary Alice and Ben Richardson
Print Buyer: Caroline Fell
Cover Image © 2004 PhotoDisc/Steve Cole

If you purchased this book within the United States or Canada you should be aware that it has been wrongfully imported without the approval of the Publisher or the Author.

Access the latest information about Addison-Wesley titles from our World Wide Web site: http://www.aw-bc.com/computing

Many of the designations used by manufacturers and sellers to distinguish their products are claimed as trademarks. Where those designations appear in this book, and Addison-Wesley was aware of a trademark claim, the designations have been printed in initial caps or all caps.

The programs and applications presented in this book have been included for their instructional value. They have been tested with care, but are not guaranteed for any particular purpose. The publisher does not offer any warranties or representations, not does it accept any liabilities with respect to the programs or applications.

ISBN 0-321-26971-3

12345678910-DOC-060504

**To my parents
Garland and Reba Brookshear**

This book presents an introductory survey of computer science. It explores the breadth of the subject while including enough depth to convey an honest appreciation for the topics involved.

Audience

I wrote this text for both computer science majors and students from other disciplines. Most computer science majors begin their studies with the illusion that computer science is only programming and Web browsing, since that is essentially all they have seen. Yet computer science is much more. Beginning computer science students need exposure to the breadth of the subject in which they are planning to major. Providing this exposure is the purpose of this book. This text gives students an overview of computer science—a foundation from which they can appreciate the relevance and inter-relationships of future courses in the field.

This same background is what students from other disciplines need to relate to the technical society in which they live. A computer science course for nonmajors should provide a fundamental understanding of the entire field rather than merely an introduction to popular software packages and the Internet. This survey approach is the model used for introductory courses in the natural sciences, and it is the model I had in mind as I wrote this text. The result is that previous editions of this book have been used successfully in courses for students over a wide range of disciplines. This edition is designed to continue that tradition.

In short, this text is ideal for an introductory computer science survey course of the type commonly referred to as CS0. Moreover, it should be of interest to anyone considering a breadth-first curriculum as discussed in such reports as "Computing Curricula 2001" and "Computing Curricula 2003: Guidelines for Associate-Degree Curricula in Computer Science," both produced by joint IEEE/ACM task forces. Indeed, since its first edition, this text has been an unofficial standard bearer of the breadth-first curriculum movement.

Organization

This text follows a bottom-up approach that progresses from the concrete to the abstract—an arrangement that results in a sound pedagogical presentation in which each topic leads to the next. It begins with the fundamentals of computer architecture (Chapters 1 and 2); progresses to software and the software development process

(Chapters 3 through 7); explores issues of data organization and data storage (Chapters 8 and 9); and closes by considering current and future applications of computer technology (Chapters 10 and 11).

While writing the text, I thought in terms of developing a plot. Consequently, I am not surprised that many students have reported reading the text in much the same way that they normally read novels. On the other hand, the text is divided into largely independent chapters and sections that can be read as isolated units or rearranged to form alternative sequences of study. Indeed, this book is often used as a text for courses that cover the material in a variety of orders. One of these alternatives begins with material from Chapters 5 and 6 (Algorithms and Programming Languages) and returns to the earlier chapters as desired. In contrast, I know of one course that starts with the material on computability from Chapter 11. In still other instances, the text has been used in "senior capstone" courses where it serves as a backbone from which students branch into projects in different areas.

For those who simply want a condensed version, I suggest the following sequence:

Section	Topic
1.1–1.4	Basics of data encoding and storage
2.1–2.3	Machine architecture and machine language
3.1–3.3	Operating systems
4.1–4.3	Networking and the Internet
5.1–5.4	Algorithms and algorithm design
6.1–6.4	Programming languages
7.1–7.2	Software engineering
8.1–8.2	Data abstractions
9.1–9.2	Database systems
10.1–10.3	Artificial intelligence
11.1–11.2	Theory of computation

In addition to the overall plot, several themes are woven throughout the text. One is that computer science is dynamic. The text repeatedly presents topics in a historical perspective, discusses the state of the art, and indicates directions of current research. Another theme is the role of abstraction and the way in which abstract tools are used to control complexity. This theme is introduced in Chapter 0 and then echoed in the context of operating system architecture, algorithm development, programming language design, software engineering, data representation, and database systems.

To Students

I was introduced to the field of computing during my tour in the U.S. Navy back in the late 1960s and early 1970s. (Yes, that makes me old—but being old is supposed to make me wise, so there's a chance this could be a good book.) I spent most of my Navy days maintaining the system software at the Navy's computer installation in London, England. After my tour was completed, I returned to school and finished my

Ph.D. (in mathematics) in 1975. I've been teaching computer science and mathematics ever since.

A lot has changed in computer science over this time, but a lot has remained the same. In particular, computer science was, and still is, fascinating. There are a lot of awesome things going on out there. The development of the Internet, progress in artificial intelligence, and the ability to collect and disseminate information in unheard-of proportions are only some of the things that will affect your life. You live in an exciting, changing world, and you have the opportunity to be a part of the action. Take it!

I'm a bit of a nonconformist (some of my friends would say more than a bit) so when I set out to write this text I didn't always follow the advice I received. In particular, many argued that certain material was too advanced for beginning students. But, I believe that if a topic is relevant, then it is relevant even if the academic community considers it to be an "advanced topic." You deserve a text that presents a complete picture of computer science—not a watered-down version containing artificially simplified presentations of only those topics that have been deemed acceptable for introductory students. Thus, I have not avoided topics. Instead I've sought better explanations. I've tried to provide enough depth to give you an honest picture of what computer science is all about. As in the case of adding spices to a recipe, you may choose to skip some of the topics in the following pages, but they are there for you to taste if you wish—and I encourage you to do so.

Finally, I should point out that in any course dealing with technology, the details you learn today may not be the details you will need to know tomorrow. The field is dynamic—that's part of the excitement. This book will give you a current picture of the subject as well as a historical perspective. With this background, you will be prepared to grow along with technology. I encourage you to start the growing process now by exploring beyond this text. Learn to learn.

Thank you for the trust you have placed in me by choosing to read my book. As an author, I have an obligation to produce a manuscript that is worth your time. I hope you find that I have lived up to this obligation.

To Instructors

There is more material in this text than can be covered normally in a single semester, so do not hesitate to skip topics that do not fit your course objectives or to rearrange the order in which you cover the chapters as you see fit. I wrote this book to be used as a course resource—not as a course definition. You will find that, although the text follows a plot, the topics are covered in an independent manner that allows you to pick and choose as you desire.

On the opening page of each chapter I have used asterisks to indicate those sections that I suggest as optional. These are sections that (in my opinion) delve more deeply into material or branch in directions you may not wish to pursue. BUT THESE ARE MERELY SUGGESTIONS. There are many alternatives. In particular, the condensed version of the text outlined earlier in this preface omits more than the sections that are marked as "optional." So, please don't get upset with me if I marked your favorite topic as optional. Just consider it a mistake on my part and cover the topics you want.

I also suggest that you consider covering some topics as reading assignments or encourage students to read the material not included in your course. I think we underrate students if we assume that we have to explain everything in class. We should be helping them learn to learn on their own.

I have already explained that the text follows a bottom-up, concrete-to-abstract organization, but I want to expand on this a bit. As academics, we too often assume that students will appreciate our perspective of a subject—often one that we have developed over many years of working in a particular field. As teachers, I think we do better by presenting material from the student's perspective. This is why the text starts with data representation/storage, machine architecture, and machine language. These are topics to which students readily relate—they can see the computer's components, they can hold them, and most students will have bought and used them. By starting the course with these topics, I see the students discovering answers to many of the "why" questions they have been carrying for years and also learning to view the course as practical rather than theoretical. From this beginning, it is natural to move on to the more abstract issues of algorithm discovery, design, representation, and complexity that those of us in the field see as the main topics in the course.

I think students learn a lot more implicitly than we teach them explicitly, and the lessons they learn implicitly are often better absorbed. This is significant when it comes to "teaching" problem solving. I think students learn to solve problems by solving problems—not by studying problem-solving. So I have included numerous problems throughout the text. I encourage you to use them and to expand on them.

Other topics that I place in this category are professionalism, ethics, and social responsibility. I do not believe that this material should be presented as an isolated subject. Instead, it should surface when it is relevant, which is the approach I have taken in this text. You will find that Sections 0.6, 3.5, 4.5, 7.1, 7.8, 9.7, and 10.7 present such topics as security, privacy, liability, and social awareness in the context of operating systems, networking, database systems, software engineering, and artificial intelligence. You will also find that each chapter includes a collection of questions called Social Issues that challenge students to think about the relationship between the material in the text and the society in which they live.

Thank you for considering my text for your course. Whether you do or do not decide that it is right for your situation, I hope that you find it to be a contribution to the computer science education literature.

Pedagogical Features

This text is the product of many years of teaching. As a result, it is rich in pedagogical aids. Paramount is the abundance of problems to enhance the student's participation—over 1,000 in this eighth edition (1,007 to be precise). These are classified as Questions/Exercises, Chapter Review Problems, and Social Issues. The Questions/Exercises appear at the end of each section. They review the material just discussed, extend the previous discussion, or hint at related topics to be covered later. The answers to these questions are in Appendix F.

The Chapter Review Problems appear at the end of each chapter (except for the introductory chapter). They are designed to serve as "homework" problems since they cover the material from the entire chapter and are not answered in the text.

Also at the end of each chapter are the questions in the Social Issues category. They are designed for thought and discussion. Many of them can be used to launch research assignments culminating in short written or oral reports.

Each chapter also ends with a list called Additional Reading that contains references to other materials relating to the subject of the chapter.

New to the Eighth Edition

This eighth edition reflects some significant alterations from previous editions. The chapter that covered both operating systems and networking in previous editions has become two chapters—Operating Systems (Chapter 3) and Networks and the Internet (Chapter 4), which gives the expanding field of networking its proper status. The chapter on file structures has been removed, and its material has been dispersed among the other chapters where it is relevant. (If you're looking for the material covering the fundamentals of sequential, indexed, and hash files, it has been condensed and is now contained in an optional section in the chapter on database systems.)

Another substantial enhancement to the eighth edition is the expansion of the book's companion web site (www.aw-bc.com/brookshear). This web site is further discussed below under the heading "Supplements."

Less significant changes in the eighth edition include the following: Much of Chapter 0 has been rewritten. Some of the material in Chapter 1 has been rearranged to consolidate the coverage of binary notation. The chapter on programming languages (now Chapter 6) has been streamlined. The subsection on design patterns in Chapter 7 (Software Engineering) has been rewritten to include component architecture. The emphasis (as well as the title) of the chapter on data structures has been changed to data abstractions (now Chapter 8). A section on data mining has been added to Chapter 9 (Database Systems). The beginning of Chapter 10 (Artificial Intelligence) has been rewritten from the perspective of agents, and the subsection on robotics has been updated. The last section in Chapter 11 (Theory of Computation) now discusses public key encryption in terms of the RSA algorithm rather than the knapsack problem. And, of course, numerous small changes have been made throughout the text to provide clear, up-to-date, and relevant coverage of topics.

I have enjoyed working on this eighth edition. I hope you like it.

Supplements

A variety of supplemental materials for this text are available at the book's companion web site: www.aw-bc.com/brookshear. The following are accessible to all readers:

- Chapter-by-chapter activities that extend topics in the text and provide opportunities to explore related topics;
- Software simulators for the example machine used throughout Chapter 2; and

- Laboratory manuals that teach the rudiments of either C++ or Java in a context compatible with the text.

In addition, the following supplements are available to qualified instructors. Please contact your Addison-Wesley sales representative, or send email to aw.cse@aw.com, for information on how to access them:

- An Instructor's Guide with answers to the Chapter Review Problems;
- PowerPoint Lecture Notes; and
- A Test Bank

You may also want to check out my personal web site at http://mscs.mu.edu/~glennb. It is not very formal (and it is subject to my whims and sense of humor), but I tend to keep some information there that you may find helpful.

Acknowledgments

First, I thank those of you who have supported this book by reading it and using it in previous editions. I am honored.

With each new edition, the list of those who have contributed to the book as reviewers and consultants grows. Today this list includes J. M. Adams, C. M. Allen, D. C. S. Allison, B. Auernheimer, P. Bankston, M. Barnard, P. Bender, K. Bowyer, P. W. Brashear, C. M. Brown, B. Calloni, M. Clancy, R. T. Close, C. L. Cocking, D. H. Cooley, L. D. Cornell, M. J. Crowley, F. Deek, M. Dickerson, M. J. Duncan, R. Eastman, S. Fox, N. E. Gibbs, D. E. Hamilton, J. D. Harris, D. Hascom, L. Heath, P. B. Henderson, L. Hunt, M. Hutchenreuther, L. A. Jehn, E. L. Kisling, K. Korb, G. Krenz, J. Liu, T. J. Long, C. May, W. McCown, S. J. Merrill, K. Messersmith, J. C. Moyer, M. Murphy, J. P. Myers, Jr., D. S. Noonan, S. Olariu, G. Rice, N. Rickert, C. Riedesel, J. B. Rogers, G. Saito, W. Savitch, R. Schlafly, J. C. Schlimmer, D. R. Scott, S. Sells, G. Sheppard, Z. Shen, J. C. Simms, M. C. Slattery, J. Slimick, J. A. Slomka, D. Smith, J. Solderitsch, R. Steigerwald, L. Steinberg, C. A. Struble, W. J. Taffe, J. Talburt, P. Tonellato, P. Tromovitch, E. D. Winter, E. Wright, M. Ziegler, and one anonymous contributor. To these individuals I give my sincere thanks.

A special thank you goes to Roger Eastman, who is responsible for the student activities/projects you will find at the book's companion web site. Roger has demonstrated a lot of creativity in developing these materials. I think you will like the results.

I also thank the people at Addison-Wesley who have contributed to this project. They have done a great job. They have pushed me when I needed pushing, criticized me when I needed criticizing, and praised me on those rare occasions when I was right, and they felt it was safe to tell me. They are a great bunch to work with—and good friends as well.

I am also grateful to my wife Earlene and daughter Cheryl who have been tremendous sources of encouragement over the years. Cheryl, of course, grew up and left home several years ago. But Earlene is still stuck with me and says she plans to stick it out—even if I continue to go through these crazy periods when I write books. I'm thankful that she looks out for me. On the morning of December 11, 1998, I survived a heart attack because she got me to the hospital in time. (For those of you in the

younger generation I should explain that surviving a heart attack is sort of like getting an extension on a homework assignment.)

Finally, I thank my parents, to whom this book is dedicated. I close with the following endorsement whose source shall remain anonymous: "Our son's book is really
good. Everyone should read it."

J. G. B.

CONTENTS

INTRODUCTION

Computer science is the discipline that seeks to build a scientific foundation for such topics as computer design, computer programming, information processing, algorithmic solutions of problems, and the algorithmic process itself. It provides the underpinnings for today's computer applications as well as the foundations for tomorrow's applications. This breadth means that we cannot become knowledgeable in computer science by studying only a few topics as isolated subjects or by merely learning how to use the computing tools of today. Rather, to understand the science of computing, we must grasp the scope and dynamics of a wide range of topics.

This book is designed to provide such a background. It presents a comprehensive introduction to the subjects that constitute a typical university computer science curriculum. The book can therefore serve as a foundation for beginning computer science students or as a source for other students seeking an introduction to the science behind today's computer-oriented society.

0.1 The Role of Algorithms

We begin with the most fundamental concept of computer science—that of an algorithm. Informally, an **algorithm** is a set of steps that defines how a task is performed. (We will be more precise later in Chapter 5.) For example, there are algorithms for cooking (called recipes), for finding your way through a strange city (more commonly called directions), for operating washing machines (usually displayed on the inside of the washer's lid or perhaps on the wall of a laundromat), for playing music (expressed in the form of sheet music), and for performing magic tricks (Figure 0.1).

Before a machine such as a computer can perform a task, an algorithm for performing that task must be discovered and represented in a form that is compatible with the machine. A representation of an algorithm is called a **program.** For the convenience of humans, computer programs are usually printed on paper or displayed on computer screens. For the convenience of machines, programs are encoded in a manner compatible with the technology of the machine. The process of developing a program, encoding it in machine compatible form, and inserting it into a machine is called **programming.** Programs, and the algorithms they represent, are collectively referred to as **software,** in contrast to the machinery itself, which is known as **hardware.**

The study of algorithms began as a subject in mathematics. Indeed, the search for algorithms was a significant activity of mathematicians long before the development of today's computers. The goal was to find a single set of directions that described how all problems of a particular type could be solved. One of the best known examples of this early research is the long division algorithm for finding the quotient of two multiple-digit numbers. Another example is the Euclidean algorithm, discovered by the ancient Greek mathematician Euclid, for finding the greatest common divisor of two positive integers (Figure 0.2).

Once an algorithm for performing a task has been found, the performance of that task no longer requires an understanding of the principles on which the algorithm is based. Instead, the performance of the task is reduced to the process of merely following directions. (We can follow the long division algorithm to find a quotient or the Euclidean algorithm to find a greatest common divisor without understanding why the algorithm works.) In a sense, the intelligence required to solve the problem at hand is encoded in the algorithm.

It is through this ability to capture and convey intelligence (or at least intelligent behavior) by means of algorithms that we are able to build machines that perform useful tasks. Consequently, the level of intelligence displayed by machines is limited by the intelligence that can be conveyed through algorithms. Only if we find an algorithm that directs the performance of a task can we construct a machine to perform that task. In turn, if no algorithm exists for solving a problem, then the solution of that problem lies beyond the capabilities of machines.

Identifying the limitations of algorithmic capabilities solidified as a subject in mathematics in the 1930s with the publication of Kurt Gödel's incompleteness theorem. This theorem essentially states that in any mathematical theory encompassing our traditional arithmetic system, there are statements that can be neither proved nor disproved. In short, any complete study of our arithmetic system lies beyond the capabilities of algorithmic activities.

Figure 0.1

An algorithm for a magic trick

Effect: The performer places some cards from a normal deck of playing cards face down on a table and mixes them thoroughly while spreading them out on the table. Then, as the audience requests either red or black cards, the performer turns over cards of the requested color.

Secret and Patter:

Step 1. From a normal deck of cards, select ten red cards and ten black cards. Deal these cards face up in two piles on the table according to color.

Step 2. Announce that you have selected some red cards and some black cards.

Step 3. Pick up the red cards. Under the pretense of aligning them into a small deck, hold them face down in your left hand and, with the thumb and first finger of your right hand, pull back on each end of the deck so that each card is given a slightly *backward* curve. Then place the deck of red cards face down on the table as you say, "Here are the red cards in this stack."

Step 4. Pick up the black cards. In a manner similar to that in step 3, give these cards a slight *forward* curve. Then return these cards to the table in a face-down deck as you say, "And here are the black cards in this stack."

Step 5. Immediately after returning the black cards to the table, use both hands to mix the red and black cards (still face down) as you spread them out on the tabletop. Explain that you are thoroughly mixing the cards.

Step 6. As long as there are face-down cards on the table, repeatedly execute the following steps:

  6.1. Ask the audience to request either a red or a black card.

  6.2. If the color requested is red and there is a face-down card with a concave appearance, turn over such a card while saying, "Here is a red card."

  6.3. If the color requested is black and there is a face-down card with a convex appearance, turn over such a card while saying, "Here is a black card."

  6.4. Otherwise, state that there are no more cards of the requested color and turn over the remaining cards to prove your claim.

Figure 0.2

The Euclidean algorithm for finding the greatest common divisor of two positive integers

Description: This algorithm assumes that its input consists of two positive integers and procedes to compute the greatest common divisor of these two values.

Procedure:

Step 1. Assign M and N the value of the larger and smaller of the two input values, respectively.

Step 2. Divide M by N, and call the remainder R.

Step 3. If R is not 0, then assign M the value of N, assign N the value of R, and return to step 2; otherwise, the greatest common divisor is the value currently assigned to N.

This realization shook the foundations of mathematics, and the study of algorithmic capabilities that ensued was the beginning of the field known today as computer science. Indeed, it is the study of algorithms that forms the core of computer science.

0.2 The Origins of Computing Machines

Today's computers have an extensive genealogy. One of the earlier computing devices was the abacus. Its history has been traced as far back as the ancient Greek and Roman civilizations. The machine is quite simple, consisting of beads strung on rods that are in turn mounted in a rectangular frame (Figure 0.3). As the beads are moved back and forth on the rods, their positions represent stored values. It is in the positions of the beads that this "computer" represents and stores data. For control of an algorithm's execution, the machine relies on the human operator. Thus the abacus alone is merely a data storage system; it must be combined with a human to create a complete computational machine.

In more recent years, the design of computing machines was based on the technology of gears. Among the inventors were Blaise Pascal (1623–1662) of France, Gottfried Wilhelm Leibniz (1646–1716) of Germany, and Charles Babbage (1792–1871) of England. These machines represented data through gear positioning, with data being input mechanically by establishing initial gear positions. Output from Pascal's and Leibniz's machines was achieved by observing the final gear positions in much the same way that we read the numbers on a car's odometer. Babbage, on the other hand, envisioned machines that would print results of computations on paper so that the possibility of transcription errors would be eliminated.

Figure 0.3

An abacus

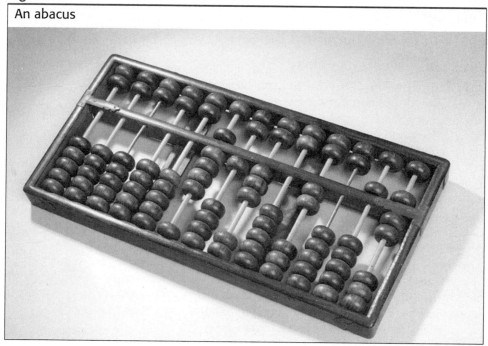

As for the ability to follow an algorithm, we can see a progression of flexibility in these machines. Pascal's machine was built to follow only the addition algorithm. Consequently, the appropriate sequence of steps was embedded into the structure of the machine itself. In a similar manner, Leibniz's machine had its algorithms firmly embedded in its architecture, although it offered a variety of arithmetic operations from which the operator could select. Babbage's Difference Engine (of which only a demonstration model was constructed) could be modified to perform a variety of calculations, but his Analytical Engine (the construction for which he never received funding) was designed to read instructions in the form of holes in paper cards. Thus Babbage's Analytical Engine was programmable. In fact, Augusta Ada Byron, who published a paper in which she demonstrated how Babbage's Analytical Engine could be programmed to perform various computations, is often identified today as the world's first programmer.

The idea of communicating an algorithm via holes in paper was not originated by Babbage. He got the idea from Joseph Jacquard (1752–1834), who, in 1801, had developed a weaving loom in which the steps to be performed during the weaving process were determined by patterns of holes in paper cards. In this manner, the algorithm followed by the loom could be changed easily to produce different woven designs. Another beneficiary of Jacquard's idea was Herman Hollerith (1860–1929), who applied the concept of representing information as holes in paper cards to speed up the tabulation process in the 1890 U.S. census. (It was this work by Hollerith that led to the creation of IBM.) Such cards ultimately came to be known as punched cards and survived as a popular means of communicating with computers well into the 1970s.

Augusta Ada Byron

Ever since the U.S. Department of Defense named a programming language in her honor, Augusta Ada Byron, Countess of Lovelace, has been the subject of much commentary in the computing community. Ada Byron lived a somewhat tragic life of less than 37 years (1815–1852) that was complicated by poor health and the fact that she was a nonconformist in a society that limited the professional role of women. She became fascinated by the machines of Charles Babbage when she witnessed a demonstration of a prototype of his Difference Engine in 1833. Her contribution to computer science involved her translation from French into English of a paper discussing Babbage's designs for the Analytical Engine. To this translation, Babbage encouraged her to attach an addendum describing applications of the engine and containing examples of how the engine could be programmed to perform various tasks. Babbage's enthusiasm for Ada Byron's work (he made numerous suggestions and apparently contributed some of the examples) was motivated by his hope that its publication would lead to financial backing for the construction of his Analytical Engine. (The daughter of Lord Byron, Ada Byron held celebrity status with potentially significant financial connections.) This backing never materialized, but Ada Byron's addendum has survived and is considered to contain the first examples of computer programs. Thus, Augusta Ada Byron is recognized today as the world's first programmer.

Indeed, the technique lives on today as witnessed by the voting issues raised in the 2000 U.S. presidential election.

The technology of the time was unable to produce the complex gear-driven machines of Pascal, Leibniz, and Babbage in a financially feasible manner. But with the advances in electronics in the early 1900s, this barrier was overcome. Examples of this progress include the electromechanical machine of George Stibitz, completed in 1940 at Bell Laboratories, and the Mark I, completed in 1944 at Harvard University by Howard Aiken and a group of IBM engineers (Figure 0.4). These machines made heavy use of electronically controlled mechanical relays. In this sense they were obsolete almost as soon as they were built, because other researchers were applying the technology of vacuum tubes to construct totally electronic computers. The first of these machines was apparently the Atanasoff–Berry machine, constructed during the period from 1937 to 1941 at Iowa State College (now Iowa State University) by John Atanasoff and his assistant, Clifford Berry. Another was a machine called Colossus, built under the direction of Tommy Flowers in England to decode German messages during the latter part of World War II. (Actually, as many as ten of these machines were apparently built, but military secrecy and issues of national security kept their existence from becoming part of the "computer family tree.") Other, more flexible machines, such as the ENIAC (electronic numerical integrator and calculator) developed by John Mauchly and J. Presper Eckert at the Moore School of Electrical Engineering, University of Pennsylvania, soon followed.

Figure 0.4

The Mark I computer

From that point on, the history of computing machines is largely that of advancing technology, including the invention of transistors and the subsequent development of integrated circuits, the establishment of communication satellites, and advances in optic technology. Today, desktop-size machines (as well as their smaller, portable cousins known as laptops) have more computing power than the room-size machines of the 1940s and can exchange information quickly via global communication systems.

The origins of these small machines can be traced to the computer hobbyists who began to experiment with homemade computers shortly after the development of the large research machines of the 1940s. It was within this "underground" of hobby activity that Steve Jobs and Stephen Wozniak built a commercially viable home computer and, in 1976, established Apple Computer, Inc., to manufacture and market their products. Other companies that marketed similar products were Commodore, Heathkit, and Radio Shack. Although these products were popular among computer hobbyists, they were not widely accepted by the business community, which continued to look to the well-established IBM for the majority of its computing needs.

In 1981, IBM introduced its first desktop computer, called the personal computer, or PC, whose underlying software was developed by a struggling young company known as Microsoft. The PC was an instant success and legitimized the desktop computer as an established commodity in the minds of the business community. Today, the term *PC* is widely used to refer to all those machines (from various manufacturers) whose design has evolved from IBM's initial desktop computer, most of which continue to be marketed with software from Microsoft. At times, however, the term *PC* is used interchangeably with the generic terms *desktop* or *laptop*.

Babbage's Difference Engine

The machines designed by Charles Babbage were truly the forerunners of modern computer design. If technology been able to produce his machines in an economically feasible manner and if the data processing demands of commerce and government been on the scale of today's requirements, Babbage's ideas could have led to the computer revolution in the 1800s. As it was, only a demonstration model of his Difference Engine was constructed in his lifetime. This machine determined numerical values by computing "successive differences." We can gain an insight to this technique by considering the problem of computing the squares of the integers. We begin with the knowledge that the square of 0 is 0, the square of 1 is 1, the square of 2 is 4, and the square of 3 is 9. With this, we can determine the square of 4 in the following manner. We first compute the differences of the squares we already know: $1^2 - 0^2 = 1$, $2^2 - 1^2 = 3$, and $3^2 - 2^2 = 5$. Then we compute the differences of these results: $3 - 1 = 2$, and $5 - 3 = 2$. Note that these differences are both 2. Assuming that this consistency continues (mathematics can show that it does) we conclude that the difference between the value $(4^2 - 3^2)$ and the value $(3^2 - 2^2)$ must also be 2. Hence $(4^2 - 3^2)$ must be 2 greater than $(3^2 - 2^2)$, so $4^2 - 3^2 = 7$ and thus $4^2 = 3^2 + 7 = 16$. Now that we know the square of 4, we could continue our procedure to compute the square of 5 based on the values of 1^2, 2^2, 3^2, and 4^2. (Although a more in-depth discussion of successive differences is beyond the scope of our current study, students of calculus may wish to observe that the preceding example is based on the fact that the second derivative of $y = x^2$ is a straight line.)

The availability of desktop and laptop computers has brought computer technology to the forefront of today's society. Computer technology is so prevalent now that knowing how to use it is fundamental to being a member of modern society. In particular, it is by means of this technology that millions of individuals gain access to the global connection system known as the Internet, a system that is influencing lifestyles and commerce on a worldwide basis.

0.3 The Science of Algorithms

Conditions such as limited data storage capabilities and intricate, time-consuming programming procedures restricted the complexity of the algorithms to which early computing machines were applied. However, as these limitations began to disappear, machines were applied to increasingly larger and more complex tasks. As attempts to express the composition of these tasks in algorithmic form began to tax the abilities of the human mind, more and more research efforts were directed toward the study of algorithms and the programming process.

It was in this context that the theoretical work of mathematicians began to pay dividends. As a consequence of Gödel's incompleteness theorem, mathematicians had already been investigating those questions regarding algorithmic processes that advancing technology was now raising. With that, the stage was set for the emergence of a new discipline known as *computer science.*

Today, this new discipline has established itself as the science of algorithms. The scope of this science is broad, drawing from such diverse subjects as mathematics, engineering, psychology, biology, business administration, and linguistics. In the chapters that follow, we will discuss many of the topics of this science. In each case, our goal will be to introduce the central ideas in the subject, the current topics of research, and some of the techniques being applied to advance knowledge in the area.

As we progress through our study, it is easy to lose track of the overall picture. We therefore pause to collect our thoughts by identifying some questions that define the science of computing and provide the focus for its study.

- Which problems can be solved by algorithmic processes?
- How can the discovery of algorithms be made easier?
- How can the techniques of representing and communicating algorithms be improved?
- How can our knowledge of algorithms and technology be applied to provide better machines?
- How can the characteristics of different algorithms be analyzed and compared?

Note that the theme common to all these questions is the study of algorithms (Figure 0.5).

0.4 Abstraction

The concept of abstraction so permeates the study of computer science and the design of computer systems that it behooves us to address it in this preliminary chapter. The term **abstraction,** as we are using it here, refers to the distinction between the external properties of an entity and the details of the entity's internal composition. It is abstraction that allows us to ignore the internal details of a complex device such as a computer, automobile, or microwave oven and use it as a single, comprehensible unit. Moreover, it is by means of abstraction that such complex systems are designed and manufactured in the first place. Computers, automobiles, and microwave ovens are constructed from components, each of which is constructed from smaller components.

Figure 0.5

The central role of algorithms in computer science

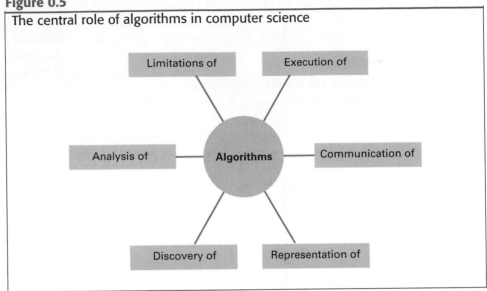

Each component represents a level of abstraction at which the use of the component is isolated from the details of the component's internal composition.

It is by applying abstraction, then, that we are able to construct, analyze, and manage large, complex computer systems, which would be overwhelming if viewed in their entirety at a detailed level. At each level of abstraction, we view the system in terms of components, called **abstract tools,** whose internal composition we ignore. This allows us to concentrate on how each component interacts with other components at the same level and how the collection as a whole forms a higher level component. Thus we are able to comprehend the part of the system that is relevant to the task at hand rather than being lost in a sea of details.

We emphasize that abstraction is not limited to science and technology. It is an important simplification technique with which our society has created a lifestyle that would otherwise be impossible. Few of us understand how the various conveniences of daily life are actually implemented. We eat food and wear clothes that we cannot produce by ourselves. We use electrical devices without understanding the underlying technology. We use the services of others without knowing the details of their professions. With each new advancement, a small part of society chooses to specialize in its implementation while the rest of us learn to use the results as abstract tools. In this manner, society's warehouse of abstract tools expands, and society's ability to advance further increases.

Abstraction is a recurring theme in our study. We will learn that computing equipment is constructed in levels of abstract tools. We will also see that the development of large software systems is accomplished in a modular fashion in which each module is used as an abstract tool in larger modules. Moreover, abstraction plays an important role in the task of advancing computer science itself, allowing researchers to focus attention on particular areas within a complex field. In fact, the organization of this text reflects this characteristic of the science. Each chapter, which focuses on a particular area within the science, is surprisingly independent of the others, yet together the chapters form a comprehensive overview of a vast field of study.

0.5 An Outline of Our Study

This text follows a bottom up approach to the study of computer science, beginning with such hands-on topics as computer hardware and leading to the more abstract topics such as algorithm complexity and computability. The result is that our study follows a pattern of building larger and larger abstract tools as our understanding of the subject expands.

We begin by considering topics dealing with the design and construction of machines for executing algorithms. In Chapter 1 (Data Storage) we look at how information is encoded and stored within modern computers, and in Chapter 2 (Data Manipulation) we investigate the basic internal operation of a simple computer. Although part of this study involves technology, the general theme is technology independent. That is, such topics as digital circuit design, data encoding and compression systems, and computer architecture are relevant over a wide range of technology and promise to remain relevant regardless of the direction technology leads.

In Chapter 3 (Operating Systems) we study the software that controls the overall operation of a computer. This software is called an operating system. It is a computer's operating system that controls the interface between the machine and its outside world, protecting the machine and the data stored within from unauthorized access, allowing a computer user to request the execution of applications, and coordinating the internal activities required to fulfill the user's requests.

In Chapter 4 (Networks and the Internet) we study how computers are connected to each other to form computer networks and how networks are connected to form internets. This study leads to topics such as network protocols, the Internet's structure and internal operation, and the World Wide Web.

Chapter 5 (Algorithms) introduces the study of algorithms from a more formal perspective. We investigate how algorithms are discovered, identify several fundamental algorithmic structures, develop elementary techniques for representing algorithms, and introduce the subjects of algorithm efficiency and correctness.

In Chapter 6 (Programming Languages) we consider the subject of algorithm representation and the program development process. Here we find that the search for better programming techniques has led to a variety of programming methodologies or paradigms, each with its own set of programming languages. We investigate these paradigms and languages as well as consider issues of grammar and language translation.

Chapter 7 (Software Engineering) introduces the branch of computer science known as software engineering, which deals with the problems encountered when developing large software systems. The underlying theme is that the design of large software systems is a complex task that embraces problems not addressed by traditional engineering principles. Thus, the subject of software engineering has become an important field of research within computer science, drawing from such diverse fields as engineering, project management, personnel management, programming language design, and even architecture.

In the next two chapters we look at ways data can be organized within a computer system. In Chapter 8 (Data Abstractions) we introduce techniques traditionally used for organizing data in a computer's main memory and then trace the evolution of data abstraction from the concept of primitives to today's object-oriented techniques. In Chapter 9 (Database Systems) we consider methods traditionally used for organizing data in a computer's mass storage and investigate how extremely large and complex database systems are implemented.

In Chapter 10 (Artificial Intelligence) we learn that in order to develop more useful machines computer science has turned to the study of human intelligence for leadership. The hope is that by understanding how our own minds reason and perceive, we will be able to design algorithms that mimic these processes and thus transfer these capabilities to machines. The result is the area of computer science known as artificial intelligence, which leans heavily on research in such areas as psychology, biology, and linguistics.

Having stretched our imagination with the developments in artificial intelligence, we investigate the limitations of algorithms (and thus machines) in Chapter 11 (Theory of Computation). Here we identify some problems that cannot be solved algorithmically (and therefore lie beyond the capabilities of machines) as well as learn that the solutions to many other problems require such enormous time or space that they are also unsolvable from a practical perspective. Thus, it is through this study that we are able to grasp the scope and limitations of algorithmic systems.

In each chapter our goal is to explore to a depth that gives you a true understanding of the subject. We want to develop a working knowledge of computer science—a knowledge that will allow you to understand the technical society in which you live and to provide a foundation from which you can learn on your own as science and technology advance.

0.6 Social Repercussions

Advances in science and technology are blurring many distinctions on which our society has based decisions in the past and are even challenging many of society's principles. What is the difference between the presence of intelligent behavior and the presence of intelligence itself? When does life begin? When does it end? What is the difference between a plant and an animal? Is there life in other solar systems?

Computer science is generating such questions in a variety of contexts. In law, questions arise regarding the degree to which software can be owned and the rights and liabilities that accompany that ownership. In ethics, individuals are faced with numerous options that challenge the traditional principles on which their behavior is based. In government, questions arise regarding the extent to which computer technology and its applications should be regulated. And, throughout society, questions abound concerning whether new computer applications represent new freedoms or new controls.

Resolving such dilemmas in a rational manner requires a basic knowledge in the relevant science or technology. If a society is to make sound decisions regarding the storage and disposal of nuclear waste, its members must comprehend the effects of radiation, understand what is required to protect against its dangers, and calculate a realistic estimate about the time span over which the radiation risk will persist. Likewise, to judge whether governments or companies should be allowed to develop large, integrated databases containing information about its citizens or customers, members of society must have a basic understanding of the capabilities, limitations, and ramifications of database technology.

This text provides the background from which you can approach such issues in an informed manner. In fact, some sections of the text are devoted explicitly to social, ethical, and legal issues themselves. For example, we discuss matters of privacy in relation to the Internet and database technology, and issues of software ownership in relation to software development. Although not a part of computer science itself, these topics are important for lay audiences as well as for those contemplating careers in computing or computer related fields.

However, factual knowledge alone does not necessarily provide solutions to many of the questions generated by today's advances in computer science. There is often no single correct answer, and many valid solutions are compromises between opposing (and perhaps equally valid) views. Thus, finding solutions often requires the ability to listen, to recognize other points of view, to carry on a rational debate, and to alter one's own opinions as new insights are gained. With this in mind, each chapter of this text ends with a collection of questions called Social Issues. These are not necessarily questions to be answered. Instead, they are questions to be considered. In many cases, an answer that may appear obvious at first will cease to satisfy you as you explore alternatives. We close this introduction with a collection of such questions that relate to computing issues in general.

Social Issues

The following questions are provided to help you investigate some of the ethical/social/legal issues associated with the field of computing. The goal is not merely to answer these questions. You should also consider why you answered as you did and whether your justifications are consistent from one question to the next.

1. The premise that our society is *different* from what it would have been without the computer revolution is generally accepted. Is our society *better* than it would have been without the revolution? Is our society worse? Would your answer differ if your position within society were different?

2. Is it acceptable to participate in today's technical society without making an effort to understand the basics of that technology? For instance, do members of a democracy, whose votes often determine how technology will be supported and used, have an obligation to try to understand that technology? Does your answer depend on which technology is being considered? For example, is your answer the same when considering nuclear technology as when considering computer technology?

3. By using cash in financial transactions, individuals have traditionally had the option to manage their financial affairs without service charges. However, as more of our economy is becoming automated, financial institutions are implementing service charges for access to these automated systems. Is there a point at which these charges unfairly restrict an individual's access to the economy? For example, suppose an employer pays employees only by check, and all financial institutions were to place a service charge on check cashing and depositing. Would the employees be unfairly treated? What if an employer insists on paying only via direct deposit?

4. In the context of interactive television, to what extent should a company be allowed to retrieve information from children (perhaps via an interactive game format) regarding the household? For example, should a company be allowed to obtain a child's report on his or her parents' buying patterns? What about information about the child?

5. To what extent should a government regulate computer technology and its applications? Consider, for example, the issues mentioned in Questions 3 and 4. What justifies governmental regulation?

6. To what extent will our decisions regarding technology in general, and computer technology in particular, affect future generations?

7. As technology advances, our educational system is constantly challenged to reconsider the level of abstraction at which topics are presented. Many questions take the form of whether a skill is still necessary or whether students should be allowed to rely on an abstract tool. Students of trigonometry are no longer taught how to find the values of trigonometric functions using tables. Instead, they use calculators as abstract tools to find these values. Some argue that long division should also give way to abstraction. What other subjects are involved with similar controversies? Will the use of video technology someday remove the need to read? Do automated spelling checkers eliminate the need for spelling skills?

8. Assume that the concept of public libraries is largely based on the premise that all citizens in a democracy must have access to information. As more information is stored and disseminated via computer technology, does access to this technology become a right of every individual? If so, should public libraries be the channel by which this access is provided?

9. What ethical concerns arise in a society that relies on the use of abstract tools? Are there cases in which it is unethical to use a product or service without understanding how it works? Without knowing how it is produced? Or, without understanding the byproducts of its use?

10. As our economy becomes more automated, it becomes easier for a government to monitor its citizens' financial activities. Is that good or bad?

11. Which technologies that were imagined by George Orwell (Eric Blair) in his novel *1984* have actually become reality? Are they being used in the manner in which Orwell predicted?

12. Researchers in the field of ethics have developed various theories in an effort to analyze ethical decisions. One theory is that decisions should be based on consequences.

For instance, within this sphere is Utilitarianism, which argues that the "correct" decision is the one that produces the greatest benefit for the largest population. Another theory is duty-based rather than consequence-based. It argues that the "correct" decision is the one that respects the rights of individuals. Do your answers to the preceding questions indicate that you tend to follow duty-based or consequence-based ethics?

Additional Reading

Dejoie, D., G. Fowler, and D. Paradice. *Ethical Issues in Information Systems*. Boston: Boyd and Fraser, 1991.

Edgar, S. L. *Morality and Machines*. Sudbury, MA: Jones and Bartlett, 1997.

Forester, T., and P. Forrison. *Computer Ethics: Cautionary Tales and Ethical Dilemmas*. Cambridge, MA: MIT Press, 1990.

Goldstine, J. J. *The Computer from Pascal to von Neumann*. Princeton: Princeton University Press, 1972.

Johnson, D. G. *Computer Ethics*, 3rd ed. Englewood Cliffs, NJ: Prentice-Hall, 2001.

Kizza, J. M. *Ethical and Social Issues in the Information Age*. New York: Springer-Verlag, 1998.

Mollenhoff, C. R. *Atanasoff: Forgotten Father of the Computer*. Ames: Iowa State University Press, 1988.

Neumann, P. G. *Computer Related Risks*. Reading, MA: Addison-Wesley, 1995.

Randell, B. *The Origins of Digital Computers*. New York: Springer-Verlag, 1973.

Spinello, R. A. and H. T. Tavani. *Readings in CyberEthics*. Sudbury, MA: Jones and Bartlett, 2001.

Swade, D. *The Difference Engine*. New York: Viking, 2000.

Woolley, B. *The Bride of Science, Romance, Reason, and Byron's Daughter*. New York: McGraw-Hill, 1999.

Data Storage

In this chapter, we consider topics associated with data representation and the storage of data within a computer. At times we will discuss issues of technology, since these matters are often reflected in the external characteristics of today's machines. However, most of our discussion will deal with topics that will be germane to computer design well after today's technologies have been replaced with those of tomorrow.

1.1 Bits and Their Storage

Inside today's computers information is encoded as patterns of 0s and 1s. These digits are called **bits** (binary digits). Although you may be inclined to associate bits with numeric values, they are really only symbols whose meaning depends on the application at hand. Sometimes patterns of bits are used to represent numeric values; sometimes they represent other symbols such as characters in an alphabet and punctuation; sometimes they represent images; and sometimes they represent sounds. Storing a bit within a machine requires a device that can be in one of two states, such as a switch (on or off), an electronically controlled relay (activated or not), or other devices, as we will see. One state is used to represent 0, the other to represent 1.

Boolean Operations

Let us consider the operations AND, OR, and XOR (exclusive or) as summarized in Figure 1.1. These operations are similar to the arithmetic operations TIMES and PLUS because they combine a pair of values (the operation's input) to produce a third value (the operation's output). In contrast to arithmetic operations, however, the only digits manipulated by the AND, OR, and XOR operations are 0 and 1. In this context we think of the digit 0 as representing the value *false* and the digit 1 representing the value *true*. Operations that manipulate true/false values are called **Boolean operations,** in honor of the mathematician George Boole (1815–1864), who was a pioneer in the field of mathematics called logic.

The Boolean operation AND is designed to reflect the truth or falseness of a statement formed by combining two smaller, or simpler, statements with the conjunction *and.* Such statements have the generic form

> *P* AND Q

where *P* represents one statement and Q represents another—for example,

> Kermit is a frog AND Miss Piggy is an actress.

The inputs to the AND operation represent the truth or falseness of the compound statement's components; the output represents the truth or falseness of the compound statement itself. Since a statement of the form P AND Q is true only when both of its components are true, we conclude that 1 AND 1 should be 1, whereas all other cases should produce an output of 0, in agreement with Figure 1.1.

In a similar manner, the OR operation is based on compound statements of the form

> *P* OR Q

where, again, *P* represents one statement and Q represents another. Such statements are true when at least one of their components is true, which agrees with the OR operation depicted in Figure 1.1.

There is not a single conjunction in the English language that captures the meaning of the XOR operation. XOR produces an output of 1 (true) when one of its inputs is 1 (true) and the other is 0 (false). For example, a statement of the form *P* XOR Q means "either *P* or Q but not both."

Figure 1.1

The Boolean operations AND, OR, and XOR (exclusive or)

The AND operation

$$\begin{array}{l}\phantom{\text{AND }}0\\ \text{AND }\underline{0}\\ \phantom{\text{AND }}0\end{array} \qquad \begin{array}{l}\phantom{\text{AND }}0\\ \text{AND }\underline{1}\\ \phantom{\text{AND }}0\end{array} \qquad \begin{array}{l}\phantom{\text{AND }}1\\ \text{AND }\underline{0}\\ \phantom{\text{AND }}0\end{array} \qquad \begin{array}{l}\phantom{\text{AND }}1\\ \text{AND }\underline{1}\\ \phantom{\text{AND }}1\end{array}$$

The OR operation

$$\begin{array}{l}\phantom{\text{OR }}0\\ \text{OR }\underline{0}\\ \phantom{\text{OR }}0\end{array} \qquad \begin{array}{l}\phantom{\text{OR }}0\\ \text{OR }\underline{1}\\ \phantom{\text{OR }}1\end{array} \qquad \begin{array}{l}\phantom{\text{OR }}1\\ \text{OR }\underline{0}\\ \phantom{\text{OR }}1\end{array} \qquad \begin{array}{l}\phantom{\text{OR }}1\\ \text{OR }\underline{1}\\ \phantom{\text{OR }}1\end{array}$$

The XOR operation

$$\begin{array}{l}\phantom{\text{XOR }}0\\ \text{XOR }\underline{0}\\ \phantom{\text{XOR }}0\end{array} \qquad \begin{array}{l}\phantom{\text{XOR }}0\\ \text{XOR }\underline{1}\\ \phantom{\text{XOR }}1\end{array} \qquad \begin{array}{l}\phantom{\text{XOR }}1\\ \text{XOR }\underline{0}\\ \phantom{\text{XOR }}1\end{array} \qquad \begin{array}{l}\phantom{\text{XOR }}1\\ \text{XOR }\underline{1}\\ \phantom{\text{XOR }}0\end{array}$$

The operation NOT is another Boolean operation. It differs from AND, OR, and XOR because it has only one input. Its output is the opposite of that input; if the input of the operation NOT is true, then the output is false, and vice versa. Thus, if the input of the NOT operation is the truth or falseness of the statement

Fozzie is a bear

then the output would represent the truth or falseness of the statement

Fozzie is not a bear.

Gates and Flip-Flops

A device that produces the output of a Boolean operation when given the operation's input values is called a **gate.** Gates can be constructed from a variety of technologies such as gears, relays, and optic devices. Today's computers usually implement gates as small electronic circuits in which the digits 0 and 1 are represented as voltage levels. We need not concern ourselves with such details, however. For our purposes, it suffices to represent gates in their symbolic form, as shown in Figure 1.2. Note that the AND, OR, XOR, and NOT gates are represented by distinctively shaped diagrams, with the input values entering on one side and the output exiting on the other.

Gates such as these provide the building blocks from which computers are constructed. One important step in this direction is depicted in the circuit in Figure 1.3. This is a particular example from a collection of circuits known as flip-flops. A **flip-flop** is a circuit that produces an output value of 0 or 1 that remains constant until a temporary pulse from another circuit causes it to shift to the other value. In other

Figure 1.2

A pictorial representation of AND, OR, XOR, and NOT gates as well as their input and output values

AND

Inputs	Output
0 0	0
0 1	0
1 0	0
1 1	1

OR

Inputs	Output
0 0	0
0 1	1
1 0	1
1 1	1

NAND ⟹Do‒

NOR ⟹Do

XOR

Inputs	Output
0 0	0
0 1	1
1 0	1
1 1	0

NOT

Inputs	Output
0	1
1	0

Figure 1.3

A simple flip-flop circuit

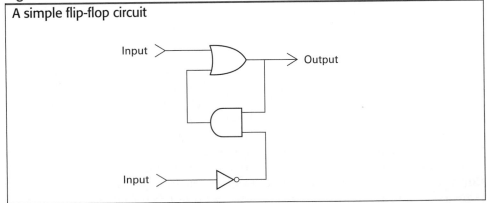

words, the output will flip or flop between two values under control of external stimuli. As long as both inputs in the circuit in Figure 1.3 remain 0, the output (whether 0 or 1) will not change. However, temporarily placing a 1 on the upper input will force the output to be 1, whereas temporarily placing a 1 on the lower input will force the output to be 0.

Let us consider this claim in more detail. Without knowing the current output of the circuit in Figure 1.3, suppose that the upper input is changed to 1 while the lower input remains 0 (Figure 1.4a). This will cause the output of the OR gate to be 1, regardless of the other input to this gate. In turn, both inputs to the AND gate will now be 1, since the other input to this gate is already 1 (obtained by passing the lower input of the flip-flop through the NOT gate). The output of the AND gate will then become 1, which means that the second input to the OR gate will now be 1 (Figure 1.4b). This guarantees that the output of the OR gate will remain 1, even when the upper input to the flip-flop is changed back to 0 (Figure 1.4c). In summary, the flip-flop's output has become 1, and this output value will remain after the upper input returns to 0.

Figure 1.4

Setting the output of a flip-flop to 1

a. 1 is placed on the upper input.

b. This causes the output of the OR gate to be 1 and, in turn, the output of the AND gate to be 1.

c. The 1 from the AND gate keeps the OR gate from changing after the upper input returns to 0.

In a similar manner, temporarily placing the value 1 on the lower input will force the flip-flop's output to be 0, and this output will persist after the input value returns to 0.

The significance of a flip-flop from our perspective is that it is ideal for the storage of a bit within a computer. The value stored in it is the output value of the flip-flop. Other circuits can easily adjust this value by sending pulses to the flip-flop's inputs, and other circuits can respond to the stored value by using the flip-flop's output as their inputs.

There are, of course, other ways to build a flip-flop. One alternative is shown in Figure 1.5. If you experiment with this circuit, you will find that, although it has a different internal structure, its external properties are the same as those of Figure 1.3. This leads us to our first example of the role of abstract tools. When designing a flip-flop, an engineer considers the alternative ways in which a flip-flop can be constructed using gates as building blocks. Then, once flip-flops and other basic circuits have been designed, the engineer can use those circuits as building blocks to construct more complex circuitry. In turn, the design of computer circuitry takes on a hierarchical structure, each level of which uses the lower level components as abstract tools.

Other Storage Techniques

In the 1960s, bits were stored in computers using small donut-shaped rings of magnetic material, called **cores,** threaded on wires. By passing electric current through the wires, each core could be magnetized in one of two directions. Later, the direction of the magnetic field could be detected by observing its effect on an electric current passing through the center of the core. Thus a core provided a means of storing a bit—a 1 was represented by a magnetic field in one direction, a 0 was represented by a magnetic field in the other. Such systems are obsolete today due to their size and power requirements.

A more recent method of storing a bit is the capacitor, which consists of two small metallic plates positioned parallel to each other with a small distance between them. If a voltage source is connected to the plates—positive to one plate and negative to the other—the charges from the voltage source will distribute themselves on

Figure 1.5

Another way of constructing a flip-flop

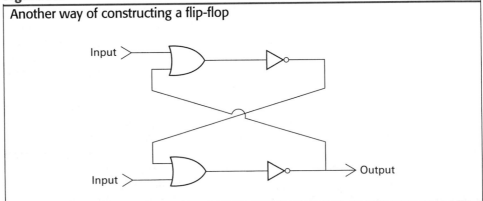

the plates. Then, when the voltage source is removed, these charges will be left on the plates. If the plates are later connected, current will flow through the connection and the charge will be neutralized. Thus a capacitor can be in one of two states, charged or discharged, one of which can be used to represent a 0, the other to represent a 1. Today's technology is capable of constructing millions of tiny capacitors along with their related circuitry on a single wafer (called a **chip**). In turn, the capacitor has become a popular technology for bit storage within machines.

Still more modern technologies allow bits to be stored in devices whose size is measured in angstroms. (An angstrom is less than the diameter of a hydrogen atom.) An example is flash memory, which is the technology used to stored images in digital cameras. Using flash memory, bits are stored by trapping electrons in tiny chambers of silicon dioxide, each of which has a diameter of roughly 90 angstroms. The binary digits are represented by full and empty chambers.

Cores, flip-flops, capacitors, and flash memory not only represent advances in miniaturization, they also provide examples of storage systems with different degrees of volatility. A core will retain its magnetic field indefinitely. A flip-flop loses the data entrusted to it when its power source is turned off. The charges stored on tiny capacitors are even more fragile. They tend to dissipate on their own, even while the circuitry to which they are attached is functioning. Thus the charge on a capacitor has to be replenished regularly by a circuit known as a refresh circuit. In recognition of this volatility, computer memory (Section 1.2) constructed from such technology is often called **dynamic memory.** The tiny chambers in flash memory will hold their electrons for many years, which makes miniature flash memory systems a popular technology for storing permanently recorded programs in devices such as electronic toys, telephones, and general purpose computers (as we will see in Section 3.2). In these applications, the contents of the chambers are never altered but instead are only read, leading to storage systems called **read only memory (ROM).**

Hexadecimal Notation

When considering the internal activities of a computer, we must deal with strings of bits, some of which can be quite long. A long string of bits is often called a **stream.** Unfortunately, streams are difficult for the human mind to comprehend. Merely transcribing the pattern 101101010011 is tedious and error prone. To simplify the representation of such bit patterns, therefore, we usually use a shorthand notation called **hexadecimal notation,** which takes advantage of the fact that bit patterns within a machine tend to have lengths in multiples of four. In particular, hexadecimal notation uses a single symbol to represent a pattern four bits, meaning that a string of twelve bits can be represented by only three symbols.

Figure 1.6 presents the hexadecimal encoding system. The left column displays all possible bit patterns of length four; the right column shows the symbol used in hexadecimal notation to represent the bit pattern to its left. Using this system, the bit pattern 10110101 is represented as B5. This is obtained by dividing the bit pattern into substrings of length four and then representing each substring by its hexadecimal equivalent—1011 is represented by B, and 0101 is represented by 5. In this manner, the 16-bit pattern 1010010011001000 can be reduced to the more palatable form A4C8.

Figure 1.6

The hexadecimal coding system

Bit pattern	Hexadecimal representation
0000	0
0001	1
0010	2
0011	3
0100	4
0101	5
0110	6
0111	7
1000	8
1001	9
1010	A
1011	B
1100	C
1101	D
1110	E
1111	F

We will use hexadecimal notation extensively in the next chapter. There you will come to appreciate its efficiency.

Questions/Exercises

1. What input bit patterns will cause the following circuit to produce an output of 1?

Inputs ——— Output

2. In the text, we claimed that placing a 1 on the lower input of the flip-flop in Figure 1.3 (while holding the upper input at 0) will force the flip-flop's output to be 0. Describe the sequence of events that occurs within the flip-flop in this case.

3. Assuming that both inputs to the flip-flop in Figure 1.5 are 0, describe the sequence of events that occurs when the upper input is temporarily set to 1.

4. It is often necessary to coordinate the activities of various parts of a circuit. This is accomplished by connecting a pulsating signal (called a *clock*) to those parts of the circuit that require coordination. As the clock alternates between the values 0 and 1, it activates the various circuit components. Below is an example of one part of such a circuit that involves the flip-flop shown in Figure 1.3. For what clock values will the flip-flop be shielded from the effects of the circuit's input values? For what clock values will the flip-flop respond to the circuit's input values?

5. a. If the output of an OR gate is passed through a NOT gate, the combination computes the Boolean operation called NOR that has an output of 1 only when both its inputs are 0. The symbol for a NOR gate is the same as an OR gate except that it has a circle at its output. Below is a circuit containing an AND gate and two NOR gates. What Boolean operation does the circuit compute?

b. If the output of an AND gate is passed through a NOT gate, the combination computes the Boolean operation called NAND that has an output of 0 only when both its inputs are 1. The symbol for a NAND gate is the same as an AND gate except that it has a circle at its output. Below is a circuit containing NAND gates. What Boolean operation does the circuit compute?

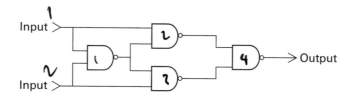

6. Use hexadecimal notation to represent the following bit patterns:
   a. 0110101011110010   b. 111010000101010100010111   c. 01001000

7. What bit patterns are represented by the following hexadecimal patterns?
   a. 5FD97   b. 610A   c. ABCD   d. 0100

1.2 Main Memory

For the purpose of storing data, a computer contains a large collection of circuits, each capable of storing a single bit. This bit reservoir is known as the machine's **main memory.**

Memory Organization

The circuits with which bits are stored in a machine's main memory are arranged in manageable units called **cells,** with a typical cell size being eight bits. (A string of eight bits is called a **byte.** Thus, a typical memory cell has a capacity of one byte.) Small computers used in such household devices as microwave ovens may have main memories consisting of only a few hundred cells, whereas large computers may have billions of cells in their main memories.

Although there is no left or right within a machine, we normally envision the bits within a memory cell as being arranged in a row. The left end of this row is called the **high-order end,** and the right end is called the **low-order end.** The last bit at the high-order end is called either the high-order bit or the **most significant bit** in reference to the fact that if the contents of the cell were interpreted as representing a numeric value, this bit would be the most significant digit in the number. Similarly, the bit at the right end is referred to as the low-order bit or the **least significant bit.** Thus we may represent the contents of a byte-size memory cell as shown in Figure 1.7.

To identify individual cells in a machine's main memory, each cell is assigned a unique "name," called its **address.** The system is analogous to, and uses the same terminology as, the technique of identifying houses in a city by addresses. In the case of memory cells, however, the addresses used are entirely numeric. To be more precise, we envision all the cells being placed in a single row and numbered in this order starting with the value zero. Such an addressing system not only gives us a way of uniquely identifying each cell but also associates an order to the cells (Figure 1.8), giving us phrases such as "the next cell" or "the previous cell."

An important consequence of assigning an order to both the cells in main memory and the bits within each cell is that the entire collection of bits within a machine's main memory is essentially ordered in one long row. Pieces of this long row can therefore be used to store bit patterns that may be longer than the length of a single cell. In particular, we can still store a string of 16 bits merely by using two consecutive memory cells.

Figure 1.7

The organization of a byte-size memory cell

High-order end   0 1 0 1 1 0 1 0   Low-order end

Most significant bit   Least significant bit

Figure 1.8

Memory cells arranged by address

To complete the main memory of a machine, the circuitry that actually holds the bits is combined with the circuitry required to allow other circuits to store and retrieve data from the memory cells. In this way, other circuits can get data from the memory by electronically asking for the contents of a certain address (called a read operation), or they can record information in the memory by requesting that a certain bit pattern be placed in the cell at a particular address (called a write operation).

Because a machine's main memory is organized as individual, addressable cells, the cells can be accessed independently as required. That is, the cells in a machine's main memory can be accessed in random order—which explains why a machine's main memory is referred to as **random access memory (RAM).** When constructed from dynamic memory technology, it is often called **DRAM** (pronounced "DEE–ram") meaning Dynamic RAM. This random accessibility of individual bytes in a machine's main memory is in stark contrast to the mass storage systems that we will discuss in the next section, in which long strings of bits must be manipulated as amalgamated blocks.

Measuring Memory Capacity

As we will learn in the next chapter, it is convenient to design main memory systems in which the total number of cells is a power of two. In turn, the size of the memories in early computers were often measured in 1024 (which is 2^{10}) cell units. Since 1024 is close to the value 1000, many in the computing community adopted the prefix *kilo* in reference to this unit. Thus the term *kilobyte* (abbreviated KB) was used to refer to 1024 bytes, and a machine with 4096 memory cells was said to have a 4KB memory (4096 = 4 × 1024). As memories became larger, this terminology grew to include the prefixes *mega* for 1,048,576 (which is 2^{20}) and *giga* for 1,073,741,824 (which is 2^{30}), and units such as MB (megabyte) and GB (gigabyte) became popular.

Unfortunately, this application of prefixes represents a misuse of terminology because these prefixes are already used in other fields in reference to units that are powers of ten. For example, when measuring distance, *kilometer* refers to 1000 meters, and when measuring radio frequencies, *megahertz* refers to 1,000,000 hertz. Moreover, some manufacturers of computer equipment have been known to use the prefix *mega* to refer to units of 1,024,000 (so that a megabyte would be 1000KB). Needless to say, these discrepancies have led to confusion and misunderstandings over the years.

To clarify matters, a proposal has been made to reserve the prefixes *kilo, mega,* and *giga* for units that are powers of ten, and to introduce the new prefixes *kibi* (short for kilobinary and abbreviated Ki), *mebi* (short for megabinary and abbreviated Mi), and *gibi* (short for gigabinary and abbreviated Gi) in reference to the corresponding units that are powers of two. Under this system, the term *kibibyte* (KiB) would refer to 1024 bytes, whereas *kilobyte* (KB) would refer to 1000 bytes. Whether these prefixes become a part of the popular vernacular remains to be seen. For now, the traditional "misuse" of the prefixes *kilo, mega,* and *giga* remains ingrained in the computing community, and thus we will follow this tradition in our study. However, the proposed prefixes *kibi, megi,* and *gibi* do represent an attempt to solve a growing problem, and one would be wise to interpret terms such as *kilobyte* and *megabyte* with caution in the future.

Questions/Exercises

1. If the memory cell whose address is 5 contains the value 8, what is the difference between writing the value 5 into cell number 6 and moving the contents of cell number 5 into cell number 6?

2. Suppose you want to interchange the values stored in memory cells 2 and 3. What is wrong with the following sequence of steps:

   Step 1. Move the contents of cell number 2 to cell number 3.
   Step 2. Move the contents of cell number 3 to cell number 2.

   Design a sequence of steps that correctly interchanges the contents of these cells.

3. How many bits would be in the memory of a computer with 4KB (more precisely KiB) memory?

1.3 Mass Storage

Due to the volatility and limited size of a computer's main memory, most computers have additional memory devices called **mass storage systems,** which include magnetic disks, CDs, and magnetic tapes. The advantages of mass storage systems over main memory include less volatility, large storage capacities, low cost, and in many cases, the ability to remove the storage medium from the machine for archival purposes.

The terms *on-line* and *off-line* are often used to describe devices that can be either attached to or detached from a machine. **On-line** means that the device or information is connected and readily available to the machine without human intervention. **Off-line** means that human intervention is required before the device or information can be accessed by the machine—perhaps because the device must be turned on, or the medium holding the information must be inserted into some mechanism.

A major disadvantage of mass storage systems is that they typically require mechanical motion and therefore require significantly more time to store and retrieve data than a machine's main memory, where all activities are performed electronically.

Magnetic Disks

One of the most common forms of mass storage in use today is the magnetic disk, in which a thin spinning disk with magnetic coating is used to hold data. Read/write heads are placed above and/or below the disk so that as the disk spins, each head traverses a circle, called a **track,** around the disk's upper or lower surface. By repositioning the read/write heads, different concentric tracks can be accessed. In many cases, a disk storage system consists of several disks mounted on a common spindle, one on top of the other, with enough space for the read/write heads to slip between the platters. In such cases, the read/write heads move in unison. Each time the read/write heads are repositioned, a new set of tracks—which is called a **cylinder**—becomes accessible.

Since a track can contain more information than we would normally want to manipulate at any one time, each track is divided into arcs called **sectors** on which information is recorded as a continuous string of bits (Figure 1.9). Each track on a traditional disk contains the same number of sectors, and each sector contains the same number of bits. (Thus the bits within a sector are more compactly stored on the tracks nearer the center of the disk than those on the tracks near the outer edge.)

Thus, a disk storage system consists of many individual sectors, each of which can be accessed as an independent string of bits. The number of tracks per surface and the number of sectors per track vary greatly from one disk system to another. Sector sizes tend to be no more than a few KB; sectors of 512 bytes or 1024 bytes are common.

Figure 1.9

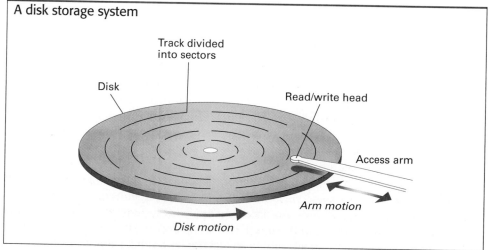

A disk storage system

Track divided into sectors

Disk

Read/write head

Access arm

Arm motion

Disk motion

The location of tracks and sectors is not a permanent part of a disk's physical structure. Instead, they are marked magnetically through a process called **formatting** (or initializing) the disk. This process is usually performed by the disk's manufacturer, resulting in what are known as formatted disks. Most computer systems can also perform this task. Thus, if the format information on a disk is damaged, the disk can be reformatted, although this process destroys all the information that was previously recorded on the disk.

The capacity of a disk storage system depends on the number of disks used and the density in which the tracks and sectors are placed. Lower-capacity systems consist of a single plastic disk known as a diskette or, in those cases in which the disk is flexible, by the less prestigious title of floppy disk. (Today's 3½-inch diameter floppy disks are housed in rigid plastic cases, which do not constitute as flexible a package as their older 5¼-inch diameter cousins that were housed in paper sleeves.) Diskettes are easily inserted and removed from their corresponding read/write units and are easily stored. As a consequence, diskettes are often used for off-line storage of information. The generic 3½-inch diskette is capable of holding 1.44MB of data, but nongeneric diskettes are available with much higher capacities. An example is the Zip disk system from Iomega Corporation, which provides storage capacities up to several hundred MB on a single rigid diskette.

High-capacity disk systems, capable of holding many gigabytes, consist of perhaps five to ten rigid disks mounted on a common spindle. The fact that the disks used in these systems are rigid leads them to be known as hard-disk systems, in contrast to their floppy counterparts. To allow for faster rotation speeds, the read/write heads in these systems do not touch the disk but instead "float" just off the surface. The spacing is so close that even a single particle of dust could become jammed between the head and disk surface, destroying both (a phenomenon known as a *head crash*). Thus hard-disk systems are housed in cases that are sealed at the factory.

Several measurements are used to evaluate a disk system's performance: (1) **seek time** (the time required to move the read/write heads from one track to another); (2) **rotation delay** or **latency time** (half the time required for the disk to make a complete rotation, which is the average amount of time required for the desired data to rotate around to the read/write head once the head has been positioned over the desired track); (3) **access time** (the sum of seek time and rotation delay); and (4) **transfer rate** (the rate at which data can be transferred to or from the disk).

Hard-disk systems generally have significantly better characteristics than floppy systems. Since the read/write heads do not touch the disk surface in a hard-disk system, one finds rotation speeds of several thousand revolutions per minute, whereas disks in floppy-disk systems rotate on the order of 300 revolutions per minute. Consequently, transfer rates for hard-disk systems, usually measured in megabytes per second, are much greater than those associated with floppy-disk systems, which tend to be measured in kilobytes per second.

Since disk systems require physical motion for their operation, both hard and floppy systems suffer when compared to speeds within electronic circuitry. Delay times within an electronic circuit are measured in units of nanoseconds (billionths of a second) or less, whereas seek times, latency times, and access times of disk systems are measured in milliseconds (thousandths of a second). Thus the time required to retrieve information from a disk system can seem like an eternity to an electronic circuit awaiting a result.

Compact Disks

Another popular data storage technology is the compact disk (CD). These disks are 12 centimeters (approximately 5 inches) in diameter and consist of reflective material covered with a clear protective coating. Information is recorded on them by creating variations in their reflective surfaces. This information can then be retrieved by means of a laser beam that monitors irregularities on the reflective surface of the CD as it spins.

CD technology was originally applied to audio recordings using a recording format known as CD-DA (compact disk-digital audio), and the CDs used today for computer data storage use essentially the same format. In particular, information on these CDs is stored on a single track that spirals around the CD like a groove in an old-fashioned record; however, unlike old-fashioned records, the track on a CD spirals from the inside out (Figure 1.10). This track is divided into units called sectors, each with its own identifying markings and a capacity of 2KB of data, which equates to $^1/_{75}$ of a second of music in the case of audio recordings.

Information is stored on a CD at a uniform linear density over the entire spiraled track, which means that more information is stored in a loop around the outer portion of the spiral than in a loop around the inner portion. In turn, more sectors will be read in a single revolution of the disk when the laser beam is scanning the outer portion of the spiraled track than when the beam is scanning the inner portion. Thus, to obtain a uniform rate of data transfer, CD-DA players are designed to vary the rotation speed depending on the location of the laser beam. However, most CD drives used for computer data storage spin at a faster, constant speed and thus must accommodate variations in data transfer rates.

As a consequence of such design decisions, CD storage systems perform best when dealing with long, continuous strings of data, as when reproducing music. In contrast, when an application requires access to items of data in a random manner, the approach used in magnetic disk storage (individual, concentric tracks) outperforms the spiral approach used in CDs.

Figure 1.10

CD storage format

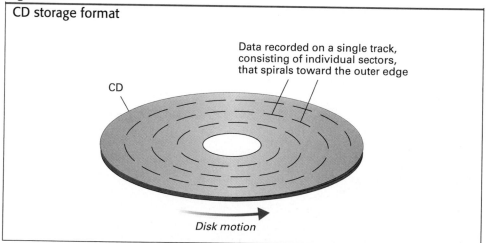

Traditional CDs have capacities in the range of 600 to 700MB. However, newer DVDs (Digital Versatile Disks), which are constructed from multiple, semi-transparent layers that can be distinguished by a precisely focused laser, provide storage capacities on order of several GB. Such disks are capable of storing lengthy multimedia presentations, including entire motion pictures.

Magnetic Tape

An older form of mass storage device uses magnetic tape (Figure 1.11). Here, information is recorded on the magnetic coating of a thin plastic tape that is wound on a reel for storage. To access the data, the tape is mounted in a device called a tape drive that typically can read, write, and rewind the tape under control of the computer. Tape drives range in size from small cartridge units, called streaming tape units, which use tape similar in appearance to that in stereo systems to older, large reel-to-reel units. Although the capacity of these devices depends on the format used, most can hold many gigabytes.

Modern streaming tape systems divide a tape into segments, each of which is magnetically marked by a formatting process similar to that of disk storage devices. Each of these segments contains several tracks that run parallel to one another lengthwise on the tape. These tracks can be accessed independently, meaning that the tape ultimately consists of numerous individual strings of bits in a manner similar to the sectors on a disk.

A major disadvantage of magnetic tape technology is that moving between different positions on a tape can be very time-consuming owing to the significant amount of tape that must be moved between the reels. Thus tape systems have much longer data access times than magnetic disk systems in which different sectors can be accessed by short movements of the read/write head. In turn, tape systems are not popular for on-line data storage. Instead, magnetic tape technology is used in off-line archival data storage applications where its high capacity, reliability, and cost efficiency

Figure 1.11

A magnetic tape storage mechanism

are beneficial, although advances in alternative technologies such as DVD are rapidly challenging this last vestige of magnetic tape.

File Storage and Retrieval

Information is stored in mass storage systems in large units called **files.** A typical file may consist of a complete text document, a photograph, a program, or a collection of data about the employees in a company. The physical properties of mass storage devices dictate that these files be stored and retrieved in multiple byte units. For example, each sector on a magnetic disk must be manipulated as one continuous string of bits. A block of data conforming to the physical characteristics of a storage device is called a **physical record.** Thus, a file stored in mass storage will typically consist of many physical records.

In contrast to this division into physical records, a file often has natural divisions determined by the information represented. For example, a file containing information regarding a company's employees would consist of multiple units, each consisting of the information about one employee. These naturally occurring blocks of data are called **logical records.** Moreover, logical records often consist of smaller units called **fields.** For example, a logical record containing information about an employee would probably consist of fields such as name, address, employee identification number, etc.

Logical record sizes rarely match the physical record size dictated by a mass storage device. In turn, one may find several logical records residing within a single physical record or perhaps a logical record split between two or more physical records (Figure 1.12). The result is that a certain amount of unscrambling is associated with retrieving data from mass storage systems. A common solution to this problem is to set aside an area of main memory that is large enough to hold several physical records and to use this memory space as a regrouping area. That is, blocks of data compatible

Figure 1.12

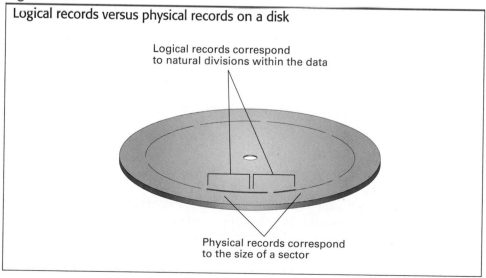

Logical records versus physical records on a disk

Logical records correspond
to natural divisions within the data

Physical records correspond
to the size of a sector

with physical records can be transferred between this main memory area and the mass storage system, while the data residing in the main memory area can be referenced in terms of logical records.

An area of memory used in this manner is called a **buffer.** In general, a buffer is a storage area used to hold data on a temporary basis, usually during the process of being transferred from one device to another. For example, modern printers contain memory circuitry of their own, a large part of which is used as a buffer for holding portions of a document that have been received by the printer but not yet printed.

Finally we should note that main memory, magnetic disks, compact disks, and magnetic tape exhibit decreasing degrees of random access to data. The addressing system used in main memory allows rapid random access to individual bytes of data. Magnetic disks provide random access only to entire sectors of data. Moreover, retrieving a sector involves seek and rotation delays. Compact disks also provide random access to individual sectors, but the delays encountered are greater than those for magnetic disks due to the additional time required to locate the spiraling track and to adjust the rotation speed of the disk. Finally, magnetic tape offers little in the way of random access. Modern tape systems mark positions on the tape so that different segments of the tape can be referenced individually, but the physical structure of the tape dictates that the retrieval time for segments far down the tape will be significant.

Questions/Exercises

1. What advantage does a hard-disk system gain from the fact that its disks spin faster than disks in a floppy-disk system?

2. When recording data on a multiple-disk storage system, should we fill a complete disk surface before starting on another surface, or should we first fill an entire cylinder before starting on another cylinder?

3. Why should the data in a reservation system that is constantly being updated be stored on a magnetic disk instead of on tape?

4. Sometimes, when modifying a document with a word processor, adding text does not increase the apparent size of the file in mass storage, but at other times the addition of a single symbol can increase the apparent size of the file by several hundred bytes. Why?

1.4 Representing Information as Bit Patterns

Having considered techniques for storing bits, we now consider how information can be encoded as bit patterns. Our study focuses on popular methods for encoding text, numerical data, images, and sound. Each of these systems has repercussions that are often visible to a typical computer user. Our goal is to understand enough about these techniques so that we can recognize their consequences for what they are.

Representing Text

Information in the form of text is normally represented by means of a code in which each of the different symbols in the text (such as the letters of the alphabet and punctuation marks) is assigned a unique bit pattern. The text is then represented as a long string of bits in which the successive patterns represent the successive symbols in the original text.

In the 1940s and 1950s, many such codes were designed and used in connection with different pieces of equipment, producing a corresponding proliferation of communication problems. To alleviate this situation, the **American National Standards Institute (ANSI,** pronounced "AN–see") adopted the **American Standard Code for Information Interchange (ASCII,** pronounced "AS–kee"). This code uses bit patterns of length seven to represent the upper- and lowercase letters of the English alphabet, punctuation symbols, the digits 0 through 9, and certain control information such as line feeds, carriage returns, and tabs. Today, ASCII is often extended to an eight-bit-per-symbol format by adding a 0 at the most significant end of each of the seven-bit patterns. This technique not only produces a code in which each pattern fits conveniently into a typical byte-size memory cell but also provides 128 additional bit patterns (those obtained by assigning the extra bit the value 1) that can represent symbols excluded in the original ASCII. Unfortunately, because vendors tend to use their own interpretations for these extra patterns, data in which these patterns appear often are not easily transported from one vendor's application to another.

Appendix A shows a portion of ASCII in an eight-bit-per-symbol format, and Figure 1.13 demonstrates that, in this system, the bit pattern

01001000   01100101   01101100   01101100   01101111   00101110

represents the message "Hello."

Although ACSII has been the dominant code for many years, other more extensive codes, capable of representing documents in a variety of languages, are now competing for popularity. One of these, **Unicode,** was developed through the cooperation of several of the leading manufacturers of hardware and software and is rapidly gaining support in the computing community. This code uses a unique pattern of 16 bits to represent each symbol. As a result, Unicode consists of 65,536 different bit patterns—enough to allow text written in such languages as Chinese, Japanese, and Hebrew to be represented.

Standards for a code that could compete with Unicode have been developed by the **International Organization for Standardization** (also known as **ISO,** in reference to the Greek word *isos,* meaning equal). Using patterns of 32 bits, this encoding system has the potential of representing billions of different symbols.

Figure 1.13

The message "Hello." in ASCII

01001000	01100101	01101100	01101100	01101111	00101110
H	e	l	l	o	.

The American National Standards Institute

The American National Standards Institute (ANSI) was founded in 1918 by a small consortium of engineering societies and government agencies as a nonprofit federation to coordinate the development of voluntary standards in the private sector. Today, ANSI membership includes more than 1300 businesses, professional organizations, trade associations, and government agencies. ANSI is headquartered in New York and represents the United States as a member body in the ISO. The Web site for the American National Standards Institute is at `http://www.ansi.org`.

Similar organizations in other countries include Standards Australia (Australia), Standards Council of Canada (Canada), China State Bureau of Quality and Technical Supervision (China), Deutsches Institur für Normung (Germany), Japanese Industrial Standards Committee (Japan), Dirección General de Normas (Mexico), State Committee of the Russian Federation for Standardization and Metrology (Russia), Swiss Association for Standardization (Switzerland), and British Standards Institution (United Kingdom).

A file consisting only of a long sequence of symbols encoded using ASCII or Unicode is often called a **text file.** It is important to distinguish between simple text files that are manipulated by utility programs called editors and the more elaborate files produced by word processors. Both consist of textual material. However, a text file contains only a character-by-character encoding of the text, whereas a file produced by a word processor contains numerous proprietary codes representing changes in fonts, alignment information, etc. Moreover, word processors may even use proprietary codes rather than a standard such as ASCII or Unicode for representing the text itself.

Representing Numeric Values

Storing information as encoded characters is inefficient when the information being recorded is purely numeric. To see why, consider the problem of storing the value 25. If we insist on storing it as encoded symbols in ASCII using one byte per symbol, we need a total of 16 bits. Moreover, the largest number we could store using 16 bits is 99. However, as we will shortly see, by using **binary notation** we can store any integer in the range from 0 to 65535 in these 16 bits. Thus, binary notation (or variations of it) is used extensively for encoded numeric data for computer storage.

Binary notation is a way of representing numeric values using only the digits 0 and 1 rather than the digits 0, 1, 2, 3, 4, 5, 6, 7, 8, and 9 as in the traditional decimal, or base ten, system. We will study the binary system more thoroughly in Section 1.5. For now, all we need is an elementary understanding of the system. For this purpose consider an old-fashioned car odometer whose display wheels contain only the digits 0 and 1 rather than the traditional digits 0 through 9. The odometer starts with a reading of all 0s, and as the car is driven for the first few miles, the rightmost 0 rotates to a 1. Then, as that 1 rotates back to a 0, it causes a 1 to appear to its left, producing the pattern 10. The 0 on the right then rotates to a 1, producing 11. Now the rightmost 1 rotates back to 0, causing the 1 to its left to rotate to a 0 as well. This in turn causes another 1 to appear in the third column, producing the pattern 100. In short, as we drive the car we see the following sequence of odometer readings:

```
0000
0001
0010
0011
0100
0101
0110
0111
1000
```

This sequence consists of the binary representations of the integers zero through eight. Although tedious, we could extend this counting technique to discover that the bit pattern consisting of sixteen 1s represents the value 65535, which confirms our claim that any integer in the range from 0 to 65535 can be encoded using 16 bits.

Due to this efficiency, it is common to store numeric information in a form of binary notation rather than in encoded symbols. We say "a form of binary notation" because the straightforward binary system just described is only the basis for several numeric storage techniques used within machines. Some of these variations of the binary system are discussed later in this chapter. For now, we merely note that a system called two's complement notation (see Section 1.6) is common for storing whole numbers because it provides a convenient method for representing negative numbers as well as positive. For representing numbers with fractional parts such as $4\frac{1}{2}$ or $\frac{3}{4}$, another technique, called floating-point notation (see Section 1.7), is used.

ISO—The International Organization for Standardization

The International Organization for Standardization (more commonly called ISO) was established in 1947 as a worldwide federation of standardization bodies, one from each country. Today, it is headquartered in Geneva, Switzerland and has more than 100 member bodies as well as numerous correspondent members. (A correspondent member is usually a standardization body from a country that does not have a nationally recognized standardization body. Such members cannot participate directly in the development of standards but are kept informed of ISO activities.) ISO maintains a Web site at http://www.iso.ch.

Representing Images

Today's computer applications involve more than just text and numeric data. They include pictures, audio, and video. In comparison to character and numeric storage systems, the techniques for representing data of these additional forms are in their infancy and consequently are not as standardized across the data processing community.

Popular techniques for representing images can be classified into two categories: **bit map techniques** and **vector techniques.** In the case of bit map techniques, an image is considered to be a collection of dots, each of which is called a **pixel,** short for "picture element." A black and white image is then represented as a long string of bits representing the rows of pixels in the image, where each bit is either 1 or 0 depending on whether the corresponding pixel is black or white. In the case of color images, each pixel is represented by a combination of bits indicating the color of that pixel. When bit map techniques are used, the resulting bit pattern is called a bit map, meaning that the bit pattern representing the image is little more than a map of the image.

Many of today's computer peripherals, such as facsimile machines, video cameras, and scanners, convert color images into bit map form. These devices generally record the color of each pixel as three components—a red component, a green component, and a blue component—corresponding to the three primary colors. One byte is used to represent the intensity of each color component. In turn, three bytes of storage are required to represent a single pixel in the original image. This three-component-per-pixel approach also corresponds to the way in which many computer screens display images. These devices display a myriad of pixels, each consisting of three components—one red, one green, and one blue—as is readily apparent via close inspection of the screen. (You might prefer to use a magnifying glass.)

The three-byte-per-pixel format means that an image consisting of 1024 rows of 1024 pixels (a typical photograph) requires several megabytes of storage, which exceeds the capacity of a typical floppy disk. In Section 1.8, we will consider two popular techniques (GIF and JPEG) that are used to compress such images into more manageable sizes.

One disadvantage of bit map techniques is that an image cannot be rescaled easily to any arbitrary size. Essentially, the only way to enlarge the image is to make the pixels bigger, which leads to a grainy appearance. (This is the technique called "digital zoom" used in digital cameras as opposed to "optical zoom" that is obtained by adjusting the camera lens.) Vector techniques provide a means of overcoming this scaling problem. Using this approach, an image is represented as a collection of lines and curves. Such a description leaves the details of how the lines and curves are drawn to the device that ultimately produces the image rather than insisting that the device reproduce a particular pixel pattern.

The various fonts available on today's printers and monitors are usually encoded using vector techniques in order to provide flexibility in character size, resulting in **scalable fonts.** For example, TrueType (developed by Microsoft and Apple Computer) is a system for describing how symbols in text are to be drawn. Likewise, PostScript (developed by Adobe Systems) provides a means of describing characters as well as more general pictorial data. Vector representations are also popular in computer-aided design (CAD) systems in which line drawings of three-dimensional objects are displayed and manipulated on computer screens. However, vector techniques are not able to provide the photographic quality images that are available via bit maps. This is why bit map techniques are used in today's digital cameras.

Representing Sound

The most generic method of encoding audio information for computer storage and manipulation is to sample the amplitude of the sound wave at regular intervals and record the series of values obtained. For instance, the series 0, 1.5, 2.0, 1.5, 2.0, 3.0, 4.0, 3.0, 0 would represent a sound wave that rises in amplitude, falls briefly, rises to a higher level, and then drops back to 0 (Figure 1.14). This technique, using a sample rate of 8000 samples per second, has been used for years in long-distance voice telephone communication. The voice at one end of the communication is encoded as numeric values representing the amplitude of the voice every eight-thousandth of a second. These numeric values are then transmitted over the communication line to the receiving end, where they are used to reproduce the sound of the voice.

Although 8000 samples per second may seem to be a rapid rate, it is not sufficient for high-fidelity music recordings. To obtain the quality sound reproduction obtained by today's musical CDs, a sample rate of 44,100 samples per second is used. The data obtained from each sample are represented in 16 bits (32 bits for stereo recordings). Consequently, each second of music recorded in stereo requires more than a million bits.

An alternative encoding system known as Musical Instrument Digital Interface (MIDI, pronounced "MID–ee") is widely used in the music synthesizers found in electronic keyboards, for video game sound, and for sound effects accompanying Web sites. By encoding directions for producing music on a synthesizer rather than encoding the sound itself, MIDI avoids the large storage requirements of the sampling technique. More precisely, MIDI encodes what instrument is to play which note for what duration of time, which means that a clarinet playing the note D for two seconds can

Figure 1.14

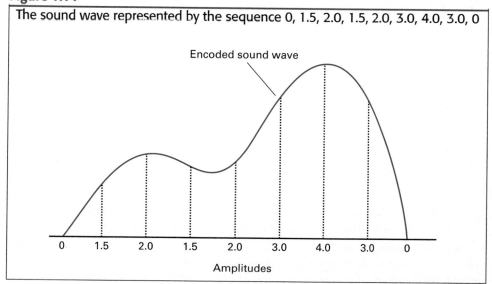

The sound wave represented by the sequence 0, 1.5, 2.0, 1.5, 2.0, 3.0, 4.0, 3.0, 0

Encoded sound wave

| 0 | 1.5 | 2.0 | 1.5 | 2.0 | 3.0 | 4.0 | 3.0 | 0 |

Amplitudes

be encoded in three bytes rather than more than two million bits when sampled at a rate of 44,100 samples per second.

In short, MIDI can be thought of as a way of encoding the sheet music read by a performer rather than the performance itself, and in turn, a MIDI "recording" can sound significantly different when performed on different synthesizers.

Questions/Exercises

1. Here is a message encoded in ASCII using eight bits per symbol. What does it say?
   01000011 01101111 01101101 01110000 01110101 01110100
   01100101 01110010 00100000 01010011 01100011 01101001
   01100101 01101110 01100011 01100101

2. In the ASCII code, what is the relationship between the codes for an uppercase letter and the same letter in lowercase?

3. Encode these sentences in ASCII:
   a. Where are you?
   b. "How?" Cheryl asked.
   c. 2 + 3 = 5.

4. Describe a device from everyday life that can be in either of two states, such as a flag on a flagpole that is either up or down. Assign the symbol 1 to one of the states and 0 to the other, and show how the ASCII representation for the letter b would appear when stored with such bits.

5. Convert each of the following binary representations to its equivalent base ten form:
   a. 0101   b. 1001   c. 1011
   d. 0110   e. 10000   f. 10010

6. Convert each of the following base ten representations to its equivalent binary form:
   a. 6   b. 13   c. 11
   d. 18   e. 27   f. 4

7. What is the largest numeric value that could be represented with three bytes if each digit were encoded using one ASCII pattern per byte? What if binary notation were used?

8. An alternative to hexadecimal notation for representing bit patterns is *dotted decimal notation* in which each byte in the pattern is represented by its base ten equivalent. In turn, these byte representations are separated by periods. For example, 12.5 represents the pattern 0000110000000101 (the byte 00001100 is represented by 12, and 00000101 is represented by 5), and the pattern 1000100000001000000000111 is represented by 136.16.7. Represent each of the following bit patterns in dotted decimal notation.
   a. 0000111100001111   b. 001100110000000010000000   c. 0000101010100000

9. What is an advantage of representing images via vector techniques as opposed to bit map techniques? What about bit map techniques as opposed to vector techniques?

10. Suppose a stereo recording of one hour of music is encoded using a sample rate of 44,100 samples per second as discussed in the text. How does the size of the encoded version compare to the storage capacity of a CD?

1.5 The Binary System

In Section 1.4 we saw that binary notation is a means of representing numeric values using only the digits 0 and 1 rather than the ten digits 0 through 9 that are used in the more common base ten notational system. It is time now to look at binary notation more thoroughly.

Binary Notation

Recall that in the base ten system, each position in a representation is associated with a quantity. In the representation 375, the 5 is in the position associated with the quantity one, the 7 is in the position associated with ten, and the 3 is in the position associated with the quantity one hundred (Figure 1.15a). Each quantity is ten times that of the quantity to its right. The value represented by the entire expression is obtained by multiplying the value of each digit by the quantity associated with that digit's position and then adding those products. To illustrate, the pattern 375 represents (3 × hundred) + (7 × ten) + (5 × one).

The position of each digit in binary notation is also associated with a quantity, except that the quantity associated with each position is twice the quantity associated with the position to its right. More precisely, the rightmost digit in a binary representation is associated with the quantity one (2^0), the next position to the left is associated with two (2^1), the next is associated with four (2^2), the next with eight (2^3), and so on. For example, in the binary representation 1011, the rightmost 1 is in the position associated with the quantity one, the 1 next to it is in the position associated with two, the 0 is in the position associated with four, and the leftmost 1 is in the position associated with eight (Figure 1.15b).

To extract the value represented by a binary representation, we follow the same procedure as in base ten—we multiply the value of each digit by the quantity associated

Figure 1.15

The base ten and binary systems

a. Base ten system

3 7 5 — Representation

Hundred / Ten / One — Position's quantity

b. Base two system

1 0 1 1 — Representation

Eight / Four / Two / One — Position's quantity

with its position and add the results. For example, the value represented by 100101 is 37, as shown in Figure 1.16. Note that since binary notation uses only the digits 0 and 1, this multiply-and-add process reduces merely to adding the quantities associated with the positions occupied by 1s. Thus the binary pattern 1011 represents the value eleven, because the 1s are found in the positions associated with the quantities one, two, and eight.

In Section 1.4 we learned how to count in binary notation, which allowed us to encode small integers. For finding binary representations of large values, you may prefer the approach described by the algorithm in Figure 1.17. Let us apply this algorithm to the value thirteen (Figure 1.18). We first divide thirteen by two, obtaining a quotient of six and a remainder of one. Since the quotient was not zero, Step 2 tells us to divide the quotient (six) by two, obtaining a new quotient of three and a remainder of zero. The newest quotient is still not zero, so we divide it by two, obtaining a quotient of one and a remainder of one. Once again, we divide the newest quotient (one) by two, this time obtaining a quotient of zero and a remainder of one. Since we have now acquired a quotient of zero, we move on to Step 3, where we learn that the binary representation of the original value (thirteen) is 1101.

Figure 1.16

Decoding the binary representation 100101

Binary Addition

To add two integers represented in binary notation, we begin, just as we did with base ten in elementary school, by memorizing the addition facts (Figure 1.19). Using these

Figure 1.17

An algorithm for finding the binary representation of a positive integer

Step 1.   Divide the value by two and record the remainder.

Step 2.   As long as the quotient obtained is not zero, continue to divide the newest quotient by two and record the remainder.

Step 3.   Now that a quotient of zero has been obtained, the binary representation of the original value consists of the remainders listed from right to left in the order they were recorded.

Figure 1.18

Applying the algorithm in Figure 1.15 to obtain the binary representation of thirteen

facts, we add two values as follows: First, add the digits in the right-hand column, write the least significant digit of this sum under the column, carry the more significant digit of the sum (if there is one) to the next column to the left, and proceed by adding that column. For example, to solve the problem

        00111010
      +00011011

we begin by adding the rightmost 0 and 1; we obtain 1, which we write below the column. Now we add the 1 and 1 from the next column, obtaining 10. We write the 0 from this 10 under the column and carry the 1 to the top of the next column. At this point, our solution looks like this:

             1
        00111010
      +00011011
              01

Figure 1.19

The binary addition facts

$$
\begin{array}{cccc}
  0 &   1 &   0 &   1 \\
+ 0 & + 0 & + 1 & + 1 \\
\hline
  0 &   1 &   1 &   10
\end{array}
$$

We add the 1, 0, and 0 in the next column, obtain 1, and write the 1 under this column. The 1 and 1 from the next column total 10; we write the 0 under the column and carry the 1 to the next column. Now our solution looks like this:

```
       1
  00111010
 +00011011
      0101
```

The 1, 1, and 1 in the next column total 11; we write the low-order 1 under the column and carry the other 1 to the top of the next column. We add that 1 to the 1 and 0 already in that column to obtain 10. Again, we record the low-order 0 and carry the 1 to the next column. We now have

```
       1
  00111010
 +00011011
    010101
```

Now we add the 1, 0, and 0 from the next to the last column, obtaining 1, which we record below the column with nothing to carry. Finally, we add the last column, which yields 0, and record this under the column. Our final solution is this:

```
  00111010
 +00011011
  01010101
```

Fractions in Binary

To extend binary notation to accommodate fractional values, we use a **radix point** in the same role as the decimal point in decimal notation. That is, the digits to the left of the point represent the integer part of the value and are interpreted as in the binary system discussed previously. The digits to its right represent the fractional part of the value and are interpreted in a manner similar to the other bits, except their positions are assigned fractional quantities. That is, the first position to the right of the radix is assigned the quantity $\frac{1}{2}$, the next position the quantity $\frac{1}{4}$, the next $\frac{1}{8}$, and so on. Note that this is merely a continuation of the rule stated previously: Each position is assigned a quantity twice the size of the one to its right. With these quantities assigned to the bit positions, decoding a binary representation containing a radix point requires the same procedure as used without a radix point. In particular, we multiply each bit value by the quantity assigned to that bit's position in the representation. To illustrate, the binary representation 101.101 decodes to $5\frac{5}{8}$, as shown in Figure 1.20.

For addition, the techniques applied in the base ten system are also applicable in binary. That is, to add two binary representations having radix points, we merely align the radix points and apply the same addition process as before. For example, 10.011 added to 100.11 produces 111.001, as shown here:

Figure 1.20

Decoding the binary representation 101.101

```
    0010.011
+   100.110
    0111.001
```

Questions/Exercises

1. Convert each of the following binary representations to its equivalent base ten form:

    a. 101010   b. 100001   c. 10111

    d. 0110   e. 11111

2. Convert each of the following base ten representations to its equivalent binary form:

    a. 32   b. 64   c. 96

    d. 15   e. 27

3. Convert each of the following binary representations to its equivalent base ten form:

    a. 11.01   b. 101.111   c. 10.1

    d. 110.011   e. 0.101

4. Express the following values in binary notation:

    a. $4\frac{1}{2}$ b. $2\frac{3}{4}$ c. $1\frac{1}{8}$

    d. $\frac{5}{16}$ e. $5\frac{5}{8}$

5. Perform the following additions in binary notation:

    a. 11011   b. 1010.001   c. 11111   d. 111.11

       +1100   +1.101   +0001   +00.01

1.6 Storing Integers

Mathematicians have long been interested in numeric notational systems, and many of their ideas have turned out to be very compatible with the design of digital circuitry. In this section we consider two of these notational systems, two's complement notation and excess notation, which are used for representing integer values in computing equipment. These systems are based on the binary system but have additional properties that make them more compatible with computer design. With these advantages, however, come disadvantages as well. Our goal is to understand these properties and how they affect computer usage.

Two's Complement Notation

The most popular system for representing integers within today's computers is **two's complement notation.** This system uses a fixed number of bits to represent each of the values in the system. In today's equipment, it is common to use a two's complement system in which each value is represented by a pattern of 32 bits. Such a large system allows a wide range of numbers to be represented but is awkward for demonstration purposes. Thus, to study the properties of two's complement systems, we will concentrate on smaller systems.

Figure 1.21 shows two complete two's complement systems—one based on bit patterns of length three, the other based on bit patterns of length four. Such a system is constructed by starting with a string of 0s of the appropriate length and then counting in binary until the pattern consisting of a 0 followed by 1s is reached. These patterns represent the values 0, 1, 2, 3, ... The patterns representing negative values are obtained by starting with a string of 1s of the appropriate length and then counting backward in binary until the pattern consisting of a 1 followed by 0s is reached. These patterns represent the values –1, –2, –3, ... (If counting backward in binary is difficult for you, merely start at the very bottom of the table with the pattern consisting of a 1 followed by 0s, and count up to the pattern consisting of all 1s.)

Note that in a two's complement system, the leftmost bit of a bit pattern indicates the sign of the value represented. Thus, the leftmost bit is often called the **sign bit.** In a two's complement system, negative values are represented by the patterns whose sign bits are 1; nonnegative values are represented by patterns whose sign bits are 0.

In a two's complement system, there is a convenient relationship between the patterns representing positive and negative values of the same magnitude. They are identical when read from right to left, up to and including the first 1. From there on, the patterns are complements of one another. (The **complement** of a pattern is the pattern obtained by changing all the 0s to 1s and all the 1s to 0s; 0110 and 1001 are complements.) For example, in the four-bit system in Figure 1.21 the patterns representing 2 and –2 both end with 10, but the pattern representing 2 begins with 00, whereas the pattern representing –2 begins with 11. This observation leads to an algorithm for converting back and forth between bit patterns representing positive and negative values of the same magnitude. We merely copy the original pattern from right to left until a 1 has been copied, then we complement the remaining bits as they are copied (Figure 1.22).

Figure 1.21

Two's complement notation systems

a. Using patterns of length three

Bit pattern	Value represented
011	3
010	2
001	1
000	0
111	−1
110	−2
101	−3
100	−4

b. Using patterns of length four

Bit pattern	Value represented
0111	7
0110	6
0101	5
0100	4
0011	3
0010	2
0001	1
0000	0
1111	−1
1110	−2
1101	−3
1100	−4
1011	−5
1010	−6
1001	−7
1000	−8

Understanding these basic properties of two's complement systems also leads to an algorithm for decoding two's complement representations. If the pattern to be decoded has a sign bit of 0, we need merely read the value as though the pattern were a binary representation. For example, 0110 represents the value 6, because 110 is binary for 6. If the pattern to be decoded has a sign bit of 1, we know the value represented

Figure 1.22

Coding the value -6 in two's complement notation using four bits

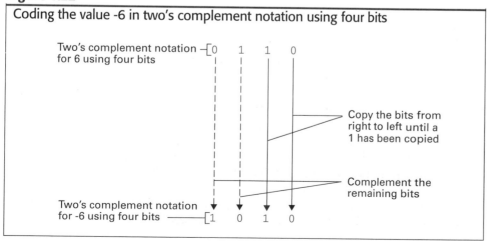

Two's complement notation for 6 using four bits   0 1 1 0

Copy the bits from right to left until a 1 has been copied

Complement the remaining bits

Two's complement notation for -6 using four bits   1 0 1 0 is negative, and all that remains is to find the magnitude of the value. We do this by copying the original pattern from right to left until a 1 has been copied, then complementing the remaining bits as they are copied, and finally decoding the pattern obtained as though it were a binary representation.

For example, to decode the pattern 1010, we first recognize that since the sign bit is 1, the value represented is negative. Hence, we convert the pattern to 0110, recognize that this represents 6, and conclude that the original pattern represents –6.

Addition in Two's Complement Notation

To add values represented in two's complement notation, we apply the same algorithm that we used for binary addition, except that all bit patterns, including the answer, are the same length. This means that when adding in a two's complement system, any extra bit generated on the left of the answer by a final carry must be truncated. Thus "adding" 0101 and 0010 produces 0111, and "adding" 0111 and 1011 results in 0010 (0111 + 1011 = 10010, which is truncated to 0010).

With this understanding, consider the three addition problems in Figure 1.23. In each case, we have translated the problem into two's complement notation (using bit patterns of length four), performed the addition process previously described, and decoded the result back into our usual base ten notation.

Observe that if we were to use the traditional techniques taught in elementary school, the third problem would require an entirely different process (subtraction) than the previous problems. On the other hand, by translating the problems into two's complement notation, we can compute the answer in all cases by applying the same addition algorithm. This is a major benefit of two's complement notation: Addition of any combination of signed numbers can be accomplished using the same algorithm and thus the same circuitry.

In contrast to elementary schoolchildren, who must first learn to add and later to subtract, a machine using two's complement notation needs to know only how to add and negate. For example, the subtraction problem 7 – 5 is the same as the addition problem

Figure 1.23

Addition problems converted to two's complement notation

Problem in base ten	Problem in two's complement	Answer in base ten
3 + 2	0011 + 0010 0101	5
–3 + –2	1101 + 1110 1011	–5
7 + –5	0111 + 1011 0010	2

7 + (–5). Consequently, if a machine were asked to subtract 5 (stored as 0101) from 7 (stored as 0111), it would first change the 5 to –5 (represented as 1011) and then perform the addition process of 0111 + 1011 to obtain 0010, which represents 2, as follows:

$$
\begin{array}{ccccc}
7 & & 0111 & & 0111 \\
\underline{-5} & \rightarrow & \underline{-0101} & \rightarrow & \underline{+1011} \\
& & & & 0010 \quad \rightarrow \quad 2
\end{array}
$$

We see, then, that when two's complement notation is used to represent numeric values, a circuit for addition combined with a circuit for negating a value is sufficient for solving both addition and subtraction problems. (Such circuits are shown and explained in Appendix B.)

The Problem of Overflow

One problem we have avoided in the preceding examples is that, in any two's complement system, there is a limit to the size of the values that can be represented. When using two's complement with patterns of four bits, the value 9 has no pattern associated with it, which means that we cannot hope to obtain the correct answer to the problem 5 + 4. In fact, the result would appear as –7. Such an error is called **overflow,** the problem that occurs when the value to be represented falls outside the range of values that can be represented. When using two's complement notation, this might occur when adding two positive values or when adding two negative values. In either case, the condition can be detected by checking the sign bit of the answer. That is, an overflow is indicated if the addition of two positive values results in the pattern for a negative value or if the sum of two negative values appears to be positive.

Of course, because most machines manipulate longer bit patterns than we have used in our examples, larger values can be manipulated without causing an overflow. Today, it is common to use patterns of 32 bits for storing values in two's complement notation, allowing for positive values as large as 2,147,483,647 to accumulate before overflow occurs. If still larger values are needed, longer bit patterns can be used or perhaps the units of measure can be changed. For instance, finding a solution in terms of miles instead of inches results in smaller numbers being used and might still provide the accuracy required.

The point is that computers can make mistakes. So, the person using the machine must be aware of the dangers involved. One problem is that computer programmers and users become complacent and ignore the fact that small values can accumulate to produce large numbers. For example, in the past it was common to use patterns of 16 bits for representing values in two's complement notation, which meant that overflow would not occur until the value $2^{15} = 32,768$ was reached. On September 19, 1989, a hospital computer system malfunctioned after years of reliable service. Close inspection revealed that this date was 32,768 days after January 1, 1900. What do you think the problem turned out to be?

Excess Notation

Another method of representing integer values is **excess notation.** Each of the values in an excess notation system is represented by a bit pattern of the same length. To establish an excess system, we first select the pattern length to be used, then write down all the different bit patterns of that length in the order they would appear if we were counting in binary. Next, we observe that the first pattern with a 1 as its most significant bit appears approximately halfway through the list. We pick this pattern to represent zero; the patterns following this are used to represent 1, 2, 3, . . . ; and the patterns preceding it are used for –1, –2, –3, ... The resulting code, when using patterns of length four, is shown in Figure 1.24. There we see that the value 5 is represented by the pattern 1101 and –5 is represented by 0011. (Note that the difference between an excess system and a two's complement system is that the sign bits are reversed.)

The system represented in Figure 1.24 is known as excess eight notation. To understand why, first interpret each of the patterns in the code using the traditional binary system and then compare these results to the values represented in the excess notation. In each case, you will find that the binary interpretation exceeds the excess notation interpretation by the value 8. For example, the pattern 1100 normally represents the value 12, but in our excess system it represents 4; 0000 normally represents 0, but in the excess system it represents –8. In a similar manner, an excess system based on patterns of length five would be called excess 16 notation, because the pattern 10000, for instance, would be used to represent 0 rather than representing its usual value of 16. Likewise, you may want to confirm that the three-bit excess system would be known as excess four notation (Figure 1.25).

Figure 1.24

An excess eight conversion table

Bit pattern	Value represented
1111	7
1110	6
1101	5
1100	4
1011	3
1010	2
1001	1
1000	0
0111	–1
0110	–2
0101	–3
0100	–4
0011	–5
0010	–6
0001	–7
0000	–8

Figure 1.25

An excess notation system using bit patterns of length three

Bit pattern	Value represented
111	3
110	2
101	1
100	0
011	−1
010	−2
001	−3
000	−4

Questions/Exercises

1. Convert each of the following two's complement representations to its equivalent base ten form:

   a. 00011   b. 01111   c. 11100

   d. 11010   e. 00000   f. 10000

2. Convert each of the following base ten representations to its equivalent two's complement form using patterns of eight bits:

   a. 6   b. −6   c. −17

   d. 13   e. −1   f. 0

3. Suppose the following bit patterns represent values stored in two's complement notation. Find the two's complement representation of the negative of each value:

   a. 00000001   b. 01010101   c. 11111100

   d. 11111110   e. 00000000   f. 01111111

4. Suppose a machine stores numbers in two's complement notation. What are the largest and smallest numbers that could be stored if the machine uses bit patterns of the following lengths?

   a. four   b. six   c. eight

5. In the following problems, each bit pattern represents a value stored in two's complement notation. Find the answer to each problem in two's complement notation by performing the addition process described in the text. Then check your work by translating the problem and your answer into base ten notation.

a. 0101	b. 0011	c. 0101	d. 1110	e. 1010
+0010	+0001	+1010	+0011	+1110

6. Solve each of the following problems in two's complement notation, but this time watch for overflow and indicate which answers are incorrect because of this phenomenon.

a. 0100	b. 0101	c. 1010	d. 1010	e. 0111
+0011	+0110	+1010	+0111	+0001

7. Translate each of the following problems from base ten notation into two's complement notation using bit patterns of length four, then convert each problem to an equivalent addition problem (as a machine might do), and perform the addition. Check your answers by converting them back to base ten notation.

   a. 6   b. 3   c. 4   d. 2   e. 1
   $-(-1)$ -2 -6 $-(-4)$ -5

8. Can overflow ever occur when adding values in two's complement notation when one value is positive and the other is negative? Explain your answer.

9. Convert each of the following excess eight representations to its equivalent base ten form without referring to the table in the text:

   a. 1110   b. 0111   c. 1000
   d. 0010   e. 0000   f. 1001

10. Convert each of the following base ten representations to its equivalent excess eight form without referring to the table in the text:

    a. 5   b. −5   c. 3
    d. 0   e. 7   f. −8

11. Can the value 9 be represented in excess eight notation? What about representing 6 in excess four notation? Explain your answer.

Analog Versus Digital

Prior to the 21st century, many researchers debated the pros and cons of digital versus analog technology. In a digital system, a value is encoded as a series of digits and then stored using several devices, each representing one of the digits. In an analog system, each value is stored in a single device that can represent any value within a continuous range.

Let us compare the two approaches in terms of buckets of water. To simulate a digital system, we could agree to let an empty bucket represent the digit 0 and a full bucket represent the digit 1. Then we could store a numeric value in a row of buckets using floating-point notation (see Section 1.7). In contrast, we could simulate an analog system by partially filling a single bucket to the point at which the water level represented the numeric value being represented. At first glance, the analog system may appear to be more accurate since it would not suffer from the truncation errors inherent in the digital system. However, any movement of the bucket in the analog system could cause errors in detecting the water level, whereas a significant amount of sloshing would have to occur in the digital system before the distinction between a full bucket and an empty bucket would be blurred. Thus the digital system would be less sensitive to error than the analog system. This robustness is a major reason why many applications that were originally based on analog technology (such as telephone communication, audio recordings, and television) are shifting to digital technologies.

1.7 Storing Fractions

In contrast to the storage of integers, the storage of a value with a fractional part requires that we store not only the pattern of 0s and 1s representing its binary representation but also the position of the radix point. A popular way of doing this is based on scientific notation and is called **floating-point notation.**

Floating-Point Notation

Let us explain floating-point notation with an example using only one byte of storage. Although machines normally use much longer patterns, this eight-bit format is representative of actual systems and serves to demonstrate the important concepts without the clutter of long bit patterns.

We first designate the high-order bit of the byte as the sign bit. Once again, a 0 in the sign bit will mean that the value stored is nonnegative, and a 1 will mean that the value is negative. Next, we divide the remaining seven bits of the byte into two groups, or fields, the **exponent field** and the **mantissa field.** Let us designate the three bits following the sign bit as the exponent field and the remaining four bits as the mantissa field. Figure 1.26 illustrates how the byte is divided.

We can explain the meaning of the fields by considering the following example. Suppose a byte contains the bit pattern 01101011. Analyzing this pattern with the preceding format, we see that the sign bit is 0, the exponent is 110, and the mantissa is 1011. To decode the byte, we first extract the mantissa and place a radix point on its left side, obtaining

.1011

Next, we extract the contents of the exponent field (110) and interpret it as an integer stored using the three-bit excess method (see again Figure 1.25). Thus the pattern in the exponent field in our example represents a positive 2. This tells us to move the radix in our solution to the right by two bits. (A negative exponent would mean to move the radix to the left.) Consequently, we obtain

10.11

which is the binary representation for $2\frac{3}{4}$. Next, we note that the sign bit in our example is 0; the value represented is thus nonnegative. We conclude that the byte 01101011 represents $2\frac{3}{4}$.

Figure 1.26

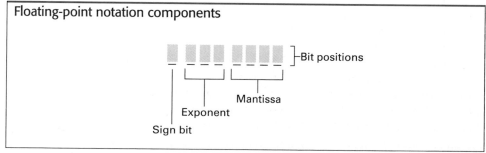

Floating-point notation components

As another example, consider the byte 10111100. We extract the mantissa to obtain

.1100

and move the radix one bit to the left, since the exponent field (011) represents the value −1. We therefore have

.01100

which represents $\frac{3}{8}$. Since the sign bit in the original pattern is 1, the value stored is negative. We conclude that the pattern 10111100 represents $-\frac{3}{8}$.

To store a value using floating-point notation, we reverse the preceding process. For example, to encode $1\frac{1}{8}$, first we express it in binary notation and obtain 1.001. Next, we copy the bit pattern into the mantissa field from left to right, starting with the leftmost 1 in the binary representation. At this point, the byte looks like this:

_ _ _ _ 1 0 0 1

We must now fill in the exponent field. To this end, we imagine the contents of the mantissa field with a radix point at its left and determine the number of bits and the direction the radix must be moved to obtain the original binary number. In our example, we see that the radix in .1001 must be moved one bit to the right to obtain 1.001. The exponent should therefore be a positive one, so we place 101 (which is positive one in excess four notation) in the exponent field. Finally, we fill the sign bit with 0 because the value being stored is nonnegative. The finished byte looks like this:

0 1 0 1 1 0 0 1

There is a subtle point you may have missed when filling in the mantissa field. The rule is to copy the bit pattern appearing in the binary representation from left to right, starting with the leftmost 1. To clarify, consider the process of storing the value $\frac{3}{8}$, which is .011 in binary notation. In this case the mantissa will be

_ _ _ _ 1 1 0 0

It will not be

_ _ _ _ 0 1 1 0

This is because we fill in the mantissa field *starting with the leftmost 1* that appears in the binary representation. This rule eliminates the possibility of multiple representations for the same value. It also means that the representation for all nonzero values will have a mantissa that starts with 1. This representation is said to be in **normalized form.** Note that the value zero must be a special case; its floating-point representation is a bit pattern of all 0s.

Truncation Errors

Let us consider the annoying problem that occurs if we try to store the value $2\frac{5}{8}$ with our one-byte floating-point system. We first write $2\frac{5}{8}$ in binary, which gives us 10.101. But when we copy this into the mantissa field, we run out of room, and the rightmost

1 STORING FRACTIONS 55

1 (which represents the last ⅛) is lost (Figure 1.27). If we ignore this problem for now and continue by filling in the exponent field and the sign bit, we end up with the bit pattern 01101010, which represents 2½ instead of 2⅝. What has occurred is called a **truncation error,** or **round-off error**—meaning that part of the value being stored is lost because the mantissa field is not large enough.

The significance of such errors can be reduced by using a longer mantissa field. In fact, most computers manufactured today use at least 32 bits for storing values in floating-point notation instead of the 8 bits we have used here. This also allows for a longer exponent field at the same time. Even with these longer formats, however, there are still times when more accuracy is required.

Another source of truncation errors is a phenomenon that you are already accustomed to in base ten notation: the problem of nonterminating expansions, such as those found when trying to express ⅓ in decimal form. Some values cannot be accurately expressed regardless of how many digits we use.

The difference between our normal base ten notation and binary notation is that more values have nonterminating representations in binary than in decimal notation. For example, the value one-tenth is nonterminating when expressed in binary. Imagine the problems this might cause the unwary person using floating-point notation to store and manipulate dollars and cents. In particular, if the dollar is used as the unit of measure, the value of a dime could not be stored accurately. A solution in this case is to manipulate the data in units of pennies so that all values are integers that can be accurately stored using a method such as two's complement.

Truncation errors and their related problems are an everyday concern for people working in the area of numerical analysis. This branch of mathematics deals with the problems involved when doing actual computations that are often massive and require significant accuracy.

Figure 1.27

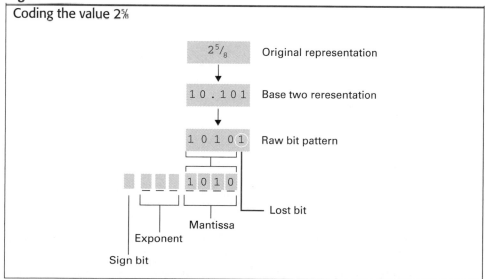

Coding the value 2⅝

The following is an example that would warm the heart of any numerical analyst. Suppose we are asked to add the following three values using our one-byte floating-point notation defined previously:

$$2\tfrac{1}{2} + \tfrac{1}{8} + \tfrac{1}{8}$$

If we add the values in the order listed, we first add $2\tfrac{1}{2}$ to $\tfrac{1}{8}$ and obtain $2\tfrac{5}{8}$, which in binary is 10.101. Unfortunately, because this value cannot be stored accurately (as seen previously), the result of our first step ends up being stored as $2\tfrac{1}{2}$ (which is the same as one of the values we were adding). The next step is to add this result to the last $\tfrac{1}{8}$. Here again a truncation error occurs, and our final result turns out to be the incorrect answer $2\tfrac{1}{2}$.

Now let us add the values in the opposite order. We first add $\tfrac{1}{8}$ to $\tfrac{1}{8}$ to obtain $\tfrac{1}{4}$. In binary this is .01; so the result of our first step is stored in a byte as 00111000, which is accurate. We now add this $\tfrac{1}{4}$ to the next value in the list, $2\tfrac{1}{2}$, and obtain $2\tfrac{3}{4}$, which we can accurately store in a byte as 01101011. The result this time is the correct answer.

In summary, when adding numeric values, the order in which they are added can be important. The problem is that if a very large number is added to a very small number, the small number may be truncated. Thus, the general rule for adding multiple values is to add the smaller values together first, in hopes that they will accumulate to a value that is significant when added to the larger values. This was the phenomenon experienced in the preceding example.

Designers of today's commercial software packages do a good job of shielding the uneducated user from problems such as this. In a typical spreadsheet system, correct answers will be obtained unless the values being added differ in size by a factor of 10^{16} or more. Thus, if you found it necessary to add one to the value

10,000,000,000,000,000

you may get the answer

10,000,000,000,000,000

rather than

10,000,000,000,000,001

Such problems are significant in applications (such as navigational systems) in which minor errors can be compounded in additional computations and ultimately produce significant consequences, but for the typical PC user this degree of accuracy is quite sufficient.

Questions/Exercises

1. Decode the following bit patterns using the floating-point format discussed in the text:
   a. 01001010   b. 01101101   c. 00111001
   d. 11011100   e. 10101011

2. Encode the following values into the floating-point format discussed in the text. Indicate the occurrence of truncation errors.
   a. $2\tfrac{3}{4}$ b. $5\tfrac{1}{4}$ c. 3/4   d. $-3\tfrac{1}{2}$ e. $-4\tfrac{3}{8}$

3. In terms of the floating-point format discussed in the text, which of the patterns 01001001 and 00111101 represents the larger value? Describe a simple procedure for determining which of two patterns represents the larger value.

4. When using the floating-point format discussed in the text, what is the largest value that can be represented? What is the smallest positive value that can be represented?

1.8 Data Compression

For the purpose of storing or transferring data, it is often helpful (and sometimes mandatory) to reduce the size of the data involved. The technique for accomplishing this is called **data compression.** We begin this section by considering some generic data compression methods and then look at some approaches designed specifically for compressing images.

Generic Data Compression Techniques

Numerous data compression techniques have been developed, each with its own best-case and worst-case scenarios. The method called **run-length encoding** produces its best results when the data being compressed consist of long sequences of the same value. Indeed, run-length encoding is the process of replacing such sequences with a code indicating the value that is repeated and the number of times it occurs in the sequence. For example, less space is required to indicate that a bit pattern consists of 253 ones, followed by 118 zeros, followed by 87 ones than to actually list all 458 bits.

In some cases, the information involved consists of blocks of data, each of which differs slightly from the preceding one. An example would be consecutive frames of a motion picture. In these cases, techniques using **relative encoding** are helpful. Their approach is to record the differences between consecutive data blocks rather than entire blocks; that is, each block is encoded in terms of its relationship to the previous block.

Another approach to reducing the size of data is **frequency-dependent encoding,** a system in which the length of the bit pattern used to represent a data item is inversely related to the frequency of the item's use. Such codes are examples of variable-length codes, meaning that items are represented by patterns of different lengths as opposed to codes such as Unicode, in which all symbols are represented by 16 bits. More precisely, in the English language the letters *e, t, a,* and *i* are used more frequently than the letters *z, q,* and *x.* So, when constructing a code for text in the English language, space can be saved by using short bit patterns to represent the former letters and longer bit patterns to represent the latter ones. The result would be a code in which English text would have shorter representations than would be obtained with uniform-length codes such as ASCII or Unicode. David Huffman is credited with discovering an algorithm that is commonly used for developing frequency-dependent codes, and it is common practice to refer to codes developed in this manner as **Huffman codes.** In turn, most frequency-dependent codes in use today are Huffman codes.

Although we have introduced run-length encoding, relative encoding, and frequency-dependent encoding as generic compression techniques, each tends to have its own application realm. In contrast, systems based on **Lempel-Ziv encoding** (named after its creators, Abraham Lempel and Jacob Ziv) are more truly general-purpose compression systems. For example, users of the Internet (Chapter 3) have most likely seen, and perhaps used, utility software that uses Lempel-Ziv techniques to produce compressed files known as zip files.

Lempel-Ziv encoding systems are examples of **adaptive dictionary encoding.** Here the term *dictionary* refers to the collection of building blocks from which the message being compressed is constructed. If we wanted to compress text in the English language, the building blocks might be the alphabetic characters. If we wanted to compress data already encoded as a string of 0s and 1s, the building blocks might be the digits 0 and 1. In an adaptive dictionary encoding system, the dictionary is allowed to change during the encoding process. For example, in the case of English text, after encoding part of a message, we might decide to add *ing* and *the* to the dictionary. Then any future occurrence of *ing* or *the* could be encoded as a single reference to the dictionary instead of three. Lempel-Ziv encoding systems apply clever and efficient ways to adapt the dictionary during the encoding (or compression) process.

As an example, let us consider how we could compress a message using the particular Lempel-Ziv system known as LZ77. We would start by actually quoting the initial part of the message. Then we would represent the rest of the message as a sequence of triples (consisting of two integers followed by a symbol from the message), each of which describes how the next part of the message should be constructed from the preceding parts. (Thus the dictionary from which the message is constructed consists of the message itself.)

For example, consider the compressed message

xyxxyzy (5, 4, x)

consisting of the initial segment *xyxxyzy* followed by the triple (5, 4, *x*). The string *xyxxyzy* is the part of the message that is already in decompressed form. To decompress the rest of the message, we must decode the triple (5, 4, *x*) as summarized in Figure 1.28. The first number of the triple tells us how far to count backward in the decompressed string. In our case, we count backward five symbols, which leads us to the second *x* from the left in the decompressed string. We now begin appending to the end of the decompressed string the symbols found at this position. The second number in the triple tells us how many consecutive symbols to append. In our case this number is 4, so we append the symbols *xxyz* to the end of the decompressed string to obtain

xyxxyzyxxyz

Finally, the last entry in the triple should be placed at the end of the extended string. In our example, this symbol is *x*, so we complete the decompression process by adding this symbol to the end of the extended string. This produces

xyxxyzyxxyzx

which is the decompressed message.

Figure 1.28

Decompressing xyxxyzy (5, 4, x)

        a. Count backward 5 symbols.
          x y x x y z y

        b. Identify the four-bit segment to be appended
           to the end of the string.
          x y x x y z y

        c. Copy the four-bit segment onto the end of the message.
          x y x x y z y x x y z

        d. Add the symbol identified in the triple to the
           end of the message.
          x y x x y z y x x y z x

Now suppose the compressed version of the message was

    xyxxyzy (5, 4, x) (0, 0, w) (8, 6, y)

We would begin by decompressing the first triple as before to obtain

    xyxxyzyxxyzx (0, 0, w) (8, 6, y)

We would then decompress the second triple to obtain

    xyxxyzyxxyzxw (8, 6, y)

Note that the triple (0, 0, w) was used because the symbol w had not yet appeared in the message. Finally, decompressing the third triple would produce the decompressed message

    xyxxyzyxxyzxwzyxxyzy

To compress a message using LZ77, we could first quote a beginning segment of the message and then search through the pattern quoted to find the longest segment that agrees with the remaining message to be compressed. This would be the pattern referenced in the first triple. Future triples would be formed by a similar process.

Finally, you may have noted that our examples do not reflect very much compression since the triples involved have represented only short segments. When applied to long bit patterns, however, it is reasonable that long segments will be represented by single triples—resulting in significant data compression.

Compressing Images

In Section 1.4, we saw that the bit map images produced by today's image digitizers tend to represent images in a three-byte-per-pixel format, which leads to large, unmanageable bit maps. Many compression schemes have been developed specifically to reduce these storage requirements. One system known as GIF (short for Graphic Interchange Format and pronounced Giff by some and Jiff by others) was developed by CompuServe. It approaches the problem by reducing the number of colors that can be assigned to a pixel to only 256, which means that the value of each pixel can be represented in a single byte rather than requiring three. Each of the 256 potential pixel values is associated with a red-green-blue combination by means of a table known as the palette. By changing the palette associated with an image, we can change the colors appearing in the image.

One of the colors in a GIF image palette is normally assigned the value "transparent," which means that the background is allowed to show through any region assigned this "color." This option, combined with the relative simplicity of the GIF system, makes GIF a logical choice in computer action games in which multiple images move around on the screen.

Another compression system for color images is JPEG (pronounced "JAY-peg"). It is a standard developed by the Joint Photographic Experts Group (hence the standard's name) within ISO. JPEG has proved to be an effective standard for representing color photographs and is the standard adopted by manufacturers of today's digital cameras.

The JPEG standard actually encompasses several methods of image representation, each with its own goals. For example, in those situations that require the utmost in precision, JPEG provides a "lossless" mode whose name implies that no information is lost in the process of encoding the picture. In JPEG's lossless mode, space is saved by storing the difference between consecutive pixels rather than the pixel intensities themselves—the theory being that, in most cases, the amount by which adjacent pixels differ can be represented by shorter bit patterns than the values of the pixels. (This is an example of relative encoding.) These differences are then encoded using a variable-length code to further conserve storage space.

Unfortunately, the use of JPEG's lossless mode does not lead to bit maps with sizes that are manageable with today's technology and thus it is seldom used. Instead, most applications use JPEG's baseline standard. Here each pixel is again represented by three components, but these consist of a brightness component and two color components. Roughly speaking, if we were to look at only the brightness components of an image, we would see a gray version of the original image since these components represent only the pixels' luminance.

The purpose of distinguishing between luminance and color is that the human eye is more sensitive to changes in brightness than to changes in color. Consider, for example, two blue backgrounds that are identical except that one contains a very small bright dot whereas the other contains a very small green dot of the same brightness as the blue background. Your eye would more readily find the bright dot than the green dot. JPEG's baseline standard takes advantage of this phenomenon by encoding each brightness component but dividing the image into four-pixel blocks and recording only the average color of each block. Thus, the final representation preserves sudden changes in brightness but tends to blur sudden changes in color. The benefit is that each four-pixel block is represented by only 6 values (4 brightness values and 2 color values) rather than the 12 values that would be required in a 3-value-per-pixel system.

Additional space is saved by recording data that indicate how the various brightness and color components change rather than their actual values. Here, as in JPEG's lossless mode, the motivation is that as an image is scanned, the degree to which nearby pixel values differ can be recorded using fewer bits than would be required if the actual values were recorded. (Actually, these changes are encoded by applying a mathematical technique known as the discrete cosine transform whose details need not concern us here.) The final bit pattern is further compressed by applying a variable-length encoding system.

In short, JPEG's baseline standard can encode high-quality color images using bit patterns that are in the range of one-twentieth the size required by the three-byte-per-pixel format produced by most scanners. This is why it is growing in popularity. Other techniques, however, have advantages in certain applications. GIF, for example, does a better job of representing images consisting of blocks of uniform colors with sharp edges (such as color cartoons) than does JPEG.

In closing, we should note that research in data compression represents a wide and active field. We have discussed only two of many techniques for compressing images. Moreover, there are many strategies for compressing audio and video. For example, techniques similar to those used in JPEG's baseline standard have been adopted by the Motion Picture Experts Group (MPEG) within ISO to establish standards for encoding (compressing) motion video. The underlying theme is to start a picture sequence with an image similar to JPEG's baseline and then to represent the rest of the sequence using relative encoding techniques.

Questions/Exercises

1. Below is a message that was compressed using LZ77. What is the decompressed string?
   101101011 (7, 5, 0) (12, 10, 1) (18, 13, 0)

2. Even though we did not concentrate on the algorithm for compressing data based on LZ77, try compressing the message
   bbabbbaabababaababaababaaa

3. In this section we claimed that GIF is better than JPEG when representing color cartoons. Explain why.

4. At most, how many bytes would be required to represent a 1024 by 1024 pixel image using GIF? What if JPEG's baseline standard were used?

5. What characteristic of the human eye does JPEG's baseline standard exploit?

6. Identify a troubling phenomenon that is common when encoding numeric information, images, and sound as bit patterns.

1.9 Communication Errors

When information is transferred back and forth among the various parts of a computer, or transmitted from the earth to the moon and back, or, for that matter, merely left in storage, a chance exists that the bit pattern finally retrieved may not be identical to the original one. Particles of dirt or grease on a magnetic recording surface or a malfunctioning circuit may cause data to be incorrectly recorded or read. Moreover, in the case of some technologies, background radiation can alter patterns stored in a machine's main memory.

To resolve such problems, a variety of encoding techniques have been developed to allow the detection and even the correction of errors. Today, because these techniques are largely built into the internal components of a computer system, they are not apparent to the personnel using the machine. Nonetheless, their presence is important and represents a significant contribution to scientific research. It is fitting, therefore, that we investigate some of these techniques that lie behind the reliability of today's equipment.

Parity Bits

A simple method of detecting errors is based on the principle that if each bit pattern being manipulated has an odd number of 1s and a pattern is found with an even number of 1s, an error must have occurred.

To use this principle, we need a system in which each pattern contains an odd number of 1s. This is easily obtained by first adding an additional bit, the **parity bit,** to each pattern in a system already available (perhaps at the high-order end). (Thus the eight-bit ASCII code becomes a nine-bit code, or a 16-bit pattern representing a value in two's complement notation becomes a 17-bit pattern.) In each case, we assign the value 1 or 0 to this new bit so that the entire resulting pattern has an odd number of 1s. As Figure 1.29 shows, the ASCII code for A becomes 101000001 (parity bit 1) and the ASCII for F becomes 001000110 (parity bit 0). Although the eight-bit pattern for A has an even number of 1s and the eight-bit pattern for F has an odd number of 1s, both the nine-bit patterns have an odd number of 1s. Once our encoding system has been modified in this way, a pattern with an even number of 1s indicates that an error has occurred and that the pattern being manipulated is incorrect.

The particular parity system just described is called **odd parity,** because we designed our system so that each pattern would contain an odd number of 1s. Another technique used is **even parity.** In such a system, each pattern is designed to contain an even number of 1s, and thus an error is signaled by the occurrence of a pattern with an odd number of 1s.

Today it is not unusual to find parity bits being used in a computer's main memory. Although we envision these machines as having memory cells of eight bits, in reality they may have nine-bit cells, one bit of which is used as a parity bit. Each time an eight-bit pattern is given to the memory circuitry for storage, the circuitry adds a

Figure 1.29

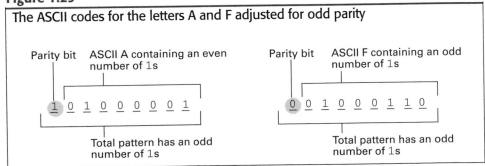

The ASCII codes for the letters A and F adjusted for odd parity

parity bit and stores the resulting nine-bit pattern. When the pattern is later retrieved, the circuitry checks the parity of the nine-bit pattern. If this does not indicate an error, then the memory removes the parity bit and confidently returns the remaining eight-bit pattern. Otherwise, the memory returns the eight data bits with a warning that the pattern being returned may not be the same pattern that was originally entrusted to memory.

Long bit patterns are often accompanied by a collection of parity bits making up a **checkbyte.** Each bit within the checkbyte is a parity bit associated with a particular collection of bits scattered throughout the pattern. For instance, one parity bit may be associated with every eighth bit in the pattern starting with the first bit, while another may be associated with every eighth bit starting with the second bit. In this manner, a collection of errors concentrated in one area of the original pattern is more likely to be detected, since it will be in the scope of several parity bits. Variations of this checkbyte concept lead to error detection schemes known as checksums and cyclic redundancy checks (CRC).

Error-Correcting Codes

Although the use of a parity bit allows the detection of an error, it does not provide the information needed to correct the error. Many people are surprised that **error-correcting codes** can be designed so that errors can be not only detected but also corrected. After all, intuition says that we cannot correct errors in a received message unless we already know the information in the message. However, a simple code with such a corrective property is presented in Figure 1.30.

To understand how this code works, we first define the **Hamming distance** (named after R. W. Hamming, who pioneered the search for error-correcting codes after becoming frustrated with the lack of reliability of the early relay machines of the 1940s) between two patterns to be the number of bits in which the two differ. For example, the Hamming distance between A and B in the code in Figure 1.30 is four, and the Hamming distance between B and C is three. The important feature of this code is that any two patterns are separated by a Hamming distance of at least three.

Figure 1.30

An error-correcting code

Symbol	Code
A	000000
B	001111
C	010011
D	011100
E	100110
F	101001
G	110101
H	111010

If a single bit is modified by a malfunctioning device, the error can be detected since the result will not be a legal pattern. (We must change at least three bits in any pattern before it will look like another legal pattern.)

If a single error has occurred in a pattern from Figure 1.30, we can also figure out what the original pattern was. After all, the modified pattern will be a Hamming distance of only one from its original form but at least two from any of the other legal patterns. To decode a message, we simply compare each received pattern with the patterns in the code until we find one that is within a distance of one from the received pattern. We consider this to be the correct symbol for decoding. For example, suppose we receive the bit pattern 010100. If we compare this pattern to the patterns in the code, we obtain the table in Figure 1.31. Thus, we can conclude that the character transmitted must be a D because this is the closest match.

You will observe that using this technique with the code in Figure 1.30 actually allows us to detect up to two errors per pattern and to correct one error. If we designed the code so that each pattern was a Hamming distance of at least five from each of the others, we would be able to detect up to four errors per pattern and correct up to two. Of course, the design of efficient codes associated with large Hamming distances is not a straightforward task. In fact, it constitutes a part of the branch of mathematics called algebraic coding theory, which is a subarea of linear algebra and matrix theory.

Error-correcting techniques are used extensively to increase the reliability of computing equipment. For example, they are often used in high-capacity magnetic disk drives to reduce the possibility that flaws in the magnetic surface will corrupt data. Moreover, a major distinction between the original CD format used for audio disks and the later format used for computer data storage is in the degree of error correction involved. CD-DA format incorporates error-correcting features that reduce the error rate to only one error for two CDs. This is quite adequate for audio recordings, but a company using CDs to supply software to customers would find that flaws in 50 percent of the disks would be intolerable. Thus, additional error-correcting features are employed in CDs used for data storage, reducing the probability of error to one in 20,000 disks.

Figure 1.31

Decoding the pattern 010100 using the code in Figure 1.30

Character	Distance between the received pattern and the character being considered
A	2
B	4
C	3
D	1 Smallest distance
E	3
F	5
G	2
H	4

Questions/Exercises

1. The following bytes were originally encoded using odd parity. In which of them do you know that an error has occurred?
   a. 10101101   b. 10000001   c. 00000000
   d. 11100000   e. 11111111

2. Could errors have occurred in a byte from Question 1 without your knowing it? Explain your answer.

3. How would your answers to Questions 1 and 2 change if you were told that even parity had been used instead of odd?

4. Encode these sentences in ASCII using odd parity by adding a parity bit at the high-order end of each character code:
   a. Where are you?
   b. "How?" Cheryl asked.
   c. 2 + 3 = 5.

5. Using the error-correcting code presented in Figure 1.30, decode the following messages:
   a. 001111 100100 001100
   b. 010001 000000 001011
   c. 011010 110110 100000 011100

6. Construct a code for the characters A, B, C, and D using bit patterns of length five so that the Hamming distance between any two patterns is at least three.

Chapter Review Problems

(Asterisked problems are associated with optional sections.)

1. Determine the output of each of the following circuits, assuming that the upper input is 1 and the lower input is 0.

a.

b.

c.

2. For each of the following circuits, identify the input combinations that produce an output of 1.

a.

b.

c.

3. In each circuit below, the rectangles represent the same type of gate. Based on the input and output information given, identify whether the gate involved is an AND, OR, or XOR.

a.

b.

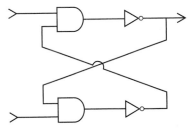

c.

4. Assume that both of the inputs in the circuit below are 1. Describe what would happen if the upper input were temporarily changed to 0. Describe what would happen if the lower input were temporarily changed to 0. Redraw the circuit using NAND gates.

5. The following table represents the addresses and contents (using hexadecimal notation) of some cells in a machine's main memory. Starting with this memory arrangement, follow the sequence of instructions and record the final contents of each of these memory cells:

Address	Contents
00	AB
01	53
02	D6
03	02

Step 1. Move the contents of the cell whose address is 03 to the cell at address 00.
Step 2. Move the value 01 into the cell at address 02.
Step 3. Move the value stored at address 01 into the cell at address 03.

6. How many cells can be in a computer's main memory if each cell's address can be represented by two hexadecimal digits? What if four hexadecimal digits are used?

7. What bit patterns are represented by the following hexadecimal notations?
   a. CB   b. 67   c. A9   d. 10   e. FF

8. What is the value of the most significant bit in the bit patterns represented by the following hexadecimal notations?
   a 7F   b FF   c 8F   d 1F

9. Express the following bit patterns in hexadecimal notation:
   a. 101010101010
   b. 110010110111
   c. 000011101011

10. Suppose a PC has 512 MB of main memory. What percent of that memory space would be required to store an image containing 1024 pixels per row and 1024 pixels per column if each pixel required three bytes of storage?

11. Suppose a picture is represented on a monitor screen by a rectangular array containing 1024 columns and 768 rows of pixels. If eight bits are required to encode the color and intensity of each pixel, how many byte-size memory cells are required to hold the entire picture?

12. a. Identify two advantages that a machine's main memory has over disk storage.
    b. Identify two advantages that disk storage has over a machine's main memory.

13. Suppose you are about to use your personal computer to write a term paper that you estimate will be 40 pages of text. Your machine has a disk drive for 3½-inch floppy disks with a capacity of 1.44MB per disk. If your term paper is encoded in ASCII, will it fit on one of these disks? If so, how many such papers can be

stored on one disk? If not, how many disks are required to hold your 40-page paper? Does your answer change significantly if your paper is encoded in Unicode?

14. Suppose that only 50GB of your personal computer's 120GB hard-disk drive is empty. Would it be reasonable to use CDs to store all the material you have on the drive as a backup? Explain your answer.

15. If each sector on a disk contains 512 bytes, how many sectors are required to store a single page of text (perhaps 50 lines of 100 characters) if each character is represented in Unicode?

16. A typical 3½-inch floppy disk has a capacity of 1.44MB. How does this compare to the size of a 400-page novel in which each page contains 3500 characters?

17. How long is the latency time of a typical hard-disk drive spinning at 60 revolutions per second?

18. What is the average access time for a hard disk spinning at 60 revolutions per second with a seek time of 10 milliseconds?

19. Suppose a typist could type 60 words per minute continuously day after day. How long would it take the typist to fill a CD whose capacity is 640MB? Assume one word is five characters and each character requires one byte of storage.

20. Here is a message in ASCII. What does it say?
01010111 01101000 01100001 01110100
00100000 01100100
01101111 01100101 01110011 00100000
01101001 01110100
00100000 01110011 01100001 01111001
00111111

21. The following is a message encoded in ASCII using one byte per character and then represented in hexadecimal notation. What is the message?
68657861646563696D616C

22. Encode the following sentences in ASCII using one byte per character.

a. $^{100}/_5 = 20$
b. To be or not to be?
c. The total cost is $7.25.

23. Express your answers to the previous problem in hexadecimal notation.

24. List the binary representations of the integers from 6 to 16.

25. a. Write the number 26 by representing the 2 and 6 in ASCII.
b. Write the number 26 in binary representation.

26. What values have binary representations in which only one of the bits is 1? List the binary representations for the smallest six values with this property.

*27. Encode the following sentences in ASCII using one byte per character. Use the most significant bit of each byte as an (odd) parity bit.
a. $^{100}/_5 = 20$
b. To be or not to be?
c. The total cost is $7.25.

*28. The following message was originally transmitted with odd parity in each short bit string. In which strings have errors definitely occurred?
11001 11011 10110 00000 11111 10001
10101 00100 01110

*29. Suppose a 24-bit code is generated by representing each symbol by three consecutive copies of its ASCII representation (for example, the symbol A is represented by the bit string 010000010100000101000001). What error-correcting properties does this new code have?

*30. Using the error-correcting code described in Figure 1.30, decode the following words:
a. 111010 110110
b. 101000 100110 001100
c. 011101 000110 000000 010100
d. 010010 001000 001110 101111 000000 110111 100110
e. 010011 000000 101001 100110

*31. Convert each of the following binary representations to its equivalent base ten representation:
a. 111   b. 0001   c. 10101
d. 10001   e. 10011   f. 000000

g. 100   h. 1000   i. 10000
j. 11001   k. 11010   l. 11011

*32. Convert each of the following base ten representations to its equivalent binary representation:
   a. 7   b. 11   c. 16   d. 15   e. 33

*33. Convert each of the following excess 16 representations to its equivalent base ten representation:
   a. 10000   b. 10011   c. 01101
   d. 01111   e. 10111

*34. Convert each of the following base ten representations to its equivalent excess four representation:
   a. 0   b. 3   c. –3   d. –1   e. 1

*35. Convert each of the following two's complement representations to its equivalent base ten representation:
   a. 01111   b. 10011   c. 01101
   d. 10000   e. 10111

*36. Convert each of the following base ten representations to its equivalent two's complement representation in which each value is represented in seven bits:
   a. 12   b. –12   c. –1   d. 0   e. 8

*37. Perform each of the following additions assuming the bit strings represent values in two's complement notation. Identify each case in which the answer is incorrect because of overflow.
   a. 00101   b. 11111   c. 01111
   +01000   +00001   +00001

   d. 10111   e. 00111   f. 00111
   +11010   +00111   +01100

   g. 11111   h. 01010   i. 01000
   +11111   +00011   +01000

   j. 01010
   +10101

*38. Solve each of the following problems by translating the values into two's complement notation (using patterns of five bits), converting any subtraction problem to an equivalent addition problem, and performing that addition. Check your work by converting your answer to base ten notation. (Watch out for overflow.)

   a. 7   b. 7   c. 12
   +1   –1   –4

   d. 8   e. 12   f. 5
   –7   +4   +11

*39. Convert each of the following binary representations into its equivalent base ten representation:
   a. 11.01   b. 100.0101   c. 0.1101
   d. 1.0   e. 10.001

*40. Express each of the following values in binary notation:
   a. $5\frac{1}{4}$ b. $\frac{1}{16}$ c. $7\frac{7}{8}$ d. $1\frac{3}{4}$ e. $6\frac{5}{8}$

*41. Decode the following bit patterns using the floating-point format described in Section 1.7:
   a. 01011010   b. 11001000
   c. 00101100   d. 10111001

*42. Encode the following values using the eight-bit floating-point format described in Section 1.7. Indicate each case in which a truncation error occurs.
   a. $\frac{1}{2}$ b. $7\frac{1}{2}$ c. $-3\frac{3}{4}$ d. $\frac{5}{32}$ e. $\frac{31}{32}$

*43. What is the best approximation to the square root of 2 that can be expressed in the eight-bit floating-point format described in Section 1.7? What value is actually obtained if this approximation is squared by a machine using this floating-point format?

*44. What is the best approximation to the value one-tenth that can be represented using the eight-bit floating-point format described in Section 1.7?

*45. Explain how errors can occur when measurements using the metric system are recorded in floating-point notation. For example, what if 110 cm was recorded in units of meters?

*46. Using the eight-bit floating-point format described in Section 1.7, what would be the result of computing the sum $\frac{1}{8} + \frac{1}{8} + \frac{1}{8} + 2\frac{1}{2}$ from left to right? How about from right to left?

*47. What answer would be given to each of the following problems by a machine using the eight-bit floating-point format described in Section 1.7?

a. $1\frac{1}{2} + \frac{3}{16} =$

b. $3\frac{1}{4} + 1\frac{1}{8} =$

c. $2\frac{1}{4} + 1\frac{1}{8} =$

*48. In each of the following addition problems, interpret the bit patterns using the eight-bit floating-point format presented in Section 1.7, add the values represented, and encode the answer in the same floating-point format. Identify those cases in which truncation errors occur.

a. 01011100
   +01101000

b. 01011000
   +01011000

c. 01111000
   +00011000

d. 01101010
   +00111000

*49. One of the bit patterns 01011 and 11011 represents a value stored in excess 16 notation and the other represents the same value stored in two's complement notation.

a. What can be determined about this common value?

b. What is the relationship between a pattern representing a value stored in two's complement notation and the pattern representing the same value stored in excess notation when both systems use the same bit pattern length?

*50. The three bit patterns 01101000, 10000010, and 00000010 are representations of the same value in two's complement, excess, and the eight-bit floating-point format presented in Section 1.7, but not necessarily in that order. What is the common value, and which pattern is in which notation?

*51. In each of the following cases, the different bit strings represent the same value but in different numeric encoding systems that we have discussed. Identify each value and the encoding systems used to represent it.

a. 11111010 0011 1011

b. 11111101 01111101 11101100

c. 1010 0010 01101000

*52. Which of the following bit patterns are not valid representations in an excess 16 notation system?

a. 01001   b. 101   c. 010101

d. 00000   e. 1000   f. 000000

g. 1111

*53. Which of the following values cannot be represented accurately in the floating-point format introduced in Section 1.7?

a. $6\frac{1}{2}$ b. 9   c. $\frac{13}{16}$ d. $\frac{17}{32}$ e. $\frac{15}{16}$

*54. If you doubled the length of the bit strings being used to represent integers in binary from four bits to eight bits, what change would be made in the value of the largest integer you could represent? What if you were using two's complement notation?

*55. What would be the hexadecimal representation of the largest memory address in a memory consisting of 4MB if each cell had a one-byte capacity?

*56. Using gates, design a circuit with four inputs and one output such that the output is 1 or 0 depending on whether the four-bit input pattern has odd or even parity, respectively.

*57. The following message was compressed using LZ77. Decompress the message.

abr (3, 1, c) (2, 1, d) (7, 3, a)

Why is the compressed message longer than the decompressed version?

*58. The following message was compressed using LZ77. Decompress the message.

0100101 (4, 3, 0) (8, 7, 1) (17, 9, 1) (8, 6, 1)

*59. Here is a part of a message that was compressed using LZ77. Based on the information given, how long was the original message?

xyz (_, 3, y) (_, 6, z)

*60. Write a set of directions explaining how to compress a string using LZ77.

*61. Write a set of directions explaining how to decompress a string using LZ77.

Social Issues

The following questions are provided to help you understand some of the ethical/social/legal issues associated with the field of computing. The goal is not merely to answer these questions. You should also consider why you answered as you did and whether your justifications are consistent from one question to the next.

1. A truncation error has occurred in a critical situation, causing extensive damage and loss of life. Who is liable, if anyone? The designer of the hardware? The designer of the software? The programmer who actually wrote that part of the program? The person who decided to use the software in that particular application? What if the software had been corrected by the company that originally developed it, but that update had not been purchased and applied in the critical application? What if the software had been pirated?

2. Is it acceptable for an individual to ignore the possibility of truncation errors and their consequences when developing his or her own applications?

3. Was it ethical to develop software in the 1970s using only two digits to represent the year (such as using 76 to represent the year 1976), ignoring the fact that the software would be flawed as the turn of the century approached? Is it ethical today to use only three digits to represent the year (such as 982 for 1982 and 015 for 2015)? What about using only four digits?

4. Many argue that encoding information often dilutes or otherwise distorts the information, since it essentially forces the information to be quantified. They argue that a questionnaire in which subjects are required to record their opinions by responding within a scale from one to five is inherently flawed. To what extent is information quantifiable? Can the pros and cons of different locations for a waste disposal plant be quantified? Is the debate over nuclear power and nuclear waste quantifiable? Is it dangerous to base decisions on averages and other statistical analysis? Is it ethical for news agencies to report polling results without including the exact wording of the questions? Is it possible to quantify the value of a human life? Is it acceptable for a company to stop investing in the improvement of a product, even though additional investment could lower the possibility of a fatality relating to the product's use?

5. With the development of digital cameras, the ability to alter or fabricate photographs is being placed within the capabilities of the general public. What changes will this bring to society? What ethical and legal issues could arise?

6. Should there be a distinction in the rights to collect and disseminate data depending on the form of the data? That is, should the right to collect and disseminate photographs, audio, or video be the same as the right to collect and disseminate text?

7. Whether intentional or not, a report submitted by a journalist usually reflects that journalist's bias. Often by changing only a few words, a story can be given either a positive or negative connotation. (Compare "The majority of those surveyed did not believe that . . ." to "A significant portion of those surveyed agreed that . . . ") Is there a difference between altering a story (by leaving out certain points or carefully selecting words) and altering a photograph?

8. Suppose that the use of a data compression system results in the loss of subtle but significant items of information. What liability issues might be raised? How should they be resolved?

Additional Reading

Gibbs, S. J., and D. C. Tsichritzis. *Multimedia Programming.* Reading, MA: Addison-Wesley, 1995.

Hamacher, V. C., Z. G. Vranesic, and S. G. Zaky. *Computer Organization,* 5th ed. New York: McGraw-Hill, 2002.

Kay, D. C., and J. R. Levine. *Graphics File Formats,* 2nd ed. New York: McGraw-Hill, 1995.

Knuth, D. E. *The Art of Computer Programming,* vol. 2, 3rd ed. Reading, MA: Addison Wesley Longman, 1998.

Miano, J. *Compressed Image File Formats.* New York: ACM Press, 1999.

Sayood, K. *Introduction to Data Compression,* 2nd ed. San Francisco: Morgan Kaufmann, 2000.

Data Manipulation

In Chapter 1 we studied topics relating to the storage of data and a computer's memory. In addition to storing data, a computer must manipulate the data as directed by an algorithm. To accomplish this, the machine must have a means of performing operations on data and a means of coordinating the sequence of these operations. A mechanism called the central processing unit (CPU) handles these tasks. This chapter concentrates on the study of this unit and related topics.

2.1 Computer Architecture

The circuitry in a computer that performs operations (such as addition and subtraction) on data is not directly connected to the storage cells in the machine's main memory. Instead, this circuitry is isolated in a part of the computer called the **central processing unit,** or **CPU** (often referred to as merely the processor). In the machines of the mid-twentieth century, CPUs were large units comprised of perhaps several racks of electronic circuitry that reflected the significance of the unit. Today, however, technology has shrunk these devices drastically. For example, the Pentium processor, made by Intel and used in many PCs, is a small flat square (approximately two inches by two inches) whose connecting pins plug into a socket mounted on the machine's main circuit board (called the **motherboard**). In fact, the Pentium processor itself is usually hard to see because it is mounted under a small cooling fan.

A CPU consists of two parts: the **arithmetic/logic unit,** which contains the circuitry that performs data manipulation, and the **control unit,** which contains the circuitry for coordinating the machine's activities. For temporary storage of information, the CPU contains cells, or **registers,** that are similar to main memory cells. These registers can be classified as either **general-purpose registers** or **special-purpose registers.** We will discuss some of the special-purpose registers in Section 2.3. For now, we are concerned only with the general-purpose registers.

General-purpose registers serve as temporary holding places for data being manipulated by the CPU. These registers hold the inputs to the arithmetic/logic unit's circuitry and provide storage space for results produced by that unit. To perform an operation on data stored in main memory, the control unit transfers the data from memory into the general-purpose registers, informs the arithmetic/logic unit which registers hold the data, activates the appropriate circuitry within the arithmetic/logic unit, and tells the arithmetic/logic unit which register should receive the result.

For the purpose of transferring bit patterns, a machine's CPU and main memory are connected by a collection of wires called a **bus** (Figure 2.1). Through this bus, the CPU extracts (reads) data from main memory by supplying the address of the pertinent memory cell along with a read signal. In a similar manner, the CPU places (writes) data in memory by providing the address of the destination cell and the data to be stored together with a write signal.

Based on this design, the task of adding two values stored in main memory involves more than the mere execution of the addition operation. The process involves the combined efforts of both the control unit, which coordinates the transfer of information between main memory and the registers within the CPU, and the arithmetic/logic unit, which performs the operation of addition when instructed to do so by the control unit.

The complete process of adding two values stored in memory might be broken down into the five steps listed in Figure 2.2. In short, the data must be transferred from main memory to the CPU, the values must be added within the CPU, and the result must be stored in a memory cell.

Early computers were not known for their flexibility—the steps that each device executed were built into the control unit as a part of the machine. Such a system is

Figure 2.1

CPU and main memory connected via a bus

analogous to an old fashioned music box that always plays the same tune when what is needed today is the flexibility of a CD changer. To gain more flexibility, some of the early electronic computers were designed so that the control unit could be conveniently rewired. This flexibility was accomplished by means of a pegboard arrangement similar to old telephone switchboards in which the ends of jumper wires were plugged into holes.

Figure 2.2

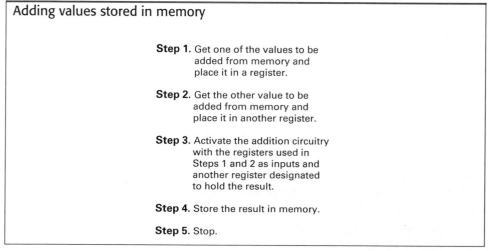

Adding values stored in memory

Step 1. Get one of the values to be added from memory and place it in a register.

Step 2. Get the other value to be added from memory and place it in another register.

Step 3. Activate the addition circuitry with the registers used in Steps 1 and 2 as inputs and another register designated to hold the result.

Step 4. Store the result in memory.

Step 5. Stop.

Cache Memory

It is instructive to compare the memory facilities within a computer in relation to their functionality. Registers are used to hold the data immediately applicable to the operation at hand; main memory is used to hold data that will be needed in the near future; and mass storage is used to hold data that will likely not be needed in the near future. Many machines are designed with an additional memory level, called cache memory. **Cache memory** is a portion (perhaps several hundred KB) of high-speed memory located within the CPU itself. In this special memory area, the machine attempts to keep a copy of that portion of main memory that is of current interest. In this setting, data transfers that normally would be made between registers and main memory are made between registers and cache memory. Any changes made to cache memory are then transferred to main memory at a more opportune time. The result is a CPU that can execute its machine cycle more rapidly because it is not delayed by main memory communication.

A breakthrough (credited, apparently incorrectly, to John von Neumann) came with the realization that a program, just like data, can be encoded and stored in main memory. If the control unit is designed to extract the program from memory, decode the instructions, and execute them, the program that the machine follows can be changed merely by changing the contents of the computer's memory instead of rewiring the control unit.

The idea of storing a computer's program in its main memory is called the **stored-program concept,** has become the standard approach used today—so standard, in fact, that it seems obvious. What made it difficult originally was that everyone thought of programs and data as different entities: Data were stored in memory; programs were part of the control unit. The result was a prime example of not seeing the forest for the trees. It is easy to be caught in such ruts, and the development of computer science might still be in many of them today without our knowing it. Indeed, part of the excitement of the science is that new insights are constantly opening doors to new theories and applications.

Questions/Exercises

1. What sequence of events do you think would be required to move the contents of one memory cell in a computer to another memory cell?

2. What information must the CPU supply to the main memory circuitry to write a value into a memory cell?

3. Mass storage, main memory, and general-purpose registers are all storage systems. What is the difference between how they are used?

2.2 Machine Language

To apply the stored-program concept, CPUs are designed to recognize instructions encoded as bit patterns. This collection of instructions along with the encoding system is called the **machine language**. An instruction expressed in this language is called a machine-level instruction or, more commonly, a **machine instruction.**

The Instruction Repertoire

The list of machine instructions that a typical CPU must be able to decode and execute is quite short. Indeed, once a machine can perform certain elementary but well-chosen tasks, adding more features does not increase the machine's theoretical capabilities. In other words, beyond a certain point, additional features may increase such things as convenience but add nothing to the machine's fundamental capabilities.

The degree to which machine designs should take advantage of this fact has lead to two philosophies of CPU architecture. One is that a CPU should be designed to execute a minimal set of machine instructions. This approach leads to what is called a **reduced instruction set computer (RISC).** The argument in favor of RISC architecture is that such a machine is efficient and fast. On the other hand, others argue in favor of CPUs with the ability to execute a large number of complex instructions, even though many of them are technically redundant. The result of this approach is known as a **complex instruction set computer (CISC).** The argument in favor of CISC architecture is that the more complex CPU is easier to program because a single instruction can be used to accomplish a task that would require a multi-instruction sequence in a RISC design.

Both CISC and RISC processors are commercially available. The Pentium series of processors, developed by Intel, are examples of CISC architecture; the PowerPC series of processors, developed by Apple Computer, IBM, and Motorola are examples of RISC architecture.

When discussing the instructions in a machine's repertoire, it is helpful to recognize that they can be classified into three categories: (1) the data transfer group, (2) the arithmetic/logic group, and (3) the control group.

Data Transfer

The data transfer group consists of instructions that request the movement of data from one location to another. Steps 1, 2, and 4 in Figure 2.2 fall into this category. We should note that using terms such as *transfer* or *move* to identify this group of instructions is actually a misnomer. It is rare that the data being transferred is erased from its original location. The process involved in a transfer instruction is more like copying the data rather than moving it. Thus terms such as *copy* or *clone* better describe the actions of this group of instructions.

While on the subject of terminology, we should mention that special terms are used when referring to the transfer of data between the CPU and main memory. A request to fill a general-purpose register with the contents of a memory cell is commonly referred to as a LOAD instruction; conversely, a request to transfer the contents of a register to a memory cell is called a STORE instruction. In Figure 2.2, Steps 1 and 2 are LOAD instructions, and Step 4 is a STORE instruction.

An important group of instructions within the data transfer category consists of the commands for communicating with devices outside the CPU-main memory context (printers, keyboards, monitors, disk drives, etc.). Since these instructions handle the input/output (I/O) activities of the machine, they are called I/O instructions and are sometimes considered as a category in their own right. On the other hand, Section 2.6 describes how these I/O activities can be handled by the same instructions that request data transfers between the CPU and main memory. Thus, we shall consider the I/O instructions to be a part of the data transfer group.

Arithmetic/Logic

The arithmetic/logic group consists of the instructions that tell the control unit to request an activity within the arithmetic/logic unit. Step 3 in Figure 2.2 falls into this group. As its name suggests, the arithmetic/logic unit is capable of performing operations other than the basic arithmetic operations. Some of these additional operations are the Boolean operations AND, OR, and XOR, introduced in Chapter 1, that we will discuss in more detail later in this chapter. These operations are often used for manipulating individual bits within a general-purpose register without disturbing the rest of the register. Another collection of operations available within most arithmetic/logic units allows the contents of registers to be moved to the right or the left within the register. These operations are known as either SHIFT or ROTATE operations, depending on whether the bits that "fall off the end" of the register are merely discarded (SHIFT) or are used to fill the holes left at the other end (ROTATE).

Control

The control group consists of those instructions that direct the execution of the program rather than the manipulation of data. Step 5 in Figure 2.2 falls into this category, although it is an extremely elementary example. This group contains many of the more interesting instructions in a machine's repertoire, such as the family of JUMP (or BRANCH) instructions used to direct the control unit to execute an instruction other than the next one in the list. These JUMP instructions appear in two varieties: unconditional jumps and conditional jumps. An example of the former would be the instruction "Skip to Step 5"; an example of the latter would be, "If the value obtained is 0, then skip to Step 5." The distinction is that a conditional jump results in a "change of venue" only if a certain condition is satisfied. As an example, the sequence of instructions in Figure 2.3 represents an algorithm for dividing two values where Step 3 is a conditional jump that protects against the possibility of division by zero.

An Illustrative Machine Language

Let us now consider how the instructions of a typical computer are encoded. The machine that we will use for our discussion is described in Appendix C and summarized in Figure 2.4. It has 16 general-purpose registers and 256 main memory cells, each with a capacity of eight bits. For referencing purposes, we label the registers with the values 0 through 15 and address the memory cells with the values 0 through 255. For convenience we think of these labels and addresses as values represented in base two and compress the resulting bit patterns using hexadecimal notation. Thus, the registers are labeled 0 through F, and the memory cells are addressed 00 through FF.

Figure 2.3

Dividing values stored in memory

Step 1. LOAD a register with a value from memory.

Step 2. LOAD another register with another value from memory.

Step 3. If this second value is zero, JUMP to Step 6.

Step 4. Divide the contents of the first register by the second register and leave the result in a third register.

Step 5. STORE the contents of the third register in memory.

Step 6. STOP.

The encoded version of a machine instruction typically consists of two parts: the **op-code** (short for operation code) field and the **operand** field. The bit pattern appearing in the op-code field indicates which of the elementary operations, such as STORE, SHIFT, XOR, and JUMP, is requested by the instruction. The bit patterns found in the operand field provide more detailed information about the operation specified by the op-code. For example, in the case of a STORE operation, the information in the operand field indicates which register contains the data to be stored and which memory cell is to receive the data.

Figure 2.4

The architecture of the machine described in Appendix C

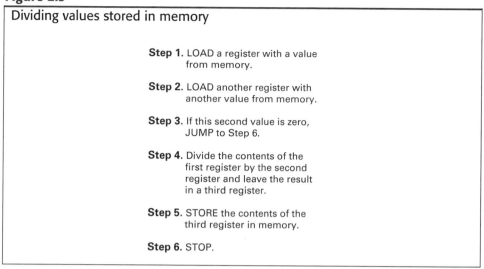

Figure 2.5

The composition of an instruction for the machine in Appendix C

The entire machine language of our illustrative machine (Appendix C) consists of only 12 basic instructions. Each of these instructions is encoded using a total of 16 bits, represented by four hexadecimal digits (Figure 2.5). The op-code for each instruction consists of the first four bits or, equivalently, the first hexadecimal digit. Note (Appendix C) that these op-codes are represented by the hexadecimal digits 1 through C. In particular, the table in Appendix C shows us that an instruction beginning with the hexadecimal digit 3 refers to a STORE instruction, and an instruction beginning with hexadecimal A refers to a ROTATE instruction.

The operand field of each instruction in our illustrative machine consists of three hexadecimal digits (12 bits), and in each case (except for the HALT instruction, which needs no further refinement) clarifies the general instruction given by the op-code. For example (Figure 2.6), if the first hexadecimal digit of an instruction were 3 (the op-code for storing the contents of a register), the next hexadecimal digit of the instruction would indicate which register is to be stored, and the last two hexadecimal digits would indicate which memory cell is to receive the data. Thus the instruction 35A7 (hexadecimal) translates to the statement "STORE the bit pattern found in register 5 in the memory cell whose address is A7."

Figure 2.6

Decoding the instruction 35A7

As another example, the op-code 7 (hexadecimal) requests that the contents of two registers be ORed. (We will see what it means to OR two registers in Section 2.4. For now we are interested merely in how instructions are encoded.) In this case, the next hexadecimal digit indicates where the result should be placed, while the last two hexadecimal digits of the operand field are used to indicate which two registers are to be ORed. Thus the instruction 70C5 translates to the statement "OR the contents of register C with the contents of register 5 and leave the result in register 0."

A subtle distinction exists between our machine's two LOAD instructions. Here we see that the op-code 1 (hexadecimal) identifies an instruction that loads a register with the contents of a memory cell, whereas the op-code 2 (hexadecimal) identifies an instruction that loads a register with a particular value. The difference is that the operand field in an instruction of the first type contains an address, whereas in the second type the operand field contains the actual bit pattern to be loaded.

Note that the machine has two ADD instructions: one for adding two's complement representations and one for adding floating-point representations. This distinction results from the fact that adding bit patterns that represent values encoded in two's complement notation requires different activities within the arithmetic/logic unit from adding values encoded in floating-point notation.

We close this section with Figure 2.7, which contains an encoded version of the instructions in Figure 2.2. We have assumed that the values to be added are stored in two's complement notation at memory addresses 6C and 6D and the sum is to be placed in the memory cell at address 6E.

Figure 2.7

An encoded version of the instructions in Figure 2.2

Encoded instructions	Translation
156C	Load register 5 with the bit pattern found in the memory cell at address 6C.
166D	Load register 6 with the bit pattern found in the memory cell at address 6D.
5056	Add the contents of register 5 and 6 as though they were two's complement representation and leave the result in register 0.
306E	Store the contents of register 0 in the memory cell at address 6E.
C000	Halt.

Questions/Exercises

1. Why might the term *move* be considered an incorrect name for the operation of moving data from one location in a machine to another?

2. In the text, JUMP instructions were expressed by identifying the destination explicitly by stating the name (or step number) of the destination within the JUMP instruction (for example, "Jump to Step 6"). A drawback of this technique is that if an instruction name (number) is later changed, we must be sure to find all jumps to that instruction and change that name also. Describe another way of expressing a JUMP instruction so that the name of the destination is not explicitly stated.

3. Is the instruction "If 0 equals 0, then jump to Step 7" a conditional or unconditional jump? Explain your answer.

4. Write the example program in Figure 2.7 in actual bit patterns.

5. The following are instructions written in the machine language described in Appendix C. Rewrite them in English.
   a. 368A   b. BADE   c. 803C   d. 40F4

6. What is the difference between the instructions 15AB and 25AB in the machine language of Appendix C?

7. Here are some instructions in English. Translate each of them into the machine language of Appendix C.
   a. LOAD register number 3 with the hexadecimal value 56.
   b. ROTATE register number 5 three bits to the right.
   c. AND the contents of register A with the contents of register 5 and leave the result in register 0.

Who Invented What?

Awarding a single individual credit for an invention is always a dubious undertaking. Thomas Edison is credited with inventing the incandescent lamp, but other researchers were developing similar lamps, and in a sense he was lucky to be the one to obtain the patent. The Wright brothers are credited with inventing the airplane, but they benefited from the research of others, and to some degree, they were pre-empted by Leonardo da Vinci, who toyed with the idea of flying machines in the fifteenth century. Even Leonardo's designs were apparently based on earlier ideas. Of course, in these cases the designated inventor still has legitimate claims to the credit bestowed. In other cases, history seems to have awarded credit inappropriately—an example is the stored-program concept. Without a doubt, John von Neumann was a brilliant scientist who deserves credit for numerous contributions. But the contribution for which popular history has chosen to credit him, the stored-program concept, was apparently developed by researchers led by J. P. Eckert at the Moore School of Electrical Engineering at the University of Pennsylvania. John von Neumann was merely the first to publish work reporting the idea and thus computing lore selected him as the inventor.

2.3 Program Execution

A computer follows a program stored in its memory by copying the instructions from memory into the control unit as needed. Once in the control unit, each instruction is decoded and obeyed. The order in which the instructions are fetched from memory corresponds to the order in which the instructions are stored in memory unless otherwise specified by a JUMP instruction.

To understand how the overall execution process takes place, it is necessary to take a closer look at the control unit inside the CPU. Within this unit are two special-purpose registers: the **program counter** and the **instruction register** (see again Figure 2.4). The program counter contains the address of the next instruction to be executed, thereby serving as the machine's way of keeping track of where it is in the program. The instruction register is used to hold the instruction being executed.

The control unit performs its job by continually repeating an algorithm that guides it through a three-step process known as the **machine cycle.** The steps in the machine cycle are fetch, decode, and execute (Figure 2.8). During the fetch step, the control unit requests that main memory provide it with the instruction that is stored at the address indicated by the program counter. Since each instruction in our machine is two bytes long, this fetch process involves retrieving the contents of two memory cells from main memory. The control unit places the instruction received from memory in its instruction register and then increments the program counter by two so that the counter contains the address of the next instruction stored in memory. Thus the program counter will be ready to be used during the next fetch.

Figure 2.8

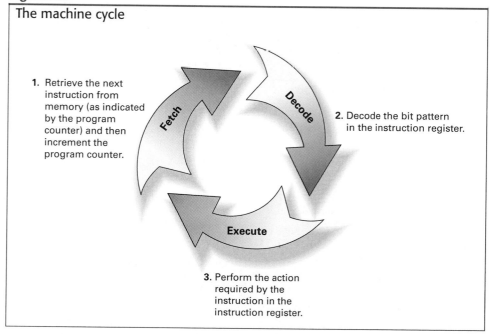

The machine cycle

1. Retrieve the next instruction from memory (as indicated by the program counter) and then increment the program counter.

Fetch

Decode

2. Decode the bit pattern in the instruction register.

Execute

3. Perform the action required by the instruction in the instruction register.

With the instruction now in the instruction register, the control unit decodes the instruction, which involves breaking the operand field into its proper components based on the instruction's op-code.

The control unit then executes the instruction by activating the appropriate circuitry to perform the requested task. For example, if the instruction is a load from memory, the control unit causes the load to occur; if the instruction is for an arithmetic operation, the control unit activates the appropriate circuitry in the arithmetic/logic unit with the correct registers as inputs.

Once the instruction in the instruction register has been executed, the control unit again begins the machine cycle with the fetch step. Observe that since the program counter was incremented at the end of the previous fetch, it again provides the control unit with the correct address.

A somewhat special case is the execution of a JUMP instruction. Consider, for example, the instruction B258 (Figure 2.9), which means "JUMP to the instruction at address 58 (hexadecimal) if the contents of register 2 is the same as that of register 0." In this case, the execute step of the machine cycle begins with the comparison of registers 2 and 0. If they contain different bit patterns, the execute step terminates and the next machine cycle begins. If, however, the contents of these registers are equal, the machine places the value 58 (hexadecimal) in its program counter during the execute step. In this case, then, the next fetch step finds 58 in the program counter, so the instruction at that address will be the next instruction to be fetched and executed.

Note that if the instruction had been B058, then the decision of whether the program counter should be changed would depend on whether the contents of register 0 was equal to that of register 0. But these are the same registers and thus must have equal content. In turn, any instruction of the form B0XY will cause a jump to be executed to the memory location XY.

Figure 2.9

Decoding the instruction B258

An Example of Program Execution

Let us follow the machine cycle applied to the program presented in Figure 2.7 that retrieves two values from main memory, computes their sum, and stores that total in a main memory cell. We first need to put the program somewhere in memory. For our example, suppose the program is stored in consecutive addresses, starting at address A0 hexadecimal. With the program stored in this manner, we can cause the machine to execute it by placing the address (A0) of the first instruction in the program counter and starting the machine (Figure 2.10).

The control unit begins the fetch step of the machine cycle by extracting the instruction stored at location A0 in main memory and placing this instruction (156C) in its instruction register (Figure 2.11a). Notice that, in our machine, instructions are 16 bits (two bytes) long. Thus the entire instruction to be fetched occupies the memory cells at both address A0 and A1. The control unit is designed to take this into account so it retrieves the contents of both cells and places the bit patterns received in the instruction register, which is 16 bits long. The control unit then adds two to the program counter so that this register contains the address of the next instruction (Figure 2.11b). At the end of the fetch step of the first machine cycle, the program counter and instruction register contain the following data:

Program Counter: A2
Instruction Register: 156C

Figure 2.10

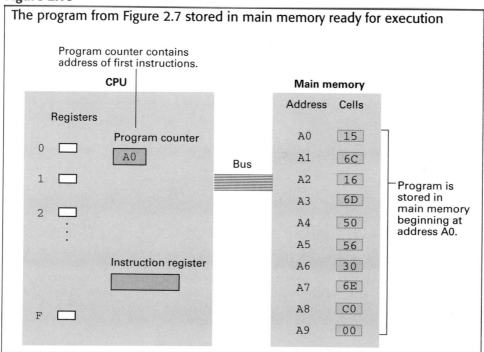

The program from Figure 2.7 stored in main memory ready for execution

Figure 2.11

Performing the fetch step of the machine cycle

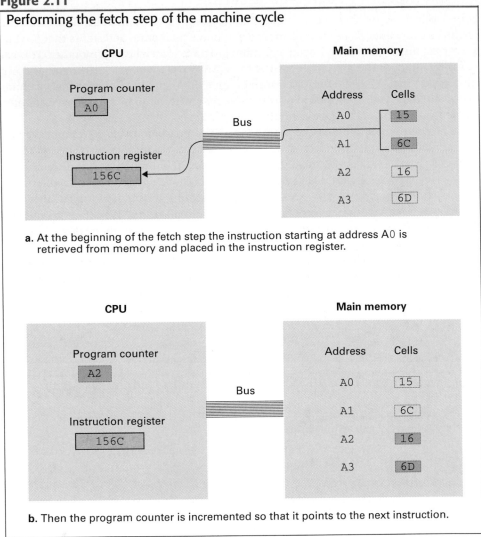

a. At the beginning of the fetch step the instruction starting at address A0 is retrieved from memory and placed in the instruction register.

b. Then the program counter is incremented so that it points to the next instruction.

Next, the control unit analyzes the instruction in its instruction register and concludes that it is to load register 5 with the contents of the memory cell at address 6C. This load activity is performed during the execution step of the machine cycle, and the control unit then begins the next cycle.

This cycle begins by fetching the instruction 166D from the two memory cells starting at address A2. The control unit places this instruction in the instruction register and increments the program counter to A4. The values in the program counter and instruction register therefore become the following:

Program Counter: A4
Instruction Register: 166D

Now the control unit decodes the instruction 166D and determines that it is to load register 6 with the contents of memory address 6D. It then executes the instruction. It is at this time that register 6 is actually loaded.

Since the program counter now contains A4, the control unit extracts the next instruction starting at this address. The result is that 5056 is placed in the instruction register, and the program counter is incremented to A6. The control unit now decodes the contents of its instruction register and executes it by activating the two's complement addition circuitry with inputs being registers 5 and 6.

During this execution step, the arithmetic/logic unit performs the requested addition, leaves the result in register 0 (as requested by the control unit), and reports to the control unit that it has finished. The control unit then begins another machine cycle. Once again, with the aid of the program counter, it fetches the next instruction (306E) from the two memory cells starting at memory location A6 and increments the program counter to A8. This instruction is then decoded and executed. At this point, the sum is placed in memory location 6E.

The next instruction is fetched starting from memory location A8, and the program counter is incremented to AA. The contents of the instruction register (C000) are now decoded as the halt instruction. Consequently, the machine stops during the execute step of the machine cycle, and the program is completed.

In summary, we see that the execution of a program stored in memory involves the same process you and I might use if we needed to follow a detailed list of instructions. Whereas we might keep our place by checking the instructions off as we do them, the computer keeps its place by using the program counter. After determining which instruction to execute next, we would read the instruction and extract its meaning. Then, we would perform the task requested and return to the list for the next instruction in the same manner that the machine executes the instruction in its instruction register and then continues with another fetch.

Programs Versus Data

Many programs can be stored simultaneously in a computer's main memory, as long as they occupy different locations. Which program will be run when the machine is started can then be determined merely by setting the program counter appropriately.

One must keep in mind, however, that because data are also contained in main memory and encoded in terms of 0s and 1s, the machine alone has no way of knowing what is data and what is program. If the program counter is assigned the address of data instead of the address of the desired program, the computer, not knowing any better, extracts the data bit patterns as though they were instructions and executes them. The final result depends on the data involved.

We should not conclude that providing programs and data with a common appearance in a machine's memory is bad. In fact, it has proved a useful attribute because it allows one program to manipulate other programs (or even itself) the same as it would data. Imagine, for example, a program that modifies itself in response to its interaction with its environment and thus exhibits the ability to learn, or perhaps a program that writes and executes other programs in order to solve problems presented to it.

Questions/Exercises

1. Suppose the memory cells from addresses 00 to 05 in the machine described in Appendix C contain the (hexadecimal) bit patterns given in the following table:

Address	Contents
00	14
01	02
02	34
03	17
04	C0
05	00

If we start the machine with its program counter containing 00, what bit pattern is in the memory cell whose address is hexadecimal 17 when the machine halts?

2. Suppose the memory cells at addresses B0 to B8 in the machine described in Appendix C contain the (hexadecimal) bit patterns given in the following table:

Address	Contents
B0	13
B1	B8
B2	A3
B3	02
B4	33
B5	B8
B6	C0
B7	00
B8	0F

    a. If the program counter starts at B0, what bit pattern is in register number 3 after the first instruction has been executed?

    b. What bit pattern is in memory cell B8 when the halt instruction is executed?

3. Suppose the memory cells at addresses A4 to B1 in the machine described in Appendix C contain the (hexadecimal) bit patterns given in the following table:

Address	Contents
A4	20
A5	00
A6	21
A7	03
A8	22
A9	01
AA	B1
AB	B0
AC	50
AD	02
AE	B0
AF	AA
B0	C0
B1	00

When answering the following questions, assume that the machine is started with its program counter containing A4.

a. What is in register 0 the first time the instruction at address AA is executed?

b. What is in register 0 the second time the instruction at address AA is executed?

c. How many times is the instruction at address AA executed before the machine halts?

4. Suppose the memory cells at addresses F0 to F9 in the machine described in Appendix C contain the (hexadecimal) bit patterns described in the following table:

Address	Contents
F0	20
F1	C0
F2	30
F3	F8
F4	20
F5	00
F6	30
F7	F9
F8	FF
F9	FF

If we start the machine with its program counter containing F0, what does the machine do when it reaches the instruction at address F8?

Comparing Computer Power

When shopping for a personal computer, you will find that clock speeds are often used to compare machines. A computer's **clock** is a circuit, called an oscillator, which generates pulses that are used to coordinate the machine's activities—the faster this oscillating circuit generates pulses, the faster the machine performs its machine cycle. Clock speeds are measured in hertz (abbreviated as Hz) with one Hz equal to one cycle (or pulse) per second. Typical clock speeds in desktop computers are in the range of a few hundred MHz (older models) to several GHz. (MHz is short for megahertz, which is a million Hz. GHz is short for gigahertz, which is 1000 MHz.)

Unfortunately, different CPU designs may perform different amounts of work in one clock cycle, and thus clock speed alone fails to be relevant when comparing machines with different CPUs. If comparing a machine based on a PowerPC to one based on a Pentium, it would be more meaningful to compare performance by means of **benchmarking,** which is the process of comparing the performance of different machines when executing the same program, known as a benchmark. By selecting benchmarks representing different types of applications, comparisons can be obtained that are meaningful for various market segments. The best machine for one application may not be the best for another.

2.4 Arithmetic/Logic Instructions

As indicated earlier, the arithmetic/logic group of instructions consists of instructions requesting arithmetic, logic, and shift operations. In this section, we look at these operations more closely.

Logic Operations

We introduced the logic operations AND, OR, and XOR (exclusive or) in Chapter 1 as operations that combine two input bits to produce a single output bit. These operations can be extended to operations that combine two strings of bits to produce a single output string by applying the basic operation to individual columns. For example, the result of ANDing the patterns 10011010 and 11001001 results in

```
      10011010
AND   11001001
      10001000
```

where we have merely written the result of ANDing the two bits in each column at the bottom of the column. Likewise, ORing and XORing these patterns would produce

```
      10011010              10011010
OR    11001001       XOR    11001001
      11011011              01010011
```

One of the major uses of the AND operation is for placing 0s in one part of a bit pattern while not disturbing the other part. Consider, for example, what happens if the byte 00001111 is the first operand of an AND operation. Without knowing the contents of the second operand, we still can conclude that the four most significant bits of the result are 0s. Moreover, the four least significant bits of the result are a copy of that part of the second operand, as shown in the following example:

```
      00001111
AND   10101010
      00001010
```

This use of the AND operation is an example of the process called **masking.** Here one operand, called the **mask,** determines which part of the other operand will affect the result. In the case of the AND operation, masking produces a result that is a partial replica of one of the operands, with 0s occupying the nonduplicated positions.

Such an operation is useful when manipulating a **bit map,** a string of bits in which each bit represents the presence or absence of a particular object. We have already encountered bit maps in the context of representing images, where each bit is associated with a pixel. As another example, a string of 52 bits, in which each bit is associated with a particular playing card, can be used to represent a poker hand by assigning 1s to those 5 bits associated with the cards in the hand and 0s to all the others. Likewise, a bit map of 52 bits, of which 13 are 1s, can be used to represent a hand of bridge, or a bit map of 32 bits can be used to represent which of 32 ice cream flavors are available.

Suppose, then, that an eight-bit memory cell is being used as a bit map, and we want to find out whether the object associated with the third bit from the high-order end is present. We merely need to AND the entire byte with the mask 00100000, which produces a byte of all 0s if and only if the third bit from the high-order end of the bit map is itself 0. A program can then act accordingly by following the AND operation with a conditional branch instruction. Moreover, if the third bit from the high-order end of the bit map is a 1, and we want to change it to a 0 without disturbing the other bits, we can AND the bit map with the mask 11011111 and then store the result in place of the original bit map.

Where the AND operation can be used to duplicate a part of a string while placing 0s in the nonduplicated part, the OR operation can be used to duplicate a part of a bit string while putting 1s in the nonduplicated part. For this we again use a mask, but this time we indicate the bit positions to be duplicated with 0s and use 1s to indicate the nonduplicated positions. For example, ORing any byte with 11110000 produces a result with 1s in its most significant four bits while its remaining bits contain a copy of the least significant four bits of the other operand, as demonstrated by the following example:

```
  11110000
OR 10101010
  11111010
```

Consequently, whereas the mask 11011111 can be used with the AND operation to force a 0 in the third bit from the high-order end of an eight-bit bit map, the mask 00100000 can be used with the OR operation to force a 1 in that position.

A major use of the XOR operation is in forming the complement of a bit string. For example, note the relationship between the second operand and the result in the following example:

```
   11111111
XOR 10101010
   01010101
```

XORing any byte with a byte of 1s produces the complement of the first byte.

In the machine language described in Appendix C, op-codes 7, 8, and 9 are used for the logic operations OR, AND, and XOR, respectively. Each requests that the corresponding logic operation be performed between the contents of two designated registers and that the result be placed in another designated register. For example, the instruction 7ABC requests that the result of ORing the contents of registers B and C be placed in register A.

Rotation and Shift Operations

The operations in the class of rotation and shift operations provide a means for moving of bits within a register and are often used in solving alignment problems, such as preparing a byte for future use in masking operations or manipulating the mantissa of floating-point representations. These operations are classified by the direction of motion (right or left) and whether the process is circular. Within these classification guidelines are numerous variations with mixed terminology. Let us take a quick look at the ideas involved.

If we consider starting with a byte of bits and shifting its contents one bit to the right or the left, we might imagine the bit on one end falling off the edge and a hole appearing at the other end. What happens with this extra bit and the hole is the distinguishing feature among the various shift operations. One technique is to place the extra bit in the hole at the other end. The result is a **circular shift,** also called a **rotation.** Thus, if we perform a right circular shift on a byte-size bit pattern eight times, we obtain the same bit pattern we started with.

Another technique is to discard the bit that falls off the edge and always fill the hole with a 0. The term **logical shift** is often used to refer to these operations. Such shifts to the left can be used for multiplying two's complement representations by two. After all, shifting binary digits to the left corresponds to multiplication by two, just as a similar shift of decimal digits corresponds to multiplication by ten. Moreover, division by two can be accomplished by shifting the binary string to the right. In either shift, care must be taken to preserve the sign bit when using certain notational systems. Thus, we often find right shifts that always fill the hole (which occurs at the sign bit position) with its original value. Shifts that leave the sign bit unchanged are sometimes called **arithmetic shifts.**

Among the variety of shift and rotate instructions possible, the machine language described in Appendix C contains only a right circular shift instruction, designated by op-code A. In this case the first hexadecimal digit in the operand specifies the register to be rotated, and the rest of the operand specifies the number of bits to be rotated. Thus the instruction A501 means "Rotate the contents of register 5 to the right by 1 bit." In particular, if register 5 originally contained the bit pattern A3, then it would contain D1 after this instruction is executed (Figure 2.12). (You may wish to experiment with how other shift and rotate instructions can be produced with combinations of the instructions provided in the machine language of Appendix C. For example, since a register is eight bits long, a right circular shift of three bits produces the same result as a left circular shift of five bits.)

Arithmetic Operations

Although we have already mentioned the arithmetic operations of add, subtract, multiply, and divide, a few loose ends should still be connected. First, as we have mentioned, this collection of operations can often be generated from the single add operation and a negation process. For this reason, some small computers are designed with only the add or perhaps only the add and subtract instructions.

We should also mention that numerous variations exist for each arithmetic operation. We have already alluded to this in relation to the add operations available on our machine in Appendix C. In the case of addition, for example, if the values to be added are stored in two's complement notation, the addition process must be performed as a straightforward binary add. However, if the operands are stored as floating-point values, the addition process must extract the mantissa of each, shift them right or left according to the exponent fields, check the sign bits, perform the addition, and translate the result into floating-point notation. Thus, although both operations are considered addition, the action of the machine is not the same.

Figure 2.12

Rotating the bit pattern A3 one bit to the right

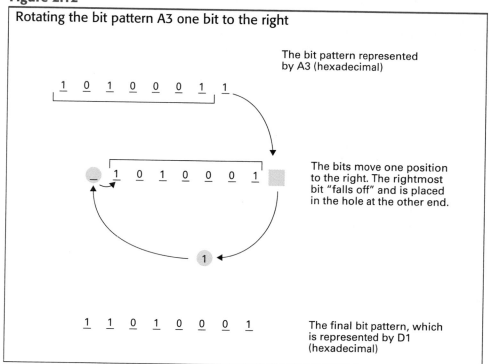

1 0 1 0 0 0 1 1   The bit pattern represented by A3 (hexadecimal)

1 0 1 0 0 0 1   The bits move one position to the right. The rightmost bit "falls off" and is placed in the hole at the other end.

1 1 0 1 0 0 0 1   The final bit pattern, which is represented by D1 (hexadecimal)

Questions/Exercises

1. Perform the indicated operations.

  a.   01001011   b.   10000011   c.   11111111
    AND 10101011   AND 11101100   AND 00101101

  d.   01001011   e.   10000011   f.   11111111
    OR 10101011   OR 11101100   OR 00101101

  g.   01001011   h.   10000011   i.   11111111
    XOR 10101011   XOR 11101100   XOR 00101101

2. Suppose you want to isolate the middle three bits of a seven-bit string by placing 0s in the other four bits without disturbing the middle three bits. What mask must you use together with what operation?

3. Suppose you want to complement the three middle bits of a seven-bit string while leaving the other four bits undisturbed. What mask must you use together with what operation?

4. a. Suppose you XOR the first two bits of a string of bits and then continue down the string by successively XORing each result with the next bit in the string. How is your result related to the number of 1s appearing in the string?

  b. How does this problem relate to determining what the appropriate parity bit should be when encoding a message?

5. It is often convenient to use a logical operation in place of a numeric one. For example, the logical operation AND combines two bits in the same manner as multiplication. Which logical operation is almost the same as adding two bits, and what goes wrong in this case?

6. What logical operation together with what mask can you use to change ASCII codes of lowercase letters to uppercase? What about uppercase to lowercase?

7. What is the result of performing a three-bit right circular shift on the following bit strings:
   a. 01101010   b. 00001111   c. 01111111

8. What is the result of performing a one-bit left circular shift on the following bytes represented in hexadecimal notation? Give your answer in hexadecimal form.
   a. AB   b. 5C   c. B7   d. 35

9. A right circular shift of three bits on a string of eight bits is equivalent to a left circular shift of how many bits?

10. What bit pattern represents the sum of 01101010 and 11001100 if the patterns represent values stored in two's complement notation? What if the patterns represent values stored in the floating-point format discussed in Chapter 1?

11. Using the machine language of Appendix C, write a program that places a 1 in the most significant bit of the memory cell whose address is A7 without modifying the remaining bits in the cell.

12. Using the machine language of Appendix C, write a program that copies the middle four bits from memory cell E0 into the least significant four bits of memory cell E1, while placing 0s in the most significant four bits of the cell at location E1.

2.5 Communicating with Other Devices

The main memory and CPU form the core of a computer. In this section, we investigate how this core, which we will refer to as the computer, communicates with peripheral devices such as disk storage systems, printers, keyboards, mice, monitors, and even other computers.

Communication via Controllers

Communication between a computer and other devices is normally handled through an intermediary device known as a **controller.** In the case of a personal computer, a controller has the physical form of a circuit board that plugs into a slot on the computer's motherboard. From there the controller connects via cables to peripheral devices within the computer case or perhaps to a connector on the back of the computer where external devices can be attached. These controllers are often small computers within themselves, each with its own memory circuitry and CPU that performs a program directing the activities of the controller.

A controller converts messages and data back and forth between forms compatible with the internal characteristics of the computer and those of the peripheral device to which it is attached. Thus each controller is designed for a particular type of device. This is why a new controller is sometimes purchased along with a new peripheral device. The controller that was used for an old disk drive may not be compatible with a new drive.

When a controller is plugged into one of the slots on the computer's motherboard, it is electronically connected to the same bus that connects the computer's CPU and main memory (Figure 2.13). From this position each controller is able to monitor the signals being sent between the CPU and main memory as well as to inject its owns signals onto the bus.

In particular, the CPU is able to communicate with the controllers attached to that bus in the same manner that it communicates with main memory. To send a bit pattern to a controller, the bit pattern is first constructed in one of the CPU's general-purpose registers. Then an instruction similar to a STORE instruction is executed by the CPU to "store" the bit pattern in the controller. Likewise, to receive a bit pattern from a controller, an instruction similar to a LOAD instruction is used. In some computer designs additional op-codes are provided in the machine language for these operations. Instructions with these op-codes are called I/O instructions. I/O instructions identify the various controllers by an addressing system similar to that of main memory. In particular, each controller is assigned a unique set of addresses (I/O addresses) that are used in the I/O instructions to identify the pertinent controller. The set of addresses assigned to a controller are collectively called a **port** because they represent a "location" through which information enters and leaves the computer. Since these I/O addresses may be identical in appearance to main memory addresses, buses for computers with this design contain a signal indicating whether the message currently being transmitted on the bus is for main memory or a controller. Thus, in response to an I/O instruction to send the contents of a register to a particular controller, the CPU will react in a manner similar to an instruction to send a bit pattern to a memory location, except that it will indicate on the bus that the bit pattern is for a controller rather than memory.

Figure 2.13

Controllers attached to a machine's bus

An alternative to extending the machine language to include special op-codes for I/O instructions is to use the same LOAD and STORE op-codes that are already provided for communication with main memory. In these cases, each controller is designed to respond to references to a unique set of addresses (again called a port) while main memory is designed to ignore references to these locations. Thus when the CPU sends a message on the bus to store a bit pattern at a memory location that is assigned to a controller, the bit pattern is actually "stored" in the controller rather than main memory. Likewise, if the CPU tries to read data from such a memory location, as in a LOAD instruction, it will receive a bit pattern from the controller rather than from memory. Such a communication system is called **memory-mapped I/O** because the computer's input/output devices appear to be in various memory locations (Figure 2.14).

Since a controller is attached to a computer's bus, it can carry on its own communication with main memory during those nanoseconds in which the CPU is not using the bus. This ability of a controller to access main memory is known as **direct memory access (DMA),** and it is a significant asset to a computer's performance. For instance, to retrieve data from a sector of a disk, the CPU can send requests encoded as bit patterns to the controller attached to the disk asking the controller to read the sector and place the data in a specified block of main memory cells. The CPU can then continue with other tasks while the controller performs the read operation and deposits the data in main memory via DMA. Thus two activities will be performed at the same time. The CPU will be executing a program and the controller will be overseeing the transfer of data between the disk and main memory. In this manner, the computing resources of the CPU are not wasted during the relatively slow data transfer.

The use of DMA also has the detrimental effect of increasing the amount of communication being handled by a computer's bus. Bit patterns must move between the CPU and main memory, between the CPU and each controller, and between each controller and main memory. Coordination of all this activity on the bus is a major design issue. Even with excellent designs, the central bus can become an impediment as the CPU and the controllers compete for bus access. This impediment is known as the **von Neumann bottleneck** because it is a consequence of the underlying **von Neumann architecture** in which a CPU fetches its instructions from memory over a central bus.

Finally, we should note that the transfer of data between two computer components is rarely a one-way affair. Even though we may think of a printer as a device that receives data, the truth is that a printer also sends data back to the computer. After

Figure 2.14

A conceptual representation of memory-mapped I/O

Bus Design

The design of a computer's bus has long been a delicate matter. The wires in a poorly designed bus can act as small antennas—picking up stray transmission signals (radio, television, etc.) and disrupting communication between the machine's CPU, memory, and peripheral devices. Moreover, the length of the bus (perhaps six inches in a desktop computer) is significantly longer than the length of the "wires" within the CPU itself (measured in microns). Thus the time required for signals to travel over the bus is much greater than that required for signals to be transferred within the CPU. The result is that bus technology is in a constant race to keep up with CPU technology. Today's personal computers reflect a variety of bus designs that differ in such features as the amount of data that can be transferred simultaneously, the rate at which the signals on the bus can be changed, and the physical properties of the connections between the bus and controller cards.

all, a computer can produce and send characters to a printer much faster than the printer can print them. If a computer blindly sent data to a printer, the printer could quickly fall behind, resulting in lost data. Thus a process such as printing a document involves a constant two-way dialogue in which the computer and the peripheral device exchange information about the device's status and coordinate their activities (a process known as **handshaking**).

Handshaking often involves a **status word,** which is a bit pattern that is generated by the peripheral device and sent to the controller. The bits in the status word reflect the conditions of the device. For example, in the case of a printer, the value of the least significant bit of the status word may indicate whether the printer is out of paper, while the next bit may indicate whether the printer is ready for additional data. Depending on the system, the controller may respond to this status information itself or make it available to the CPU. In either case, either the program within the controller or the program being executed by the CPU can be designed to delay sending data to the printer until the appropriate status information is received.

Data Communication Rates

The rate at which bits are transferred from one computing component to another is measured in **bits per second (bps).** Common units include **Kbps** (kilo-bps, equal to 1000 bps), **Mbps** (mega-bps, equal to 1 million bps), and **Gbps** (giga-bps, equal to 1 billion bps). The maximum rate available in a particular case depends on the type of the communication path and the technology used in its implementation. This maximum rate is often loosely equated to the communication path's **bandwidth.** That is, to say that a communication path has a high bandwidth means that the communication path has the ability to transfer bits at a high rate. Unfortunately, this is an imprecise use of the term since a "high transfer rate" could mean different rates in different settings.

There are two basic types of communication paths: parallel and serial. These terms refer to the manner in which the bit patterns are transferred with respect to each other. In the case of **parallel communication**, several bits are transferred at the same time, each on a separate line. Such a technique is capable of transferring data rapidly but requires a relatively complex communication path. Examples include a computer's internal bus and much of the communication between the computer and its peripheral devices, such as mass storage systems and printers. In these cases, rates measured in Mbps and higher are common.

In contrast, **serial communication** is based on transferring only one bit at a time. This technique tends to be slower but requires a simpler data path because all the bits are transferred over the same line, one after the other. Serial communication is typically used for communication between different computers, where the simpler data path proves to be economical.

For example, existing telephone lines are inherently serial communication systems because they transfer tones one after the other. Communication between computers over these lines is accomplished by first converting bit patterns into audible tones by means of a **modem** (short for *modulator-demodulator*), transferring these tones serially over the telephone system, and then converting the tones back into bits by another modem at the destination.

In reality, simply representing bit patterns by tones of different frequencies (known as frequency-shift keying) is used only for low-speed communication of no more than 1200 bps. To achieve transfer rates of 2400 bps, 9600 bps, and higher, modems combine changes in a tone's frequency, amplitude (volume), and phase (the degree to which the transmission of the tone is delayed). To achieve still higher rates, data compression techniques are often applied, producing apparent transfer rates of up to 57.6 Kbps.

These transfer rates appear to be the limit to what can be achieved within the frequency range for which traditional telephone lines were designed (up to 3 KHz), yet they fall short of the rates required by today's communication needs. Transferring

Variable-Length Instructions

To simplify explanations in the text, the machine language described in Appendix C uses a fixed size (two bytes) for all instructions. Thus, to fetch an instruction, the CPU always retrieves the contents of two consecutive memory cells and increments its program counter by two. In reality, most machine languages use instructions of different lengths. The Pentium series, for example, has instructions that range from single-byte instructions to multiple-byte instructions whose length depends on the exact use of the instruction. CPUs with such machine languages determine the length of the incoming instruction by the instruction's opcode. That is, the CPU first fetches the op-code of the instruction and then, based on the bit pattern received, knows how many more bytes to fetch from memory to obtain the rest of the instruction.

graphics at 57.6 Kbps can become exasperating, and transferring video by this method is slow beyond reason. Thus new technologies are continually being developed to provide higher transfer rates to customers who might otherwise use traditional telephone lines. One of these technologies is known as DSL (Digital Subscriber Line), which takes advantage of the fact that existing telephone lines are actually capable of handling a wider frequency range than that used by traditional voice communication. These systems normally obtain transfer rates of about 1.5 Mbps but can provide rates as high as 6 Mbps in one direction if the capabilities in the other direction are restricted. The exact performance depends on the version of DSL being used and the length of the line from the telephone company's operation center, which is typically limited to no more than 3.5 miles. Other technologies that compete with DSL include cable, as used in cable television systems, which can achieve rates as high as 40 Mbps, and optic fibers, whose transfer rates fall in the Mbps and Gbps range.

Questions/Exercises

1. Assume that the machine described in Appendix C uses memory-mapped I/O and that the address B5 is the location within the printer port to which data to be printed should be sent.
   a. If register 7 contains the ASCII code for the letter A, what machine language instruction should be used to cause that letter to be printed at the printer?
   b. If the machine executes a million instructions per second, how many times can this character be sent to the printer in one second?
   c. If the printer is capable of printing five traditional pages of text per minute, will it be able to keep up with the characters being sent to it in (b)?

2. Suppose that the hard disk on your personal computer rotates at 3000 revolutions a minute, that each track contains 16 sectors, and that each sector contains 1024 bytes. Approximately what communication rate is required between the disk drive and the disk controller if the controller is going to receive bits from the disk drive as they are read from the spinning disk?

3. Estimate how long would it take to transfer a 300-page novel encoded in ASCII at a transfer rate of 57,600 bps.

2.6 Other Architectures

To broaden our perspective, let us consider some alternatives to the traditional machine architecture we have discussed so far.

Pipelining

Electric pulses travel through a wire no faster than the speed of light. Since light travels approximately 1 foot in a nanosecond (one billionth of a second), it requires at least 2 nanoseconds for the control unit in the CPU to fetch an instruction from a memory cell that is 1 foot away. (The read request must be sent to memory, requiring at least 1 nanosecond, and the instruction must be sent back to the control unit, requiring at least another nanosecond.) Consequently, to fetch and execute an instruction in such a machine requires several nanoseconds—

which means that increasing the execution speed of a machine ultimately becomes a miniaturization problem. Although fantastic advances have been made in this area, there appears to be a limit.

In an effort to solve this dilemma, computer engineers concentrate on throughput rather than merely execution speed, where **throughput** refers to the total amount of work the machine can accomplish in a given amount of time rather than how long it takes to do one task.

One example of how a computer's throughput can be increased without requiring an increase in execution speed involves **pipelining,** which is the technique of allowing the steps in the machine cycle to overlap. In particular, while one instruction is being executed, the next instruction can be fetched, which means that more than one instruction can be in "the pipe" at any one time, each at a different stage of being processed. In turn, the total throughput of the machine is increased even though the time required to fetch and execute each individual instruction remains the same. (Of course, when a JUMP instruction is reached, any gain that would have been obtained by prefetching is not realized because the instructions in "the pipe" are not the ones needed after all.)

Modern machine designs push the pipelining concept beyond our simple example. They are often capable of fetching several instructions at the same time and actually executing more than one instruction at a time when those instructions do not rely on each other.

Multiprocessor Machines

Pipelining can be viewed as a first step toward **parallel processing,** which is the performance of several activities at the same time. However, true parallel processing requires more than one processing unit, resulting in computers known as multiprocessor machines.

A variety of computers today are designed with this idea in mind. One strategy is to attach several processing units, each resembling the CPU in a single-processor machine, to the same main memory. In this configuration, the processors can proceed independently yet coordinate their efforts by leaving messages to one another in the common memory cells. For instance, when one processor is faced with a large task, it can store a program for part of that task in the common memory and then request another processor to execute it. The result is a machine in which different instruction sequences are performed on different sets of data, which is called a **MIMD** (multiple-instruction stream, multiple-data stream) architecture, as opposed to the more traditional **SISD** (single-instruction stream, single-data stream) architecture.

A variation of multiple-processor architecture is to link the processors together such that they execute the same sequence of instructions in unison, each with its own set of data. This leads to a **SIMD** (single-instruction stream, multiple-data stream) architecture. Such machines are useful in applications in which the same task must be applied to each set of similar items within a large block of data.

Another approach to parallel processing is to construct large computers as conglomerates of smaller machines, each with its own memory and CPU. Within such an architecture, each of the small machines is coupled to its neighbors so that tasks assigned to the whole system can be divided among the individual machines. Thus if a task assigned to one of the internal machines can be broken into independent subtasks, that machine can ask its neighbors to perform these subtasks concurrently. The original task can then be completed in much less time than would be required by a single-processor machine.

In Chapter 10 we will study yet another multiprocessor architecture, artificial neural networks, whose design is based on theories of biological neural systems. These machines consist of many elementary processors, or processing units, each of whose output is merely a simple reaction to its combined inputs. These simple processors are linked to form a network in which the outputs of some processors are used as inputs to others. Such a machine is programmed by adjusting the extent to which each processor's output is allowed to influence the reaction of those processors to which it is connected. This simulates the theory that biological neural networks learn to produce a particular reaction to a given stimulus by adjusting the chemical composition of the junctions (synapses) between neurons, which in turn adjusts the ability of one neuron to affect the actions of others.

Proponents of artificial neural networks argue that, although technology is approaching the ability to construct electronic circuitry with roughly as many switching circuits as there are neurons in the human brain (neurons are believed to be nature's switching circuits), the capabilities of today's machines still fall far short of those of the human mind. This, they argue, is a result of the inefficient use of a traditional computer's components as dictated by the von Neumann architecture. After all, if a machine is constructed with a lot of memory circuitry supporting a few processors, then most of its circuitry is destined to be idle most of the time. In contrast, much of the human mind can be active at any given moment.

Thus computer designs are expanding the basic CPU-main memory model and in some cases breaking away from it altogether in order to develop more useful machines.

Questions/Exercises

1. Referring back to Question 3 of Section 2.3, if the machine used the pipeline technique discussed in the text, what will be in "the pipe" when the instruction at address AA is executed? Under what conditions would the pipelining technique not prove beneficial at this point in the program?

2. What conflicts must be resolved when running the program in Question 4 of Section 2.3 on a pipeline machine?

3. Suppose there were two "central" processing units attached to the same memory and executing different programs. Furthermore, suppose that one of these processors needs to add one to the contents of a memory cell at roughly the same time that the other needs to subtract one from the same cell. (The net effect should be that the cell ends up with the same value with which it started.)
   a. Describe a sequence in which these activities would result in the cell's ending up with a value one less than its starting value.
   b. Describe a sequence in which these activities would result in the cell's ending up with a value one greater than its starting value.

Chapter Review Problems

(Asterisked problems are associated with optional sections.)

1. Give a brief definition of each of the following:
   a. Register   b. Cache memory
   c. Main memory   d. Mass storage

2. Suppose a block of data is stored in the memory cells of the machine described in Appendix C from address B9 to C1, inclusive. How many memory cells are in this block? List their addresses.

3. What is the value of the program counter in the machine described in Appendix C immediately after executing the instruction B0BA?

4. Suppose the memory cells at addresses 00 through 05 in the machine described in Appendix C contain the following bit patterns:

Address	Contents
00	21
01	04
02	31
03	00
04	C0
05	00

   Assuming that the program counter initially contained 00, record the contents of the program counter, instruction register, and memory cell at address 00 at the end of each fetch phase of the machine cycle until the machine halts.

5. Suppose three values x, y, and z are stored in a machine's memory. Describe the sequence of events (loading registers from memory, saving values in memory, and so on) that leads to the computation of $x + y + z$. How about $(2x) + y$?

6. The following are instructions written in the machine language described in Appendix C. Translate them into English.
   a. 407E   b. 8008   c. A403
   d. 2835   e. B3AD

7. Suppose a machine language is designed with an op-code field of four bits. How many different instruction types can the language contain? What if the op-code field is increased to eight bits?

8. Translate the following instructions from English into the machine language described in Appendix C.
   a. LOAD register 7 with the hexadecimal value 66.
   b. LOAD register 7 with the contents of memory cell 66.
   c. AND the contents of registers F and 2 leaving the result in register 0.
   d. ROTATE register 4 three bits to the right.
   e. JUMP to the instruction at memory location 31 if the contents of register 0 equals the value in register B.

9. Classify each of the following instructions (in the machine language of Appendix C) in terms of whether its execution changes the contents of the memory cell at location 3B, retrieves the contents of the memory cell at location 3B, or is independent of the contents of the memory cell at location 3B.
   a. 153B b. 253B c. 353B
   d. 3B3B e. 403B

10. Suppose the memory cells at addresses 00 through 03 in the machine described in Appendix C contain the following bit patterns:

Address	Contents
00	24
01	05
02	C0
03	00

   a. Translate the first instruction into English.
   b. If the machine is started with its program counter containing 00, what bit pattern is in register 4 when the machine halts?

11. Suppose the memory cells at addresses 00 through 05 in the machine described in Appendix C contain the following bit patterns:

Address	Contents
00	10
01	04
02	30
03	45
04	C0
05	00

When answering the following questions, assume that the machine starts with its program counter equal to 00.
a. Translate the instructions that are executed into English.
b. What bit pattern is in the memory cell at address 45 when the machine halts?
c. What bit pattern is in the program counter when the machine halts?

12. Suppose the memory cells at addresses 00 through 09 in the machine described in Appendix C contain the following bit patterns:

Address	Contents
00	1A
01	02
02	2B
03	02
04	9C
05	AB
06	3C
07	00
08	C0
09	00

Assume that the machine starts with its program counter equal to 00.
a. What will be in the memory cell at address 00 when the machine halts?
b. What bit pattern will be in the program counter when the machine halts?

13. Suppose the memory cells at addresses 00 through 0D in the machine described in Appendix C contain the following bit patterns:

Address	Contents
00	20
01	03
02	21
03	01
04	40
05	12
06	51
07	12
08	B1
09	0C
0A	B0
0B	06
0C	C0
0D	00

Assume that the machine starts with its program counter equal to 00.
a. What bit pattern will be in register 1 when the machine halts?
b. What bit pattern will be in register 0 when the machine halts?
c. What bit pattern is in the program counter when the machine halts?

14. Suppose the memory cells at addresses F0 through FD in the machine described in Appendix C contain the following (hexadecimal) bit patterns:

Address	Contents
F0	20
F1	00
F2	21
F3	01
F4	23
F5	05
F6	B3
F7	FC
F8	50
F9	01
FA	B0
FB	F6
FC	C0
FD	00

If we start the machine with its program counter equal to F0, what is the value in register 0 when the machine finally executes the halt instruction at location FC?

15. If the machine in Appendix C executes an instruction every microsecond (a millionth of a second), how long does it take to complete the program in Problem 14?

16. Suppose the memory cells at addresses 20 through 28 in the machine described in Appendix C contain the following bit patterns:

Address	Contents
20	12
21	20
22	32
23	30
24	B0
25	21
26	20
27	C0
28	00

Assume that the machine starts with its program counter equal to 20.

a. What bit patterns will be in registers 0, 1, and 2 when the machine halts?

b. What bit pattern will be in the memory cell at address 30 when the machine halts?

c. What bit pattern will be in the memory cell at address B0 when the machine halts?

17. Suppose the memory cells at addresses AF through B1 in the machine described in Appendix C contain the following bit patterns:

Address	Contents
AF	B0
B0	B0
B1	AF

What would happen if we started the machine with its program counter equal to AF?

18. Suppose the memory cells at addresses 00 through 05 in the machine described in Appendix C contain the following (hexadecimal) bit patterns:

Address	Contents
00	25
01	B0
02	35
03	04
04	C0
05	00

If we start the machine with its program counter equal to 00, when does the machine halt?

19. In each of the following cases, write a short program in the machine language described in Appendix C to perform the requested activities. Assume that each of your programs is placed in memory starting at address 00.

a. Move the value at memory location 8D to memory location B3.

b. Interchange the values stored at memory locations 8D and B3.

c. If the value stored in memory location 45 is 00, then place the value CC in memory location 88; otherwise, put the value DD in memory location 88.

20. A popular game among computer hobbyists is core wars—a variation of battleship. (The term *core* originates from an early memory technology in which 0s and 1s were represented as magnetic fields in little rings of magnetic material.) The game is played between two opposing programs, each stored in different locations of the same computer's memory. The computer is assumed to alternate between the two programs, executing an instruction from one followed by an instruction from the other. The goal of each program is to destroy the other by writing extraneous data on top of it; however, neither program knows the location of the other.

a. Write a program in the machine language of Appendix C that approaches the game in a defensive manner by being as small as possible.

b. Write a program in the language of Appendix C that tries to avoid any attacks from the opposing program by moving to different locations. More precisely, write your program to start at location 00, copy itself to location 70, and then jump to this new copy.

c. Extend the program in (b) to continue relocating to new memory locations. In particular, make your program move to location 70, then to E0 (=70 + 70), then to 60 (=70 + 70 + 70), etc.

21. Write a program in the machine language of Appendix C to compute the sum of the two's complement values stored at memory locations A1, A2, A3, and A4. Your program should store the total at memory location A5.

22. Suppose the memory cells at addresses 00 through 05 in the machine described in Appendix C contain the following (hexadecimal) bit patterns:

Address	Contents
00	20
01	C0
02	30
03	04
04	00
05	00

What happens if we start the machine with its program counter equal to 00?

23. What happens if the memory cells at addresses 06 and 07 of the machine described in Appendix C contain the bit patterns B0 and 06, respectively, and the machine is started with its program counter containing the value 06?

24. Suppose the following program, written in the machine language of Appendix C, is stored in main memory beginning at address 30 (hexadecimal). What task will the program perform when executed?

2003
2101
2200
2310
1400
3410
5221
5331
3239
333B
B248
B038
C000

25. Summarize the steps involved when the machine described in Appendix C performs an instruction with op-code B. Express your answer as a set of directions as though you were telling the CPU what to do.

*26. Summarize the steps involved when the machine described in Appendix C performs an

instruction with op-code 5. Express your answer as a set of directions as though you were telling the CPU what to do.

*27. Summarize the steps involved when the machine described in Appendix C performs an instruction with op-code 6. Express your answer as a set of directions as though you were telling the CPU what to do.

*28. Suppose the registers 4 and 5 in the machine described in Appendix C contain the bit patterns 3C and C8, respectively. What bit pattern is left in register 0 after executing each of the following instructions:
a. 5045   b. 6045   c. 7045
d. 8045   e. 9045

*29. Using the machine language described in Appendix C, write programs to perform each of the following tasks:
a. Copy the bit pattern stored in memory location 66 into memory location BB.
b. Change the least significant four bits in the memory cell at location 34 to 0s while leaving the other bits unchanged.
c. Copy the least significant four bits from memory location A5 into the least significant four bits of location A6 while leaving the other bits at location A6 unchanged.
d. Copy the least significant four bits from memory location A5 into the most significant four bits of A5. (Thus, the first four bits in A5 will be the same as the last four bits.)

*30. Perform the indicated operations:

a.   111000
AND 101001

b.   000100
AND 101010

c.   000100
AND 010101

d.   111011
AND 110101

e.   111000
OR 101001

f.   000100
OR 101010

g.   000100
OR 010101

h.   111011
OR 110101

i.   111000
XOR 101001

j.   000100
XOR 101010

k.   000100
XOR 010101

l.   111011
XOR 110101

*31. Identify both the mask and the logical operation needed to accomplish each of the following objectives:
   a. Put 0s in the middle four bits of an eight-bit pattern without disturbing the other bits.
   b. Complement a pattern of eight bits.
   c. Complement the most significant bit of an eight-bit pattern without changing the other bits.
   d. Put a 1 in the most significant bit of an eight-bit pattern without disturbing the other bits.
   e. Put 1s in all but the most significant bit of an eight-bit pattern without disturbing the most significant bit.

*32. Identify a logical operation (along with a corresponding mask) that, when applied to an input string of eight bits, produces an output string of all 0s if and only if the input string is 10000001.

*33. Describe a sequence of logical operations (along with their corresponding masks) that, when applied to an input string of eight bits, produces an output byte of all 0s if the input string both begins and ends with 1s. Otherwise, the output should contain at least one 1.

*34. What would be the result of performing a four-bit left circular shift on the following bit patterns?
   a. 10101   b. 11110000   c. 001
   d. 101000   e. 00001

*35. What would be the result of performing a one-bit right circular shift on the following bytes represented in hexadecimal notation (give your answers in hexadecimal notation)?
   a. 3F   b. 0D   c. FF   d. 77

*36. What single instruction in the machine language of Appendix C could be used to accomplish a three-bit left circular shift of register B?

*37. Write a program in the machine language of Appendix C that reverses the contents of the memory cell at address 8C.

*38. Can a printer, printing 40 characters per second, keep up with a string of ASCII characters (one byte per symbol) arriving serially at the rate of 300 bps? What about 1200 bps?

*39. Suppose a person is typing 30 words per minute at a keyboard. (A word is considered to be five characters.) If a machine executes 50 instructions every microsecond (millionth of a second), how many instructions does the machine execute during the time between the typing of two consecutive characters?

*40. How many bits per second must a keyboard transmit to keep up with a typist typing 30 words per minute? (Assume each character is encoded in ASCII along with a parity bit and each word consists of five characters.)

*41. A communication system capable of transmitting any sequence of eight different states at the rate of at most 300 states per second could be used to transfer information at what rate in bits per second?

*42. Suppose the machine described in Appendix C communicates with a printer using the technique of memory-mapped I/O. Suppose also that address FF is used to send characters to the printer, and address FE is used to receive information about the printer's status. In particular, suppose the least significant bit at the address FE indicates whether the printer is ready to receive another character (with a 0 indicating "not ready" and a 1 indicating "ready"). Starting at address 00, write a machine language routine that waits until the printer is ready for another character and then sends the character represented by the bit pattern in register 5 to the printer.

*43. Write a program in the machine language described in Appendix C that places 0s in all the memory cells from address A0 through C0 but is small enough to fit in the memory cells from address 00 through 13 (hexadecimal).

*44. Suppose a machine has 20GB of storage space available on a hard disk and receives data over a telephone connection at the rate of 14,400 bps. At this rate, how long would it take to fill the available storage space?

*45. Suppose a communication line is being used to transmit data serially at 14,400 bps. If a burst of interference lasts .01 second, how many data bits would be affected?

*46. Suppose you are given 32 processors, each capable of finding the sum of two multidigit numbers in a millionth of a second. Describe how parallel processing techniques can be applied to find the sum of 64 numbers in only six-millionths of a second. How much time does a single processor require to find this same sum?

*47. Summarize the difference between a CISC architecture and a RISC architecture.

*48. Identify two approaches to increasing throughput.

*49. Describe how the average of a collection of numbers can be computed more rapidly with a multiprocessor machine than a single-processor machine.

Social Issues

The following questions are provided to help you understand some of the ethical/social/legal issues associated with the field of computing. The goal is not merely to answer these questions. You should also consider why you answered as you did and whether your justifications are consistent from one question to the next.

1. Suppose a computer manufacturer develops a new machine architecture. To what extent should the company be allowed to own that architecture? What policy would be best for society?

2. In a sense, the year 1923 marked the birth of what many now call *planned obsolescence*. This was the year that General Motors, led by Alfred Sloan, introduced the automobile industry to the concept of model years. The idea was to increase sales by changing styling rather than necessarily introducing a better automobile. Sloan is quoted as saying, "We want to make you dissatisfied with your current car so you will buy a new one." To what extent is this marketing ploy used today in the computer industry?

3. We often think in terms of how computer technology has changed our society. Many argue, however, that this technology has often kept changes from occurring by allowing old systems to survive and, in some cases, become more entrenched. For example, would the dominance of the New York Stock Exchange or the U.S. government's role in society have survived without computer technology? To what extent would centralized authority be present today had computer technology not been available? To what extent would we be better or worse off without computer technology?

4. Is it ethical for an individual to take the attitude that he or she does not need to know anything about the internal details of a machine because someone else will build it, maintain it, and fix any problems that arise? Does your answer depend on whether the machine is a computer, automobile, nuclear power plant, or toaster?

5. Suppose a manufacturer produces a computer chip and later discovers a flaw in its design. Suppose further that the manufacturer corrects the flaw in future production but decides to keep the original flaw a secret and does not recall the chips already shipped, reasoning that none of the chips already in use are being used in an application in which the flaw will have consequences. Is anyone hurt by the manufacturer's decision?

6. Does advancing technology provide cures for heart disease or is it a source of a sedentary life style that contributes to heart disease?

7. It is easy to imagine financial or navigational disasters that may occur as the result of arithmetic errors due to overflow and truncation problems. What consequences could result from errors in image storage systems due to loss of image details (perhaps in fields such as reconnaissance or medical diagnosis)?

Additional Reading

Carpinelli, J. D. *Computer Systems Organization and Architecture*. Reading, MA: Addison Wesley, 2001.

Hamacher, V. C., Z. G. Vranesic, and S. G. Zaky. *Computer Organization,* 5th ed. New York: McGraw-Hill, 2002.

Knuth, D. E. *The Art of Computer Programming,* vol. 1, 3rd ed. Reading, MA: Addison Wesley Longman, 1998.

Tanenbaum, A. S. *Structured Computer Organization*, 4th ed. Upper Saddle River, NJ: Prentice Hall, 1999.

Operating Systems

Today's computer applications often require a single machine to perform activities that may compete with one another for the machine's resources. For example, many computers are charged with the task of serving several users at the same time. Even in a single-user situation such as a PC, the user may require simultaneous activities such as playing music from a CD while editing a document and perhaps even printing another document. These demands require a high degree of coordination to ensure that unrelated activities do not interfere with one another and that communication between related activities is efficient and reliable. This coordination is handled by a software package known as an operating system. In this chapter we discuss fundamental concepts relating to operating systems.

3.1 The Evolution of Operating Systems

An **operating system** is the software that controls the overall operation of a computer. It provides the means by which a user can store and retrieve files, provides the interface by which a user can request the execution of programs, and provides the environment necessary to execute the program. Perhaps the best known example of an operating system is Windows, which is provided by Microsoft and widely used by PCs. Another well established example is Unix, which is a popular choice for computers that must serve numerous users at the same time.

Today's operating systems are large, complex software packages that have evolved over time. The computers of the 1940s and 1950s were not very flexible or efficient. Machines occupied entire rooms. Program execution required significant preparation of equipment in terms of mounting tapes, placing punched cards in the card reader, setting switches, and so on. The execution of each program, called a *job,* was handled as an isolated activity—the machine was prepared for executing the program, the program was executed, and then all the tapes, punched cards, etc. had to be retrieved before the next program preparation could begin. When several users needed to share a machine, sign-up sheets were provided so that users could reserve the machine for blocks of time. During the time period allocated to a user, the machine was totally under that user's control. The session usually began with program setup, followed by short periods of program execution. It was often completed in a hurried effort to do just one more thing ("It will only take a minute") while the next user was impatiently starting to set up.

In such an environment, operating systems began as systems for simplifying program setup and for streamlining the transition between jobs. One early development was the separation of users and equipment, which eliminated the physical transition of people in and out of the computer room. For this purpose a computer operator was hired to operate the machine. Anyone wanting a program run was required to submit it, along with any required data and special directions about the program's requirements, to the operator and return later for the results. The operator, in turn, loaded these materials into the machine's mass storage where a program called the operating system could read and execute them one at a time. This was the beginning of **batch processing**—the execution of jobs by collecting them in a single batch, then executing them without further interaction with the user.

In batch processing systems, the jobs residing in mass storage wait for execution in a **job queue** (Figure 3.1). A **queue** is a storage organization in which objects (in this case, jobs) are ordered in **first-in, first-out (FIFO)** fashion. That is, the objects are removed from the queue in the order in which they arrived. In reality, most job queues do not rigorously follow the FIFO structure, since most operating systems provide for consideration of job priorities. As a result, a job waiting in the job queue can be bumped by a higher-priority job.

In early batch processing systems, each job was accompanied by a set of instructions explaining the steps required to prepare the machine for that particular job. These instructions were coded in a job control language (JCL) and stored with the job in the job queue. When the job was selected for execution, the operating system

Figure 3.1

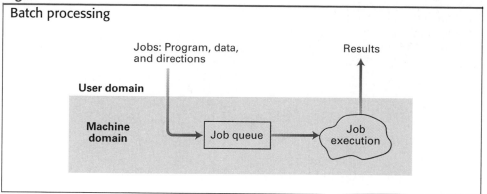

Batch processing

Jobs: Program, data, and directions

Results

User domain

Machine domain

Job queue

Job execution

printed these instructions at a printer where they could be read and followed by the computer operator. This communication between the computer operator and the operating system is still seen today, as witnessed by PC operating systems that report such errors as "no dialtone," "disk drive not accessible," and "printer not responding." However, in the PC environment we do not think of the person using the machine as the "computer operator." In fact, the position of computer operator has essentially become obsolete even in the case of large computer installations. Instead, institutions hire system administrators to manage the computer system—obtaining and overseeing the installation of new equipment and software, enforcing local regulations such as the issuing of new accounts and establishing the disk space limits for the various users, and coordinating efforts to resolve problems that arise in the system—rather than operating machines in a hands-on manner. Indeed, with today's modern operating systems, large computer installations often run unattended.

The major drawback to traditional batch processing is that the user has no interaction with the program once it is submitted to the job queue. This approach is acceptable for some applications, such as payroll processing, in which the data and all processing decisions are established in advance. However, it is not acceptable when the user must interact with the program during its execution. Examples include reservation systems in which reservations and cancellations must be reported as they occur; word processing systems in which documents are developed in a dynamic write and rewrite manner; and computer games in which interaction with the machine is the central feature of the game.

To accommodate these needs, new operating systems were developed that allowed the execution of programs that carried on a dialogue with the user through remote terminals or workstations—a feature known as **interactive processing** (Figure 3.2). These interactive systems required that the actions of the computer be coordinated with the actions of the user. (Using a word processor would be frustrating if the machine did not respond to requests promptly.) Providing computer services in such a timely manner became known as **real-time processing.**

Figure 3.2

Interactive processing

Programs, data, directions, and results

User domain

Machine domain

Program execution

If interactive systems had been required to serve only one user at a time, real-time processing would have been no problem. But computers were expensive, so each machine had to serve more than one user. In turn, it was common for several users to seek interactive service of a machine at the same time, and real-time considerations presented obstacles. If the operating system for such a multiuser environment insisted on executing only one job at a time, only one user would receive satisfactory real-time service.

A solution to this problem was to design the operating system so that it rotated the various jobs in and out of execution by a process called **time-sharing,** which is the technique of dividing time into intervals, or time slices, and then restricting the execution of a job to only one time slice at a time. At the end of each time slice, the current job is temporarily set aside and another is allowed to execute during the next time slice. By rapidly shuffling the jobs back and forth in this manner, the illusion of several jobs executing simultaneously is created. Depending on the types of jobs being executed, early time-sharing systems were able to provide acceptable real-time processing to as many as 30 users at the same time. Today, time-sharing is used in single-user as well as multiuser systems, although in the former it is usually called **multitasking,** in reference to the illusion of more than one task being performed simultaneously.

Another dimension to multitasking was added by the development of multiprocessor machines. In such machines multitasking is accomplished by assigning different tasks to different processors rather than by sharing the time of a single processor. In turn the operating system is charged with the job of assigning activities to the processors in the machine. This job involves problems of **load balancing** (dynamically allocating tasks to the various processors so that all processors are used efficiently) as well as **scaling** (breaking tasks into a number of subtasks compatible with the number of processors available).

Thus operating systems have grown from simple programs that retrieved and executed programs one at a time into complex systems that coordinate multiple activities. In turn, operating system design has become a significant subject in computer science.

Questions/Exercises

1. Identify examples of queues. In each case, indicate any situations that violate the FIFO structure.

2. Which of the following would require real-time processing?
   a. Printing mailing labels
   b. Playing a computer game
   c. Displaying letters on a monitor screen as they are typed at the keyboard
   d. Executing a program that predicts the state of next year's economy

3. What is the difference between real-time processing and interactive processing?

4. What is the difference between time-sharing and multitasking?

3.2 Operating System Architecture

To understand the composition of a typical operating system, we first consider the complete spectrum of software found within a typical computer system. Then we will concentrate on the operating system itself.

A Software Survey

We approach our survey of the software found on a typical computer system by presenting a scheme for classifying software. Such classification schemes invariably place similar software units in different classes in the same manner as the assignment of time zones dictates that nearby communities must set their clocks an hour apart even though there is no significant difference between the occurrence of sunrise and sunset. Moreover, in the case of software classification, the dynamics of the subject and the lack of a definitive authority lead to contradictory terminology. For example, users of Microsoft's Windows operating systems will find program groups called "Accessories" and

Beneficial Uniformity or Detrimental Monopoly?

At first glance, it seems reasonable that the use of a single, standard operating system across a wide range of machines would be a good thing. Such a standard would mean that operating skills learned on one computer could easily be transferred to other machines. Moreover, developers of application software would not have to develop products that were compatible with multiple operating system designs. However, these arguments overlook many of the realities of today's society. The producer of a universal operating system would have tremendous power in the marketplace. If misused, this power could potentially be more harmful than beneficial to the users of computers. Many of these issues have been documented by the parties involved in antitrust lawsuits against Microsoft in the United States and Europe.

"Administrative Tools" that include software from both our application and utility classes. The following classification should therefore be viewed as a means of gaining a foothold in a complex, dynamic subject rather than as a statement of universally accepted fact.

Let us begin by dividing a machine's software into two broad categories: **application software** and **system software** (Figure 3.3). Application software consists of the programs for performing tasks particular to the machine's utilization. A machine used to maintain the inventory for a manufacturing company will contain different application software from that found on a machine used by an electrical engineer. Examples of application software include spreadsheets, database systems, desktop publishing systems, accounting systems, program development software, and games.

In contrast to application software, system software performs those tasks that are common to computer systems in general. In a sense, the system software provides the infrastructure that the application software requires, in much the same manner as a nation's infrastructure (government, roads, utilities, financial institutions, etc.) provides the foundation on which its citizens rely for their individual lifestyles.

Within the class of system software are two categories, one is the operating system itself and the other consists of software units collectively known as **utility software.** The majority of an installation's utility software consists of programs for performing activities that are fundamental to computer installations but not included in the operating system. In a sense, utility software consists of software units that extend the capabilities of the operating system. For example, the ability to format a disk or to copy a file is often not implemented within the operating system itself but instead is provided by means of a utility program. Other instances of utility software include software to compress and decompress data, software for playing audio recordings, and software for handling network communication.

Figure 3.3

Software classification

By implementing certain activities as utility software, the design of an operating system can be less complex than it would be otherwise. Moreover, the routines implemented as utility software can be customized more readily to the needs of a particular installation. Indeed, it is common to find companies or individuals who have modified, or added to, the utility software that was originally provided with their machine's operating system.

The distinction between application software and utility software is often vague. From our point of view, the difference is whether the package is part of the software infrastructure. Thus a new application may evolve into a utility if it becomes a fundamental tool. The distinction between utility software and the operating system is equally vague. In particular, anti-trust lawsuits in the United States and Europe have been founded on questions regarding whether units called browsers and media players are components of Microsoft's operating systems or actually utilities that Microsoft has included merely to squash competition.

Components of an Operating System

Let us focus now on components that are well within the domain of operating systems. The portion of an operating system that communicates with the user, or users, of the machine is often called the **shell.** Modern shells perform this task by means of a **graphical user interface** (**GUI**—pronounced "GOO–ee") in which objects to be manipulated, such as files and programs, are represented pictorially on the monitor screen as icons. These systems allow users to issue commands by pointing to and clicking these icons on the screen by means of a hand-held device called a mouse. Older shells communicate with users through textual messages using a keyboard and monitor screen.

Although an operating system's shell plays an important role in establishing a machine's functionality, this shell is merely an interface between a user and the real heart of the operating system (Figure 3.4). This distinction between the shell and the

Figure 3.4

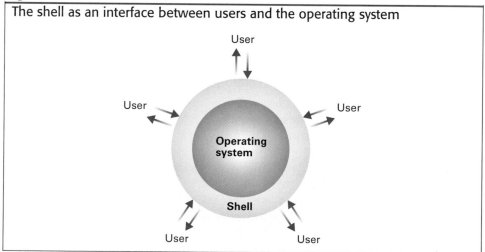

The shell as an interface between users and the operating system

BIOS

In addition to the bootstrap, the ROM in a PC contains a collection of routines for performing fundamental input/output activities such as receiving information from the keyboard, displaying messages on the computer screen, and reading data from mass storage. Being stored in ROM, these routines can be used by the bootstrap to perform I/O activities before the operating system becomes functional. For example, they are used to communicate with the computer user before the boot process actually begins and to report errors during bootstrapping. Collectively these routines form a basic input/output system (BIOS, pronounced "BYE–os"). Thus the term BIOS actually refers only to a portion of the software in a computer's ROM, although the term is widely used today in reference to the entire collection of software stored in ROM and sometimes to the ROM itself.

internal parts of the operating system is emphasized by the fact that some operating systems allow a user to select among different shells to obtain the most compatible interface for that particular user. Users of the UNIX operating system, for example, can select among a variety of shells including the Borne shell, the C shell, and the Korn shell. Early versions of Microsoft Windows were essentially replacement shells for MS-DOS, which was an operating system that used a text based shell in which users had to type instructions to the operating system via the keyboard.

A major component within today's GUI shells is the **window manager,** which allocates blocks of space on the screen, called windows, and keeps track of which application is associated with each window. When an application wants to display something on the screen, it notifies the window manager, and the window manager places the desired image in the window assigned to the application. In turn, when a mouse button is clicked, it is the window manager that computes the mouse's location on the screen and notifies the appropriate application of the mouse action.

In contrast to an operating system's shell, the internal part of an operating system is often called its **kernel.** An operating system's kernel contains those software components that perform the very basic functions required by the computer installation. One such unit is the **file manager,** whose job is to coordinate the use of the machine's mass storage facilities. More precisely, the file manager keeps records of all the files stored in mass storage, including where each file is located, which users are allowed to access the various files, and which portions of mass storage are available for new files or extensions to existing files.

For the convenience of the machine's users, most file managers allow files to be grouped into a bundle called a **directory** or **folder.** This approach allows a user to organize his or her files according to their purposes by placing related files in the same directory. Moreover, by allowing directories to contain other directories, called subdirectories, a hierarchical organization can be constructed. For example, a user may create a directory called MyRecords that contains subdirectories called FinancialRecords, Medical-Records, and HouseHoldRecords. Within each of these subdirectories could be files that fall within that particular category. A chain of directories within directories is called a directory **path.** Paths are often expressed by listing the directories along the path separated by slashes. For instance, `animals/prehistoric/dinosaurs` would represent the path starting at the directory named `animals`, passing through its subdirectory named `prehistoric`, and terminating in the sub-subdirectory `dinosaurs`.

Any access to a file by other software units is obtained at the discretion of the file manager. The procedure begins by requesting that the file manager grant access to the file through a procedure known as opening the file. If the file manager approves of the requested access, it provides the information needed to find and manipulate the file. This information is stored in an area of main memory called a **file descriptor.** It is by referencing the information in this file descriptor that individual operations are performed on the file.

Another component of the kernel consists of a collection of **device drivers,** which are the software units that communicate with the controllers (or at times, directly with peripheral devices) to carry out operations on the peripheral devices attached to the machine. Each device driver is uniquely designed for its particular type of device (such as a printer, disk drive, magnetic tape unit, or monitor) and translates generic requests into the more technical steps required by the device assigned to that driver. For example, a device driver for a printer contains the software for reading and decoding that particular printer's status word as well as all the other handshaking details. Thus, other software components do not have to deal with those technicalities in order to print a file. Instead, the other components can merely rely on the device driver software to print the file, and let the device driver take care of the details. In this manner, the design of the other software units can be independent of the unique characteristics of particular devices. The result is a generic operating system that can be customized for particular peripheral devices by merely installing the appropriate device drivers.

Still another component of an operating system's kernel is the **memory manager,** which is charged with the task of coordinating the machine's use of main memory. Such duties are minimal in an environment in which the machine is asked to perform only one task at a time. In these cases, the program for performing the current task is placed in main memory, executed, and then replaced by the program for performing the next task.

Linux

For the computer enthusiast who wants to experiment with the internal components of an operating system, there is Linux. Linux is an operating system originally designed by Linus Torvalds while a student at the University of Helsinki. It is a nonproprietary product and thus available, along with its source code (see Chapter 6) and documentation, without charge. Because it is freely available in source code form, it has become popular among computer hobbyists, students of operating systems, and programmers in general. Moreover, Linux is recognized as one of the most reliable operating systems available today. For this reason, several companies now package and market versions of Linux in an easily useable form, and these products are now beginning to challenge the long-established commercial operating systems on the market. You can learn more about Linux from the Web site at http://www.linux.org.

However, in multiuser or multitasking environments in which the machine is asked to address many needs at the same time, the duties of the memory manager are extensive. In these cases, many programs and blocks of data must reside in main memory concurrently, each in an area of memory set aside for it by the memory manager. As the needs of different activities come and go, the memory manager must find places to fulfill their memory requirements and keep track of those memory areas no longer occupied.

The task of the memory manager is complicated further when the total main memory space required exceeds the space actually available in the machine. In this case the memory manager may create the illusion of additional memory space by rotating programs and data back and forth between main memory and mass storage. Suppose, for example, that a main memory of 512MB is required but only 256MB is actually available. To create the illusion of the larger memory space, the memory manager would divide the required space into units called **pages** and store the contents of these pages in mass storage. (A typical page size is no more than a few kilobytes.) As different pages are actually required in main memory, the memory manager would exchange them for pages that are no longer required, and thus the other software units could execute as though there were actually 512MB of main memory in the machine. This large illusionary memory space is called **virtual memory.**

Also within the kernel of an operating system are the **scheduler** and **dispatcher,** which we study in the next section. For now we merely note that in a time-sharing system the scheduler determines which activities are to be considered for execution and the dispatcher controls the allocation of time slices to these activities.

Getting It Started

We have seen that an operating system provides the software infrastructure required by other software units, but we have not considered how the operating system itself gets started. This is accomplished through a procedure known as **boot strapping** (often shortened to **booting**) that is performed by the machine each time it is turned on. It is this procedure that transfers the operating system from mass storage (where it is permanently stored) into main memory (which is essentially empty when the machine is first turned on). To understand the boot strap process, we begin by considering the machine's CPU.

A CPU is designed so that its program counter starts with a particular predetermined address each time the CPU is turned on. It is at this location that the CPU expects to find the first instruction to be executed. But a computer changes the contents of its memory as it executes programs, and in fact most of the main memory in today's computers is constructed from technologies that "forget" the bit patterns entrusted to them when the machine is turned off. In this sense, most of the main memory is said to be volatile.

So to ensure that the CPU finds the correct instructions when it is first turned on, a portion of memory is constructed in such a way that its content is permanent. Such memory is known as **read-only memory (ROM).** As an analogy, you can think of storing bit patterns in ROM as blowing tiny fuses, although the technology used is more advanced and actually reversible. More precisely, the technology (called flash memory) used for ROM in most PCs today is the same as that used to store images in

Figure 3.5

The booting process

Step 1: Machine starts by executing the bootstrap program already in memory. Operating system is stored in mass storage.

Step 2: Bootstrap program directs the transfer of the operating system into main memory and then transfers control to it.

digital cameras. The point is that ROM maintains the data entrusted to it whether the machine is on or off.

The portion of main memory constructed from ROM contains a small program, called the **bootstrap.** It is this program that is executed automatically when the machine is turned on. It directs the CPU to transfer programs and data from a predetermined location in mass storage into the volatile area of main memory (Figure 3.5). In most cases this material is the operating system. Once the operating system has been placed in main memory, the bootstrap directs the CPU to execute a jump instruction to that area of memory. At this point, the operating system takes over and begins controlling the machine's activities.

In most personal computers, the bootstrap is designed to try to extract the operating system from a floppy disk first. If the bootstrap does not find a floppy disk inserted in the machine, the bootstrap will automatically try to extract the operating system from the machine's hard disk. If, however, a floppy disk is found and that disk does not contain a copy of the operating system, the bootstrap will pause with an error message to the machine's operator. You have probably experienced this phenomenon if you have turned on a personal computer with data disks already inserted in the machine's floppy disk drives.

Questions/Exercises

1. List the components of a typical operating system and summarize the role of each in a single phrase.

2. What is the difference between application software and utility software?

3. What is virtual memory?

4. Summarize the booting procedure.

3.3 Coordinating the Machine's Activities

In this section we consider how an operating system coordinates the execution of application software, utility software, and units within the operating system itself. We begin with the concept of a process.

The Concept of a Process

One of the most fundamental concepts of modern operating systems is the distinction between a program and the activity of executing a program. The former is merely a static set of directions, whereas the latter is a dynamic activity whose properties change as time progresses. This activity is known as a **process.** A process encompasses the current status of the activity, called the **process state.** This state includes the current position in the program being executed (the value of the program counter) as well as the values in the other CPU registers and the associated memory cells. Roughly speaking, the process state is a snapshot of the machine at that time. At different times during the execution of a program (at different times in a process) different snapshots (different process states) will be observed.

To emphasize the distinction between a program and a process, we note that a single program can be associated with more than one process at the same time. For example, in a multiuser, time-sharing system two users may wish to edit different documents. Both activities may use the same editing program, but each would be a separate process with its own set of data and its own rate of progress. In this situation an operating system could keep only one copy of the editor program in main memory and allow each process to use it during its time slice.

In a typical time-sharing computer installation, many processes are normally competing for time slices. These processes include the execution of application and utility programs as well as portions of the operating system itself. It is the task of the operating system to coordinate these processes. Coordination involves ensuring that each process has the resources (peripheral devices, space in main memory, access to files, and access to a CPU) that it needs, that independent processes do not interfere with one another, and that processes that need to exchange information are able to do so.

Process Administration

The tasks associated with coordinating the execution of processes are handled by the scheduler and dispatcher within the operating system's kernel. The scheduler maintains a record of the processes present in the computer system, introduces new processes to this pool, and removes processes from the pool that are complete. Thus when a user requests the execution of an application, it is the scheduler that adds the execution of that application to the pool of current tasks, or when an application terminates, it is the scheduler that removes the execution of that application from the pool.

To keep track of all the processes, the scheduler maintains a block of information in main memory called the **process table.** Each time a new task is assigned to the machine, the scheduler creates a process for that task by placing a new entry in the process table. This entry contains such information as the memory area assigned to the process (obtained from the memory manager), the priority of the process, and whether the process is ready or waiting. A process is **ready** if it is in a state in which its progress can continue; it is **waiting** if its progress is currently delayed until some external event occurs, such as the completion of a disk access or the arrival of a message from another process.

The dispatcher is the component of the kernel that ensures that the scheduled processes are actually executed. In a time-sharing system this task is accomplished by dividing time into short segments, each called a **time slice** or **quantum** (typically no more than 50 milliseconds), and then switching the CPU's attention among the processes as each is allowed to execute for no longer than one time slice (Figure 3.6). The procedure of changing from one process to another is called a **process switch** (or a **context switch**).

Each time a process begins its time slice, the dispatcher initiates a timer circuit that will measure the next quantum. At the end of the time slice, the timer circuit generates a signal called an **interrupt.** The CPU reacts to this signal in much the same way that you react when interrupted from a task. You stop what you are doing, record where you are in the task, and take care of the interrupting entity. When the CPU receives an interrupt signal, it completes its current machine cycle, saves its position in the current process (we will return to this step in a moment), and begins executing a program, called the **interrupt handler,** which is stored at a predetermined location in main memory. Having saved the state of the current process, the dispatcher will be able to restart the process later when it is time to give the process another time slice.

In our time-sharing scenario, the interrupt handler is a part of the dispatcher. Thus the effect of the interrupt signal is to preempt the current process and transfer control back to the dispatcher. At this point, the dispatcher allows the scheduler to update the process table (for instance, the priority of the process that has just completed its time slice may need to be lowered and the priorities of other processes may need to be raised). The dispatcher then selects the process from the process table that

Figure 3.6

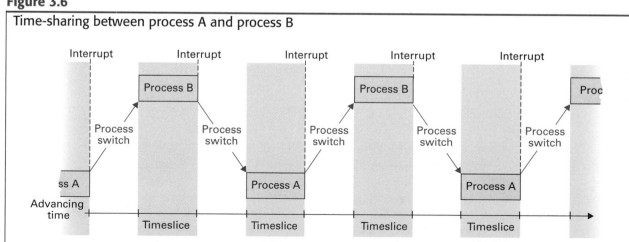

Time-sharing between process A and process B

has the highest priority among the ready processes, restarts the timer circuit, and allows the selected process to begin its time slice.

Paramount to the success of a time-sharing system is the ability to stop, and later restart, a process. If you are interrupted while reading a book, your ability to continue reading at a later time depends on your ability to remember your location in the book as well as the information that you had accumulated to that point. In short, you must be able to re-create the environment that was present immediately prior to the interruption. In the case of a process, the environment that must be re-created is the process's state. Recall that this state includes the value of the program counter as well as the contents of the registers and pertinent memory cells. Machines designed for time-sharing systems incorporate the task of saving this information as part of the CPU's reaction to the interrupt signal. These machines also tend to have machine-language instructions for reloading a previously saved state. Such machine features simplify the task of the dispatcher when performing a process switch and exemplify how the design of modern machines is influenced by the needs of today's operating systems.

In closing, we should note that the use of time-sharing has been found to increase the overall efficiency of a machine. This is somewhat counterintuitive since the shuffling of processes required by time-sharing introduces an overhead. However, without time-sharing a computer system spends much of its time waiting for peripheral devices to complete tasks or for a user to make the next request. Time-sharing allows this lost time to be given to another process. For example, if a process executes an I/O request, such as a request to retrieve data from a disk, the time slice of that process will be terminated, since the process would merely waste the remaining time waiting for the controller to perform the request. In this case, the scheduler will update the process table to reflect the process's waiting status, and the dispatcher will assign a new time slice to a process that is ready. Later (perhaps several hundred milliseconds), when the I/O request has been completed, the scheduler will reclassify the process as ready, and thus that process will again compete for a time slice. Hence, progress on one task can be made while another task is waiting. In turn, a collection of tasks will often be completed in less time when executed in a time-sharing environment than when executed in a sequential manner.

Questions/Exercises

1. Summarize the difference between a program and a process.

2. Summarize the steps performed by the CPU when an interrupt occurs.

3. In a time-sharing system, how can high-priority processes be allowed to run faster than others?

4. If each quantum in a time-sharing system is 50 milliseconds and each context switch requires at most a microsecond, how many processes can the machine service in a single second?

5. If each process uses its complete quantum in the machine in Exercise 4, what fraction of the machine's time is spent actually performing processes? What would this fraction be if each process executes an I/O request after only a microsecond of its quantum?

3.4 Handling Competition Among Processes

An important task of an operating system is the allocation of the machine's resources to the processes in the system. Here we are using the term *resource* in a broad sense, including the machine's peripheral devices as well as features within the machine itself. The file manager allocates access to files as well and allocates disk space for the construction of new files; the memory manager allocates memory space; the scheduler allocates space in the process table; and the dispatcher allocates time slices. As with many problems in computer systems, this allocation task may appear simple on the surface. Below the surface, however, lie several problems that can lead to malfunctions in a poorly designed system. Remember, a machine does not think for itself; it merely follows directions. Thus to construct reliable operating systems, we must develop algorithms that cover every possible contingency, regardless of how minuscule it may appear.

Semaphores

Consider a time-sharing operating system controlling the activities of a machine with a single printer. If a process needs to print its results, it must request that the operating system give it access to the printer's device driver. At this point, the operating system must decide whether to grant this request, depending on whether the printer is already being used by another process. If it is not, the operating system should grant the request and allow the process to continue; otherwise, the operating system should deny the request and perhaps classify the process as a waiting process until the printer becomes available. Indeed, if two processes were given simultaneous access to the machine's printer, the results would be worthless to both.

To control access to the printer, the operating system must keep track of whether the printer has been allocated. One approach to this task would be to use a flag, which in this context refers to a bit in memory whose states are often referred to as *set* and *clear*, rather than 1 and 0. A clear flag (value 0) indicates that the printer is available and a set flag (value 1) indicates that the printer is currently allocated. On the surface this approach seems to hold no unforeseen problems. The operating system merely checks the flag each time a request for printer access is made. If it is clear, the request is granted and the operating system sets the flag. If the flag is set, the operating system makes the requesting process wait. Each time a process finishes with the printer, the operating system either allocates the printer to a waiting process or, if no process is waiting, merely clears the flag.

Although this solution looks good at first glance, it has a problem. The task of testing and possibly setting the flag may require several machine instructions. It is therefore possible for the task to be interrupted after a clear flag has been detected but before the flag has been set. The following scenario could therefore take place.

Suppose the printer is currently available, and a process requests use of it. The flag is checked and found to be clear, indicating that the printer is available. However, at this point, the process is interrupted and another process begins its time slice. It too requests the use of the printer. Again, the flag is checked and found still clear because the previous process was interrupted before the operating system had time to set the flag. Consequently, the operating system allows the second process to begin using the printer. Later, the original process resumes execution where it left off, which is immediately after the operating system found the flag to be clear. Thus the operating system continues by granting the original process access to the printer. Two processes are now using the same printer.

The solution to this problem is to insist that the task of testing and possibly setting the flag must be completed without interruption. One approach is to use the interrupt disable and interrupt enable instructions provided in most machine languages. When executed, an interrupt disable instruction causes future interrupts to be blocked, whereas an interrupt enable instruction causes the CPU to resume responding to interrupt signals. Thus if the operating system starts the flag-testing routine with a disable interrupt instruction and ends it with an enable interrupt instruction, no other activity can interrupt the routine once it starts.

Another approach is to use the **test-and-set** instruction that is available in many machine languages. This instruction directs the CPU to retrieve the value of a flag, note the value received, and then set the flag all within a single machine instruction. The advantage here is that since the CPU always completes an instruction before recognizing an interrupt, the task of testing and setting the flag cannot be split when it is implemented as a single instruction.

A properly implemented flag, as just described, is called a **semaphore,** in reference to the railroad signals used to control access to sections of track. In fact, semaphores are used in software systems in much the same way as they are in railway systems. Corresponding to the section of track that can contain only one train at a time is a sequence of instructions that can be executed by only one process at a time. Such a sequence of instructions is called a **critical region.** The requirement that only one process at a time be allowed to execute a critical region is known as **mutual exclusion.** In summary, a common way of obtaining mutual exclusion to a critical region is to guard the critical region with a semaphore. To enter the critical region, a process must find the semaphore clear and then set the semaphore before entering the critical region; then upon exiting the critical region, the process must clear the semaphore. If the semaphore is found in its set state, the process trying to enter the critical region must wait until the semaphore has been cleared.

Deadlock

Another problem that can arise during resource allocation is **deadlock,** the condition in which two or more processes are blocked from progressing because each is waiting for a resource that is allocated to another. For example, one process may have access to the machine's printer but be waiting for the tape drive, while another process has access to the tape drive but is waiting for the printer. Another example occurs in systems in which processes are allowed to create new processes (an action called **forking**) to perform subtasks. If the scheduler has no space left in the process table and each process in the system must create an additional process before it can complete its task, then no process can continue. Such conditions, as in other settings (Figure 3.7), can severely degrade a system's performance.

Figure 3.7

A deadlock resulting from competition for nonshareable railroad intersections

Analysis of deadlock has revealed that it cannot occur unless all three of the following conditions are satisfied:

1. There is competition for nonshareable resources.
2. The resources are requested on a partial basis; that is, having received some resources, a process will return later to request more.
3. Once a resource has been allocated, it cannot be forcibly retrieved.

The point of isolating these conditions is that the deadlock problem can be removed by attacking any one of the three. In general, techniques that attack the third condition tend to fall in the category known as deadlock detection and correction schemes. In these cases, the occurrence of deadlock is considered so remote that no effort is made to avoid the problem. Instead, the approach is to detect it should it occur and then correct it by forcibly retrieving some of the allocated resources. Our example of a full process table falls in this class. When initially setting up a computer system, the system administrator will usually establish a process table that is large enough for that particular installation. If, however, deadlock should occur due to a full table, the administrator merely uses his or her powers as "super user" to remove (the technical term is *kill*) some of the processes, which releases space in the process table so that the remaining processes can continue their tasks.

Techniques that attack the first two conditions tend to be known as deadlock avoidance schemes. One, for example, attacks the second condition by requiring each process to request all its resources at one time. Another perhaps more imaginative technique attacks the first condition, not by removing the competition directly but by converting nonshareable resources into shareable ones. For example, suppose the resource in question is a printer and a variety of processes require its use. Each time a process requests the printer, the operating system grants the request. However, instead of connecting the process to the printer's device driver, the operating system connects it to a device driver that stores the information to be printed in mass storage rather than sending it to the printer. Thus each process, thinking it has access to the printer, executes in its normal way. Later, when the printer is available, the operating system can transfer the data from mass storage to the printer. In this manner, the operating system has made the nonshareable resource appear shareable by creating the illusion of more than one printer. This technique of holding data for output at a later but more convenient time is called **spooling** and is quite popular on systems of all sizes.

We have introduced spooling as a technique for granting multiple processes access to a common resource—a theme that has many variations. For example, a file manager could grant several processes access to the same file if the processes are merely reading data from the file, but conflicts can occur if more than one process tries to alter a file at the same time. Thus a file manager may allocate file access according to the needs of the processes, allowing several processes to have read access but only one having write access at any given time. Other systems may divide the file into pieces so that different processes can alter different parts of the file concurrently. Additional problems must still be resolved, however. How, for example, should those processes with only read access to a file be notified when a process with write access alters the file?

Questions/Exercises

1. Suppose process A and process B are sharing time on the same machine, and each needs the same nonshareable resource for short periods of time. (For example, each process may be printing a series of independent, short reports.) Each process may then repeatedly acquire the resource, release it, and later request it again. What is a drawback to controlling access to the resource in the following manner:

   Begin by assigning a flag the value 0. If process A requests the resource and the flag is 0, grant the request. Otherwise, make process A wait. If process B requests the resource and the flag is 1, grant the request. Otherwise, make process B wait. Each time process A finishes with the resource, change the flag to 1. Each time process B finishes with the resource, change the flag to 0.

2. Suppose a two-lane road converges to one lane to pass through a tunnel. To coordinate the use of the tunnel, the following signal system has been installed:

   A car entering either end of the tunnel causes red lights above the tunnel entrances to be turned on. As the car exits the tunnel, the lights are turned off. If an approaching car finds a red light on, it waits until the light is turned off before entering the tunnel.

   What is the flaw in this system?

3. Suppose the following solutions have been proposed for removing the deadlock that occurs on a single-lane bridge when two cars meet. Identify which condition for deadlock given in the text is removed by each solution.
   a. Do not let a car onto the bridge until the bridge is empty.
   b. If cars meet, make one of them back up.
   c. Add a second lane to the bridge.

4. Suppose we represent each process in a time-sharing system with a dot and draw an arrow from one dot to another if the process represented by the first dot is waiting for a resource being used by the second. Mathematicians call the resulting picture a *directed graph*. What property of the directed graph is equivalent to deadlock in the system?

3.5 Security

We normally associate the concept of security with protection against malicious activity, but in the global sense, reliability is a security issue as well. If a flaw in the file manager causes the loss of part of a file, the file was not secure. If a flaw in an operating system leads to a system failure (often called a system crash), causing the loss of an hour's worth of typing, we would argue that our work was not secure. Thus the topic of security encompasses the avoidance of design flaws, which is the goal of the field of computer science known as software engineering—a topic we will address in Chapter 7.

For security in the sense of guarding against malicious behavior, an operating system is challenged with threats that come from outside the machine as well as threats from within. An example of an exterior threat is an unauthorized user trying to gain access to the machine. An example of a threat from within is a process in a time-sharing system trying to access cells in main memory that are not assigned to it.

The most common means of dealing with the problem of unauthorized user access is to require each potential user to provide a password as a part of the **login** procedure, which is a sequence of transactions in which the user establishes initial contact with a computer's operating system and identifies himself or herself. Unfortunately, passwords can be obtained covertly by various means. Some computer users simply share their passwords with friends—a practice with questionable ethics. In other cases passwords are stolen. One approach to stealing passwords is to exploit flaws within a machine's operating system to obtain its password records. Another is to design a program that simulates the local system's login procedure so that users, thinking they are communicating with the operating system, type their passwords, which are then recorded by the program. Still another way of obtaining passwords is to try the most obvious passwords and see if they work. For example, users who fear forgetting their passwords may use their own names as passwords. Dates such as birthdays are also popular password choices.

In an effort to thwart those playing the guess-the-password game, operating systems can be designed to report any avalanche of incorrect passwords. Many operating systems are also designed to report the time that an account was last used each time a new session under that account is started. This allows users to detect any unauthorized use of their accounts. A more sophisticated defense against password guessers is to create the illusion of success (called a trapdoor) when false passwords are given and to proceed to give the intruder misinformation while trying to record the intruder's origin.

In regard to threats arising within the machine, a multitasking operating system faces numerous security issues concerning the interaction of the different processes that are sharing time. The memory manager must ensure that each process is restricted to its allotted area in main memory, the file manager must ensure that processes do not gain access to files to which they are not authorized, and the scheduler and dispatcher must work together to ensure that a single process is not allow to dominate the machine.

To ensure that processes access only the main memory cells allotted to it, CPUs designed for multitasking systems typically contain special purpose registers in which the operating system can store the upper and lower limits of a process' allotted memory area. Then, while performing the process, the CPU compares each memory reference to these registers to ensure that the reference is within the designated limits. If the reference is found to be outside the process' designated area, the CPU automatically transfers control back to the operating system (by performing an interrupt sequence) so the operating system can take appropriate action.

Embedded in this illustration is a subtle but significant problem. Without further security features a process could still gain access to memory cells outside of its designated area merely by changing the special purpose registers that contain its memory limits. That is, a process that wanted access to additional memory could merely increase the value in the register containing the upper memory limit and then proceed to use the additional memory space without approval from the operating system.

To protect against such malicious activities, certain instructions in a machine language are designated as **privileged instructions** and the CPU is designed to operate in either privileged or nonprivileged mode. When first turned on, the CPU is in privileged mode, meaning that all instructions in its repertoire are executable. However, by executing a "change privilege mode" instruction, the machine can be switched to nonprivileged mode in which the CPU will refuse to execute privileged instructions. Typical examples of privileged instructions include instructions that change the contents of memory limit registers and instructions that change the current privilege mode of the CPU. (In reality, most machine languages contain instructions with various degrees of privilege—some being more privileged than others. In turn, these machines have a variety of **privilege levels** ranging from most privileged, in which all instructions are executable, to least privileged, in which no privileged instruction is executable.)

An attempt to execute a privileged instruction when the CPU is in nonprivileged mode causes an interrupt. This interrupt converts the CPU to privileged mode but transfers control to an interrupt handler within the operating system. Thus, if the operating system switches the CPU to nonprivileged mode each time a process is given a time slice, then the operating system will be notified of any attempt by that process to execute a privileged instruction. In turn, the operating system will be in position to maintain the integrity of the computer system.

We close by observing that the use of privileged instructions and the control of the CPU's privilege levels is a complex component of an operating system's design. If a process is allowed to alter the timer that controls the system's time-sharing, that process can dominate the machine. If a process is allowed to access peripheral devices directly, then it can read files without supervision by the system's file manager. If a process is allowed to access memory cells outside its allotted area, it can read and even alter data being used by other processes. Thus, a single flaw in privilege level control can open the door to disaster from malicious programmers or from inadvertent programming errors.

Questions/Exercises

1. Give some examples of poor choices for passwords and explain why they would be poor choices.

2. Processors in Intel's Pentium series use four privilege levels. Why would the designers decide to have four levels rather than three or five?

3. If a process in a time-sharing system could access memory cells outside its allotted area, how could it gain control of the machine?

Chapter Review Problems

(Asterisked problems are associated with optional sections.)

1. List four activities of a typical operating system.

2. Summarize the distinction between batch processing and interactive processing.

3. What is the difference between interactive processing and real-time processing?

4. What is a multitasking operating system?

5. If you have a PC, identify some situations in which you can take advantage of its multitasking capabilities.

6. Based on a computer system with which you are familiar, identify two units of application software and two units of utility software. Then explain why you classified them as you did.

7. What information is contained in a process table within an operating system?

8. What is the difference between a process that is ready and a process that is waiting?

9. What is the difference between virtual memory and main memory?

10. What complications could arise in a time-sharing system if two processes require access to the same file at the same time? Are there cases in which the file manager should grant such requests? Are there cases in which the file manager should deny such requests?

11. Define load balancing and scaling in the context of multiprocessor architectures.

12. Summarize the booting process.

13. If you have a PC, record the sequence activities that you can observe when you turn it on. Then determine when the bootstrap process is looking for the disk containing the operating system and when it is actually loading the operating system into main memory.

14. Suppose a time-sharing operating system allocated time slices of 20 milliseconds and the machine executed an average of 5 instructions per microsecond. How many instructions could be executed in a single time slice?

15. Suppose a time-sharing operating system is allotting time slices of 50 milliseconds. If it normally takes 8 milliseconds to position a disk's read/write head over the desired track and another 17 milliseconds for the desired data to rotate around to the read/write head, how much of a program's time slice can be spent waiting for a read operation from a disk to take place? If the machine is capable of executing ten instructions each microsecond, how many instructions can be executed during this waiting period? (This is why when a process performs an operation with a peripheral device, a time-sharing system terminates that process's time slice and allows another process

to run while the first process is waiting for the services of the peripheral device.)

16. List five resources to which a multitasking operating system might have to coordinate access.

17. A process is said to be I/O-bound if it requires a lot of I/O operations, whereas a process that consists of mostly computations within the CPU/memory system is said to be compute-bound. If both a compute-bound process and an I/O-bound process are waiting for a time slice, which should be given priority? Why?

18. Would greater throughput be achieved by a system running two processes in a time-sharing environment if both processes were I/O-bound (refer to Problem 13) or if one was I/O-bound and the other was compute-bound? Why?

19. Write a set of directions that tells an operating system's dispatcher what to do when a process's time slice is over.

20. Identify the components of the state of a process.

21. Identify a situation in a time-sharing system in which a process does not consume the entire time slice allocated to it.

22. List in chronological order the major events that take place when a process is interrupted.

23. Answer each of the following in terms of an operating system that you use:
    a. How do you ask the operating system to copy a file from one location to another?
    b. How do you ask the operating system to show you the directory on a disk?
    c. How do you ask the operating system to execute a program?

24. Answer each of the following in terms of an operating system that you use:
    a. How does the operating system restrict access to only those who are approved users?
    b. How do you ask the operating system to show you what processes are currently in the process table?
    c. How do you tell the operating system that you do not want other users of the machine to have access to your files?

*25. Explain an important use for the test-and-set instruction found in many machine languages. Why is it important for the entire test-and-set process to be implemented as a single instruction?

*26. A banker with only $100,000 loans $50,000 to each of two customers. Later, both customers return with the story that before they can repay their loans they must each borrow another $10,000 to complete the business deals in which their previous loans are involved. The banker resolves this deadlock by borrowing the additional funds from another source and passing on this loan (with an increase in the interest rate) to the two customers. Which of the three conditions for deadlock has the banker removed?

*27. Students who want to enroll in Model Railroading II at the local university are required to obtain permission from the instructor and pay a laboratory fee. The two requirements are fulfilled independently in either order and at different locations on campus. Enrollment is limited to 20 students; this limit is maintained by both the instructor, who will grant permission to only 20 students, and the financial office, which will allow only 20 students to pay the laboratory fee. Suppose that this registration system has resulted in 19 students having successfully registered for the course, but with the final space being claimed by 2 students—one who has only obtained permission from the instructor and another who has only paid the fee. Which requirement for deadlock is removed by each of the following solutions to the problem:
    a. Both students are allowed in the course.
    b. The class size is reduced to 19, so neither of the two students is allowed to register for the course.
    c. The competing students are both denied entry to the class and a third student is given the twentieth space.
    d. It is decided that the only requirement for entry into the course is the payment of the

fee. Thus the student who has paid the fee gets into the course, and entry is denied to the other student.

*28. Explain how deadlock can occur as two pawns approach each other in a chess game. What nonshareable resources are involved? How is such deadlock normally broken?

*29. Suppose each nonshareable resource in a computer system is classified as a level 1, level 2, or level 3 resource. Moreover, suppose each process in the system is required to request the resources it needs according to this classification. That is, it must request all the required level 1 resources at once before requesting any level 2 resources. Once it receives the level 1 resources, it can request all the required level 2 resources, and so on. Can deadlock occur in such a system? Why or why not?

*30. Each of two robot arms is programmed to lift assemblies from a conveyor belt, test them for tolerances, and place them in one of two bins depending on the results of the test. The assemblies arrive one at a time with a sufficient interval between them. To keep both arms from trying to grab the same assembly, the computers controlling the arms share a common memory cell. If an arm is available as an assembly approaches, its controlling computer reads the value of the common cell. If the value is nonzero, the arm lets the assembly pass. Otherwise, the controlling computer places a nonzero value in the memory cell, directs the arm to pick up the assembly, and places the value 0 back into the memory cell after the action is complete. What sequence of events could lead to a tug-of-war between the two arms?

*31. The following is the "dining philosophers" problem that was originally proposed by E. W. Dijkstra and is now a part of computer science folklore.

Five philosophers are sitting at a round table. In front of each is a plate of spaghetti. There are five forks on the table, one between each plate. Each philosopher wants to alternate between thinking and eating. To eat, a philosopher requires possession of both the forks that are adjacent to the philosopher's plate.
Identify the possibilities of deadlock and starvation that are present in the dining philosophers problem.

*32. Identify the use of a queue in the process of spooling output to a printer.

*33. The pavement in the middle of an intersection can be considered as a nonshareable resource for which cars approaching the intersection compete. A traffic light rather than an operating system is used to control the allocation of the resource. If the light is able to sense the amount of traffic arriving from each direction and is programmed to give the green light to the heavier traffic, the lighter traffic might suffer from what is called starvation. What is meant by starvation?

*34. In what sense can a process starve if the dispatcher always assigns time slices according to a priority system in which the priority of each process remains fixed? (Hint: What is the priority of the process that just completed its time slice in comparison to the processes that are waiting, and consequently which routine gets the next time slice?)

*35. What is the similarity between deadlock and starvation? (Refer to Problem 34.) What is the difference between deadlock and starvation?

*36. What problem arises as the lengths of the time slices in a time-sharing system are made shorter and shorter? What about as they become longer and longer?

*37. As computer science has developed, machine languages have been extended to provide specialized instructions. Three such machine instructions were introduced in Section 3.4 that are used extensively by operating systems. What are these instructions?

38. How does an operating system keep a process from accessing another process's memory space?

39. Suppose a password consisted of a string of nine characters from the English alphabet (26 characters). If each possible password could be tested in a millisecond, how long would it take to test all possible passwords?

40. Why are CPUs that are designed for multitasking operating systems capable of operating in different privilege levels?

41. Identify three ways in which a process could challenge the security of a computer system if not prevented by the operating system.

Social Issues

The following questions are provided to help you understand some of the ethical/social/legal issues associated with the field of computing. The goal is not merely to answer these questions. You should also consider why you answered as you did and whether your justifications are consistent from one question to the next.

1. Suppose you are using a multiuser operating system that allows you to view the names of the files belonging to other users as well as to view the contents of those files that are not otherwise protected. Would viewing such information without permission be similar to wandering through someone's unlocked home without permission, or would it be more like reading materials placed in a common lounge such as a physician's waiting room?

2. When you have access to a multiuser computer system, what responsibilities do you have when selecting your password?

3. If a flaw in an operating system's security allows a malicious programmer to gain unauthorized access to sensitive data, to what extent should the developer of the operating system be held responsible?

4. Is it your responsibility to lock your house in such a way that intruders cannot get in, or is it the public's responsibility to stay out of your house unless invited? Is it the responsibility of an operating system to guard access to a computer and its contents, or is it the responsibility of hackers to leave the machine alone?

5. In *Walden,* Henry David Thoreau argues that we have become tools of our tools; that is, instead of benefiting from the tools that we have, we spend our time obtaining and maintaining our tools. To what extent is this true in regards to computing? For example, if you own a personal computer, how much time do you spend earning the money to pay for it, learning how to use its operating system, learning how to use its utility and application software, maintaining it, and downloading upgrades to its software in comparison to the amount of time you spend benefiting from it? When you use it, is your time well spent? Are you more socially active with or without a personal computer?

Additional Reading

Bishop, M. *Computer Security: Art and Science*. Reading, MA: Addison Wesley, 2003.

Nutt, G. *Operating Systems: A Modern Approach*, 3rd ed. Reading, MA: Addison Wesley, 2004.

Rosenoer, J. *CyberLaw, The Law of the Internet*. New York: Springer, 1997.

Silberschatz, A., P. B. Galvin, and G. Gagne. *Operating System Concepts*, 6th ed. New York: Wiley, 2001.

Tanenbaum, A. S. *Modern Operating Systems*, 2nd ed. Upper Saddle River, NJ: Prentice Hall, 2001.

Networking and the Internet

In this chapter we discuss the area of computer science that is having the most pronounced affect on society—the field of computer networking. The ability to connect computers over wide regions has spawned a proliferation of applications. In turn, the underlying software required to support such applications has grown from simple utility packages into an expanding system of network software that provides a sophisticated network-wide infrastructure. In a sense, then, network software is evolving into a network-wide operating system. In this chapter we consider some of the topics associated with this expanding field of computer science.

4.1 Network Fundamentals

The need to share information and resources among different computers has lead to linked computer systems, called **networks,** in which computers are connected so that data can be transferred from machine to machine. In fact, the concept of one large central computer serving many users has been superceded by that of many small computers connected via a network. In these networks, users share resources— such as printing capabilities, software packages, data storage facilities, and information—that are scattered throughout the system.

Network Classifications

Computer networks are often classified as either **local area networks** (**LANs**) or **wide area networks** (**WANs**). A LAN normally consists of a collection of computers in a single building or building complex. For example, the computers on a university campus or those in a manufacturing plant might be connected by a LAN. A WAN links machines that could be in neighboring cities or on opposite sides of the world.

A network's internal operation can be based either on designs that are in the public domain or on innovations owned and controlled by a particular entity such as an individual or a corporation. A network of the former type is called an **open** network; a network of the latter type is called a **closed,** or sometimes a **proprietary,** network. The Internet (a popular world-wide network of networks that we will study shortly) is an open system. In particular, communication throughout the Internet is governed by an open collection of standards known as the TCP/IP protocol suite, which we will discuss in Section 4.4. Anyone is free to use these standards without paying fees or signing license agreements. In contrast, Novell Inc. is a provider of network software that applies innovations that Novell has developed and owns. Thus networks based on Novell's products are examples of closed networks.

Still another way of classifying networks is based on the topology of the network, which refers to the pattern in which the machines are connected. Figure 4.1 represents four popular topologies: (1) ring, in which the machines are connected in a circular fashion; (2) bus, in which the machines are all connected to a common communication line called a bus; (3) star, in which one machine serves as a hub to which all the others are connected; and (4) irregular topology, in which the machines are connected in what appears to be a haphazard manner.

It is important to remember that the connections between machines in a network do not need to be physical. Wireless networks are becoming more and more common. For example, traditional radio broadcast technology, in which a transmitted signal propagates in all directions, can be used to implement a bus topology network. In this case the bus is not a physical wire but instead is a segment of the broadcast frequency spectrum.

Sometimes it becomes necessary to connect two existing networks. When the networks are compatible, this can be done by merely connecting the networks by a coupling device called a **bridge.** For example, in the case of two bus networks, it may be possible to use a bridge to serve as a connection between the two existing buses so that signals on either are relayed onto the other (Figure 4.2a). The important point is that when two networks are connected via a bridge, the result is simply a larger single network.

Figure 4.1

Network topologies

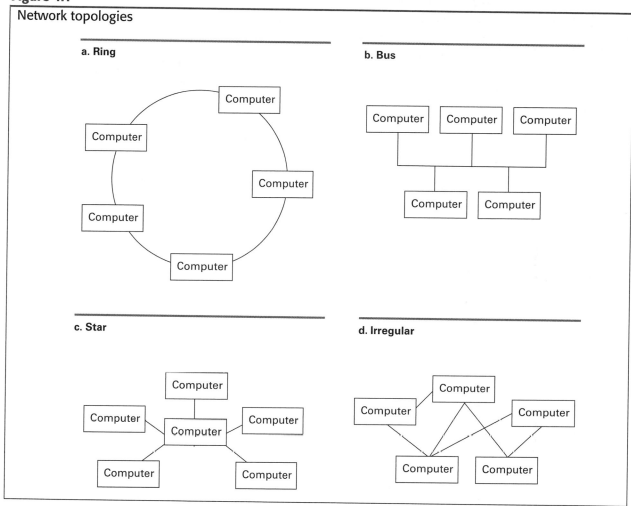

a. Ring

b. Bus

c. Star

d. Irregular

It is often necessary, however, to join two networks whose characteristics are not compatible. For instance, the characteristics of a star network would not be readily compatible with those of a bus network. In these cases the two networks can be connected in a manner that builds a network of networks, which is known as an **internet.** (Note that the generic term *internet* is distinct from the Internet. The Internet, written with an upper case I, refers to a particular, world-wide internet that we will study in the remaining sections of this chapter.) That is, in the case of an internet, the original networks maintain their individuality and continue to function as independent networks. They are merely linked so that messages in one can be transferred to the other, thus allowing a machine in one network to send a message to a machine in the other network.

The connection between two networks to form an internet is handled by a machine known as a **router,** which is a computer belonging to both networks that

Figure 4.2

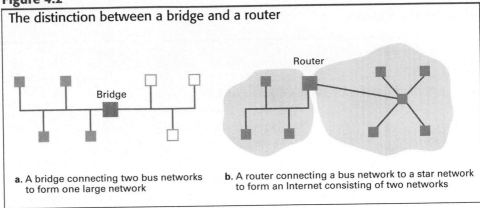

The distinction between a bridge and a router

a. A bridge connecting two bus networks to form one large network

b. A router connecting a bus network to a star network to form an Internet consisting of two networks

forwards messages in one network into the other network (Figure 4.2b). Note that the task of a router is significantly greater than that of a bridge since a router must convert between the idiosyncrasies of the two original networks—a task that often requires a certain amount of repackaging of messages.

The Client/Server Model

The various activities (or processes) executing on the different machines within a network (or even executing on the same machine via time-sharing) must often communicate with each other to coordinate their actions and to perform their designated tasks. Such communication between processes is called **interprocess communication.**

A popular convention used for interprocess communication is the **client/server model** (Figure 4.3). This model defines the basic roles played by the processes as either a **client,** which makes requests of other processes, or a **server,** which satisfies the requests made by clients.

An early application of the client/server model appeared in networks connecting all the computers in a cluster of offices. In this situation, a single, high-quality printer was attached to the network where it was available to all the machines in the network. In this case the printer played the role of a server (often called a print server), and the other machines were programmed to play the role of clients that sent print requests to the print server.

Figure 4.3

The client/server model

Client — Requests → Server
Server — Service → Client

Another early application of the client/server model was used to reduce the cost of disk storage while also removing the need for duplicate copies of records. Here one machine in a network was equipped with a high-capacity disk drive that contained all an organization's records. Other machines on the network then requested access to the records as they needed them. Thus the machine that actually contained the records played the role of a server (called a file server), and the other machines played the role of clients that requested access to the files that were stored at the file server.

Today the client/server model is used extensively in network applications as we will see in this chapter. However, the client/server model is not the only means of inter-process communication. Another model is the **peer-to-peer model,** whose properties provide insightful contrasts to the client/server model. Whereas the client/server model involves one process (the server) communicating with numerous others (clients), the peer-to-peer model involves two processes communicating as equals (Figure 4.4).

Moreover, whereas a server must execute continuously so that it is prepared to serve its clients at any time, the peer-to-peer model often involves two processes that execute on a temporary basis.

Lately, the peer-to-peer model has been popularized as a means of sharing music recordings via the Internet (often with questionable legality). Individuals, who are seeking recordings, broadcast their desire over the Internet, and those who own the items of interest contact them. Then, the items are transferred between the two parties using the peer-to-peer model. This is in contrast to earlier approaches that applied the client/server model by establishing a central "distribution center" (the server) from which clients downloaded items of interest (or at least found sources for those items).

Figure 4.4

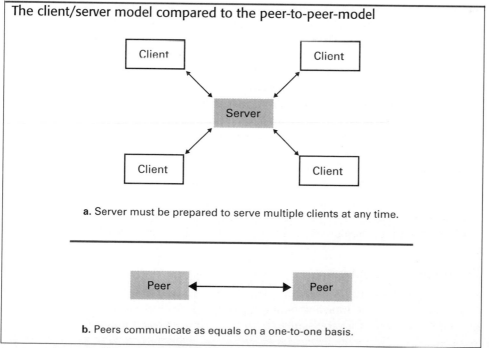

The client/server model compared to the peer-to-peer-model

a. Server must be prepared to serve multiple clients at any time.

b. Peers communicate as equals on a one-to-one basis.

Ethernet

Ethernet is a set of standards for implementing a LAN with a bus topology. Its name is derived from the original Ethernet design in which machines were connected by a coaxial cable called the ether. Originally developed in the 1970s and now standardized by IEEE as a part of the IEEE 802 family of standards, Ethernet is the most common method of networking PCs. Indeed, Ethernet controller cards for PCs are readily available and easily installed.

Today there are actually several versions of Ethernet, reflecting advances in technology and higher transfer rates. All, however, share common traits that characterize the Ethernet family. Among these are the format in which data are packaged for transmission, the use of Manchester encoding (a method of representing 0s and 1s in which a 0 is represented by a descending signal and a 1 is represented by an ascending signal) for the actual transmission of bits, and the use of CSMA/CD for controlling the right to transmit.

The central server, however, proved to be a focal point at which the music industry could enforce copyright laws, leading to the eventual dismantling of these music distribution centers. In contrast, the lack of a centralized base of operation has so far allowed systems founded on the peer-to-peer model to resist legal efforts to control them.

Compliance with interprocess communication conventions such as the client/server model leads to software units with well-defined roles. A client sends requests to servers and waits for replies; a server performs the services requested and sends replies back to the clients. The role of each process is the same whether the processes reside on the same machine or on distant machines within a network. Thus, if the components of a software system are designed using such a model, then these components can perform their tasks regardless of where they may ultimately reside in a network, meaning that the execution of the overall software system is independent of the underlying network structure.

Finally, we should note that the rules by which interprocess communication is conducted are called **protocols**. These protocols clarify the details of how a model such as the client/server model is implemented. In particular, protocols involve such things as the way (1) information within a message is encoded, (2) information is packaged and addressed for transmission, and (3) message transmission and reception is handled. By developing and adopting protocol standards, venders are able to develop products for network applications that are compatible with products from other venders. Thus, the development of protocol standards is an indispensable process in the development of networking technologies. We will encounter numerous instances of protocols throughout this chapter and explore some particular examples in Section 4.4.

Distributed Systems

With the success of networking technology, interaction between computers via networks has become common and multifaceted. Many modern software systems, such as global information retrieval systems, company-wide accounting and inventory systems, and even computer games, are designed as **distributed systems,** meaning that they consist of units executing on different computers in a network.

Early distributed systems were developed independently from scratch, but today, research is revealing a common infrastructure running throughout these systems, including such things as communication and security systems. In turn, efforts have been made to produce prefabricated systems that provide this basic infrastructure and therefore allow distributed applications to be constructed by merely developing the part of the system that is unique to the application.

One result of such undertakings is the system known as Enterprise JavaBeans (developed by Sun Microsystems) that provides an infrastructure for distributed systems while isolating the application dependent portions of a system in components called enterprise beans. Another approach is the software development environment called .NET Framework (developed by Microsoft). A goal of both systems is to simplify the task of developing complex distributed software products.

Questions/Exercises

1. What is an open network?
2. What is a router?
3. Identify some relationships in society that conform to the client/server model.
4. Identify some protocols used in society.

4.2 The Internet

The most notable example of an internet is the **Internet** (note the uppercase *I*), which originated from a research program initiated in 1973 by the US Defense Advanced Research Projects Agency (DARPA—pronounced "DAR-pa"). The goal of this program was to develop the ability to connect a variety of computer networks so that they could function as a single, reliable connected system. Today, the Internet is a worldwide combination of WANs and LANs involving millions of machines.

Internet Architecture

Conceptually, the Internet can be viewed as a collection of **domains,** each of which consists of a network or a relatively small internet operated by a single organization such as a university, company, or government institution. Each domain is an autonomous system that can be configured as the local authority desires, perhaps even as a global collection of WANs. To establish a domain in the Internet, the entity in charge of the domain must register with the Internet Corporation for Assigned Names and Numbers (ICANN), which is a nonprofit corporation established to coordinate the naming of domains, as we will learn shortly.

Once a domain has been registered, it can be attached to the existing Internet by means of a router that connects one of the networks in the domain to a network already in the Internet. This particular router is often referred to as the domain's

gateway in that it represents the domain's gate to the rest of the Internet. From the point of view of a single domain, the portion of the Internet lying outside of its gateway is sometimes called the **cloud,** in reference to the fact that the structure of the Internet outside the domain's gateway is out of the domain's control and is of minimal concern to the operation of the domain itself. Any message being transmitted to a destination within the domain is handled within the domain; any message being transmitted to a destination outside the domain is directed toward the gateway where it is sent out into the cloud.

If one "stood" at a domain's gateway and "looked out" into the cloud, one could find a variety of structures. Indeed, the Internet has grown in a somewhat haphazard way as various domains have found points at which to connect to the cloud. One popular structure, however, is for the gateways of a number of domains to be connected to form a regional network of gateways. For instance, a group of universities could choose to pool their resources to construct such a network. In turn, this regional network would be connected to a more global network to which other regional networks attach. In this manner, that portion of the cloud takes on a hierarchical structure (Figure 4.5).

It is becoming quite common for individuals and small organizations to establish domains of their own. Such small domains (often consisting of a single machine) are usually linked to the Internet via a larger domain already established by a company called an **Internet service provider** (**ISP**). In addition to providing Internet access for customer domains, these companies also offer personal access to the Internet via communication systems that already enter homes and offices (such as telephone and television). Indeed, most individuals obtain personal Internet access via an ISP by temporarily connecting their PCs as though they were machines within a domain operated by the ISP.

Figure 4.5

A typical approach to connecting to the Internet

Internet Addressing

Each machine in the Internet is assigned a unique address, called an **IP address,** that is used to identify the machine for communication purposes. Each IP address is a pattern of 32 bits consisting of two parts: a pattern identifying the domain in which the machine resides and a pattern identifying the particular machine within the domain. The part of the address identifying the domain, the **network identifier,** is assigned under the authority of ICANN at the time the domain is established and registered. Thus it is by means of this registration process that each domain in the Internet is assured of having a unique network identifier. The portion of the address that identifies a particular machine within a domain is called the **host address.** (The term **host** is often used in reference to a machine in a network in recognition of its role in hosting the requests of other machines.) The host address is assigned by the domain's local authority—usually a person with a job title such as network administrator or system administrator.

IP addresses are traditionally written in **dotted decimal notation** in which the bytes of the address are separated by periods and each byte is expressed as an integer represented in traditional base ten notation. For example, using dotted decimal notation, the pattern 5.2 would represent the two-byte bit pattern 0000010100000010, which consists of the byte 00000101 (represented by 5) followed by the byte 00000010 (represented by 2), and the pattern 17.12.25 would represent the three-byte bit pattern consisting of the byte 00010001, followed by the byte 00001100, followed by the byte 00011001. Thus a machine in the domain of the Addison-Wesley publishing company might have the IP address 192.207.177.133, where the first three bytes (192.207.177) form the network identifier (identifying the Addison-Wesley domain) and the last byte (133) is the host address (identifying a particular machine within Addison-Wesley's domain).

Addresses in bit-pattern form (even when compressed using dotted decimal notation) are rarely conducive to human consumption. For this reason each domain is also assigned a unique mnemonic address known as a **domain name.** For example, the domain name of the Addison-Wesley publishing company, is aw.com. Note that the naming system reflects the domain's classification, which in this case is commercial as indicated by the com suffix. Such a classification is called a **top-level domain** (**TLD**). There are numerous TLDs, including edu for educational institutions, gov for U.S. government institutions, org for nonprofit organizations, museum for museums, info for unrestricted use, and net, which was originally intended for Internet service providers but is now used on a much broader scale. In addition to these general TLDs, there are also two-letter TLDs for specific countries (called country-code TLDs) such as au for Australia and ca for Canada.

Once a domain has a mnemonic name, its local authority is free to extend it to obtain mnemonic names for the machines within its domain. For example, an individual machine within the domain aw.com may be identified as ssenterprise.aw.com.

We should emphasize that the dotted notation used in mnemonic addresses is not related to the dotted decimal notation used to represent addresses in bit pattern form. Instead, the sections in a mnemonic address identify the machine's location within a hierarchical classification system. In particular, the address ssenterprise.aw.com indicates that the machine known as ssenterprise is within the institution aw within the class (or TLD) of commercial domains com. In the case of large domains, a local authority may break its domain into subdomains, in which case the mnemonic addresses of the machines within the domain may be longer. For example, suppose Nowhere University was assigned the domain name `nowhereu.edu` and chose to divide its domain into subdomains. Then, a machine at Nowhere University could have an address such as `r2d2.compsc.nowhereu.edu`, meaning that the machine `r2d2` is in the subdomain `compsc` within the domain `nowhereu` within the class of educational domains `edu`.

Each domain's local authority is responsible for maintaining a directory containing the mnemonic address and the corresponding IP address of those machines within its domain. This directory is implemented on a designated machine within the domain in the form of a server, called a **name server,** that responds to requests regarding address information. Together, all the name servers throughout the Internet are part of an Internet-wide directory system that is used to convert addresses in mnemonic form into their equivalent bit-pattern forms. In particular, when a human requests that a message be sent to a destination identified in mnemonic form, this system of name servers is used to convert that mnemonic address into its equivalent IP address that is compatible with the Internet software. Normally, such a task is completed in a fraction of a second.

Electronic Mail

One of the most popular uses of the Internet has become **e-mail** (short for electronic mail), a system by which messages are transferred among Internet users. For the purpose of providing e-mail service, each domain's local authority designates a particular machine within its domain to handle the domain's e-mail activities. This machine is known as the domain's **mail server.** Every e-mail message sent from within the domain is first sent to the domain's mail server, which then sends the message on to its destination. Likewise, every e-mail message addressed to a person within the domain is received by the domain's mail server, where it is held until that person requests to see his or her incoming mail.

With the role of a domain's mail server in mind, it is easy to understand the structure of an individual's e-mail address. It consists of a symbol string identifying the individual, followed by the symbol `@`, followed by the mnemonic name of the mail server that should receive the mail. Thus the e-mail address of an individual at Addison-Wesley Inc. might appear as `shakespeare@mailroom.aw.com`. In other words, the machine known as `mailroom` within the domain `aw.com` is the mail server that handles e-mail for the person who is identified by the symbol string `shakespeare`.

It is common practice for a domain to be designed in such a way that the name of the mail server does not have to appear in the e-mail address. In these cases, e-mail addresses consist of merely a symbol string identifying the e-mail recipient, followed by the symbol `@`, followed by the mnemonic domain name. Thus, the address above would be reduced to `shakespeare@aw.com`.

The File Transfer Protocol

One means of transferring files (such as documents, photographs, or other encoded information) is to attach them to e-mail messages. However, a more efficient means is to take advantage of the **File Transfer Protocol** (**FTP**), which is a client/server pro-

Spam Filters

Spam is the name given to unwanted "junk" e-mail. For many Internet users, spam has become a serious problem so attempts have been made to write software utilities that filter incoming e-mail, discarding the messages that are determined to be spam. Many ISPs include spam filters as a part of their service.

The more simplistic approaches to filtering e-mail simply scan incoming messages looking for occurrences of particular strings of text, either in the source address or the internal text of the message itself. However, many users conclude that the most successful filters are those that use statistical analysis to classify messages. With these systems a user first "trains" the system by explicitly identifying incoming messages as worthwhile or junk. Once this training process has produced a collection of classified messages, the filter applies Baysian probability theory to determine which of the two classes each incoming message most closely matches and then classifies the new message accordingly. Most users are amazed at how accurate these filters are after only one or two training sessions.

tocol for transferring files across the Internet. To transfer a file using FTP, a user at one machine in the Internet uses a software package that implements FTP to establish contact with another machine. (The original machine plays the role of a client. The machine it contacts plays the role of a server, which is usually called an FTP server.) Once this connection is established, files can easily be transferred between the two machines in either direction.

A commonly misunderstood feature of FTP is the distinction it makes between "text files" and "binary files." The source of this distinction is that when printing a text document with early teletype devices, a new line of text required both a line feed (a vertical movement) and a carriage return (a horizontal movement), each of which is encoded individually in ASCII. (A line feed is indicated by the pattern 00001010, whereas a carriage return is indicated by 00001101.) For the sake of efficiency, many early programmers found it convenient to mark line breaks in a text file with only one of these codes. For example, if everyone agreed to mark line breaks with only a carriage return rather than both a carriage return and a line feed, then eight bits of file space would be saved for each line of text in the file. All one had to do was remember to insert a line feed each time a carriage return was reached when printing the file. These shortcuts have survived in today's systems. In particular, the UNIX operating system assumes that a line break in a text file is indicated by only a line feed, whereas systems developed by Apple Computer, Inc. use only a carriage return, and Microsoft's operating systems require both a carriage return and a line feed. The result is that when these files are transferred from one system to another, conversions must be made. This, then, is the distinction between "text files" and "binary files" in FTP. If a file is transferred as a "text file" using FTP, the required conversions will be made as part of the transfer process; if the file is transferred as a "binary file," no conversions

Internet2

Now that the Internet has shifted from a research project to a household commodity, the research community is working on a project called Internet2. Internet2 currently involves more than 200 universities working in partnership with industry and government. The goal is to develop a high bandwidth internet for the research community as well as the next generation of Internet applications such as video conferencing and remote access and control of costly state-of-the-art equipment including telescopes and MRI scanners. Someday Internet2 could popularize remote surgery performed by robot hands that mimic the hands of a distant surgeon who views the patient by video. You can learn more about Internet2 at http://www.internet2.org.

will be made. Thus even though you may think of a file produced by a word processor as being text, it should be transferred as a "binary file" since these files contain proprietary codes for representing carriage returns and line feeds that should not be altered as part of the file transfer process.

FTP has become a popular way of providing limited access to data via the Internet. Suppose, for example, that you want to allow certain people to retrieve a file while prohibiting access by anyone else. You need merely place the file in a machine with FTP server facilities and guard access to the file via a password. Then, people who know the password will be able to gain access to the file via FTP, while all others will be blocked. A machine in the Internet used in this manner is sometimes called an FTP site because it constitutes a location in the Internet at which files are available via FTP.

FTP sites are also used to provide unrestricted access to files. To accomplish this, the term *anonymous* is used as a universal password. Such sites are often referred to as **anonymous FTP** sites.

Telnet

One of the early uses of the Internet was to allow computer users to access machines from great distances. **Telnet** is a protocol system that was established for this purpose. Using telnet, a user (running telnet client software) can contact the telnet server at a distant machine and then follow that operating system's login procedure to gain access to the machine.

All communication via telnet is carried out in terms of a standard fictitious terminal, called the Network Virtual Terminal (NVT), which one envisions as consisting of a keyboard and a printer. Indeed, the telnet protocol defines a set of commands for transferring characters to and from such a device. All telnet servers are designed to communicate via these commands as though they were conversing with a NVT. In turn, all a client has to do to communicate with a telnet server is to masquerade as a NVT. Thus, the task of a telnet client is to convert the idiosyncrasies of its local system to conform with the properties of a NVT.

Having been designed prior to the development of graphical user interfaces, the telnet protocol handles only text-based messages and is therefore somewhat restricted in its applications. Nonetheless, telnet remains a popular means of communicating with machines from remote locations.

Questions/Exercises

1. What is the difference between a network identifier and a host address?

2. What are the components of the complete Internet address of a machine?

3. What bit pattern is represented by 3.4.5 in dotted decimal notation? Express the bit pattern 0001001100010000 using dotted decimal notation.

4. In what way is the structure of a mnemonic address of a machine on the Internet (such as `r2d2.compsc.nowhereu.edu`) similar to a traditional postal address? Does this same structure occur in IP addresses?

5. Name three types of servers found on the Internet and tell what each does.

4.3 The World Wide Web

The Internet has become a means of disseminating multimedia documents known as **hypertext.** These documents may contain units of text, images, sound, and video, as well as links to other hypertext documents. (The term **hypermedia** is sometimes used in recognition that hypertext has expanded to include formats other than text.) A reader of a hypertext document can follow the links associated with it by merely pointing and clicking with the mouse. For example, suppose the sentence "The orchestra's performance of 'Bolero' by Maurice Ravel was outstanding" appeared in a hypertext document and the name *Maurice Ravel* was linked to another document—perhaps giving information about the composer. A reader could choose to view that associated material by pointing to the name *Maurice Ravel* with the mouse and clicking the mouse button. Moreover, if the proper links are installed, the reader might listen to an audio recording of the concert by clicking on the name *Bolero.*

In this manner, a reader of hypertext documents can explore related documents or follow a train of thought from document to document. As portions of various documents are linked to other documents, an intertwined web of related information is formed. When implemented on a computer network, the documents within such a web can reside on different machines, forming a network-wide web. The web that has evolved on the Internet spans the entire globe and is known as the **World Wide Web** (or the **Web** for short). A hypertext document on the World Wide Web is often called a **Web page.** A collection of closely related Web pages (usually stored at the same location) is called a **Web site.**

Web Implementation

Software packages that allow users to access hypertext on the Internet fall into one of two categories: packages that play the role of clients, and packages that play the role of servers. A client package resides on the user's machine and is charged with the tasks of obtaining materials requested by the user and presenting these materials to the user in an organized manner. It is the client that provides the user interface that allows a user to browse within the Web. In turn, the client is often referred to as a **browser,** or sometimes as a Web browser. The server package (often called a **Web server**) resides on a machine containing hypertext documents to be accessed. Its task is to provide access to the documents on its machine as requested by clients. In summary, a user gains access to hypertext documents by means of a browser residing on the user's machine. This browser, playing the role of a client, obtains the documents by soliciting the services of the Web servers scattered throughout the Internet. Hypertext documents are normally transferred between browsers and Web servers using a protocol known as the **Hypertext Transfer Protocol** (**HTTP**).

In order to locate and retrieve documents on the World Wide Web, each document is given a unique address called a **Uniform Resource Locator** (**URL**). Each URL contains the information needed by a browser to contact the proper server and request the desired document. Thus to view a Web page, a person first provides his or her browser with the URL of the desired document and then instructs the browser to retrieve and display the document.

A typical URL is presented in Figure 4.6. It consists of four segments: the protocol to use to communicate with the server controlling access to the document, the mnemonic address of the machine containing the server, the directory path needed for the server to find the directory containing the document, and the name of the document itself. In short, the URL in Figure 4.6 tells a browser to contact the Web server on the computer known as ssenterprise.aw.com using HTTP and to retrieve the document named Julius_Caesar.html found within the subdirectory Shakespeare within the directory called authors.

Sometimes a URL may not explicitly contain all the segments shown in Figure 4.6. For example, if the server does not need to follow a directory path to reach the document, no directory path will appear in the URL. Moreover, sometimes a URL will con-

The World Wide Web Consortium

The World Wide Web Consortium (W3C) was formed in 1994 to promote the World Wide Web by developing protocol standards (known as W3C standards). W3C is headquartered at CERN, the high-energy particle physics laboratory in Geneva, Switzerland. CERN is where the original HTML markup language was developed as well as the HTTP protocol for transferring HTML documents over the Internet. Today W3C is the source of many standards (including standards for XML and numerous multimedia applications) that lead to compatibility over a wide range of Internet products. You can learn more about W3C via its Web site at http://www.w3.org.

Figure 4.6

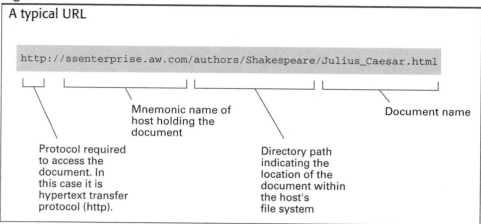

A typical URL

http://ssenterprise.aw.com/authors/Shakespeare/Julius_Caesar.html

Mnemonic name of
host holding the
document

Document name

Protocol required
to access the
document. In
this case it is
hypertext transfer
protocol (http).

Directory path
indicating the
location of the
document within
the host's
file system

sist of only a protocol and the mnemonic address of a machine. In these cases, the Web server at that machine will return a predetermined document, often called a home page, that usually describes the information available at that Web site. Such shortened URLs provide a means of contacting organizations. For example, the URL http://www.aw.com will lead to the home page of Addison-Wesley Inc., which contains links to numerous other documents relating to the company and its products. Moreover, many browsers assume that the HTTP protocol should be used if no protocol is identified. These browsers correctly retrieve the Addison-Wesley home page when given the "URL" consisting merely of www.aw.com.

Of course, a person using the Web may need to research a topic rather than retrieve a particular document. For this purpose, many Web sites (including the home pages of most ISPs) provide the services of a search engine. A **search engine** is a software package designed to help Web users identify documents pertaining to various subjects. To use a search engine, one types a collection of words or phrases that a desired document would probably contain, and then the search engine scans its records, reporting the documents whose contents contain the identified text. Improving search engine technology, including better methods for identifying relevant documents and improved systems for building and storing the underlying search engine records, is an ongoing process.

HTML

A hypertext document is similar to a traditional text file because its text is encoded character by character using a system such as ASCII or Unicode. The distinction is that a hypertext document also contains special symbols, called **tags**, that describe how the document should appear on a computer screen and which items within the document are linked to other documents. This system of tags is known as **Hypertext Markup Language** (**HTML**). Thus it is in terms of HTML that an author of a Web page describes the information that a browser needs in order to present the page on the user's screen and to find any related documents referenced by the current page.

Figure 4.7

A simple Web page

a. The page encoded using HTML.

Tag indicating beginning of document — `<html>`

Preliminaries —
`<head>`
`<title>demonstration page</title>`
`</head>`

Part of the page that will be displayed by browser —
`<body>`
`<h1>My Web Page</h1>`
`<p>Click here for another page.</p>`
`</body>`

Tag indicating end of document — `</html>`

b. The page as it would appear on a computer screen.

My Web Page

Click here for another page.

The HTML encoded version (called the **source** version) of an extremely simple yet representative Web page is shown in Figure 4.7a. Note that the tags are delimited by the symbols < and >. The Web page document consists of two sections—a head (delimited by the <head> and </head> tags) and a body (delimited by the <body> and </body> tags). The head contains preliminary information in much the same manner as the head of an interoffice memo contains the date and subject of the memo. The body contains the material to be presented on the user's screen. In this case the page consists of the heading "My Web Page" displayed prominently on the screen (The text "My Web Page" is marked as a level-one heading as indicated by the <h1> and </h1> tags) followed by the text "Click here for another page" (The text "Click here for another page" is surrounded by the tags <p> and </p> that delimit paragraphs). Figure 4.7b shows the page as it would be presented on a computer screen by a browser.

In its present form, the page in Figure 4.7 is static. Nothing will happen when the viewer clicks on the word *here*, even though the page implies that doing so will cause the browser to display another page. To cause the appropriate action, we must link the word *here* to another document.

Let us suppose that, when the word *here* is clicked, we want the browser to retrieve and display the page at the URL http://crafty.com/demo.html. To do so, we must first surround the word *here* in the source version of the page with the tags <a> and </a>, which are called anchor tags. Inside the opening anchor tag we insert the parameter

```
href = "http://crafty.com/demo.html"
```

(as shown in Figure 4.8a) indicating that the hypertext reference (href) associated with the tag is located at the URL following the equal sign. With this modification

Figure 4.8

An enhanced simple Web page

a. The page encoded using HTML.

```
<html>
<head>
<title>demonstration page</title>
</head>
<body>
<h1>My Web Page</h1>
<p>Click
    <a href="http://crafty.com/demo.html">
    here
    </a>
    for another page.</p>
</body>
</html>
```

Anchor tag containing parameter — `<a href="http://crafty.com/demo.html">`

Closing anchor tag — `</a>`

b. The page as it would appear on a computer screen.

My Web Page

Click here for another page.

the page will now appear on a computer screen as shown in Figure 4.8b. Note that this is identical to Figure 4.7b except that the word here is highlighted by color indicating that it is a link to another Web document. Clicking on such highlighted terms will cause the browser to retrieve and display the associated Web document. Thus, it is by means of anchor tags that Web documents are linked to each other.

XML

HTML is essentially a notational system by which a text document along with the document's appearance can be encoded as a simple text file. In a similar manner we can also encode nontextual material as text files—an example being sheet music. At first glance the pattern of staffs, measure bars, and notes in which music is traditionally represented does not conform to the character-by-character format dictated by text files. However, we can overcome this problem by developing an alternative notation system. More precisely, we could agree to represent the start of a staff by `<staff clef = "treble">`, the end of the staff by `</staff>`, a time signature with the form `<time> 2/4 </time>`, the beginning and ending of a measure by `<measure>` and `</measure>`, respectively, a note such as an eighth note on C as `<notes> egth C </notes>`, etc. Then the text

```
<staff clef = "treble"> <key>C minor</key>
<time> 2/4 </time>
<measure> < rest> egth </rest> <notes> egth G,
egth G, egth G </notes></measure>
<measure> <notes> hlf E </notes></measure>
</staff>
```

could be used to encode the music shown in Figure 4.9. Using such notation, sheet music could be encoded, modified, stored, and transferred over the Internet as text files. Moreover, software could be written to present the contents of such files in the form of traditional sheet music or even to play the music on a synthesizer.

Note that our sheet music encoding system encompasses the same style used by HTML. We chose to delimit the tags that identify components by the symbols < and >. We chose to indicate the beginning and end of structures (such as a staff, a string of notes, or a measure) by tags of the same name—the ending tag being designated by a slash (a `<measure>` was terminated with the tag `</measure>`). And, we chose to indicate

Figure 4.9

The first two bars of Beethoven's Fifth Symphony

special attributes within tags by expressions such as clef = "treble". This same style could be used to develop systems for representing other formats such as mathematical expressions, medical charts, and entire Web pages.

The **eXtensible Markup Language** (**XML**) is a standardized style (similar to that of our music example) for designing notational systems for representing data as text files. (Actually, XML is a simplified derivative of an older set of standards called the Standard Generalized Markup Language, better known as SGML.) Following the XML standard, notational systems called **markup languages** have been developed for representing mathematics, multimedia presentations, music, and Web pages.

XML provides a good example of how standards are designed to have wide-ranging applications. Rather than designing individual, unrelated markup languages for encoding various types of documents such as sheet music, text, and mathematics, the approach represented by XML is to develop a standard for markup languages in general. Then, by using this standard, markup languages can be developed for various applications. Markup languages developed in this manner possess a uniformity that allows them to be combined to obtain markup languages for complex applications such as text documents that contain segments of sheet music and mathematical expressions.

Finally we should note that XML allows the development of new markup languages that differ from HTML in that they emphasize semantics rather than appearance. For example, using HTML the ingredients in a recipe can be marked so that they appear as a list in which each ingredient is positioned on a separate line. But using semantic oriented tags, ingredients in a recipe could be marked as ingredients (perhaps using the tags <ingredient> and </ingredient>) rather than merely items in a list. This approach would allow search engines to identify recipes that contain or do not contain certain ingredients, which would be a substantial improvement over the current state of the art in which only recipes that do or do not contain certain words can be isolated. More precisely, if semantic tags are used, a search engine could identify recipes for lasagna that do not contain spinach, whereas a similar search based merely on word content would skip over a recipe that started with the statement "This lasagna does not contain spinach." In turn, if Internet-wide standards are established for marking documents according to semantics rather than appearance, the result would be a World Wide "Semantic" Web rather than the World Wide "Word" Web we have today.

Dynamic Web Pages

Consider now the steps that would be required for a browser to retrieve the simple Web page shown in Figure 4.8 and display it on the browser's computer screen. First, playing the role of a client, the browser would use the information in the URL (perhaps obtained from the person using the browser) to contact the Web server controlling access to the page and ask that a copy of the page be transferred to it. The server would respond by sending the text document displayed in Figure 4.8a to the browser. The browser would then interpret the HTML tags in the document to

POP3 Versus IMAP

Users of the Internet who obtain e-mail service via remote temporary connections to their Internet service provider may have heard of, and perhaps been given a choice between, POP3 (pronounced "pop–THREE") and IMAP (pronounced "EYE–map"). These are protocols by which a user at a remote computer (usually a desktop PC or a laptop) can access the messages that have been collected by a mail server and stored in the user's mailbox. POP3 stands for Post Office Protocol-version 3 and is the simpler of the two. Using POP3, a user can transfer (download) messages to his or her local computer where they can be read, stored in various folders, edited, and otherwise manipulated as the user desires. This activity is done on the user's local machine using the local machine's mass storage. IMAP, which stands for Internet Mail Access Protocol, allows a user to create folders and organize messages on the same machine as the mail server. In this manner, a user who must access his or her e-mail from different computers can maintain records on the mail server machine that are then accessible from any remote computer to which the user may have access. Thus IMAP requires a higher level of service from the ISP maintaining the mail server, and thus the ISP may charge a higher fee for IMAP service as opposed to POP3.

determine how the page should be displayed and present the document on its computer screen accordingly. The user of the browser would see an image like that depicted in Figure 4.8b. If the user then clicked the mouse over the word *here*, the browser would use the URL in the associated anchor tag to contact the appropriate server to obtain and display another Web page. In summary, the process consists of the browser merely fetching and displaying Web pages as directed by the user.

But what if we wanted a Web page with animation or perhaps a Web page with which a customer could fill out an order form and submit the order? These needs would require additional activity by either the browser or the Web server. Based on the roles played by the browser and Web server, activities performed at the browser's machine are called **client-side** activities, whereas activities performed at the Web server's machine are called **server-side** activities.

Animation on a web page is normally performed as a client-side activity. The program that directs the animation is transferred to the browser along with the Web page document. There it is executed by the browser to control the animation.

In contrast, suppose a travel agent wanted customers to be able to identify desired destinations and dates of travel, at which time the agent would present the customer with a customized Web page containing only the information pertinent to that customer's needs. In this case the travel agent's Web site would first provide a Web page that presented a customer with the available destinations. Based on this information, the customer would specify the destinations of interest and desired dates of travel (a client-side activity). This information would then be transferred back to the agent's Web site were it would be used to construct the appropriate customized Web page (a server-side activity) which would then be sent to the customer's browser.

A similar example occurs in the case of a person using the services of a search engine. Here the person specifies a topic of interest (a client-side activity) which is then transferred to the search engine where a customized Web page identifying documents of possible interest is constructed (a server-side activity) and sent back to the client.

There is a proliferation of systems for performing client and server side activities, each competing with the others for prominence. An early and still popular means of controlling client-side activities is to include programs written in the language JavaScript (developed by Netscape Communications, Inc.) within a Web document's head. From there a browser can extract the programs and follow them as needed. Another approach (developed by Sun Microsystems) is to first transfer a Web page to a browser and then transfer additional program units called applets (written in the language Java) to the browser as requested within the Web page document. Still another approach is the system Flash (a proprietary system developed and controlled by Macromedia) by which extensive multimedia client-side presentations can be implemented.

An early means of controlling server-side activities was to use a set of standards called CGI (Common Gateway Interface) by which clients could request the execution of programs stored at a server. A variation of this approach (developed by Sun Microsystems) is to allow clients to cause program units called servlets to be executed at the server side. A simplified version of the servlet approach is applicable when the requested server-side activity is the construction of a customized Web page, as in our travel agent example. In this case Web page templates called JavaServer Pages (JSP) are stored at the Web server and completed using information received from a client. A similar approach is used by Microsoft, where the templates from which customized Web pages are constructed are called Active Server Pages (ASP). In contract to these proprietary systems, PHP (originally standing for Personal Home Page but now considered to mean PHP Hypertext Processor) is an open source system for implementing server-side functionality.

Finally, we would be remiss if we did not recognize the security and ethical problems that arise from allowing clients and servers to execute programs on the other's machine. The fact that Web servers routinely transfer programs to client machines where they are executed leads to ethical questions on the server side and security questions on the client side. If the client blindly executes any program sent to it by a

The Computer Emergency Response Team

In November 1988 a worm released into the Internet caused significant disruption of service. Consequently, the US Defense Advanced Research Projects Agency (DARPA—pronounced "DAR–pa") formed the Computer Emergency Response Team (CERT—pronounced "SERT"), located at the CERT Coordination Center at Carnegie-Mellon University. The CERT is the Internet's security "watchdog." Among its duties are the investigation of security problems, the issuance of security alerts, and the implementation of public awareness campaigns to improve Internet security. The CERT Coordination Center maintains a Web site at http://www.cert.org where it posts notices of its activities.

Web server, it opens itself to malicious activities by the server. Likewise, the fact that clients can cause programs to be executed at the server leads to ethical questions on the client side and security questions on the server side. If the client is able to exploit flaws in programs stored on the server machine, it could lead to security breaches and potential damage at the server.

Questions/Exercises

1. What is a URL? What is a browser?
2. What is the difference between HTML and XML?
3. To what do the terms *client side* and *server side* refer?

4.4 Network Protocols

In Section 4.1 we met the concept of protocols in the context of client/server communication. In general, protocols are used to define the details of each activity within a network, including how messages are addressed, how the right to transmit messages is delegated among the machines, and how the duties of packaging messages for transmission and unpacking received messages are to be handled. We begin this section by considering protocols for controlling the right of a machine to transmit its own messages over a network.

Controlling Transmission Privileges

One approach to coordinating the right to transmit messages is the **token ring** protocol, which was developed by IBM in the 1970s and continues to be a popular protocol in networks based on the ring topology. In this protocol, all the machines in the network transmit messages in only one common direction (Figure 4.10), meaning

Figure 4.10

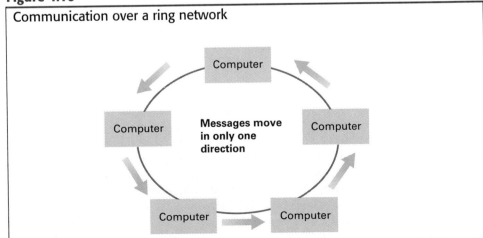

Communication over a ring network

Figure 4.11

Communication over a bus network

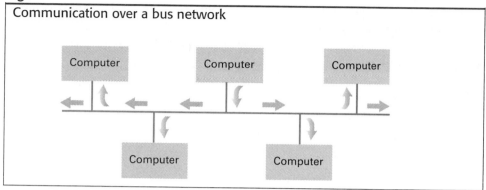

that all messages sent over the network move around the ring in the same direction by being forwarded from machine to machine. When a message reaches its destination, the destination machine keeps a copy of it and forwards a copy on around the ring. When the forwarded copy reaches the originating machine, that machine knows that the message must have reached its destination and removes the message from the ring. Of course, this system depends on intermachine cooperation. If a machine insists on constantly transmitting messages of its own rather than forwarding those of the other machines, nothing will be accomplished.

To solve this problem, a unique bit pattern, called a *token,* is passed around the ring. Possession of this token gives a machine the authority to transmit its own message; without the token, a machine is only allowed to forward messages. Normally, each machine merely relays the token in the same manner in which it relays messages. If, however, the machine receiving the token has messages of its own to introduce to the network, it transmits one message while holding the token. When this message has completed its cycle around the ring, the machine forwards the token to the next machine in the ring. Likewise, when the next machine receives the token, it can either forward the token immediately or transmit its own new message before sending the token on to the next machine. In this manner, each machine in the network has equal opportunity to introduce messages of its own as the token circles around the ring.

Another protocol for coordinating the right to transmit is found in an **Ethernet**, which is a popular version of a bus network. In an Ethernet, the right to transmit messages is controlled by a protocol known as **Carrier Sense, Multiple Access with Collision Detection (CSMA/CD)**. This protocol dictates that each message transmitted by any machine be broadcast to all the machines on the bus (Figure 4.11). Each machine monitors all the messages but keeps only those addressed to itself. To transmit a message, a machine waits until the bus is silent, and at this time it begins transmitting while continuing to monitor the bus. If another machine also begins transmitting, both machines detect the clash and pause for a brief random period of time before trying to transmit again. The result is a system similar to that used by a small group of people in a conversation. If two people start to talk at once, they both stop. The difference is that people may go through a series such as, "I'm sorry, what were you going to say?", "No, no. You go first," whereas under the CSMA/CD protocol each machine merely tries again.

The Layered Approach to Internet Software

A principal task of networking software is to provide the infrastructure required for transferring messages from one machine to another. In the Internet, this message passing activity is accomplished by means of a hierarchy of software units performing tasks analogous to those that would be performed if you were to send a gift in a package from the West Coast of the United States to a friend on the East Coast (Figure 4.12). You would first wrap the gift as a package and write the appropriate address on the outside of the package. Then, you would take the package to a shipping company such as the US Postal Service. The shipping company might place the package along with others in a large container and deliver the container to an airline, whose services it has contracted. The airline would place the container in an aircraft and transfer it to the destination city, perhaps with intermediate stops along the way. At the final destination, the airline would remove the container from the aircraft and give it to the shipping company's office at the destination. In turn, the shipping company would take your package out of the container and deliver it to the addressee.

In short, the transportation of the gift would be carried out by a three-level hierarchy: (1) the user level (consisting of you and your friend), (2) the shipping company, and (3) the airline. Each level uses the next lower level as an abstract tool. (You are not concerned with the details of the shipping company, and the shipping company is not concerned with the internal operations of the airline.) Each level in

Figure 4.12

Package-shipping example

the hierarchy has representatives at both the origin and the destination, with the representatives at the destination tending to do the reverse of their counterparts at the origin.

Such is the case with software for controlling communication over the Internet, except that the Internet software has four layers rather than three, each consisting of a collection of software routines rather than people and businesses. The four layers are known as the **application layer**, the **transport layer**, the **network layer**, and the **link layer** (Figure 4.13). All layers are present on each machine in the Internet. A message typically originates in the application layer. From there it is passed down through the transport and network layers as it is prepared for transmission, and finally transmitted by the link layer. The message is received by the link layer at the destination and passed back up the hierarchy until it is delivered to the application layer at the message's destination.

Let us investigate this process more thoroughly by tracing a message as it finds its way through the system (Figure 4.14). We begin our journey with the application layer.

The application layer consists of those software units such as clients and servers that use Internet communication to carry out their tasks. Although the names are similar, this layer is not restricted to software in the application classification presented in Section 3.2, but also includes many utility packages. For example, software for transferring files using FTP or for providing remote login capabilities using telnet have become so common that they are normally considered utility software.

The application layer uses the transport layer to send and receive messages over the Internet in much the same way that you would use a shipping company to send and receive packages. Just as it is your responsibility to provide an address compatible with the specifications of the shipping company, it is the application layer's responsibility to

Figure 4.13

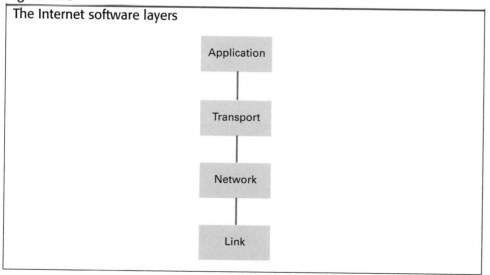

The Internet software layers

Application

Transport

Network

Link

Figure 4.14

Following a message through the Internet

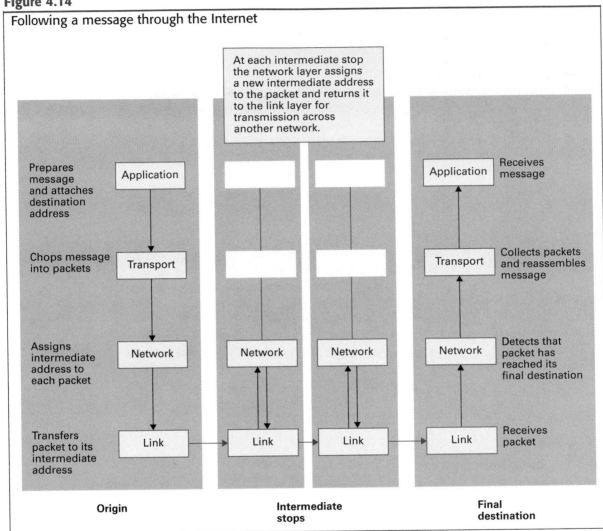

At each intermediate stop the network layer assigns a new intermediate address to the packet and returns it to the link layer for transmission across another network.

Prepares message and attaches destination address — Application — Receives message

Chops message into packets — Transport — Collects packets and reassembles message

Assigns intermediate address to each packet — Network — Network — Network — Network — Detects that packet has reached its final destination

Transfers packet to its intermediate address — Link — Link — Link — Link — Receives packet

Origin   **Intermediate stops**   **Final destination**

provide an address that is compatible with the transport layer. (To fulfill this need, the application layer may use the services of the name servers within the Internet to translate mnemonic addresses used by humans into Internet-compatible IP addresses.)

A major task of the transport layer is to accept messages from the application layer and to ensure that the messages are properly formatted for transmission over the Internet. Toward this latter goal, the transport layer divides long messages into small segments, which are transmitted over the Internet as individual units. This division is necessary because a single long message can obstruct the flow of other messages at the points on the Internet where numerous messages must cross paths. Indeed, small segments of messages can interweave at these points, whereas a long message forces others to wait while it passes (much like cars waiting for a long train to pass at a railroad crossing).

The transport layer adds sequence numbers to the small segments it produces so that the segments can be reassembled at the message's destination. Then it attaches the destination address to each segment and hands these addressed segments, known as **packets,** to the network layer. From this point, the packets are treated as individual, nonrelated messages until they reach the transport layer at their final destination. It is quite possible for the packets related to a common message to follow different paths through the Internet.

The network layer is responsible for seeing that the packets it receives are forwarded from one network within the Internet to another until they reach their final destinations. Thus it is the network layer that must deal with the Internet's topology. In particular, if a packet's path through the Internet must pass through many individual networks, it is the network layer at each intermediate stop that determines the direction in which the packet will be sent next. The decision is made as follows: If the final destination of the packet is within the current network, the network layer will send the packet there; otherwise, the network layer will send the packet to a router in the current network through which the packet can be transferred into an adjacent network. In this way, a packet destined for a machine within the current network will be sent to that machine, whereas a packet destined for a machine outside the current network will continue its network-to-network journey.

Having determined a packet's next destination, the network layer appends this address to the packet as an intermediate address and hands the packet to the link layer.

The link layer has the responsibility of transferring the packet to the intermediate address that was determined by the network layer. Thus the link layer must deal with the communication details particular to the individual network in which the machine resides. If that network is a token ring, the link layer must wait for possession of the token before transmitting. If the network uses CSMA/CD, the link layer must listen for a silent bus before transmitting. Moreover, each individual network within the Internet has its own addressing system that is independent from the addressing system used by the Internet. (Remember that the Internet is a collection of independent networks, each with its own characteristics.) Thus the link layer must translate the Internet addresses attached to the packets into the appropriate local addressing system.

Each time a packet is transmitted, it is received by the link layer at the receiving machine. There, the link layer hands the packet up to its network layer where the packet's final destination is compared to the current location. If these do not coincide, the network layer determines a new intermediate address for the packet, attaches that address to the packet, and returns the packet to the link layer for retransmission. In this manner, each packet hops from machine to machine on its way to its final destination. Note that only the link and network layers are involved at the intermediate stops during this journey (see again Figure 4.14).

If the network layer determines that an arriving packet has reached its final destination, it hands the packet to its transport layer. As the transport layer receives packets from the network layer, it extracts the underlying message segments and reconstructs the original message according to the sequence numbers that were provided by the transport layer at the message's origin. Once the message is complete, the transport layer hands it to its application layer—thus completing the message transmission process.

Determining which application should receive an incoming message is an important task of the transport layer. This is handled by assigning unique **port numbers** (not related to the I/O ports discussed in Chapter 2) to the various application units and requiring that an application sending a message append the appropriate port number to the message's address before starting the message on its journey. Then, once the message is received by the transport layer at the destination, the transport layer merely hands the message to the application layer software at the designated port number.

Users of the Internet rarely need to be concerned with port numbers since the common applications have universally accepted port numbers. For example, if a Web browser is asked to retrieve the document whose URL is http://www.zoo.org/animals/frog.html, the browser knows to contact the HTTP server at www.zoo.org via port number 80. Likewise, when transferring a file, an FTP client knows to look for the FTP server at port number 21.

In summary, communication over the Internet involves the interaction of four layers of software. The application layer deals with messages and addresses from the application's point of view. The transport layer converts these messages into packets that are compatible with the Internet and reassembles messages that are received before delivering them to the appropriate application. The network layer deals with directing the packets through the Internet. The link layer handles the actual transmission of a packet from one machine to another within a single network. With all this activity, it is somewhat amazing that the response time of the Internet is measured in milliseconds, so that many transactions appear to take place instantaneously.

The TCP/IP Protocol Suite

The demand for open networks has generated a need for published standards by which manufacturers can supply equipment and software that function properly with products from other vendors. One standard that has resulted is the Open System Interconnection (OSI) reference model, produced by the International Organization for Standardization. This standard is based on a seven-level hierarchy as opposed to the four-level hierarchy we have just described. It has become an often-quoted model because it carries the authority of an international organization, but it has been slow to replace the four-level point of view, mainly because it was established after the four-level hierarchy had already been developed, implemented, widely publicized, and proved reliable as the protocol system for the Internet.

The TCP/IP protocol suite is a collection of protocols used by the Internet to implement the four-level communication hierarchy used by the Internet. Actually, the **Transmission Control Protocol (TCP)** and the **Internet Protocol (IP)** are the names of only two of the protocols in this vast collection—so the fact that the entire collection is referred to as the TCP/IP protocol suite is rather misleading. More precisely, TCP defines a version of the transport layer. We say a *version* because the TCP/IP protocol suite provides for two ways of implementing the transport layer, the second being defined by the **User Datagram Protocol (UDP)**. This is analogous to the fact that when shipping a package, you have a choice of different shipping companies, each of which offers the same basic service but with its own unique characteristics. Thus, depending on the particular quality of service required, the application layer software may choose to send data via a TCP or UDP version of the transport layer (Figure 4.15).

There are two basic differences between TCP and UDP. The first is that before sending a message as requested by the application layer, a transport layer based on TCP sends its own message to the transport layer at the destination telling it that a message is about to be sent. It then waits for this message to be acknowledged before starting to send the application layer's message. In this manner, a TCP transport layer is said to establish a connection before sending a message. A transport layer based on UDP does not establish such a connection prior to sending a message. It merely sends the message to the address it was given and forgets about it. For all it knows, the destination machine may not even be operational. For this reason, UDP is called a connectionless protocol.

The second basic difference between TCP and UDP is that TCP transport layers at the origin and destination work together by means of acknowledgments and packet retransmissions to confirm that all segments of a message are successfully transferred to the destination. In turn, TCP is called a reliable protocol, whereas UDP, which does not offer such retransmission services, is said to be an unreliable protocol. This does not mean that UDP is a poor choice. After all, a transport layer based on UDP is more streamlined than a layer based on TCP, and thus if an application is prepared to handle the potential consequences of UDP, that option may be the better choice. For example, e-mail is normally sent via TCP, but the communication carried out by the name servers when translating addresses from mnemonic form into IP form uses UDP.

IP is the Internet's standard for the network layer. Among its features is that each time an IP network layer prepares a packet to be handed to the link layer, it appends a value called a *hop count*, or time to live, to that packet. This value is a limit to the number of times the packet should be forwarded as it tries to find its way through the

Figure 4.15

Choosing between TCP and UDP

Application layer

?

Transport layer

TCP
More "reliable" but less efficient

UDP
More efficient but less "reliable"

Internet. Each time an IP network layer forwards a packet, it decrements that packet's hop count by one. With this information, the network layer can protect the Internet from packets circling endlessly within the system. Although the Internet continues to grow on a daily basis, an initial hop count of 64 remains more than sufficient to allow a packet to find its way through the maze of LANs, WANs, and routers.

Questions/Exercises

1. What layers of the Internet software hierarchy are used to forward an incoming message to another machine?

2. What are some differences between a transport layer based on the TCP protocol and another based on the UDP protocol?

3. How does the Internet software ensure that messages are not relayed within the Internet forever?

4. What keeps a machine on the Internet from recording copies of all the messages passing through it?

4.5 Security

When a machine is connected to a network, it becomes accessible to many potential users. The problems encountered fall into two general categories: unauthorized access to information and vandalism. One approach to protecting data from unauthorized access is to encrypt the data, so that even if the data are obtained by an intruder, the information remains safe. For this purpose, a variety of encryption techniques have been developed.

One popular approach to encryption of messages sent over the Internet is called **public-key encryption.** It allows many people to send secure messages to a central receiver. Public-key encryption involves the use of two values called keys. One key, known as the public key, is used to encode messages and is known by all people authorized to generate messages; the other, known as the private key, is required to decode messages and is known by only the person who is to receive messages. Knowledge of the public key does not allow messages to be decoded. Thus, little damage is done if it falls into unauthorized hands. Knowledge of the private key is, of course, more sensitive, but it is inherently more secure than the public key because it is held by only one person. We will investigate a particular public-key encryption system at the end of Chapter 11.

There are also many legal issues regarding unauthorized access to information, some of which deal with distinguishing between authorized and unauthorized parties. For example, is an employer authorized to monitor the communication of employees? To what extent does an Internet service provider have authorized access to the information being communicated by its clients? To what extent is an Internet service provider responsible for the content of its client's communication? Such questions are challenging today's legal community.

In the United States, many of these questions are addressed by the Electronic Communication Privacy Act (ECPA) of 1986, which has its origins in legislation to control wire-tapping. Although the act is lengthy, its scope is captured in a few short excerpts. In particular, it states that

> Except as otherwise specifically provided in this chapter any person who intentionally intercepts, endeavors to intercept, or procures any other person to intercept or endeavor to intercept, any wire, oral, or electronic communication . . . shall be punished as provided in subsection (4) or shall be subject to suit as provided in subsection (5).

and

> . . . any person or entity providing an electronic communication service to the public shall not intentionally divulge the contents of any communication . . . on that service to any person or entity other than an addressee or intended recipient of such communication or an agent of such addressee or intended recipient.

In brief, the ECPA confirms an individual's right to private communication—it is illegal for unauthorized personnel to eavesdrop on another's communication, and it is illegal for an Internet service provider to release information about the communication of its clients. However, the act also states the following:

> It shall not be unlawful . . . for an officer, employee, or agent of the Federal Communications Commission, in the normal course of his employment and in discharge of the monitoring responsibilities exercised by the Commission in the enforcement of chapter 5 of title 47 of the United States Code, to intercept a wire or electronic communication, or oral communication transmitted by radio, or to disclose or use the information thereby obtained.

Thus the ECPA explicitly gives the Federal Communications Commission (FCC) the right to monitor electronic communication under some restrictions. This leads to some rather complicated issues. First, in order for the FCC to exercise its rights under the ECPA, the target communication systems must be constructed and programmed so that communications can be monitored. To establish these capabilities was the goal of the Communications Assistance for Law Enforcement Act (CALEA). It requires telecommunication carriers to modify their equipment to accommodate law enforcement taps. However, implementation of this act has proved to be complex and expensive, resulting in extensions to the deadline for compliance.

A more controversial issue involves the clash between the FCC's right to monitor communications and the public's right to use encryption. After all, if the messages being monitored are well encrypted, then tapping the communication is worthless to law enforcement agencies. Governments in the United States, Canada, and Europe are considering systems that would require the registration of ciphering keys. But we live in a world in which corporate espionage has become as significant as military espionage. Thus it is understandable that requiring the registration of ciphering keys would make many law-abiding corporations, as well as citizens, uncomfortable. How secure can the registration system be?

The problem of vandalism is exemplified by the occurrence of such afflictions as computer viruses and network worms. In general, a **virus** is a program segment that attaches itself to other programs in the computer system. For example, a virus may insert itself at the beginning of a program already in the system, so each time the host program is executed, the virus is performed first. When executed, the virus may perform malicious acts that are readily noticeable or merely search for other programs to which it can attach copies of itself. When an infected program is transferred to a new machine, perhaps via the Internet, the virus will begin to infect programs on the new machine as soon as the transferred program is executed. In this manner, the virus moves from machine to machine. In some cases, viruses are designed to spread themselves to other programs until a predetermined condition, such as the arrival of a particular date, is met and then perform more malicious vandalism. This increases the likelihood that the virus will be spread to numerous machines before it is detected.

The term **worm** normally refers to an autonomous program that transfers itself through a network, taking up residence in machines and forwarding copies of itself through the network. As in the case of viruses, these programs can be designed merely to replicate themselves or to perform additional vandalism.

One approach that can be applied to problems of both unauthorized access and vandalism is to install software that filters the traffic entering or passing through a machine. For example, the network layer could be modified to reject all traffic arriving from an entire (blacklisted) domain or specific IP addresses, or the transport layer could be altered to reject all traffic addressed to any port number that is not assigned to an preapproved application. Software of this type is called a **firewall** in that it forms a protective barrier that shields the region on one side from the dangers on the other. Often firewalls are placed on a domain's gateway so that the entire domain is protected from the perils lurking throughout the rest of the Internet. In other cases firewalls are placed on individual machines to provide a level of protection unique to a particular need.

As the popularity of computer networking and the Internet increases, the potential for damage from unauthorized access and vandalism also grows. Security breaches within the Internet have led to instances of significant financial losses, risks to national security, and numerous questions of ethics and law. Moreover, the global nature of the Internet means that remedies attempted by a single nation are limited by that nation's ability to establish and enforce treaties with other nations. Whether the affects of accidents and malicious activity can be controlled in the future remains to be seen.

Questions/Exercises

1. Technically, the term *data* refers to representations of information, whereas *information* refers to the underlying meaning. Does the use of passwords protect data or information? Does the use of encryption protect data or information?

2. What are the basic points in the ECPA?

3. Explain how the CALEA demonstrates that passing a law requiring an action may not actually get the job done.

4. What distinction is there between the types of firewalls that can be placed at a domain's gateway as opposed to an individual host within the domain.

Chapter Review Problems

(Asterisked problems are associated with optional sections.)

1. What is a protocol? Identify three protocols introduced in this chapter and describe the purpose of each.

2. Identify and describe a client/server protocol used in everyday life.

3. Describe the client/server model.

4. Identify two ways of classifying computer networks.

5. What is the difference between an open network and a closed network?

6. Define each of the following:
   a. Name server
   b. Domain
   c. Router
   d. Host

7. Encode each of the following bit patterns using dotted decimal notation.
   a. 000000010000001000000011
   b. 1000000000000000
   c. 0001100000001100

8. What bit pattern is represented by each of the followed dotted decimal patterns?
   a. 0.0
   b. 25.18.1
   c. 5.12.13.10

9. Suppose the address of a host on the Internet is quoted as 134.48.4.123. What is the 32-bit address in hexadecimal notation?

10. If a domain's network identifier is 192.207.177, how many unique IP addresses are available for referencing computers within the domain? (After you have computed the answer, you may conjecture that there might be fewer IP addresses than there are computers in the domain, and this is often the case. One solution

is to allocate IP addresses to machines only as they are needed, leading to a dynamic allocation system in which IP addresses are reassigned on a moment by moment basis as the needs of within the domain change.)

11. If a computer's mnemonic Internet address was

    batman.batcave.metropolis.gov

    what could you conjecture about the structure of the domain containing the machine?

12. Explain the components of the e-mail address

    kermit@frogs.animals.com

13. In the context of FTP, what is the distinction between a "text file" and a "binary file"?

14. What is the role of a Network Virtual Terminal in the telnet protocol?

15. Define each of the following:
    a. Hypertext
    b. HTML
    c. Browser

16. Many "lay-users" of the Internet interchange the terms *Internet* and *World Wide Web*. To what do each of the terms correctly refer?

17. When viewing a simple Web document, ask your browser to display the source version of the document. Then identify the basic structure of the document. In particular, identify the head and the body of the document and list some of the statements you find in each.

18. Using the informal XML style as presented in the text, design a markup language for representing simple algebraic expressions as text files.

19. Using the informal XML style presented in the text, design a set of tags that a word processor might use for marking the underlying text. For

example, how would a word processor indicate what text should be bold, italic, underlined, etc.?

20. Using the informal XML style presented in the text, design a set of tags that could be used to mark motion picture reviews according to the way the text items should appear on a printed page. Then design a set of tags that could be used to mark the reviews according to the meaning of the items in the text.

21. Using the informal XML style presented in the text, design a set of tags that could be used to mark articles about sporting events according to the way the text items should appear on a printed page. Then design a set of tags that could be used to mark the articles according to the meaning of the items in the text.

22. Identify the components of the following URL and describe the meaning of each.

`http://lifeforms.com/animals/movi-estars/kermit.html`

23. Identify the components of each of the following abbreviated URLs.
a. `http://www.farmtools.org/wind-mills.html`
b. `http://castles.org/`
c. `www.coolstuff.com`

24. How would the action of a browser differ if you asked it to "find the document" at the URL

`telnet://stargazer.universe.org`

as opposed to

`http://stargazer.universe.org?`

25. Give two examples of client-side activities on the Web. Give two examples of server-side activities on the Web.

26. Summarize the principles of public-key encryption.

27. What are some concerns dealing with Internet security and privacy?

28. What are the ECPA and the CALEA?

29. In what sense does the global nature of the Internet limit legal solutions to Internet problems?

*30. Suppose each computer in a ring network is programmed to transmit simultaneously in both directions those messages that originate at that station and are addressed to all the other stations belonging to the network. Moreover, suppose this is done by first acquiring access to the communication path to the machine's left, retaining this access until access to the path to the right is acquired, and then transmitting the message. Identify the deadlock that occurs if all the machines in the network try to originate such a message at the same time.

*31. What is the OSI reference model?

*32. In a network based on the bus topology, the bus is a nonshareable resource for which the machines must compete in order to transmit messages. How is deadlock controlled in this context?

*33. Token-based protocols can be used to control the right to transmit in networks that do not have a ring topology. Design a token-based protocol to control the right to transmit in a LAN with a bus topology.

*34. Describe the steps followed by a machine that wants to transmit a message in a network using the CSMA/CD protocol.

*35. List the four layers in the Internet software hierarchy and identify a task performed by each layer.

*36. Why does the transport layer chop large messages into small packets?

*37. Sending a message from the application layer on one computer to an application on another, may require the transfer of additional messages between machines. What additional communication might be necessary by the application layer? What additional communication might be necessary by the transport layer?

*38. In what way could TCP be considered a better protocol for implementing the transport layer than UDP? In what way could UDP be considered better than TCP?

*39. What does it mean to say that UDP is a connectionless protocol?

*40. At what layer in the TCP/IP protocol hierarchy could a firewall be placed to filter incoming traffic by means of
a. message content
b. source address
c. type of application

*41. Suppose you wanted to establish a firewall to filter out e-mail messages containing certain terms and phrases. Would this firewall be placed at your domain's gateway or at the domain's mail server? Explain your answer.

Social Issues

The following questions are provided to help you understand some of the ethical/social/legal issues associated with the field of computing. The goal is not merely to answer these questions. You should also consider why you answered as you did and whether your justifications are consistent from one question to the next.

1. The ability to connect computers via networks has popularized the concept of working at home. What are some pros and cons of this movement? Will it affect the consumption of natural resources? Will it strengthen families? Will it reduce "office politics"? Will those who work at home have the same career advancement opportunities as those who work on site? Will community ties be weakened? Will reduced personal contact with peers have a positive or negative effect?

2. The Internet stands on the brink of becoming an alternative to "hands on" shopping. What effect will such a shift in shopping habits have on communities? What about shopping malls? What about small shops, such as bookstores and clothing stores, in which you like to browse without buying? To what extent is buying at the lowest possible price good or bad? Is there any moral obligation to pay more for an item in order to support a local business? Is it ethical to compare products at a local store and then order your selection at a lower price via the Internet? What are the long-term consequences of such behavior?

3. To what extent should a government control its citizens' access to the Internet (or any international network) in the name of national security? What are some security issues that may occur?

4. Electronic bulletin boards allow users of networks to post messages (often anonymously) and read messages posted by others. Should the manager of such a bulletin board be held responsible for its contents? Should a telephone company be held responsible for the contents of telephone conversations? Should the manager of a grocery store be held responsible for the contents of a community bulletin board located in the store?

5. Should the use of the Internet be monitored? Should it be regulated? If so, by whom?

6. How much time do you spend accessing the Internet? Is that time well spent? Has Internet access altered your social activities? Do you find it easier to talk to people via the Internet than in person?

7. When you buy a software package for a desktop computer, the developer usually asks you to register with the developer so that you can be notified of future upgrades. This registration process is increasingly being handled via the Internet. You are usually asked to give such things as your name, address, and perhaps how you learned of the product, and then the developer's software automatically transfers this data to the developer. What ethical issues would be raised if the developer designed the registration software so that it sent additional information to the developer during the registration process? For example, the software might scan the contents of your system and report the other software packages found.

8. When you visit a Web site, that site has the capability of recording data, called cookies, on your computer indicating that you have visited that site. These cookies can then be used to identify return visitors. They also provide a record of the sites you have visited that can be accessed by other sites. Should a Web site have such a capability? Should a Web site be allowed to record cookies on your computer without your knowledge? What are possible benefits of cookies? What problems could arise from the use of cookies?

9. Does a law against an act keep the act from happening or merely make it illegal? If corporations are required to register their encryption keys, are they safe or merely protected by law? What is the difference?

10. In general, etiquette leads us to avoid calling a friend at his or her place of work for personal or social matters such as making arrangements for a weekend outing. Likewise, most of us would hesitate to call a customer at his or her home to describe a new product. In a similar manner, we mail wedding invitations to the guests' residences, whereas we mail announcements of business conferences to the attendees' work addresses. Is it proper to send personal e-mail to a friend via the mail server at the friend's place of employment?

11. To what extent should photographs be owned? Suppose a person places his or her photograph on a Web site and someone else downloads that photograph, alters it so that the subject is in a compromising situation, and circulates the altered version. What recourse should the subject of the photograph have?

Additional Reading

Bishop, M. *Computer Security: Art and Science*. Reading, MA: Addison Wesley, 2003.

Comer, D. E., and R. Droms. *Computer Networks and Internets*, 4th ed. Upper Saddle River, NJ: Prentice Hall, 2004.

Kurose, J. F., and K. W. Ross. *Computer Networking*, 2nd ed. Reading, MA: Addison Wesley, 2003.

Rosenoer, J. *CyberLaw, The Law of the Internet*. New York: Springer, 1997.

Spinello, R. A. and H. T. Tavani. *Readings in CyberEthics*. Boston: Jones and Bartlett, 2001.

Stevens, W. R. *TCP/IP Illustrated,* vol. 1. Reading, MA: Addison-Wesley, 1994.

Algorithms

We have seen that before a computer can perform a task, it must be given an algorithm telling it precisely what to do; consequently, the study of algorithms is the cornerstone of computer science. In this chapter we introduce many of the fundamental concepts of this study, including the issues of algorithm discovery and representation as well as the major control concepts of iteration and recursion. In so doing we also present a few well-known algorithms for searching and sorting.

5.1 The Concept of an Algorithm

In the introductory chapter we informally defined an algorithm as a set of steps that define how a task is performed. In this section we look more closely at this fundamental concept.

An Informal Review

We have encountered a multitude of algorithms in our study. We have found algorithms for converting numeric representations from one form to another, detecting and correcting errors in data, compressing and decompressing data files, controlling time-sharing in a multitasking environment, and many more. Moreover, we have seen that the machine cycle that is followed by a CPU is nothing more than the simple algorithm

> As long as the halt instruction has not been executed continue to execute the following steps:
>> a. Fetch an instruction.
>> b. Decode the instruction.
>> c. Execute the instruction.

As demonstrated by the algorithm describing a magic trick in Figure 0.1, algorithms are not restricted to technical activities. Indeed, they underlie even such mundane activities as shelling peas:

> Obtain a basket of unshelled peas and an empty bowl.
> As long as there are unshelled peas in the basket continue to execute the following steps:
>> a. Take a pea from the basket.
>> b. Break open the pea pod.
>> c. Dump the peas from the pod into the bowl.
>> d. Discard the pod.

In fact, many researchers believe that every activity of the human mind, including imagination, creativity, and decision making, is actually the result of algorithm execution—a conjecture we will revisit in our study of artificial intelligence (Chapter 10).

But before we proceed further, let us consider the formal definition of an algorithm.

The Formal Definition of an Algorithm

Informal, loosely defined concepts are acceptable and common in everyday life, but a science must be based on well-defined terminology. Consider, then, the formal definition of an algorithm stated in Figure 5.1.

Figure 5.1

The definition of an algorithm
An algorithm is an ordered set of unambiguous, executable steps, that defines a terminating process.

Note that the definition requires that the set of steps in an algorithm be ordered. This means that the steps in an algorithm must have a well-established structure in terms of the order in which its steps are executed. This does not mean, however, that the steps must be executed in a sequence consisting of a first step, followed by a second, and so on. Some algorithms, known as parallel algorithms, contain more than one sequence of steps, each designed to be executed by different processors in a multiprocessor machine. In such cases the overall algorithm does not possess a single thread of steps that conforms to the first-step, second-step scenario. Instead, the algorithm's structure is that of multiple threads that branch and reconnect as different processors perform different parts of the overall task. (We will revisit this concept in Section 6 of Chapter 6.) Other examples include algorithms executed by circuits such as the flip-flop in Section 1.1, in which each gate performs a single step of the overall algorithm. Here the steps are ordered by cause and effect, as the action of each gate propagates throughout the circuit.

Next, consider the requirement that an algorithm must consist of executable steps. To appreciate this condition, consider the instruction

Make a list of all the positive integers

which would be impossible to perform because there are infinitely many positive integers. Thus any set of instructions involving this instruction would not be an algorithm. Computer scientists use the term *effective* to capture the concept of being executable. That is, to say that a step is effective means that it is doable.

Another requirement imposed by the definition in Figure 5.1 is that the steps in an algorithm be unambiguous. This means that during execution of an algorithm, the information in the state of the process must be sufficient to determine uniquely and completely the actions required by each step. In other words, the execution of each step in an algorithm does not require creative skills. Rather, it requires only the ability to follow directions.

The definition in Figure 5.1 also requires that an algorithm define a terminating process, which means that the execution of an algorithm must lead to an end. The origin of this requirement is in theoretical computer science, where the goal is to answer such questions as "What are the ultimate limitations of algorithms and machines?" Here computer science seeks to distinguish between problems whose answers can be obtained algorithmically and problems whose answers lie beyond the capabilities of algorithmic systems. In this context, a line is drawn between processes that culminate with an answer and those that merely proceed forever without producing a result.

There are, however, meaningful applications for nonterminating processes, including monitoring the vital signs of a hospital patient and maintaining an aircraft's altitude in flight. Some would argue that these applications involve merely the repetition of algorithms, each of which reaches an end and then automatically repeats. Others would counter that such arguments are simply attempts to cling to an overly restrictive formal definition. In any case, the result is that the term *algorithm* is often used in applied, or informal settings in reference to sets of steps that do not necessarily define terminating processes. An example is the long-division "algorithm" that does not define a terminating process when dividing 1 by 3. Technically, such instances represent misuses of the term.

The Abstract Nature of Algorithms

It is important to emphasize the distinction between an algorithm and its representation—a distinction that is analogous to that between a story and a book. A story is abstract, or conceptual, in nature; a book is a physical representation of a story. If a book is translated into another language or republished in a different format, it is merely the representation of the story that changes—the story itself remains the same.

In the same manner, an algorithm is abstract and distinct from its representation. A single algorithm can be represented in many ways. As an example, the algorithm for converting temperature readings from Celsius to Fahrenheit is traditionally represented as the algebraic formula

$$F = (9/5)C + 32$$

But it could be represented by the instruction

Multiply the temperature reading in Celsius by $9/5$
and then add 32 to the product

or even in the form of an electronic circuit. In each case the underlying algorithm is the same; only the representations differ.

The distinction between an algorithm and its representation presents a problem when we try to communicate algorithms. A common example involves the level of detail at which an algorithm must be described. Among meteorologists, the instruction "Convert the Celsius reading to its Fahrenheit equivalent" may suffice, but a layperson, requiring a more detailed description, would argue that the instruction is ambiguous. The problem, however, is not that the underlying algorithm is ambiguous but that the algorithm is not represented in enough detail for the layperson. Thus the ambiguity is in the algorithm's representation rather than in the algorithm. In the next section we will see how the concept of primitives can be used to eliminate such ambiguity problems in an algorithm's representation.

Finally, while on the subject of algorithms and their representations, we should clarify the distinction between two other related concepts—programs and processes. A program is a representation of an algorithm. (Here we are using the term *algorithm* in its less formal sense in that many programs are representations of nonterminating "algorithms.") In fact, within the computing community the term *program* usually refers to a formal representation of an algorithm designed for computer application. We defined a *process* in Chapter 3 to be the activity of executing a program. Note, however, that to execute a program is to execute the algorithm represented by the program, so a process could equivalently be defined as the activity of executing an algorithm. We conclude that programs, algorithms, and processes are distinct, yet related, entities. A program is the representation of an algorithm, whereas a process is the activity of executing an algorithm.

Questions/Exercises

1. Summarize the distinctions between a process, an algorithm, and a program.

2. Give some examples of algorithms with which you are familiar. Are they really algorithms in the precise sense?

3. Identify some points of vagueness in our informal definition of an algorithm introduced in Section 1 of Chapter 0.

4. In what sense do the steps described by the following list of instructions fail to constitute an algorithm?
   Step 1. Take a coin out of your pocket and put it on the table.
   Step 2. Return to Step 1.

5.2 Algorithm Representation

In this section we consider issues relating to an algorithm's representation. Our goal is to introduce the basic concepts of primitives and pseudocode as well as to establish a representation system for our own use.

Algorithm Representation During Algorithm Design

The task of designing a complex algorithm requires that the designer keeps track of numerous interrelated concepts—a requirement that can exceed the capabilities of the human mind. (In an article in *Psychological Review* in 1956, George A. Miller reported research indicating that the human mind is capable of manipulating only about seven details at any one time.) Thus the designer of complex algorithms needs a way to record and recall portions of an evolving algorithm as his or her concentration requires.

During the 1950s and 1960s, flowcharts (by which algorithms are represented by geometric shapes connected by arrows) represented the state-of-the-art design tool. However, flowcharts often became tangled webs of crisscrossing arrows that made understanding the structure of the underlying algorithm difficult. Thus the use of flowcharts as design tools has given way to other representation techniques. An example is the pseudocode used in this text, by which algorithms are represented with well-defined textual structures. On the other hand, flowcharts are still beneficial when the goal is presentation rather than design. For example, Figures 5.8 and 5.9 apply flowchart notation to demonstrate the algorithmic structure represented by popular control statements.

The search for better design notations is a continuing process. In Chapter 7 we will see that the trend is to use graphical techniques to assist in the global design of large software systems, while pseudocode remains popular for designing the smaller procedural components within a system.

Primitives

The representation of an algorithm requires some form of language. In the case of humans this may be a traditional natural language (English, Spanish, Russian, Japanese) or perhaps the language of pictures, as demonstrated in Figure 5.2, which describes an algorithm for folding a bird from a square piece of paper. Often, however, such natural channels of communication lead to misunderstandings, sometimes because the terminology used may have more than one meaning. (The sentence, "Visiting grandchildren can be nerve-racking," could mean either that the grandchildren cause problems when they come to visit or that going to see them is problematic.) Problems also arise over misunderstandings regarding the level of detail required. Few readers could successfully fold a bird from the directions given in Figure 5.2, yet a student of origami would probably have little difficulty. In short, communication problems arise when the language used for an algorithm's representation is not precisely defined or when information is not given in adequate detail.

Computer science approaches these problems by establishing a well-defined set of building blocks from which algorithm representations can be constructed. Such a building block is called a **primitive.** Assigning precise definitions to these primitives

Figure 5.2

Folding a bird from a square piece of paper

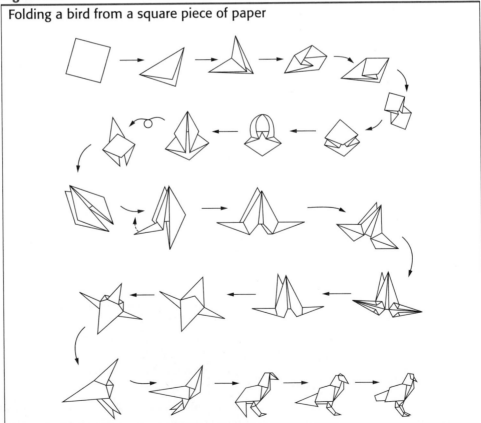

removes many problems of ambiguity, and requiring algorithms to be described in terms of these primitives establishes a uniform level of detail. A collection of primitives along with a collection of rules stating how the primitives can be combined to represent more complex ideas constitutes a programming language.

Each primitive consists of two parts: its syntax and its semantics. Syntax refers to the primitive's symbolic representation, and semantics refers to the meaning of the primitive. The syntax of *air* consists of three symbols, whereas the semantics is a gaseous substance that surrounds the world. As an example, Figure 5.3 presents some of the primitives used in origami.

To obtain a collection of primitives to use in representing algorithms for computer execution, we could turn to the individual instructions that the machine is designed to execute. If an algorithm is expressed at this level of detail, we will certainly have a program suitable for machine execution. However, expressing algorithms at this

Figure 5.3

Origami primitives

level is tedious, and so one normally uses a collection of "higher-level" primitives, each being an abstract tool constructed from the lower-level primitives provided in the machine's language. The result is a formal programming language in which algorithms can be expressed in a conceptually higher form than in the actual machine language. We will discuss such programming languages in the next chapter.

Pseudocode

For now, we forgo the introduction of a formal programming language in favor of a less formal, more intuitive notational system known as pseudocode. In general, a **pseudocode** is a notational system in which ideas can be expressed informally during the algorithm development process.

One way to obtain a pseudocode is simply to loosen the rules of the formal language in which the final version of the algorithm is to be expressed. This approach is commonly used when the target programming language is known in advance. There the pseudocode used during the early stages of program development consists of syntax-semantic structures similar to, but less formal than, those used in the target programming language.

Our goal, however, is to consider the issues of algorithm development and representation without confining our discussion to a particular programming language. Thus our approach to pseudocode is to develop a consistent, concise notation for representing recurring semantic structures. In turn, these structures will become the primitives in which we attempt to express future ideas.

One such recurring semantic structure is the assignment of values to descriptive names. For example, we will want to reference values using names such as Temperature, TotalRainfall, BankBalance, and Altitude. To establish associations between names and values, we will use the form

> *name* ← *expression*

where *name* is the descriptive name and *expression* describes the value to be associated with the name. We will read these statements as "assign *name* the value of *expression*." That is, the value of the expression is assigned to the name. For example, the statement

> RemainingFunds ← CheckingBalance + SavingsBalance

assigns the result of adding the values of CheckingBalance and SavingsBalance to the name RemainingFunds.

Another recurring semantic structure is the need to select one of two possible activities depending on the truth or falseness of some condition. Examples include:

> If the gross domestic product has increased, buy common stock; otherwise, sell common stock.
>
> Buy common stock if the gross domestic product has increased and sell it otherwise.
>
> Buy or sell common stock depending on whether the gross domestic product has increased or decreased, respectively.

Each of these statements could be rewritten to conform to the structure

> **if** (*condition*) **then** (*activity*)
> **else** (*activity*)

where we have used the key words **if**, **then**, and **else** to announce the different sub-structures within the main structure and have used parentheses to delimit the boundaries of these substructures. By adopting this syntactic structure for our pseudocode, we acquire a uniform way in which to express this common semantic structure. This, then, is what we do.

Whereas the statement

> Depending on whether or not the year is a leap year, divide the total by 366 or 365, respectively.

may possess a more creative literary style, we will consistently opt for the straight-forward

> **if** (year is leap year)
>   **then** (daily total ← total divided by 366)
>   **else** (daily total ← total divided by 365)

We also adopt the shorter syntax

> **if** (*condition*) **then** (*activity*)

for those cases not involving an else activity. Using this notation, the statement

> Should it be the case that sales have decreased, lower the price by 5%.

will be reduced to

> **if** (sales have decreased) **then** (lower the price by 5%)

Still another common semantic structure is the repeated execution of a statement or sequence of statements as long as some condition remains true. Informal examples include

> As long as there are tickets to sell, continue selling tickets.

and

> While there are tickets to sell, keep selling tickets.

For such cases, we adopt the uniform pattern

> **while** (*condition*) **do** (*activity*)

for our pseudocode. In short, such a statement means to check the condition and, if it is true, perform the activity and return to check the condition again. If, however, the condition is found to be false, move on to the next instruction following the **while** structure. Thus both of the preceding statements are reduced to

> **while** (tickets remain to be sold) **do** (sell a ticket)

Indentation often enhances the readability of a program. For example, the statement

> **if** (not raining)
>   **then** (**if** (temperature = hot)
>   **then** (go swimming)
>   **else** (play golf)
>   )
>   **else** (watch television)

is easier to comprehend than the otherwise equivalent

if (not raining) **then** (**if** (temperature = hot) **then** (go swimming)
else (play golf)) **else** (watch television)

Thus we will adopt the use of indentation in our pseudocode. (Note that we can even use indentation to align a closing parenthesis directly below its partner to simplify the process of identifying the scope of statements or phrases.)

We want to use our pseudocode to describe activities that can be used as abstract tools in other applications. Computer science has a variety of terms for such program units, including subprogram, subroutine, procedure, module, and function, each with its own variation of meaning. We will adopt the term *procedure* for our pseudocode and use this term to announce the title by which the pseudocode unit will be known. More precisely, we will begin a pseudocode unit with a statement of the form

procedure *name*

where ***name*** is the particular name of the unit. We will then follow this introductory statement with the statements that define the unit's action. For example, Figure 5.4 is a pseudocode representation of a procedure called **Greetings** that prints the message "Hello" three times.

When the task performed by a procedure is required elsewhere in our pseudocode, we will merely request it by name. For example, if two procedures were named **ProcessLoan** and **RejectApplication**, then we could request their services within an if-then-else structure by writing

if (. . .) **then** (Execute the procedure ProcessLoan)
else (Execute the procedure RejectApplication)

which would result in the execution of the procedure **ProcessLoan** if the tested condition were true or in the execution of **RejectApplication** if the condition were false.

Procedures should be designed to be as generic as possible. A procedure for sorting lists of names should be designed to sort any list—not a particular one—so it should be written in such a way that the list to be sorted is not specified in the procedure itself. Instead, the list should be referred to by a generic name within the procedure's representation.

In our pseudocode, we will adopt the convention of listing these generic names in parentheses on the same line on which we identify the procedure's name. In particular, a procedure named **Sort**, which is designed to sort any list of names, would begin with the statement

Figure 5.4

The procedure Greetings in pseudocode

procedure Greetings
Count ← 3;
while (Count > 0) **do**
    (print the message "Hello" and
    Count ← Count −1)

procedure Sort (List)

Later in the representation where a reference to the list being sorted is required, the generic name List would be used. In turn, when the services of Sort are required, we will identify which list is to be substituted for List in the procedure Sort. Thus we will write something such as

Apply the procedure Sort to the organization's membership list

and

Apply the procedure Sort to the wedding guest list

depending on our needs.

Keep in mind that the purpose of our pseudocode is to provide a means of representing algorithms in a readable, informal manner. We want a notational system that will assist us in expressing our ideas–not enslave us to rigorous, formal rules. Thus we will feel free to expand or modify our pseudocode when needed. In particular, many people find it helpful to follow a closing parenthesis with a short comment explaining which statement or phrase is being terminated. In particular, one may follow the final parenthesis in a **while** statement with the words **end while**, producing a statement such as

```
while (...) do
   ( .
     .
     .
   ) end while
```

or perhaps

```
while (...) do
   (if (...)
      then ( .
             .
             .
           ) end if
   ) end while
```

The point is that we are trying to express an algorithm in a readable form, and thus we may introduce visual aids (indentation, comments, etc.) at times to achieve this goal. Moreover, if we encounter a recurring theme that is not yet incorporated in our pseudocode, we may choose to extend our pseudocode by adopting a consistent syntax for representing the new concept.

Questions/Exercises

1. A primitive in one context may turn out to be a composite of primitives in another. For instance, our **while** statement is a primitive in our pseudocode, yet it is implemented as a composite of machine-language instructions. Give two examples of this phenomenon in a noncomputer setting.

2. In what sense is the construction of procedures the construction of primitives?

3. The Euclidean algorithm finds the greatest common divisor of two positive integers X and Y by the following process:

> As long as the value of neither X nor Y is zero, continue dividing the larger of the values by the smaller and assigning X and Y the values of the divisor and remainder, respectively. (The final value of X is the greatest common divisor.)

Express this algorithm in our pseudocode.

4. Describe a collection of primitives that are used in a subject other than computer programming.

5.3 Algorithm Discovery

The development of a program consists of two activities—discovering the underlying algorithm and representing that algorithm as a program. Up to this point we have been concerned with the issues of algorithm representation without considering the question of how algorithms are found in the first place. Yet algorithm discovery is usually the more challenging step in the software development process. After all, discovering an algorithm to solve a problem requires finding a method of solving that problem. Thus, to understand how algorithms are discovered is to understand the problem-solving process.

The Art of Problem Solving

The techniques of problem solving and the need to learn more about them are not unique to computer science but rather are topics pertinent to almost any field. The close association between the process of algorithm discovery and that of general problem solving has caused computer scientists to join with those of other disciplines in the search for better problem-solving techniques. Ultimately, one would like to reduce the process of problem solving to an algorithm in itself, but this has been shown to be impossible. (This is a result of the material in Chapter 11, where we will show that there are problems that do not have algorithmic solutions.) Thus the ability to solve problems remains more of an artistic skill to be developed than a precise science to be learned.

As evidence of the illusive, artistic nature of problem solving, the following loosely defined problem-solving phases presented by the mathematician G. Polya in 1945 remain the basic principles on which attempts to teach problem-solving skills are based today.

Phase 1. Understand the problem.

Phase 2. Devise a plan for solving the problem.

Phase 3. Carry out the plan.

Phase 4. Evaluate the solution for accuracy and for its potential as a tool for solving other problems.

Translated into the context of program development, these phases become

Phase 1. Understand the problem.

Phase 2. Get an idea of how an algorithmic procedure might solve the problem.

Phase 3. Formulate the algorithm and represent it as a program.

Phase 4. Evaluate the program for accuracy and for its potential as a tool for solving other problems.

Having presented Polya's list, we should emphasize that these phases are not steps to be followed when trying to solve a problem but rather phases that will be completed sometime during the solution process. The key word here is *followed*. You do not solve problems by following. Rather, to solve a problem, you must take the initiative and lead. If you approach the task of solving a problem in the frame of mind depicted by "Now I've finished Phase 1, it's time to move on to Phase 2," you are not likely to be successful. However, if you become involved with the problem and ultimately solve it, you most likely can look back at what you did and realize that you performed Polya's phases.

Another important observation is that Polya's phases are not necessarily completed in sequence. Contrary to the claim made by many authors, successful problem solvers often start formulating strategies for solving a problem (Phase 2) before the problem itself is entirely understood (Phase 1). Then, if these strategies fail (during Phases 3 or 4), the potential problem solver gains a deeper understanding of the intricacies of the problem and, based on this deeper understanding, can return to form other and hopefully more successful strategies.

Keep in mind that we are discussing how problems are solved—not how we would like them to be solved. Ideally, we would like to eliminate the waste inherent in the trial-and-error process just described. In the case of developing large software systems, discovering a misunderstanding as late as Phase 4 can represent a tremendous loss in resources. Avoiding such catastrophes is a major goal of software engineers (Chapter 6), who have traditionally insisted on a thorough understanding of a problem before proceeding with a solution. One could argue, however, that a true understanding of a problem is not obtained until a solution has been found. The mere fact that a problem is unsolved implies a lack of understanding. To insist on a complete understanding of the problem before proposing any solutions is therefore somewhat idealistic.

As an example, consider the following problem:

> Person A is charged with the task of determining the ages of person B's three children. B tells A that the product of the children's ages is 36. After considering this clue, A replies that another clue is required, so B tells A the sum of the children's ages. Again, A replies that another clue is needed, so B tells A that the oldest child plays the piano. After hearing this clue, A tells B the ages of the three children.
>
> How old are the three children?

At first glance the last clue seems to be totally unrelated to the problem, yet it is apparently this clue that allows A to finally determine the ages of the children. How can this be? Let us proceed by formulating a plan of attack and following this plan, even though we still have many questions about the problem. Our plan will be to trace the steps described by the problem statement while keeping track of the information available to person A as the story progresses.

The first clue given A is that the product of the children's ages is 36. This means that the triple representing the three ages is one of those listed in Figure 5.5(a). The next clue is the sum of the desired triple. We are not told what this sum is, but we are told that this information is not enough for A to isolate the correct triple; therefore the desired triple must be one whose sum appears at least twice in the table of Figure 5.5(b). But the only triples appearing in (b) with identical sums are (1,6,6) and (2,2,9), both of which produce the sum 13. This is the information available to A at the time the last clue is given. It is at this point that we finally understand the significance of the last clue. It has nothing to do with playing the piano; rather it is the fact that there is an oldest child. This rules out the triple (1,6,6) and thus allows us to conclude that the children's ages are 2, 2, and 9.

In this case, then, it is not until we attempt to implement our plan for solving the problem (Phase 3) that we gain a complete understanding of the problem (Phase 1). Had we insisted on completing phase 1 before proceeding, we would probably never have found the children's ages. Such irregularities in the problem-solving process are fundamental to the difficulties in developing systematic approaches to problem solving.

Another irregularity is the mysterious inspiration that may come to a potential problem solver who, having worked on a problem without apparent success, may at a later time suddenly see the solution while doing another task. This phenomenon was identified by H. von Helmholtz as early as 1896 and was discussed by the mathematician Henri Poincaré in a lecture before the Psychological Society in Paris. There, Poincaré described his experiences of realizing the solution to a problem he had worked on after he had set it aside and begun other projects. The phenomenon reflects a process in which a subconscious part of the mind appears to continue working and, if successful, forces the solution into the conscious mind. Today, the period between conscious work on a problem and the sudden inspiration is known as an incubation period, and its understanding remains a goal of current research.

Getting a Foot in the Door

We have been discussing problem solving from a somewhat philosophical point of view while avoiding a direct confrontation with the question of how we should go about trying to solve a problem. There are, of course, numerous problem-solving

Figure 5.5

a. Triples whose product is 36		**b. Sums of triples from part (a)**	
(1,1,36)	(1,6,6)	1 + 1 + 36 = 38	1 + 6 + 6 = 13
(1,2,18)	(2,2,9)	1 + 2 + 18 = 21	2 + 2 + 9 = 13
(1,3,12)	(2,3,6)	1 + 3 + 12 = 16	2 + 3 + 6 = 11
(1,4,9)	(3,3,4)	1 + 4 + 9 = 14	3 + 3 + 4 = 10

approaches, each of which can be successful in certain settings. We will identify some of them shortly. For now, we note that there seems to be a common thread running through these techniques, which simply stated is "get your foot in the door." As an example, let us consider the following simple problem:

Before A, B, C, and D ran a race they made the following predictions:

A predicted that B would win.
B predicted that D would be last.
C predicted that A would be third.
D predicted that A's prediction would be correct.

Only one of these predictions was true, and this was the prediction made by the winner. In what order did A, B, C, and D finish the race?

After reading the problem and analyzing the data, it should not take long to realize that since the predictions of A and D were equivalent and only one prediction was true, the predictions of both A and D must be false. Thus neither A nor D were winners. At this point we have our foot in the door, and obtaining the complete solution to our problem is merely a matter of extending our knowledge from here. If A's prediction was false, then B did not win either. The only remaining choice for the winner is C. Thus, C won the race, and C's prediction was true. Consequently, we know that A came in third. That means that the finishing order was either CBAD or CDAB. But the former is ruled out because B's prediction must be false. Therefore the finishing order was CDAB.

Of course, being told to get our foot in the door is not the same as being told how to do it. Obtaining this toehold, as well as realizing how to expand this initial thrust into a complete solution to the problem, requires creative input from the would-be problem solver. There are, however, several general approaches that have been proposed by Polya and others for how one might go about getting a foot in the door. One is to try working the problem backward. For instance, if the problem is to find a way of producing a particular output from a given input, one might start with that output and attempt to back up to the given input. This approach is typical of people trying to discover the bird-folding algorithm in the previous section. They tend to unfold a completed bird in an attempt to see how it is constructed.

Another general problem-solving approach is to look for a related problem that is either easier to solve or has been solved before and then try to apply its solution to the current problem. This technique is of particular value in the context of program development. Often the major difficulty in program development is not that of solving a particular instance of a problem but rather of finding a general algorithm that can be used to solve all instances of the problem. More precisely, if we were faced with the task of developing a program for alphabetizing lists of names, our task would not be to sort a particular list but to find a general algorithm that could be used to sort any list of names. Thus, although the instructions

Interchange the names David and Alice.
Move the name Carol to the position between Alice and David.
Move the name Bob to the position between Alice and Carol.

correctly sort the list David, Alice, Carol, and Bob, they do not constitute the general-purpose algorithm we desire. What we need is an algorithm that can sort this list as well as other lists we may encounter. This is not to say that our solution for sorting a particular list is totally worthless in our search for a general-purpose algorithm. We might, for instance, get our foot in the door by considering such special cases in an attempt to find general principles that can in turn be used to develop the desired general-purpose algorithm. In this case, then, our solution is obtained by the technique of solving a collection of related problems.

Still another approach to getting a foot in the door is to apply **stepwise refinement,** which is essentially the technique of not trying to conquer an entire task (in all its gory detail) at once. Rather, stepwise refinement proposes that one first view the problem at hand in terms of several subproblems. The idea is that by breaking the original problem into subproblems, one is able to approach the overall solution in terms of steps, each of which is easier to solve than the entire original problem. In turn, stepwise refinement proposes that these steps be decomposed into smaller steps and these smaller steps be broken into still smaller ones until the entire problem has been reduced to a collection of easily solved subproblems.

In this light, stepwise refinement is a top-down methodology in that it progresses from the general to the specific. In contrast, bottom-up methodologies progress from the specific to the general. Although contrasting in theory, the two approaches actually complement each other in practice. For instance, the decomposition of a problem proposed by the top-down methodology of stepwise refinement is often guided by the problem solver's intuition, which is working in a bottom-up mode.

Solutions produced by stepwise refinement possess a natural modular structure, and herein lies a major reason for the popularity of stepwise refinement in algorithm design. If an algorithm has a natural modular structure, then it is easily adapted to a modular representation, which is conducive to the development of a manageable program. Furthermore, the modules produced by stepwise refinement are compatible with the concept of team programming, in which several people are assigned the task of developing a software product as a team. After all, once the task of the software has been broken into subproblems (or potential modules), the personnel on the team can work independently on these subtasks without getting in each other's way.

These advantages of stepwise refinement in the context of software development have produced many followers of the technique. However, with all its good points, stepwise refinement is not the final word in algorithm discovery. Rather, it is essentially an organizational tool whose problem-solving attributes are consequences of this organization. Stepwise refinement is a natural methodology to use when organizing a nationwide political campaign, writing a term paper, or planning a sales convention. Similarly, most software development projects in the data processing community have a large organizational component. The task is not so much that of discovering a startling new algorithm as it is a problem of organizing the tasks to be performed into a coherent package. For these reasons, stepwise refinement has correctly become a major design methodology in data processing.

But stepwise refinement remains only one of many design methodologies of interest to computer scientists, and thus one should not be misled into believing that all algorithm discoveries can be achieved by means of stepwise refinement. In fact, bringing

Naming Items in Programs

In a natural language, items often have multiword names such as "cost of producing a widget" or "estimated arrival time." However, when expressing algorithms in a formal program or in a pseudocode version of a program, multiword names can complicate an algorithm's description. Experience has shown that it is better to have each item identified by a single contiguous block of text. Over the years many techniques have been used to compress multiple words into a single lexical unit to obtain descriptive names for items in programs. One is to use underlines to connect words, producing names such as `estimated_arrival_time`. Another is to use uppercase letters to help a reader comprehend a compressed multiword name. For example, one could start each word with an uppercase letter to obtain names such as `EstimatedArrivalTime`. This technique is often called **Pascal casing**, because it was popularized by users of the Pascal programming language. A variation of Pascal casing is called **camel casing,** which is identical to Pascal casing except that the first letter remains in lowercase as in `estimatedArrivalTime`. In this text we lean toward Pascal casing, but the choice is largely a matter of taste.

preconceived notions and preselected tools to the problem-solving task can sometimes mask a problem's simplicity. The ages-of-the-children problem discussed earlier in this section is an excellent example of this phenomenon. Students of algebra invariably approach the problem as a system of simultaneous equations, an approach that leads to a dead end and often traps the would-be problem solver into believing that the information given is not sufficient to solve the problem. Another example is the following:

> As you step from a pier into a boat, your hat falls into the water, unbeknownst to you. The river is flowing at 2.5 miles per hour so your hat begins to float downstream. In the meantime, you begin traveling upstream in the boat at a speed of 4.75 miles per hour relative to the water. After 10 minutes you realize that your hat is missing, turn the boat around, and begin to chase your hat down the river. How long will it take to catch up with your hat?

Most algebra students as well as pocket calculator enthusiasts approach this problem by first determining how far upstream the boat will have traveled in 10 minutes as well as how far downstream the hat will have traveled during that same time. Then, they determine how long it will take for the boat to travel downstream to this position. But, when the boat reaches this position, the hat will have floated farther downstream! Thus, the problem solver either begins to apply techniques of the calculus or becomes trapped in a cycle of computing where the hat will be each time the boat goes to where the hat was.

The problem is much simpler than this, however. The trick is to resist the urge to begin writing formulas and making calculations. Instead, we need to put these skills aside and adjust our perspective. The entire problem takes place in the river. The fact that the water is moving in relation to the shore is irrelevant. Think of the same problem posed on a large conveyer belt instead of a river. First, solve the problem with the conveyer belt stopped. If you place your hat at your feet while standing on the belt and then walk away from your hat for 10 minutes, it will take 10 minutes to return to your hat. Now turn on the conveyer belt. This means that the scenery will begin to move past the belt, but, because you are on the belt, this does not change your relationship to the belt or your hat. It will still take 10 minutes to return to your hat.

We conclude that algorithm discovery remains a challenging art that must be developed over a period of time rather than taught as a subject consisting of well-defined methodologies. To train a potential problem solver to follow certain methodologies is to quash those creative skills that should instead be nurtured.

Questions/Exercises

1. a. Find an algorithm for solving the following program: Given a positive integer n, find the list of positive integers whose product is the largest among all the lists of positive integers whose sum is n. For example, if n is 4, the desired list is 2, 2 because 2×2 is larger than $1 \times 1 \times 1 \times 1$, $2 \times 1 \times 1$, and 3×1. If n is 5, the desired list is 2, 3.
   b. What is the desired list if $n = 2001$?
   c. Explain how you got your foot in the door.

2. a. Suppose we are given a checkerboard consisting of 2^n rows and 2^n columns of squares, for some positive integer n, and a box of L-shaped tiles, each of which can cover exactly three squares on the board. If any single square is cut out of the board, can we cover the remaining board with tiles such that tiles do not overlap or hang off the edge of the board?
   b. Explain how your solution to (a) can be used to show that $2^{2n} - 1$ is divisible by 3 for all positive integers n.
   c. How are (a) and (b) related to Polya's phases of problem solving?

3. Decode the following message, then explain how you got your foot in the door.

   Pdeo eo pda yknnayp wjosan.

5.4 Iterative Structures

Our goal now is to study some of the repetitive structures used in describing algorithmic processes. In this section we discuss **iterative structures** in which a collection of instructions is repeated in a looping manner. In the next section we will introduce the technique of recursion. As a side effect, we will introduce some popular algorithms—the sequential search, the binary search, and the insertion sort. We begin by introducing the sequential search algorithm.

The Sequential Search Algorithm

Consider the problem of searching a list for the occurrence of a particular target value. We want to develop an algorithm that determines whether that value is in the list. If

Iterative Structures in Music

Musicians were using and programming iterative structures centuries before computer scientists. Indeed, the structure of a song (being composed of multiple verses, each followed by the chorus) is exemplified by the while statement

while (there is a verse remaining) **do**
    (sing the next verse;
    sing the chorus)

Moreover, the notation

is merely a composer's way of expressing the structure

N ← 1;
while (N < 3) **do**
    (play the passage;
    play the Nth ending;
    N ← N + 1)

the value is in the list, we consider the search a success; otherwise we consider it a failure. We assume that the list is sorted according to some rule for ordering its entries. For example, if the list is a list of names, we assume the names appear in alphabetical order, or if the list consists of numeric values, we assume its entries appear in order of increasing magnitude.

To get our foot in the door, we imagine how we might search a guest list of perhaps 20 entries for a particular name. In this setting we might scan the list from its beginning, comparing each entry with the target name. If we find the target name, the search terminates as a success. However, if we reach the end of the list without finding the target value, our search terminates as a failure. In fact, if we reach a name greater than (alphabetically) the target name without finding the target value, our search terminates as a failure. (Remember, the list is arranged in alphabetical order, so reaching a name greater than the target name indicates that the target does not appear in the list.) In summary, our rough idea is to continue searching down the list as long as there are more names to be investigated and the target name is greater than the name currently being considered.

In our pseudocode this process can be represented as

Select the first entry in the list as TestEntry.
while (TargetValue > TestEntry and
     there remain entries to be considered)
  do (Select the next entry in the list as TestEntry)

Upon terminating this **while** structure, one of two conditions will be true: either the target value has been found or the target value is not in the list. In either case we can detect a successful search by comparing the test entry to the target value. If they are equal, the search has been successful. Thus we add the statement

> **if** (TargetValue = TestEntry)
>   **then** (Declare the search a success.)
>   **else** (Declare the search a failure.)

to the end of our pseudocode routine.

Finally, we observe that the first statement in our routine, which selects the first entry in the list to play the role of the test entry, is based on the assumption that the list in question contains at least one entry. We might reason that this is a safe guess, but just to be sure, we can position our routine as the **else** option of the statement

> **if** (List empty)
>   **then** (Declare search a failure.)
>   **else** (. . .)

This produces the procedure shown in Figure 5.6. Note that this procedure can be used from within other procedures by using statements such as

> Apply the procedure Search to the passenger list to look for the name
> Darrel Baker.

to find out if Darrel Baker is a passenger and

> Apply the procedure Search to the list of ingredients using nutmeg as the
> target value.

to find out if nutmeg appears in the list of ingredients.

In summary, the algorithm represented by Figure 5.6 considers the entries in the sequential order in which they occur in the list. For this reason, the algorithm is called

Figure 5.6

The sequential search algorithm in pseudocode

```
            procedure Search (List, TargetValue)
        if (List empty)
            then
              (Declare search a failure)
            else
              (Select the first entry in List to be TestEntry;
              while (TargetValue > TestEntry and
                      there remain entries to be considered)
                do (Select the next entry in List as TestEntry.);
              if (TargetValue = TestEntry)
                  then (Declare search a success.)
                  else (Declare search a failure.)
              ) end if
```

the **sequential search** algorithm. Because of its simplicity, it is often used for short lists or when other concerns dictate its use. However, in the case of long lists, sequential searches are not as efficient as other techniques (as we shall soon see).

Loop Control

The repetitive use of an instruction or sequence of instructions is an important algorithmic concept. One method of implementing such repetition is the iterative structure known as the **loop,** in which a collection of instructions, called the body of the loop, is executed in a repetitive fashion under the direction of some control process. A typical example is found in the sequential search algorithm represented in Figure 5.6. Here we use a while statement to control the repetition of the single statement Select the next entry in List as TestEntry. Indeed, the while statement

> **while** (*condition*) **do** (*body*)

exemplifies the concept of a loop structure in that its execution traces the cyclic pattern

> check the *condition*
> execute the *body*
> check the *condition*
> execute the *body*
> .
> .
> .
> check the *condition*

until the condition fails.

As a general rule, the use of a loop structure produces a higher degree of flexibility than would be obtained merely by explicitly writing the body several times. For example, although the loop structure

> Execute the statement "Add a drop of sulfuric acid" three times.

is equivalent to the sequence

> Add a drop of sulfuric acid.
> Add a drop of sulfuric acid.
> Add a drop of sulfuric acid.

we cannot produce a similar sequence that is equivalent to the loop described by

> **while** (the pH level is greater than 4) **do**
>   (add a drop of sulfuric acid)

because we do not know in advance how many drops of acid will be required.

Let us now take a closer look at the composition of loop control. You may be tempted to view this part of a loop structure as having minor importance. After all, it is typically the body of the loop that actually performs the task at hand (for example, adding drops of acid)—the control activities appear merely as the overhead involved because we chose to execute the body in a repetitive fashion. However, experience has shown that the control of a loop is the more error-prone part of the structure and therefore deserves our attention.

Searching and Sorting

The sequential and binary search algorithms are only two of many algorithms for performing the search process. Likewise, the insertion sort is only one of many sorting algorithms. Other classic algorithms for sorting include the merge sort (discussed in Chapter 11), the selection sort (Question/Exercise 6 in Section 5.4), the bubble sort (Question/Exercise 7 in Section 5.4), the quick sort (which applies a divide-and-conquer approach to the sorting process), and the heap sort (which uses a clever technique for finding the entries that should be moved forward in the list). You will find discussions of these algorithms in the books listed under Additional Reading at the end of this chapter.

The control of a loop consists of the three activities initialize, test, and modify (Figure 5.7), with the presence of each being required for successful loop control. The test activity has the obligation of causing the termination of the looping process by watching for a condition that indicates termination should take place. This condition is known as the **termination condition**. It is for the purpose of this test activity that we provide a condition within each **while** statement of our pseudocode. In the case of the **while** statement, however, the condition stated is the condition under which the body of the loop should be executed—the termination condition is the negation of the condition appearing in the **while** structure. Thus, in the **while** statement of Figure 5.6, the termination condition is

(TargetValue ≤ TestEntry) or (there are no more entries to be considered)

The other two activities in the loop control ensure that the termination condition will ultimately occur. The initialization step establishes a starting condition, and the modification step moves this condition toward the termination condition. For instance, in Figure 5.6, initialization takes place in the statement preceding the **while** statement, where the current test entry is established as the first list entry. The modification step in this case is actually accomplished within the loop body, where our position of interest (identified by the test entry) is moved toward the end of the list.

Figure 5.7

Components of repetitive control	
Initialize:	Establish an initial state that will be modified toward the termination condition
Test:	Compare the current state to the termination condition and terminate the repetition if equal
Modify:	Change the state in such a way that it moves toward the termination condition

Thus, having executed the initialization step, repeated application of the modification step results in the termination condition being reached. (Either we will reach a test entry that is greater than or equal to the target value or we ultimately reach the end of the list.)

We should emphasize that the initialization and modification steps must lead to the appropriate termination condition. This characteristic is critical for proper loop control, and thus one should always double-check for its presence when designing a loop structure. Failure to make such an evaluation can lead to errors even in the simplest cases. A typical example is found in the statements

```
Number ← 1;
while (Number ≠ 6) do
  (Number ← Number + 2)
```

Here the termination condition is Number = 6. But the value of Number is initialized at 1 and then incremented by 2 in the modification step. Thus, as the loop cycles, the values assigned to Number will be 1, 3, 5, 7, 9, and so on, but never the value 6. In turn, the loop will never terminate.

There are two common loop structures that differ merely in the order in which the loop control components are executed. The first is exemplified by our pseudocode statement

while (*condition*) **do** (*activity*)

whose semantics are represented in Figure 5.8 in the form of a **flowchart.** Such charts use various shapes to represent individual steps and use arrows to indicate the order of the steps. The distinction between the shapes indicates the type of action involved in the associated step. A diamond indicates a decision and a rectangle indicates an arbitrary statement or sequence of statements. Note that the test for termination in the while structure occurs before the loop's body is executed.

Figure 5.8

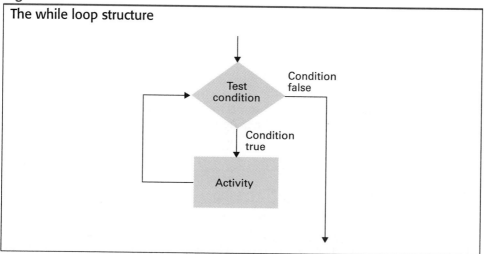

The while loop structure

Figure 5.9

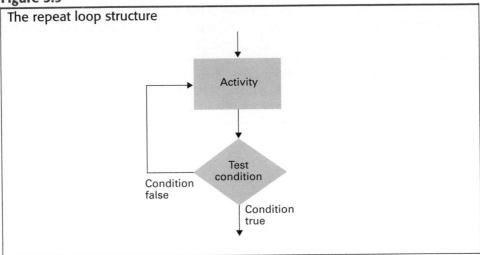
The repeat loop structure

In contrast, the structure in Figure 5.9 requests that the body of the loop be executed before the test for termination is performed. In this case, the loop's body is always performed at least once, whereas in the **while** structure, the body is never executed if the termination condition is satisfied the first time it is tested.

We use the syntactic form

repeat (*activity*) **until** (*condition*)

in our pseudocode to represent the structure shown in Figure 5.9. Thus, the statement

repeat (take a coin from your pocket)
until (there are no coins in your pocket)

assumes there is a coin in your pocket at the beginning, but

while (there is a coin in your pocket) **do**
(take a coin from your pocket)

does not.

Following the terminology of our pseudocode, we will usually refer to these structures as the **while** loop structure or the **repeat** loop structure. In a more generic context you may hear the **while** loop structure referred to as a **pretest loop** (since the test for termination is performed before the body is executed) and the **repeat** loop structure referred to as a **posttest loop** (since the test for termination is performed after the body is executed).

The Insertion Sort Algorithm

As an additional example of iterative structures, let us consider the problem of sorting a list of names into alphabetical order. But before proceeding, we should identify the constraints under which we will work. Simply stated, our goal is to sort the list "within itself."

In other words, we want to sort the list by shuffling its entries as opposed to moving the list to another location. Our situation is analogous to the problem of sorting a list whose entries are recorded on separate index cards spread out on a crowded desktop. We have cleared off enough space for the cards but are not allowed to push additional materials back to make more room. This restriction is typical in computer applications, not because the workspace within the machine is necessarily crowded like our desktop, but simply because we want to use the storage space available in an efficient manner.

Let us get a foot in the door by considering how we might sort the names on the desktop. Consider the list of names

Fred
Alex
Diana
Byron
Carol

One approach to sorting this list is to note that the sublist consisting of only the top name, Fred, is sorted but the sublist consisting of the top two names, Fred and Alex, is not. Thus we might pick up the card containing the name Alex, slide the name Fred down into the space where Alex was, and then place the name Alex in the hole at the top of the list, as represented by the first row in Figure 5.10. At this point our list would be

Alex
Fred
Diana
Byron
Carol

Now the top two names form a sorted sublist, but the top three do not. Thus we might pick up the third name, Diana, slide the name Fred down into the hole where Diana was, and then insert Diana in the hole left by Fred, as summarized in the second row of Figure 5.10. The top three entries in the list would now be sorted. Continuing in this fashion, we could obtain a list in which the top four entries are sorted by picking up the fourth name, Byron, sliding the names Fred and Diana down, and then inserting Byron in the hole (see the third row of Figure 5.10). Finally, we can complete the sorting process by picking up Carol, sliding Fred and Diana down, and then inserting Carol in the remaining hole (see the fourth row of Figure 5.10).

Having analyzed the process of sorting a particular list, our task now is to generalize this process to obtain an algorithm for sorting general lists. To this end, we observe that each row of Figure 5.10 represents the same general process: Pick up the first name in the unsorted portion of the list, slide the names greater than the extracted name down, and insert the extracted name back in the list where the hole appears. If we identify the extracted name as the pivot entry, this process can be expressed in our pseudocode as

```
Move the pivot entry to a temporary location leaving a hole in List;
while (there is a name above the hole and
          that name is greater than the pivot) do
   (move the name above the hole down into the hole
      leaving a hole above the name)
Move the pivot entry into the hole in List.
```

Figure 5.10

Sorting the list Fred, Alex, Diana, Byron, and Carol alphabetically

Next, we observe that this process should be executed repeatedly. To begin the sorting process, the pivot should be the second entry in the list and then, before each additional execution, the pivot selection should be one more entry down the list until the last entry has been positioned. That is, as the preceding routine is repeated, the initial position of the pivot entry should advance from the second entry to the third, then to the fourth, etc., until the routine has positioned the last entry in the list. Following this lead we can control the required repetition with the statements

```
N ← 2;
while (the value of N does not exceed the length of List) do
   (Select the Nth entry in List as the pivot entry;
      .
      .
      .
   N ← N + 1)
```

where N represents the position to use for the pivot entry, the **length of List** refers to the number of entries in the list, and the dots indicate the location where the previous routine should be placed.

Our complete pseudocode program is shown in Figure 5.11. In short, the program sorts a list by repeatedly removing an entry and inserting it into its proper place. It is because of this repeated insertion process that the underlying algorithm is called the **insertion sort.**

Note that the structure of Figure 5.11 is that of a loop within a loop, the outer loop being expressed by the first **while** statement and the inner loop represented by the second **while** statement. Each execution of the body of the outer loop results in the inner loop being initialized and executed until its termination condition is obtained. Thus a single execution of the outer loop's body will result in several executions of the inner loop's body.

The initialization component of the outer loop's control consists of establishing the initial value of N with the statement

```
N ← 2;
```

The modification component is handled by incrementing the value of N at the end of the loop's body with the statement

```
N ← N + 1
```

The termination condition occurs when the value of N exceeds the length of the list.

The inner loop's control is initialized by removing the pivot entry from the list and thus creating a hole. The loop's modification step is accomplished by moving entries down into the hole, thus causing the hole to move up. The termination condition consists of the hole being immediately below a name that is not greater than the pivot or of the hole reaching the top of the list.

Figure 5.11

```
The insertion sort algorithm expressed in pseudocode

procedure Sort (List)
N ← 2;
while (the value of N does not exceed the length of List) do
    (Select the Nth entry in List as the pivot entry;
     Move the pivot entry to a temporary location leaving a hole in List;
     while (there is a name above the hole and that name is greater than the pivot) do
        (move the name above the hole down into the hole leaving a hole above the name)
     Move the pivot entry into the hole in List;
     N ← N + 1
    )
```

Questions/Exercises

1. Modify the sequential search procedure in Figure 5.6 to allow for lists that are not sorted.

2. Convert the pseudocode routine

```
Z ← 0;
X ← 1;
while (X < 6) do
  (Z ← Z + X;
   X ← X + 1)
```

to an equivalent routine using a **repeat** statement.

3. Some of the popular programming languages today use the syntax

    while (. . .) do (. . .)

to represent a pretest loop and the syntax

    do (. . .) while (. . .)

to represent a posttest loop. Although elegant in design, what problems could result from such similarities?

4. Suppose the insertion sort as presented in Figure 5.11 was applied to the list Gene, Cheryl, Alice, and Brenda. Describe the organization of the list at the end of each execution of the body of the outer **while** structure.

5. Why would we not want to change the phrase **greater than** in the **while** statement in Figure 5.11 to **greater than or equal to**?

6. A variation of the insertion sort algorithm is the **selection sort.** It begins by selecting the smallest entry in the list and moving it to the front. It then selects the smallest entry from the remaining entries in the list and moves it to the second position in the list. By repeatedly selecting the smallest entry from the remaining portion of the list and moving that entry forward, the sorted version of the list grows from the front of the list, while the back portion of the list consisting of the remaining unsorted entries shrinks. Use our pseudocode to express a procedure similar to that in Figure 5.11 for sorting a list using the selection sort algorithm.

7. Another well-known sorting algorithm is the **bubble sort.** It is based on the process of repeatedly comparing two adjacent names and interchanging them if they are not in the correct order relative to each other. Let us suppose that the list in question has n entries. The bubble sort would begin by comparing (and possibly interchanging) the entries in positions n and $n - 1$. Then, it would consider the entries in positions $n - 1$ and $n - 2$, and continue moving forward in the list until the first and second entries in the list had been compared (and possibly interchanged). Observe that this pass through the list will pull the smallest entry to the front of the list. Likewise, another such pass will ensure that the next to the smallest entry will be pulled to the second position in the list. Thus, by making a total of $n - 1$ passes through the list, the entire list will be sorted. (If one watches the algorithm at work, one sees the small entries bubble to the top of the list—an observation from which the algorithm gets its name.) Use our pseudocode to express a procedure similar to that in Figure 5.11 for sorting a list using the bubble sort algorithm.

5.5 Recursive Structures

Recursive structures provide an alternative to the loop paradigm for implementing the repetition of activities. Whereas a loop involves repeating a set of instructions in a manner in which the set is completed and then repeated, recursion involves repeating the set of instructions as a subtask of itself. An example is found in processing incoming telephone calls using the call waiting feature. There, an incomplete telephone conversation is set aside while another incoming call is processed. The result is that two conversions are performed. However, they are not performed one-after-the-other as in a loop structure, but instead one is performed within the other.

The Binary Search Algorithm

As a way of introducing recursion, we consider the **binary search** algorithm, which applies a divide-and-conquer methodology to the search process. To this end, we again tackle the problem of searching to see whether a particular entry is in a sorted list, but this time we get our foot in the door by considering the procedure we follow when searching a dictionary. In this case we do not perform a sequential entry-by-entry or even a page-by-page procedure. Rather, we begin by opening the directory to a page in the area where we believe the target entry is located. If we are lucky, we will find the target value there; otherwise, we must continue searching. But at this point we will have narrowed our search considerably.

Recursive Structures in Art

The following recursive procedure can be applied to a rectangular canvas to produce drawings of the style of the Dutch painter Piet Mondrian (1872–1944), who produced paintings in which the rectangular canvas was divided into successively smaller rectangles. Try following the procedure yourself to produce drawings similar to the one shown. Begin by applying the procedure to a rectangle representing the canvas on which you are working.

procedure Mondrian (Rectangle)
if (the size of Rectangle is too large for your artistic taste)
   then (divide Rectangle into two smaller rectangles;
       apply the procedure Mondrian to one of the smaller rectangles;
       apply the procedure Mondrian to the other smaller rectangle)

Of course, in the case of searching a dictionary, we have prior knowledge of where words are likely to be found. If we are looking for the word *somnambulism,* we would start by opening to the latter portion of the dictionary. In the case of generic lists, however, we do not have this advantage, so let us agree to always start our search with the "middle" entry in the list. Here we write the word *middle* in quotation marks because the list may have an even number of entries and thus no middle entry in the exact sense. In this case, let us agree that the middle entry refers to the first entry in the second half of the list.

If the middle entry in the list is the target value, we can declare the search a success. Otherwise, we can at least restrict the search process to the first or last half of the list depending on whether the target value is less than or greater than the entry we have considered. (Remember that the list is sorted.)

To search the remaining portion of the list, we could apply the sequential search, but instead let us apply the same approach to this portion of the list that we used for the whole list. That is, we select the middle entry in the remaining portion of the list as the next entry to consider. As before, if that entry is the target value, we are finished. Otherwise we can restrict our search to an even smaller portion of the list.

This approach to the searching process is summarized in Figure 5.12, where we consider the task of searching the list on the left of the figure for the entry John. We first consider the middle entry Harry. Since our target belongs after this entry, the search continues by considering the lower half of the original list. The middle of this sublist is found to be Larry. Since our target should precede Larry, we turn our attention to the first half of the current sublist. When we interrogate the middle of that secondary sublist, we find our target John and declare the search a success. In short, our strategy is to successively divide the list in question into smaller segments until the target is found or the search is narrowed to an empty segment.

We need to emphasize this last point. If the target value is not in the original list, our approach to searching the list will proceed by dividing the list into smaller

Figure 5.12

Applying our strategy to search a list for the entry John

Figure 5.13

A first draft of the binary search technique

```
        if (List empty)
        then
         (Report that the search failed.)
        else
         [Select the "middle" entry in the List to be the TestEntry;
          Execute the block of instructions below that is
            associated with the appropriate case.
             case 1: TargetValue = TestEntry
                 (Report that the search succeeded.)
             case 2: TargetValue < TestEntry
                 (Search the portion of List preceding TestEntry for
                     TargetValue, and report the result of that search.)
             case 3: TargetValue > TestEntry
                 (Search the portion of List following TestEntry for
                     TargetValue, and report the result of that search.)
        ] end if
```

segments until the segment under consideration is empty. At this point our algorithm should recognize that the search is a failure.

Figure 5.13 is a first draft of our thoughts using our pseudocode. It directs us to begin a search by testing to see if the list is empty. If so, we are told to report that the search is a failure. Otherwise, we are told to consider the middle entry in the list. If this entry is not the target value, we are told to search either the front half or the back half of the list. Both of these possibilities require a secondary search. It would be nice to perform these searches by calling on the services of an abstract tool. In particular, our approach is to apply a procedure named **Search** to carry out these secondary searches. To complete our program, therefore, we must provide such a procedure.

But this procedure should perform the same task that is expressed by the pseudocode we have already written. It should first check to see if the list it is given is empty, and if it is not, it should proceed by considering the middle entry of that list. Thus we can supply the procedure we need merely by identifying the current routine as being the procedure named **Search** and inserting references to that procedure where the secondary searches are required. The result is shown in Figure 5.14.

Note that this procedure contains a reference to itself. If we were following this procedure and came to the instruction

Apply the procedure Search . . .

we would apply the same procedure to the smaller list that we were applying to the original one. If that search succeeded, we would return to declare our original search successful; if this secondary search failed, we would declare our original search a failure.

To see how the procedure in Figure 5.14 performs its task, let us follow it as it searches the list Alice, Bill, Carol, David, Evelyn, Fred, and George, for the target value Bill. Our search begins by selecting David (the middle entry) as the test entry under consideration. Since the target value (Bill) is less than this test entry, we are

Figure 5.14

The binary search algorithm in pseudocode

```
        procedure Search (List, TargetValue)
    if (List empty)
      then
        (Report that the search failed.)
      else
        [Select the "middle" entry in List to be the TestEntry;
         Execute the block of instructions below that is
           associated with the appropriate case.
            case 1: TargetValue = TestEntry
                (Report that the search succeeded.)
            case 2: TargetValue < TestEntry
                (Apply the procedure Search to see if TargetValue
                    is in the portion of the List preceding TestEntry,
                    and report the result of that search.)
            case 3: TargetValue > TestEntry
                (Apply the procedure Search to see if TargetValue
                    is in the portion of List following TestEntry,
                    and report the result of that search.)
        ] end if
```

instructed to apply the procedure **Search** to the list of entries preceding David—that is, the list Alice, Bill, and Carol. In so doing, we create a second copy of the search procedure and assign it to this secondary task.

We now have two copies of our search procedure being executed, as summarized in Figure 5.15. Progress in the original copy is temporarily suspended at the instruction

Apply the procedure Search to see if TargetValue is
in the portion of List preceding the TestEntry

while we apply the second copy to the task of searching the list Alice, Bill, and Carol. When we complete this secondary search, we will discard the second copy of the procedure, report its findings to the original copy, and continue progress in the original. In this way, the second copy of the procedure executes as a subordinate to the original, performing the task requested by the original module and then disappearing.

The secondary search selects Bill as its test entry because that is the middle entry in the list Alice, Bill, and Carol. Since this is the same as the target value, it declares its search to be a success and terminates.

At this point, we have completed the secondary search as requested by the original copy of the procedure, so we are able to continue the execution of that original copy. Here we are told that the result of the secondary search should be reported as the result of the original search. Thus we report that the original search has succeeded. Our process has correctly determined that Bill is a member of the list Alice, Bill, Carol, David, Evelyn, Fred, and George.

Let us now consider what happens if we ask the procedure in Figure 5.14 to search the list Alice, Carol, Evelyn, Fred, and George for the entry David. This time the original copy of the procedure selects Evelyn as its test entry and concludes that

Figure 5.15

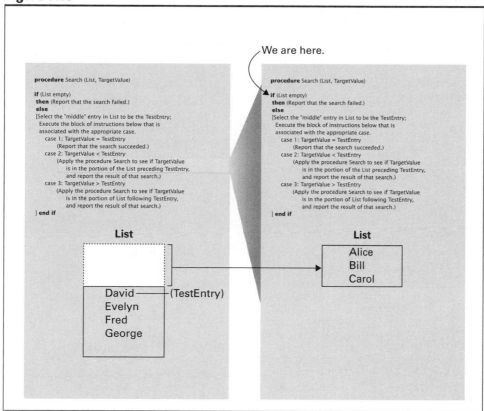

the target value must reside in the preceding portion of the list. It therefore requests another copy of the procedure to search the list of entries appearing in front of Evelyn—that is, the two-entry list consisting of Alice and Carol. At this stage our situation is as represented in Figure 5.16.

The second copy of the procedure selects Carol as its current entry and concludes that the target value must lie in the latter portion of its list. It then requests a third copy of the procedure to search the list of names following Carol in the list Alice and Carol. This sublist is empty, so the third copy of the procedure has the task of searching the empty list for the target value David. Our situation at this point is represented by Figure 5.17. The original copy of the procedure is charged with the task of searching the list Alice, Carol, Evelyn, Fred, and George, with the test entry being Evelyn; the second copy is charged with searching the list Alice and Carol, with its test entry being Carol; and the third copy is about to begin searching the empty list.

Of course, the third copy of the procedure quickly declares its search to be a failure and terminates. The completion of the third copy's task allows the second copy to continue its task. It notes that the search it requested was unsuccessful, declares its own task to be a failure, and terminates. This report is what the original copy of the procedure has been waiting for, so it can now proceed. Since the search it requested failed,

Figure 5.16

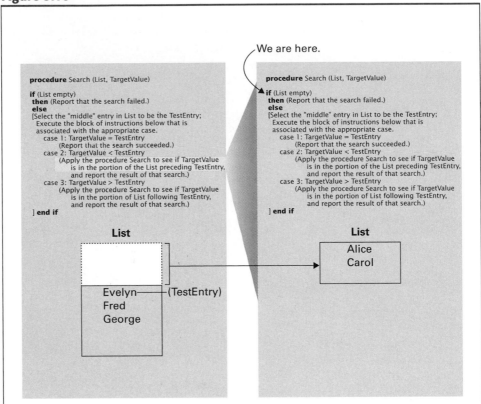

it declares its own search to have failed and terminates. Our routine has correctly concluded that David is not contained in the list Alice, Carol, Evelyn, Fred, and George.

In summary, if we were to look back at the previous examples, we could see that the process employed by the algorithm represented in Figure 5.14 is to repeatedly divide the list in question into two smaller pieces in such a way that the remaining search can be restricted to only one of these pieces. This divide-by-two approach is the reason why the algorithm is known as the binary search.

Recursive Control

The binary search algorithm is similar to the sequential search in that each algorithm requests the execution of a repetitive process. However, the implementation of this repetition is significantly different. Whereas the sequential search involves a circular form of repetition, the binary search executes each stage of the repetition as a subtask of the previous stage. This technique is known as **recursion.**

As we have seen, the illusion created by the execution of a procedure involving recursion is the existence of multiple copies of itself, each of which is called an activation of the procedure. These activations are created in a telescoping manner and

Figure 5.17

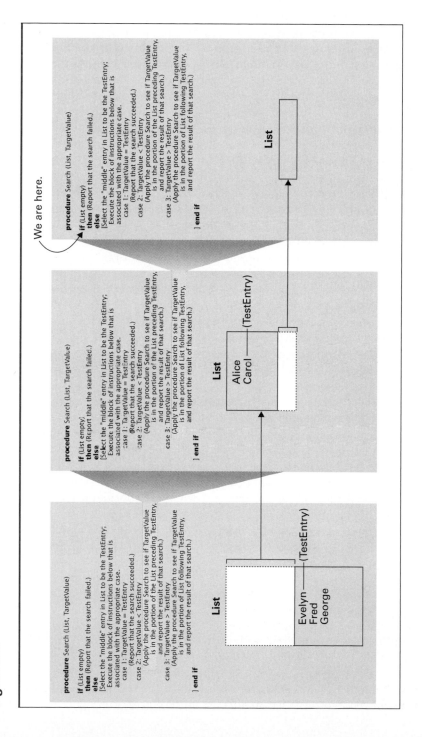

disappear as the algorithm advances. Of those activations existing at any given time, only one is actively progressing. The others are effectively in limbo, each waiting for another activation to terminate before it can continue.

Being a repetitive process, recursive systems are just as dependent on proper control as are loop structures. Just as in loop control, recursive systems are dependent on testing for a termination condition and on a design that ensures this condition will be reached. In fact, proper recursive control involves the same three ingredients—initialization, modification, and test for termination—that are required in loop control.

In general, a recursive routine is designed to test for the termination condition (often called the base or degenerative case) before requesting further activations. If the termination condition is not met, the routine creates another activation of the routine and assigns it the task of solving a revised problem that is closer to the termination condition than that assigned to the current activation. However, if the termination condition is met, a path is taken that causes the current activation to terminate without creating additional activations.

Let us see how the initialization and modification phases of repetitive control are implemented in our binary search procedure of Figure 5.14. In this case, the creation of additional activations is terminated once the target value is found or the task is reduced to that of searching an empty list. The process is initialized implicitly by being given an initial list and a target value. From this initial configuration the routine modifies the task it is assigned to that of searching a smaller list. Since the original list is of finite length and each modification step reduces the length of the list in question, we are assured that the target value ultimately is found or the task is reduced to that of searching the empty list. We can therefore conclude that the repetitive process is guaranteed to cease.

Having seen both iterative and recursive control structures, we may wonder whether the two are equivalent in power. That is, if an algorithm were designed using a loop structure, could another algorithm using only recursive techniques be designed that would solve the same problem and vice versa? Such questions are important in computer science because their answers tell us what features should be provided in a programming language in order to obtain the most powerful programming system possible. We return to these ideas in Chapter 11 where we consider some of the more theoretical aspects of computer science and its mathematical foundations. With this background, we then can prove the equivalence of iterative and recursive structures in Appendix E.

Questions/Exercises

1. What names are interrogated by the binary search (Figure 5.14) when searching for the name Joe in the list Alice, Brenda, Carol, Duane, Evelyn, Fred, George, Henry, Irene, Joe, Karl, Larry, Mary, Nancy, and Oliver?

2. What is the maximum number of entries that must be interrogated when applying the binary search to a list of 200 entries? What about a list of 100,000 entries?

5.6 Efficiency and Correctness

In this section we introduce two topics that constitute major research areas within computer science. The first of these is algorithm efficiency, and the second is algorithm correctness.

Algorithm Efficiency

Even though today's machines are capable of executing millions of instructions each second, efficiency remains a major concern in algorithm design. Often the choice between efficient and inefficient algorithms can make the difference between a practical solution to a problem and an impractical one.

Let us consider the problem of a university registrar faced with the task of retrieving and updating student records. Although the university has an actual enrollment of approximately 10,000 students during any one semester, its "current student file" contains the records of more than 30,000 students who are considered current students in the sense that they have registered for at least one course in the past few years but have not completed a degree. For now, let us assume that these records are stored in the registrar's computer as a list ordered by student identification numbers. To find any student record, the registrar would therefore search this list for a particular identification number.

We have presented two algorithms for searching such a list: the sequential search and the binary search. Our question now is whether the choice between these two algorithms makes any difference in the case of the registrar. We consider the sequential search first.

Given a student identification number, the sequential search algorithm starts at the beginning of the list and compares the entries found to the number desired. Not knowing anything about the source of the target value, we cannot conclude how far into the list this search must go. We can say, though, that after many searches we expect the average depth of the searches to be halfway through the list; some will be shorter, but others will be longer. We conclude that over a period of time, the sequential search will investigate roughly 15,000 records per search. If retrieving and checking each record for its identification number requires 10 milliseconds (10 one-thousandths of a second), such a search would require an average of 150 seconds or 2.5 minutes—an unbearably long time for the registrar to wait for a student's record to appear on a computer screen. Even if the time required to retrieve and check each record were reduced to only 1 millisecond, the search would still require an average of 15 seconds, which is still a long time to wait.

In contrast, the binary search proceeds by comparing the target value to the middle entry in the list. If this is not the desired entry, then at least the remaining search is restricted to only half of the original list. Thus, after interrogating the middle entry in the list of 30,000 student records, the binary search has at most 15,000 records still to consider. After the second inquiry, at most 7500 remain, and after the third retrieval, the list in question has dropped to no more than 3750 entries. Continuing in this fashion, we see that the target record will be found after retrieving at most 15 entries from the list of 30,000 records. Thus if each of these retrievals can be performed in 10 milliseconds, the process of searching for a particular record requires only 0.15 of a second—meaning that access to any particular student record will appear to be instantaneous from the registrar's point of view. We conclude that the choice between the sequential search algorithm and the binary search algorithm would have a significant impact in this application.

This example indicates the importance of the area of computer science known as algorithm analysis that encompasses the study of the resources, such as time or storage space, that algorithms require. A major application of such studies is the evaluation of the relative merits of alternative algorithms. In our case, we analyzed the time required by the sequential and binary search algorithms in order to determine which was the better solution in a particular application. In general such analysis is performed in a more generic context. That is, when considering algorithms for searching lists, we do not focus on a list of a particular length, but instead try to identify a formula that would indicate the algorithm's performance for lists of arbitrary lengths. Such analyses usually involve a best-case analysis, a worst-case analysis, and an average-case analysis.

Our previous analysis focused on the average-case performance of the sequential search algorithm and the worst-case performance of the binary search algorithm. Although we concentrated on a list of a particular length, it is not difficult to generalize our reasoning to lists of arbitrary lengths. In particular, when applied to a list with n entries, the sequential search algorithm will interrogate an average of $n/2$ entries, whereas the binary search algorithm will interrogate at most $lg\ n$ entries in its worst-case scenario. ($lg\ n$ represents the base two logarithm of n.)

Let us analyze the insertion sort algorithm (summarized in Figure 5.11) in a similar manner. Recall that this algorithm involves selecting a list entry, called the pivot entry, comparing this entry to those preceding it until the proper place for the pivot is found, and then inserting the pivot entry in this place. Since the activity of comparing two names dominates the algorithm, our approach will be to count the number of such comparisons that are performed when sorting a list whose length is n.

The algorithm begins by selecting the second list entry to be the pivot. It then progresses by picking successive entries as the pivot until it has reached the end of the list. In the best possible case, each pivot is already in its proper place, and thus it needs to be compared to only a single name before this is discovered. Thus, in the best case, applying the insertion sort to a list with n entries requires $n - 1$ comparisons. (The second entry is compared to one name, the third entry to one name, and so on.)

In contrast, the worst scenario is that each pivot must be compared to all the preceding entries before its proper location can be found. This occurs if the original list is in reverse order. In this case the first pivot (the second list entry) is compared to one name, the second pivot (the third list entry) is compared to two names, and so on (Figure 5.18). Thus the total number of comparisons when sorting a list of n entries is $1 + 2 + 3 + \ldots + (n - 1)$, which is equivalent to $(1/2)(n^2 - n)$. In particular, if the list contained 10 entries, the worst-case scenario of the insertion sort algorithm would require 45 comparisons.

In the average case of the insertion sort, we would expect each pivot to be compared to half of the entries preceding it. This results in half as many comparisons as were performed in the worst case, or a total of $(1/4)(n^2 - n)$ comparisons to sort a list

Figure 5.18

Applying the insertion sort in a worst-case situation

Initial list	1st pivot	2nd pivot	3rd pivot	4th pivot	Sorted list
	Comparisons made for each pivot				
Elaine	1 ⤢ Elaine	3 ⤢ David	6 ⤢ Carol	10 ⤢ Barbara	Alfred
David	David	Elaine	David	Carol	Barbara
Carol	Carol	2 Carol	5 Elaine	9 David	Carol
Barbara	Barbara	Barbara	4 Barbara	8 Elaine	David
Alfred	Alfred	Alfred	Alfred	7 Alfred	Elaine

of n names. If, for example, we use the insertion sort to sort a variety of lists of length 10, we expect the average number of comparisons per sort to be 22.5.

The significance of these results is that the number of comparisons made during the execution of the insertion sort algorithm gives an approximation of the amount of time required to execute the algorithm. Using this approximation, Figure 5.19 shows a graph indicating how the time required to execute the insertion sort algorithm increases as the length of the list increases. This graph is based on our worst-case analysis of the algorithm, where we concluded that sorting a list of length n would require at most $(\frac{1}{2})(n^2 - n)$ comparisons between list entries. On the graph, we have marked several list lengths and indicated the time required in each case. Notice that as the list lengths increase by uniform increments, the time required to sort the list

Figure 5.19

Graph of the worst-case analysis of the insertion sort algorithm

Figure 5.20

Graph of the worst-case analysis of the binary search algorithm

Time required to execute
the algorithm

Time increasing
by decreasing
increments

Length of list

Length increasing by
uniform increments

increases by increasingly greater amounts. Thus the algorithm becomes less efficient as the size of the list increases.

Let us apply a similar analysis to the binary search algorithm. Recall that we concluded that searching a list with n entries using this algorithm would require interrogating at most $lg\ n$ entries, which again gives an approximation to the amount of time required to execute the algorithm for various list sizes. Figure 5.20 shows a graph based on this analysis on which we have again marked several list lengths of uniformly increasing size and identified the time required by the algorithm in each case. Note that the time required by the algorithm increases by decreasing increments. That is, the binary search algorithm becomes more efficient as the size of the list increases.

The distinguishing factor between Figures 5.19 and 5.20 is the general shape of the graphs involved. It is the general shape of a graph, not its specifics, that reveals how well an algorithm performs for larger and larger inputs. Note that the general shape of a graph is determined by the type of the expression being graphed rather than the specifics of the expression—all linear expressions produce a straight line; all quadratic expressions produce a parabolic curve; all logarithmic expressions produce the logarithmic shape shown in Figure 5.20. It is customary to identify a shape with the simplest expression that produces that shape. In particular, we identify the parabolic shape with the expression n^2 and the logarithmic shape with the expression $lg\ n$.

We have seen that the shape of the graph obtained by comparing the time required for an algorithm to perform its task to the size of the input data reflects the efficiency characteristics of the algorithm. Thus it is common to classify algorithms according to the shapes of these graphs—normally based on the algorithm's worst-case analysis. The notation used to identify these classes is sometimes called "big-theta notation." All algorithms whose graphs have the shape of a parabola, such as the insertion sort, are classified in the class represented by $\Theta(n^2)$ (read "big theta of n squared"); all algorithms whose graphs have the shape of a logarithmic expression, such as the binary search, fall in the class represented by $\Theta(lg\ n)$ (read "big theta of $log\ n$"). Knowing the class in which a particular algorithm falls allows us to predict its performance and to compare it against other algorithms that solve the same problem. Two algorithms in $\Theta(n^2)$ will exhibit similar time requirements as the size of the inputs increase, whereas the time requirements of an algorithm in $\Theta(lg\ n)$ will not expand as rapidly as that of an algorithm in $\Theta(n^2)$.

Software Verification

Recall that the fourth phase in Polya's analysis of problem solving (Section 5.3) is to evaluate the solution for accuracy and for its potential as a tool for solving other problems. The significance of the first part of this phase is exemplified by the following example:

> A traveler with a gold chain of seven links must stay in an isolated hotel for seven nights. The rent each night consists of one link from the chain. What is the fewest number of links that must be cut so that the traveler can pay the hotel one link of the chain each morning without paying for lodging in advance?

We first realize that not every link in the chain must be cut. If we cut only the second link, we could free both the first and second links from the other five. Following this insight, we are led to the solution of cutting only the second, fourth, and sixth links in the chain, a process that releases each link while cutting only three (Figure 5.21). Furthermore, any fewer cuts leaves two links connected, so we conclude that the correct answer to our problem is three.

Upon reconsidering the problem, however, we might make the observation that when only the third link in the chain is cut, we obtain three pieces of chain of lengths one, two, and four (Figure 5.22). With these pieces we can proceed as follows:

> First morning: Give the hotel the single link.
>
> Second morning: Retrieve the single link and give the hotel the two-link piece.
>
> Third morning: Give the hotel the single link.
>
> Fourth morning: Retrieve the three links held by the hotel and give the hotel the four-link piece.

Figure 5.21

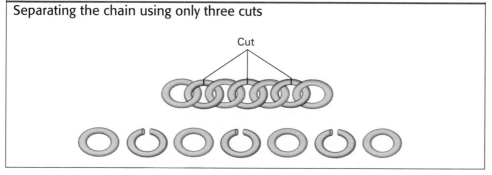

Separating the chain using only three cuts

Cut

Figure 5.22

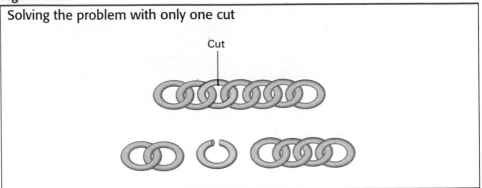

Solving the problem with only one cut

Fifth morning: Give the hotel the single link.

Sixth morning: Retrieve the single link and give the hotel the double-link piece.

Seventh morning: Give the hotel the single link.

Consequently, our first answer, which we were sure was correct, is incorrect. How, then, can we be sure that our new solution is correct? We might argue as follows: Since a single link must be given to the hotel on the first morning, at least one link of the chain must be cut, and since our new solution requires only one cut, it must be optimal.

Translated into the programming environment, this example emphasizes the distinction between a program that is believed to be correct and a program that is correct. The two are not necessarily the same. The data processing community is rich in horror stories involving software that although "known" to be correct still failed at a critical moment because of some unforeseen situation. Verification of software is therefore an important undertaking, and the search for efficient verification techniques constitutes an active field of research in computer science.

One current line of research in this area attempts to apply the techniques of formal logic to prove the correctness of a program. That is, the goal is to apply formal logic to prove that the algorithm represented by a program does what it is intended to do. The underlying thesis is that by reducing the verification process to a formal procedure, one is protected from the inaccurate conclusions that may be associated with intuitive arguments, as was the case in the gold chain problem. Let us consider this approach to program verification in more detail.

Just as a formal mathematical proof is based on axioms (geometric proofs are often founded on the axioms of Euclidean geometry, whereas other proofs may be based on the axioms of set theory), a formal proof of a program's correctness is based on the specifications under which the program was designed. To prove that a program correctly sorts lists of names, we are allowed to begin with the assumption that the program's input is a list of names, or if the program is designed to compute the average of one or more positive numbers, we assume that the input does, in fact, consist of one or more positive numbers. In short, a proof of correctness begins with the assumption that cer-

Beyond Verification of Software

Verification problems, as discussed in the text, are not unique to software. Equally important is the problem of confirming that the hardware that executes a program is free of flaws. This involves the verification of circuit designs as well as machine construction. Again, the state of the art relies heavily on testing, which, as in the case of software, means that subtle errors can find their way into finished products. Records indicate that the Mark I, constructed at Harvard University in the 1940s, contained wiring errors that were not detected for many years. A more recent example is a flaw in the floating-point portion of the early Pentium microprocessors. In both of these cases, the error was detected before serious consequences developed.

tain conditions, called **preconditions,** are satisfied at the beginning of the program's execution.

The next step in a proof of correctness is to consider how the consequences of these preconditions propagate through the program. For this purpose, researchers have analyzed various program structures to determine how a statement, known to be true before the structure is executed, is affected by executing the structure. As a simple example, if a certain statement about the value of Y is known to hold prior to executing the instruction

$$X \leftarrow Y$$

then that same statement can be made about X after the instruction has been executed. More precisely, if the value of Y is not 0 before the instruction is executed, then we can conclude that the value of X will not be 0 after the instruction is executed.

A slightly more involved example occurs in the case of an if-then-else structure such as

> **if** (*condition*) **then** (*instruction 1*)
> **else** (*instruction 2*)

Here, if some statement is known to hold before execution of the structure, then immediately before executing *instruction 1*, we know that both that statement and the condition tested are true, whereas if *instruction 2* is to be executed, we know the statement and the negation of the condition must hold.

Following rules such as these, a proof of correctness proceeds by identifying statements, called **assertions,** that can be established at various points in the program. The result is a collection of assertions, each being a consequence of the program's preconditions and the sequence of instructions that lead to the point in the program at which the assertion is established. If the assertion so established at the end of the program corresponds to the desired output specifications, we can conclude that the program is correct.

As an example, consider the typical while loop structure represented in Figure 5.23. Suppose, as a consequence of the preconditions given at point A, we can establish that a particular assertion is true each time the test for termination is performed (point B) during the repetitive process. (Such an assertion within a loop is known as a **loop invariant.**) Then, if the repetition ever terminates, execution moves to point C, where we can conclude that both the loop invariant and the termination condition hold. (The loop invariant still holds because the test for termination does not alter any values in the program, and the termination condition holds because otherwise the loop does not terminate.) If these combined statements imply the desired output, our proof of correctness can be completed merely by showing that the initialization and modification components of the loop ultimately lead to the termination condition.

You should compare this analysis to our example of the insertion sort shown in Figure 5.11. The outer loop in that program is based on the loop invariant

> Each time the test for termination is performed, the names preceding the Nth entry form a sorted list

and the termination condition is

> The value of N is greater than the length of the list.

Thus, if the loop ever terminates, we know that both conditions must be satisfied, which implies that the entire list would be sorted.

Figure 5.23

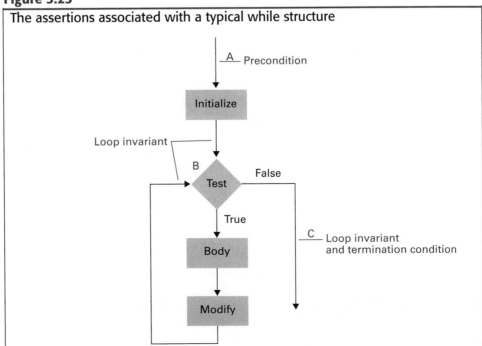

The assertions associated with a typical while structure

Unfortunately, formal program verification techniques have not been refined to the point that they can be easily applied in general applications. The result is that in most cases today, software is "verified" by testing it under various conditions—a process that is shaky at best. After all, verification by testing proves nothing more than that the program runs correctly for the cases under which it was tested. Any additional conclusions are merely projections. The errors contained in a program are often consequences of subtle oversights that are easily overlooked during testing as well. Consequently errors in a program, just as our error in the gold chain problem, can, and often do, go undetected, even though significant effort may be exerted to avoid it. A dramatic example occurred at AT&T: An error in the software controlling 114 switching stations went undetected from its installation in December 1989 until January 15, 1990, at which time a unique set of circumstances caused approximately five million calls to be unnecessarily blocked over a nine-hour period.

Questions/Exercises

1. Suppose we find that a machine programmed with our insertion sort algorithm requires an average of one second to sort a list of 100 names. How long do you estimate it takes to sort a list of 1000 names? How about 10,000 names?

2. Give an example of an algorithm in each of the following classes: $\Theta(lg\ n)$, $\Theta(n)$, and $\Theta(n^2)$.

3. List the classes $\Theta(n^2), \Theta(lg\ n), \Theta(n),$ and $\Theta(n^3)$ in decreasing order of efficiency.

4. Consider the following problem and a proposed answer. Is the proposed answer correct? Why or why not?

   Problem: Suppose a box contains three cards. One of three cards is painted black on both sides, one is painted red on both sides, and the third is painted red on one side and black on the other. One of the cards is drawn from the box, and you are allowed to see one side of it. What is the probability that the other side of the card is the same color as the side you see?

   Proposed answer: One-half. Suppose the side of the card you can see is red. (The argument would be symmetric with this one if the side were black.) Only two cards among the three have a red side. Thus the card you see must be one of these two. One of these two cards is red on the other side, while the other is black. Thus the card you can see is just as likely to be red on the other side as it is to be black.

5. The following program segment is an attempt to compute the quotient (forgetting any remainder) of two positive integers (a dividend and a divisor) by counting the number of times the divisor can be subtracted from the dividend before what is left becomes less than the divisor. For instance, $7/3$ should produce 2 because 3 can be subtracted from 7 twice. Is the program correct? Justify your answer.

```
Count ← 0;
Remainder ← Dividend;
repeat (Remainder ← Remainder − Divisor;
        Count ← Count + 1)
until (Remainder < Divisor)
Quotient ← Count.
```

6. The following program segment is designed to compute the product of two nonnegative integers X and Y by accumulating the sum of X copies of Y—that is, 3 times 4 is computed by accumulating the sum of three 4s. Is the program correct? Justify your answer.

```
Product ← Y;
Count ← 1;
while (Count < X) do
   (Product ← Product + Y;
    Count ← Count + 1)
```

7. Assuming the precondition that the value associated with N is a positive integer, establish a loop invariant that leads to the conclusion that if the following routine terminates, then Sum is assigned the value $0 + 1 + \ldots + N$.

```
Sum ← 0;
I ← 0;
while (I < N) do
   (I ← I + 1;
    Sum ← Sum + I)
```

Provide an argument to the effect that the routine does in fact terminate.

8. Suppose that both a program and the hardware that executes it have been formally verified to be accurate. Does this ensure accuracy?

Chapter Review Problems

1. Give an example of a set of steps that conforms to the informal definition of an algorithm given in the opening paragraph of Section 5.1 but does not conform to the formal definition given in Figure 5.1.

2. Explain the distinction between an ambiguity in a proposed algorithm and an ambiguity in the representation of an algorithm.

3. Describe how the use of primitives helps remove ambiguities in an algorithm's representation.

4. Select a subject with which you are familiar and design a pseudocode for giving directions in that subject. In particular, describe the primitives you would use and the syntax you would use to represent them. (If you are having trouble thinking of a subject, try sports, arts, or crafts.)

5. Does the following program represent an algorithm in the strict sense? Why or why not?

```
Count ← 0;
while (Count not 5) do
   (Count ← Count + 2)
```

6. In what sense do the following three steps not constitute an algorithm?

Step 1: Draw a straight line segment between the points with rectangular coordinates (2,5) and (6,11).
Step 2: Draw a straight line segment between the points with rectangular coordinates (1,3) and (3,6).
Step 3: Draw a circle whose center is at the intersection of the previous line segments and whose radius is two.

7. Rewrite the following program segment using a repeat structure rather than a while structure. Be sure the new version prints the same values as the original.

    Count ← 2;
    while (Count < 7) **do**
       (print the value assigned to Count and
        Count ← Count + 1)

8. Rewrite the following program segment using a while structure rather than a **repeat** structure. Be sure the new version prints the same values as the original.

    Count ← 1;
    repeat
        (print the value assigned to Count and
         Count ← Count + 1)
    until (Count = 5)

9. What must be done to translate a posttest loop expressed in the form

    repeat *(. . .)* **until** *(. . .)*

    into an equivalent posttest loop expressed in the form

    do *(. . .)* **while** *(. . .)*

10. Design an algorithm that, when given an arrangement of the digits 0, 1, 2, 3, 4, 5, 6, 7, 8, 9, rearranges the digits so that the new arrangement represents the next larger value that can be represented by these digits (or reports that no such rearrangement exists if no rearrangement produces a larger value). Thus 5647382901 would produce 5647382910.

11. Design an algorithm for finding all the factors of a positive integer. For example, in the case of the integer 12, your algorithm should report the values 1, 2, 3, 4, 6, and 12.

12. Design an algorithm for determining the day of the week of any date since January 1, 1700. For example, August 17, 2001 was a Friday.

13. What is the difference between a formal programming language and a pseudocode?

14. What is the difference between syntax and semantics?

15. The following is an addition problem in traditional base ten notation. Each letter represents a different digit. What digit does each letter represent? How did you get your foot in the door?

    $$\begin{array}{r} XYZ \\ + \ YWY \\ \hline ZYZW \end{array}$$

16. The following is a multiplication problem in traditional base ten notation. Each letter represents a different digit. What digit does each letter represent? How did you get your foot in the door?

    $$\begin{array}{r} XY \\ \times \ YX \\ \hline XY \\ YZ \\ \hline WVY \end{array}$$

17. The following is an addition problem in binary notation. Each letter represents a unique binary digit. Which letter represents 1 and which represents 0? Design an algorithm for solving problems like this.

    $$\begin{array}{r} YXX \\ + \ XYX \\ \hline XYYY \end{array}$$

18. Four prospectors with only one lantern must walk through a mine shaft. At most, two prospectors can travel together and any prospector in the shaft must be with the lantern. The prospectors, named Andrews, Blake, Johnson, and Kelly, can walk through the shaft in one minute, two minutes, four minutes, and eight minutes, respectively. When two walk together they travel at the speed of the slower prospector. How can all four prospectors get through the mine shaft in only 15 minutes? After you have solved this problem, explain how you got your foot in the door.

19. Starting with a large wine glass and a small wine glass, fill the small glass with wine and then pour that wine into the large glass. Next, fill the small glass with water and pour some of that water into the large glass. Mix the contents of the large glass, and then pour the mixture

back into the small glass until the small glass is full. Will there be more water in the large glass than there is wine in the small glass? After you have solved this problem, explain how you got your foot in the door.

20. Two bees, named Romeo and Juliet, live in different hives but have met and fallen in love. On a windless spring morning, they simultaneously leave their respective hives to visit each other. Their routes meet at a point 50 meters from the closest hive, but they fail to see each other and continue on to their destinations. At their destinations, they spend the same amount of time to discover that the other is not home and begin their return trips. On their return trips, they meet at a point that is 20 meters from the closest hive. This time they see each other and have a picnic lunch before returning home. How far apart are the two hives? After you have solved this problem, explain how you got your foot in the door.

21. Design an algorithm that, given two strings of characters, tests whether the first string appears as a substring somewhere in the second.

22. The following algorithm is designed to print the beginning of what is known as the Fibonacci sequence. Identify the body of the loop. Where is the initialization step for the loop control? The modification step? The test step? What list of numbers is produced?

```
Last ← 0;
Current ← 1;
while (Current < 100) do
  (print the value assigned to Current;
    Temp ← Last;
    Last ← Current; and
    Current ← Last + Temp)
```

23. What sequence of numbers is printed by the following algorithm if it is started with input values 0 and 1?

```
procedure MysteryWrite (Last, Current)
if (Current < 100) then
  (print the value assigned to Current;
    Temp ← Current + Last;
    apply MysteryWrite to the values Current and
      Temp)
```

24. Modify the procedure MysteryWrite in the preceding problem so that the values are printed in reverse order.

25. What letters are interrogated by the binary search (Figure 5.14) if it is applied to the list A, B, C, D, E, F, G, H, I, J, K, L, M, N, O when searching for the value J? What about searching for the value Z?

26. After performing many sequential searches on a list of 6000 entries, what would you expect to be the average number of times that the target value would have been compared to a list entry? What if the search algorithm was the binary search?

27. Identify the body of the following loop structure and count the number of times it will be executed. What happens if the test is changed to read while (Count not 6)?

```
Count ← 1;
while (Count not 7) do
  (print the value assigned to Count and
    Count ← Count + 3)
```

28. What problems do you expect to arise if the following program is implemented on a computer? (Hint: Remember the problem of round-off errors associated with floating-point arithmetic.)

```
Count ← one-tenth;
repeat
  (print the value assigned to Count and
    Count ← Count + one-tenth)
until (Count equals 1)
```

29. Design a recursive version of the Euclidean algorithm (Question 3 of Section 5.2).

30. Suppose we apply both Test1 and Test2 (defined below) to the input value 1. What is the difference in the printed output of the two routines?

procedure Test1 (Count)
if (Count not 5)
   then (print the value assigned to Count
      and apply Test1 to the value Count + 1)

procedure Test2 (Count)
if (Count not 5)
   then (apply Test2 to the value Count + 1
      and print the value assigned to Count)

31. Identify the important constituents of the control mechanism in the routines of the previous problem. In particular, what condition causes the process to terminate? Where is the state of the process modified toward this termination condition? Where is the state of the control process initialized?

32. Apply the procedure MysteryPrint (defined below) to the value 3 and record the values that are printed.

procedure MysteryPrint (N)
if (N < 0) **then** (print the value of N and
          apply the procedure MysteryPrint
            to the value N − 2)
Print the value of N + 1.

33. Apply the procedure MysteryPrint (defined below) to the value 2 and record the values that are printed.

procedure MysteryPrint (N)
if (N < 0) **then** (print the value of N and
          apply the procedure MysteryPrint
            to the value N − 2)
   else (print the value of N and
       if (N < −2) **then** (apply the
            procedure MysteryPrint to
            the value N + 1))

34. Design an algorithm to generate the sequence of positive integers (in increasing order) whose only prime divisors are 2 and 3; that is, your program should produce the sequence 2, 3, 4, 6, 8, 9, 12, 16, 18, 24, 27, ... Does your program represent an algorithm in the strict sense?

35. Answer the following questions in terms of the list: Alice, Byron, Carol, Duane, Elaine, Floyd, Gene, Henry, Iris.
  a. Which search algorithm (sequential or binary) will find the name Gene more quickly?
  b. Which search algorithm (sequential or binary) will find the name Alice more quickly?
  c. Which search algorithm (sequential or binary) will detect the absence of the name Bruce more quickly?
  d. Which search algorithm (sequential or binary) will detect the absence of the name Sue more quickly?
  e. How many entries will be interrogated when searching for the name Elaine when using the sequential search? How many will be interrogated when using the binary search?

36. The factorial of 0 is defined to be 1. The factorial of a positive integer is defined to be the product of that integer times the factorial of the next smaller nonnegative integer. We use the notation $n!$ to express the factorial of the integer n. Thus the factorial of 3 (written 3!) is $3 \times (2!) = 3 \times (2 \times (1!)) = 3 \times (2 \times (1 \times (0!))) = 3 \times (2 \times (1 \times (1))) = 6$. Design a recursive algorithm that computes the factorial of a given value.

37. a. Suppose you must sort a list of five names, and you have already designed an algorithm that sorts a list of four names. Design an algorithm to sort the list of five names by taking advantage of the previously designed algorithm.
  b. Design a recursive algorithm to sort arbitrary lists of names based on the technique used in (a).

38. The puzzle called the Towers of Hanoi consists of three pegs, one of which contains several rings stacked in order of descending diameter from bottom to top. The problem is to move the stack of rings to another peg. You are allowed to move only one ring at a time, and at no time is a ring to be placed on top of a smaller one.

Observe that if the puzzle involved only one ring, it would be extremely easy. Moreover, when faced with the problem of moving several rings, if you could move all but the largest ring to another peg, the largest ring could then be placed on the third peg, and then the problem would be to move the remaining rings on top of it. Using this observation, develop a recursive algorithm for solving the Towers of Hanoi puzzle for an arbitrary number of rings.

39. Another approach to solving the Towers of Hanoi puzzle (Problem 38) is to imagine the pegs arranged on a circular stand with a peg mounted at each of the positions of 4, 8, and 12 o'clock. The rings, which begin on one of the pegs, are numbered 1, 2, 3, and so on,

starting with the smallest ring being 1. Odd-numbered rings, when on top of a stack, are allowed to move clockwise to the next peg; likewise, even-numbered rings are allowed to move counterclockwise (as long as that move does not place a ring on a smaller one). Under this restriction, always move the largest-numbered ring that can be moved. Based on this observation, develop a nonrecursive algorithm for solving the Towers of Hanoi puzzle.

40. Develop two algorithms, one based on a loop structure and the other on a recursive structure, to print the daily salary of a worker who each day is paid twice the previous day's salary

(starting with one penny for the first day's work) for a 30-day period. What problems relating to number storage are you likely to encounter if you implement your solutions on an actual machine?

41. Design an algorithm to find the square root of a positive number by starting with the number itself as the first guess and repeatedly producing a new guess from the previous one by averaging the previous guess with the result of dividing the original number by the previous guess. Analyze the control of this repetitive process. In particular, what condition should terminate the repetition?

42. Design an algorithm that lists all possible rearrangements of the symbols in a string of five distinct characters.

43. Design an algorithm that, given a list of names, finds the longest name in the list. Determine what your solution does if there are several "longest" names in the list. In particular, what would your algorithm do if all the names had the same length?

44. Design an algorithm that, given a list of five or more numbers, finds the five smallest and five largest numbers in the list without sorting the entire list.

45. Arrange the names Brenda, Doris, Raymond, Steve, Timothy, and William in an order that requires the least number of comparisons when sorted by the insertion sort algorithm (Figure 5.11).

46. What is the largest number of entries that are interrogated if the binary search algorithm (Figure 5.14) is applied to a list of 4000 names? How does this compare to the sequential search (Figure 5.6)?

47. Use big-theta notation to classify the traditional grade school algorithms for addition and multiplication. That is, if asked to add two numbers each having n digits, how many individual additions must be performed? If requested to multiply two n-digit numbers, how many individual multiplications are required?

48. Sometimes a slight change in a problem can significantly alter the form of its solution. For example, find a simple algorithm for solving the following problem and classify it using big-theta notation:

Divide a group of people into two disjoint sub-groups (of arbitrary size) such that the difference in the total ages of the members of the two sub-groups is as large as possible.

Now change the problem so that the desired difference is as small as possible and classify your approach to the problem.

49. From the following list, extract a collection of numbers whose sum is 3165. How efficient is your approach to the problem?

26, 39, 104, 195, 403, 504, 793, 995, 1156, 1673

50. Does the loop in the following routine terminate? Explain your answer. Explain what might happen if this routine is actually executed by a computer (refer to Section 1.7).

```
X ← 1;
Y ← ½;
while (X not equal 0) do
 (X ← X – Y;
  Y ← Y ÷ 2)
```

51. The following program segment is designed to compute the product of two nonnegative integers X and Y by accumulating the sum of X copies of Y; that is, 3 times 4 is computed by accumulating the sum of three 4s. Is the program segment correct? Explain your answer.

```
Product ← 0;
Count ← 0;
repeat (Product ← Product + Y,
        Count ← Count + 1)
until (Count = X)
```

52. The following program segment is designed to report which of the positive integers X and Y is larger. Is the program segment correct? Explain your answer.

```
Difference ← X – Y;
if (Difference is positive)
 then (print "X is bigger than Y")
 else (print "Y is bigger than X")
```

53. The following program segment is designed to find the largest entry in a nonempty list of integers. Is it correct? Explain your answer.

```
TestValue ← first list entry;
CurrentEntry first list entry;
while (CurrentEntry is not the last entry) do
 (if (CurrentEntry > TestValue)
    then (TestValue CurrentEntry)
  CurrentEntry the next list entry)
```

54. a. Identify the preconditions for the sequential search as represented in Figure 5.6. Establish a loop invariant for the while structure in that program that, when combined with the termination condition, implies that upon termination of the loop, the algorithm will report success or failure correctly.

b. Give an argument showing that the while loop in Figure 5.6 does in fact terminate.

55. Based on the preconditions that X and Y are assigned nonnegative integers, identify a loop invariant for the following while structure that, when combined with the termination condition, implies that the value associated with Z upon loop termination must be X – Y.

```
Z ← X;
J ← 0;
while (J < Y) do
 (Z ← Z – 1;
  J ← J + 1)
```

Social Issues

The following questions are provided to help you understand some of the ethical/social/legal issues associated with the field of computing. The goal is not merely to answer these questions. You should also consider why you answered as you did and whether your justifications are consistent from one question to the next.

1. Since it is currently impossible to verify completely the accuracy of complex programs, under what circumstances, if any, should the creator of a program be liable for errors?

2. Suppose you have an idea and develop it into a product that many people can use. Moreover, it has required a year of work and an investment of $50,000 to develop your idea into a form that is useful to the general public. In its final form, however, the product can be used by most people without buying anything from you. What right do you have for compensation? Is it ethical to pirate computer software?

3. Suppose a software package is so expensive that it is totally out of your price range. Is it ethical to copy it for your own use? (After all, you are not cheating the supplier out of a sale because you would not have bought the package anyway.)

4. Ownership of "things" has always been an issue. Ownership of rivers, forests, oceans, etc. has been well debated. In what sense should someone or some institution be given ownership of an algorithm?

5. Suppose someone discovers an algorithm for breaking the security features in a multiuser operating system. Should that person be entitled to ownership rights to that algorithm? If so, what rights should the person have? Should algorithm ownership rights be dependent on the subject of the algorithm? Is it ethical to advertise and circulate techniques for breaking security? Does it matter what is being broken into?

6. Some people feel that new algorithms are discovered, whereas others feel that new algorithms are created. To which philosophy do you subscribe? Would the different points of view lead to different conclusions regarding ownership of algorithms and ownership rights?

7. Is it ethical to design an algorithm for performing an illegal act? Does it matter whether the algorithm is ever executed?

8. An author is paid for the motion picture rights to a novel even though the story is often altered in the film version. How much of a story has to change before it becomes a different story? What alterations must be made to an algorithm for it to become a different algorithm?

9. Educational software is now being marketed for children in the 18 months or younger age group. Proponents argue that such software provides sights and sounds that would otherwise not be available to many children. Opponents argue that it is a poor substitute for personal parent/child interaction. What is your opinion? Should you form an opinion without knowing more about the software?

Additional Reading

Aho, A. V., J. E. Hopcroft, and J. D. Ullman. *The Design and Analysis of Computer Algorithms.* Reading, MA: Addison-Wesley, 1974.

Baase, S. *Computer Algorithms: Introduction to Design and Analysis*, 3rd ed. Reading, MA: Addison-Wesley, 2000.

Cormen, T. H., C. E. Leiserson, and R. L. Rivest. *Introduction to Algorithms*, 2nd ed. New York: McGraw-Hill, 2002.

Gries, D. *The Science of Programming.* New York: Springer-Verlag, 1998.

Harbin, R. *Origami—the Art of Paper Folding.* London: Hodder Paperbacks, 1973.

Johnsonbaugh, R., and M. Schaefer. *Algorithms.* Englewood Cliffs, NJ: Prentice-Hall, 2004.

Knuth, D. E. *The Art of Computer Programming*, vol. 3, 3rd ed. Reading, MA: Addison-Wesley, 1998.

Levitin, A. V. *Introduction to the Design and Analysis of Algorithms.* Reading, MA: Addison-Wesley, 2003.

Polya, G. *How to Solve It*. Princeton, NJ: Princeton University Press, 1973.

Roberts, E. S. *Thinking Recursively*. New York: Wiley, 1986.

Programming Languages

The development of complex software systems such as operating systems, network software, and the vast array of application software available today would likely be impossible if humans were forced to write programs in machine language. Dealing with the intricate detail associated with such languages while trying to organize complex systems would be a taxing experience, to say the least. Consequently, programming languages similar to our pseudocode have been developed that allow algorithms to be expressed in a form that is both palatable to humans and easily convertible into machine language instructions. These languages allow humans to avoid the intricacies of registers, memory addresses, and machine cycles during the program development process, so that they can concentrate on the properties of the problem being solved. In this chapter we investigate the subject of programming languages.

6.1 Historical Perspective

We begin our study by tracing the historical development of programming languages.

Early Generations

As we learned in Chapter 2, programs for modern computers consist of sequences of instructions that are encoded as numeric digits. Such an encoding system is known as a machine language. Unfortunately, writing programs in a machine language is a tedious task that often leads to errors that must be located and corrected (a process known as **debugging**) before the job is finished.

In the 1940s, researchers simplified the programming process by developing notational systems by which instructions could be represented in mnemonic rather than numeric form. For example, whereas the instruction

Move the contents of register 5 to register 6

would be expressed as

4056

using the machine language introduced in Chapter 2, in a mnemonic system it might appear as

```
MOV R5, R6
```

As a more extensive example, the machine language routine

```
156C
166D
5056
306E
C000
```

that adds the contents of memory cells 6C and 6D and stores the result at location 6E (Figure 2.7 of Section 2.2) might be expressed as

```
LD R5,Price
LD R6,ShippingCharge
ADDI R0,R5 R6
ST R0,TotalCost
HLT
```

using mnemonics. (Here we have used LD, ADDI, ST, and HLT to represent *load, add, store,* and *halt.* Moreover, we have used the descriptive names `Price`, `ShippingCharge`, and `TotalCost` to refer to the memory cells at locations 6C, 6D, and 6E, respectively. Such descriptive names are often called **identifiers**.) Note that the mnemonic form, although still lacking, does a better job of representing the meaning of the routine than does the numeric form.

To convert programs written in mnemonic form into machine language, programs called **assemblers** were developed. That is, assemblers are programs that translate other programs written in mnemonic form into numeric machine-language instructions that are compatible with the machine. These translation programs are called assemblers because their task is to assemble actual machine instructions from mnemonics and identifiers.

A mnemonic system for representing programs is collectively called an **assembly language.** At the time assembly languages were first developed, they represented a giant step forward in the search for better programming techniques. In fact, assembly languages were so revolutionary that they became known as second-generation languages, the first generation being the machine languages themselves.

Although assembly languages have many advantages over their machine-language counterparts, they still fall short of providing the ultimate programming environment. After all, the primitives used in an assembly language are essentially the same as those found in the corresponding machine language. The difference is simply in the syntax used to represent them. Thus a program written in an assembly language is inherently machine dependent—that is, the instructions within the program are expressed in terms of a particular machine's attributes. In turn, a program written in assembly language cannot be easily transported to another machine design because it must be rewritten to conform to the new machine's register configuration and instruction set.

Another disadvantage of an assembly language is that a programmer, although not required to code instructions in numeric form, is still forced to think in terms of the small, incremental steps of the machine's language. The situation is analogous to designing a house in terms of boards, nails, bricks, and so on. It is true that the actual construction of the house ultimately requires a description based on these elementary pieces, but the design process is easier if we think in terms of larger units such as rooms, windows, doors, and so on.

In short, the elementary primitives in which a product must ultimately be constructed are not necessarily the primitives that should be used during the product's design. The design process is better suited to the use of high-level primitives, each representing a concept associated with a major feature of the product. Once the design is complete, these primitives can be translated to lower-level concepts relating to the details of implementation.

Following this philosophy, computer scientists began developing programming languages that were more conducive to software development than were the low-level assembly languages. The result was the emergence of a third generation of programming languages that differed from previous generations in that their primitives were both higher level (in that they expressed instructions in larger increments) and **machine independent** (in that they did not rely on the characteristics of a particular machine). The best-known early examples are FORTRAN (FORmula TRANslator), which was developed for scientific and engineering applications, and COBOL (COmmon Business-Oriented Language), which was developed by the U.S. Navy for business applications.

In general, the approach to third-generation programming languages was to identify a collection of high-level primitives (in essentially the same spirit with which we developed our pseudocode in Chapter 5) in which software could be developed. Each of these primitives was designed so that it could be implemented as a sequence of the low-level primitives available in machine languages. For example, the statement

assign TotalCost the value Price + ShippingCharge

expresses a high-level activity without reference to how a particular machine should perform the task, yet it can be implemented by the sequence of machine instructions discussed earlier. Thus our pseudocode structure

identifier ← expression

is a potential high-level primitive.

Once this collection of high-level primitives had been identified, a program, called a **translator,** was written that translated programs expressed in these high-level primitives into machine-language programs. Such a translator was similar to the second-generation assemblers, except that it often had to compile several machine instructions into short sequences to simulate the activity requested by a single high-level primitive. Thus these translation programs were often called **compilers.**

An alternative to translators, called **interpreters,** emerged as another means of implementing third-generation languages. These programs were similar to translators except that they executed the instructions as they were translated instead of recording the translated version for future use. That is, rather than producing a machine-language copy of a program that would be executed later, an interpreter actually executed a program from its high-level form.

As a side issue we should note that the task of promoting third-generation programming languages was not as easy as might be imagined. The thought of writing programs in a form similar to a natural language was so revolutionary that many in managerial positions fought the notion at first. Grace Hopper, who is recognized as the developer of the first compiler, often told the story of demonstrating a translator for a third-generation language in which German terms, rather than English, were used. The point was that the programming language was constructed around a small set of primitives that could be expressed in a variety of natural languages with only simple modifications to the translator. But she was surprised to find that many in the audience were shocked that, in the years following World War II, she would be teaching a computer to "understand" German. Today we know that understanding a natural language involves much, much more than responding to a few rigorously defined primitives. Indeed, **natural languages** (such as English, German, and Latin) are distinguished from **formal languages** (such as programming languages) in that the latter are precisely defined by grammars (Section 6.4) whereas the former evolved over time without formal grammatical analysis (Section 10.6).

Machine Independence and Beyond

With the development of third-generation languages, the goal of machine independence was largely achieved. Since the statements in a third-generation language did not refer to the attributes of any particular machine, they could be compiled as easily for one machine as for another. A program written in a third-generation language could theoretically be used on any machine simply by applying the appropriate compiler.

Reality, however, has not proven to be this simple. When a compiler is designed, particular characteristics of the underlying machine are sometimes reflected as conditions on the language being translated. For example, the different ways in which

Cross-Platform Software

A typical application program must rely on the operating system to perform many of its tasks. It may require the services of the window manager to communicate with the computer user, or it may use the file manager to retrieve data from mass storage. Unfortunately, different operating systems dictate that requests for these services be made in different ways. Thus for programs to be transferred and executed across networks and internets involving different machine designs and different operating systems, the programs must be operating-system independent as well as machine independent. The term cross-platform is used to reflect this additional level of independence. That is, cross-platform software is software that is independent of an operating system's design as well as the machine's hardware design and is therefore executable throughout a network.

machines handle I/O operations have historically caused the "same" language to have different characteristics, or dialects, on different machines. Consequently, it is often necessary to make at least minor modifications to a program to move it from one machine to another.

Compounding this problem of portability is the lack of agreement in some cases as to what constitutes the correct definition of a particular language. To aid in this regard, the American National Standards Institute and the International Organization for Standardization have adopted and published standards for many of the popular languages. In other cases, informal standards have evolved because of the popularity of a certain dialect of a language and the desire of other compiler writers to produce compatible products. However, even in the case of highly standardized languages, compiler designers often provide features, sometimes called *language extensions,* that are not part of the standard version of the language. If a programmer takes advantage of these features, the program produced will not be compatible with environments using a compiler from a different vendor.

In the overall history of programming languages, the fact that third-generation languages fell short of true machine independence is actually of little significance for two reasons. First, they were close enough to being machine independent that software could be transported from one machine to another with relative ease. Second, the goal of machine independence turned out to be only a seed for more demanding goals. Indeed, the realization that machines could respond to such high-level statements as

> assign TotalCost the value Price + ShippingCharge

led computer scientists to dream of programming environments that would allow humans to communicate with machines in terms of abstract concepts rather than forcing them to translate these concepts into machine-compatible form. Moreover, computer scientists wanted machines that could perform much of the algorithm discovery process rather than just algorithm execution. The result has been an ever-expanding spectrum of programming languages that challenges a clear-cut classification in terms of generations.

Figure 6.1

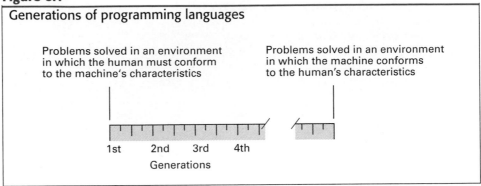

Generations of programming languages

Problems solved in an environment in which the human must conform to the machine's characteristics

Problems solved in an environment in which the machine conforms to the human's characteristics

1st   2nd   3rd   4th

Generations

Programming Paradigms

The generation approach to classifying programming languages is based on a linear scale (Figure 6.1) on which a language's position is determined by the degree to which the user of the language is freed from the world of computer gibberish and allowed to think in terms associated with the problem. In reality, the development of programming languages has not progressed in this manner but has developed along different paths as alternative approaches to the programming process (different paradigms) have surfaced and been pursued. Consequently, the historical development of programming languages is better represented by a multiple-track diagram as shown in Figure 6.2, in which different paths resulting from different paradigms are shown to emerge and progress independently. In particular, the figure presents four

Figure 6.2

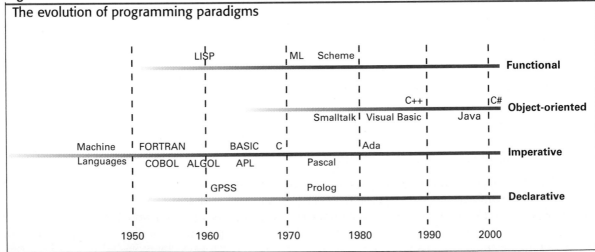

The evolution of programming paradigms

paths representing the functional, object-oriented, imperative, and declarative paradigms, with various languages associated with each paradigm positioned in a manner that indicates their births relative to other languages. It does not imply that one language necessarily evolved from a previous one.

We should note that although the paradigms identified in Figure 6.2 are called *programming* paradigms, these alternatives have ramifications beyond the programming process. They represent fundamentally different approaches to building solutions to problems and therefore affect the entire software development process. In this sense, the term *programming paradigm* is a misnomer. A more realistic term would be *software development paradigm.*

The **imperative paradigm,** also known as the **procedural paradigm,** represents the traditional approach to the programming process. It is the paradigm on which our pseudocode of Chapter 5 is based as well as the machine language discussed in Chapter 2. As the name suggests, the imperative paradigm defines the programming process to be the development of a sequence of commands that, when followed, manipulate data to produce the desired result. Thus the imperative paradigm tells us to approach the programming process by finding an algorithm to solve the problem at hand and then expressing that algorithm as a sequence of commands.

In contrast to the imperative paradigm is the **declarative paradigm,** which asks a programmer to describe the problem rather than find an algorithmic solution to the problem. The approach to a declarative programming system is to discover and implement a general problem-solving algorithm first. Once this is done, problems can be solved merely by stating them in a form that is compatible with this algorithm and then applying the algorithm. In such an environment the task of a programmer becomes that of developing a precise statement of the problem rather than of discovering an algorithm for solving the problem.

A major obstacle in developing a programming environment based on the declarative paradigm is the discovery of the underlying problem-solving algorithm. For this reason early declarative programming languages tended to be special-purpose in nature, designed for use in particular applications. For example, the declarative approach has been used for many years to simulate a system (political, economic, environmental, etc.) in order to test hypotheses or to obtain predictions. In these settings the underlying algorithm is essentially the process of simulating the passage of time by repeatedly recomputing values of parameters (gross domestic product, trade deficit, and so on) based on the previously computed values. Thus, implementing a declarative language for such simulations requires that one first implement an algorithm that performs this repetitive procedure. Then, the only task required of a programmer using the system is to describe the situation to be simulated. In this manner, a weather forecaster does not need to develop an algorithm for forecasting the weather but merely describes the current weather status, allowing the underlying simulation algorithm to produce weather predictions for the near future.

A tremendous boost was given to the declarative paradigm with the discovery that the subject of formal logic within mathematics provides a simple problem-solving algorithm suitable for use in a general-purpose declarative programming system.

The result has been increased attention to the declarative paradigm and the emergence of logic programming, a subject discussed in Section 6.7.

The **functional paradigm** views the process of program development as connecting predefined "black boxes," each of which accepts inputs and produces outputs, in such a way as to produce the required input-to-output relationship. Mathematicians refer to such "boxes" as functions, which is the reason this approach is called the functional paradigm. The primitives of a functional programming language consist of elementary functions from which the programmer must construct the more elaborate functions required to solve the problem at hand. Thus a programmer using the functional paradigm approaches the problem of software development as finding a way to connect the elementary, primitive functions so as to produce a system that computes the desired results. In short, the programming process under the functional paradigm is that of constructing functions as nested complexes of simpler functions.

As an example, Figure 6.3 shows how a function for balancing your checkbook can be constructed from two simpler functions. One of these, called Find_sum, accepts values as its input and produces the sum of those values as its output. The other, called Find_diff, accepts two input values and computes their difference. The structure displayed in Figure 6.3 can be represented in the LISP programming language (a prominent functional programming language) by the expression

```
(Find_diff  (Find_sum Old_balance Credits)(Find_sum Debits))
```

Figure 6.3

A function for checkbook balancing constructed from simpler functions

The nested structure of this expression reflects the fact that the inputs to the function `Find_diff` are produced by two applications of `Find_sum`. The first application of `Find_sum` produces the result of adding all the `Credits` to the `Old_balance`. The second application of `Find_sum` computes the total of all `Debits`. Then, the function `Find_diff` uses these results to obtain the new checkbook balance.

As another example, suppose we had a function called `Sort` that sorts a list of numbers and another called `First` that retrieves the first entry from a list. Then the expression

```
(First (Sort List))
```

would retrieve the smallest entry in List. Here the nested structure indicates that the output of `Sort` is the input to `First`. That is, the list is sorted, and then the first entry is extracted from the sorted list.

To appreciate the distinction between the functional and imperative paradigms, consider the analogy of a system of factories required to produce consumer goods. Under the functional paradigm, the entire system of factories would be viewed as one large (although geographically diverse) factory that receives shipments of raw materials and ultimately produces a consumer product. The individual factories would be seen merely as components of the larger system that are connected together so that outputs from some are connected to inputs of others, allowing materials to flow through the system in a predefined manner.

In contrast, the imperative paradigm would view the manufacturing of consumer goods as a system of individual factories, each performing its own computation and producing a product that is stored for later consumption. Under the imperative paradigm the system might be expressed as:

WarehouseA ← the result of applying procedure SteelFactory to IronOre, Limestone, and Coal;
WarehouseB ← the result of applying procedure FrameFactory to the contents of WarehouseA;

.
.
.

We see, then, that the imperative paradigm produces a system in which each factory is independently asked to produce its goods, which are then stored in a warehouse until needed by another factory. In contrast, the functional paradigm results in a system in which the factories operate in unison with the output of one factory being directly connected as an input to another. Thus, the functional paradigm leads to a system in which materials are shipped to their destination as they are produced, whereas the imperative paradigm leads to a system of warehouses.

The **object-oriented paradigm**, which is associated with the programming process called **object-oriented programming (OOP),** is another approach to the software development process. In this approach, units of data are viewed as active "objects" rather than the passive units envisioned by the traditional imperative paradigm. To clarify, consider a list of names. In the traditional imperative paradigm, this list is considered merely a collection of data. Any program accessing this list must contain the algorithms for performing the required manipulations. Thus the list is passive in the sense that it is maintained by a controlling program rather than having the responsibility of maintaining itself. In the object-oriented approach, however, the list is constructed as an object consisting of the list together with a collection of procedures for manipulating the list. This may include procedures for inserting a new entry in the list, deleting an entry from the list, detecting if the list is empty, and sorting the list. In turn, a program accessing the list does not need to contain algorithms for performing these tasks. Instead, it makes use of the procedures provided in the object. In a sense, rather than sorting the list as in the imperative paradigm, the program asks the list to sort itself.

As another example of the object-oriented approach, consider the task of developing a graphical user interface. Here the icons that appear on the screen are implemented as objects. Each of these objects encompasses a collection of procedures describing how that object is to respond to the occurrence of various events, such as being selected by a click of the mouse button or being dragged across the screen by the mouse. Thus the entire system is constructed as a collection of objects, each of which knows how to respond to certain events.

Many of the advantages of an object-oriented design are consequences of the modular structure that emerges as a natural by-product of the object-oriented philosophy. Each object is implemented as a separate, well-defined unit. Once the properties of an entity have been defined in this manner, that definition can be reused each time an occurrence of that entity is required. In turn, proponents of object-oriented programming argue that the object-oriented paradigm provides a natural environment for the "building block" approach to software development. They envision software libraries of object definitions from which new software systems can be constructed in the same way that many traditional products are constructed from off-the-shelf components.

In closing, we should note that the procedures within an object that describe how the object should respond to various messages are essentially small imperative program units. Thus most object-oriented languages contain many of the features found in imperative languages. For instance, the popular object-oriented language C++ was developed by adding object-oriented features to the imperative language known as C, and since Java and C# are derivatives of C++, they too have inherited this imperative core. In Sections 6.2 and 6.3 we will explore many of these imperative features, and in so doing, we will be discussing concepts that permeate a vast majority of today's object-oriented software. Then, in Section 6.5, we will consider features that are unique to the object-oriented paradigm.

 ## Questions/Exercises

1. In what sense is a program in a third-generation language machine independent? In what sense is it still machine dependent?

2. What is the difference between an assembler and a compiler?

3. We can summarize the imperative programming paradigm by saying that it places emphasis on describing a process that leads to the solution of the problem at hand. Give a similar summary of the declarative, functional, and object-oriented paradigms.

4. In what sense are the third-generation programming languages at a higher level than the earlier generations?

6.2 Traditional Programming Concepts

In this section we consider some of the concepts found in imperative and object-oriented programming languages. For this purpose we will draw examples from the languages Ada, C, C++, C#, FORTRAN, and Java. FORTRAN and C are third-generation imperative languages. C++ is an object-oriented language that was developed as an extension of the language C. Java and C# are object-oriented languages derived from C++. (Java was developed by Sun Microsystems, whereas C# is a product of Microsoft.) Ada was originally designed as a third-generation imperative language containing many object-oriented characteristics. Its newest version, however, more fully embraces the object-oriented paradigm.

Appendix D contains a brief background of each of these languages as well as an example of how the insertion sort algorithm could be implemented in each. You may wish to refer to this appendix as you read this section. Keep in mind, however, that our purpose is to develop an understanding of the basic features found in programming languages. Our use of specific languages is merely to show how the features discussed may actually be implemented. Thus you should not allow yourself to become entangled in the details of any single language.

Even though we are including object-oriented languages such as C++, Java, and C# among our example languages, we will approach this section as though we were writing a program in the imperative paradigm, because many units within an object-

Programming Language Cultures

As with natural languages, users of different programming languages tend to develop cultural differences and often debate the merits of their perspectives. Sometimes these differences are significant, for instance, when different programming paradigms are involved. In other cases, the distinctions are subtle. For example, whereas the text distinguishes between procedures and functions (Section 6.3), C programmers refer to both as functions. This is because a procedure in a C program is thought of as a function that does not return a value. A similar example is that C++ programmers refer to a procedure within an object as a member function, whereas the generic term for this is method. This discrepancy can be traced to the fact that C++ was developed as an extension of C. Another cultural difference is that programs in Ada are normally typeset with reserved words in bold—a tradition that is not widely practiced by users of C, C++, C#, FORTRAN, or Java.

The text of this book attempts to be language neutral by using generic terminology. However, each specific example is presented in a form that is compatible with the style of the language involved. As you encounter these examples, you should keep in mind that they are presented as examples of how generic ideas appear in actual languages—not as a means of teaching the details of a particular language. Try to look at the forest rather than the trees.

oriented program (such as the procedures describing how an object should react to an outside stimulus) are essentially short imperative programs. Later, in Section 6.5, we will focus on features unique to the object-oriented paradigm.

Statements in our example programming languages tend to fall into three categories: declarative statements, imperative statements, and comments. **Declarative statements** define customized terminology that is used later in the program, such as the names used to reference data items; **imperative statements** describe steps in the underlying algorithms; and **comments** enhance the readability of a program by explaining its esoteric features in a more human-compatible form. Normally, an imperative program (or an imperative program unit such as a procedure) begins with a collection of declarative statements describing the data to be manipulated by the program. This preliminary material is followed by imperative statements that describe the algorithm to be executed (Figure 6.4). Comment statements are dispersed as needed to clarify the program. Let us, then, begin our presentation with concepts associated with declaration statements.

Variables and Data Types

As suggested in Section 6.1, high-level programming languages allow locations in main memory to be referenced by descriptive names rather than by numeric addresses. Such a name is known as a **variable,** in recognition of the fact that by changing the value stored at the location, the value associated with the name changes as the program executes. Our example languages require that variables be established via declarative statements prior to being used in the program. These declarative statements also require that the programmer describe the type of data that will be stored at the memory location associated with the variable.

Such a type is known as a **data type** and encompasses both the manner in which the data item is encoded and the operations that can be performed on that data. For example, the type **integer** refers to numeric data consisting of whole numbers, probably stored using two's complement notation. Operations that can be performed on

Figure 6.4

The composition of a typical imperative program or program unit

Program

The first part consists of declaration statements describing the data that is manipulated by the program.

The second part consists of imperative statements describing the action to be performed.

integer data include the traditional arithmetic operations and comparison of relative size, such as determining whether one value is greater than another. The type **real** (sometimes called **float**) refers to numeric data that may contain values other than whole numbers, probably stored in floating-point notation. Operations performed on data of type real are similar to those performed on data of type integer. Note, however, that the activity required for adding two items of type real differs from that for adding two items of type integer.

Suppose, then, that we wanted to use the variable WeightLimit in a program to refer to an area of main memory containing a numeric value encoded in two's complement notation. In the languages C, C++, Java, and C# we would use the statement

```
int WeightLimit;
```

which means "The name WeightLimit will be used later in the program to refer to a memory area containing a value stored in two's complement notation." Multiple variables of the same type can normally be declared in the same declaration statement. For example, the statement

```
int Height, Width;
```

would declare both Height and Width to be variables of type integer. Moreover, most languages allow a variable to be assigned an initial value when it is declared. Thus,

```
int WeightLimit = 100;
```

would not only declare WeightLimit to be a variable of type integer but also assign it the starting value 100.

Other common data types include character and Boolean. The type **character** refers to data consisting of symbols, probably stored using ASCII or Unicode. Operations performed on such data include comparisons such as determining whether one symbol occurs before another in alphabetical order, testing to see whether one string of symbols appears inside another, and concatenating one string of symbols at the end of another to form one long string.

The type **Boolean** refers to data items that can take on only the values true or false. Operations on data of type Boolean include inquiries as to whether the current value is true or false. For example, if the variable EndOfList was declared to be of type Boolean, then a statement of the form

```
if (EndOfList) then (...) else (...)
```

would be reasonable.

The data types that are included as primitives in a programming language are called **primitive data types**. The types integer, real/float, character, and Boolean are common primitives. Other data types that have not yet become widespread primitives include images, audio, video, and hypertext. However, types such as GIF, JPEG, and HTML may soon become as common as integer and real.

Figure 6.5 presents some declaration statements expressed in the language C and its derivatives C++, C#, and Java. The variables Length and Width are declared to be of type float/real, the variables Price, Tax, and Total are declared to be of type integer, and the variable Symbol is declared to be of type character. In Section 6.4 we will see how a translator uses the knowledge that it gathers from such declaration statements to help it translate a program from a high-level language into machine language. For now, we note that such information can be used to identify errors. For example, a statement requesting the addition of two variables that were declared to be of type character would probably represent an error.

Data Structure

In addition to data type, variables in a program are often associated with **data structure**—that is, the conceptual shape or arrangement of data. For example, text is normally viewed as a long string of characters whereas sales records may be viewed as a rectangular table of numeric values, where each row represents the sales made by a particular employee and each column represents the sales made on a particular day.

One common data structure is the **homogeneous array,** which is a block of values of the same type such as a one-dimensional list, a two-dimensional table with rows and columns, or tables with higher dimensions. To establish such an array in a program, most programming languages require that the declaration statement establishing the name of the array also specify the length of each dimension of the array. For example, Figure 6.6 displays the conceptual structure declared by the statement

```
int Scores[2][9];
```

in the language C, which means "The variable Scores will be used in the following program unit to refer to a two-dimensional array of integers having two rows and nine columns." The same statement in FORTRAN would be written as

```
INTEGER Scores(2,9)
```

Once a homogeneous array has been declared, it can be referenced elsewhere in the program by its name, or an individual component can be identified by means of integer values called **indices** that specify the row, column, and so on, desired. However, the range of these indices varies from language to language. For example, in C (and its derivatives C++, Java, and C#) indices start at 0, meaning that the entry in the second row and fourth column of the array called Scores (as defined above) would be referenced by Scores[1][3], and the entry in the first row and first column would be Scores[0][0]. In contrast, indices start at 1 in a FORTRAN program

Figure 6.5

Variable declarations in C, C++, C#, and Java

```
float Length, Width;
int Price, Tax, Total;
char Symbol;
```

Figure 6.6

A two-dimensional array with two rows and nine columns

Scores

Scores (2,4) in FORTRAN where indices start at one.

Scores [1][3] in C and its derivatives where indices start at zero.

so the entry in the second row and fourth column would be referenced by Scores(2,4) (see again Figure 6.6).

In contrast to a homogeneous array in which all data items are the same type, a **heterogeneous array** is a block of data in which different elements can have different types. For instance, a block of data referring to an employee may consist of an entry called Name of type character, an entry called Age of type integer, and an entry called SkillRating of type real. Figure 6.7 shows how such an array would be declared in C as well as depicts the conceptual structure that the declaration describes.

A component within a heterogeneous array is usually referenced by the name of the array, followed by a period and the component name. For example, the Age component in the array Employee in Figure 6.7 would be referenced by Employee.Age.

In Chapter 8 we will see how conceptual structures such as arrays are actually implemented inside a computer. In particular, we will learn that the data contained

Figure 6.7

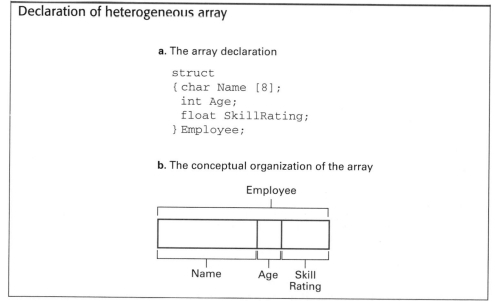

Declaration of heterogeneous array

a. The array declaration

```
struct
{ char Name [8];
  int Age;
  float SkillRating;
} Employee;
```

b. The conceptual organization of the array

Employee

Name   Age   Skill
                   Rating

in an array may be scattered over a wide area of main memory or mass storage. This is why we refer to data structure as being the *conceptual* shape or arrangement of data. Indeed, the actual arrangement within the machine's storage system may be quite different from its conceptual arrangement.

Constants and Literals

Sometimes a fixed, predetermined value is used in a program. For example, a program for controlling air traffic in the vicinity of a particular airport may contain numerous references to that airport's altitude above sea level. When writing such a program, one can include this value, say 645 feet, literally each time it is required. Such an explicit appearance of a value is called a **literal.** The use of literals leads to program statements such as

    EffectiveAlt ← Altimeter + 645

where `EffectiveAlt` and `Altimeter` are assumed to be variables and 645 is a literal.

Often, the use of literals is not good programming practice because literals can mask the meaning of the statements in which they appear. How, for instance, can a reader of the preceding statement know what the value 645 represents? Moreover, literals can complicate the task of modifying the program should it become necessary. If our air traffic program is moved to another airport, all references to the airport's altitude must be changed. If the literal 645 is used in each reference to that altitude, each such reference throughout the program must be located and changed. The problem is compounded if the literal 645 also occurs in reference to a quantity other than the airport's altitude. How do we know which occurrences of 645 to change and which to leave alone?

To solve these problems, programming languages allow descriptive names to be assigned to specific, nonchangeable values. Such a name is called a **constant.** As an example, in C++ and C#, the declarative statement

    const int AirportAlt = 645;

associates the identifier `AirportAlt` with the fixed value 645 (which is considered to be of type integer). The similar concept in Java is expressed by

    final int AirportAlt = 645;

Following such declarations, the descriptive name `AirportAlt` can be used in lieu of the literal 645. Using such a constant in our pseudocode, the statement

    EffectiveAlt ← Altimeter + 645

could be rewritten as

    EffectiveAlt ← Altimeter + AirportAlt

which better represents the meaning of the statement. Moreover, if such constants are used in place of literals and the program is moved to another airport whose altitude is 267 feet, then changing the single declarative statement in which the constant is defined is all that is needed to convert all references to the airport's altitude to the new value.

Assignment Statements

Once the special terminology to be used in a program (such as the variables and constants) has been declared, a programmer can begin to describe the algorithms involved. This is done by means of imperative statements. The most basic imperative statement is the **assignment statement,** which requests that a value be assigned to a variable (or more precisely, stored in the memory area identified by the variable). Such a statement normally takes the syntactic form of a variable, followed by a symbol representing the assignment operation, and then by an expression indicating the value to be assigned. The semantics of such a statement are that the expression is to be evaluated and the result stored as the value of the variable. For example, the statement

        Z = X + Y;

in C, C++, C#, and Java requests that the sum of X and Y be assigned to the variable Z. In some other languages (such as Ada) the equivalent statement would appear as

        Z := X + Y;

Note that these statements differ only in the syntax of the assignment operator, which in C, C++, C#, and Java is merely an equal sign but in Ada is a colon followed by an equal sign. Perhaps a better notation for the assignment operator is found in APL, a language that was designed by Kenneth E. Iverson in 1962. (APL stands for A Programming Language.) It uses an arrow to represent assignment. Thus, the preceding assignment would be expressed as

        Z ← X + Y

in APL (as well as in our pseudocode of Chapter 5).

Much of the power of assignment statements comes from the scope of expressions that can appear on the right side of the statement. In general, any algebraic expression can be used, with the arithmetic operations of addition, subtraction, multiplication, and division typically represented by the symbols +, –, *, and /, respectively. Languages differ, however, in the manner in which these expressions are interpreted. For example, the expression 2 * 4 + 6 / 2 could produce the value 14 if it is evaluated from right to left, or 7 if evaluated from left to right. These ambiguities are normally resolved by rules of **operator precedence,** meaning that certain operations are given precedence over others. The traditional rules of algebra dictate that multiplication and division have precedence over addition and subtraction. That is, multiplications and divisions are performed before additions and subtractions. Following this convention, the preceding expression would produce the value 11. In most languages, parentheses can be used to override the language's operator precedence. Thus 2 * (4 + 6) / 2 would produce the value 10.

Many programming languages allow the use of one symbol to represent more than one operation. In these cases the meaning of the symbol is determined by the data type of the operands. For example, the symbol + traditionally indicates addition when its operands are numeric, but in some languages, such as Java, the symbol indicates concatenation when its operands are character strings. That is, the result of the expression

```
        "abra" + "cadabra"
```

is *abracadabra*. Such multiple use of an operation symbol is called **overloading**.

Control Statements

A **control statement** is an imperative statement that alters the execution sequence of the program. Of all the programming statements, those from this group have probably received the most attention and generated the most controversy. The major villain is the simplest control statement of all, the goto statement. It provides a means of directing the execution sequence to another location that has been labeled for this purpose by a name or number. It is therefore nothing more than a direct application of the machine-level JUMP instruction. The problem with such a feature in a high-level programming language is that it allows programmers to write rat's nests like

```
        goto 40
    20  Apply procedure Evade
        goto 70
    40  if (KryptoniteLevel < LethalDose) then goto 60
        goto 20
    60  Apply procedure RescueDamsel
        70...
```

when a single statement such as

```
    if (KryptoniteLevel < LethalDose)
        then (apply procedure RescueDamsel)
        else (apply procedure Evade)
```

does the job.

To avoid such complexities, modern languages are designed with control statements that allow a certain branching structure to be expressed within a single statement. The choice of which control statements to incorporate into a language is a design decision. The object is to provide a language that not only allows algorithms to be expressed in a readable form but also assists the programmer in obtaining such readability. This is done by restricting the use of those features that have historically led to sloppy programming while encouraging the use of better-designed features. The result is the practice known as **structured programming,** which encompasses an organized design methodology combined with the appropriate use of the language's control statements. The idea is to produce a program that can be readily comprehended and shown to meet its specifications.

Figure 6.8 presents some common branching structures and the control statements provided in various programming languages for representing those structures. Note that the first two structures are those that we have already encountered in Chapter 5. They are represented by the if-then-else and while statements in our pseudocode. The third structure, known as the case structure, can be viewed as an extension of the if-then-else structure. Whereas the if-then-else allows a choice between two options, the case allows a selection between many options.

Figure 6.8

Control structures and their representations in C, C++, C#, and Java

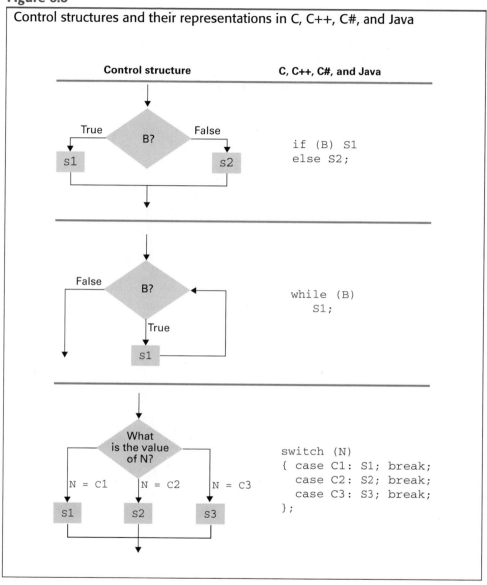

Another common structure, often called the **for** structure, and its representation in the more popular object-oriented languages is shown in Figure 6.9. This is a loop structure similar to that of the **while** statement in our pseudocode. The difference is that all the initialization, modification, and termination of the loop is incorporated into a single statement. Such a statement is convenient when the body of the loop is to be performed once for each value within a specific range. In particular, the statements in Figure 6.9 direct that the loop body be performed repeatedly—first with the value of Count being 1, then with the value of Count being 2, and again with the value of Count being 3.

Figure 6.9

The for loop structure and its representation in C++, C#, and Java

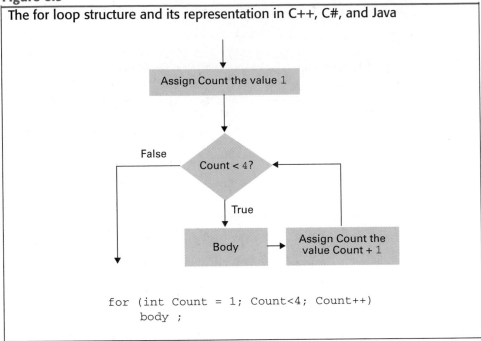

```
for (int Count = 1; Count<4; Count++)
      body ;
```

The point to be made from the examples we have cited is that common branching structures appear, with slight variations, throughout the gamut of imperative and object-oriented programming languages. A somewhat surprising result from theoretical computer science is that only a few of these structures are needed to ensure that a programming language provides a means of expressing a solution to any problem that has an algorithmic solution. We will investigate this claim in Chapter 11. For now, we merely point out that learning a programming language is not an endless task of learning different control statements. Most of the control structures found in today's programming languages are essentially variations of those we have identified here.

Comments

No matter how well a programming language is designed and how well the language's features are applied in a program, additional information is usually helpful or mandatory when a human tries to read and understand the program. For this reason, programming languages provide ways of inserting explanatory statements, called **comments,** within a program. These statements are ignored by a translator, and therefore their presence or absence does not affect the program from a machine's point of view. The machine-language version of the program produced by a translator will be the same with or without comments, but the information provided by these statements constitutes an important part of the program from a human's point of view. Without such documentation, large, complex programs can easily thwart the comprehensive powers of a human programmer.

Visual Basic

Visual Basic is an object-oriented programming language that was developed by Microsoft as a tool with which users of Microsoft's Windows operating system could develop their own GUI applications. Actually, Visual Basic is more than a language—it is an entire software development package that allows a programmer to construct a graphical user interface (GUI) from predefined components (such as buttons, check boxes, text boxes, scroll bars, etc.) and to customize these components by describing how they should react to various events. In the case of a button, for example, the programmer would describe what should happen when that button is clicked. In Chapter 7, we will learn that this strategy of constructing software from predefined components represents the current trend in software development techniques.

The popularity of the Windows operating system combined with the convenience of the Visual Basic development package has promoted Visual Basic to a widely used programming language. Whether this prominence will continue now that Microsoft has introduced C# remains to be seen.

There are two common ways of inserting comments within a program. One is to delimit the entire comment by special markers, one at the beginning of the comment and one at the end. The other is to mark the beginning of the comment and allow the comment to occupy the remainder of the line to the right of the marker. We find examples of both these techniques in C++, C#, and Java. They allow comments to be bracketed by /* and */, but they also allow a comment to begin with // and extend through the remainder of the line. Thus both

```
/* This is a comment. */
```

and

```
// This is a comment.
```

are valid comment statements.

A few words are in order about what constitutes a meaningful comment. Beginning programmers, when told to use comments for internal documentation, tend to follow a program statement such as

```
ApproachAngle = SlipAngle + HyperSpaceIncline;
```

with a comment such as "Calculate ApproachAngle by adding HyperSpaceIncline and SlipAngle." Such redundancy adds length rather than clarity to a program. The purpose of a comment is to explain the program, not to repeat it. A more appropriate comment in this case might be to explain why ApproachAngle is being calculated (if that is not obvious). For example, the comment, "ApproachAngle is used later to compute ForceFieldJettisonVelocity and is not needed after that," is more helpful than the previous one.

Additionally, comments that are scattered among a program's statements can sometimes hamper a human's ability to follow the program's flow and thus make it harder to comprehend the program than if no comments had been included. A good approach is to collect comments that relate to a single program unit into one place, perhaps at the beginning of the unit. This provides a central place where the reader of the program unit can look for explanations. It also provides a location in which the purpose and general characteristics of the program unit can be described. If this format is adopted for all program units, the written program is given a degree of uniformity in which each unit consists of a block of explanatory statements followed by the formal presentation of the program unit. Such uniformity in a program enhances its readability.

Questions/Exercises

1. Why is the use of a constant considered better programming style than the use of a literal?

2. What is the difference between a declarative statement and an imperative statement?

3. List some common data types.

4. Identify some common control structures found in imperative and object-oriented programming languages.

5. What is the difference between a homogeneous array and a heterogeneous array?

6.3 Procedural Units

In previous chapters we have seen advantages to breaking large programs into manageable units. In this section we focus on the concept of a procedure. Procedures provide the basic technique for obtaining a modular representation of a program in an imperative language. Moreover, in object-oriented languages, it is by means of procedures that programmers specify how objects should respond to various stimuli.

Procedures

A **procedure,** in its generic sense, is a set of instructions for performing a task that can be used as an abstract tool by other program units. Control is transferred to the procedure at the time its services are required and then returned to the original program unit after the procedure has finished (Figure 6.10). The process of transferring control to a procedure is often referred to as *calling* or *invoking* the procedure. We will refer to a program unit that requests the execution of a procedure as the *calling* unit.

In many respects a procedure is a miniature program, consisting of declaration statements that describe variables used in the procedure followed by imperative statements that describe the steps to be performed when the procedure is executed. As a

Figure 6.10

The flow of control involving a procedure

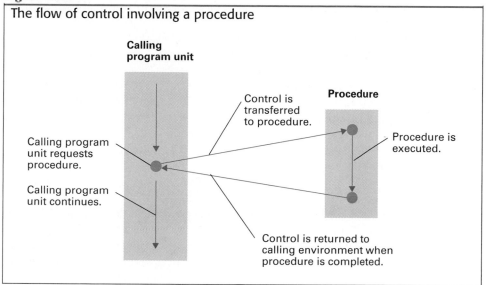

general rule, a variable declared within a procedure is a **local variable,** meaning that it can be referenced only within that procedure. This eliminates any confusion that might occur if two procedures, written independently, happen to use variables of the same name. (Variables that are not restricted to a particular part of a program are called **global variables** in that they are accessible throughout the program. Most languages provide a means of declaring both local and global variables.)

In our example programming languages, procedures are defined in much the same way as in our pseudocode of Chapter 5. The definition begins with a statement, known as the **procedure's header,** that identifies, among other things, the name of the procedure. Following this header are the statements that define the procedure's details.

However, in contrast to our informal pseudocode of Chapter 5 in which we requested the execution of a procedure by a statement such as "Apply the procedure DeactivateKrypton," most modern programming languages allow procedures to be called by merely stating the procedure's name. For example, if GetNames, SortNames, and WriteNames were the names of procedures for acquiring, sorting, and printing a list of names, then a program to get, sort, and print the list could be written as

```
GetNames;
SortNames;
WriteNames;
```

rather than

```
Apply the procedure GetNames.
Apply the procedure SortNames.
Apply the procedure WriteNames.
```

Note that by assigning each procedure a name that indicates the action performed by the procedure, this condensed form appears as a sequence of commands that reflect the meaning of the program.

Parameters

Procedures are often written using generic terms that are made specific when the procedure is applied. For example, Figure 5.11 of the preceding chapter presents a pseudocode version of a procedure for sorting lists that is expressed in terms of a generic list rather than a specific list. In our pseudocode, we agreed to identify such generic terms within parentheses in the procedure's header. Thus the procedure in Figure 5.11 begins with the header

procedure Sort (List)

and then proceeds to describe how the list is to be sorted using the term List to refer to the list being sorted. If we want to apply the procedure to sort a wedding guest list, we need merely follow the directions in the procedure, assuming that the generic term List refers to the wedding guest list. If however we want to sort a membership list, we need merely interpret the generic term List as referring to the membership list.

Such generic terms within procedures are called **parameters.** More precisely, the terms used within the procedure are called **formal parameters** and the precise meanings assigned to these formal parameters when the procedure is applied are called **actual parameters.** In a sense, the formal parameters represent slots in the procedure into which actual parameters are plugged when the procedure is requested.

In general, programming languages follow the format of our pseudocode for identifying the formal parameters in a procedure. That is, most programming languages require that, when defining a procedure, the formal parameters be listed in parentheses in the procedure's header. As an example, Figure 6.11 presents the definition of a procedure named `ProjectPopulation` as it might be written in the programming language C. The procedure expects to be given a specific yearly growth rate when it is called. Based on this rate, the procedure computes the projected population of a species, assuming an initial population of 100, for the next 10 years, and stores these values in a global array called `Population`.

Most programming languages also use parenthetical notation to identify the actual parameters when a procedure is called. That is, the statement requesting the execution of a procedure consists of the procedure name followed by a list of the actual parameters enclosed in parentheses. Thus a statement such as

```
ProjectPopulation (0.03);
```

might be used in a C program to call the procedure `ProjectPopulation` of Figure 6.11 using a `GrowthRate` of 0.03.

When more than one parameter is involved, the actual parameters are associated, entry by entry, with the formal parameters listed in the procedure's header—the first actual parameter is associated with the first formal parameter, etc. Then, the values of the actual parameters are effectively transferred to their corresponding formal parameters, and the procedure is executed.

Figure 6.11

The procedure ProjectPopulation written in the programming language C

Starting the head with the term "void" is the way that a C programmer specifies that the program unit is a procedure rather than a function. We will learn about functions shortly.

The formal parameter list. Note that C, as with many programming languages, requires that the data type of each parameter be specified.

```
void   ProjectPopulation   (float GrowthRate)

{ int Year;        This declares a local variable
                   named Year.


Population[0] = 100.0;
for (Year = 0; Year =< 10; Year++)
Population[Year+1] = Population[Year] + (Population[Year] * GrowthRate);
}
```

These statements describe how the populations are to be computed and stored in the global array named Population.

To emphasize this point, suppose the procedure PrintCheck was defined with a header such as

        procedure PrintCheck(Payee, Amount)

where Payee and Amount are formal parameters used within the procedure to refer to the person to whom the check is to be payable and the amount for which the check is to be paid, respectively. Then, calling the procedure with the statement

        PrintCheck("John Doe", 150)

would cause the procedure to be executed with the formal parameter Payee being associated with the actual parameter John Doe and the formal parameter Amount being associated with the value 150. However, calling the procedure with the statement

        PrintCheck(150, "John Doe")

would cause the value 150 to be assigned to the formal parameter Payee and the name John Doe to be assigned to the formal parameter Amount, which would lead to erroneous results.

The task of transferring data between actual and formal parameters is handled in a variety of ways by different programming languages. In some languages a duplicate of the data represented by the actual parameters is produced and given to the procedure. Using this approach, any alterations to the data made by the procedure are reflected only in the duplicate—the data in the calling program unit are never changed.

Figure 6.12

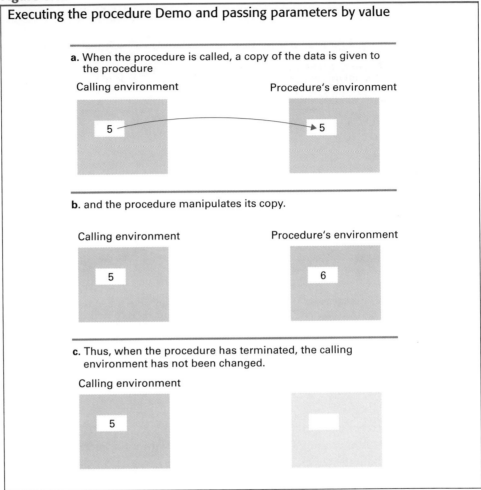

Executing the procedure Demo and passing parameters by value

a. When the procedure is called, a copy of the data is given to the procedure

Calling environment   Procedure's environment

5   5

b. and the procedure manipulates its copy.

Calling environment   Procedure's environment

5   6

c. Thus, when the procedure has terminated, the calling environment has not been changed.

Calling environment

5

We often say that such parameters are **passed by value.** Note that passing parameters by value protects the data in the calling unit from being mistakenly altered by a poorly designed procedure. For example, if the calling unit passed an employee's name to a procedure, it would not want the procedure to change that name.

Unfortunately, passing parameters by value is inefficient when the parameters represent large blocks of data. A more efficient technique is to give the procedure direct access to the actual parameters by telling it the addresses of the actual parameters in the calling program unit. In this case we say that the parameters are **passed by reference.** Note that passing parameters by reference allows the procedure to modify the data residing in the calling environment. Such an approach would be desirable in the case of a procedure for sorting a list since the point of calling such a procedure would be to cause changes in the list.

As an example, let us suppose that the procedure Demo was defined as

Figure 6.13

Executing the procedure Demo and passing parameters by reference

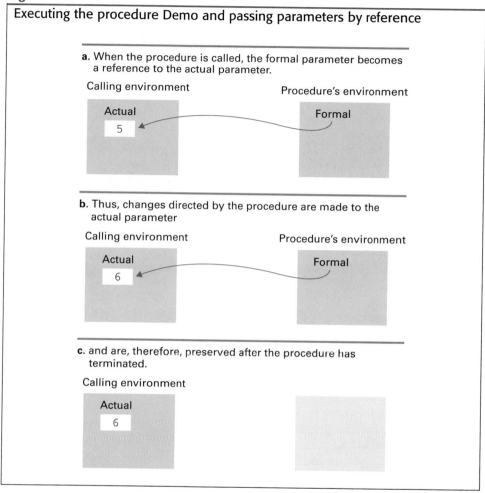

a. When the procedure is called, the formal parameter becomes a reference to the actual parameter.

Calling environment   Procedure's environment

Actual   Formal

5

b. Thus, changes directed by the procedure are made to the actual parameter

Calling environment   Procedure's environment

Actual   Formal

6

c. and are, therefore, preserved after the procedure has terminated.

Calling environment

Actual

6

```
procedure Demo (Formal)
    Formal ← Formal + 1;
```

Moreover, suppose that the variable Actual was assigned the value 5 and we called Demo with the statement

```
Demo(Actual)
```

Then, if parameters were passed by value, the change to Formal in the procedure would not be reflected in the variable Actual (Figure 6.12). But, if parameters were passed by reference, the value of Actual would be incremented by one (Figure 6.13).

Different programming languages provide different parameter-passing techniques, but in all cases the use of parameters allows a procedure to be written in a generic sense and applied to specific data at the appropriate time.

Event-Driven Software Systems

In the text, we have considered cases in which procedures are activated as the result of statements elsewhere in the program that explicitly call the procedure. There are cases, however, in which procedures are activated implicitly by the occurrence of an event. Examples are found in GUIs where the procedure that describes what should happen when a button is clicked is not activated by a call from another program unit, but instead is activated as the result of the button being clicked. Software systems in which procedures are activated by events rather than explicit requests are called **event-driven** systems. In short, an event-driven software system consists of procedures that describe what should happen as the result of various events. When the system is executed, these procedures lie dormant until their respective event occurs—then they become active, perform their task, and return to dormancy.

Functions

Let use pause to consider a slight variation of the procedure concept that is found in many programming languages. At times the purpose of a procedure is to produce a value rather than perform an action. (Consider the subtle distinction between a procedure whose purpose is to estimate the number of widgets that will be sold as opposed to a procedure for sorting lists—the emphasis in the former is to produce a value, the emphasis in the latter is to perform an action.) In these cases, the "procedure" may be implemented as a function. Here the term **function** refers to a program unit similar to a procedure except that a value is transferred back to the calling program unit as "the value of the function." That is, as a consequence of executing the function, a value will be computed and sent back to the calling program unit. This value can then be stored in a variable for later reference or used immediately in a computation. For example, a C, C++, Java, or C# programmer might write

```
ProjectedJanSales = EstimatedSales(January);
```

to request that the variable `ProjectedJanSales` be assigned the result of applying the function `EstimatedSales` to determine how many widgets are expected to be sold in January. Or, the programmer might write

```
if (LastJanSales < EstimatedSales(January)) ...
    else ...
```

to cause different actions to be performed depending on whether this January's sales are expected to be better than those of last January. Note that in the second case, the value computed by the function was never stored.

Functions are defined within a program in much the same way as procedures. The difference is that a function header usually begins by specifying the data type of the value that is to be returned, and the function definition usually ends with a return

Figure 6.14

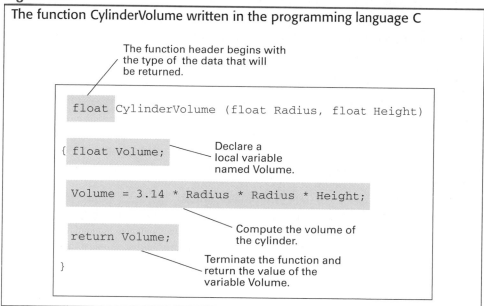

The function CylinderVolume written in the programming language C

The function header begins with the type of the data that will be returned.

```
float CylinderVolume (float Radius, float Height)

{ float Volume;

  Volume = 3.14 * Radius * Radius * Height;

  return Volume;

}
```

Declare a local variable named Volume.

Compute the volume of the cylinder.

Terminate the function and return the value of the variable Volume.

statement in which the value to be returned is specified. Figure 6.14 presents a definition of a function named `CylinderVolume` as it might be written in the language C. (Actually, a C programmer would use a more succinct form, but we will use this somewhat verbose version for pedagogical reasons.) When called, the function receives specific values for the formal parameters `Radius` and `Height` and returns the result of computing the volume of a cylinder with those dimensions. Thus the function could be used elsewhere in the program in a statement such as

```
Cost = CostPerVolUnit * CylinderVolume(3.45, 12.7);
```

to determine the cost of the contents of a cylinder with radius 3.45 and height 12.7.

Questions/Exercises

1. What is the difference between a global variable and a local variable?
2. What is the difference between a procedure and a function?
3. Why do many programming languages implement I/O operations as if they were calls to procedures?
4. What is the difference between a formal parameter and an actual parameter?
5. When writing in modern programming languages, programmers tend to use verbs for names of procedures and nouns for names of functions. Why?

6.4 Language Implementation

In this section we investigate the process of converting a program written in a high-level language into a machine-executable form.

The Translation Process

The process of converting a program from one language to another is called **translation.** The program in its original form is the **source program;** the translated version is the **object program.** The translation process consists of three activities—lexical analysis, parsing, and code generation—that are performed by units in the translator known as the **lexical analyzer, parser,** and **code generator** (Figure 6.15).

Lexical analysis is the process of recognizing which strings of symbols from the source program represent a single entity. For example, the three symbols 153 should not be interpreted as a 1, a 5, and a 3 but should be recognized as representing a single numeric value. Likewise, a word appearing in the program, although composed of individual symbols, should be interpreted as a single unit. Most humans perform lexical analysis with little conscious effort. When asked to read aloud, we pronounce words rather than individual characters.

Thus the lexical analyzer reads the source program symbol by symbol, identifying which groups of symbols represent single units, and classifying those units according to whether they are numeric values, words, arithmetic operators, and so on. As each unit is classified, the lexical analyzer generates a bit pattern known as a **token** to represent the unit and hands the token to the parser. During this process, the lexical analyzer skips over all comment statements.

Thus the parser views the program in terms of lexical units (tokens) rather than individual symbols. It is the parser's job to group these units into statements. Indeed, parsing is the process of identifying the grammatical structure of the program and recognizing the role of each component. It is the technicalities of parsing that cause one to hesitate when reading the sentence

The man the horse that won the race threw was not hurt.

(Try this one: "That that is is. That that is not is not. That that is not is not that that is."!)

Figure 6.15

The translation process

Source program → Lexical analyzer → Parser → Code generator → Object program

To simplify the parsing process, early programming languages insisted that each program statement be positioned in a particular manner on the printed page. Such languages were known as **fixed-format languages.** Today, most programming languages are **free-format languages,** meaning that the positioning of statements is not critical. Their advantage lies in a programmer's ability to organize the written program in a way that enhances readability from a human's point of view. In these cases it is common to use indentation to help a reader grasp the structure of a statement. Rather than writing

```
if Cost < CashOnHand then pay with cash else use
credit card
```

a programmer might write

```
if Cost < CashOnHand
   then pay with cash
   else use credit card
```

For a machine to parse a program written in a free-format language, the syntax of the language must be designed so that the structure of a program can be identified regardless of the spacing used in the source program. To this end, most free-format languages use punctuation marks such as semicolons to mark the end of a statement, as well as **key words** such as if, then, and else to mark the beginning of individual phrases. These key words are often **reserved words,** meaning that they cannot be used by the programmer for other purposes within the program.

The parsing process is based on a set of syntax rules that define the syntax of the programming language. One way of expressing these rules is by means of **syntax diagrams,** which are pictorial representations of a program's grammatical structure. Figure 6.16 shows a syntax diagram of the if-then-else statement from our pseudocode in Chapter 4. This diagram indicates that an if-then-else structure begins with the word **if**, followed by a *Boolean expression*, followed by the word **then**, followed by a *Statement*. This combination may or may not be followed by the word **else** and a *Statement*. Notice that terms that actually appear in an if-then-else statement are enclosed in ovals, whereas terms that require further description, such as *Boolean expression* and *Statement*, are enclosed in rectangles. Terms that require further description (those in rectangles) are called **nonterminals;** terms that appear in ovals are called **terminals.** In a complete description of a language's syntax the nonterminals are described by additional diagrams.

Figure 6.16

A syntax diagram of our if-then-else pseudocode statement

Figure 6.17

Syntax diagrams describing the structure of a simple algebraic expression

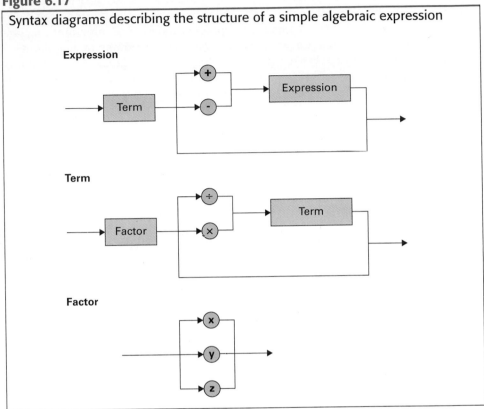

As a more complete example, Figure 6.17 presents a set of syntax diagrams that describes the syntax of a structure called *Expression*, which is intended to be the structure of simple arithmetic expressions. The first diagram describes an *Expression* as consisting of a *Term* that may or may not be followed by a + or – symbol followed by another *Expression*. The second diagram describes a *Term* as consisting of either a single *Factor* or a *Factor* followed by a × or ÷ symbol, followed by another *Term*. Finally, the last diagram describes a *Factor* as one of the symbols x, y, or z.

The manner in which a particular string conforms to a set of syntax diagrams can be represented in a pictorial form by a **parse tree,** as demonstrated in Figure 6.18, which presents a parse tree for the string

    x + y × z

based on the set of diagrams in Figure 6.17. Note that the tree starts at the top with the nonterminal *Expression* and at each level shows how the nonterminals at that level are decomposed until the symbols in the string itself are obtained. In particular, the figure shows that the string x + y × z consists of a *Term* (which turns out to be the *Factor* x), followed by the + symbol, followed by an *Expression* (which turns out to be the *Term* y × z).

Figure 6.18

The parse tree for the string x + y × z based on the syntax diagrams in Figure 6.17

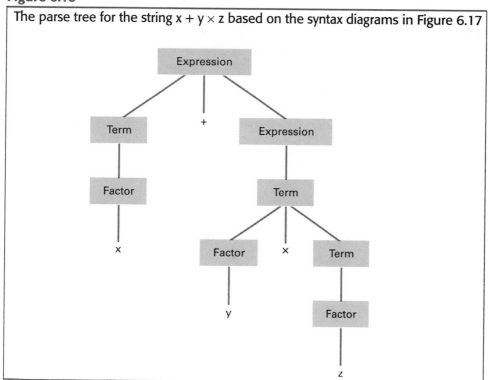

The process of parsing a program is essentially that of constructing a parse tree for the source program. Indeed, a parse tree represents the parser's understanding of the program's grammatical composition. For this reason the syntax rules describing a program's grammatical structure must not allow two distinct parse trees for one string, since this would lead to ambiguities within the parser. Such flaws can be quite subtle. In fact, the rule in Figure 6.16 contains such a flaw. It allows both the parse trees in Figure 6.19 for the single statement

```
if B1 then if B2 then S1 else S2
```

Note that these interpretations are significantly different. The first implies that statement S2 is to execute if B1 is false; the second implies that S2 is to execute only if B1 is true and B2 is false.

The syntax definitions of formal programming languages are designed to avoid such ambiguities. In our pseudocode we avoid such problems by using parentheses. In particular, we might write

```
if B1
   then (if B2 then S1)
   else S2
```

and

```
if B1
   then (if B2 then S1
               else S2)
```

to distinguish between the two possible interpretations.

Figure 6.19

Two distinct parse trees for the statement if B1 then if B2 then S1 else S2

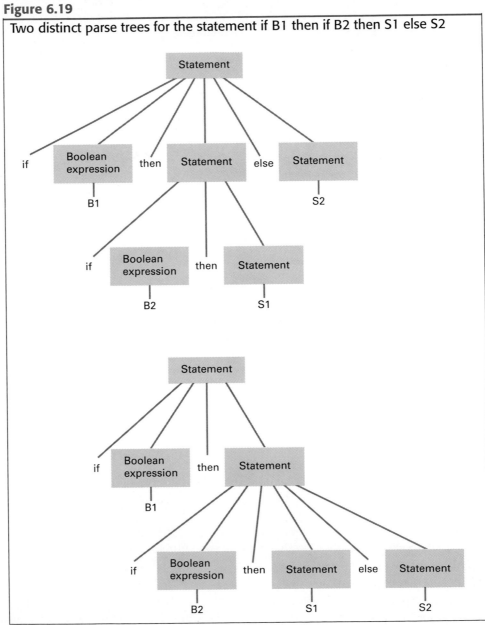

As a parser analyzes the declarative statements in a program, it records the information in these statements in a table called the **symbol table.** Thus the symbol table contains such information as which variables have been declared and what data types and data structures are associated with those variables. The parser then relies on this information when analyzing imperative statements such as

    z ← x + y;

In particular, to determine the meaning of the symbol +, the parser must know the data type associated with x and y. If x is of type real and y is of type character, then adding x and y makes little sense and should be reported as an error. If x and y are both of type integer, then the parser will request that the code generator build a machine-language instruction using the machine's integer addition op-code; if both are of type real, the parser will request that the floating-point addition op-code be used.

The preceding program statement may be meaningful when the data types involved are not the same. For instance, if x is integer and y is real, the concept of addition is still applicable. In this case the parser may choose to have the code generator build the instructions to convert one value to the other type and then perform the addition. Such implicit conversion between types is called **coercion.**

Coercion is frowned upon by many language designers. They argue that the need for coercion usually indicates a flaw in the program's design and therefore should not be accommodated by the parser. The result is that most modern languages are **strongly typed,** which means that all activities requested by a program must involve data of agreeable types without coercion. Parsers for these languages report all type conflicts as errors.

The final activity in the translation process is code generation, which is the process of constructing the machine-language instructions to implement the statements recognized by the parser. This process involves numerous issues, one being that of producing efficient code. For example, consider the task of translating the two-statement sequence

    x ← y + z;
    w ← x + z;

These statements could be translated as individual statements. Such a single-statement approach, however, would not produce an efficient product. The code generator should recognize that once the first statement has been executed, the values of x and z will already be in the CPU's general-purpose registers and therefore should not be loaded from memory before executing the second statement. Implementing insights such as this is called **code optimization** and is an important task of the code generator.

Finally, note that the steps of lexical analysis, parsing, and code generation are not carried out in a strict sequential order. Instead, these activities are intertwined. The lexical analyzer begins by reading characters from the source program and identifying the first token. It hands this token to the parser. Each time the parser receives a token from the lexical analyzer, it analyzes the grammatical structure being read. At this point it may request another token from the lexical analyzer or, if the parser recognizes that a complete phrase or statement has been read, it calls on the code generator to produce the proper machine instructions. Each such request causes the code generator to build machine instructions that are added to the object program. In turn, the task of translating a program from one language to another conforms naturally to the object-oriented paradigm. The source program, lexical analyzer, parser, code generator, and object program are objects that interact by sending messages back and forth as each object goes about performing its task (Figure 6.20).

Linking and Loading

The object program produced by the translation process, although expressed in machine language, is rarely in a form that can be executed directly by the machine. One reason is that most programming environments allow the modules of a program to be developed and translated as individual units at different times (which supports the modular construction of software). Thus the object program produced from a single translation process is often only one of several pieces of a complete program, each piece of which requests services from the others in order to accomplish the task of the entire system. Even when a complete program is developed and translated as a single unit, its object program is rarely prepared to stand alone at execution time because it most likely contains requests for services from utility software available through the operating system or from the operating system itself. Thus an object program is actually a machine-language program containing several loose ends that must be connected to other object programs before an executable program is obtained.

In the past, the task of making these connections was performed by a program called a **linker** that was executed explicitly as a step in the program development process. Its job was to link several object programs (the result of previous and separate translations), operating system routines, and other utility software to produce a complete, executable

Figure 6.20

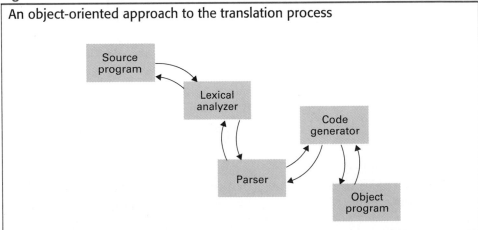

An object-oriented approach to the translation process

program (sometimes called a **load module**) that was in turn stored as a file in the machine's mass storage system. Today the linking process is usually disguised as a part of the translation process or delayed until a request is made to execute the program.

Once a load module has been constructed, it must be placed in memory by a program called a **loader,** which is often part of the operating system's scheduler (Section 3.3), before it can be executed. The significance of this step is most pronounced in multitasking systems. There, since a program must share memory with other programs being executed, the exact memory area available to the program is not known until it is time to load the program. In this setting, the task of the loader is to place the program in the memory area allotted by the operating system and make any last-minute (last-microsecond) adjustments that might be needed once the exact memory location of the program is known. (A jump instruction in the program must jump to the correct address within the program.) The desire to minimize these final adjustments by the loader has encouraged the development of techniques by which explicit references to memory addresses within a program can be avoided, resulting in program units (called **relocatable modules**) that, without modification, execute correctly regardless of where they are placed in memory.

In summary, the complete task of preparing a high-level-language program for execution consists of the three-step sequence of translate, link, and load, as represented in Figure 6.21. Once the translate and link steps have been completed, the program can be repeatedly loaded and executed without returning to the source version. If, however, a change is necessary to the program, it is made to the source program, and then the modified source program is translated and linked to produce a new load module containing the change.

Software Development Packages

The software units used in the software development process are usually grouped into a package that functions as one integrated software development system. Such a system would be classified as application software in the classification scheme of Section 3.2. By using this application package, a programmer gains ready access to an editor for writing programs, a translator for converting the programs into machine language, and a variety of debugging tools that allow the programmer to trace the execution of a malfunctioning program to discover where it goes astray.

The advantages of using such an integrated system are numerous. Perhaps the most obvious is that a programmer can move back and forth between the editor and

Figure 6.21

The complete program preparation process

Source program → Translate → Object program → Link → Load module → Load → Executable program

Implementation of Java

In the case of an animated Web page, the software that controls the animation is transferred across the Internet along with the page. If this software is supplied in source program form, additional delays will result upon viewing the page because the software will have to be translated into the proper machine language before it is executed. However, supplying the software in machine-language form would mean that a different version of the software would have to be provided depending on the machine language used by the client computer.

Sun Microsystems has resolved this problem by designing a universal "machine language" called bytecode into which Java source programs can be translated. Although bytecode is not really a machine language, it can be executed quickly by any machine using an appropriate interpreter. Such interpreters are a standard part of today's browser software. Thus if the software for controlling a Web page is written in Java and translated into bytecode, then this bytecode version can be transferred to the browsers viewing the Web page where they can provide efficient animation.

debugging tools with ease, as changes to the program are made and tested. Moreover, many software development packages allow related program units that are under development to be linked in such a way that access to related units is simplified. Some packages maintain records regarding which program units within a group of related units have been altered since the last benchmark was made. Such capabilities are quite advantageous in the development of large software systems in which many interrelated units are developed by different programmers.

On a smaller scale, the editors in software development packages are often customized to the programming language being used. Such an editor will usually provide automatic line indentation that is the de facto standard for the target language and in some cases may recognize and automatically complete key words after the programmer has typed only the first few characters. Moreover, the editor may highlight keywords within source programs (perhaps with color) so that they stand out, making the programs easier to read.

In the next chapter we will learn that software developers are increasingly searching for ways by which new software systems can be constructed from prefabricated blocks called components—leading to a new software development model called component architecture. Software development packages based on the component architecture model often use graphical interfaces in which components can be represented as icons on the monitor screen. In this setting a programmer (or component assembler) selects desired components with a mouse. A selected component can then be customized by means of the package's editor and then attached to other components by pointing and clicking with the mouse. Such packages combined with the component architecture model represent a major step forward in the search for better software development tools.

Questions/Exercises

1. Describe the three major steps in the translation process.

2. What is a symbol table?

3. Draw the parse tree for the expression

```
x × y + x + z
```

based on the syntax diagrams in Figure 6.17.

4. Describe the strings that conform to the structure Chacha according to the following syntax diagrams.

6.5 Object-Oriented Programming

In Section 6.1 we saw that the object-oriented paradigm entails the development of active program units called **objects,** each of which contains procedures describing how that object should respond to various stimuli. The object-oriented approach to a problem is to identify the objects involved and describe them as self-contained units. In turn, object-oriented programming languages provide statements for expressing these ideas. In this section we will introduce some of these statements as they appear in the languages C++, Java, and C#, which are three of the more prominent object-oriented languages today.

Classes and Objects

Consider the task of developing a computer game in which the player must protect the Earth from falling meteors by shooting them with high-power lasers. Each laser contains a finite internal power source that is partially consumed each time the laser is fired. Once this source is depleted, the laser becomes useless. Each laser should be able to respond to the commands to aim further to the right, aim further to the left, and to fire its laser beam.

In the object-oriented paradigm, each laser in the computer game would be implemented as an object that contains a record of its remaining power as well as procedures for modifying its aim and firing its laser beam. Since all the laser objects have the same properties, they can be built from the same template. In the object-oriented paradigm such a template is called a **class.** In the languages C++, Java, and C# a class is described by a statement of the form

```
class Name
{
    .
    .
    .
}
```

where *Name* is the name by which the class can be referenced elsewhere in the program. It is within the braces that the properties of the class are described.

In particular, a class named `LaserClass` describing the structure of a laser in our computer game is outlined in Figure 6.22. (A more complete description of the class will be given later in Figure 6.24.) Any object built from this template will contain a variable named `RemainingPower` of type integer and three procedures named `turnRight`, `turnLeft`, and `fire`, which describe the steps to be performed to accomplish the corresponding action. A variable that resides within an object, such as `RemainingPower`, is called an **instance variable** and the procedures within an object are called **methods** (or member functions in the C++ vernacular). Note that in Figure 6.22 the instance variable `RemainingPower` is described using a declaration statement similar to those discussed in Section 6.2 and the methods are described in a form reminiscent of procedures and functions as discussed in Section 6.3. After all, declarations of instance variables and descriptions of methods are basically imperative programming concepts.

Once we have described the class `Laser4` in our game program, we can declare three variables `Laser1`, `Laser2`, and `Laser3` to be of "type" `LaserClass` by a statement of the form

```
LaserClass Laser1, Laser2, Laser3;
```

Note that this is the same format as the statement

```
int x, y, z;
```

Figure 6.22

The structure of a class describing a laser weapon in a computer game

```
class LaserClass

{   int RemainingPower = 100;          Description of the data
                                       that will reside inside of
    void turnRight ( )                 each object of this "type."

    { ... }

    void turnLeft ( )                  Methods describing how an
                                       object of this "type" should
    { ... }                            respond to various messages

    void fire ( )

    { ... }

}
```

that would be used to create three variables named x, y, and z of type integer, as we learned early in Section 6.2. Both consist of the name of a "type" followed by a list of the variables being declared. The difference is that any entity assigned to x will be constructed according to the predefined integer template (a primitive type), whereas any entity assigned to Laser1 will be constructed according to the class template Laser-Class defined within the program.

In the language C++ the preceding declaration statement actually creates three objects of "type" LaserClass and assigns them to the variables Laser1, Laser2, and Laser3. However, in Java and C# the statement merely creates the variables, which can then be assigned values. To actually create an object of "type" LaserClass and assign it to Laser1, one would use the statement

```
LaserClass Laser1 = new LaserClass();
```

which not only declares the variable Laser1 to be of type LaserClass but also creates a new object using the LaserClass template and assigns it to Laser1. Here, again, the form of the statement is similar to that used to declare variables of predefined types. For example, the statement

```
int x = 3;
```

not only declares the variable x to be of type integer but also assigns the new variable the value 3.

Whether we are programming in C++, Java, or C#, after creating objects and assigning them the names Laser1, Laser2, and Laser3, we could continue our game program by writing statements that activate the appropriate methods within these objects (in object-oriented vernacular, this is called sending messages to the objects) as required. In particular, we could cause Laser1 to execute its fire method using the statement

```
Laser1.fire();
```

Or, we could cause the object Laser2 to execute its turnLeft method via the statement

```
Laser2.turnLeft();
```

Before moving on, we should pause to emphasize the distinction between a class and an object. A class is a template from which objects are constructed. One class can be used to create numerous objects. We often refer to an object as an **instance** of the class from which it was constructed. Thus, in our computer game Laser1, Laser2, and Laser3 are used to refer to instances of the class LaserClass.

Constructors

When an object is constructed, often some customizing activities need to be performed. For example, in our meteor computer game we might want the different lasers to have different initial power settings, which would mean that the instance variables named RemainingPower within the various objects should be given different starting values. Such initialization needs are handled by special methods, called **constructors,** within the class that are executed automatically when an object is constructed from the class. A constructor is identified within a class definition by the fact that it is a method with the same name as the class.

Figure 6.23 presents an extension of the LaserClass definition originally shown in Figure 6.22. Note that it contains a constructor in the form of a method named Laser-Class. This method assigns the instance variable RemainingPower the value it receives as its parameter. Thus, when an object is constructed from this class, this method will be executed, causing RemainingPower to be initialized at the appropriate setting.

The actual parameters to be used by a constructor are identified in a parameter list in the statement causing the creation of the object. Thus, based on the class definition in Figure 6.23, a C++ programmer would write

```
LaserClass Laser1(50), Laser2(100);
```

to create two objects of type LaserClass—one known as Laser1 with an initial power reserve of 50, the other known as Laser2 with an initial power reserve of 100. Java and C# programmers would accomplish the same task with the statements

```
LaserClass Laser1 = new LaserClass(50);
LaserClass Laser2 = new LaserClass(100);
```

Figure 6.23

A class with a constructor

```
class  LaserClass
{ int RemainingPower;

{ LaserClass (InitialPower)
  { RemainingPower = InitialPower;
  }

  void turnRight (  )
  { ... }

  void turnLeft (  )
  { ... }

  void fire (  )
  { ... }

}
```

Constructor assigns a value to Remaining Power when an object is created.

Additional Features

Let us now suppose we want to enhance our meteor computer game so that a player who reaches a certain score will be rewarded by recharging some of the lasers to their original power setting. These lasers will have the same properties as the other lasers except that they will be rechargeable.

To simplify the description of objects with similar yet different characteristics, object-oriented languages allow one class to encompass the properties of another through a system known as **inheritance.** As an example, suppose we were using Java to develop our game program. We could first use the class statement described previously to define a class called `LaserClass` that described those properties that are common to all lasers in the program. Then we could use the statement

```
class RechareableLaser extends LaserClass
{
        .
        .
        .
}
```

to describe another class called `RechargeableLaser`. (C++ and C# programmers would merely replace the word `extends` with a colon.) Here the `extends` clause indicates that this class is to inherit the features of the class `LaserClass` as well as contain those features appearing within the braces. In our case, these braces would contain a new method (perhaps named `recharge`) that would describe the steps required to reset the instance variable `RemainingPower` to its original value. Once these classes were defined, we could use the statement

```
LaserClass Laser1, Laser2;
```

to declare `Laser1` and `Laser2` to be variables referring to traditional lasers, and use the statement

```
RechargeableLaser Laser3, Laser4;
```

to declare `Laser3` and `Laser4` to be variables referring to lasers having the additional properties described in the `RechargeableLaser` class.

The use of inheritance leads to the existence of a variety of objects with similar yet different characteristics, which in turn leads to a phenomenon reminiscent of overloading, which we met in Section 6.2. (Recall that overloading refers to the use of a single symbol, such as $+$, for representing different operations depending on the type of its operands.) Suppose that an object-oriented graphics package consists of a variety of objects, each representing a shape (circle, rectangle, triangle, and so on). A particular image may consist of a collection of these objects. Each object knows its size, location, and color as well as how to respond to messages telling it, for example, to move to a new location or to draw itself on the monitor screen. To draw an image, we merely send a "draw yourself" message to each object in the image. However, the routine used to draw an object varies according to the shape of the object—drawing a square is not the same process as drawing a circle. This customized interpretation of a message is known as **polymorphism;** the message is said to be polymorphic.

Another characteristic associated with object-oriented programming is **encapsulation,** which refers to restricting access to an object's internal properties. To say that certain features of an object are *encapsulated* means that only the object itself is able to access them. Features that are encapsulated are said to be private. Features that are accessible from outside the object are said to be public.

As an example, let us return to our `LaserClass` originally outlined in Figure 6.22. Recall that it described an instance variable `RemainingPower` and three methods `turnRight`, `turnLeft`, and `fire`. These methods are to be accessed by other program units to cause an instance of `LaserClass` to perform the appropriate action. But the value of `RemainingPower` should only be altered by the instance's internal methods. No other program unit should be able to access this value directly. To enforce these rules we need merely designate `RemainingPower` as private and `turnRight`, `turnLeft`, and `fire` as public as shown in Figure 6.24. With these designations inserted, any attempt to access the value of `RemainingPower` from outside the object in which it resides will be identified as an error when the program is translated—forcing the programmer to correct the problem before proceeding.

Figure 6.24

Our LaserClass definition using encapsulation as it would appear in a Java or C# program

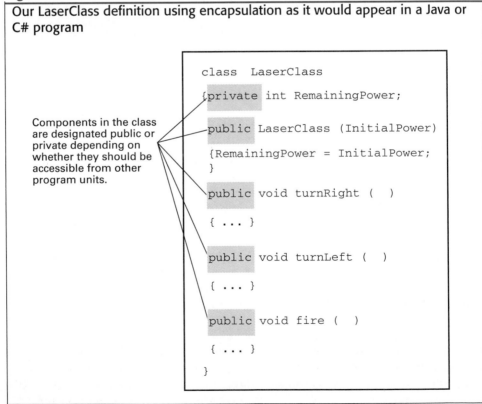

Components in the class are designated public or private depending on whether they should be accessible from other program units.

```
class  LaserClass

{private int RemainingPower;

public LaserClass (InitialPower)

{RemainingPower = InitialPower;
}

public void turnRight (  )

{ ... }

public void turnLeft (  )

{ ... }

public void fire (  )

{ ... }

}
```

Questions/Exercises

1. What is the difference between an object and a class?

2. What classes of objects other than `LaserClass` might be found in the computer game example used in this section? What instance variables in addition to RemainingPower might be found in the class `LaserClass`?

3. Suppose the classes `PartTimeEmployee` and `FullTimeEmployee` inherited the properties of the class `Employee`. What are some features that you might expect to find in each class?

4. What is a constructor?

5. Why are some items within a class designated as private?

6.6 Programming Concurrent Activities

Suppose we were asked to design a program to produce animation for an action computer game involving multiple attacking enemy spaceships. One approach would be to design a single program that would control the entire animation screen. Such a program would be charged with drawing each of the spaceships, which (if the animation is to appear realistic) would mean that the program would have to keep up with the individual characteristics of numerous spacecraft. An alternate approach would be to design a program to control the animation of a single spaceship whose characteristics are determined by parameters assigned at the beginning of the program's execution. Then, the animation could be constructed by creating multiple activations of this program, each with its own set of parameters. By executing these activations simultaneously, we could obtain the illusion of many individual spaceships streaking across the screen at the same time.

Such simultaneous execution of multiple activations is called **parallel processing** or **concurrent processing.** True parallel processing requires multiple CPUs, one to execute each activation. When only one CPU is available, the illusion of parallel processing is obtained by allowing the activations to share the time of the single processor, as discussed in Chapter 3.

Programming languages for expressing programs involving parallel processing were originally designed for use in developing operating systems. However, as our introductory example shows, many modern computer applications are more easily solved in the context of parallel processing than in the more traditional context involving a single sequence of instructions. In turn, newer programming languages provide syntax for expressing the semantic structures involved in parallel computations. The design of such a language requires the identification of these semantic structures and the development of a syntax for representing them.

Each programming language tends to approach the parallel processing paradigm from its own point of view, resulting in different terminology. For example, what we have informally referred to as an activation is called a task in the Ada vernacular and a thread in Java. That is, in an Ada program, simultaneous actions are performed by creating multiple *tasks,* whereas in Java one creates multiple *threads.*

In either case, the result is that multiple activities are generated and executed in much the same way as processes under the control of a multitasking operating system. Thus we will adopt the policy of referring to an activation, task, or thread as a process.

Perhaps the most basic action that must be expressed in a program involving parallel processing is that of creating new processes. If we want multiple activations of the spaceship program to be executed at the same time, we need a syntax for saying so. Such spawning of new processes is usually handled in a manner similar to that of requesting the execution of a traditional procedure. The difference is that, in the traditional setting, the program unit that requests the activation of a procedure does not progress any further until the requested procedure terminates (recall Figure 6.10), whereas in the parallel context the requesting program unit continues with its remaining statements while the requested procedure performs its task (Figure 6.25). Thus to create multiple spaceships streaking across the screen, we would write a main program that simply generates multiple activations of the spaceship program, each provided with the parameters describing the distinguishing characteristics of that spaceship.

A more complex issue associated with parallel processing involves handling communication between processes. For instance, in our spaceship example, the processes representing the different spaceships would need to communicate their locations among themselves in order to coordinate their activities. In other cases one process may need to wait until another reaches a certain point in its computation, or one process may need to stop another one until the first has accomplished a particular task.

Such communication needs have long been a topic of study among computer scientists, and many of the newer programming languages reflect the various approaches to the interprocess communication problem. As an example, let us consider the communication problems encountered when two processes manipulate the same data. (This example is presented in more detail in the optional Section 3.4.) In particular, if each of two processes that are executing concurrently need to add the value three to a common item of data, a method is needed to ensure that one process is allowed to complete its transaction before the other is allowed to perform its task. Otherwise they could both start their individual computations with the same initial value, which would mean that the final result would be incremented by only three rather than six. Data that can be accessed by only one process at a time is said to have mutually exclusive access.

One approach to solving this problem is to write the program units that describe the processes involved so that when a process is using shared data, it blocks other processes from accessing that data until such access is safe. (This is the approach described in the optional Section 3.4, where we identified the portion of a process that accesses shared data as a critical region.) Experience has shown that this approach has the drawback of distributing the task of ensuring mutual exclusion throughout various parts of the program—each program unit accessing the data must be properly designed to enforce mutual exclusion and thus a mistake in a single segment can corrupt the entire system. For this reason many argue that a better solution is to embody the data item with the ability to control access to itself. In short, instead of relying on the processes that access the data to guard against multiple access, the data

Figure 6.25

Spawning processes

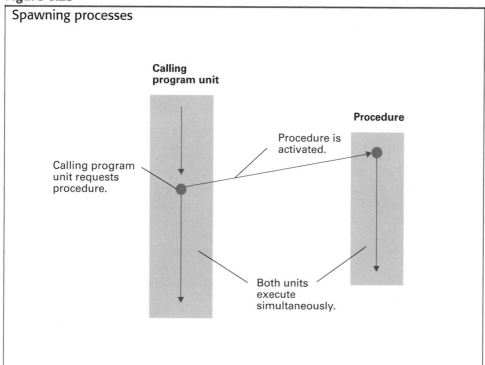

item itself is assigned this responsibility. The result is that control of access is concentrated at a single point in the program rather than dispersed among many program units.[1] A data item augmented with the ability to control access to itself is often called a **monitor.**

We see then that the design of programming languages for parallel processing involves developing ways to express such things as the creation of processes, the pausing and restarting of processes, the identification of critical regions, and the composition of monitors.

In closing, we should note that although animation provides an interesting setting in which to explore the issues of parallel computing, it is only one of many fields that benefit from parallel processing techniques. Other areas include weather forecasting, air traffic control, simulation of complex systems (from nuclear reactions to pedestrian traffic), computer networking, and database maintenance.

---

[1]*This problem has a natural solution in object-oriented programming languages where the processes that access data are collected in the same object as the data. In particular, you may wish to explore the use of the synchronize command in Java.*

Questions/Exercises

1. What are some properties that would be found in a programming language for concurrent processing that would not be found in a more traditional language?

2. Describe two methods for insuring mutually exclusive access to data.

6.7 Declarative Programming

Earlier we claimed that formal logic provides a general problem-solving algorithm around which a declarative programming system can be constructed. In this section we investigate this claim by first introducing the rudiments of the algorithm and then taking a brief look at a declarative programming language based on it.

Logical Deduction

Suppose we know that either Kermit is on stage or Kermit is sick, and we are told that Kermit is not on stage. We could then conclude that Kermit must be sick. This is an example of a deductive-reasoning principle called **resolution.**

To better understand this principle, let us first agree to represent simple statements by single letters and the negation of a statement by the symbol $\neg$. For instance, we might represent the statement "Kermit is a prince" by A and "Miss Piggy is an actress" by B. Then, the expression

A OR B

would mean "Kermit is a prince or Miss Piggy is an actress" and

B AND $\neg A$

would mean "Miss Piggy is an actress and Kermit is not a prince." We will use an arrow to indicate "implies." For example, the expression

$A \rightarrow B$

means "Kermit is a prince implies that Miss Piggy is an actress."

In its general form, the resolution principle states that from two statements of the form

P OR Q

and

R OR $\neg Q$

we can conclude the statement

P OR R

In this case we say that the two original statements resolve to form the third statement, which we call the **resolvent.** It is important to observe that the resolvent is a logical consequence of the original statements. That is, if the original statements are true, the resolvent must also be true. (If Q is true, then R must be true; but if Q is false, then P must be true. Thus regardless of the truth or falseness of Q, either P or R must be true.)

We will represent the resolution of two statements pictorially as shown in Figure 6.26, where we write the original statements with lines projecting down to their resolvent. Note that resolution can be applied only to pairs of statements that appear in **clause form**—that is, statements whose elementary components are connected by the Boolean operation OR. Thus

$$P \ \text{OR} \ Q$$

is in clause form, whereas

$$P \rightarrow Q$$

is not. The fact that this potential problem poses no serious concern is a consequence of a theorem in mathematical logic that states that any statement expressed in the first-order predicate logic (a system for representing statements with extensive expressive powers) can be expressed in clause form. We will not pursue this important theorem here, but for future reference we observe that the statement

$$P \rightarrow Q$$

is equivalent to the clause form statement

$$Q \ \text{OR} \ \neg P$$

A collection of statements is said to be **inconsistent** if it is impossible for all the statements to be true at the same time. In other words, an inconsistent collection of statements is a collection of statements that are self-contradictory. A simple example would be a statement of the form P combined with the statement $\neg P$. Logicians have shown that repeated resolution provides a systematic method of confirming the inconsistency of a set of inconsistent clauses. The rule is that if repeated application of resolution produces the empty clause (the result of resolving a clause of the form P with a clause of the form $\neg P$), then the original collection of statements must be inconsistent. As an example, Figure 6.27 demonstrates that the collection of statements

Figure 6.26

Resolving the statements (P OR Q) and (R OR $\neg Q$) to produce (P OR R)

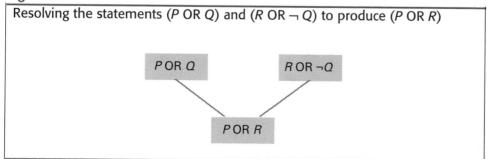

Figure 6.27

Resolving the statements (P OR Q), (R OR ¬Q), ¬R, and ¬P

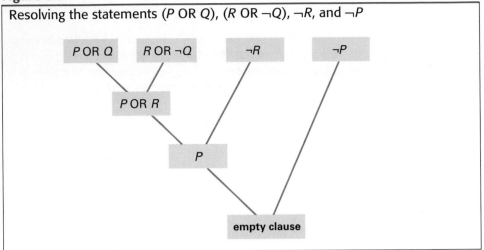

$$P \ OR \ Q \qquad R \ OR \ \neg Q \qquad \neg R \qquad \neg P$$

is inconsistent.

Suppose now that we want to confirm that a collection of statements implies the statement P. To imply the statement P is the same as contradicting the statement $\neg P$. Thus, to demonstrate that the original collection of statements implies P, all we need to do is apply resolution to the original statements together with the statement $\neg P$ until an empty clause occurs. Upon obtaining an empty clause, we can conclude that statement $\neg P$ is inconsistent with the original statements, and thus the original statements must imply P.

One final point remains before we are ready to apply resolution in an actual programming environment. Suppose we have the two statements

```
(Mary is at X) → (Mary's lamb is at X)
```

where X represents any location and

```
Mary is at home
```

In clause form the two statements become

```
(Mary's lamb is at X) OR ¬(Mary is at X)
```

and

```
(Mary is at home)
```

which at first glance do not have components that can be resolved. On the other hand, the components (Mary is at home) and ¬(Mary is at X) are quite close to being opposites of each other. The solution is to recognize that Mary is at X, being a statement about locations in general, is a statement about *home* in particular. Thus a special case of the first statement is

        (Mary's lamb is at home) OR ¬(Mary is at home)

which can be resolved with the statement

        (Mary is at home)

to produce the statement

        (Mary's lamb is at home)

The process of assigning values to variables (such as assigning the value *home* to *X*) so that resolution can be performed is called **unification.** It is this process that allows general statements to be applied to specific applications in a deduction system.

Prolog

The programming language Prolog (short for PROgramming in LOGic) is a declarative programming language whose underlying problem-solving algorithm is based on repeated resolution. A program in Prolog consists of a collection of initial statements upon which the underlying algorithm bases its deductive reasoning. The components from which these statements are constructed are called **predicates.** A predicate consists of a predicate identifier followed by a parenthetical statement listing the predicate's arguments. A single predicate represents a fact about its arguments, and its identifier is usually chosen to reflect this underlying semantics. Thus if we want to express the fact that Bill is Mary's parent, we can use the predicate form

        parent(bill, mary).

Note that the arguments in this predicate start with lowercase letters, even though they represent proper nouns. This is because Prolog distinguishes between constants and variables by insisting that constants begin with lowercase letters and variables begin with uppercase letters.

Statements in a Prolog program are either facts or rules, each of which is terminated by a period. A fact consists of a single predicate. For example, the fact that a turtle is faster than a snail could be represented by the Prolog statement

        faster(turtle, snail).

and the fact that a rabbit is faster than a turtle could be represented by

        faster(rabbit, turtle).

A Prolog rule is an "implies" statement. However, instead of writing such a statement in the form X → Y, a Prolog programmer writes "Y if X," except that the symbol :- (a colon followed by a dash) is used in place of the word *if.* Thus the rule "X is old implies X is wise" may be expressed by a logician as

        old(X) → wise(X)

but would be expressed in Prolog as

```
wise(X) :- old(X).
```

As another example, the rule

```
(faster(X, Y) AND faster(Y, Z)) → faster(X, Z)
```

would be expressed in Prolog as

```
faster(X, Z) :- faster(X, Y), faster(Y, Z).
```

The comma separating faster(X, Y) and faster(Y, Z) represents the conjunction AND. Although rules such as these are not in clause form, they are allowed in Prolog because they can be easily converted into clause form.

Keep in mind that the Prolog system does not know the meaning of the predicates in a program; it simply manipulates the statements in a totally symbolic manner according to the resolution inference rule. Thus it is up to the programmer to describe all the pertinent features of a predicate in terms of facts and rules. In this light, Prolog facts tend to be used to identify specific instances of a predicate, whereas rules are used to describe general principles. This is the approach followed by the preceding statements regarding the predicate faster. The two facts describe particular instances of "fasterness" while the rule describes a general property. Note that the fact that a rabbit is faster than a snail, though not explicitly stated, is a consequence of the two facts combined with the rule.

When developing software using Prolog, the task of a programmer is to develop the collection of facts and rules that describe the information that is known. These facts and rules constitute the set of initial statements to be used in the deductive system. Once this collection of statements is established, conjectures (called goals in Prolog terminology) can be proposed to the system—usually by typing them at a computer's keyboard. When such a goal is presented to a Prolog system, the system applies resolution to try to confirm that the goal is a consequence of the initial statements. Based on our collection of statements describing the relationship faster, each of the goals

```
faster(turtle, snail).
faster(rabbit, turtle).
faster(rabbit, snail).
```

could be so confirmed because each is a logical consequence of the initial statements. The first two are identical to facts appearing in the initial statements, whereas the third requires a certain degree of deduction by the system.

More interesting examples are obtained if we provide goals whose arguments are variables rather than constants. In these cases Prolog tries to derive the goal from the initial statements while keeping track of the unifications required to do so. Then, if the goal is obtained, Prolog reports these unifications. For example, consider the goal

```
faster(W, snail).
```

In response to this, Prolog reports

```
faster(turtle, snail).
```

Indeed, this is a consequence of the initial statements and agrees with the goal via unification. Furthermore, if we asked Prolog to tell us more, it finds and reports the consequence

```
faster(rabbit, snail).
```

In contrast, we can ask Prolog to find instances of animals that are slower than a rabbit by proposing the goal

```
faster(rabbit, W).
```

In fact, if we started with the goal

```
faster(V, W).
```

Prolog ultimately reports all the `faster` relationships that can be derived from the initial statements. Thus a single Prolog program can be used to confirm that a particular animal is faster than another, to find those animals that are faster than a given animal, to find those animals that are slower than a given animal, or to find all faster relationships. This versatility is one of the features that has captured the imagination of computer scientists.

Questions/Exercises

1. Which of the statements *R, S, T, U,* and *V* are logical consequences of the collection of statements ($\neg R$ OR *T* OR *S*), ($\neg S$ OR *V*), ($\neg V$ OR *R*), (*U* OR $\neg S$), (*T* OR $\neg U$), and (*S* OR *V*)?

2. Is the following collection of statements consistent? Explain your answer.

    P OR *Q* OR *R* $\neg R$ OR *Q*   *R* OR $\neg P$ $\neg Q$

3. Suppose a Prolog program consisted of the statements

    ```
    thriftier(carol, john).
    thriftier(bill, sue).
    thriftier(sue, carol).
    thriftier(X,Z) :- thriftier(X,Y), thriftier(Y,Z).
    ```

    List the results that can be produced from each of the following goals:
    a. `thriftier(sue, V).`
    b. `thriftier(U, carol).`
    c. `thriftier(U,V).`

4. Complete the two rules at the end of the Prolog program below so that the predicate `mother(X, Y)` means X is the mother of Y and the predicate `father(X, Y)` means if X is the father of Y.

    ```
    female(carol).
    female(sue).
    male(bill).
    male(john).
    parent(john, carol).
    parent(sue, carol).
    mother(X,Y) :-
    father(X,Y) :-
    ```

Chapter Review Problems

(Asterisked problems are associated with optional sections.)

1. What does it mean to say that a programming language is machine independent?

2. Translate the following pseudocode program into the machine language described in Appendix C.

```
x ← 0;
while (x < 3) do
   (x ← x + 1)
```

3. Translate the statement

```
Halfway ← Length + Width
```

into the machine language of Appendix C, assuming that Length, Width, and Halfway are all represented in floating-point notation.

4. Translate the high-level statement

```
if (X equals 0)
   then Z ← Y + W
   else Z ← Y + X
```

into the machine language of Appendix C, assuming that W, X, Y, and Z are all values represented in two's complement notation, each using one byte of memory.

5. Why was it necessary to identify the type of data associated with the variables in Problem 4 in order to translate the statements? Why do many high-level programming languages require the programmer to identify the type of each variable at the beginning of a program?

6. Name and describe four different programming paradigms.

7. Suppose the function f expects two numeric values as its parameters and returns the smaller of the two values as its output value. If w, x, y, and z represent numeric values, what is the result returned by $f(f(w,x), f(y,z))$?

8. Suppose f is a function that returns the result of reversing the string of symbols given as its input, and g is a function that returns the concatenation of the two strings given as its input. If x is the string abcd, what is returned by $g(f(x),x)$?

9. Suppose you are going to write an object-oriented program for maintaining your financial records. What data should be stored inside the object representing your checking account? To what messages should that object be able to respond? What are other objects that might be used in the program?

10. Summarize the distinction between a machine language and an assembly language.

11. Design an assembly language for the machine described in Appendix C.

12. John Programmer argues that the ability to declare constants within a program is not necessary because variables can be used instead. For example, our example of AirportAlt in Section 6.2 can be handled by declaring AirportAlt to be a variable and then assigning it the required variable at the beginning of the program. Why is this not as good as using a constant?

13. Summarize the distinction between declarative statements and imperative statements.

14. Explain the differences between a literal, a constant, and a variable.

15. a. What is operator precedence?

    b. Depending on operator precedence, what values could be associated with the expression $6 + 2 \times 3$?

16. What is structured programming?

17. What is the difference between the meaning of the "equals" symbol in the statement

```
if (X = 5) then ( . . . )
```

as opposed to the assignment statement

```
X = 2 + Y
```

18. Draw a flowchart representing the structure expressed by the following statement.

```
for (int x = 2; x < 8; ++x)
{ . . . }
```

19. Draw a flowchart representing the structure expressed by the following statement.

```
switch (suit)
  {case "clubs": bid(1);
   case "diamonds": bid(2);
   case "hearts": bid(3);
   case "spades": bid(4);
  }
```

20. If you are familiar with written music, analyze musical notation as a programming language. What are the control structures? What is the syntax for inserting program comments? What music notation has semantics similar to the for statements in Figure 6.9?

21. Rewrite the following program segment using a single case statement instead of nested if-then-else statements.

```
if (W = 5)
  then (Z ← 7)
  else (if (W = 6)
          then (Y ← 7)
          else (if (W = 7)
                  then (X ← 7)
                )
        )
```

22. Summarize the following rat's-nest routine with a single if-then-else statement:

```
       if X > 5 then goto 80
       X = X + 1
       goto 90
80     X = X + 2
90     stop
```

23. Summarize the basic control structures found in imperative and object-oriented programming languages for performing each of the following activities:
   a. Determining which command should be executed next.

   b. Repeating a collection of commands.
   c. Changing a variable's value.

24. Summarize the distinction between a translator and an interpreter.

25. Suppose the variable X in a program was declared to be of type integer. What error would occur when executing the program statement

   X ← 2.5

26. What does it mean to say that a programming language is strongly typed?

27. Why would a large array probably not be passed to a procedure by value?

28. Suppose the procedure modify is defined by

   procedure Modify (Y)
   Y ← 7;
   print the value of Y.

   If parameters are passed by value, what will be printed when the following program segment is executed? What if parameters are passed by reference?

   X ← 5;
   apply the procedure Modify to X;
   print the value of X;

29. Suppose the procedure modify is defined by

   procedure Modify (Y)
   Y ← 9;
   print the value of X;
   print the value of Y.

   Also suppose that X is a global variable. If parameters are passed by value, what will be printed when the following program segment is executed? What if parameters are passed by reference?

   X ← 5;
   apply the procedure Modify to X;
   print the value of X;

30. Sometimes an actual parameter is passed to a procedure by producing a duplicate for use by the procedure (as when the parameter is passed by value), but when the procedure is completed

the value in the procedure's copy is transferred to the actual parameter before the calling procedure continues. In such cases the parameter is said to be passed by value-result. What would be printed by the program segment in Problem 28 if parameters were passed by value-result?

31. What ambiguity exists in the statement

X ← 3 + 2 × 5

32. Suppose a small company has five employees and is planning to increase the number to six. The following are excerpts from two equivalent programs used by the company that must be altered to reflect the change in the number of employees. Both programs are written in the C++ language. Indicate what changes must be made to each program. What complications arise in the case of Program 1 that are avoided by the use of constants in Program 2?

Program 1

```
          .
          .
          .
DailySalary = TotalSal/5;
AvgSalary = TotalSal/5;
DailySales = TotalSales/5;
AvgSales = TotalSales/5;
          .
          .
          .
```

Program 2

```
          .
          .
          .
const int NumEmpl = 5;
const int DaysWk = 5;
          .
          .
          .
DailySalary = TotalSal/DaysWk;
AvgSalary = TotalSal/NumEmpl;
DailySales = TotalSales/DaysWk;
AvgSales = TotalSales/NumEmpl;
          .
          .
          .
```

33. Draw a syntax diagram representing the structure of the while statement in the pseudocode of Chapter 4.

34. Design a set of syntax diagrams to describe the syntax of telephone numbers in your locality. For instance, in the United States telephone numbers consist of an area code, followed by a regional code, followed by a four digit number such as (444) 555–1234.

35. Design a set of syntax diagrams to describe simple sentences in your native language.

36. Design a set of syntax diagrams to describe different ways of representing dates such as month/day/year or month day, year.

37. Design a set of syntax diagrams that describes the grammatical structure of "sentences" that consist of occurrences of the word yes followed by the same number of the word no. For example, "yes yes no no" would be such a sentence, whereas "no yes," "yes no no," and "yes no yes" would not.

38. Give an argument to the effect that a set of syntax diagrams cannot be designed that describes the grammatical structure of "sentences" that consist of occurrences of the word yes, followed by the same number of occurrences of the word no, followed by the same number of occurrences of the word maybe. For example, "yes no maybe" and "yes yes no no maybe maybe" would be such sentences, whereas "yes maybe," "yes no no maybe," and "maybe no" would not.

39. Write a sentence describing the structure of a string as defined by the syntax diagram below. Then, draw the parse tree for the string xxyxx.

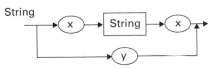

40. Add syntax diagrams to those in Question 4 of Section 6.4 to obtain a set of diagrams that defines the structure Dance to be either a Chacha or a Waltz, where a Waltz consists of one or more copies of the pattern forward diagonal close

or

backward diagonal close

41. Draw the parse tree for the expression

x × y + y ÷ x

based on the syntax diagrams in Figure 6.17.

42. What code optimization could be performed by a code generator when building the machine code representing the statement

if (X = 5) **then** (Z ← X + 2)
       else (Z ← X + 4)

43. Simplify the following program segment

Y ← 5;
if (Y = 7)
  then (Z ← 8)
  else (Z ← 9)

44. Simplify the following program segment

while (X not equal to 5) **do**
  (X ← 5)

*45. In an object-oriented programming environment, how are types and classes similar? How are they different?

*46. Describe how inheritance might be used to develop classes describing various types of buildings.

*47. What is the difference between the public and private parts of a class?

*48. a. Give an example of a situation in which an instance variable should be private.
b. Give an example of a situation in which an instance variable should be public.
c. Give an example of a situation in which a method should be private.
d. Give an example of a situation in which a method should be public.

*49. Describe some objects that might be found in a program for simulating the pedestrian traffic in a hotel lobby. Include explanations of the actions some of the objects should be able to perform.

*50. Draw a diagram (similar to Figure 6.27) representing the resolutions needed to show that the collection of statements (Q OR ¬R), (T OR R), ¬P, (P OR ¬T), and (P OR ¬Q) are inconsistent.

*51. Is the collection of statements ¬R, (T OR R), (P OR ¬Q), (Q OR ¬T), and (R OR ¬P) consistent? Explain your answer.

*52. What conclusions can Prolog find if faced with the goal

bigger(X, lassie).

and the initial statements

bigger(rex, lassie).
bigger(fido, rex).
bigger(spot, rex).
bigger(X,Z) :- bigger(X,Y),
bigger (Y,Z).

*53. What conclusions can Prolog find if faced with the goal

eq(X,Y).

and the initial statements

grteq(a,b).
grteq(b,c).
grteq(c,a).
grteq(U,W) :- grteq(U,V),
grteq(V,W).
eq(X,Y) :- grteq(X,Y),
grteq(Y,X).

*54. What problem would be encountered if the following program segment was executed on a machine in which values are represented in the eight-bit floating-point format described in Section 1.7?

X ← 0.01;
while (X not equal to 1.00) **do**
  (print the value of X;
   X ← X + 0.01)

Social Issues

The following questions are provided to help you understand some of the ethical/social/legal issues associated with the field of computing. The goal is not merely to answer these questions. You should also consider why you answered as you did and whether your justifications are consistent from one question to the next.

1. In general, copyright laws support ownership rights associated with the expression of an idea but not for the idea itself. As a result, a paragraph in a book is copyrightable but the ideas expressed in the paragraph are not. How should this right extend to source programs and the algorithms they express? To what extent should a person who knows the algorithms used in a commercial software package be allowed to write his or her own program expressing those same algorithms and market this version of the software?

2. By using a high-level programming language a programmer is able to express algorithms using words such as *if*, *then*, and *while*. To what extent does the computer understand the meaning of those words? Does the ability to respond correctly to the use of words imply an understanding of the words? How do you know when another person has understood what you said?

3. Should a person who develops a new and useful programming language have a right to profit from the use of that language? If so, how can that right be protected? To what extent can a language be owned? To what extent should a company have the right to own the creative, intellectual accomplishments of its employees.

4. To what extent is a programmer who helps develop a violent computer game responsible for any consequences of that game? Should children's access to violent computer games be restricted? If so, how and by whom? What about other groups in society, such as convicted criminals?

5. With a deadline approaching, is it acceptable for a programmer to forgo documentation via comment statements to get a program running on time? (Beginning students are often surprised to learn how important documentation is considered among professional software developers.)

6. Much of the research in programming languages has been to develop languages that allow programmers to write programs that can be easily read and understood by humans. To what extent should a programmer be required to use such capabilities? That is, to what extent is it good enough for the program to perform correctly even though it is not well written from a human perspective?

7. Suppose an amateur programmer writes a program for his or her own use and in doing so is sloppy in the program's construction. The program does not use the programming language features that would make it more readable, it is not efficient, and it contains shortcuts that take advantage of the particular situation in which the programmer intends to use the program. Over time the programmer gives copies of the program to friends who want to use it themselves, and these friends give it to their friends. To what extent is the programmer liable for problems that may occur?

8. To what extent should a computer professional be knowledgeable in the various programming paradigms? Some companies insist that all software developed in that company be written in the same, predetermined programming language. Does your answer to the original question change if the professional works for such a company?

Additional Reading

Aho, A. V., R. Sethi, and J. D. Ullman. *Compilers: Principles, Techniques, and Tools.* Reading, MA: Addison-Wesley, 1986.

Barnes, J. *Programming in Ada 95,* 2nd ed. Reading, MA: Addison-Wesley, 1998.

Clocksin, W. F., and C. S. Mellish. *Programming in Prolog,* 5th ed. New York: Springer-Verlag, 2003.

Graham, P., *ANSI Common Lisp.* Englewood Cliffs, NJ: Prentice-Hall, 1996.

Hamburger, H., and D. Richards. *Logic and Language Models for Computer Science.* Englewood Cliffs, NJ: Prentice-Hall, 2002.

Kelley, A., and I. Pohl. *C by Dissection: The Essentials of C Programming,* 4th ed. Reading, MA: Addison-Wesley, 2001.

Metcalf, M., and J. Reid. *Fortran 90/95 Explained,* 2nd ed. Oxford, England: Oxford University Press, 1999.

Noonan, R., and A. Tucker. *Programming Languages: Principles and Paradigms.* Burr Ridge, IL: McGraw-Hill, 2002.

Pohl, I. *C# by Dissection: The Essentials of C# Programming.* Reading, MA: Addison-Wesley, 2003.

Pratt, T. W., and M. V. Zelkowitz. *Programming Languages, Design and Implementation,* 4th ed. Englewood Cliffs, NJ: Prentice-Hall, 2001.

Savitch, W. *Problem Solving with C++,* 4th ed. Reading, MA: Addison-Wesley, 2003.

Savitch, W. *Absolute Java.* Reading, MA: Addison-Wesley, 2004.

Sebesta, R. W. *Concepts of Programming Languages,* 6th ed. Reading, MA: Addison-Wesley, 2004.

Wu, C. T. *An Introduction to Object-Oriented Programming with Java,* 3rd ed. Burr Ridge, IL: McGraw-Hill, 2004.

CHAPTER 7

Software Engineering

In this chapter we consider the overall process of software development and maintenance. The subject is called *software engineering* because software development is an engineering process. However, software engineering has many characteristics that make it unique within the engineering discipline.

Our discussion concerns large software systems. The problems faced when developing such systems are more than enlarged versions of those problems faced when writing small programs. For instance, the development of such systems requires the efforts of more than one person over an extended period of time during which the requirements of the proposed system may be altered and the personnel assigned to the project may change. Consequently, software engineering includes topics such as personnel and project management that are more readily associated with business management than computer science. We, however, will focus on topics readily related to computer science.

7.1 The Software Engineering Discipline

To appreciate the problems involved in software engineering, it is helpful to select a large complex device (an automobile, a multistory office building, or perhaps a cathedral) and imagine being asked to design it and then to supervise its construction. How can you estimate the cost in time, money, and other resources to complete the project? How can you divide the project into manageable pieces? How can you ensure that the pieces produced are compatible? How can those working on the various pieces communicate? How can you measure progress? How can you cope with the wide range of detail (the selection of the doorknobs, the design of the gargoyles, the availability of blue glass for the stained glass windows, the strength of the pillars, the design of the duct work for the heating system)? Questions of the same scope must be answered during the development of a large software system.

Since engineering is a well-established field, you might think that there is a wealth of previously developed engineering techniques that can be useful in answering such questions. This reasoning is partially true, but it overlooks the many distinctions between the properties of software and those of other fields of engineering.

One such distinction deals with the ability to construct systems from generic prefabricated components. Traditional fields of engineering have long benefited from the ability to use "off-the-shelf" components as building blocks when constructing complex devices. The designer of a new car does not have to design the engine, radio, air conditioner, and door locks. Instead, the designer uses previously designed versions of these components. In the context of software, however, previously designed components tend to be domain specific—that is, their internal design is dependent on a specific application. To reuse such a component would therefore require that it be redesigned. The result is that complex software systems have historically been built from scratch.

Another distinction between software engineering and traditional engineering deals with the role of tolerances. Traditional areas of engineering deal with the development of products that are acceptable as long as they perform their task within certain bounds.

Association for Computing Machinery

The Association for Computing Machinery (ACM) was founded in 1947 as an international scientific and educational organization dedicated to advancing the arts, sciences, and applications of information technology. It is headquartered in New York and includes numerous special interest groups (SIGs) focusing on such topics as computer architecture, artificial intelligence, biomedical computing, computers and society, computer science education, computer graphics, hypertext/hypermedia, operating systems, programming languages, simulation and modeling, and software engineering. The ACM's Web site is at http://www.acm.org. Its Code of Ethics and Professional Conduct can be found at http://www.acm.org/constitution/code.html.

A washing machine that cycles through its wash–rinse–spin cycle within a 2 percent tolerance of the desired time is acceptable. Software, in contrast, performs either correctly or incorrectly. An accounting system that is accurate only to within a 2 percent tolerance is not acceptable.

Still another distinction relates to the lack of quantitative systems, called **metrics,** for measuring the properties of software. The quality of a mechanical device is often measured in terms of the mean time between failures, which is a measurement of how well the device endures wear and tear. Software, in contrast, does not wear out, so this method of measuring quality does not carry over into software engineering.

The inability to measure software properties in a quantitative manner is one of the major reasons that software engineering has not yet found a rigorous footing in the same sense as mechanical and electrical engineering. Whereas these subjects are founded on the established science of physics, software engineering is still searching for its roots. In a sense, the state of software engineering today is similar to that of mechanical engineering in the early seventeenth century before Isaac Newton and others discovered that properties such as mass, acceleration, and force could be measured and related to each other mathematically.

Thus research in software engineering is currently progressing on two levels: Some researchers, sometimes called practitioners, work toward developing techniques for immediate application, while others, called theoreticians, search for underlying principles and theories on which more stable techniques can someday be constructed. Being based on a subjective foundation, many methodologies developed and promoted by practitioners in the past have been replaced by other approaches that may themselves become obsolete with time. Meanwhile, progress by theoreticians continues to be evasive.

The need for progress by both practitioners and theoreticians is enormous. Our society has become addicted to computer systems and their associated software. Our economy, health care, government, law enforcement, transportation, and defense depend on large software systems. Yet there continue to be major problems with the reliability of these systems. Software errors have caused such disasters and near disasters as the rising moon being interpreted as a nuclear attack, the loss of $5 million by the Bank of New York in only one day, the loss of the *Mariner 18* space probe, radiation overdoses that have killed and paralyzed, and the simultaneous disruption of telephone communications over large regions.

While science continues to search for methods of developing better-quality software, professional organizations have contributed their efforts indirectly by promoting high standards of ethics and professional conduct among their membership. For example, the Association of Computing Machinery (ACM) and the Institute of Electrical and Electronics Engineers (IEEE) have adopted codes of professional conduct and ethics that enhance the professionalism of software developers and counter nonchalant attitudes toward each individual's responsibilities.

In the remainder of this chapter we discuss some of the fundamental principles of software engineering (such as the software life cycle and modularity), look at some of the directions in which software engineering is moving (such as design patterns and open source development), and witness the affects that the object-oriented paradigm has had on the field.

Questions/Exercises

1. Why would the number of lines in a program not be a good measure of the complexity of the program?

2. What technique can be used to determine how many errors are in a unit of software?

3. Suggest a metric for measuring software quality. What weaknesses does your metric have?

4. Identify another field that, like software engineering, is still struggling to find its scientific foundation and thus continues to apply techniques developed largely by practitioners rather than theoreticians.

7.2 The Software Life Cycle

The most fundamental concept in software engineering is the software life cycle.

The Cycle as a Whole

The software life cycle is shown in Figure 7.1. This figure represents the fact that once software is developed, it enters a cycle of being used and modified that continues for the rest of the software's life. Such a pattern is common for many manufactured products as well. The difference is that, in the case of other products, the modification phase is more accurately called a repair or maintenance phase because other products tend to move from being used to being modified as their parts become worn.

Software, on the other hand, does not wear out. Instead, software moves into the modification phase because errors are discovered, because changes in the software's application occur that require corresponding changes in the software, or because changes made during a previous modification are found to induce problems elsewhere in the software.

Regardless of why software enters the modification phase, the process requires that a person (often not the original author) study the underlying program and its documentation until the program, or at least the pertinent part of the program, is understood. Otherwise, any modification could introduce more problems than it solves. Acquiring this understanding can be a difficult task, even when the software is well-designed and documented. In fact, it is often within this phase that a piece of

Figure 7.1

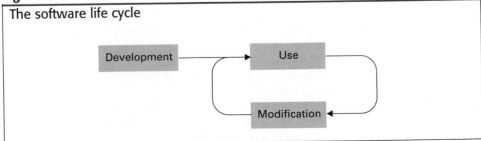

The software life cycle

software is finally discarded under the pretense (too often true) that it is easier to develop a new system from scratch than to modify the existing package successfully.

Experience has shown that a little effort during the development of software can make a tremendous difference when modifications in the software are required. For example, in our discussion of data description statements in Chapter 6 we saw how the name `AirportAlt` might be used in lieu of the nondescriptive value 645 in a program and reasoned that if a change became necessary, it would be easier to change the value associated with the name instead of finding and changing numerous occurrences of the value 645. In turn, most of the research in software engineering focuses on the development stage of the software life cycle, with the goal being to take advantage of this effort-versus-benefit leverage.

The Traditional Development Phase

The major stages within the development phase of the software life cycle are analysis, design, implementation, and testing (Figure 7.2).

Analysis

The development phase of the software life cycle begins with analysis—a major goal being to identify what the proposed system should accomplish. If the system is to be a generic product sold in a competitive market, this analysis would involve a broad-based investigation to identify the needs of potential customers. If, however, the system is to be designed for a specific user, then the process would be a more narrow investigation.

As the needs of the potential user are identified, they are compiled to form a set of **requirements** that the new system must satisfy. These requirements are stated in terms of the application rather than in the technical terminology of the data processing community. One requirement might be that access to data must be restricted to authorized personnel. Another might be that the data must reflect the

Figure 7.2

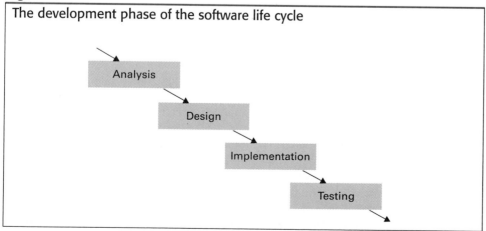

The development phase of the software life cycle

Institute of Electrical and Electronics Engineers

The Institute of Electrical and Electronics Engineers (IEEE, pronounced "i-triple-e") is an organization of electrical, electronics, and manufacturing engineers that was formed in 1963 as the result of merging the American Institute of Electrical Engineers (founded in 1884 by 25 electrical engineers, including Thomas Edison) and the Institute of Radio Engineers (founded in 1912). Today, IEEE's operation center is located in Piscataway, New Jersey. The Institute includes numerous technical societies such as the Aerospace and Electronic Systems Society, the Lasers and Electro-Optics Society, the Robotics and Automation Society, the Vehicular Technology Society, and (most important for our study) the Computer Society. Among its activities, the IEEE is involved in the development of standards. In particular, IEEE's efforts led to the standards used in most computers today for representing values in floating-point format.

You will find the IEEE's Web page at http://www.ieee.org, the IEEE Computer Society's Web page at http://www.computer.org, and the IEEE's Code of Ethics at http://www.ieee.org/about/whatis/code.html.

current state of the inventory as of the end of the last business day. Still another might be that the arrangement of the data as displayed on the computer screen must adhere to the format of the paper forms currently in use.

After the system requirements are identified, they are converted into more technical **specifications.** For example, the requirement that data be restricted to authorized personnel might become the specification that the system will not respond until an approved eight-digit password has been typed at the keyboard or that data will be displayed in encrypted form unless preprocessed by a routine known only to authorized personnel.

Design

Whereas analysis concentrates on *what* the proposed system should do, design concentrates on *how* the system will accomplish those goals. It is here that the structure of the software system is established.

It is a well-established principle that the best structure for a large software system is a modular one. It is by means of this modular decomposition that the implementation of large systems becomes a possibility. Without such a breakdown, the technical details required in the implementation of a large system would exceed a human's comprehensive powers. With a modular design, however, only the details pertaining to the module under consideration need be mastered. This same modular design is also conducive to future maintenance because it allows changes to be made on a modular basis. (If a change is to be made to the way each employee's health benefits are calculated, then only modules dealing with health benefits need be considered.)

There are, however, distinctions regarding the concept of a module. If one approaches the design task in terms of the traditional imperative paradigm, modules consist of procedures, and the development of a modular design takes the form of identifying the various tasks that the proposed system must perform. In contrast, if one approaches the design task from the object-oriented perspective, modules are seen as objects, and the design process becomes that of identifying the entities (objects) in the proposed system as well as how these entities should behave.

Implementation

Implementation involves the actual writing of programs, creation of data files, and development of databases. It is at this point that we see the distinction between the tasks of a **software analyst** (sometimes referred to as a system analyst) and a **programmer.** The former is a person involved with the entire development process with an emphasis on analysis and design steps. The later is a person involved primarily with the implementation step. In its narrowest interpretation, a programmer is charged with writing programs that implement the specifications produced by a software analyst.

Having made this distinction, we should note again that there is no central authority controlling the use of terminology throughout the computing community. Many who carry the title of software analyst are essentially programmers, and many with the title programmer (or perhaps senior programmer) are actually software analysts in the full sense of the term. This blurring of terminology is founded in the fact that today the steps in the software development process are often intermingled, as we will soon see.

Testing

Testing is closely associated with implementation, because each module of the system is normally tested as it is implemented. Indeed, each module in a well-designed system can be tested independently of the other modules by using simplified versions of the other modules, sometimes called stubs, to simulate the interaction between the target module and the rest of the system. Of course, this testing of components gives way to overall system testing as the various modules are completed and combined.

Unfortunately, the testing and debugging of a system is extremely difficult to perform successfully. Experience has shown that large software systems can contain numerous errors, even after significant testing. Many of these errors may go undetected for the life of the system, but others may cause major malfunctions. The elimination of such errors is one of the goals of software engineering. The fact that they are still prevalent means that a lot of research remains to be done.

Recent Trends

Early approaches to software engineering insisted on performing analysis, design, implementation, and testing in a strictly sequential manner. The feeling was that too much was at risk during the development of a large software system to allow for variations. As a result, software engineers insisted that the entire analysis of the system be completed before beginning the design and, likewise, that the design be completed before beginning implementation. The result was a development process now referred to as the **waterfall model,** an analogy to the fact that the development process was allowed to flow in only one direction.

You will notice a similarity between the four problem-solving phases identified by Polya (Section 4.3) and the analysis, design, implementation, and testing phases of software development. After all, to develop a large software system is to solve a problem. On the other hand, the traditional waterfall approach to software development is in stark contrast to the "free-wheeling," trial-and-error process that is often vital to creative problem solving. Whereas the waterfall approach seeks to establish a highly structured environment in which development progresses in a sequential fashion, creative problem solving seeks a nonstructured environment in which one can drop previous plans of attack to pursue sparks of intuition without explaining why.

In recent years, software engineering techniques have begun to reflect this underlying contradiction as illustrated by the emergence of the **incremental model** for software development. Following this model, the desired software system is constructed in increments—the first being a simplified version of the final product with limited functionality. Once this version has been tested and perhaps evaluated by the future user, more features are added and tested in an incremental manner until the system is complete. For example, if the system being developed is a student records system for a university registrar, the first increment may incorporate only the ability to view student records from a small sample of the entire record system. Once that version is operational, additional features, such as the ability to add and update records, would be added in a stepwise manner.

The incremental model is evidence of the trend in software development toward **prototyping** in which incomplete versions of the proposed system, called **prototypes,** are built and evaluated. In the case of the incremental model these prototypes evolve into the complete, final system—a process known as **evolutionary prototyping.** In other cases, the prototypes may be discarded in favor of a fresh implementation of the final design. This approach is known as **throwaway prototyping.** An example that normally falls within this throwaway category is rapid prototyping in which a simple example of the proposed system is quickly constructed in the early stages of development. Such a prototype may consist of only a few screen images that give an indication of how the system will interact with the user and what capabilities it will have. The goal is not to produce a working version of the product but to obtain a demonstration tool that can be used to clarify communication between the parties involved. For example, rapid prototypes have proved advantageous in ironing out system requirements during the analysis stage or as aids during sales presentations to potential clients.

Today software engineering methodologies range over a wide spectrum of philosophies. On one end is the traditional waterfall model characterized somewhat by the image of managers and programmers working in individual offices—each performing a well-defined portion of the overall software development task. On the other end is the model (fondly referred to as **extreme programming**) in which a team of less than a dozen individuals share a communal work space where they freely share ideas and assistance as they incrementally develop a software package via repeated daily cycles of designing, implementing, and testing.

Another development in software engineering has been the application of computer technology to the software development process itself, resulting in what is called

computer-aided software engineering (CASE). These computerized systems are known as CASE tools and include project planning tools (that assist in cost estimation, project scheduling, and personnel allocation), project management tools (that assist in monitoring the progress of the development project), documentation tools (that assist in writing and organizing documentation), prototyping and simulation tools (that assist in the development of prototypes), interface design tools (that assist in the development of GUIs), and programming tools (that assist in writing and debugging programs). Some of these tools are little more than the word processors, spreadsheet systems, and e-mail communication systems used in other applications. Others are quite sophisticated packages designed primarily for the software engineering environment. For example, some CASE tools include code generators that, when given specifications for a part of a system, produce high-level language programs that implement that part of the system.

Questions/Exercises

1. What is the difference between system requirements and system specifications?
2. Summarize each of the four stages (analysis, design, implementation, and testing) within the development phase of the software life cycle.
3. Summarize the distinction between the traditional waterfall model of software development and the newer prototyping paradigm.

7.3 Modularity

One of the key statements in Section 7.2 was that to modify software one must understand the program or at least the pertinent parts of the program. Gaining such an understanding is often difficult enough in the case of small programs and would be close to impossible when dealing with large software systems if it were not for **modularity**—that is, the division of software into manageable units, each of which performs only a part of the overall task.

Modular Implementation

Modularity can be achieved in a variety of forms. In Chapters 5 and 6 we saw how modules can be formed in terms of procedures and used as building blocks (abstract tools) in the construction of larger systems. In Chapter 6 we also met modularity in the context of the object-oriented paradigm. In this case modules take the form of objects, each with its own internal organization that is independent of the contents of other objects. In fact, it is this inherent modular structure that has led to the rise in popularity of the object-oriented approach to software development.

The **structure chart** is the traditional tool for representing a modular structure obtained by means of procedures. In such a chart, each module (procedure) is represented by a rectangle, and dependencies between modules are represented by

Figure 7.3

A structure chart for a simple Internet "mail order" business

arrows connecting the rectangles. The structure chart in Figure 7.3 represents such a modular structure for an Internet "mail-order" business in which customers contact the company's Web site to browse through the catalogue and place orders. The chart indicates that the module named OverseeWebSite uses the modules ProcessIncomingCustomer, OverseeBrowsing, and ProcessOrder as abstract tools to accomplish its task. More precisely, the procedure OverseeWebSite calls the procedure ProcessIncomingCustomer to carry out the steps required to obtain identifying information about customers as they contact the site. It then calls the procedure OverseeBrowsing to allow the customer to view the catalogue and produce an order. Once an order has been produced, OverseeWebSite calls the procedure ProcessOrder to oversee the shipment and billing activities.

Whereas structure charts are used to represent the procedural organization of a software system, **class diagrams** are often used to represent an object-oriented system's structure in terms of the classes of objects and the relationships between these classes. Figure 7.4 is a simple class diagram of our Internet ordering system. It indicates that the system is composed of three types of objects, Customer, Catalogue,

Figure 7.4

A class diagram for a simple Internet "mail order" business

and `OrderForm`, that are related by the relationships called `CurrentlyBrowsing` and `CurrentlyConstructing`. The underlying idea is that an object of the type `Customer` contains the data and procedures regarding a particular customer, an object of type `Catalogue` contains the data and procedures required to present the company's products to customers, and an object of type `OrderForm` contains the data and procedures for keeping track of the items the associated customer wants to order. The relationship `CurrentlyBrowsing` represents the association between customers and the catalogue. (A customer may be browsing through the company's catalogue.) The relationship `CurrentlyConstructing` represents the relationship between a customer and his or her order form. (A customer may be constructing an order.) The numbers appearing at the ends of the line representing the relationship `CurrentlyConstructing` indicate that only one customer can be associated with an order form and vice versa. Such a one-to-one relationship is different from the many-to-one relationship `CurrentlyBrowsing` in which the notation indicates that many customers may be browsing through a single catalogue at the same time. (We will return to these ideas when we discuss entity-relationship diagrams in Section 7.5.)

In recent years, significant progress has been made toward establishing a standard notational system for representing object-oriented designs—the most prominent example being the **Unified Modeling Language (UML),** which is a system for representing a variety of object-oriented concepts. The notation used in the class diagram in Figure 7.4 is based on UML conventions.

Software Engineering in the Real World

The following scenario is typical of the problems encountered by real-world software engineers. Company XYZ hires a software-engineering firm to develop and install a company-wide integrated software system to handle the company's data processing needs. As a part of the system produced by Company XYZ, a network of PCs is used to provide employees access to the company-wide system. Thus each employee finds a PC on his or her desk. Soon these PCs are used not only to access the new data management system but also as customizable tools with which each employee increases his or her productivity. For example, one employee may develop a spreadsheet program that streamlines that employee's tasks. Unfortunately, such customized applications may not be well designed or thoroughly tested and may involve features that are not completely understood by the employee. As the years go by, the use of these ad hoc applications becomes integrated into the company's internal business procedures. Moreover, the employees who developed these applications may be promoted, transferred, or quit the company, leaving others behind using a program they do not understand. The result is that what started out as a well-designed, coherent system can become dependent on a patchwork of poorly designed, undocumented, and error-prone applications.

Coupling

We have introduced modularity as a way of obtaining manageable software. The idea is that a future modification will likely apply to only a few of the modules so that one's attention can be restricted to that portion of the system during the modification process. This, of course, depends on the assumption that changes in one module will not unknowingly affect other modules in the system. Consequently, a goal when designing a modular system should be to maximize independence between modules. Working against this objective is the fact that some connection between modules is necessary for them to form a coherent system. This connection is referred to as inter-module **coupling.** The goal of maximizing independence therefore corresponds to minimizing coupling.

Intermodule coupling actually occurs in several forms. One form is **control coupling,** which occurs when a module passes control to another, as in the transfer/return relationship associated with procedures. Another form is **data coupling,** which refers to the sharing of data between modules.

The structure chart in Figure 7.3 already represents the control coupling in a procedural approach to our Web site example. Data coupling is traditionally represented in a structure chart with additional arrows, as represented in Figure 7.5. This chart indicates the data items that are passed to a module when its services are requested and those data items that are passed back to the original module when the requested task is completed. In particular, the chart indicates that the module `OverseeWebSite` will receive information about each customer from the procedure `ProcessIncomingCustomer` and will pass this information to the procedure `OverseeBrowsing`. Moreover, this procedure will report the order form produced, which will be passed on to the procedure `ProcessOrder`.

Figure 7.5

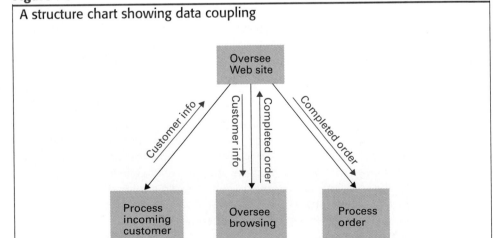

A structure chart showing data coupling

The minimalization of data coupling is one of the main benefits of the object-oriented approach. After all, one of the motivating concepts of an object is that of collecting the routines that manipulate a particular item of data into a single module. Thus, in an object-oriented system, most intermodule coupling takes the form of interobject communication, which is usually implemented as control coupling. That is, a request for an object to perform a task is essentially a request for the execution of a method (procedure) within the object. The request thus results in control being passed to the object in a manner similar to control being passed to a procedure in the imperative paradigm.

One way of representing interobject communication in an object-oriented design is to add the information to a class diagram to form a **collaboration diagram**—which is essentially a class diagram that also shows how the various objects in the system collaborate with each other. A simple collaboration diagram (using UML-compatible notation) for our Internet "mail-order" business is shown in Figure 7.6. It indicates that an object of type Customer may send a message to an OrderForm object telling it to add an item to the order and that an object of type Catalogue may send a message to a Customer object containing information about particular merchandise.

Regardless of the type of coupling involved, a programmer should strive to make that coupling apparent in the final written program. Coupling that is disguised is known as **implicit coupling** and is the cause of many software errors. A common form of implicit coupling is obtained by the use of **global data**—data elements that are automatically available to the modules throughout a system, as opposed to local data elements that are accessible only within a particular module unless explicitly passed to another. Most high-level languages provide methods for implementing both

Figure 7.6

A collaboration diagram of a simple Internet "mail order" business

global and local data. The problem associated with global data is that changes to the data often occur as side effects of executing a module rather than being explicitly indicated. (In software vernacular, the term **side effect** refers to an action performed by the software that is not readily apparent from the written program.) In turn, a person reading the program may not realize that a module alters a global unit unless he or she reads the internal details of the module. This degrades the module's usefulness as an abstract tool. (Here, then, is an example where comment statements should be used to help a reader understand a program.)

Cohesion

Just as important as minimizing the coupling between modules is maximizing the internal binding within each module. The term **cohesion** refers to this internal binding or, in other words, the degree of relatedness of a module's internal parts. To appreciate the importance of cohesion, we must look beyond the initial development of a system and consider the entire software life cycle. If it becomes necessary to make changes in a module, the existence of a variety of activities within it can confuse what would otherwise be a simple process. Thus, in addition to seeking low intermodule coupling, software designers strive for high intramodule cohesion.

A weak form of cohesion is known as **logical cohesion.** This is the cohesion within a module induced by the fact that its internal elements perform activities logically similar in nature. For example, consider a module that performs all of a system's communication with the outside world. The "glue" that holds such a module together is that all the activities within the module deal with communication. However, the topics of the communication can vary greatly. Some may deal with obtaining data, while others deal with reporting errors.

A stronger form of cohesion is known as **functional cohesion,** which means that all the parts of the module are focused around the performance of a single activity. The module OverseeBrowsing in Figure 7.3 is not functionally cohesive if it contains the details of communicating with the customer, retrieving and displaying information about products, and constructing the customer's order. However, if these details are isolated in other modules and used as abstract tools, each step in the OverseeBrowsing module can be presented in the overall context of overseeing the actions associated with the browsing process, thus making the module more functionally cohesive.

In object-oriented designs, entire objects are usually only logically cohesive since the methods within an object often perform loosely related activities—the only common bond being that they are activities performed by the same object. For example, in our Internet business example, each order form object would probably contain a method for adding an item to the order, deleting an item from the order, and submitting the order. Such an object would therefore form only a logically cohesive module. However, a software designer should strive to make each individual method within an object functionally cohesive. That is, even though the object in its entirety is only logically cohesive, each method within an object should perform only one functionally cohesive task (Figure 7.7).

Figure 7.7

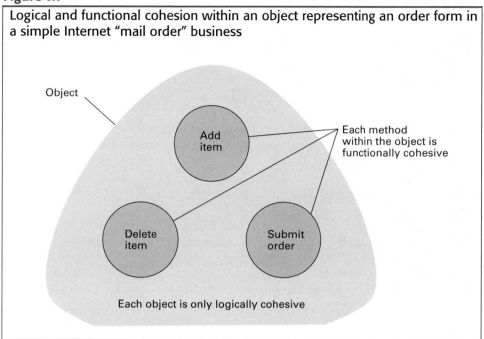

Logical and functional cohesion within an object representing an order form in a simple Internet "mail order" business

Object

Add
item

Delete
item

Submit
order

Each method
within the object is
functionally cohesive

Each object is only logically cohesive

Questions/Exercises

1. How does a novel differ from an encyclopedia in terms of the degree of coupling between its units such as chapters, sections, or entries? What about cohesion?

2. A sporting event is often divided into units. For example, a baseball game is divided into innings and a tennis match is divided into sets. Analyze the coupling between such "modules." In what sense are such units cohesive?

3. Is the goal of maximizing cohesion compatible with minimizing coupling? That is, as cohesion increases, does coupling naturally tend to decrease?

4. Extend the collaboration diagram in Figure 7.6 to include other messages that should be passed between objects of type `Customer` and `Catalogue`.

7.4 Design Methodologies

The development of methodologies for designing software systems is a major quest within software engineering. We have already met some of the topics in this area, including the waterfall model and prototyping. In this section we explore additional topics as well as some directions of current research.

Top-Down Versus Bottom-Up

Perhaps the most well-known strategy associated with system design is the top-down methodology. The point of this methodology is that one should not try to solve a complex problem in a single step. Instead, one should begin by breaking the problem into smaller, more manageable subproblems. Then, one should proceed by breaking these subproblems into still smaller problems. In this manner, a complex problem becomes a collection of simpler problems whose solutions collectively solve the original problem.

The result of top-down design tends to be a hierarchical system of refinements that often can be translated directly into a modular structure that is compatible with the imperative programming paradigm. The solutions to the smallest problems in the hierarchy become procedural modules that perform simple tasks and are used as abstract tools by more superior modules to solve the more complex problems in the system.

In contrast to the top-down design methodology is the bottom-up approach, in which one starts the design of a system by identifying individual tasks within the system and then considers how solutions to these tasks can be used as abstract tools in the solution to more complex problems. For many years, this approach was considered inferior to the top-down design paradigm. Today, however, the bottom-up methodology has gained support. One reason for this shift is that the top-down methodology seeks a solution in which a dominant module uses submodules, each of which relies on subsubmodules, and so on. However, the best design for many systems is not of a hierarchical nature. For example, a design consisting of two or more modules interacting as equals, as exemplified by the client/server model or systems involving general parallel processing applications, may be a better solution than a design consisting of a superior module that relies on subordinates to perform its task.

Another reason for increased interest in bottom-up design is that it is more consistent with the goal of building complex software systems from preconstructed, off-the-shelf components—an approach that is a current trend in software engineering.

Design Patterns

In an effort to find ways by which software can be constructed from off-the-shelf components, software engineers have turned to the field of architecture for inspiration. Of particular interest is the book *A Pattern Language* by Christopher Alexander et al., which describes a set of patterns for designing communities. Each pattern consists of the statement of a problem followed by a proposed solution. The problems are intended to be universal, and the proposed solutions are generic in the sense that they address the universal nature of the problem rather than merely proposing a solution for a particular case.

For example, one pattern, called Quiet Backs, addresses the need to escape the commotion of a business center for short periods of refreshment. The proposed solution is to design "quiet backs" into business districts. In some cases, the district could be designed around a main street to which all buildings face—thus providing for quiet side streets behind the buildings. In other cases, "quiet backs" can be obtained by means of parks, rivers, or cathedrals.

The important point for our discussion is that Alexander's work attempted to identify universal problems and provide templates for solving them. Today, many software engineers are applying this same approach to the design of large software systems. In particular, they are using design patterns as a means of providing generic building blocks with which software systems can be constructed.

It is in this context that the object-oriented programming paradigm is proving especially useful. Since objects form complete, self-contained units that have clearly defined interfaces with their environments, they make perfect candidates for building blocks. Once an object has been designed to fulfill a certain role, it can be used to fulfill that role in any program requiring that service. Moreover, those who read the optional Section 6.5 understand that through inheritance, object-oriented programming environments allow programmers to define new types of objects that extend the properties of previously defined objects. In this sense, then, prefabricated object definitions can be easily customized to conform to the needs of a specific application.

It is not surprising, then, that the object-oriented programming languages C++, Java, and C# are accompanied by collections of prefabricated "templates" from which programmers can easily implement objects for performing certain roles. In particular, C++ is associated with the C++ Standard Template Library; the Java programming environment, provided by Sun Microsystems, is accompanied by the Java Application Programmer Interface (API); and C# programmers have access to the .NET Framework Class Library, provided by Microsoft. All three collections are essentially collections of design patterns that are ultimately implemented as objects.

Yet another step in applying design patterns to software development is the emerging field known as **component architecture** in which software is constructed from units called components that may consist of more than one object. The component architecture model replaces the traditional programmer by a "component assembler" who constructs software systems from components that are often displayed as icons in a graphical interface. Rather than be involved with the internal programming of the components, a component assembler merely selects pertinent components from collections of predefined components and then "connects" them to obtain the desired functionality.

Both Sun Microsystems and Microsoft provide tools with which component assemblers can construct software. In Sun's product, components are called Java Beans, in keeping with the Java theme from which the Java programming language was named. Microsoft's approach is packaged in the software development environment known as .NET (pronounced "dot–NET").

With all the excitement that has been generated in the software engineering community over design patterns and component architecture, it is interesting to note that Alexander was not pleased with the results of his patterns in architecture. In short, he found that the systems designed from his patterns were lacking in character, and his work since the early 1980s has focused on ways to capture this evasive quality. However, software engineers argue that the goal in software development does not involve such qualities as beauty and character, but instead accuracy and efficiency. Thus, they continue, design patterns will prove to be more successful in the field of software engineering than in architecture. The successes achieved thus far strongly support this conjecture.

Open-Source Development

Meaningful advances sometimes develop in cultures outside of the mainstream, where they may evolve into well-defined doctrines before finally being recognized as important contributions by the more formal establishment. For example, jazz is now recognized as a valuable contribution to the world of music, much of modern art was originally scorned by critics, and someday golf may become an Olympic sport.

Such is the case of a rather ad hoc technique for developing software that has been used for years by computer enthusiasts and is now being recognized as a legitimate software development methodology. Actually, the technique is a form of evolutionary prototyping—the distinction being that the prototyping is carried out in a public forum. The methodology is called **open-source development** although a better name might be public evolutionary prototyping.

In a sense, open-source development is an extension of beta testing (Section 7.6)—but it allows the "beta testers" to modify the software and report these modifications rather than merely report problems as in traditional beta testing. The entire process is as follows: The original author writes an initial version of the software (usually to fulfill his or her own needs) and posts the source code and its documentation on the Internet. From there it can be downloaded and used by others. Since these other users have the source code and documentation, they are able to modify or enhance the software to fit their own needs or to correct errors that they find. They report these changes to the original author, who incorporates them into the posted version of the software. This extended version is therefore available for further modifications. In practice, it is possible for a software package to evolve through several extensions in a single week.

Because the participants of open-source development are not organized among themselves and do not receive financial gain, one might think that they would not be dedicated enough to produce large, high-quality software systems. However, this conjecture has proven to be false. The Linux operating system, which is recognized as one of the most reliable operating systems available, is a prime example. In fact, Linus Torvald, the original creator of Linux, could be considered the father of open-source development since it was via this methodology that he guided the early development of Linux.

One problem that keeps open-source development from becoming a more popular software development methodology is that it is difficult for a single entity to maintain ownership of the final product. After all, open-source development requires that the software's source code be widely circulated, making legal controls difficult to enforce.

Another problem is that it has proven difficult for managers trained in the business community to embrace the "hands-off" style that is apparently required to allow open-source development to succeed. Open-source development seems to rely on a free-wheeling environment in which an individual's enthusiasm is nourished by expressing creative skills and achieving an inner feeling of accomplishment and pride. But managers have shown a tendency to exercise a level of control that dampens this enthusiasm. For example, a manager may want to hold back parts of the software system in order to maintain ownership, but open-source development relies on providing complete software systems that an individual will download, use, and ultimately modify according to his or her needs. In other cases a manager may delay the release of new versions of the software to avoid embarrassing errors when, in reality, it is the discovery of such errors that whets the appetite of many open-source contributors.

Regardless of whether open-source development becomes a popular model for developing commercial software, it should be recognized as an existing and viable methodology that deserves the attention of researchers in the field of software engineering. Learning more about what makes open-source development work in some situations yet fail in others should provide insights that contribute to the field at large.

Questions/Exercises

1. Would you be following a top-down methodology if you attempted to solve a picture puzzle merely by pouring the pieces out on a table and trying to piece them together? Would your answer change if you looked at the puzzle box to see what the entire picture was supposed to look like?

2. Identify some software structures that we have discussed in earlier chapters that could be considered design patterns.

3. What role in the software engineering process do design patterns play?

4. What is the difference between a traditional programmer and a component assembler?

5. What is the distinction between traditional evolutionary prototyping and open-source development?

7.5 Tools of the Trade

Software engineering has produced a variety of notational systems to aid in the system analysis and design process. Of these, we have already met structure charts, class diagrams, and collaboration diagrams. Another is the **dataflow diagram,** which is a pictorial representation of the data paths in a system. That is, a dataflow diagram identifies the origin, destination, and processing points of data in a system. The various symbols in such a diagram have specific meanings: Arrows represent data paths, bold lines represent data sources and destinations, circles (fondly called *bubbles* by many software engineers) represent locations of data manipulation, and two parallel straight lines represent data storage. In each case, the symbol is labeled with the name

Figure 7.8

A dataflow diagram of a simple Internet "mail order" business

of the entity represented. A dataflow diagram for our simple Internet "mail-order" business is shown in Figure 7.8.

The dataflow approach to software development originated in the context of the imperative programming paradigm. The idea was that by following the data paths through the proposed system, we discover where data units merge, split, or are otherwise altered. Because computational activity is needed at these locations in the system, such activities, or groupings of activities, should form the procedural modules of the system. Consequently, concentrating on flow of data helps us discover a modular structure for a system.

Although developed with the imperative paradigm in mind, dataflow analysis has found use in object-oriented environments as well. In particular, identifying the items of data in a system helps to identify objects, and identifying changes made to data helps to identify the actions these objects should perform.

Another tool used in the analysis and design of software systems is the **entity-relationship diagram,** which is a pictorial representation of the items of information (entities) within the system and the relationships between these pieces of information. As an example, let us consider part of an entity-relationship diagram for a software system for maintaining information about professors, students, and classes at a university.

We first identify the data entities involved. They include the entity Professor, which we think of as representing a single professor at the university; the entity Student, which represents a single student; and the entity Class, which represents a section of a given course. With each occurrence of the Professor entity is associated a name, address, employee identification number, salary, and so on; with each occurrence of the Student entity is associated a name, address, student identification number, grade point average, and so on; and with each occurrence of the Class entity is associated a course identification (History 101), semester and year, classroom, time of day, and so on.

System Design Tragedies

The need for good design disciplines is exemplified by the problems encountered in the Therac-25, which was a computer-based electron-accelerator radiation-therapy system used by the medical community in the middle 1980s. Flaws in the machine's design contributed to six cases of radiation overdose—three of these resulted in death. The flaws included (1) a poor design for the machine's interface that allowed the operator to begin radiation before the machine had adjusted for the proper dosage, and (2) poor coordination between the design of the hardware and the software that resulted in the absence of certain safety features.

In more recent cases, poor design has led to wide-spread power outages, severance of telephone service, major errors in financial transactions, loss of space probes, and disruption of the Internet. You can learn more about such problems through the Risks Forum (Web page is at http://catless.ncl.as.uk/Risks).

Having identified the entities in our system, we now consider the relationships among the entities. We first note that each professor teaches classes and each student attends classes. We therefore identify the relationship between the entities Professor and Class as the relationship Teaches and that between the entities Student and Class as the relationship Attends. (Note that entities are referred to by nouns, whereas relationships are referenced by verbs.)

To represent these entities and relationships, we use the entity-relationship diagram in Figure 7.9. Here each entity is represented by a rectangle and each relationship is represented by a diamond. The diagram shows that professors are related to classes by means of the relationship Teaches and students are related to classes by means of the relationship Attends.

There is, however, a different structure associated with the two relationships in our example. The relationship between Professor and Class is a **one-to-many relationship** in that each professor teaches several classes but each class is taught by only one professor. In contrast, the relationship between Student and Class is a **many-to-many relationship** because each student attends several classes and each class is attended by several students. Other examples of one-to-many and many-to-many relationships can be found between authors and books. The traditional relationship between authors and novels is a one-to-many relationship since a novelist

Figure 7.9

An entity-relationship diagram

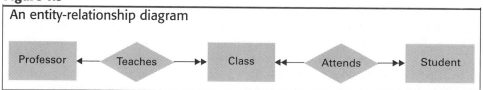

Figure 7.10

One-to-one, one-to-many, and many-to-many relationships between entities of types X and Y

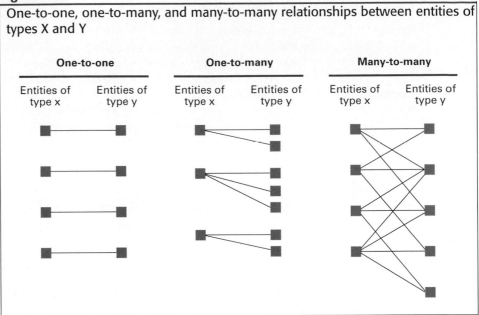

may write many novels but each novel has a single author. On the other hand, the relationship between textbook authors and textbooks is a many-to-many relationship because a single textbook often has multiple authors.

Still another type of relationship is the **one-to-one relationship**, an example of which appears in Figure 7.6. There each Customer is associated with only one OrderForm and each OrderForm is associated with only one Customer. In summary, there are three fundamental types of relationships that may occur among entities—one-to-one, one-to-many (or many-to-one depending on the point of view), and many-to-many, as summarized in Figure 7.10.

The type of each relationship appearing in an entity-relationship diagram is often represented by pointers on the lines connecting relationships to entities. In particular, a single pointer toward an entity indicates that only one occurrence of that entity is involved in each occurrence of the relationship, whereas a double pointer indicates that more than one occurrence of the entity may be involved. Thus the pointer toward the entity Professor in Figure 7.9 indicates that only one professor teaches a class, while the double pointer toward the entity Class in the Teaches relationship indicates that each professor may teach more than one class.

Among the various tools used by software engineers in the past, entity-relationship diagrams appear to be the most likely to survive the shift to object-oriented methodologies. This is because the identification of entities is essentially the identification of objects, and the classification of entity relationships is the first step toward identifying the relationships and communication paths required between objects. Indeed, the traditional entity-relationship diagram is readily recognizable as the predecessor of the UML class diagram (Figure 7.4) used in object-oriented design environments.

Still another tool in the development of a software system is the **data dictionary,** which is a central repository of information about the data items appearing throughout the system. This information includes the identifier used to reference each item; what constitutes valid entries in each item (Will the item always be numeric or perhaps always alphabetic? What will be the range of values that might be assigned to this item?); where the item is stored (Will the item be stored in a file or a database and, if so, which one?); and where the item is referenced in the software (Which modules will require the item's information?).

Several goals are associated with the development of a data dictionary. One is to enhance communication between the potential user of the system and the analyst charged with the task of converting the user's needs into requirements and specifications. It would be discouraging to find, after the system has been implemented, that part numbers are not really numeric or that the size of the inventory exceeds the maximum allowed by the system. The process of constructing a data dictionary helps avoid such misunderstandings.

Another goal associated with the data dictionary is to establish uniformity throughout the system. It is usually by means of constructing the dictionary that redundancies and contradictions surface. For example, the item referred to as `PartNumber` in the inventory records may be the same as the `PartId` in the sales records. Moreover, the personnel department may use the item `Name` to refer to an employee while inventory records may contain the item `Name` in reference to a part.

Finally, we should mention CRC (class-responsibility-collaboration) cards that are useful in the design of object-oriented systems. A CRC card is essentially a traditional index card on which the description of an object is written. The methodology of CRC cards is for the designer to produce a card for each object in the proposed system and then to use the cards to represent the objects in a simulation of the proposed system—perhaps on a desktop or via a "theatrical" experiment in which each member of the design team holds a card and plays the role of the object as described by that card. Such theatrical simulations (often called **structured walkthroughs**) have been found useful in identifying flaws in a design prior to the design's implementation.

Questions/Exercises

1. Suppose that a receptionist receives requests for appointments. The response to a request is either a schedule for a future appointment or an immediate appointment. Draw a dataflow diagram representing this part of the receptionist's job.

2. Draw an entity-relationship diagram representing airline companies, flights flown by each company, and the passengers on the various flights.

3. What would be the distinction between implementing a one-to-one relationship and a one-to-many relationship?

7.6 Testing

In Section 5.6 we discussed techniques for verifying the correctness of algorithms in a mathematically rigorous manner but concluded that most software today is "verified" by means of testing. Unfortunately, testing is an inexact science at best. We cannot declare that a piece of software is correct via testing unless we run enough tests to exhaust all possible scenarios. But, even in simple programs, there are often billions of different paths that may be traversed. Thus, testing all possible paths through a complex program is an impossible task.

On the other hand, software engineers have developed testing methodologies that improve the odds of revealing errors in software, even when all paths cannot be tested. One of these is based on the observation that errors in software tend to be clumped. That is, experience has shown that a small number of modules within a large software system tend to be more problematic than the rest. Thus, by identifying these modules and testing them more thoroughly, more of the system's errors can be discovered than if all modules were tested in a uniform, less-thorough manner. This is an instance of the proposition known as the **Pareto principle,** in reference to the economist and sociologist Vilfredo Pareto (1848–1923) who observed that a small part of Italy's population controlled most of Italy's wealth. In general, the Pareto principle states that results can often be increased most rapidly by applying efforts in a concentrated area.

Another software testing methodology, called **basis path testing,** is to develop a set of test data that insures that each instruction in the software is executed at least once. Techniques using an area of mathematics known as graph theory have been developed for identifying such sets of test data. Thus, although it may be impossible to insure that every path through a software system is tested, it is possible to insure that every statement within the system is executed at least once during the testing process.

Techniques based on the Pareto principle and basis path testing rely on knowledge of the internal composition of the software being tested. They therefore fall within the category called **glass-box testing**—meaning that the software tester is aware of the interior structure of the software and uses this knowledge when designing the test. In contrast is the category called **black-box testing,** which refers to tests that do not rely on knowledge of the software's interior composition. In short, black-box testing is performed from the user's point of view. In black-box testing, one is not concerned with how the software goes about its task but merely with whether the software performs correctly in terms of accuracy and timeliness.

One methodology that is often associated with black-box testing, called **boundary value analysis,** is to identify boundary points within the software's specifications and test the software at these boundary points. For example, if the software is supposed to accept input values within a specified range, then the software would be tested at the lowest and highest values in that range, or if the software is supposed to coordinate multiple activities, then the software would be tested on a collection of the most demanding activities.

Another black-box testing methodology is to apply redundancy. Following this approach, two software systems for performing the same task are developed independently by different teams or even different companies. Then, the two systems are tested by applying them to the same data and comparing their results. Errors are indicted by discrepancies. Such redundancy techniques are often applied in space exploration systems.

Another methodology that falls within the black-box category is being used increasingly by developers of software aimed at the PC market (sometimes referred to as "shrink-wrapped" software in recognition of its packaging). This is to supply a segment of the intended audience with a preliminary version of the software, called a **beta version.** The goal is to learn how the software performs in real-life situations before the final version of the product is solidified and released to the market.

The advantages of such **beta testing** extend far beyond the traditional discovery of errors. General customer feedback (both positive and negative) is obtained that may assist in refining market strategies. Moreover, early distribution of beta software assists other software developers in designing compatible products. For example, in the case of a new operating system, the distribution of a beta version encourages the development of compatible utility software so that the final operating system ultimately appears on store shelves surrounded by companion products. Finally, the existence of beta software can generate a feeling of anticipation within the marketplace—an atmosphere that increases publicity and sales.

Questions/Exercises

1. When testing software, is a successful test one that does or does not find errors?

2. What techniques would you propose using to identify the modules within a system that should receive more thorough testing than others?

3. What would be a good test to perform on a software package that was designed to sort a list of no more than 100 entries?

7.7 Documentation

A software system is of little use unless people can learn to use and maintain it. Hence, documentation is an important part of a software package, and its development is, in turn, an important topic in software engineering.

Documentation of a software package is normally produced for two purposes. One is to explain the features of the software and describe how to use them. This is known as **user documentation** because it is designed to be read by the user of the software. Hence, user documentation tends to be nontechnical.

Today, user documentation is recognized as an important marketing tool. Good user documentation (combined with a well-designed user interface) makes a software package accessible and thus increases its sales. Recognizing this, many software developers hire technical writers to produce this part of their product, or they provide preliminary versions of their products to independent authors so that how-to books are available in book stores when the software itself is released to the public.

User documentation traditionally takes the form of a physical book or booklet, but in many cases the same information is included as part of the software itself. This allows a user to refer to the documentation while using the software. In this case the information may be broken into small units, sometimes called help packages, which may appear on the monitor screen automatically if the user dallies too long between commands.

The other purpose of documentation is to describe the software's internal composition so that the system can be maintained later in its life cycle. Documentation of this type is known as **system documentation** and is inherently more technical than user documentation. A major component of system documentation is the source version of all the programs in the system. It is important that these programs be presented in a readable format, which is why software engineers support the use of well-designed, high-level programming languages, the use of comment statements for annotating a program, and a modular design that allows each module to be presented as a coherent unit. In fact, most companies that produce software products have adopted conventions for their employees to follow when writing programs. These include indentation conventions for organizing a program on the written page, naming conventions to establish a distinction between names of variables, constants, objects, classes, etc., and documentation conventions to ensure that all programs are sufficiently documented. Such conventions establish uniformity throughout a company's software, which ultimately simplifies the software maintenance process.

Another component of system documentation is a record of the design documents describing the system's specifications and how these specifications were obtained. Creating this documentation is an ongoing process that starts with the initial analysis during the software's development. Being an ongoing process, the creation of this documentation leads to a conflict between the goals of software engineering and human nature. It is highly likely that the initial specifications and the initial software design will change during the development process. At issue is the temptation to make these changes without updating the earlier design documents. The result is a strong possibility that the documents will be incorrect and hence their use in the final documentation misleading.

Herein lies an important benefit of CASE tools. They make such tasks as redrawing diagrams and updating data dictionaries much easier than with the older manual methods. Consequently, updates are more likely to be made and the final documentation is more likely to be accurate.

We close by emphasizing that the example of updating documents is only one of many instances in which software engineering must cope with the faults of human nature. Others include the inevitable personality conflicts, jealousies, and ego clashes that arise when people work together. Thus, as we have mentioned before, the subject of software engineering covers much more than those subjects directly associated with computer science.

Questions/Exercises

1. In what forms can software be documented?

2. At what phase (or phases) in the software life cycle is documentation prepared?

3. Which is more important, a program or its documentation?

7.8 Software Ownership and Liability

Most would agree that a company or individual should be allowed to recoup, and profit from, the investment needed to develop quality software. Without a means of protecting this investment, few would be willing to undertake the task of producing the software our society desires. But questions of software ownership and ownership rights can fall between the cracks of well-established copyright and patent laws. These laws were developed to allow the developer of a "product" to release that product to the public while protecting his or her ownership rights, but the characteristics of software have repeatedly challenged the courts in their efforts to apply copyright and patent principles to issues of software ownership.

Copyright laws were originally established to protect an author's rights to literary works. In this case, the value of the product is in how ideas are expressed rather than in the ideas themselves. The value in a poem is in the rhythm, style, and format of the poem rather than the subject matter; the value of a novel is in the author's presentation of the story rather than the story itself. Thus a poet's or a novelist's investment can be protected by giving him or her ownership of that particular expression of the idea, but not the idea itself. Another person is free to express the same idea as long as that expression does not have "substantial similarity" to that of the original.

In short, copyright laws were developed to protect form rather than function, but the value of software is often in its function rather than its form. Thus a straightforward application of copyright law would tend not to protect a software developer's investment. In general, courts have recognized this problem and have been receptive to attempts to give software developers fair protection under existing copyright law. The problem is in establishing the meaning of "substantial similarity" in the case of software.

It would be frivolous to claim that two programs were substantially similar merely because they perform the same task. To do so would lead to the conclusion that there could be only one operating system since the task of any operating system is to coordinate the machine's activities and its allocation of resources. But what if the underlying structure (as represented by structure charts or collaboration diagrams) of two programs is the same? This may or may not indicate plagiarism. If, for example, the common structure was the result of applying a well-known design pattern, then the similarity may merely reflect that both programs were well designed. Likewise, the fact that two programs carry out a task in the same manner may simply reflect the reality that there is an obvious algorithm for the particular application rather than a breach of copyright.

To tackle such problems, courts have applied techniques called filtering to separate similarities that do not indicate copyright infringement from those that may. In terms of software, some of the items that have been argued for filtration (and thus not subject to copyright protection) include features determined by standards, characteristics that are essentially dictated by logical consequences of the program's purpose, and components that are a part of the public domain. (This approach to determining substantial similarity is the fundamental idea behind more precise procedures known in legal jargon as successive filtration and the abstractions test.)

So, if similarities in these areas would not constitute copyright infringement, what type of similarities would? Some plaintiffs have successfully argued that the look and feel of a software system should be protected under copyright law. Although the phrase *look and feel* was not used until 1985, the concept has its roots as early as the 1960s when IBM introduced its System/360 series of computers. This series consisted of a variety of machines ranging from designs for small-business applications to large machines for businesses with significant needs. All these machines were supplied with operating systems that communicated with their environments in essentially the same manner. That is, the entire series of machines had a standardized interface with the user. In turn, as a business grew, it could change to a larger machine in the 360 series without major reprogramming and retraining efforts. Indeed, the look (meaning the appearance projected by the system software) and the feel (meaning the manner in which the user interacted with the system software) were the same for all machines in the 360 series.

Today, the advantages of standardized interfaces are well recognized and sought after throughout the software spectrum. When the interface designed by one company becomes popular, it becomes advantageous for competing companies to design their systems to look and feel like the well-known one. This similarity makes it easier for users of the well-known system to convert to the competitor's system, even though the interior designs of the two systems may be quite different. Companies facing such competitive practices have sought protection under copyright laws by claiming ownership of the look and feel of the original system. After all, the look and feel of a software package has many of the characteristics of the properties protected by copyright laws.

An early test of the look and feel argument was in 1987, when Lotus Development Corporation sued Mosaic Software, claiming that the latter had copied the look and feel of the Lotus 1–2–3 spreadsheet system. The suit was successful. In more recent cases, however, look and feel arguments have met with mixed results. If, for example, a defendant can convince a court that the look and feel of a system is so common that it has become a standard in the public domain, then the look and feel becomes subject to filtration and would not be protected by copyright.

Software is somewhat unique in that it is a commodity to which both copyright and patent law has been applied—a fact that has made courts reluctant at times to interpret copyright protection too broadly for fear of overlapping patent law.

As with copyright, patents also suffer fundamental problems when used to protect software ownership rights. One obstacle is the long-standing principle that no one can own natural phenomena such as laws of physics, mathematical formulas, and thoughts—a collection that, courts have often held, include algorithms. There are, however, increasing numbers of cases in which software developers have successfully obtained patents, one example being the encryption algorithm known as RSA that is heavily used in many of today's public key encryption systems.

Another drawback to the use of patents to protect software ownership rights is that obtaining a patent is an expensive and time-consuming process, often involving several years. During this time a software product could become obsolete, and until the patent is granted the applicant has only questionable authority to exclude others from appropriating the product.

Copyright and patent laws are designed to protect the rights of creators and inventors so that they will be more likely to make their achievements known to the public. In contrast, trade secret laws provide a means of restricting the distribution of ideas. Designed to maintain ethical conduct between competing businesses, these laws protect against improper disclosure or wrongful appropriation of a company's internal accomplishments. Companies often attempt to protect their trade secrets by means of written nondisclosure agreements in which personnel with access to company secrets agree not to disclose their knowledge to others. Courts have generally upheld such agreements.

To protect themselves against liability, software developers often accompany their product with disclaimers in which they state the limitations of their liability. Such statements as "In no event will Company X be liable for any damages arising out of the use of this software" are common. Courts, however, rarely recognize a disclaimer if the plaintiff can show negligence on the part of the defendant. Thus liability cases tend to focus on whether the defendant used a level of care compatible with the product being produced. A level of care that might be deemed acceptable in the case of developing a word processing system may be considered negligent when developing software to control a nuclear reactor. Consequently, one of the best defenses against software liability claims is to apply sound software engineering principles during the software's development, using a level of care compatible with the software's application.

Questions/Exercises

1. What test can be applied to decide whether one program is substantially similar to another?
2. In what ways are copyright, patent, and trade secret laws designed to benefit society?
3. To what extent are disclaimers not recognized by the courts?

Chapter Review Problems

(Asterisked problems are associated with optional sections.)

1. Give an example of how efforts in the development of software can pay dividends later in software maintenance.

2. What is evolutionary prototyping?

3. In each of the following cases identify whether the process more closely follows the waterfall model or the evolutionary prototyping model. Explain your answers.
   a. The construction of a large building.
   b. Learning through scientific research.
   c. Writing a term paper.
   d. Obtaining a formal education in a university.
   e. Obtaining an informal education through life experience.

4. Summarize how the use of CASE tools has changed the software development process.

5. Explain how the lack of metrics for measuring certain software properties affects the software engineering discipline.

6. Suppose you had a metric for measuring the complexity of a software system. Would that metric be cumulative? That is, would the

complexity of a complete system be the sum of the complexities of its parts? Explain your answer.

7. Suppose you had a metric for measuring the complexity of a software system. Would that metric be commutative in the sense that the complexity of a complete system would be the same if it were originally developed with feature X and had feature Y added later or if it were originally developed with feature Y and had feature X added later? Explain your answer.

8. How does software engineering differ from other, more traditional fields of engineering such as electrical and mechanical engineering?

9. a. Identify a disadvantage of the traditional waterfall model for software development.
   b. Identify an advantage of the traditional waterfall model for software development.

10. How does the establishment of codes of ethics and professional conduct aid in the development of quality software?

11. Describe how the use of constants rather than literals can simplify software maintenance.

12. What is the difference between coupling and cohesion? Which should be minimized and which should be maximized? Why?

13. Select an object from everyday life and analyze its components in terms of functional or logical cohesion.

14. Which of the following statements is an argument for coupling, and which is an argument for cohesion:
   a. For a student to learn, the subject should be presented in well-organized units with specific goals.
   b. A student does not really understand a subject until the subject's overall scope and relationship with other subjects has been grasped.

15. In the text, we mentioned control coupling but did not pursue it. Contrast the coupling between two program units obtained by a simple goto statement with the coupling obtained by a procedure call.

*16. In an object-oriented program, what does declaring an instance variable to be public or private indicate about data coupling?

*17. Identify a complication in relation to data coupling that can occur in the context of parallel processing.

18. Answer the following questions in relation to the accompanying structure chart:

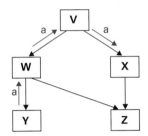

   a. To which module does module Y return control?
   b. To which module does module Z return control?
   c. Are modules W and X linked via control coupling?
   d. Are modules W and X linked via data coupling?
   e. What data is shared by both module W and module Y?
   f. In what way are modules Y and X related?

19. In relation to the structure chart in the previous problem, what stubs are necessary to test module V? What characteristics might these stubs have?

20. Answer the following questions in relation to the accompanying structure chart:

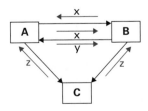

   a. What is different between the way modules A and B use data items x and y?

b. If one of the modules was in charge of obtaining data item z from a user at a remote terminal, which module would that apparently be?

21. Draw a simple class diagram representing the relationship between magazine publishers, magazines, and subscribers.

22. Extend the class diagram you drew for the previous problem to a collaboration diagram.

23. What is the difference between a class diagram and a collaboration diagram?

24. What is UML?

25. It is important to understand that a class diagram represents relationships among classes, which are the templates from which objects are constructed. To clarify the point, suppose there are three customers currently shopping at the Internet mail-order business described in Section 7.3. Using rectangles to represent objects, draw a diagram depicting the objects and their relationships that would be present under the system proposed in Figure 7.4.

26. Using a structure chart, represent the procedural structure of an online inventory/customer records system for a mail-order business. What modules in your system must be modified because of changes in sales tax laws? What if the length of the postal system's ZIP code changes?

27. Design an object-oriented solution to the previous problem and represent it by a class diagram.

28. What problems could arise during the modification stage if a large program was designed in such a way that all of its data elements were global?

29. Identify some design patterns in fields other than architecture and software engineering.

30. Summarize the role of design patterns in software engineering.

31. To what extent are the control structures in a typical high-level programming language (if-then-else, while, etc.) small-scale design patterns?

32. Draw a dataflow diagram depicting the registration process at a university.

33. Contrast the information represented in dataflow diagrams with that given in structure charts.

34. What is the difference between a one-to-many relationship and a many-to-many relationship?

35. Give an example of a one-to-many relationship that is not mentioned in this chapter. Give an example of a many-to-many relationship that is not mentioned in this chapter.

36. Draw an entity-relationship diagram representing the relationships between the cooks, waitresses, customers, and cashiers in a restaurant.

37. Draw an entity-relationship diagram representing the relationships between magazines, publishers of magazines, and subscribers to magazines.

38. In each of the following cases, identify whether the activity relates to a structure chart, a dataflow diagram, an entity-relationship diagram, or a data dictionary.
   a. Identifying the data pertinent to the system to be developed.
   b. Identifying the relationship between the various items of data appearing in the system.
   c. Identifying the characteristics of each item of data in the system.
   d. Identifying which items of data are shared among the various parts of the system.

39. What is the difference between a class diagram and an entity-relationship diagram?

40. Summarize the distinction between top-down and bottom-up design strategies.

41. Which of the following involve the Pareto principle?
   a. One obnoxious person can spoil the party for everyone.
   b. Each radio station concentrates on a particular format such as hard rock music, classical music, or talk.
   c. In an election, candidates are wise to focus their campaigns on the segment of the electorate that has voted in the past.

42. Do software engineers expect large software systems to be homogeneous or heterogeneous in error content? Explain your answer.

43. Basis path testing is a methodology by which every *instruction* in a program is executed at least once. How does this differ from ensuring that every *path* is executed at least once?

44. What is the difference between black-box testing and glass-box testing?

45. Give some analogies of black-box and glass-box testing that occur in fields other than software engineering.

46. How does open-source development differ from beta testing? (Consider glass-box testing versus black-box testing.)

47. Is open-source development a top-down or bottom-up methodology? Explain your answer.

48. Suppose that 100 errors were intentionally placed in a large software system before the system was subjected to final testing. Moreover, suppose that 200 errors were discovered and corrected during this final testing, of which 50 errors were from the group intentionally placed in the system. If the remaining 50 known errors are then corrected, how many unknown errors would you estimate are still in the system? Explain why.

49. In what way do traditional copyright laws fail to safeguard the investments of software developers?

50. In what way do traditional patent laws fail to safeguard the investments of software developers?

Social Issues

The following questions are provided to help you understand some of the ethical/social/legal issues associated with the field of computing. The goal is not merely to answer these questions. You should also consider why you answered as you did and whether your justifications are consistent from one question to the next.

1. a. Mary Analyst has been assigned the task of designing a system with which medical records will be stored on a computer that is connected to a large network. Her concerns regarding security have been overruled for financial reasons, and she has been told to proceed with the project using a security system that she feels is inadequate. What should she do? Why?

   b. Suppose that Mary Analyst developed the system as she was told, and now she is aware that the medical records are being observed by unauthorized personnel. What should she do? To what extent is she liable for the breach of security?

   c. Suppose that instead of obeying her employer, Mary Analyst refuses to proceed with the system and blows the whistle by making the flawed design public, resulting in a financial hardship for the company and the loss of many innocent employees' jobs. Were Mary Analyst's actions correct? What if it turns out that, being only a part of the overall design team, Mary Analyst was unaware that sincere efforts were being made elsewhere within the company to develop a valid security system that would be applied to the system on which Mary was working. How does this change your judgment of Mary's actions? (Remember, Mary's view of the situation is the same as before.)

2. When large software systems are developed by many people, how should liabilities be assigned? Is there a hierarchy of responsibility? Are there degrees of liability?

3. We have seen that large, complex software systems are often developed by many individuals, few of which may have a complete picture of the entire project. Is it ethically proper for an employee to contribute to a project without full knowledge of its function?

4. To what extent is someone responsible for how his or her accomplishments are ultimately applied by others?

5. In the relationship between a computer professional and a client, is it the professional's responsibility to implement the client's desires or to direct the client's desires? What if the professional foresees that a client's desires could lead to unethical consequences? For example, the client may wish to cut corners for the sake of efficiency, but the professional may foresee a potential source of erroneous data or misuse of the system if those shortcuts are taken. If the client insists, is the professional free of responsibility?

6. In many societies free competition is seen as benefiting the public good in that it leads to better products and lower prices. What happens, though, if technology begins to advance so rapidly that new inventions are superseded before the inventor has time to profit from the invention?

7. Is the computer revolution contributing to, or helping to solve, the world's energy problems?

8. Will society continue to find new applications for technology? What, if anything, would reverse society's dependency on technology? What would be the result of a society that continues to find new applications for technology and never reverses that trend?

Additional Reading

Alexander, C., S. Ishikawa, and M. Silverstein. *A Pattern Language*. New York: Oxford Univ. Press, 1977.

Beck, K. *Extreme Programming Explained*. Boston, MA: Addison-Wesley, 2000.

Braude, E. *Software Design: From Programming to Architecture*. New York: Wiley, 2004.

Brooks, F. P. *The Mythical Man-Month*, Anniversary ed. Boston, MA: Addison Wesley Longman, 1995.

Fenton, N. E., and S. L. Pfleeger. *Software Metrics: A Rigorous and Practical Approach*, 2nd ed. Boston, MA: PWS, 1997.

Gamma, E., R. Helm, R. Johnson, and J. Vlissides. *Design Patterns: Elements of Reusable Object-Oriented Software*. Reading, MA: Addison-Wesley, 1995.

Pfleeger, S. L. *Software Engineering: Theory and Practice*, 2nd ed. Upper Saddle River, NJ: Prentice-Hall, 2001.

Pooley, R., and P. Stevens. *Using UML: Software Engineering with Objects and Components*, revised ed. Reading, MA: Addison-Wesley, 2000.

Pressman, R. S. *Software Engineering: A Practitioner's Approach*, 5th ed. New York: McGraw-Hill, 2001.

Schach, S. R. *Classical and Object-Oriented Software Engineering*, 5th ed. New York: McGraw-Hill, 2002.

Sommerville, I. *Software Engineering*, 6th ed. Reading, MA: Addison-Wesley, 2001.

CHAPTER 8

Data Abstractions

A computer's main memory is organized as individual cells identified by consecutive addresses. However, it is often convenient to associate other arrangements with these cells. For example, weekly sales records are more naturally viewed in a tabular form in which sales of different items on different days are arranged in rows and columns. In this chapter we consider how such organizations are simulated within a machine's main memory. The goal is to allow the user of the data to think in terms of abstract organizations rather than the data's actual organization.

8.1 Data Structure Fundamentals

We begin this chapter by introducing some basic data structures and then isolating three fundamental topics associated with their study: abstraction, the distinction between static and dynamic structures, and the concept of a pointer.

Basic Data Structures

We introduced the concept of data structure in Section 6.2 where we learned that the term refers to the conceptual organization of data. There we also learned about the data structure known as a homogeneous array. Recall that a **homogeneous array** is a "rectangular" block of data whose entries are of the same type. In particular, a two-dimensional homogeneous array consists of rows and columns in which positions are identified by pairs of indices—the first index identifies the row associated with the position, the second index identifies the column.

Other basic data structures that will serve as useful examples in this chapter include lists and trees. A **list** is a collection of data whose entries are arranged sequentially. The beginning of a list is called the **head** of the list. The end of a list is called the **tail.** Examples include guest lists, shopping lists, class enrollment lists, and inventory lists.

There are two special types of lists known as stacks and queues. A **stack** is a list in which entries are removed and inserted only at the head (an analogy being a stack of books on a table). Thus the last entry placed in a stack will always be the first entry removed—an observation that leads to stacks being known as **last-in, first-out (LIFO)** structures. The head of a stack is called the **top** of the stack. The tail of a stack is called its **bottom** or **base**. Removing an entry from the top of a stack is called **popping** an entry. Inserting a new entry at the top of a stack is called **pushing** an entry.

A **queue** is a list in which entries are removed at the head and new entries are inserted at the tail (an analogy being a queue, or line, of people waiting to buy tickets at the theater). Thus, in contrast to stacks, the first entry inserted in the queue will be the first entry removed, meaning that queues are **first-in, first-out (FIFO)** structures.

Figure 8.1

An example of an organization chart

Finally, a **tree** is a collection of data whose entries have a hierarchical organization similar to that of an organization chart of a typical company (Figure 8.1). Here, the president is represented at the top, with lines branching down to the vice presidents, who are followed by regional managers, and so on. To this intuitive definition of a tree structure we impose one additional constraint, which (in terms of an organization chart) is that no individual in the company reports to two different superiors. That is, different branches of the organization do not merge at a lower level. (We have already seen examples of trees in Chapter 6 where they appeared in the form of parse trees.)

Each position in a tree is called a **node** (Figure 8.2). The node at the top is called the **root node** (if we turned the drawing upside down, this node would represent the base or root of the tree). The nodes at the other extreme are called **terminal nodes** (or sometimes **leaf nodes**). If we select any node in a tree, we find that this node together with those nodes below it also have the structure of a tree. We call these smaller structures **subtrees.** At times we refer to tree structures as though each node gives birth to those nodes immediately below it. In this sense, we often speak of a node's ancestors or descendants. We refer to its immediate descendants as its **children** and its immediate ancestor as its **parent.** Moreover, we speak of nodes with the same parent as being **siblings.** A tree in which each parent has no more than two children is called a **binary tree.** Finally, we often refer to the number of nodes in the longest path from the root to a leaf as the **depth** of the tree. In other words, the depth of a tree is the number of horizontal layers within it.

Figure 8.2

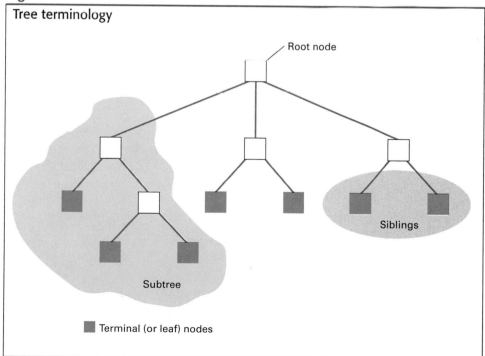

Tree terminology

Root node

Siblings

Subtree

■ Terminal (or leaf) nodes

Abstraction Again

The data structures defined above are structures that are often associated with data stored in a computer's main memory. However, a computer's main memory is not organized as stacks, queues, and trees but is instead organized sequentially as a collection of addressable cells. Thus, all other structures must be simulated. How this simulation is accomplished is the subject of this chapter. For now we merely point out that organizations such as stacks, queues, and trees are abstract tools that are created so that users of the data can be shielded from the details of actual data storage (memory cells and addresses) and can be allowed to access information as though it were stored in a more convenient form.

The term *user* in this context does not necessarily refer to a human; instead, the meaning of the word depends on our perspective at the time. If we are thinking in terms of a person using a PC to maintain bowling league records, then the user is a human. In this case, the application software would be responsible for presenting the data in an abstract form convenient to the human—perhaps as a collection of tables. If we are thinking in terms of a server on the Internet, then the user might be a client. In this case, the server would be responsible for presenting data in an abstract form convenient to the client. If we are thinking in terms of the modular structure of a program, then the user would be any module requiring access to the data. In this case, the module containing the data would be responsible for presenting the data in an abstract form convenient to the other modules. In each of these scenarios, the common thread is that the user, regardless of its constitution, has the privilege of accessing data as an abstract tool.

Static Versus Dynamic Structures

An important distinction when constructing abstract organizations of data is whether the structure being simulated is static or dynamic—whether the shape or size of the structure changes over time. For example, if the abstract tool is a list of names, it is important to consider whether the list will remain a fixed size throughout its existence or expand and shrink as names are added and deleted.

As a general rule, static structures are more easily managed than dynamic ones. If a structure is static, we need merely to provide a means of accessing the various data items in the structure and perhaps a means of changing the values at designated locations. But, if the structure is dynamic, we must also deal with the problems of adding and deleting data entries as well as finding the memory space required by a growing data structure. In the case of a poorly designed structure, excessive growth could dictate that the entire structure be transferred to another memory area where more space is available—a process that could be time consuming.

Pointers

Recall that the various cells in a machine's main memory are identified by numeric addresses. Being numeric values, these addresses themselves can be encoded and stored in memory cells. A **pointer** is a storage area that contains the address in memory at which a piece of information is stored. In the case of data structures, pointers are used to record the location where data items are stored. That is, if at one memory location (a pointer) we store the address at which an item of data is located, then

Figure 8.3

Novels arranged by title but linked according to authorship

the contents of that pointer can be used later to find and retrieve the item. In a sense, the pointer points to the data.

We have already encountered the concept of a pointer in our study of CPUs in Chapter 2. There we found that a register called a program counter is used to hold the address of the next instruction to be executed. Thus, the program counter plays the role of a pointer. In fact, another name for a program counter is **instruction pointer.** The URLs used to link hypertext documents can also be considered examples of the pointer concept, except that URLs are pointers to locations on the Internet rather than to locations in main memory.

As an example of the application of pointers, suppose we have a list of novels stored in a computer's memory alphabetically by title. Although convenient in many applications, this arrangement makes it difficult to find all the novels by a particular author, because they are scattered throughout the list. To solve this problem, we can reserve an additional memory cell within each block of cells representing a novel and use this cell as a pointer to another block representing a book by the same author. In this manner the novels with common authorship can be linked in a loop (Figure 8.3). Once we find one novel by a given author, then we can find all the others by following the pointers from one book to another.

Many modern programming languages include pointers as a primitive data type. That is, they allow the declaration, allocation, and manipulation of pointers, in ways reminiscent of integers and character strings. Using such a language, a programmer can design elaborate networks of data within a machine's memory where pointers are used to link related items to each other.

Questions/Exercises

1. Give examples (outside of computer science) of each of the following structures: list, stack, queue, and tree.

2. Suppose a tree has four nodes A, B, C, and D. If A and C are siblings and D's parent is A, which nodes are leaf nodes? Which node is the root?

3. Describe an application that you would expect to involve a static data structure. Then describe an application that you would expect to involve a dynamic data structure.

4. Describe contexts outside of computer science in which the pointer concept occurs.

8.2 Implementing Data Structures

Let us now consider ways in which the data structures introduced in the previous section can be stored in a computer's main memory.

Storing Homogeneous Arrays

Suppose we want to store and manipulate a sequence of 24 hourly temperature readings, each of which requires one memory cell of storage space. Moreover, suppose we want to identify these readings by their positions in the sequence. That is, we want to be able to access the first reading or the fifth reading. In short, we want to manipulate the sequence as though it were a one-dimensional array.

We can obtain this goal merely by storing the readings in a sequence of 24 memory cells with consecutive addresses. Then, if the address of the first cell in the sequence is x, the location of any particular temperature reading can be computed by subtracting one from the index of the desired reading and then adding the result to x. In particular, the fourth reading would be located at address $x + (4 - 1)$, as shown in Figure 8.4.

This technique is used by most translators of high-level programming languages. When the translator encounters a declaration statement such as

```
int Readings[24];
```

declaring that the term `readings` is to refer to a one-dimensional array of integer values, then the translator arranges for 24 consecutive memory cells to be set aside. Later, if it encounters the assignment statement

```
Readings[4] ← 67;
```

requesting that the value 67 be placed in the fourth entry of the array `Readings`, it builds the sequence of machine instructions required to place the value 67 in the memory cell at address $x + (4 - 1)$, where x is the address of the first cell in the block associated with the array `readings`. In this manner, the programmer is allowed to

Figure 8.4

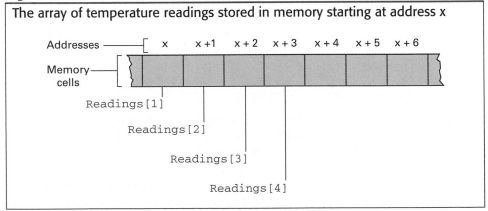

The array of temperature readings stored in memory starting at address x

write the program as though the temperature readings were actually stored in a one-dimensional array. (Caution: In the languages C, C++, C#, and Java, the fourth reading is referenced by `Readings[3]`. See Question/Exercise 3 at the end of this section.

Now suppose we want to record the sales made by a company's sales force during a one-week period. In this case, we might envision the data arranged in a two-dimensional array, where the values across each row indicate the sales made by a particular employee, and the values down a column represent all the sales made during a particular day.

To accommodate this need, we first recognize that the array is static in the sense that its size does not vary as updates are made. We can therefore calculate the amount of storage area needed for the entire array and reserve a block of contiguous memory cells of that size. Next, we store the data in the array row by row. Starting at the first cell of the reserved block, we store the values from the first row of the array into consecutive memory locations; following this, we store the next row, then the next, and so on (Figure 8.5). Such a storage system is said to use **row major order** in contrast to **column major order,** in which the array is stored column by column.

With the data stored in this manner, let us consider how we could find the value in the third row and fourth column of the array. Envision that we are at the first location in the reserved block of memory. Starting at this location, we find the data in the first row of the array followed by the second, then the third, and so on. To get to the third row, we must move beyond both the first and second rows. Since each row contains five entries (one for each day of the week from Monday through Friday), we must move beyond a total of 10 entries to reach the first entry of the third row. From there, we must move beyond another three entries to reach the entry in the fourth column of the row. Altogether, to reach the entry in the third row and fourth column, we must move beyond 13 entries from the beginning of the block.

Figure 8.5

A two-dimensional array with four rows and five columns stored in row major order

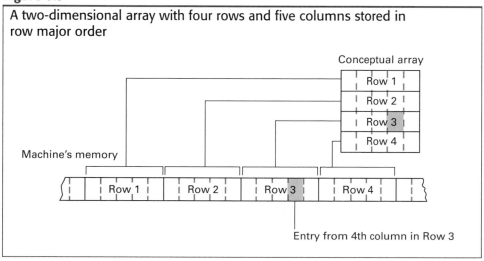

Implementing Contiguous Lists

The primitives for constructing and manipulating arrays that are provided in most high-level programming languages are convenient tools for constructing and manipulating contiguous lists. If the entries of the list are all the same primitive data type, then the list is nothing more than a one-dimensional homogeneous array. A slightly more involved example is a list of ten names, each of which is no longer than eight characters, as discussed in the text. In this case, a programmer could construct the contiguous list as a two-dimensional array of characters with ten rows and eight columns, which would produce the structure represented in Figure 8.6 (assuming that the array is stored in row-major order).

Many high-level languages incorporate features that encourage such implementations of lists. For example, if the two-dimensional array of characters proposed above were called `MemberList`, then the expression `MemberList[3, 5]` normally would refer to the single character in the third row and fifth column, but some languages use the expression `MemberList[3]` to refer to the entire third row, which would be the third entry in the list.

The preceding calculation can be generalized to obtain a formula for converting references in terms of row and column positions into actual memory addresses. In particular, if we let c represent the number of columns in an array (which is the number of entries in each row), then the address of the entry in the ith row and jth column will be

$$x + (c \times (i - 1)) + (j - 1)$$

where x is the address of the cell containing the entry in the first row and first column. That is, we must move beyond $i - 1$ rows, each of which contains c entries, to reach the ith row and then $j - 1$ more entries to reach the jth entry in this row. In our prior example $c = 5$, $i = 3$, and $j = 4$, so if the array were stored starting at address x, then the entry in the third row, fourth column would be at address $x + (5 \times (3 - 1)) + (4 - 1) = x + 13$. The expression $(c \times (i - 1)) + (j - 1)$ is sometimes called the **address polynomial.**

Once again, this is the technique used by most translators of high-level programming languages. When faced with the declaration statement

```
int Sales[8, 5];
```

declaring that the term `Sales` is to refer to a two-dimensional array of integer values with 8 rows and 5 columns, the translator arranges for 40 consecutive memory cells to be set aside. Later, if it encounters the assignment statement

```
Sales[3, 4] ← 5;
```

requesting that the value 5 be placed in the entry at the third row and fourth column of the array `Sales`, it builds the sequence of machine instructions required to place the value 5 in the memory cell whose address is $x + 5(3 - 1) + (4 - 1)$, where x is the address of the first cell in the block associated with the array `Sales`. In this manner, the programmer is allowed to write the program as though the sales were actually stored in a two-dimensional array.

Storing Lists

Let us now consider techniques for storing a list of names in a computer's main memory. One strategy is to store the entire list in a single block of memory cells with consecutive addresses. Assuming that each name is no longer than eight letters, we can divide the large block of cells into a collection of subblocks, each containing eight cells. Into each subblock we can store a name by recording its ASCII code using one cell per letter. If the name alone does not fill all the cells in the subblock allocated to it, we can merely fill the remaining cells with the ASCII code for a space. Using this system requires a block of 80 consecutive memory cells to store a list of 10 names.

The storage system just described is summarized in Figure 8.6. The significant point is that the entire list is stored in one large block of memory, with successive entries following each other in contiguous memory cells. Such an organization is referred to as a **contiguous list.**

A contiguous list is a convenient storage structure for implementing static lists but has disadvantages in the case of dynamic lists where the deletion and insertion of names can lead to a time consuming shuffling of entries. In a worst case scenario, the addition of entries could create the need to move the entire list to a new location to obtain an available block of contiguous cells large enough for the expanded list.

These problems can be simplified if we allow the individual entries in a list to be stored in different areas of memory rather than together in one large, contiguous block. To explain, let us reconsider our example of storing a list of names (where each name is no more than eight characters long). This time we store each name in a block of nine contiguous memory cells. The first eight of these cells are used to hold the name itself, and the last cell is used as a pointer to the next name in the list. Following this lead, the list can be scattered among several small nine-cell blocks linked together by pointers. Because of this linkage system, such an organization is called a **linked list.**

Figure 8.6

Names stored in memory as a contiguous list

Contiguous block of memory cells

First name stored here

Second name stored here

Last name stored here

Figure 8.7

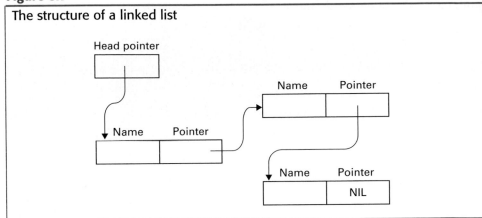

The structure of a linked list

To keep track of the beginning of a linked list, we set aside another pointer in which we save the address of the first entry. Since this pointer points to the beginning, or head, of the list, it is called the **head pointer.**

To mark the end of a linked list, we use a **NIL pointer,** which is merely a special bit pattern placed in the pointer cell of the last entry to indicate that no further entries are in the list. For example, if we agree never to store a list entry at address 0, the value zero will never appear as a legitimate pointer value and can therefore be used as the NIL pointer.

The final linked list structure is represented by the diagram in Figure 8.7, in which we depict the scattered blocks of memory used for the list by individual rectangles. Each rectangle is labeled to indicate its composition. Each pointer is represented by an arrow that leads from the pointer itself to the pointer's addressee. Traversing the list involves following the head pointer to find the first entry. From

Figure 8.8

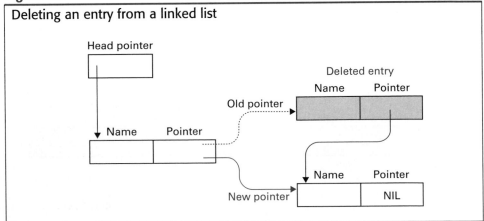

Deleting an entry from a linked list

there, we follow the pointers stored with the entries to hop from one entry to the next until the NIL pointer is reached.

To appreciate the advantages of a linked list over a contiguous one, consider the task of deleting an entry. In a contiguous list this would create a hole that must be filled by moving other entries. However, in the case of a linked list, an entry can be deleted by changing a single pointer. This is done by changing the pointer that formerly pointed to the deleted entry so that it points to the entry following the deleted entry (Figure 8.8). From then on, when the list is traversed, the deleted entry is passed by because it no longer is part of the chain.

Inserting a new entry in a linked list is only a little more involved. We first find an unused block of memory cells large enough to hold the new entry and a pointer. Here we store the new entry and fill in the pointer with the address of the entry in the list that should follow the new entry. Finally, we change the pointer associated with the entry that should precede the new entry so that it points to the new entry (Figure 8.9). After we make this change, the new entry will be found in the proper place each time the list is traversed.

Storing Stacks and Queues

When storing stacks and queues, an organization similar to a contiguous list is often used. In the case of a stack, a block of contiguous memory cells large enough to accommodate the stack when it grows and shrinks is reserved. (Determining the size of this block can often be a critical decision. If too little room is reserved, the stack ultimately exceeds the allotted storage space; however, if too much room is reserved, memory space will be wasted.) One end of this block is designated as the stack's base. It is here that the first entry pushed on the stack is stored, with each additional entry placed next to its predecessor as the stack grows toward the other end of the reserved block.

Figure 8.9

Inserting an entry into a linked list

Figure 8.10

A stack in memory

Observe that as entries are pushed and popped, the location of the top of the stack will move back and forth within the reserved block of memory cells. To keep track of this location, its address is stored in an additional memory cell known as the **stack pointer.** That is, the stack pointer is a pointer to the top of the stack.

Figure 8.11

A queue implementation with head and tail pointers. Note how the queue crawls through memory as entries are inserted and removed.

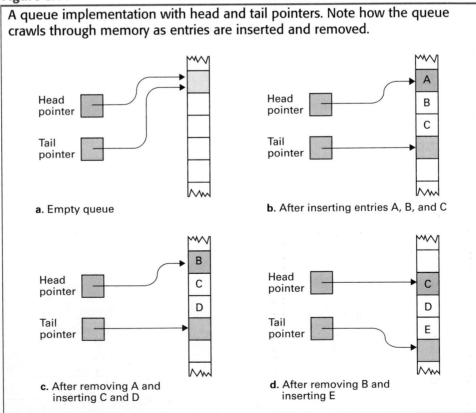

A Problem with Pointers

Just as the use of flowcharts led to tangled algorithm designs (Chapter 5), and the haphazard use of `goto` statements led to poorly designed programs (Chapter 6), undisciplined use of pointers has been found to produce needlessly complex and error-prone data structures. To bring order to this chaos, many programming languages restrict the flexibility of pointers. For example, Java does not allow pointers in their general form. Instead, it allows only a restricted form of pointers called references. One distinction is that a reference cannot be modified by an arithmetic operation. For example, if a Java programmer wanted to advance the reference `Next` to the next entry in a contiguous list, he or she would use a statement equivalent to

        redirect Next to the next list entry

whereas a C programmer would use a statement equivalent to

        assign Next the value Next + 1.

Note that the Java statement better reflects the underlying goal. Moreover, to execute the Java statement, there must be another list entry, but if `Next` already pointed to the last entry in the list, the C statement would result in `Next` pointing to something outside the list—a common error for beginning, and even seasoned, C programmers.

The complete system, as illustrated in Figure 8.10, works as follows: To push a new entry on the stack, we first adjust the stack pointer to point to the vacancy just beyond the top of the stack and then place the new entry at this location. To pop an entry from the stack, we read the data pointed to by the stack pointer and then adjust the pointer to point to the next entry down on the stack.

The traditional implementation of a queue is similar to that of a stack. Again we reserve a block of contiguous cells in the machine's main memory large enough to hold the queue at its projected maximum size. However, in the case of a queue we need to perform operations at both ends of the structure, so we set aside two memory cells to use as pointers instead of only one as we did for a stack. One of these pointers, called the **head pointer,** keeps track of the head of the queue; the other, called the **tail pointer,** keeps track of the tail. When the queue is empty, both of these pointers point to the same location (Figure 8.11). Each time an entry is inserted, it is placed in the location pointed to by the tail pointer, and then the tail pointer is adjusted to point toward the next unused location. In this manner, the tail pointer is always pointing to the first vacancy at the tail of the queue. Removing an entry from the queue involves extracting the entry pointed to by the head pointer and then adjusting the head pointer to point toward the next entry in the queue.

A problem with the storage system as described thus far is that, as entries are inserted and removed, the queue crawls slowly through memory like a glacier (see again Figure 8.11). Thus we need a mechanism for containing the queue within its reserved block of memory. The solution is simple. We let the queue migrate toward the other end of the block. When the tail of the queue reaches the end of the block, we start inserting additional entries back at the original end of the block, which by this time is vacant. Likewise, when the last entry in the block finally becomes the head of the queue and this entry is removed, the head pointer is adjusted back to the beginning of the block where other entries are, by this time, waiting. In this manner, the queue chases itself around within the block rather than wandering off through memory. This technique results in an implementation that is called a **circular queue.**

Storing Binary Trees

For the purpose of discussing tree storage techniques, we restrict our attention to binary trees, which we recall are trees in which each node has at most two children. Such trees normally are stored in memory using a linked structure similar to that of linked lists. However, rather than each entry consisting of two components (the data followed by a next-entry pointer), each entry (or node) of the binary tree contains three components: (1) the data, (2) a pointer to the node's first child, and (3) a pointer to the node's second child. Although there is no left or right inside a machine, it is helpful to refer to the first pointer as the **left child pointer** and the other pointer as the **right child pointer** in reference to the way we would draw the tree on paper. Thus each node of the tree is represented by a short, contiguous block of memory cells with the format shown in Figure 8.12.

Storing the tree in memory involves finding available blocks of memory cells to hold the nodes and linking these nodes according to the desired tree structure. Each pointer must be set to point to the left or right child of the pertinent node or assigned the NIL value if there are no more nodes in that direction of the tree. (This means that a terminal node is characterized by having both of its pointers assigned NIL.) Finally, we set aside a special memory location, called a **root pointer,** where we store the address of the root node. It is this root pointer that provides initial access to the tree.

An example of this linked storage system is presented in Figure 8.13, where a conceptual binary tree structure is exhibited along with a representation of how that tree might actually appear in a computer's memory. Note that the actual arrangement of the nodes within main memory may be quite different from the conceptual arrangement within the tree. However, by following the root pointer, one can find the root node and then trace any path down the tree by following the appropriate pointers from node to node.

Figure 8.12

The structure of a node in a binary tree

| Cells containing the data | Left child pointer | Right child pointer |

Figure 8.13

The conceptual and actual organization of a binary tree using a linked storage system

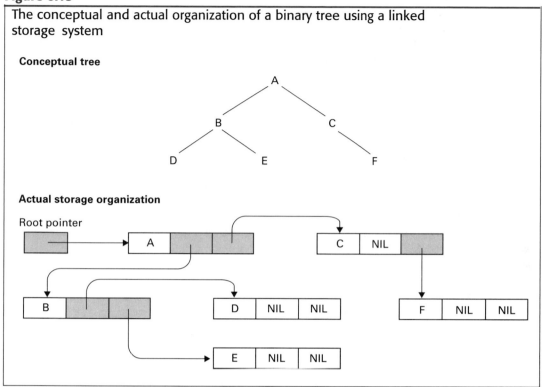

An alternative to storing a binary tree as a linked structure is to use a single, contiguous block of memory cells for the entire tree. Using this approach, we store the tree's root node in the first cell of the block. (For simplicity, we assume that each node of the tree requires only one memory cell.) Then we store the left child of the root in the second cell, store the right child of the root in the third cell, and in general, continue to store the left and right children of the node found in cell n in the cells $2n$ and $2n + 1$, respectively. Cells within the block that represent locations not used by the tree are marked with a unique bit pattern that indicates the absence of data. Using this technique, the same tree shown in Figure 8.13 would be stored as shown in Figure 8.14. Note that the system is essentially that of storing the nodes across successively lower levels of the tree as segments, one after the other. That is, the first entry in the block is the root node, followed by the root's children, followed by the root's grandchildren, and so on.

In contrast to the linked structure described earlier, this alternative storage system provides an efficient method for finding the parent or sibling of any node. The location of a node's parent can be found by dividing the node's position in the block by 2 while discarding any remainder (the parent of the node in position 7 would be the node in position 3). The location of a node's sibling can be found by adding 1 to

Figure 8.14

A tree stored without pointers

the location of a node in an even-numbered position or subtracting 1 from the location of a node in an odd-numbered position. For example, the sibling of the node in position 4 is the node in position 5, while the sibling of the node in position 3 is the node in position 2. Moreover, this storage system makes efficient use of space when the binary tree is approximately balanced (in the sense that both subtrees below the root node have the same depth) and full (in the sense that they do not have long, thin branches). For trees without these characteristics, though, the system can become quite inefficient, as shown in Figure 8.15.

Manipulating Data Structures

In this section, we have seen that the way data structures are actually stored in a computer's memory is not the same as the conceptual structure envisioned by the user. A two-dimensional array is not actually stored as a two-dimensional rectangular block; a stack is not actually stored as stack; and a list or a tree may actually consist of small pieces scattered over a large area of memory.

Hence, to allow the user to access the structure as an abstract tool, we must shield the user from the complexities of the actual storage system. In the case of homogeneous arrays, we have seen how a translator accomplishes this by using the address polynomial to convert references in terms of rows and columns into memory cell addresses. In the case of lists, stacks, queues, and trees, we can complete the abstract tool by providing procedures that perform tasks such as inserting new entries and deleting old entries.

Figure 8.15

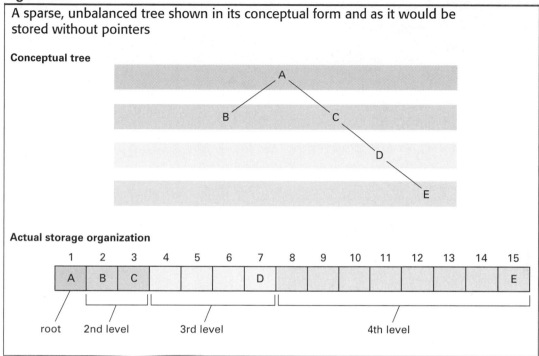

A sparse, unbalanced tree shown in its conceptual form and as it would be stored without pointers

Each of these procedures performs its task while shielding the user from the details of the underlying storage system. For example, J. W. Brown could be inserted in the list of students enrolled in Physics 208 merely by executing a procedure call such as

```
insert("Brown, J.W.", Physics208)
```

or the value 253 could be pushed on a stack called PagesToCheck using

```
push(253, PagesToCheck)
```

As a more detailed example, Figure 8.16 presents a procedure named PrintList for printing a linked list of names. This procedure assumes that the first entry of the list

Figure 8.16

A procedure for printing a linked list

```
procedure PrintList (List)
CurrentPointer ← head pointer of List.
while (CurrentPointer is not NIL) do
   (Print the name in the entry pointed to by CurrentPointer;
    Observe the value in the pointer cell of the List entry
    pointed to by CurrentPointer, and reassign CurrentPointer
    to be that value.)
```

is pointed to by a pointer called the head pointer and that each entry in the list consists of two pieces: a name and a pointer to the next entry. Once this procedure has been developed, it can be used to print a linked list as an abstract tool without being concerned for the steps actually required to print the list. For example, to obtain a printed class list for Economics 301, a user need only perform the procedure call

```
PrintList (Economics301)
```

to obtain the desired results.

Questions/Exercises

1. Show how the array below would be arranged in main memory when stored in row major order.

5	3	7
4	2	8
1	9	6

2. Give a formula for finding the entry in the ith row and jth column of a two-dimensional array if it is stored in column major order rather than row major order.

3. In the C, C++, and Java programming languages, indices of arrays start at 0 rather than at 1. Thus the entry in the first row, fourth column of an array named Array is referenced by Array[0][3]. In this case, what address polynomial is used by the translator to convert references of the form Array[i][j] into memory addresses?

4. What condition indicates that a linked list is empty?

5. Modify the procedure in Figure 8.16 so that it stops printing once a particular name has been printed.

6. Based on the technique of this section for implementing a stack in a contiguous block of cells, what condition indicates that the stack is empty?

7. Describe how a stack can be implemented in a high-level language in terms of a one-dimensional array.

8. When a queue is implemented in a circular fashion as described in this section, what is the relationship between the head and tail pointers when the queue is empty? What about when the queue is full? How can one detect whether a queue is full or empty?

9. Draw a diagram representing how the tree below appears in memory when stored using the left and right child pointers, as described in this section. Then, draw another diagram

showing how the tree would appear in contiguous storage using the alternative storage system described in this section.

8.3 A Short Case Study

Let us consider a case study involving the storage of a list of names in alphabetical order. We assume that the operations to be performed on this list are the following:

search for the presence of an entry,
print the list in alphabetical order, and
insert a new entry

Our goal is to develop a storage system along with a collection of procedures to perform these operations—thus producing a complete abstract tool.

We begin by considering options for storing the list. If the list were stored according to the linked list model, we would need to search the list in a sequential fashion, a process that, as we discussed in Chapter 5, could be very inefficient if the list becomes long. We will therefore seek an implementation that allows us to use the binary search algorithm (Chapter 5) for our search procedure. To apply this algorithm, our storage system must allow us to find the middle entry of successively smaller portions of the list. Our solution is to store the list as a binary tree. We make (1) the middle list entry the root node, (2) the middle of the remaining first half of the list the root's left child, and (3) the middle of the remaining second half the root's right child. The middle entries of each remaining fourth of the list become the children of the root's children and so forth. For example, the tree in Figure 8.17 represents the list of letters A, B, C, D, E, F, G, H, I, J, K, L, and M. (We consider the larger of the middle two entries as the middle when the part of the list in question contains an even number of entries.)

Figure 8.17

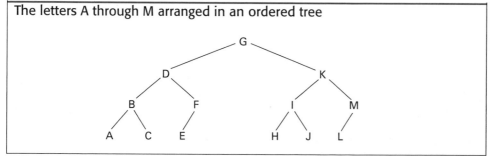

The letters A through M arranged in an ordered tree

Figure 8.18

The binary search as it would appear if the list were implemented as a linked binary tree

```
procedure Search(Tree, TargetValue)

if (root pointer of Tree = NIL)
  then
    (declare the search a failure)
  else
    (execute the block of instructions below that is
    associated with the appropriate case)
    case 1: TargetValue = value of root node
        (Report that the search succeeded)
    case 2: TargetValue < value of root node
        (Apply the procedure Search to see if
          TargetValue is in the subtree identified
          by the root's left child pointer and
          report the result of that search)
    case 3: TargetValue > value of root node
        (Apply the procedure Search to see if
          TargetValue is in the subtree identified
          by the root's right child pointer and
          report the result of that search)
  ) end if
```

To search the list stored in this manner, we compare the target value to the root node. If the two are equal, our search has succeeded. If they are not equal, we move to the left or right child of the root, depending on whether the target is less than or greater than the root, respectively. There we find the middle of the portion of the list that is necessary to continue the search. This process of comparing and moving to a child continues until we find the target value (meaning that our search was successful) or we reach a NIL pointer without finding the target value (meaning that our search was a failure).

Figure 8.18 shows how this search process can be expressed in the case of a linked tree structure. Note that this procedure is merely a refinement of the procedure in Figure 5.14, which is our original statement of the binary search. The distinction is largely cosmetic. Instead of stating the algorithm in terms of searching successively smaller segments of the list, we now state the algorithm in terms of searching successively smaller subtrees (Figure 8.19).

Having stored our "list" as a binary tree, you may think that the process of printing the list in alphabetical order would now be difficult. However, to print the list in alphabetical order, we merely need to print the left subtree in alphabetical order, print the root node, and then print the right subtree in alphabetical order (Figure 8.20). After all, the left subtree contains those elements that are less than the root node, while the right subtree contains the elements larger than the root. A sketch of our logic so far looks like this:

```
if (tree not empty)
then (print the left subtree in alphabetical order;
        print the root node;
        print the right subtree in alphabetical order)
```

Figure 8.19

The successively smaller trees considered by the procedure in Figure 8.18 when searching for the letter J

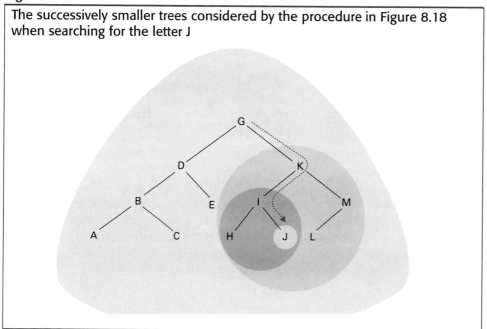

This outline involves the tasks of printing the left subtree and the right subtree in alphabetical order, both of which are essentially smaller versions of our original task. That is, solving the problem of printing a tree involves the smaller task of printing subtrees, which suggests a recursive approach to our tree printing problem.

Figure 8.20

Printing a search tree in alphabetical order

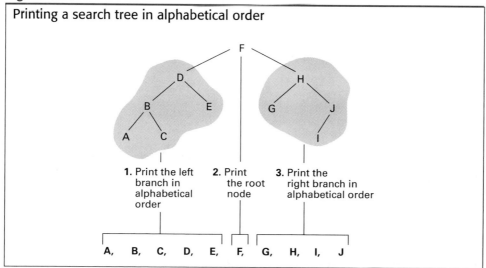

Figure 8.21

A procedure for printing the data in a binary tree

procedure PrintTree (Tree)

if (Tree is not empty)
    then (Apply the procedure PrintTree to the tree that
               appears as the left branch in Tree;
           Print the root node of Tree;
           Apply the procedure PrintTree to the tree that
               appears as the right branch in Tree)

Following this lead, we can expand our initial idea into a complete pseudocode procedure for printing our tree as shown in Figure 8.21. We have assigned the routine the name **PrintTree** and then requested the services of **PrintTree** for printing the left and right subtrees. Note that the termination condition of the recursive process (reaching an empty subtree) is guaranteed to be reached, because each successive activation of the routine operates on a smaller tree than the one causing the activation.

Figure 8.22

Inserting the entry M into the list B, E, G, H, J, K, N, P stored as a tree

a. Search for the new entry until its absence is detected

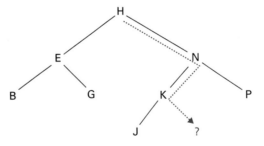

b. This is the position in which the new entry should be attached

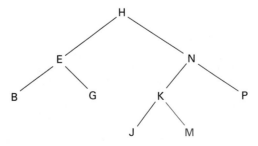

The task of inserting a new entry in the tree is also easier than it may appear at first. Your intuition may lead you to believe that insertions might require cutting the tree open to allow room for new entries, but actually the node being added can always be attached as a new leaf, regardless of the value involved. To find the proper place for a new entry, we move down the tree along the path that we would follow if we were searching for that entry. Since the entry is not in the tree, our search will lead to a NIL pointer. At this point we will have found the proper location for the new node (Figure 8.22). Indeed, the point we will have found is the location to which a search for the new data would lead.

A procedure expressing this process in the case of a linked tree structure is shown in Figure 8.23. It searches the tree for the value being inserted (called NewValue) and then places a new leaf node containing NewValue at the proper location. Note that if the entry being inserted is actually found in the tree during the search, no insertion is made.

We conclude that a software package consisting of a linked binary tree structure together with our procedures for searching, printing, and inserting provides a complete package that could be used as an abstract tool by our hypothetical application. Indeed, when properly implemented, this package could be used without concern for the actual underlying storage structure. The user could envision a list of names stored in alphabetical order, whereas the reality would be that the "list" entries are actually scatted among blocks of memory cells that are linked as a binary tree.

Figure 8.23

A procedure for inserting a new entry in a list stored as a binary tree

```
        procedure Insert(Tree, NewValue)

    if (root pointer of Tree − NIL)
      (set the root pointer to point to a new leaf
          containing NewValue)
      else (execute the block of instructions below that is
          associated with the appropriate case)
          case 1: NewValue = value of root node
              (Do nothing)
          case 2: NewValue < value of root node
              (if (left child pointer of root node = NIL)
                      then (set that pointer to point to a new
                          leaf node containing NewValue)
                      else (apply the procedure Insert to insert
                          NewValue into the subtree identified
                          by the left child pointer)
          case 3: NewValue > value of root node
              (if (right child pointer of root node = NIL)
                      then (set that pointer to point to a new
                          leaf node containing NewValue)
                      else (apply the procedure Insert to insert
                          NewValue into the subtree identified
                          by the right child pointer)
        ) end if
```

Questions/Exercises

1. Draw a binary tree that you could use to store the list R, S, T, U, V, W, X, Y, and Z for future searching.

2. Indicate the path traversed by the binary search algorithm in Figure 8.18 when applied to the tree in Figure 8.17 when searching for the entry J. What about the entry P?

3. Draw a diagram representing the status of activations of the recursive tree-printing algorithm in Figure 8.21 at the time node K is printed within the ordered tree in Figure 8.17.

4. Describe how a tree structure in which each node has as many as 26 children could be used to encode the correct spelling of words in the English language.

8.4 Customized Data Types

In Chapter 6 we introduced the concept of a data type and discussed such elementary types as integer, real, character, and Boolean. These data types are provided in most programming languages as primitive data types. In this section we consider ways in which a programmer can define his or her own data types to fit more closely the needs of a particular application.

User-Defined Data Types

Expressing an algorithm is often easier if data types other than those provided as primitives in the programming language are available. For this reason, many modern programming languages allow programmers to define additional data types, using the primitive types as building blocks. These "home-made" data types are known as **user-defined data types.**

For example, suppose we wanted to develop a program involving numerous variables, each with the same heterogeneous structure consisting of a name, age, and skill rating. One approach would be to define each variable separately as a heterogeneous structure (Section 6.2). A better approach, however, would be to define the heterogeneous structure to be a new (user-defined) data type and then to use that new type as though it were a primitive.

For example, we could adopt the pseudocode statement of the form

```
define type EmployeeType to be
{char  Name[8];
 int   Age;
 real  SkillRating;
}
```

to define a new type, called **EmployeeType,** that consists of the heterogeneous structure containing components called **Name** (of type character), **Age** (of type integer), and **SkillRating** (of type real). This new data type could then be used to declare variables in the same way as a primitive data type. In particular, in the same way that most programming languages allow the variable x to be declared as an integer using the statement

    int x;

the variable Employee could be declared to be of the type EmployeeType with the statement

    EmployeeType Employee;

From then on in the program, the variable Employee would refer to an entire block of memory cells containing the name, age, and skill rating of an employee. Individual items within the block could be referenced by expressions such as Employee.name and Employee.age. Moreover, the statement

    EmployeeType DistManager, SalesRep1, SalesRep2;

could be used to declare the three variables DistManager, SalesRep1, and SalesRep2 to be of type EmployeeType just as the statement

    float Sleeve, Waist, Neck;

is normally used to declare the variables Sleeve, Waist, and Neck to be of the primitive type float.

It is important to distinguish between a user-defined data type and an actual item of that type. The latter is referred to as an **instance** of the type. A user-defined data type is essentially a template that is used in constructing instances of the type. It describes the properties that all instances of that type have but does not itself constitute an occurrence of that type (the same as a cookie-cutter is a template from

Garbage Collection

As dynamic data structures grow and shrink, storage space is used and released. The process of reclaiming unused storage space for future use is known as **garbage collection.** Garbage collection is required in numerous settings. The memory manager within an operating system must perform garbage collection as it allocates and retrieves memory space. The file manager performs garbage collection as files are stored in and deleted from the machine's mass storage. Moreover, any process running under the control of the dispatcher may need to perform garbage collection within its own allotted memory space.

Garbage collection involves some subtle problems. In the case of linked structures, each time a pointer to a data item is changed, the garbage collector must decide whether to reclaim the storage space to which the pointer originally pointed. The problem becomes especially complex in intertwined data structures involving multiple paths of pointers. Inaccurate garbage collection routines can lead to loss of data or to inefficient use of storage space. For example, if garbage collection fails to reclaim storage space, the available space will slowly dwindle away, a phenomenon known as a **memory leak.**

which cookies are made but is not itself a cookie). In the preceding example, the user-defined data type EmployeeType was used to construct three instances of that type, known as DistManager, SalesRep1, and SalesRep2.

Abstract Data Types

Although the concept of a user-defined data type is advantageous, it falls short of allowing the creation of new data types in the full sense. A complete data type consists of two parts: (1) a predetermined storage system (such as a two's complement system in the case of the type integer and a floating-point system in the case of type real) and (2) a collection of predefined operations (such as addition and subtraction). In particular, the primitive data types in a programming language are associated with primitive operations. If a programmer declares a variable to be of a primitive type, the programmer can begin applying primitive operations to that variable without further definitions.

Traditional user-defined data types, however, merely allow programmers to define new storage systems. They do not also provide operations to be performed on data with these structures. To clarify, suppose we wanted to create and use several stacks of integer values within a program. Our approach might be to implement each stack as a homogeneous array of 20 integer values. The bottom entry in the stack would be placed (pushed) in the first array position, and additional stack entries would be placed (pushed) into successively higher entries in the array (see Question/Exercise 7 in Section 8.2). An additional integer variable would be used as the stack pointer. It would hold the index of the array entry into which the next stack entry should be pushed. Thus each stack would consist of a homogeneous array containing the stack itself and an integer playing the role of the stack pointer.

To implement this plan, we could first establish a user-defined type called StackType with a statement of the form

```
define type StackType to be
{int StackEntries[20];
 int StackPointer = 0;
}
```

(Note that, following the lead of languages such as C, C++, C#, and Java, we are assuming that the indices for the array StackEntries range from 0 to 19, so we have initialized StackPointer to the value 0.) Having made this declaration, we could then declare stacks called StackOne, StackTwo, and StackThree via the statement

```
StackType StackOne, StackTwo, StackThree;
```

At this point, each of the variables StackOne, StackTwo, and StackThree would reference a unique block of memory cells used to implement an individual stack.

But what if we now want to push the value 25 onto StackOne? We would like to avoid the details of the array structure underlying the stack's implementation and merely use the stack as an abstract tool—perhaps by using a procedure call similar to

```
push(25, StackOne)
```

But such a statement would not be available unless we also defined an appropriate procedure named push. Other operations we would like to perform on variables of type StackType would include popping entries off the stack, checking to see if the stack is empty, and checking to see if the stack is full—all of which would require definitions of additional procedures. In short, our definition of the data type StackType has not included all the properties we would like to have associated with the type.

We could solve this problem by expanding our **define type** statement to include procedures as well as data descriptions. For example, we could write

```
define type StackType to be
{int StackEntries[20];
 int StackPointer = 0;
 procedure push(value)
   {StackEntries[StackPointer] = value;
    StackPointer = StackPointer + 1;
    }
 procedure pop . . .

}
```

which is intended to mean that the type StackType is associated with procedures called push, pop, etc. as well as data called StackEntries and StackPointer. (For the sake of simplicity we have included a very innocent version of the procedure push. In reality the procedure should ensure that the stack is not full before trying to insert an additional entry.)

With this extended definition of the type StackType, we could declare StackOne, StackTwo, and StackThree to be stacks with the statement

StackType StackOne, StackTwo, StackThree;

Then we could push entries onto these stacks with statements such as

StackOne.push(25);

which means to execute the push procedure associated with StackOne using the value 25 as the actual parameter.

User-defined data types that include definitions of operations are called **abstract data types.** Thus, as opposed to the more elementary user-defined data types, abstract data types are complete data types, and their appearance in such languages as Ada in the 1980s represented a significant step forward in the evolutionary process of programming language design. Today, object-oriented languages provide for extended versions of abstract data types called classes, as we will see in the next section.

Questions/Exercises

1. What is the difference between a data type and an instance of that type?
2. What is the difference between a user-defined data type and an abstract data type?
3. Describe an abstract data type for implementing a list.
4. Describe an abstract data type for implementing checking accounts.

8.5 Classes and Objects

As we learned in Chapter 6, the object-oriented paradigm leads to systems composed of units called objects that interact with each other to accomplish tasks. Each object is an entity that responds to messages received from other objects. Objects are described by templates known as classes.

In many respects, these classes are actually descriptions of abstract data types (whose instances are called objects). In fact, the statements used to define classes in popular object-oriented programming languages are strikingly similar to the **define type** statement introduced in the previous section. For example, Figure 8.24 shows how a class known as StackOfIntegers can be defined in the languages Java and C#. (The equivalent class definition in C++ has the same structure but slightly different syntax.) Note the similarity between this class and the **define type** statement used in the previous section to describe the abstract data type **StackType**. It describes the class/type as containing an array of integers called StackEntries, an integer used to identify the top of the stack within the array called StackPointer, and procedures for manipulating the stack.

Using this class as a template, an object named StackOne can be created in a Java or C# program by the statement

        StackOfIntegers StackOne = new StackOfIntegers();

or in a C++ program by the statement

        StackOfIntegers StackOne();

Later in the programs, the value 106 can be pushed onto StackOne using the statement

        StackOne.push(106);

Figure 8.24

A stack of integers implemented in Java and C#

```
  class StackOfIntegers
  {private int[] StackEntries = new int[20];
   private int StackPointer = 0;


   public void push(int NewEntry)
   {if (StackPointer < 20)
      StackEntries[StackPointer++] = NewEntry;
   }

   public int pop()
   {if (StackPointer > 0) return StackEntries[--StackPointer];
    else return 0;
   }
  }
```

The Standard Template Library

The data structures discussed in this chapter have become standard programming structures—so standard, in fact, that many programming environments treat them very much like primitives. One example is found in the C++ programming environment, which is enhanced by the Standard Template Library (STL). The STL contains a collection of predefined classes that describe popular data structures. Consequently, by incorporating the STL into a C++ program, the programmer is relieved from the task of describing these structures in detail. Instead, he or she needs merely to declare identifiers to be of these types in the same manner that we declared StackOne to be of type StackOfIntegers in Section 8.5.

or the top entry from StackOne can be retrieved in the variable OldValue using the statement

```
OldValue = StackOne.pop();
```

These features are essentially the same as those associated with abstract data types. There are, however, distinctions between classes and abstract data types. The former is an extension of the latter. For instance, as we learned in Section 6.5, object-oriented languages allow classes to inherit properties from other classes and to contain special methods called constructors that customize individual objects when they are created. Moreover, classes are normally associated with varying degrees of encapsulation (Section 6.5), allowing the internal properties of their instances to be protected from misguided shortcuts. And, finally, a class may be used as a means of grouping related procedures, and therefore a class may consist only of procedure definitions. In this sense, we could call a class an abstract type rather than an abstract data type.

We conclude that the concepts of classes and objects represent another step in the evolution of techniques for representing data abstractions in programs. It is, in fact, the ability to define and use abstractions in a convenient manner that has led to the popularity of the object-oriented programming paradigm.

Questions/Exercises

1. In what ways are abstract data types and classes similar? In what ways are they different?
2. What is the difference between a class and an object?
3. Describe a class that would be used as a template for constructing objects of type queue-of-integers.

8.6 Pointers in Machine Language

So far in this chapter we have introduced pointers and have shown how they are used in constructing data structures. In this section we consider how pointers are handled in machine language.

Suppose that we want to write a program in the machine language described in Appendix C to pop an entry off the stack as described in Figure 8.10 and place that entry in a general-purpose register. In other words, we want to load a register with the contents of the memory cell that contains the entry on top of the stack. Our machine language provides two instructions for loading registers: one with op-code 2, the other with op-code 1. Recall that in the case of op-code 2, the operand field contains the data to be loaded, and in the case of op-code 1, the operand field contains the address of the data to be loaded.

Since we do not know what the contents will be, we cannot use op-code 2 to obtain our goal. Moreover, we cannot use op-code 1, since we do not know what the address will be. After all, the address of the top of the stack will vary as the program is executed. We do know the address of the stack pointer. That is, we know the location of the address of the data we want to load. What we need, then, is a third op-code for loading a register, in which the operand contains the address of a pointer to the data to be loaded.

The designer of the machine in Appendix C might use op-code D to accomplish this goal. The language could be designed so that an instruction of the form DRXY would mean to load register R with the contents of the memory cell whose address is found at address XY (Figure 8.25). Thus if the stack pointer is in the memory cell at

Figure 8.25

Our first attempt at expanding the machine language in Appendix C to take advantage of pointers address AA, then the instruction D5AA would cause the data at the top of the stack to be loaded into register 5.

This instruction, however, does not complete the pop operation. We must also subtract one from the stack pointer so that it points to the new top of the stack. This means that, following the load instruction, our machine language program would have to load the stack pointer into a register, subtract one from it, and store the result back in memory.

By using one of the registers as the stack pointer instead of a memory cell, we could reduce this movement of the stack pointer back and forth between registers and memory. But this would mean that we must redesign the load instruction so that it expects the pointer to be in a register rather than in main memory. Thus, instead of the earlier approach, the designer of the machine might define an instruction with op-code D to have the form DR0S, which would mean to load register R with the contents of the memory cell pointed to by register S (Figure 8.26). Then, a complete pop operation could be performed by following this instruction with an instruction to subtract one from the value stored in register S.

Note that a similar instruction is needed to implement a push operation. The machine designer might therefore extend the language described in Appendix C further by introducing the op-code E so that an instruction of the form ER0S would mean to store the contents of register R in the memory cell pointed to by register S. Again, to complete the push operation, this instruction would be followed by an instruction to add one to the value in register S.

With these extensions, the machine language described in Appendix C would exhibit three addressing techniques. In the first, the instruction's operand contains the data involved as demonstrated by op-code 2. In the second, the instruction's operand

Figure 8.26

Loading a register from a memory cell that is located by means of a pointer stored in a register contains the address of the data involved as demonstrated by op-codes 1 and 3. In the third, the instruction's operand contains the location of the address of the data involved as demonstrated by op-codes D and E. These techniques are known as **immediate addressing, direct addressing,** and **indirect addressing,** respectively. All three are common in today's machine languages.

Questions/Exercises

1. Suppose the machine language described in Appendix C has been extended as suggested at the end of this section. Moreover, suppose register 8 contains the pattern DB, the memory cell at address DB contains the pattern CA, and the cell at address CA contains the pattern A5. What bit pattern will be in register 5 immediately after executing each of the following instructions?
   a. 25A5   b. 15CA   c. D508

2. Using the extensions described at the end of this section, write a complete machine language routine to perform a pop operation. Assume that the stack is implemented as shown in Figure 8.10, the stack pointer is in register F, and the top of the stack is to be popped into register 5.

3. Using the extensions described at the end of this section, write a program to copy the contents of five contiguous memory cells starting at address A0 to the five cells starting at address B0. Assume your program starts at address 00.

4. In the chapter, we introduced a machine instruction of the form DR0S. Suppose we extended this form to DRXS, meaning "Load register R with the data pointed to by the value in register S plus the value X." Thus the pointer to the data is obtained by retrieving the value in register S and then incrementing that value by X. The value in register S is not altered. (If register F contained 04, then the instruction DE2F would load register E with the contents of the memory cell at address 06. The value of register F would remain 04.) What advantages would this instruction have? What about an instruction of the form DRTS—meaning "Load register R with the data pointed to by the value in register S incremented by the value in register T"?

Chapter Review Problems

(Asterisked problems are associated with optional sections.)

1. Draw pictures showing how the array below appears in a machine's memory when stored in row major order and in column major order:

A	B	C	D
E	F	G	H
I	J	K	L

2. Suppose an array with six rows and eight columns is stored in row major order starting at address 20 (base ten). If each entry in the array requires only one memory cell, what is the address of the entry in the third row and fourth column? What if each entry requires two memory cells?

3. Rework Problem 2 assuming column major order rather than row major order.

4. What complications are imposed if one tries to implement a dynamic list using a traditional homogeneous array?

5. Describe a method for storing three-dimensional homogeneous arrays. What addressing formula would be used to locate the entry in the ith plane, jth row, and the kth column?

6. Suppose the list of letters A, B, C, E, F, and G is stored in a contiguous block of memory cells. What activities are required to insert the letter D in the list, assuming that the list's alphabetical order is to be maintained?

7. The table below represents the contents of some cells in a computer's main memory along with the address of each cell represented. Note that some of the cells contain letters of the alphabet, and each such cell is followed by an empty cell. Place addresses in these empty cells so that each cell containing a letter together with the following cell form an entry in a linked list in which the letters appear in alphabetical order. (Use zero for the NIL pointer.) What address should the head pointer contain?

Address	Contents
11	C
12	
13	G
14	
15	E
16	
17	B
18	
19	U
20	
21	F
22	

8. The following table represents a portion of a linked list in a computer's main memory. Each entry in the list consists of two cells: The first contains a letter of the alphabet; the second contains a pointer to the next list entry. Alter the pointers so that the letter N is no longer in the list. Then replace the letter N with the letter G and alter the pointers so that the new letter appears in the list in its proper place in alphabetical order.

Address	Contents
30	J
31	38
32	B
33	30
34	X
35	46
36	N
37	40
38	K
39	36
40	P
41	34

9. The table below represents a linked list using the same format as in the preceding problems. If the head pointer contains the value 44, what name is represented by the list? Change the pointers so that the list contains the name Jean.

Address	Contents
40	N
41	46
42	I
43	40
44	J
45	50
46	E
47	00
48	M
49	42
50	A
51	40

10. Which of the following routines correctly inserts NewEntry immediately after the entry called PreviousEntry in a linked list? What is wrong with the other routine?

Routine 1

1. Copy the value in the pointer field of PreviousEntry into the pointer field of NewEntry.
2. Change the value in the pointer field of PreviousEntry to the address of NewEntry.

Routine 2

1. Change the value in the pointer field of PreviousEntry to the address of NewEntry.
2. Copy the value in the pointer field of PreviousEntry into the pointer field of NewEntry.

11. Design a procedure for concatenating two linked lists (that is, placing one before the other to form a single list).

12. Design a procedure for combining two sorted contiguous lists into a single sorted contiguous list. What if the lists are linked?

13. Design a procedure for reversing the order of a linked list.

14. a. Design an algorithm for printing a linked list in reverse order using a stack as an auxiliary storage structure.
   b. Design a recursive procedure to perform this same task without making explicit use of a stack. In what form is a stack still involved in your recursive solution?

15. Sometimes a single linked list is given two different orders by attaching two pointers to each entry rather than one. Fill in the table below so that by following the first pointer after each letter one finds the name Carol, but by following the second pointer after each letter one finds the letters in alphabetical order. What values belong in the head pointer of each of the two lists represented?

Address	Contents
60	O
61	
62	
63	C
64	
65	
66	A
67	
68	
69	L
70	
71	
72	R
73	
74	

16. The table below represents a stack stored in a contiguous block of memory cells, as discussed in the text. If the base of the stack is at address 10 and the stack pointer contains the value 12, what value is retrieved by a pop instruction? What value is in the stack pointer after the pop operation?

Address	Contents
10	F
11	C
12	A
13	B
14	E

17. Draw a table showing the final contents of the memory cells if the instruction in Problem 16 had been to push the letter D on the stack rather than to pop a letter. What would the value in the stack pointer be after the push instruction?

18. Design a procedure to remove the bottom entry from a stack so that the rest of the stack is retained.

19. Design a procedure to compare the contents of two stacks.

20. Suppose you were given two stacks containing data. If you were only allowed to move entries one at a time from one stack to another, what rearrangements of the original data would be possible? What arrangements would be possible if you were given three stacks?

21. Suppose you were given three stacks containing data and you were only allowed to move entries one at a time from one stack to another. Design an algorithm for reversing two adjacent entries on one of the stacks.

22. Suppose we want to create a stack of names that vary in length. Why is it advantageous to store the names in separate areas of memory and then build the stack out of pointers to these names rather than allowing the stack to contain the names themselves?

23. Does a queue crawl through memory in the direction of its head or its tail?

24. Suppose you wanted to implement a "queue" in which new entries had priorities associated with them. Thus a new entry should be placed in front of those entries with lower priorities. Describe a storage system for implementing such a "queue" and justify your decisions.

25. Suppose the entries in a queue require one memory cell each, the head pointer contains the value 11, and the tail pointer contains the value 17. What are the values of these pointers after one entry is inserted and two are removed?

26. a. Suppose a queue implemented in a circular fashion is in the state shown in the diagram below. Draw a diagram showing the structure after the letters G and R are inserted, three letters are removed, and the letters D and P are inserted.

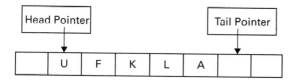

   b. What error occurs in part (a) if the letters G, R, D, and P are inserted before any letters are removed?

27. Describe how an array could be used to implement a queue in a high-level language.

28. Suppose you were given two queues containing data and you were only allowed to move one entry at a time from the head of a queue to the tail of either. Design an algorithm for reversing two adjacent entries in one of the queues.

29. The table below represents a tree stored in a machine's memory. Each node of the tree consists of three cells. The first cell contains the data (a letter), the second contains a pointer to the node's left child, and the third contains a pointer to the node's right child. A value of 0 represents a NIL pointer. If the value of the root pointer is 55, draw a picture of the tree.

Address	Contents
40	G
41	0
42	0
43	X
44	0
45	0
46	J
47	49
48	0
49	M
50	0
51	0
52	F
53	43
54	40
55	W
56	46
57	52

30. The table below represents the contents of a block of cells in a computer's main memory. Note that some of the cells contain letters of the alphabet, and each of those cells is followed by two blank cells. Fill in the blank cells so that the memory block represents the tree that follows. Use the first cell following a letter as the pointer to that node's left child and the next cell as the pointer to the right child. Use 0 for NIL pointers. What value should be in the root pointer?

Address	Contents
30	C
31	
32	
33	H
34	
35	
36	K
37	
38	
39	E
40	

```
41
42        G
43
44
45        P
46
47
```

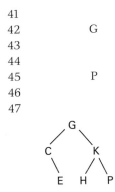

31. Design a nonrecursive algorithm to replace the recursive one represented in Figure 8.18.

32. Design a nonrecursive algorithm to replace the recursive one represented in Figure 8.21. Use a stack to control any backtracking that may be necessary. (The term *backtracking* refers to the process of backing out of a system in the opposite order from which the system was entered. A classic example is the process of retracing steps to find one's way out of a forest. In this problem, backtracking involves finding one's way back up the tree in order to pursue another branch.)

33. Apply the recursive tree-printing algorithm of Figure 8.21 to the tree represented in Problem 29. Draw a diagram representing the nested activations of the algorithm (and the current position in each) at the time node X is printed.

34. While keeping the root node the same and without changing the physical location of the data elements, change the pointers in the tree of Problem 29 so the tree-printing algorithm of Figure 8.21 prints the nodes alphabetically.

35. Draw a diagram showing how the binary tree below appears in memory when stored without pointers using a block of contiguous memory cells as described in Section 8.6.

36. Suppose the contiguous cells representing a binary tree as described in Section 8.6 contained the values A, B, C, D, E, F, and F, respectively. Draw a picture of the tree.

37. Give an example in which you might want to implement a list (the conceptual structure) as a tree (the actual underlying structure). Give an example in which you might want to implement a tree (the conceptual structure) as a list (the actual underlying structure).

38. The linked tree structures discussed in the text contained pointers that allow one to move down the tree from parents to children. Describe a pointer system that would allow movement up the tree from children to parents. What about movement among siblings?

39. Describe a data structure suitable for representing a board configuration during a chess game.

40. Identify the trees below whose nodes would be printed in alphabetical order by the algorithm in Figure 8.21.

41. Modify the procedure in Figure 8.21 to print the "list" in reverse order.

42. Describe a tree structure that can be used to store the genealogical history of a family. What operations are performed on the tree? If the tree is implemented as a linked structure, what pointers should be associated with each node? Design procedures to perform the operations you identified above, assuming that the tree is implemented as a linked structure with the pointers you just described. Using your storage system, explain how one could find all the siblings of a person.

43. Design a procedure for finding and deleting a given value from a tree ordered in the fashion of Figure 8.17.

44. In the traditional implementation of a tree, each node is constructed with a separate pointer for each possible child. If the node has fewer children than pointers, some of its pointers are simply set to NIL. But such a node can never have more children than pointers, and thus this design limits the maximum number of children a node can have. Describe how a tree could be implemented without limiting the number of children a node could have.

45. Using the define type pseudocode statement introduced in Section 8.4, define a user-defined data type representing data regarding an employee of a company (such as name, address, job assignment, pay scale, etc.).

46. Using the define type pseudocode statement introduced in Section 8.4, sketch a definition of an abstract data type representing a list of names. In particular, what structure would contain the list and what procedures would be provided to manipulate the list? (You do not need to include detailed descriptions of the procedures.)

47. Using the define type pseudocode statement introduced in Section 8.4, sketch a definition of an abstract data type representing a queue. Then give pseudocode statements showing how instances of that type could be created and how entries could be inserted in and deleted from those instances.

48. a. What is the difference between a user-defined data type and a primitive data type?

b. What is the difference between an abstract data type and a user-defined data type?

49. Identify the data structures and methods that might appear in an abstract data type representing an address book.

50. Identify the data structures and methods that might appear in an abstract data type representing a simple spacecraft in a video game.

*51. Modify Figure 8.24 so that the class defines a queue rather than a stack.

*52. Using instructions of the form DR0S and ER0S as described at the end of Section 8.8, write a complete machine language routine to push an entry onto a stack implemented as shown in Figure 8.10. Assume that the stack pointer is in register F and that the entry to be pushed is in register 5.

*53. Suppose each entry in a linked list consisted of one memory cell of data followed by a pointer to the next list entry. Moreover, suppose that a new entry located at memory address A0 is to be inserted between the entries at locations B5 and C4. Using the language described in Appendix C and the additional op-codes D and E as described at the end of Section 8.6, write a machine-language routine to perform the insertion.

*54. What advantages does an instruction of the form DR0S as described in Section 8.6 have over an instruction of the form DRXY? What advantage does the form DRXS as described in Question/Exercise 4 of Section 8.6 have over the form DR0S?

Social Issues

The following questions are provided to help you understand some of the ethical/social/legal issues associated with the field of computing. The goal is not merely to answer these questions. You should also consider why you answered as you did and whether your justifications are consistent from one question to the next.

1. Suppose a software analyst develops a data organization that allows for efficient manipulation of data in a particular application. How can the rights to that data structure be protected? Is a data structure the expression of an idea (like a poem) and therefore protected by copyright or do data structures fall through the same legal loopholes as algorithms? What about patent law?

2. To what extent is incorrect data worse than no data?

3. In many application programs, the size to which a stack can grow is determined by the amount of memory available. If the available space is consumed, then the software is designed to produce a message such as "stack overflow" and terminate. In most cases this error never occurs, and the user is never aware of it. Who is liable if such an error occurs and sensitive information is lost? How could the software developer minimize his or her liability?

4. In a data structure based on a pointer system, the deletion of an item usually consists of changing a pointer rather than erasing memory cells. Thus when an entry in a linked list is deleted, the deleted entry actually remains in memory until its memory space is required by other data. What ethical and security issues result from this persistence of deleted data?

5. It is easy to transfer data and programs from one computer to another. Thus it is easy to transfer the knowledge held by one machine to many machines. In contrast, it sometimes takes a long time for a human to transfer knowledge to another human. For example, it takes time for a human to teach another human a new language. What implications could this contrast in knowledge transfer rate have if the capabilities of machines begin to challenge the capabilities of humans?

6. The use of pointers allows related data to be linked in a computer's memory in a manner reminiscent of the way many believe information is associated in the human mind. How are such links in a computer's memory similar to links in a brain? How are they different? Is it ethical to attempt to build computers that more closely mimic the human mind?

7. Has the popularization of computer technology produced new ethical issues or simply provided a new context in which previous ethical theories are applicable?

8. Suppose the author of an introductory computer science textbook wants to include program examples to demonstrate concepts in the text. However, to obtain clarity many of the examples must be simplified versions of what would actually be used in professional quality software. The author knows that the examples could be used by unsuspecting readers and ultimately could find their way into significant software applications in which more robust techniques would be more appropriate. Should the author use the simplified examples, insist that all examples be robust even if doing so decreases their demonstrative value, or refuse to use such examples unless clarity and robustness can both be obtained?

Additional Reading

Carrano, F. M., and J. Prichard. *Data Abstraction and Problem Solving with Java: Walls and Mirrors.* Reading, MA: Addison-Wesley, 2004.

Main, M., and W. Savitch. *Data Structures and Other Objects Using C++*, 2nd ed. Reading, MA: Addison-Wesley, 2003.

Shaffer, C. A. *Practical Introduction to Data Structures and Algorithm Analysis*, 2nd ed. Upper Saddle River, NJ: Prentice-Hall, 2001.

Weiss, M. A. *Data Structures and Problem Solving Using Java*, 2nd ed. Reading, MA: Addison-Wesley, 2002.

CHAPTER

9

Database Systems

In this chapter we investigate database systems and learn how abstraction is used to allow database users to find and extract useful information from large complex data collections. We also introduce the subject of data mining—a rapidly growing field closely associated with database technology. As a side issue, Section 9.5 presents the principles of traditional file structures, many of which are tools underlying today's multidimensional database implementations.

9.1 Database Fundamentals

The term **database** refers to a collection of data that is multidimensional since internal links between its entries make the information accessible from a variety of perspectives. This is in contrast to a traditional file system (Section 9.5), sometimes called a **flat file,** which is a one-dimensional storage system because it presents its information from a single point of view. Whereas a flat file containing information about composers and their compositions might provide a list of compositions arranged by composer, a database might present all the works by a single composer, all the composers who wrote a particular type of music, and perhaps the composers who wrote variations of another composer's work.

The Role of Schemas

Historically, as computing machinery found broader uses in information management, each application tended to be implemented as a separate system with its own collection of data. Payroll was processed using the payroll file, the personnel department maintained its own employee records, and inventory was managed via an inventory file. This meant that much of the information required by an organization was duplicated throughout the company, while many different but related items were stored in separate systems. In this setting, database systems emerged as a means of integrating the information stored and maintained by a particular organization (Figure 9.1). With such a system, both payroll and mailing newsletters could be processed from the same records used by the personnel department.

Of course along with the benefits of data integration come disadvantages. One is the potential of sensitive data being accessed by unauthorized personnel. Someone

Distributed Databases

With the advancement of networking capabilities, database systems have grown to encompass databases, known as distributed databases, that consist of data residing on different machines. For instance, an international corporation may store and maintain local employee records at local sites yet link those records via a network to create a single distributed database.

A distributed database may contain fragmented and/or replicated data. The first case is exemplified by the previous employee-records example in which different fragments of the database are stored in different locations. In the second case, duplicates of the same database component are stored at different locations. Such replication may occur as a means of reducing information retrieval time. Both cases pose problems not present in more traditional centralized databases—how to disguise the distributed nature of the database so that it functions as a coherent system or how to ensure that replicated portions of a database remain duplicates of each other as updates occur. In turn, the study of distributed databases is a current area of research.

Figure 9.1

A file versus a database organization

a. File-oriented information system

b. Database-oriented information system

working on the organization's newsletter might need access to employee names and addresses but should not have access to payroll data; similarly, an employee processing payroll should not have access to the other financial records of the corporation. Thus the ability to control access to the information in the database is often as important as the ability to share it.

To provide different users access to different information within a database, database systems often rely on schemas and subschemas. A **schema** is a description of the entire database structure that is used by the database software to maintain the database. A **subschema** is a description of only that portion of the database pertinent to a particular user's needs. For example, a schema for a university database would indicate that each student record contains such items as the current address and phone number of that student in addition to the student's academic record. Moreover, it would indicate that each student record is linked to the record of the student's faculty adviser. In turn, the record for each faculty member would contain the person's address, employment history, and so on. Based on this schema, a linkage system would be maintained that ultimately connected the information about a student to the employment history of a faculty member.

To keep the university's registrar from using this linkage to obtain privileged information about the faculty, the registrar's access to the database must be restricted to a subschema whose description of the faculty records does not include employment history. Under this subschema, the registrar could find out which faculty member is a particular student's adviser but could not obtain access to additional information about that faculty member. In contrast, the subschema for the payroll department would provide the employment history of each faculty member but would not include the linkage between students and advisers. Thus the payroll department could modify a faculty member's salary but could not obtain the names of the students advised by that person.

Database Management Systems

A typical database application involves two software layers—an application layer and a database management layer (Figure 9.2). The application software handles the communication with the database user (usually a person but sometimes another piece of software). Thus it is the application software that determines the overall system's external characteristics. It may, for example, communicate with the user through a question-and-answer dialogue or a fill-in-the-blanks scenario. It may use a text-based format or a graphical user interface (GUI).

The application software does not directly manipulate the database. The actual manipulation of the database is accomplished by another software layer called the **database management system (DBMS).** Once the application software has determined what action the user is requesting, it uses the DBMS as an abstract tool to achieve the results. If the request is to add or delete data, it is the DBMS that actually alters the database. If the request is to retrieve information, it is the DBMS that actually performs the required searches.

Figure 9.2

The conceptual layers of a database implementation

This dichotomy between the application software and the DBMS has several benefits. One is that it allows for the construction and use of abstract tools, which we have repeatedly found to be a major simplifying concept in software design. If the details of how the database is actually stored are isolated within the DBMS, the design of the application software can be greatly simplified. In particular, with a well-designed DBMS the application software does not have to be concerned with whether the database is stored on a single machine or scattered among many machines within a network as a **distributed database.**

A second advantage of separating the application software from the DBMS is that such an organization provides a means for controlling access to the database. By dictating that the DBMS perform all access to the database, the DBMS can enforce the restrictions imposed by the various subschemas. In particular, the DBMS can use the entire database schema for its internal needs but can require that the application software employed by each user remain within the bounds described by that user's subschema.

Still another reason for separating the user interface and actual data manipulation into two different software layers is to achieve **data independence**—the ability to change the organization of the database itself without changing the application software. For example, the personnel department might need to add an additional field to each employee's record to indicate whether the corresponding employee chose to participate in the company's new health insurance program. If the application software dealt directly with the database, such a change in the data's format could require modifications to all application programs dealing with the same database. As a result, the change instigated by the personnel department would cause changes to the payroll program as well as to the program for printing mailing labels for the company's newsletter.

The separation between application software and a DBMS removes the need for such reprogramming. To implement a change in the database required by a single user, one needs to change only the overall schema and the subschemas of those users involved in the change. The subschemas of all the other users remain the same, so their application software, which is based on the unaltered subschemas, does not need to be modified.

Finally, we should note that the application and the database management layers often reside on separate machines and communicate via a network, with the application layer playing the role of a client, and the database management layer playing the role of a server.

Database Models

We have repeatedly seen how abstraction can be used to hide internal complexities. Database management systems provide yet another example. They hide the complexities of a database's internal structure, allowing the user of the database to imagine that the information stored in the database is arranged in a more useful format. In particular, a DBMS contains routines that translate commands stated in terms of a conceptual view of the database into the actions required by the actual data storage system. This conceptual view of the database is called a **database model.**

In the following sections we will consider both the relational database model and the object-oriented database model. In the case of the relational database model, the conceptual view of the database is that of a collection of tables consisting of rows and columns. For example, information about a company's employees might be viewed as a table containing a row for each employee and columns labeled name, address, employee identification number, etc. In turn, the DBMS would contain routines that would allow the application software to select certain entries from a particular row of the table or perhaps to report the range of values found in the salary column—even though the information is not actually stored in rows and columns.

These routines form the abstract tools used by the application software to access the database. More precisely, application software is often written in one of the general-purpose programming languages, such as those discussed in Chapter 6. These languages provide the basic ingredients for algorithmic expressions but lack instructions for manipulating a database. However, a program written in one of these languages can use the routines provided by the DBMS as prewritten subroutines—in effect extending the capabilities of the language in a manner that supports the conceptual image of the database model.

The search for better database models is an ongoing process. The goal is to find models that allow complex data systems to be conceptualized easily, lead to concise ways of expressing requests for information, and produce efficient database management systems.

Questions/Exercises

1. Identify two departments in a manufacturing plant that would have different uses for the same or similar inventory information. Then, describe how the subschema for the two departments might differ.

2. What is the purpose of a database model?

3. Summarize the roles of the application software, the DBMS, and the actual data-manipulating routines in retrieving information from a database.

9.2 The Relational Model

In this section we look more closely at the relational database model. It portrays data as being stored in rectangular tables, called **relations** that are similar to the format in which information is displayed by spreadsheet programs. For example, the relational model allows information regarding the employees of a firm to be represented by a relation such as that shown in Figure 9.3.

A row in a relation is called a **tuple** (some say "TOO-pul," others say "TU-pul"). In the relation of Figure 9.3, tuples consist of the information about a particular employee. Columns in a relation are referred to as **attributes** because each entry in a column describes some characteristic, or attribute, of the entity represented by the corresponding tuple.

Figure 9.3

A relation containing employee information

Empl Id	Name	Address	SSN
25X15	Joe E. Baker	33 Nowhere St.	111223333
34Y70	Cheryl H. Clark	563 Downtown Ave.	999009999
23Y34	G. Jerry Smith	1555 Circle Dr.	111005555
•	•	•	•
•	•	•	•
•	•	•	•

Issues of Relational Design

The first step in designing a relational database is to design the relations making up the database. Although this may appear to be a simple task, many subtleties are waiting to trap the unwary designer.

Suppose that in addition to the information contained in the relation of Figure 9.3, we want to include information about the jobs held by the employees. We may want to include a job history associated with each employee that consists of such attributes as job title (secretary, office manager, floor supervisor), a job identification code (unique to each job), the skill code associated with each job, the department in which the job exists, and the period during which the employee held the job in terms of a starting date and termination date. (We use an asterisk as the termination date if the job represents the employee's current position.)

One approach to this problem is to extend the relation in Figure 9.3 to include these attributes as additional columns in the table, as shown in Figure 9.4. However,

Figure 9.4

A relation containing redundancy

Empl Id	Name	Address	SSN	Job Id	Job Title	Skill Code	Dept	Start Date	Term Date
25X15	Joe E. Baker	33 Nowhere St.	111223333	F5	Floor manager	FM3	Sales	9-1-2002	9-30-2003
25X15	Joe E. Baker	33 Nowhere St.	111223333	D7	Dept. head	K2	Sales	10-1-2003	*
34Y70	Cheryl H. Clark	563 Downtown Ave.	999009999	F5	Floor manager	FM3	Sales	10-1-2002	*
23Y34	G. Jerry Smith	1555 Circle Dr.	111005555	S25X	Secretary	T5	Personnel	3-1-1999	4-30-2001
23Y34	G. Jerry Smith	1555 Circle Dr.	111005555	S26Z	Secretary	T6	Accounting	5-1-2001	*
•	•	•	•	•	•	•	•	•	•
•	•	•	•	•	•	•	•	•	•
•	•	•	•	•	•	•	•	•	•

Figure 9.5

An employee database consisting of three relations

EMPLOYEE relation

Empl Id	Name	Address	SSN
25X15	Joe E. Baker	33 Nowhere St.	111223333
34Y70	Cheryl H. Clark	563 Downtown Ave.	999009999
23Y34	G. Jerry Smith	1555 Circle Dr.	111005555
•	•	•	•
•	•	•	•
•	•	•	•

JOB relation

Job Id	Job Title	Skill Code	Dept
S25X	Secretary	T5	Personnel
S26Z	Secretary	T6	Accounting
F5	Floor manager	FM3	Sales
•	•	•	•
•	•	•	•
•	•	•	•

ASSIGNMENT relation

Empl Id	Job Id	Start Date	Term Date
23Y34	S25X	3-1-1999	4-30-2001
34Y70	F5	10-1-2002	*
23Y34	S26Z	5-1-2001	*
•	•	•	•
•	•	•	•
•	•	•	•

close examination of the result reveals several problems. One is a lack of efficiency due to redundancy. The relation no longer contains one tuple for each employee but rather one tuple for each assignment of an employee to a job. If an employee has advanced in the company through a sequence of several jobs, several tuples in the new relation must contain the same information about the employee (name, address, identification number, and Social Security number). For example, the personal information about Baker and Smith is repeated because they have held more than one job. Moreover, when a particular position has been held by numerous employees, the department associated with that job along with the appropriate skill code must be repeated in each tuple representing an assignment of the job. For example, the description of the floor manager job is duplicated because more than one employee has held this position.

Another, perhaps more serious, problem with our extended relation surfaces when we consider deleting information from the database. Suppose for example that Joe E. Baker is the only employee to hold the job identified as D7. If he were to leave the company and be deleted from the database represented in Figure 9.4, we would lose the information about job D7. After all, the only tuple containing the fact that job D7 requires a skill level of K2 is the tuple relating to Joe Baker.

You might argue that the ability to erase only a portion of a tuple could solve the problem, but this would in turn introduce other complications. For instance, should the information relating to job F5 also be retained in a partial tuple, or does this information reside elsewhere in the relation? Moreover, the temptation to use partial tuples is a strong indication that the design of the database can be improved.

The cause of all these problems is that we have combined more than one concept into a single relation. As proposed, the extended relation in Figure 9.4 contains information dealing directly with employees (name, identification number, address, Social Security number), information about the jobs available in the company (job identification, job title, department, skill code), and information regarding the relationship between employees and jobs (start date, termination date). Based on this observation, we can solve our problems by redesigning the system using three relations—one for each of the preceding topics. We can keep the original relation in Figure 9.3 (which we now call the **EMPLOYEE** relation) and insert the additional information in the form of the two new relations called **JOB** and **ASSIGNMENT**, which produces the database in Figure 9.5.

A database consisting of these three relations contains the pertinent information about employees in the **EMPLOYEE** relation, about available jobs in the **JOB** relation, and about job history in the **ASSIGNMENT** relation. Additional information is implicitly available by combining the information from different relations. For instance, if we know an employee's identification number, we can find the departments in which that employee has worked by first finding all the jobs that employee has held using the **ASSIGNMENT** relation and then finding the departments associated with those jobs

Database Systems for PCs

Personal computers are used in a variety of applications, ranging from elementary to sophisticated. In elementary "database" applications, such as storing Christmas card lists or maintaining bowling league records, spreadsheet systems are often used in lieu of database software since the application calls for little more than the ability to store, print, and sort data. There are, however, quite sophisticated database systems available for the PC market, one of which is Microsoft's Access. This is a complete relational database system as described in Section 9.2 as well as chart- and report-generation software. Access provides an excellent example of how the principles presented in this text form the backbone of popular products on the market today.

Figure 9.6

Finding the departments in which employee 23Y34 has worked

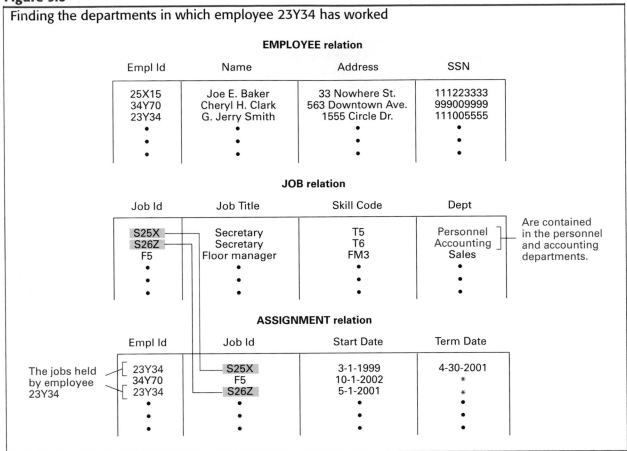

by means of the JOB relation (Figure 9.6). Through processes such as these, any information that could be obtained from the single large relation can be obtained from the three smaller relations without the problems previously cited.

Unfortunately, dividing information into various relations is not always as trouble-free as in the preceding example. For instance, compare the original relation in Figure 9.7, with attributes EmplId, JobTitle, and Dept, to the proposed decomposition into two relations. At first glance, the two-relation system may appear to contain the same information as the single-relation system, but, in fact, it does not. Consider for example the problem of finding the department in which a given employee works. This is easily done in the single-relation system by interrogating the tuple containing the employee identification number of the target employee and extracting the corresponding department. However, in the two-relation system, the desired information is not necessarily available. We can find the job title of the target employee and a department having such a job but this does not necessarily mean that the target employee works in that particular department, because several departments may have jobs with the same title.

Figure 9.7

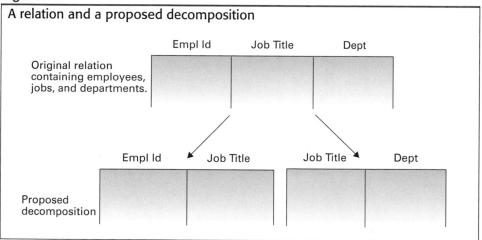

A relation and a proposed decomposition

Original relation containing employees, jobs, and departments.

Empl Id   Job Title   Dept

Proposed decomposition

Empl Id   Job Title   Job Title   Dept

We see, then, that sometimes decomposing a relation into smaller relations causes the loss of information, and sometimes it does not. (The former is called a **lossless decomposition**—or sometimes a **nonloss decomposition.**) The study of such relational characteristics is an important topic in computer science. The goal is to identify the relational characteristics that can lead to problems in database design and find ways to reorganize those relations to remove these problematic characteristics.

Relational Operations

Now that you have a basic understanding of how data can be organized in terms of the relational model, it is time to see how information can be extracted from a database consisting of relations. We begin with a look at some operations that we may want to perform on relations.

At times we need to select certain tuples from a relation. To retrieve the information about an employee, we must select the tuple with the appropriate identification attribute value from the **EMPLOYEE** relation, or to obtain a list of the job titles in a certain department, we must select the tuples from the **JOB** relation having that department as their department attribute. The result of this selection is another relation consisting of the tuples selected from the parent relation. The outcome of selecting information about a particular employee results in a relation containing only one tuple from the **EMPLOYEE** relation. The outcome of selecting the tuples associated with a certain department probably results in several tuples from the **JOB** relation.

In short, one operation we may want to perform on a relation is to select tuples possessing certain characteristics and to place these selected tuples in a new relation. To express this operation, we adopt the syntax

NEW ← SELECT from EMPLOYEE where Emplld = "34Y70"

Figure 9.8

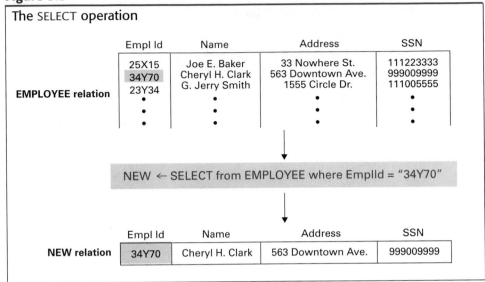

The SELECT operation

The semantics of this statement is to create a new relation called **NEW** containing those tuples (there should be only one in this case) from the relation **EMPLOYEE** whose EmplId attribute equals **34Y70** (Figure 9.8).

Figure 9.9

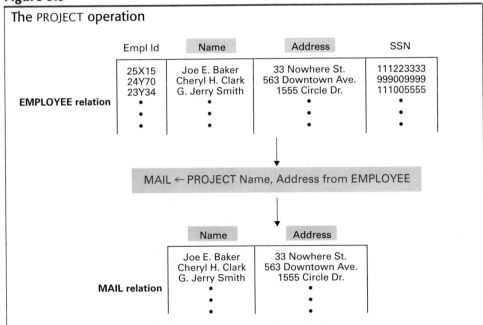

The PROJECT operation

In contrast to the **SELECT** operation, which extracts rows from a relation, the **PRO-JECT** operation extracts columns. Suppose, for example, that in searching for the job titles in a certain department, we had already **SELECT**ed the tuples from the **JOB** relation that pertained to the target department and placed these tuples in a new relation called **NEW1**. The list we are seeking is the **JobTitle** column within this new relation. The **PROJECT** operation allows us to extract this column (or columns if required) and place the result in a new relation. We express such an operation as

NEW2 ← PROJECT JobTitle from NEW1

The result is the creation of another new relation (called **NEW2**) that contains the single column of values from the **JobTitle** column of relation **NEW1**.

As another example of the **PROJECT** operation, the statement

MAIL ← PROJECT Name, Address from EMPLOYEE

can be used to obtain a listing of the names and addresses of all employees. This list is in the newly created (two-column) relation called **MAIL** (Figure 9.9).

The third operation we introduce is the **JOIN** operation. It is used to combine different relations into one relation. The **JOIN** of two relations produces a new relation whose attributes consist of the attributes from the original relations (Figure 9.10). The names of these attributes are the same as those in the original relations except that each is prefixed by the relation of its origin. (If relation **A** containing attributes **V** and **W** is JOINed with relation **B** containing attributes **X**, **Y**, and **Z**, then the result has five attributes named **A.V**, **A.W**, **B.X**, **B.Y**, and **B.Z**.) This naming convention ensures that the attributes in the new relation have unique names, even though the original relations may have attribute names in common.

Figure 9.10

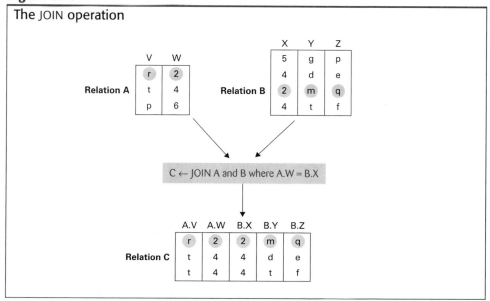

The JOIN operation

The tuples (rows) of the new relation are produced by concatenating tuples from the two original relations (see again Figure 9.10). Which tuples are actually joined to form tuples in the new relation is determined by the condition under which the JOIN is constructed. One such condition is that designated attributes have the same value. This, in fact, is the case represented in Figure 9.10, where we demonstrate the result of executing the statement

C ← JOIN A and B where A.W = B.X

In this example, a tuple from relation A should be concatenated with a tuple from relation B in exactly those cases where the attributes W and X in the two tuples are equal. Thus the concatenation of the tuple (r, 2) from relation A with the tuple (2, m, q) from relation B appears in the result because the value of attribute W in the first equals the value of attribute X in the second. On the other hand, the result of concatenating the tuple (r, 2) from relation A with the tuple (5, g, p) from relation B does not appear in the final relation because these tuples do not share common values in attributes W and X.

As another example, Figure 9.11 represents the result of executing the statement

C ← JOIN A and B where A.W < B.X

Note that the tuples in the result are exactly those in which attribute W in relation A is less than attribute X in relation B.

Let us now see how the JOIN operation can be used with the database of Figure 9.5 to obtain a listing of all employee identification numbers along with the department in which each employee works. Our first observation is that the information required is distributed over more than one relation, and thus the process of retrieving the

Figure 9.11

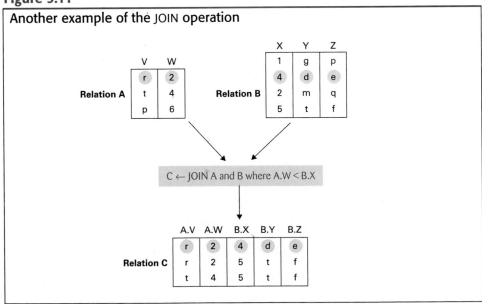

Another example of the JOIN operation

information must entail more than SELECTions and PROJECTions. In fact, the tool we need is the statement

> NEW1 ← JOIN ASSIGNMENT and JOB where ASSIGNMENT.JobId = JOB.JobId

that produces the relation NEW1, as shown in Figure 9.12. From this relation, our problem can be solved by first SELECTing those tuples in which ASSIGNMENT.TermDate equals "∗" (which indicates "still employed") and then PROJECTing the attributes ASSIGNMENT.EmplId and JOB.Dept. In short, the information we need can be obtained from the database in Figure 9.5 by executing the statements

> NEW1 ← JOIN ASSIGNMENT and JOB where ASSIGNMENT.JobId = JOB.JobId
> NEW2 ← SELECT from NEW1 where ASSIGNMENT.TermDate = "∗"
> LIST ← PROJECT ASSIGNMENT.EmplId, JOB.Dept from NEW2

SQL

Now that we have introduced the basic relational operations, let us reconsider the overall structure of a database system. Remember that a database is actually stored in a mass storage system. To relieve the application programmer from the details of

Figure 9.12

An application of the JOIN operation

such systems, a database management system is provided that allows the application software to be written in terms of a database model, such as the relational model. The DBMS accepts commands in terms of the model and converts them into actions relative to the actual storage structure. This conversion is handled by a collection of routines within the DBMS that are used by the application software as abstract tools. Thus a DBMS based on the relational model would include routines to perform the **SELECT**, **PROJECT**, and **JOIN** operations, which could then be called from the application software. In this manner the application software can be written as though the database were actually stored in the simple tabular form of the relational model.

Today's relational database management systems do not necessarily provide routines to perform the **SELECT**, **PROJECT**, and **JOIN** operations in their raw form. Instead, they provide routines that may be combinations of these basic steps. An example is the language SQL (Structured Query Language), which forms the backbone of most relational database query systems. For example, SQL is the underlying language in the relational database system MySQL (pronounced "My–S–Q–L") used by many database servers. One reason for SQL's popularity is that the American National Standards Institute has standardized it. Another reason is that it was originally developed and marketed by IBM and has thus benefited from a high level of exposure. In this section we explain how relational database queries are expressed in SQL.

Although we are about to find that a query stated in SQL is expressed in an imperative-sounding form, the reality is that it is essentially a declarative statement. You should read an SQL statement as a description of the information desired rather than a sequence of activities to be performed. The significance of this is that SQL relieves application programmers from the burden of developing algorithms for manipulating relations—they need merely to describe the information desired.

For our first example of an SQL statement, let us reconsider our last query in which we developed a three-step process for obtaining all employee identification numbers along with their corresponding departments. In SQL this entire query could be represented by the single statement

```
select EmplId, Dept
from ASSIGNMENT, JOB
where ASSIGNMENT.JobId = JOB.JobId
   and ASSIGNMENT.TermDate = '*'
```

As indicated by this example, each SQL query statement can contain three clauses: a select clause, a from clause, and a where clause. Roughly speaking, such a statement is a request for the result of forming the **JOIN** of all the relations listed in the from clause, **SELECT**ing those tuples that satisfy the conditions in the where clause, and then PROJECTing those tuples listed in the select clause. (Note that the terminology is somewhat reversed since the select clause in an SQL statement identifies the attributes used in the **PROJECT** operation.) Let us consider some simple examples.

The statement

```
select Name, Address
from EMPLOYEE
```

produces a listing of all employee names and addresses contained in the relation
EMPLOYEE. Note that this is merely a PROJECT operation.

The statement

```
select EmplId, Name, Address, SSNum
from EMPLOYEE
where Name = 'Cheryl H. Clark'
```

produces all the information from the tuple associated with Cheryl H. Clark in the
EMPLOYEE relation. This is essentially a SELECT operation.

The statement

```
select Name, Address
from EMPLOYEE
where Name = 'Cheryl H. Clark"
```

produces the name and address of Cheryl H. Clark as contained in the EMPLOYEE relation. This is a combination of SELECT and PROJECT operations.

The statement

```
select EMPLOYEE.Name, ASSIGNMENT.StartDate
from EMPLOYEE, ASSIGNMENT
where EMPLOYEE.EmplId = ASSIGNMENT.EmplId
```

produces a listing of all employee names and their dates of initial employment. Note
that this is the result of JOINing the relations EMPLOYEE and ASSIGNMENT and then
SELECTing and PROJECTing the appropriate tuples and attributes as identified in the
where and select clauses.

We close by noting that SQL encompasses statements for defining the structure
of relations, creating relations, and modifying the contents of relations as well as performing queries. For example, the following are examples of the insert into,
delete from, and update statements.

The statement

```
insert into EMPLOYEE
values ('42Z12', 'Sue A. Burt', '33 Fair St.',
        '444661111')
```

adds a tuple to the EMPLOYEE relation containing the values given;

```
delete from EMPLOYEE
where Name = 'G. Jerry Smith'
```

removes the tuple relating to G. Jerry Smith from the EMPLOYEE relation; and

```
update EMPLOYEE
set Address = '1812 Napoleon Ave.'
where Name = 'Joe E. Baker'
```

changes the address in the tuple associated with Joe E. Baker in the EMPLOYEE relation.

Questions/Exercises

1. Answer the following questions based on the partial information given in the EMPLOYEE, JOB, and ASSIGNMENT relations in Figure 9.5:
   a. Who is the secretary in the accounting department with experience in the personnel department?
   b. Who is the floor manager in the sales department?
   c. What job does G. Jerry Smith currently hold?

2. Based on the EMPLOYEE, JOB, and ASSIGNMENT relations presented in Figure 9.5, write a sequence of relational operations to obtain a list of all job titles within the personnel department.

3. Based on the EMPLOYEE, JOB, and ASSIGNMENT relations presented in Figure 9.5, write a sequence of relational operations to obtain a list of employee names along with the employees' departments.

4. Convert your answers to Questions 2 and 3 into SQL.

5. How does the relational model provide for data independence?

6. How are the different relations in a relational database tied together?

9.3 Object-Oriented Databases

One of the newer areas in database research involves applying the object-oriented paradigm to the construction of a database. The result is an **object-oriented database** consisting of objects that are linked to each other to reflect their relationships. For example, an object-oriented implementation of the employee database from the previous section could consist of three classes (types of objects): EMPLOYEE, JOB, and ASSIGNMENT. An object from the EMPLOYEE class could contain such entries as EmplId, Name, Address, and SSNum; an object from the class JOB could contain such entries as JobId, JobTitle, SkillCode, and Dept; and each object from the class ASSIGNMENT could contain entries such as StartDate and TermDate.

A conceptual representation of such a database is shown in Figure 9.13 where the links between the various objects are represented by lines connecting the related objects. If we focus on an object of type EMPLOYEE, we find it linked to a collection of objects of type ASSIGNMENT representing the various assignments that that particular employee has held. In turn, each of these objects of type ASSIGNMENT is linked to an object of type JOB representing the job associated with that assignment. Thus all the assignments of an employee can be found by following the links from the object representing that employee. Similarly, all the employees who have held a particular job can be found by following the links from the object representing that job.

The links between objects in an object-oriented database are normally maintained by the DBMS, so the details of how these links are implemented are not a concern of the programmer writing application software. Instead, when a new object is added to the database, the application software merely specifies the other objects to which it should be linked. The DBMS then creates any linkage system that may be required

Figure 9.13

The associations between objects in an object-oriented database

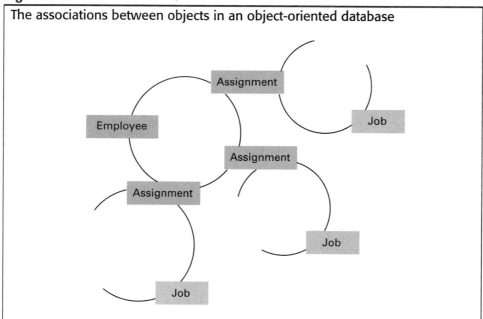

to record these associations. In particular, a DBMS may link the objects representing the assignments of a given employee in a manner similar to a linked list.

Another task of an object-oriented DBMS is to provide permanent storage for the objects entrusted to it—a requirement that may seem obvious but is inherently distinct from the manner in which objects are normally treated. Normally, when an object-oriented program is executed, the objects created during the program's execution are discarded when the program terminates. In this sense the objects are considered transient. But objects that are created and added to a database must be saved after the program that created them terminates. Such objects are said to be **persistent.** Thus creating persistent objects is a significant departure from the norm.

Proponents of object-oriented databases offer numerous arguments to show why the object-oriented approach to database design is better than the relational approach. One argument points out that the object-oriented approach allows the entire software system (application software, DBMS, and the database itself) to be designed in the same paradigm. This is in contrast to the historically common practice of using an imperative programming language to develop application software for interrogating a relational database. Inherent in such a task is the clash between imperative and relational paradigms. This distinction is subtle at our level of study but the difference has been the source of many software errors over the years. Even at our level, we can appreciate that an object-oriented database combined with an object-oriented application program produces a homogeneous image of objects throughout the system communicating with each other. On the other hand, a relational database combined with an imperative application program conjures an image of two inherently different organizations trying to find a common interface.

To appreciate another advantage that object-oriented databases have over their relational counterparts, consider the problem of storing employee names in a relational database. If an entire name is stored as a single attribute in a relation, then inquiries regarding only last names are awkward. However, if the name is stored as three separate attributes—allowing for a first name, middle name, and last name—then it becomes awkward to deal with people whose names do not conform to the first-name, middle-name, family-name template. In an object-oriented database, these issues can be hidden within the object that holds the employee's name. An employee's name can be stored as an intelligent object that is capable of reporting the related employee's name in a variety of formats. Thus, from outside these objects, it would be just as easy to deal with last names only as with entire names, maiden names, or nicknames. The details involved with each perspective would be encapsulated within the objects.

This ability to encapsulate the technicalities of different data formats is advantageous in other cases as well. In a relational database, the attributes in a relation are part of the overall design of the database, and thus the types associated with these attributes permeate the entire DBMS. (Variables for temporary storage must be declared to be the appropriate type, and procedures for manipulating data of the various types must be designed.) Thus, extending a relational database to include attributes of new types (audio and video) can be problematic. In particular, a variety of procedures throughout the database design might need to be expanded to incorporate these new data types. In an object-oriented design, however, the same procedures used to retrieve an object representing an employee's name can be used to retrieve an object representing a motion picture because the distinctions in type can be hidden within the objects involved. Thus the object-oriented approach appears to be more compatible with the construction of multimedia databases—a feature that is already proving to be a great advantage.

Still another advantage the object-oriented paradigm offers to database design is the potential for storing intelligent objects rather than merely data. That is, an object can contain methods describing how it should respond to messages regarding its contents and relationships. For example, each object of the class **EMPLOYEE** in Figure 9.13 could contain methods for reporting and updating the information in the object as well as a method for reporting that employee's job history and perhaps a method for changing that employee's job assignment. Likewise, each object from the **JOB** class could have a method for reporting the specifics of the job and perhaps a method for reporting those employees who have held that particular job. Thus to retrieve an employee's job history, we would not need to write an external procedure describing how the information is to be obtained. Instead, we could merely ask the appropriate employee object to report its job history. The ability to construct databases whose components are able to respond to inquiries intelligently offers an exciting array of possibilities beyond those of more traditional relational databases.

Questions/Exercises

1. What methods would be contained in an instance of an object from the **ASSIGNMENT** class in the employee database discussed in this section?

2. Identify some classes, as well as some of their internal characteristics, that can be used in an object-oriented database dealing with a warehouse inventory.

3. Identify an advantage that an object-oriented database can have over a relational database.

9.4 Maintaining Database Integrity

Inexpensive database management systems for personal use are relatively simple systems. They tend to have a single objective—to shield the user from the technical details of the database implementation. The databases maintained by these systems are relatively small and generally contain information whose loss or corruption would be inconvenient rather than disastrous. When a problem does arise, the user can usually correct the erroneous items directly or reload the database from a backup copy and manually make the modifications required to bring that copy up to date. This process may be inconvenient, but the cost of avoiding the inconvenience tends to be greater than the inconvenience itself. In any case, the inconvenience is restricted to only a few people, and any financial loss is generally limited.

In the case of large, multiuser, commercial database systems, however, the stakes are much higher. The cost of incorrect or lost data can be enormous and can have devastating consequences. In these environments, a major role of the DBMS is to maintain the database's integrity by guarding against problems such as operations that for some reason are only partially completed or different operations that may interact inadvertently to cause inaccurate information in the database. It is this role of a DBMS that we address in this section.

The Commit/Rollback Protocol

A single transaction, such as the transfer of funds from one bank account to another, the cancellation of an airline reservation, or the registration of a student in a university course may involve multiple steps at the database level. For example, a transfer of funds between bank accounts requires that the balance in one account be decremented and the balance in the other be incremented. Between such steps the information in the database may be inconsistent. Indeed, funds are missing during the brief period after the first account has been decremented but before the other has been incremented. Likewise, when reassigning a passenger's seat on a flight, there may be an instant when the passenger has no seat or an instant when the passenger list appears to be one passenger greater than it actually is.

In the case of large databases that are subject to heavy transaction loads, it is highly likely that a random snapshot will find the database in the middle of some transaction. A request for the execution of a transaction or an equipment malfunction will therefore likely occur at a time when the database is in an inconsistent state.

Let us first consider the problem of a malfunction. The goal of the DBMS is to ensure that such a problem will not freeze the database in an inconsistent state. This is often accomplished by maintaining a log containing a record of each transaction's activities in a nonvolatile storage system, such as a disk. Before a transaction is allowed to alter the database, the alteration to be performed is first recorded in the log. Thus the log contains a permanent record of each transaction's actions.

The point at which all the steps in a transaction have been recorded in the log is called the **commit point.** It is at this point that the DBMS has the information it needs to reconstruct the transaction on its own if that should become necessary. At this point the DBMS becomes committed to the transaction in the sense that it accepts the responsibility of guaranteeing that the transaction's activities will be reflected in the database. In the case of an equipment malfunction, the DBMS can use the information in its log to reconstruct the transactions that have been completed (committed) since the last backup was made.

If problems should arise before a transaction has reached its commit point, the DBMS may find itself with a partially executed transaction that cannot be completed. In this case the log can be used to **roll back** (undo) the activities actually performed by the transaction. In the case of a malfunction, for instance, the DBMS could recover by rolling back those transactions that were incomplete (noncommitted) at the time of the malfunction.

Rollbacks of transactions are not restricted, however, to the process of recovering from equipment malfunctions. They are often a part of a DBMS's normal operation. For example, a transaction may be terminated before it has completed all its steps due to an attempt to access privileged information, or it may be involved in a deadlock in which competing transactions find themselves waiting for data being used by the other. In these cases, the DBMS can use the log to roll back a transaction and thus avoid an erroneous database due to incomplete transactions.

To emphasize the delicate nature of DBMS design, we should note that there are subtle problems lurking within the rollback process. The rolling back of one transaction may affect database entries that have been used by other transactions. For example, the transaction being rolled back may have updated an account balance, and another transaction may have already based its activities on this updated value. This may mean that these additional transactions must also be rolled back, which may adversely affect still other transactions. The result is the problem known as **cascading rollback.**

Locking

We now consider the problem of a transaction being executed while the database is in a state of flux from another transaction, a situation that can lead to inadvertent interaction between the transactions and produce erroneous results. For instance, the problem known as the **incorrect summary problem** can arise if one transaction is in the middle of transferring funds from one account to another when another transaction tries to compute the total deposits in the bank. This could result in a total that is either too large or too small depending on the order in which the transfer steps are performed. Another possibility is known as the **lost update problem,** which is exemplified by two transactions, each of which makes a deduction from the same account. If one transaction reads the account's current balance at the point when the other has just read the balance but has not yet calculated the new balance, then both transactions will base their deductions on the same initial balance. In turn, the effect of one of the deductions will not be reflected in the database.

To solve such problems, a DBMS could force transactions to execute in their entirety on a one-at-a-time basis by holding each new transaction in a queue until those preceding it have completed. But a transaction often spends a lot of time waiting for disk operations to be performed. By interweaving the execution of transactions, the time during which one transaction is waiting can be used by another transaction to process data it has already retrieved. Most large database management systems therefore contain a scheduler to coordinate time-sharing among transactions in much the same way that a time-sharing operating system coordinates interweaving of processes (Section 3 of Chapter 3).

To guard against such anomalies as the incorrect summary problem and the lost update problem, these schedulers incorporate a **locking protocol** in which the items within a database that are currently being used by some transaction are marked as such. These marks are called locks; marked items are said to be locked. Two types of locks are common—**shared locks** and **exclusive locks.** They correspond to the two types of access a transaction may require to a data item—shared access and exclusive access. If a transaction is not going to alter the data item, then it requires shared access, meaning that other transactions are also allowed to view the data item. However, if the transaction is going to alter the item, it must have exclusive access, meaning that it must be the only transaction with access to the item.

In a locking protocol, each time a transaction requests access to a data item, it must also tell the DBMS the type of access it requires. If a transaction requests shared access to a data item that is either unlocked or locked with a shared lock, that access is granted and the item is marked with a shared lock. If, however, the requested item is already marked with an exclusive lock, the additional access is denied. If a transaction requests exclusive access to a data item, that request is granted only if the item has no lock associated with it. In this manner, a transaction that is going to alter a data item protects that item from other transactions by obtaining exclusive access. At the same time, several transactions can share access to a data item if none of them are going to change it. Of course, once a transaction is finished with an item, it notifies the DBMS, and the associated lock is removed.

Various algorithms are used to handle the case in which a transaction's access request is rejected. One algorithm is that the transaction is merely forced to wait until the requested item becomes available. This approach, however, can lead to deadlock, since two transactions that require exclusive access to the same two data items could block each other's progress if each obtains exclusive access to one of the items and then insists on waiting for the other. To avoid such deadlocks, some database management systems give priority to older transactions. That is, if an older transaction requires access to a data item that is locked by a younger transaction, the younger transaction is forced to release all of its data items, and its activities are rolled back (based on the log). Then, the older transaction is given access to the data item it required, and the younger transaction is forced to start again. If a younger transaction is repeatedly preempted, it will grow older in the process and ultimately become one of the older transactions. This protocol, known as the **wound-wait protocol** (old transactions wound young transactions, young transactions wait for old ones), ensures that every transaction will ultimately be allowed to complete its task.

Questions/Exercises

1. What is the difference between a transaction that has reached its commit point and one that has not?

2. How could a DBMS guard against extensive cascading rollback?

3. Show how the uncontrolled interweaving of two transactions, one deducting $100 from an account and the other deducting $200 from the same account, could produce final balances of $100, $200, and $300, assuming that the initial balance is $400.

4. a. Summarize the possible results of a transaction requesting shared access to an item in a database.

   b. Summarize the possible results of a transaction requesting exclusive access to an item in a database.

5. Describe a sequence of events that would lead to deadlock among transactions performing operations on a database system.

6. Describe how the deadlock in your answer to Question 5 could be broken. Would your solution require use of the database management system's log? Explain your answer.

9.5 Traditional File Structures

In this section we digress from our study of mutidimensional database systems to consider traditional file structures. These structures represent the historical beginning of data storage and retrieval systems from which current database technology has evolved. In turn, many of the techniques developed for these structures (such as indexing and hashing) are important tools in the construction of today's massive, complex databases.

Sequential Files

A **sequential file** is a file that is accessed in a serial manner from its beginning to its end as though the information in the file were arranged in one long row. Examples include audio files, video files, files containing programs, and files containing textual documents. In fact, most of the files created by a typical personal computer user are sequential files.

   The data in a sequential file must be recorded in mass storage in such a way that the sequential nature of the file is preserved. If the mass storage system is itself sequential (as in the case of a tape or CD), this is a straightforward undertaking. We need merely record the file on the storage medium according to the sequential properties of the medium. Then, processing the file is the task of merely reading and processing the file's contents in the order in which it is found. This is exactly the process followed when playing audio CDs, where the music is stored as a sequential file sector by sector along one continuous spiraling track.

In the case of disk storage, however, the file would be scattered over different sectors that could be retrieved in a variety of orders. To preserve the proper order, most operating systems maintain a list of the sectors on which the file is stored. This list is recorded as part of the disk's directory system on the same disk as the file. By means of this list, the operating system can retrieve the sectors in the proper sequence as though the file were stored sequentially, even though the file is actually distributed over various portions of the disk.

Inherent in processing a sequential file is the need to detect when the end of the file is reached. Generically, we refer to the end of a sequential file as the **end-of-file (EOF)**. There are a variety of ways of identifying the EOF. One is to place a special record, called a **sentinel**, at the end of the file. Another is to use the information in the operating system's directory system to identify a file's EOF.

A classic example involving sequential files is payroll processing in a small company. Here we imagine a sequential file consisting of a series of logical records, each of which contains the information about an employee's pay (name, employee identification number, pay scale, etc.) from which checks must be printed on a routine basis. As each employee record is retrieved, that employee's pay is calculated, and the appropriate check produced. The activity of processing such a sequential file is exemplified by the statement

while (the EOF has not been reached) **do**
(retrieve the next record from the file and process it)

Each logical record within a file is often uniquely identified by means of a particular field within the record (perhaps the employee's identification number in the case of a payroll file). Such an identifying field is called a **key field.** The value held in a key field is called a **key.** Arranging the records in a sequential file according to keys can greatly reduce processing time. For example, suppose that processing payroll requires that each employee record must be updated to reflect the information on that employee's time sheet. If both the file containing the time sheets and the file containing the employee records are in the same order according to the same key field, then this updating process can be handled by accessing both files sequentially—using the time sheet retrieved from one file to update the corresponding record from the other file. This is a significant improvement over the repeated searching process that would be required if the files were not in corresponding order. Thus updating classic sequential files is typically handled in multiple steps. First, the new information (such as the collection of time sheets) is recorded in a sequential file known as a transaction file, and this transaction file is sorted to match the order of the file to be updated, which is called the master file. Then, the records in the master file are updated by retrieving the records from both files sequentially.

A slight variation of this updating process is the process of merging two sequential files to form a new file containing the records from the two originals. The records in the input files are assumed to be arranged in ascending order according to a common key

Figure 9.14

A procedure for merging two sequential files

procedure MergeFiles (InputFileA, InputFileB, OutputFile)

if (both input files at EOF) **then** (Stop, with OutputFile empty)
if (InputFileA not at EOF) **then** (Declare its first record to be its current record)
if (InputFileB not at EOF) **then** (Declare its first record to be its current record)
while (neither input file at EOF) **do**
    (Put the current record with the "smaller" key field value in OutputFile;
    if (that current record is the last record in its corresponding input file)
      then (Declare that input file to be at EOF)
      else (Declare the next record in that input file to be the file's current record)
)
Starting with the current record in the input file that is not at EOF,
    copy the remaining records to OutputFile.

field, and it is also assumed that the files are to be merged in a manner that produces an output file whose keys are also in ascending order. The classic merge algorithm is summarized in Figure 9.14. The underlying theme is to build the output file as the two input files are scanned sequentially (Figure 9.15).

In closing note that a text file is merely a sequential file in which each logical record is a single symbol encoded using ASCII or Unicode. This simple structure is often the underlying framework used for implementing more elaborate sequential files such as an employee records file. One only needs to establish a uniform format for representing the information about each employee as a string of text, encode the information according to that format, and then record the resulting employee records one after another as one single string of text. For example, one could construct a simple employee file by agreeing to enter each employee record as a string of 31 characters, consisting of a field of 25 characters containing the employee's name (filled with enough blanks to complete the 25-character field), followed by a field of 6 characters representing the employee's identification number. The final file would be a long string of encoded characters in which each 31-character block represents the information about a single employee (Figure 9.16). Information would be retrieved from the file in terms of logical records consisting of 31-character blocks. Within each of these blocks, individual fields would be identified according to the uniform format with which the blocks were constructed.

Indexed Files

Sequential files are ideal for storing data that will be processed in the order in which the file's entries are stored. However, such files are inefficient when records within the file must be retrieved in an unpredictable order. In such situations what is needed is a way to identify the location of the desired logical record quickly. A popular solution is to use an index for the file in much the same way that an index in a book is used to locate topics within the book. Such a file system is called an **indexed file.**

Figure 9.15

Applying the merge algorithm (Letters are used to represent entire records.
The particular letter indicates the value of the record's key field.)

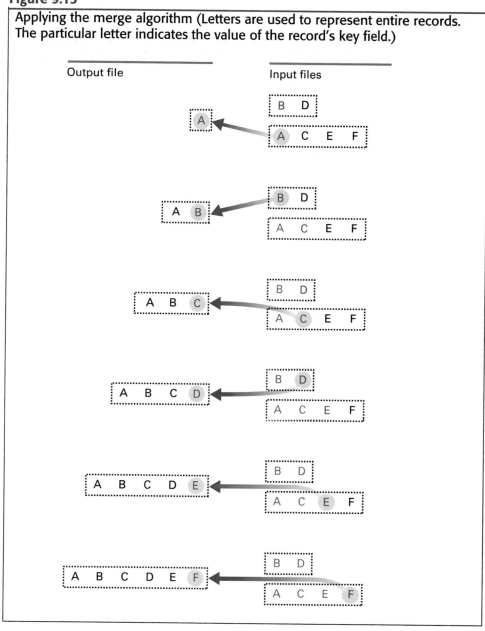

An index for a file contains a list of the keys stored in the file along with entries indicating where the record containing each key is stored. Thus to find a particular record, one finds the identifying key in the index and then retrieves the block of information stored at the location associated with that key.

Figure 9.16

The structure of a simple employee file implemented as a text file

File consists of a sequence of blocks each containing 31 characters.

File

Each block consists of a 25 character field containing an employee's name followed by a six character field containing the employee's identification number.

Logical record

| K | I | M | B | E | R | L | Y | | A | N | N | | D | A | W | S | O | N | | | | | | | 3 | 8 | 5 | 1 | 7 | 2 |

Employee's name

Employee's identification number

A file's index is normally stored as a separate file on the same mass storage device as the indexed file. The index is usually transferred to main memory before file processing begins so that it is easily accessible when access to records in the file is required (Figure 9.17).

A classic example of an indexed file occurs in the context of maintaining employee records. Here an index can be used to avoid lengthy searches when retrieving an individual record. In particular, if the file of employee records is indexed by employee identification numbers, then an employee's record can be retrieved quickly when the

Figure 9.17

Opening an indexed file

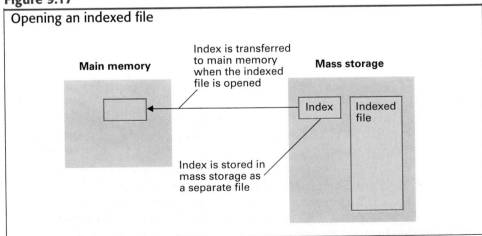

Main memory

Index is transferred to main memory when the indexed file is opened

Mass storage

Index

Indexed file

Index is stored in mass storage as a separate file

Authentication via Hashing

Hashing is much more than a means of constructing efficient data storage systems. For example, hashing can be used as a means of authenticating messages transferred over the Internet. The underlying theme is to hash the message (in a secret way) and encrypt the value obtained. This value is then transferred with the message. To authenticate the message, the receiver hashes the message received (in the same secret way) and confirms that the value produced agrees with the original value. If the value obtained does not agree with the original value, the message is assumed to be corrupted. In this light, most error detection techniques can be viewed as an application of hashing. For example, the parity system merely hashes each bit pattern to a 0 or a 1 and sends the result along with the pattern to be used in the authentication process.

employee's identification number is known. Another example is found on audio CDs where an index is used to allow relatively quick access to individual recordings.

Over the years numerous variations of the basic index concept have been used. One variation constructs an index in a hierarchical manner so that the index takes on a layered or tree structure. A prominent example is the hierarchical directory system used by most operating systems for organizing file storage. In such a case, the directories, or folders, play the role of indexes, each containing links to its subindexes. From this perspective, the entire file system is merely one large indexed file.

Hash Files

Although indexing provides relatively quick access to entries within a data storage structure, it does so at the expense of index maintenance. **Hashing** is a technique that provides similar access without such overhead. As in the case of an indexed system, hashing allows a record to be located by means of a key value. But, rather than looking up the key in an index, hashing identifies the location of the record directly from the key.

A hash system can be summarized as follows: The data storage space is divided into several sections, called **buckets,** each of which is capable of holding several records. The records are dispersed among the buckets according to an algorithm (called the **hash function**) that converts key values into bucket numbers. Each record is stored in the bucket identified by this process. Therefore, a record that has been placed in the storage structure can be retrieved by first applying the hash function to the record's identifying key to determine the appropriate bucket, then retrieving the contents of that bucket, and finally searching through the data retrieved for the desired record.

Hashing is not only used as a means of retrieving data from mass storage but also as a means of retrieving items from large blocks of data stored in main memory. When hashing is applied to a storage structure in mass storage, the result is called a **hash file.** When applied to a storage structure within main memory, the result is usually called a **hash table.**

Let us apply the hashing technique to the classic employee file in which each record contains information about a single employee in a company. First, we establish several available areas of mass storage that will play the role of buckets. The number of buckets and the size of each bucket are design decisions that we will consider later. For now, let us assume that we have created 41 buckets, which we refer to as bucket number 0, bucket number 1, through bucket number 40.

Let us assume that an employee's identification number will be used as the key for identifying the employee's record. Our next task, then, is to develop a hash function for converting these keys into bucket numbers. Although the employee identification "numbers" may have the form 25X3Z or J2X35 and are therefore not numeric, they are stored as bit patterns, and we can interpret the bit patterns as numbers. Using this numeric interpretation, we can divide any key by the number of buckets available and record the remainder, which in our case will be an integer in the range from 0 to 40. Thus we can use the remainder of this division process to identify one of the 41 buckets (Figure 9.18).

Using this as our hash function, we proceed to construct the file by considering each record individually, applying our divide-by-41 hash function to its key to obtain a bucket number, and then storing the record in that bucket (Figure 9.19). Later, if we need to retrieve a record, we need merely apply our hash function to the record's key to identify the appropriate bucket and then search that bucket for the record in question.

At this point let us reconsider our decision to divide the storage area into 41 buckets. First, note that to obtain an efficient hash system, the records being stored should be distributed evenly among the buckets. If a disproportionate number of keys happen to hash to the same bucket (a phenomenon called **clustering**), then a disproportionate number of records will be stored in a single bucket. In turn, retrieving a

Figure 9.18

Hashing the key field value 25X3Z to one of 41 buckets

Figure 9.19

The rudiments of a hashing system

Remainders

When divided by 41, the key field values of 14, 55, and 96 each produce a remainder of 14. Thus these records are stored in bucket 14.

95 136   96 14 55   343   Buckets in mass storage
#13   #14   #15   #16

record from that bucket could require a time consuming search, causing the loss of any benefits gained by hashing.

Now observe that if we had chosen to divide the storage area into 40 buckets rather than 41, our hash function would have involved dividing the keys by the value 40 rather than 41. But, if a dividend and a divisor both have a common factor, that factor will be present in the remainder as well. In particular, if the keys to the entries stored in our hash file happened to be multiples of 5 (which is also a divisor of 40), then the factor of 5 would appear in the remainders when divided by 40, and the entries would cluster in those buckets associated with the remainders 0, 5, 10, 15, 20, 25, 30, and 35. Similar situations would occur in the case of keys that are multiples of 2, 4, 8, 10, and 20, because they are all also factors of 40. Consequently, we choose to divide the storage area into 41 buckets because the choice of 41, being a prime number, eliminated the possibility of common factors and therefore reduced the chance of clustering.

Unfortunately, the possibility of clustering can never be completely eliminated—only reduced. Even with a well-designed hash function, it is highly likely that two keys will hash to the same value, a phenomenon called a **collision,** early in the file construction process. To understand why, consider the following scenario.

Suppose that we have found a hash function that arbitrarily distributes records among 41 buckets, that our storage system is empty, and that we are going to insert new records one at a time. When we insert the first record, it will be placed in an empty bucket. However, when we insert the next record, only 40 of the 41 buckets are still empty, so the probability that the second record will be placed in an empty bucket is only 40/41. Assuming that the second record is placed in an empty bucket, the third record finds only 39 empty buckets, and thus the probability of it being placed in one of them is 39/41. Continuing this process, we find that if the first seven records are placed in empty buckets, the eighth record has a 34/41 probability of being placed in one of the remaining empty buckets.

This analysis allows us to compute the probability that all the first eight records will be placed in empty buckets—it is the product of the probabilities of each record being placed in an empty bucket, assuming that the preceding entries were so placed. This probability is

$$(41/41)(40/41)(39/41)(38/41) \ . \ . \ . \ (34/41) = .482$$

The point is that the result is less than one-half. That is, it is more likely than not that when distributing records among 41 buckets a collision will have occurred by the time the eighth record is stored.

The high probability of collisions indicates that, regardless of how well-chosen a hash function may be, any hash system must be designed with clustering in mind. In particular, it is possible that a bucket may fill up and overflow. One approach to this problem would be to allow the buckets to expand in size. Another approach is to allow buckets to spill into an overflow area that has been reserved for that purpose. In any case the problem of clustering and overflowing buckets can significantly degrade the performance of a hash file.

Research has shown that, as a general rule, hash files perform well as long as the ratio of the number of records to the total record capacity of the file (a ratio known as the **load factor**) remains below 50 percent. However, if the load factor begins to creep above 75 percent, the system's performance generally degrades (clustering raises its ugly head, causing some buckets to fill and possibly overflow). For this reason, a hash storage system is usually reconstructed with a larger capacity if its load factor approaches the 75 percent value. We conclude that the efficiency of record retrieval obtained by implementing a hash system is not gained without cost—one cost being less economic use of storage space.

Questions/Exercises

1. Follow the merge algorithm presented in Figure 9.14, assuming that one input file contains records with key field values equal to B and E while the other contains A, C, D, and F.
2. The merge algorithm is the heart of a popular sort algorithm called the merge sort. Can you discover this algorithm? (*Hint:* Any nonempty file can be considered to be a collection of one-entry files.)
3. Is being sequential a physical or conceptual property of a file?
4. What are the steps required when retrieving a record from an indexed file?
5. Explain how a poorly chosen hash function can result in a hash storage system becoming little more than a sequential file.

6. Suppose a hash storage system is constructed using the division hash function as presented in the text but with six storage buckets. For each of the following key values, identify the bucket in which the record with that key is placed. What goes wrong and why?

a. 24   b. 30   c. 3   d. 18   e. 15
f. 21   g. 9   h. 39   i. 27   j. 0

7. How many people must be gathered together before the odds are that two members of the group will have birthdays on the same day of the year? How does this problem relate to the material in this section?

9.6 Data Mining

A rapidly expanding subject that is closely associated with database technology is **data mining,** which consists of techniques for discovering patterns in collections of data. Data mining has become an important tool in numerous areas including marketing, inventory management, quality control, loan risk management, fraud detection, and investment analysis. Data mining techniques even have applications in what might seem unlikely settings as exemplified by their use in identifying the functions of particular genes encoded in DNA molecules and characterizing properties of organisms.

Data mining activities differ from traditional database interrogation since data mining seeks to identify previously unknown patterns as opposed to traditional database inquiries that merely ask for the retrieval of stored facts. Moreover, data mining is practiced on static data collections, called **data warehouses,** rather than "online" operational databases that are subject to frequent updates. These warehouses are often "snapshots" of databases or collections of databases. They are used in lieu of the actual operational databases because finding patterns in a static system is easier than in a dynamic one.

We should also note that the subject of data mining is not restricted to the domain of computing but has tentacles that extend far into statistics. In fact, many would argue that since data mining had its origins in attempts to perform statistical analysis on large diverse data collections, it is an application of statistics rather than a field of computer science.

Two common forms of data mining are class description and class discrimination. Class description deals with identifying properties that characterize a given group of data items, whereas class discrimination deals with identifying properties that divide two groups. For example, class description techniques would be used to identify characteristics of people who buy small economical vehicles, whereas class discrimination techniques would be used to find properties that distinguish customers who shop for used cars from those who shop for new ones.

Another form of data mining is cluster analysis, which seeks to discover classes. Note that this differs from class description, which seeks to discover properties of members within classes that are already identified. More precisely, cluster analysis tries to find properties of data items that lead to the discovery of groupings. For example, when analyzing information about people who have viewed a particular motion picture, cluster analysis may find that, by considering the age of the viewers, the customer base breaks down into two age groups—a 4 to 10 age group and a 25 to 40 age group. (Perhaps the motion picture attracted children and their parents?)

Bioinformatics

Advances in database technology and data mining techniques are expanding the repertoire of tools available to biologists in research areas involving the identification of patterns and the classification of organic compounds. The result is a new field within biology called bioinformatics. Having originated in endeavors to decode DNA, bioinformatics now encompasses such tasks as cataloguing proteins and understanding sequences of protein interactions (called biochemical pathways). Although normally considered to be a part of biology, bioinformatics is an example of how computer science is influencing and even becoming ingrained in other fields.

Still another form of data mining, association analysis, looks for links between data groups. It is association analysis that may reveal that customers who buy potato chips also buy beer and soda or that people who shop during the traditional weekday work hours also draw retirement benefits.

Outlier analysis is another form of data mining. It tries to identify data entries that do not comply with the norm. Outlier analysis can be used to identify errors in data collections, to identify credit card theft by detecting sudden deviations from a customer's normal purchase patterns, and perhaps to identify potential terrorists by recognizing unusual behavior.

Finally, the form of data mining called sequential pattern analysis tries to identify patterns of behavior over time. For example, sequential pattern analysis may reveal trends in economic systems such as equity markets or in environmental systems such as climate conditions.

As indicated by our last example, results from data mining can be used to predict future behavior. If an entity possesses the properties that characterize a class, then the entity will probably behave like members of that class. However, many data mining projects are aimed at merely gaining a better understanding of the data, as witnessed by the use of data mining in unraveling the mysteries of DNA. In any case, the scope of data mining applications is potentially enormous, and thus data mining promises to be an active area of research for years to come.

Moreover, database technology and data mining are close cousins, and thus research in one will have repercussions in the other. Database techniques are used extensively to give data warehouses the capability of presenting data in the form of data cubes (data viewed from multiple perspectives) that make data mining possible. In turn, as researchers in data mining improve techniques for implementing data cubes, these results will pay dividends in the field of database design.

In closing, we should recognize that successful data mining encompasses much more than the identification of patterns within a collection of data. Intelligent judgment must be applied to determine whether those patterns are significant or merely coincidences. The fact that a particular convenience store has sold a high number of winning lottery tickets should probably not be considered significant to someone planning to buy a lottery ticket, but the discovery that customers who buy snack food also tend to buy frozen dinners might constitute meaningful information to a grocery store manager. Likewise, data mining encompasses a vast number of ethical issues involving the rights of individuals represented in the data warehouse, the accuracy and use of the conclusions drawn, and even the appropriateness of data mining in the first place.

Questions/Exercises

1. Why is data mining not conducted on "online" databases?
2. Give an additional example of a pattern that might be found by each of the types of data mining identified in the text.
3. Identify some different perspectives that a data cube may allow in mining sales data.
4. How does data mining differ from traditional database inquiries?

9.7 Social Impact of Database Technology

In the past, collections of data were processed manually, meaning that relationships between information scattered throughout large collections were essentially undiscoverable. For example, the reading habits of a library's patrons may have been buried within the library's records, but unraveling it would have been a time-consuming process. Today, however, most library records are automated, and in some cases, profiles of an individual's reading habits are within easy reach. It is now feasible for libraries to provide such information to marketing firms, law enforcement agencies, political parties, employers, and private individuals.

This example is representative of the potential problems that permeate the entire spectrum of database applications. Technology has made it easy to collect enormous amounts of data and to merge or compare different data collections to obtain relationships that would otherwise remain buried in the heap. The ramifications, both positive and negative, are enormous.

Consequently, data collection is now conducted on a massive scale. In some cases the process is readily apparent; in others it is subtle. Examples of the first case occur when one is explicitly asked to provide information. This may be done in a voluntary manner, as in surveys or contest registration forms, or it may be done in an involuntary manner, such as when imposed by government regulations. Sometimes whether it is voluntary or not depends on one's point of view. Is providing personal information when applying for a loan voluntary or involuntary? The distinction depends on whether receiving the loan is a convenience or a necessity. To use a credit card at some retailers now requires that you allow your signature to be recorded in a digitized format. Again, providing the information is either voluntary or involuntary depending on your situation.

More subtle cases of data collection avoid direct communication with the subject. Examples include a credit company that records the purchasing practices of the holders of its credit cards, sites on the World Wide Web that record the identities of those who visit the site, and social activists who record the license plate numbers on the cars parked in a targeted institution's parking lot. In these cases the subject of the data collection may not be aware that information is being collected and less likely to be aware of the existence of the databases being constructed.

Sometimes the underlying data-collection activities are self-evident if one merely stops to think. For example, a grocery store may offer discounts to its regular customers who register in advance with the store. The registration process may involve the issuance of identification cards that must be presented at the time of purchase to obtain the discount. The result is that the store is able to compile a record of the customers' purchases—a record whose value far exceeds the value of the discounts awarded.

Of course, the force driving this boom in data collection is the value of the data, which is amplified by advances in database technology that allow data to be linked in ways that reveal information that would otherwise remain obscure. For example, the purchasing patterns of credit card holders can be classified and cross-listed to obtain customer profiles of immense marketing value. Subscription forms for bodybuilding magazines can be mailed to those who have recently purchased exercise equipment, whereas similar forms for dog obedience magazines can be targeted toward those who have recently purchased dog food. Alternative ways of combining information are sometimes very imaginative. Welfare records have been compared to criminal records to find and apprehend parole violators, and in 1984 the Selective Service in the United States used the birthday registration list from a popular ice cream retailer to identify citizens who had failed to register for the military draft.

There are several approaches that can be taken to protect society from abusive use of databases. One is to apply legal remedies. Unfortunately, passing a law against an action does not stop the action from occurring but merely makes the action illegal. A prime example in the United States is the Privacy Act of 1974 whose purpose was to protect citizens from abusive use of government databases. One provision of this act required government agencies to publish notice of their databases in the Federal Register to allow citizens to access and correct their personal information. However, government agencies have been slow to comply with this provision. This does not necessarily imply malicious intent. In many cases the problem has been one of bureaucracy. But, the fact that a bureaucracy may be constructing personnel databases that it is unable to identify is not reassuring.

Another, and perhaps more powerful, approach to controlling database abuse is public opinion. Databases will not be abused if the penalties outweigh the benefits; and the penalty businesses fear the most is adverse public opinion—this goes right to the bottom line. In the early 1990s it was public opinion that ultimately stopped major credit bureaus from selling mailing lists for marketing purposes. More recently, America Online (a major Internet service provider) buckled under public pressure against its policy of selling customer-related information to telemarketers. Even government agencies have bowed to public opinion. In 1997 the Social Security Administration in the United States modified its plan to make social security records available via the Internet when public opinion questioned the security of the information. In these cases results were obtained in days—a stark contrast to the extended time periods associated with legal processes.

Of course, in many cases database applications are beneficial to both the holder and the subject of the data, but in all cases there is a loss of privacy that should not be taken lightly. Privacy issues are serious when the information is accurate, but they become gigantic when the information is erroneous. Imagine the feeling of hopelessness if you realized that your credit rating was adversely affected by erroneous information. Imagine how your problems would be amplified in an environment in which this misinformation was readily shared with other institutions.

Privacy problems are, and will be, a major side effect of advancing technology in general and database techniques in particular. The solutions to these problems will require an educated, alert, and active citizenry.

Questions/Exercises

1. Should law enforcement agencies be given access to databases for the purpose of identifying individuals with criminal tendencies, even though the individuals may not have committed a crime?

2. Should insurance companies be given access to databases for the purpose of identifying individuals with potential medical problems, even though the individuals have not shown any symptoms?

3. Suppose you were financially comfortable. What benefits could you derive if this information were shared among a variety of institutions? What penalties could you suffer from the distribution of this same information? What if you were financially uncomfortable?

4. What role does a free press have in controlling database abuse? (For example, to what extent does the press affect public opinion?)

Chapter Review Problems

(Asterisked problems are associated with optional sections.)

1. Summarize the distinction between a flat file and a database.

2. What is meant by data independence?

3. What is the role of a DBMS in the layered approach to a database implementation?

4. What is the difference between a schema and a subschema?

5. Identify two benefits of separating application software from the DBMS.

6. Identify the level within a database system (user, programmer of application software, designer of the DBMS software) at which each of the following concerns or activities occur:

   a. How should data be stored on a disk to maximize efficiency?

   b. Is there a vacancy on flight 243?

   c. Could a relation be stored as a sequential file?

   d. How many times should a user be allowed to mistype a password before the conversation is terminated?

e. How can the PROJECT operation be implemented?

7. Describe how the following information about airlines, flights (for a particular day), and passengers would be represented in a relational database:

Airlines: Clear Sky, Long Hop, and Tree Top

Flights for Clear Sky: CS205, CS37, and CS102

Flights for Long Hop: LH67 and LH89

Flights for Tree Top: TT331 and TT809

Smith has reservations on CS205 (seat 12B), CS37 (seat 18C), and LH 89 (seat 14A).

Baker has reservations on CS37 (seat 18B) and LH89 (seat 14B).

Clark has reservations on LH67 (seat 5A) and TT331 (seat 4B).

8. To what extent is the order in which SELECT and PROJECT operations are applied to a relation significant? That is, under what conditions will SELECTing and then PROJECTing produce the same results as first PROJECTing and then SELECTing?

9. In terms of the relations shown below, what is the appearance of the relation RESULT after executing each of these instructions:

X relation

U	V	W
A	Z	5
B	D	3
C	Q	5

Y relation

R	S
3	J
4	K

a. RESULT ← PROJECT W from X
b. RESULT ← SELECT from X where W = 5
c. RESULT ← PROJECT S from Y
d. RESULT ← JOIN X and Y where X.W Y.R

10. Using the commands SELECT, PROJECT, and JOIN, write a sequence of instructions to answer each of the following questions about parts and their manufacturers in terms of the following database:

PART relation

PartName	Weight
Bolt 2X	1
Bolt 2Z	1.5
Nut V5	0.5

MANUFACTURER relation

CompanyName	PartName	Cost
Company X	Bolt 2Z	.03
Company X	Nut V5	.01
Company Y	Bolt 2X	.02
Company Y	Nut V5	.01
Company Y	Bolt 2Z	.04
Company Z	Nut V5	.01

a. Which companies make Bolt 2Z?
b. Obtain a list of the parts made by Company X along with each part's cost.
c. Which companies make a part with weight 1?

11. Answer Problem 10 using SQL.

12. Using commands such as SELECT, PROJECT, and JOIN, write sequences to answer the following questions about the information in the EMPLOYEE, JOB, and ASSIGNMENT relations in Figure 9.5:

a. Obtain a list of the names and addresses of the company's employees.
b. Obtain a list of the names and addresses of those who have worked or are working in the personnel department.
c. Obtain a list of the names and addresses of those who are working in the personnel department.

13. Answer the previous problem using SQL.

14. Design a relational database containing information about music composers, their lives, and their compositions. (Avoid redundancies similar to those in Figure 9.4.)

15. Design a relational database containing information about music performers, their recordings, and the composers of the music they recorded. (Avoid redundancies similar to those in Figure 9.4.)

16. Design a relational database containing information about manufacturers of computing equipment and their products. (Avoid redundancies similar to those in Figure 9.4.)

17. Design a relational database containing information about publishers, magazines, and subscribers, in which the relationships among these entities are represented by the following entity-relationship diagram. (Avoid redundancies similar to those in Figure 9.4.)

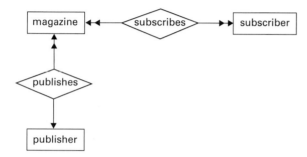

18. Design a relational database containing information about parts, suppliers, and customers. Each part may be supplied by several suppliers and ordered by many customers. Each supplier may supply many parts and have many customers. Each customer may order many parts from many suppliers; in fact, the same part may be ordered from more than one supplier. (Avoid redundancies similar to those in Figure 9.4.)

19. What inconvenience may arise because of our decision to combine the month, day, and year into a single attribute in the relational database in Figure 9.5?

20. Write a sequence of instructions (using the operations SELECT, PROJECT, and JOIN) to retrieve the JobId, StartDate, and TermDate for each job in the accounting department from the relational database described in Figure 9.6.

21. Answer the previous problem using SQL.

22. Write a sequence of instructions (using the operations SELECT, PROJECT, and JOIN) to retrieve the Name, Address, JobTitle, and Dept of every current employee from the relational database described in Figure 9.5.

23. Answer the previous problem using SQL.

24. Write a sequence of instructions (using the operations SELECT, PROJECT, and JOIN) to retrieve the Name and JobTitle of each current employee from the relational database described in Figure 9.5.

25. Answer the previous problem using SQL.

26. What is the difference in the information supplied by the single relation

a.

Name	Department	TelephoneNumber
Jones	Sales	555-2222
Smith	Sales	555-3333
Baker	Personnel	555-4444

and the two relations

b.

Name	Department
Jones	Sales
Smith	Sales
Baker	Personnel

c.

Department	TelephoneNumber
Sales	555-2222
Sales	555-3333
Personnel	555-4444

27. Design a relational database containing information about automobile parts and their subparts. Be sure to allow for the fact that one part may contain smaller parts and at the same time be contained in still larger parts.

28. Based on the database represented in Figure 9.5, state the question that is answered by the following program segment:

```
TEMP ← SELECT from ASSIGNMENT
    where TermDate = "*"
RESULT ← PROJECT JobId, StartDate from TEMP
```

29. Translate the query in the previous problem into SQL.

30. Based on the database represented in Figure 9.5, state the question that is answered by the following program segment:

```
TEMP1 ← JOIN EMPLOYEE and ASSIGNMENT
    where EMPLOYEE.EmplId = ASSIGNMENT.EmplId
TEMP2 ← SELECT from TEMP1
    where TermDate = "*"
RESULT ← PROJECT name, StartDate from TEMP2
```

31. Translate the query in the previous problem into SQL.

32. Based on the database represented in Figure 9.5, state the question that is answered by the following program segment:

```
TEMP1 ← JOIN EMPLOYEE and JOB
    where EMPLOYEE.EmplId = JOB.EmplId
TEMP2 ← SELECT from TEMP1
    where Dept = "SALES"
RESULT ← PROJECT Name from TEMP2
```

33. Translate the query in the previous problem into SQL.

34. Translate the SQL statement

```
select JOB.JobTitle
from ASSIGNMENT, JOB
where ASSIGNMENT.JobId = JOB.JobId
and ASSIGNMENT.EmplId = "34Y70"
```

into a sequence of SELECT, PROJECT, and JOIN operations.

35. Translate the SQL statement

```
select ASSIGNMENT.StartDate
from ASSIGNMENT, EMPLOYEE
where ASSIGNMENT.EmplId =
EMPLOYEE.EmplId
and EMPLOYEE.Name = "Joe E. Baker"
```

into a sequence of SELECT, PROJECT, and JOIN operations.

36. Describe the effect that the following SQL statement would have on the database in Problem 10.

```
insert into MANUFACTURER
values ('Company Z', 'Bolt 2X', .03)
```

37. Describe the effect that the following SQL statement would have on the database in Problem 10.

```
update MANUFACTURER
set Cost = .03
where CompanyName = 'Company Y'
and PartName = 'Bolt 2X'
```

*38. Identify some of the objects that you would expect to find in an object-oriented database used to maintain a grocery store's inventory. What methods would you expect to find within each of these objects?

*39. Identify some of the objects that you would expect to find in an object-oriented database used to maintain records of a library's holdings. What methods would you expect to find within each of these objects?

*40. What incorrect information is generated by the following schedule of transactions T1 and T2?

T1 is designed to compute the sum of accounts A and B; T2 is designed to transfer $100 from account A to account B. T1 begins by retrieving the balance of account A; then, T2 performs its transfer; and finally, T1 retrieves the balance of account B and reports the sum of the values it has retrieved.

*41. Explain how the locking protocol described in the text would resolve the error produced in Problem 40.

*42. What effect would the wound-wait protocol have on the sequence of events in Problem 40 if T1 was the younger transaction? If T2 was the younger transaction?

*43. Suppose one transaction tries to add $100 to an account whose balance is $200 while another tries to withdraw $100 from the same account. Describe an interweaving of these transactions that would lead to a final balance of $100. Describe an interweaving of these transactions that would lead to a final balance of $300.

*44. What is the difference between a transaction having exclusive access and one having shared access to an item in a database and why is the distinction important?

*45. The problems discussed in Section 9.4 involving concurrent transactions are not limited to database environments. What similar problems would arise when accessing a document with word processors? (If you have a PC with a word processor, try to access the same document with two activations of the word processor and see what happens.)

*46. Suppose a sequential file contains 50,000 records and 5 milliseconds is required to interrogate an entry. How long should we expect to wait when retrieving a record from the middle of the file?

*47. List the steps that are executed in the merge algorithm in Figure 9.14 if one of the input files is empty at the start.

*48. Modify the algorithm in Figure 9.14 to handle the case in which both input files contain a record with the same key field value. Assume that these records are identical and that only one should appear in the output file.

*49. Design a system by which a file stored on a disk can be processed as a sequential file with either of two different orderings.

*50. Describe how a sequential file containing information about a magazine's subscribers could be constructed using a text file as the underlying structure.

*51. Design a technique by which a sequential file whose logical records are not a consistent size could be implemented as a text file. For example, suppose you wanted to construct a sequential file containing information about novelists in which each logical record contained information about a novelist as well as a list of that author's works.

*52. What advantages does an indexed file have over a hash file? What advantages does a hash file have over an indexed file?

*53. The chapter drew parallels between a traditional file index and the file directory system maintained by an operating system. In what ways does an operating system's file directory differ from a traditional index?

*54. If a hash file is partitioned into 10 buckets, what is the probability of at least two of three arbitrary records hashing to the same section? (Assume the hash function gives no bucket priority over the others.) How many records must be stored in the file until it is more likely for collisions to occur than not?

*55. Solve the previous problem, assuming that the file is partitioned into 100 buckets instead of 10.

*56. If we are using the division technique discussed in this chapter as a hash function and the file storage area is divided into 23 buckets, which section should we search to find the record whose key, when interpreted as a binary value, reduces to the integer 124?

*57. Compare the implementation of a hash file to that of a homogeneous two-dimensional array. How are the roles of the hash function and the address polynomial similar?

*58. Give one advantage that
   a. a sequential file has over an indexed file.
   b. a sequential file has over a hash file.
   c. an indexed file has over a sequential file.
   d. an indexed file has over a hash file.
   e. a hash file has over a sequential file.
   f. a hash file has over an indexed file.

*59. In what way is a sequential file similar to a linked list?

Social Issues

The following questions are provided to help you understand some of the ethical/social/legal issues associated with the field of computing. The goal is not merely to answer these questions. You should also consider why you answered as you did and whether your justifications are consistent from one question to the next.

1. In the United States, DNA records of all federal prisoners are now stored in a database for use in criminal investigations. Would it be ethical to release this information for other purposes—for example, for genetic research? If so, for what purposes? If not, why not? What are the pros and cons in each case?

2. To what extent should a university be allowed to release information about its students? What about their names and addresses? What about grade distributions without identifying the students? Is your answer consistent with your answer to Question 1?

3. What restrictions are appropriate regarding the construction of databases about individuals? What information does a government have a right to hold regarding its citizens? What information does an insurance company have a right to hold regarding its clients? What information does a company have a right to hold regarding its employees? Should controls in these settings be implemented and, if so, how?

4. Is it proper for a credit card company to sell the purchasing patterns of its clients to marketing firms? Is it acceptable for a sports car mail order business to sell its mailing list to a sports car magazine? Is it acceptable for the Internal Revenue Service to sell the names and addresses of those taxpayers with significant capital gains to stockbrokers? If you cannot answer with an unqualified yes or no, what would you propose as an acceptable policy?

5. To what extent is the designer of a database responsible for how the information in that database is used?

6. Suppose a database mistakenly allows unapproved access to information in the database. If that information is obtained and used adversely, to what degree do the database designers share responsibility for the misuse of the information? Does your answer depend on the amount of effort required by the perpetrator to discover the flaw in the database design and obtain the unauthorized information?

7. The prevalence of data mining raises numerous issues of ethics and privacy. Is your privacy infringed if data mining reveals certain characteristics about the overall population of your community? Does the use of data mining promote good business practice or bigotry? To what extent is it proper to force citizens to participate in a census, knowing that more information will be extracted from the data than is explicitly requested by the individual questionnaires? Does data mining give marketing firms an unfair advantage over unsuspecting audiences? To what extent is profiling good or bad?

8. Many libraries offer a reference service so that patrons can enlist the assistance of a librarian when searching for information. Will the existence of the Internet and database technology render this service obsolete? If so, would that be a step forward or backward? If not, why not? How will the existence of the Internet and database technology affect the existence of libraries themselves?

Additional Reading

Date, C. J. *An Introduction to Database Systems,* 8th ed. Reading, MA: Addison-Wesley, 2004.

Dunham, M. H. *Data Mining*. Upper Saddle River, NJ: Prentice Hall, 2003.

Ramakrishnan, R. *Database Management Systems,* 3rd ed. New York: McGraw-Hill, 2003.

Silberschatz, A., H. Korth, and S. Sudarshan. *Database Systems Concepts*, 4th ed. New York: McGraw-Hill, 2002.

Ullman, J. D. and J. D. Widom. *A First Course in Database Systems*, 2nd ed. Upper Saddle River, NJ: Prentice Hall, 2002.

Artificial Intelligence

Artificial Intelligence is the field of computer science that seeks to build autonomous machines—machines that can carry out complex tasks without human intervention. This goal requires that machines be able to perceive and reason, both of which fall within the category of commonsense activities that, although natural for the human mind, are apparently quite difficult for machines. The result is that, although fascinating progress has been made, the field of artificial intelligence is still in its infancy when compared to its goals. In this chapter we explore some of the topics in this vast area of research.

10.1 Intelligence and Machines

The field of artificial intelligence is quite large and merges with other subjects such as psychology, neurology, mathematics, linguistics, and electrical and mechanical engineering. To focus our thoughts, then, we begin by considering the concept of an agent and the types of intelligent behavior that an agent may exhibit. Indeed, much of the research in artificial intelligence can be categorized in terms of an agent's behavior.

Intelligent Agents

An **agent** is a "device" that responds to stimuli from its environment. Most agents have sensors by which they receive data from their environments and actuators by which they can affect their environments. Examples of sensors include microphones, cameras, and air sampling devices. Examples of actuators include grippers, legs, wings, and speech synthesizers. It is natural to envision an agent as an individual machine such as a robot, although an agent may take the form of merely a single program whose execution shares time with other tasks on a multitasking computer. In particular, clients and servers in a network could be considered agents that send and receive massages by means of their "actuators" and "sensors."

The goal of artificial intelligence is to build agents that behave intelligently. This means that the actions of the agent's actuators must be rational responses to the data received though its sensors. In the simplest case, these responses might be reflex actions in which each action is a predetermined response to the input data.

Higher levels of response are required to obtain more "intelligent" behavior. For example, we might empower an agent with knowledge of its environment and require that the agent adjust its actions accordingly. Throwing a baseball is largely a reflex action but determining how and where to throw the ball requires knowledge of the current environment. (There is one out with runners on first and third.) How such real-world knowledge can be stored, updated, accessed, and ultimately brought to influence the decision making process continues to be a challenging problem in artificial intelligence.

Another level of response is required if we want the agent to seek a goal such as winning a game of chess or maneuvering through a crowded passageway. Such goal directed behavior requires that the agent's response, or sequence of responses, be the result of deliberately forming a plan of action or selecting the best action among the current options. We will explore some results of research in goal directed behavior in Section 10.3.

In some cases an agent's responses may improve over time as the agent learns. This could take the form of developing **procedural knowledge** (learning "how") or storing **declarative knowledge** (learning "what"). Learning procedural knowledge usually involves a trial and error process by which an agent learns appropriate actions by being punished for poor actions and rewarded for good ones. Following this approach, agents have been developed that, over time, improve their abilities in competitive games such as checkers and chess. Learning declarative knowledge usually takes the form of expanding or altering the "facts" in an agent's store of knowledge. For example, a baseball player must repeatedly adjust his or her database of knowledge (there is still just one out, but now runners are on first and second) from which rational responses to future events are determined.

To produce rational responses to stimuli, an agent must "understand" the stimuli received by its sensors. That is, an agent must be able to extract information from the data produced by its sensors, or in other words, an agent must be able to perceive. In some cases this is a straightforward process. Signals obtained from a gyroscope are easily encoded in forms compatible with calculations for determining responses. But in other cases extracting information from input data is difficult. Examples include understanding speech and images. Likewise, agents must be able to formulate their responses in terms compatible with their actuators. This may be a straightforward process or it may require an agent to formulate responses as complete spoken sentences—meaning that the agent must generate speech. In turn, such topics as image processing and analysis, natural language understanding, and speech generation are important areas of research.

The agent attributes that we have identified here represent past as well as current areas of research. Of course, they are not totally independent of each other. Ultimately, we would like to develop agents that possess all of them, producing agents that understand the data received from their environments and develop new response patterns through a learning process whose goal is to maximize the agent's abilities. However, by isolating various types of rational behavior and pursuing them independently, researchers gain a toehold that can later be combined with progress in other areas to produce more intelligent agents.

We close this subsection by introducing an agent that will provide a context for our discussion in Sections 10.2 and 10.3. The agent is designed to solve the eight-puzzle, which consists of eight square tiles labeled 1 through 8 mounted in a frame capable of holding a total of nine such tiles in three rows and three columns (Figure 10.1). Among the tiles in the frame is a vacancy into which any of the adjacent tiles can be pushed, allowing the tiles in the frame to be scrambled. The problem posed is to move the tiles in a scrambled puzzle back to their initial positions (Figure 10.1).

Figure 10.1

The eight-puzzle in its solved configuration

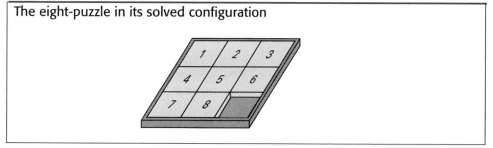

Our agent takes the form of a box equipped with a gripper, a video camera, and a finger with a rubber end so that it does not slip when pushing something (Figure 10.2). When the agent is first turned on, its gripper begins to open and close as if asking for the puzzle. When we place a scrambled eight-puzzle in the gripper, the gripper closes on the puzzle. After a short time the machine's finger lowers and begins pushing the tiles around in the frame until they are back in their original positions. At this point the machine releases the puzzle and turns itself off.

This puzzle-solving machine exhibits two of the agent attributes that we have identified. First, it must be able to perceive in the sense that it must extract the current puzzle state from the image it receives from its camera. We will address issues of understanding images in Section 10.2. Second, it must develop and implement a plan for obtaining a goal. We will address these issues in Section 10.3.

Performance Versus Simulation

In the final analysis, the behavior of an agent is judged to be intelligent (or rational) by observing its input-response patterns. This leads to two approaches to research in artificial intelligence. One is **performance oriented** in which the researcher tries to maximize the performance of the agent. The other is **simulation oriented** in which the researcher is more interested in how the responses are produced than in the efficiency of the agent. Performance oriented research is common in cases when the immediate goal is to produce a product. Simulation oriented research is more compatible with long-term research and development projects in which the goal is to expand our understanding of a subject. Both play important roles in the advancement of artificial intelligence.

Figure 10.2

Our puzzle-solving machine

The Origins of Artificial Intelligence

The quest to build machines that mimic human behavior has a long history, but many would agree that the modern field of artificial intelligence has its origins in 1950. This was the year that Alan Turing published the article *Computing Machinery and Intelligence* in which he proposed that machines could be programmed to exhibit intelligent behavior. The name of the field—*artificial intelligence*—was coined a few years later in the now legendary proposal written by John McCarthy who suggested that a "study of artificial intelligence be carried out during the summer of 1956 at Dartmouth College" to explore "the conjecture that every aspect of learning or any other feature of intelligence can in principle be so precisely described that a machine can be made to simulate it."

As an example, consider the fields of natural language processing and linguistics. These fields are closely related and benefit from research in each other, yet the underlying goals are different. Linguists are interested in learning how humans process language, whereas researchers in the field of natural language processing are interested in developing machines that can manipulate natural language. Thus, linguists operate in simulation-oriented mode—building systems whose goals are to test theories. In contrast, researchers in natural language processing operate in performance-oriented mode—building systems to perform tasks. Systems produced in this latter mode (such as document translators and systems by which machines respond to verbal commands) rely heavily on knowledge gained by linguists but often apply "shortcuts" that happen to work in the restricted environment of the particular system.

As an elementary example, consider the task of developing a shell for an operating system that receives instructions from the outside world through verbal English commands. In this case, the shell (an agent) does not need to worry about the entire English language. More precisely, the shell does not need to distinguish between the various meanings of the word *copy* (Is it a noun or a verb? Should it carry the connotation of plagiarism?). Instead, the shell needs merely to distinguish the word *copy* from other commands such as *rename* and *delete*. Thus the shell could perform its task just by matching its inputs to predetermined audio patterns. The performance of such a system may be satisfactory but it would not be aesthetically pleasing to a linguist.

The Turing Test

In the past the **Turing test** (proposed by Alan Turing in 1950) has served as a benchmark in measuring progress in the field of artificial intelligence. Turing's proposal was to allow a human, whom we call the interrogator, to communicate with a test subject by means of a typewriter system, without being told whether the test subject was a human or a machine. In this environment, a machine would be declared to behave intelligently if the interrogator was not able to distinguish it from a human. Turing predicted that by the year 2000 machines would have a 30 percent chance of passing a five-minute Turing test—a conjecture that has turned out to be surprisingly accurate.

A well-known example of a Turing test scenario arose as a result of the program DOCTOR (a version of the more general system called ELIZA) developed by Joseph Weizenbaum in the mid–1960s. This interactive program was designed to project the image of a Rogerian analyst conducting a psychological interview; the computer played the role of the analyst while the user played the patient. Internally, all that DOCTOR did was restructure the statements made by the patient according to some well-defined rules and direct them back to the patient. For example, in response to the statement "I am tired today," DOCTOR might have replied with "Why do you think you're tired today?" If DOCTOR was unable to recognize the sentence structure, it merely responded with something like "Go on" or "That's very interesting."

Weizenbaum's purpose in developing DOCTOR dealt with the study of natural language communication. From this point of view, the subject of psychotherapy played the secondary role of providing an environment (or a domain of discourse) in which the program could function. To Weizenbaum's dismay, however, several psychologists proposed using the program for actual psychotherapy. (The Rogerian thesis is that the patient, not the analyst, should lead the discussion during the therapeutic session, and thus, they argued, a computer could possibly conduct a discussion as well as a therapist could.) Moreover, DOCTOR projected the image of comprehension so strongly that many who "communicated" with it found themselves relating intimate thoughts and feelings and, in many cases, actually becoming subservient to the machine's question-and-answer dialogue. In a sense, DOCTOR passed the Turing test. The result was that ethical, as well as technical, issues were raised, and Weizenbaum became an advocate for maintaining human dignity in a world of advancing technology.

Questions/Exercises

1. Identify several types of "intelligent" actions that might be made by an agent.

2. A plant placed in a dark room with a single light source grows toward the light. Is this an intelligent response? Does the plant possess intelligence? What, then, is your definition of intelligence?

3. Suppose a vending machine is designed to dispense various products depending on which button is pressed. Would you say that such a machine is "aware" of which button is pressed? What, then, is your definition of awareness?

4. If a machine passes the Turing test, would you agree that it is intelligent? If not, would you agree that it appears to be intelligent?

10.2 Understanding Images

Let us now return to the issues posed by the puzzle-solving machine introduced in the previous section. The opening and closing of the gripper on the machine presents no serious problem, and the ability to detect the presence of the puzzle in the gripper during this process is straightforward because our application requires very

Strong AI Versus Weak AI

The conjecture that machines can be programmed to exhibit intelligent behavior is known as **weak AI** and is accepted, to varying degrees, by a wide audience today. However, the conjecture that machines can be programmed to possess intelligence and, in fact, consciousness, which is known as **strong AI,** is widely debated. Opponents of strong AI argue that a machine is inherently different from a human and thus can never feel love, tell right from wrong, and think about itself in the same way that a human does. However, proponents of strong AI argue that the human mind is constructed from small components that individually are not human and are not conscious but, when combined, are. Why, they argue, would the same phenomenon not be possible with machines?

The problem in resolving the strong AI debate is that such attributes as intelligence and consciousness are internal characteristics that cannot be identified directly. As Alan Turing pointed out, we credit other humans with intelligence because they behave intelligently—even though we cannot observe their internal mental states. Are we, then, prepared to grant the same latitude to a machine if it exhibits the external characteristics of consciousness? Why or why not?

little precision. (Some automatic garage door openers are able to detect and react to the presence of an obstacle in the doorway when closing.) Even the problem of focusing the camera on the puzzle can be handled simply by designing the gripper to position the puzzle at a particular predetermined position for viewing. Consequently, the first intelligent behavior required by the machine is the extraction of information through a visual medium.

It is important to realize that the problem faced by our machine when looking at the puzzle is not that of merely producing and storing an image. Technology has been able to do this for years as in the case of traditional photography and television systems. Instead, the problem is to understand the image in order to extract the current status of the puzzle (and perhaps later to monitor the movement of the tiles). This is a significant distinction from the activity of a television receiver that simply transforms the image from one medium to another with no conceptual understanding of the image. In short, our machine must demonstrate the ability to perceive.

In the case of our puzzle-solving machine, the possible interpretations of the puzzle image are relatively limited. We can assume that what appears is always an image containing the digits 1 through 8 in a well-organized pattern. The problem is merely to extract the arrangement of these digits. For this, we imagine that the picture of the puzzle has been encoded in terms of bits in the computer's memory, with each bit representing the brightness level of a particular pixel. Assuming a uniform size of the image (the machine holds the puzzle at a predetermined location in front of the camera), our machine can detect which tile is in which position by comparing the different sections of the picture to prerecorded templates consisting of the bit patterns produced by the individual digits used in the puzzle. As matches are found, the condition of the puzzle is revealed.

This technique of recognizing images is one method used in optical character readers. It has the drawback, however, of requiring a certain degree of uniformity for the style, size, and orientation of the symbols being read. In particular, the bit pattern produced by a physically large character does not match the template for a smaller version of the same symbol, even though the shapes are the same. Moreover, you can imagine how the problems increase in difficulty when trying to process handwritten material.

Another approach to the problem of character recognition is based on matching the geometric characteristics rather than the exact appearance of the symbols. In such cases the digit 1 might be characterized as a single vertical line, 2 might be an opened curved line joined with a horizontal straight line across the bottom, and so on. This method of recognizing symbols involves two steps: the first is to extract the features from the image being processed, the second is to compare the features to those of known symbols. As with the template-matching approach, this technique for recognizing characters is not foolproof. For instance, minor errors in the image can produce a set of entirely different geometric features, as in the case of distinguishing between an O and a C or, in the case of the eight-puzzle, a 3 and an 8.

We are fortunate in our puzzle application because we do not need to understand images of general three-dimensional scenes. Consider, for example, the advantage we have by being assured that the shapes to be recognized (the digits 1 through 8) are isolated in different parts of the picture rather than appearing as overlapping images, as is common in more general settings. In a general photograph, for instance, one is faced not only with the problem of recognizing an object from different angles but also with the fact that some portions of the object may be hidden from view.

The task of understanding general images is usually approached as a two-step process: (1) **image processing**, which refers to identifying characteristics of the image, and (2) **image analysis**, which refers to the process of understanding what these characteristics mean. We have already observed this dichotomy in the context of recognizing symbols by means of their geometric features. In that situation, we found image processing represented by the process of identifying the geometric features found in the image and image analysis represented by the process of identifying the meaning of those features.

Image processing entails numerous subjects. One is edge enhancement, which is the process of applying mathematical techniques to clarify the boundaries between regions in an image. In a sense, edge enhancement is an attempt to convert a photograph into a line drawing. Another activity in image analysis is known as region finding. This is the process of identifying those areas in an image that have common properties such as brightness, color, or texture. Such a region probably represents a section of the image that belongs to a single object. (It is the ability to recognize regions that allows computers to add color to old-fashioned black and white motion pictures.) Still another activity within the scope of image processing is smoothing, which is the process of removing flaws in the image. Smoothing keeps errors in the image from confusing the other image-processing steps, but too much smoothing can cause the loss of important information as well.

Smoothing, edge enhancement, and region finding are all steps toward identifying the various components in an image. Image analysis is the process of finding what these components represent and ultimately what the image means. Here one faces such problems as recognizing partially obstructed objects from different perspectives. One approach to image analysis is to start with an assumption about what the image might be and then try to associate the components in the image with the objects whose presence is conjectured. This appears to be an approach applied by humans. For instance, we sometimes find it hard to recognize an unexpected object in a setting in which our vision is blurred, but once we have a clue what the object might be, we can easily identify it.

The problems associated with general image analysis are enormous, and much research in the area remains to be done. Tasks that are performed quickly and apparently easily by the human mind continue to lie beyond the capabilities of machines. On the other hand, there are indications that alternative machine architectures may someday overcome the problems that elude us today (see Section 10.4).

Questions/Exercises

1. How do the requirements of a video system on a robot differ if the robot itself uses them to control its activities rather than relaying them to a human who controls the robot remotely?

2. What tells you that the following drawing is nonsense? How can this insight be programmed into a machine?

3. How many blocks are in the stack represented below? How could a machine be programmed to answer such questions accurately?

10.3 Reasoning

Let us now use our puzzle-solving machine to explore basic techniques for developing agents with elementary reasoning abilities.

Production Systems

Once our puzzle-solving machine has deciphered the positions of the tiles from the visual image, its task becomes that of figuring out what moves are required to solve the puzzle. An approach to this problem that might come to mind is to preprogram the machine with solutions to all possible arrangements of the tiles. Then, the machine's task would merely be to select and execute the proper program. However, the eight-puzzle has thousands of different configurations, so the idea of providing an explicit solution for each is certainly not inviting and probably not even possible when time and storage constraints are considered. We are thus forced to program the machine so that it can construct solutions to the eight-puzzle on its own. That is, the machine must be programmed to perform elementary reasoning activities.

The development of reasoning abilities within a machine has been a topic of research for many years. One of the results of this research is the recognition that a large class of reasoning problems have common characteristics. These common characteristics are isolated in a system known as a **production system,** which consists of three main components:

1. *A collection of states.* Each **state** is a situation that might occur in the application environment. The beginning state is called the **start** (or initial) **state;** the desired state (or states) is called the **goal state.** (In our case, a state is a configuration of the eight-puzzle; the start state is the configuration of the puzzle when handed to the machine; the goal state is the configuration of the solved puzzle, as shown in Figure 10.1.)

2. *A collection of productions (rules or moves).* A **production** is an operation that can be performed in the application environment to move from one state to another. Each production may be associated with preconditions; that is, conditions may exist that must be present in the environment before a production can be applied. (Productions in our case are the movements of tiles. Each movement of a tile has the precondition that the vacancy must be next to the tile in question.)

3. *A control system.* The **control system** consists of the logic that solves the problem of moving from the start state to the goal state. At each step in the process the control system must decide which of those productions whose preconditions are satisfied should be applied next. (Given a particular state in our eight-puzzle example, there would be several tiles next to the vacancy and therefore several applicable productions. The control system must decide which tile to move.)

Note that the task assigned to our puzzle-solving machine can be formulated in the context of a production system. In this setting the control system takes the form of a program. This program inspects the current state of the eight-puzzle, identifies a sequence of productions that leads to the goal state, and executes this sequence. It is therefore our task to design a control system for solving the eight-puzzle.

An important concept in the development of a control system is that of a **state graph,** which is a convenient way of representing, or at least conceptualizing, all the states, productions, and preconditions in a production system. Here the term *graph* refers to a structure that mathematicians would call a **directed graph,** meaning a collection of locations called **nodes** connected by arrows. A state graph consists of a collection of nodes representing the states in the system connected by arrows representing the productions that shift the system from one state to another. Two nodes are connected by an arrow in the state graph if and only if there is a production in the production system that transforms the system from the state at the origin of the arrow to the state at the destination of the arrow. Preconditions are implicitly represented by the absence of arrows between certain nodes.

We should emphasize that just as the number of possible states prevented us from explicitly providing predesigned solutions to the eight-puzzle, the problem of magnitude prevents us from explicitly representing the entire state graph. A state graph is then a way of conceptualizing the problem at hand but not something that we would consider expressing in its entirety. Nonetheless, you may find it helpful to consider (and possibly extend) the portion of the state graph for the eight-puzzle displayed in Figure 10.3.

When viewed in terms of the state graph, the problem faced by the control system becomes that of finding a sequence of arrows that leads from the start state to the goal state. After all, this sequence of arrows represents a sequence of productions that solves the original problem. Thus, regardless of the application, the task of the control system can be viewed as that of finding a path through a state graph. This universal view of control systems is the prize that we obtain by analyzing problems requiring reasoning in terms of production systems. If a problem can be characterized in terms of a production system, then its solution can be formulated in terms of searching for a path.

To emphasize this point, let us consider how other tasks can be framed in terms of production systems and thus as control systems finding paths through state graphs. One of the classic problems in artificial intelligence is playing games such as chess.

Figure 10.3

A small portion of the eight-puzzle's state graph

Figure 10.4

Deductive reasoning in the context of a production system

Start state

Socrates is a man.
All men are humans.
All humans are mortal.

Socrates is a man.
All men are humans. ⟧ => Socrates is a human.

Socrates is a man.
All men are humans.
All humans are mortal.
Socrates is a human.

Intermediate state

Socrates is a man.
All men are humans.
All humans are mortal.
Socrates is a human.
Socrates is mortal.

All humans are mortal.
Socrates is a human. ⟧ => Socrates is mortal.

Goal state

These games involve moderate complexity in a well-defined context and hence provide an ideal environment for testing theories. In chess the states of the underlying production system are the possible board configurations, the productions are the moves of the pieces, and the control system is embodied in the players (human or otherwise). The start node of the state graph represents the board with the pieces in their initial positions. Branching from this node are arrows leading to those board configurations that can be reached after the first move in a game; branching from each of these nodes one finds those configurations reachable by the next move; and so on. With this formulation, we can imagine a game of chess as consisting of two players, each trying to find a path through a large state graph to a goal node of his or her own choosing.

Perhaps a less obvious example of a production system is the problem of drawing logical conclusions from given facts. The productions in this context are the rules of logic that allow new statements to be formed from old ones. For example, the statements "All super heroes are noble" and "Superman is a superhero" can be combined to produce "Superman is noble." Similarly, "Batman and Robin are smart" can be restated as "Neither Batman nor Robin is not smart." States in such a system consist of collections of statements known to be true at particular points in the deduction process: The start state is the collection of basic statements (often called axioms) from which conclusions are to be drawn, and a goal state is any collection of statements that contain the proposed conclusion.

As an example, Figure 10.4 shows the portion of a state graph that might be traversed when the conclusion "Socrates is mortal" is drawn from the collection of statements "Socrates is a man," "All men are humans," and "All humans are mortal." There we see the body of knowledge shifting from one state to another as the reasoning process applies appropriate productions to generate additional statements.

Search Trees

We have seen that the control system's job involves searching the state graph to find a path from the start node to the goal. A simple method of performing this search is to traverse each of the arrows leading from the start state and in each case record the destination state, then traverse the arrows leaving these new states and again record the results, and so on. Our search for the goal spreads out from the start state like a drop of dye in water. This process continues until one of the new states is the goal, at which point a solution has been found, and the control system needs merely to apply the productions along the discovered path from the start state to the goal.

The effect of this strategy is to build a tree, called a **search tree,** that consists of the part of the state graph that has been investigated by the control system. The root node of the search tree is the start state, and the children of each node are those states reachable from the parent by applying one production. Each arc between nodes in a search tree represents the application of a single production, and each path from the root to a leaf represents a path between the corresponding states in the state graph.

The search tree that would be produced when solving the eight-puzzle from the configuration shown in Figure 10.5 is illustrated in Figure 10.6. The leftmost branch of this tree represents an attempt to solve the problem by first moving the 6 tile up, the center branch represents the approach of moving the 2 tile to the right, and the rightmost branch represents moving the 5 tile down. Furthermore, the search tree shows that if we do begin by moving the 6 tile up, then the only production allowable next is to move the 8 tile to the right. (Actually, at that point we could also move the 6 tile down but that would merely reverse the previous production and thus be an extraneous move.)

The goal state occurs in the last level of the search tree of Figure 10.6. Since this indicates that a solution has been found, the control system can terminate its search

Figure 10.5

An unsolved eight-puzzle

1	3	5
4	2	
7	8	6

Figure 10.6

A sample search tree

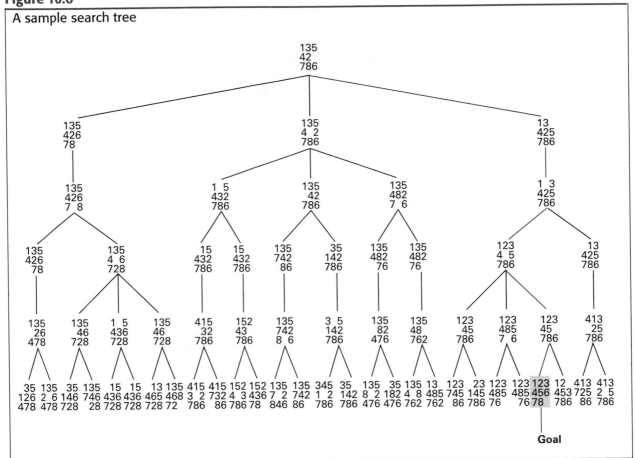

procedure and begin constructing the instruction sequence that will be used to solve the puzzle in the external environment. This turns out to be the simple process of walking up the search tree from the location of the goal node while pushing the productions represented by the tree arcs on a stack as they are encountered. Applying this technique to the search tree in Figure 10.6 produces the stack of productions in Figure 10.7. The control system can now solve the puzzle in the outside world by executing the instructions as they are popped from this stack.

There is one more observation that we should make. Recall that the trees we discussed in Chapter 7 use a pointer system that points *down* the tree, thereby allowing us to move from a parent node to its children. In the case of a search tree, however, the control system must be able to move from a child to its parent as it moves *up* the tree from the goal state to the start state. Such trees are constructed with their pointer systems pointing up rather than down. That is, each child node contains a pointer to its parent rather than the parent nodes containing pointers to their children. (In some applications, both sets of pointers are used to allow movement in the tree in both directions).

Figure 10.7

Productions stacked for later execution

Top of stack —— Move the 5 tile down.

Move the 3 tile right.

Move the 2 tile up.

Move the 5 tile left.

Move the 6 tile up.

Heuristics

For our example in Figure 10.6, we chose a starting configuration that produces a manageable search tree. In contrast, the search tree generated in an attempt to solve a more complex problem could grow much larger. In a game of chess, there are 20 possible first moves so the root node of the search tree in such a case would have 20 children rather than the 3 in the case of the eight-puzzle. Moreover, a game of chess can easily consist of 30 to 35 pairs of moves rather than the 5 straightforward ones in our example. Even in the case of the eight-puzzle, the search tree can become quite large if the goal is not quickly reached. As a result, developing a full search tree can become as impractical as representing the entire state graph.

One strategy for countering this problem is to change the order in which the search tree is constructed. Rather than building it in a **breadth-first** manner (meaning that the tree is constructed layer by layer), we can pursue the more promising paths to greater depths and consider the other options only if these original choices turn out to be false leads. This results in a **depth-first** construction of the search tree, meaning that the tree is constructed by building vertical paths rather than horizontal layers.

The depth-first approach is similar to the strategy that we as humans would apply when faced with the eight-puzzle. We would rarely pursue several options at the same time, as modeled by the breadth-first approach. Instead, we probably would select the option that appeared most promising and follow it first. Note that we said *appeared* most promising. We rarely know for sure which option is best at a particular point. We merely follow our intuition, which may, of course, lead us astray. Nonetheless, the use of such intuitive information seems to give humans an advantage over the brute-force methods in which each option was given equal attention, and it would therefore seem prudent to apply intuitive methods in automated control systems.

To this end, we need a way of identifying which of several states appears to be the most promising. Our approach is to use a **heuristic,** which is a quantitative value associated with each state that attempts to measure the "distance" from that state to the nearest goal. In a sense, a heuristic is a measure of projected cost. Given a choice between two states, the one with the smaller heuristic value is the one from which a goal can apparently be reached with the least cost. This state, therefore, would represent the direction we should pursue.

A heuristic should have two characteristics. First, it should constitute a reasonable estimate of the amount of work remaining in the solution if the associated state were reached. This means that it can provide meaningful information when selecting among options—the better the estimate provided by the heuristic, the better will be the decisions that are based on the information. Second, the heuristic should be easy to compute. This means that its use has a chance of benefiting the search process rather than of becoming a burden. (In contrast, although the actual number of moves required to reach the goal from the given state is an excellent piece of information to have when making decisions, computing this information involves finding the actual solution first.)

A simple heuristic in the case of the eight-puzzle would be to estimate the "distance" to the goal by counting the number of tiles that are out of place—the conjecture being that a state in which four tiles are out of place is farther from the goal (and therefore less appealing) than a state in which only two tiles are out of place. However, this heuristic does not take into account how far out of position the tiles are. If the two tiles are far from their proper positions, many productions could be required to move them across the puzzle.

A slightly better heuristic, then, is to measure the distance each tile is from its destination and add these values to obtain a single quantity. A tile immediately adjacent to its final destination would be associated with a distance of one, whereas a tile whose corner touches the square of its final destination would be associated with a distance of two (because it must move at least one position vertically and another position horizontally). This heuristic is easy to compute and produces a rough estimate of the number of moves required to transform the puzzle from its current state to the goal. For instance, the heuristic value associated with the configuration in Figure 10.8 is seven (because tiles 2, 5, and 8 are each a distance of one from their final destinations while tiles 3 and 6 are each a distance of two from home). In fact, it actually takes seven moves to return this puzzle configuration to the solved configuration.

Now that we have a heuristic for the eight-puzzle, the next step is to incorporate it into our decision-making process. Recall that a human faced with a decision tends to select the option that appears closest to the goal. Thus our search procedure should consider the heuristic of each leaf node in the tree and pursue the search from a leaf node

Figure 10.8

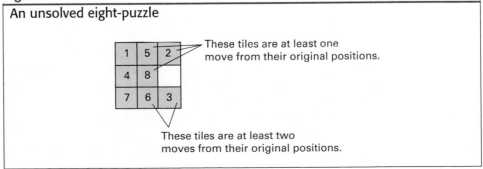

An unsolved eight-puzzle

Figure 10.9

An algorithm for a control system using heuristics

Establish the start node of the state graph as the root of the
  search tree and record its heuristic value.
while (the goal node has not been reached) **do**
  [Select the leftmost leaf node with the smallest heuristic
    value of all leaf nodes.
  To this selected node attach as children those nodes that
    can be reached by a single production.
  Record the heuristic of each of these new nodes next
    to the node in the search tree
  ]
Traverse the search tree from the goal node up to the root,
  pushing the production associated with each arc traversed
  onto a stack.
Solve the original problem by executing the productions as they
  are popped off the stack.

associated with the smallest value. This is the strategy adopted in Figure 10.9, which presents an algorithm for developing a search tree and executing the solution obtained.

Let us apply this algorithm to the eight-puzzle, starting from the initial configuration in Figure 10.5. First, we establish this initial state as the root node and record its heuristic value, which is five. Then, the first pass through the body of the **while** structure instructs us to add the three nodes that can be reached from the initial state, as shown in Figure 10.10. Note that we have recorded the heuristic value of each leaf node in parentheses beneath the node.

The goal node has not been reached, so we again pass through the body of the **while** structure, this time extending our search from the leftmost node ("the leftmost

Figure 10.10

The beginnings of our heuristic search

Heuristic values

Figure 10.11

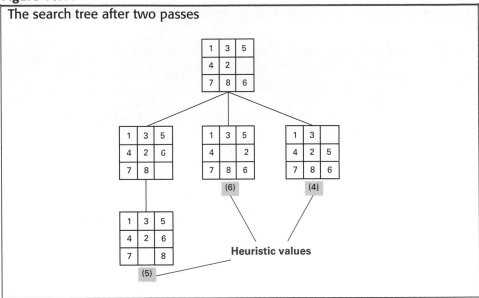

The search tree after two passes

leaf node with the smallest heuristic value"). After this, the search tree has the form displayed in Figure 10.11.

The heuristic value of the leftmost leaf node is now five, indicating that this branch is perhaps not a good choice to pursue after all. The algorithm picks up on this

Figure 10.12

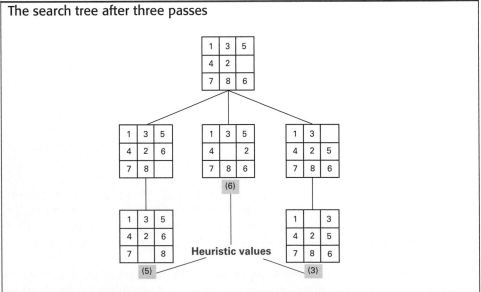

The search tree after three passes

Figure 10.13

The complete search tree formed by our heuristic system

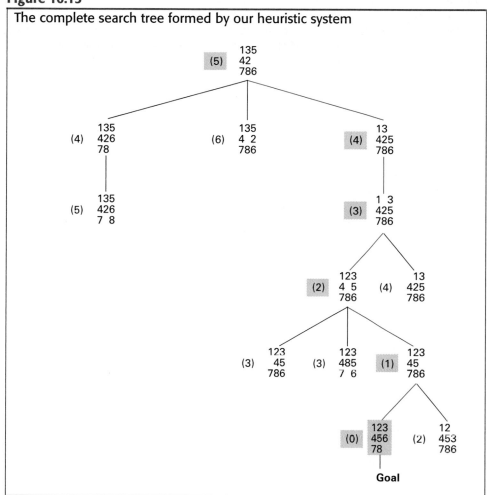

Goal

and in the next pass through the loop instructs us to expand the tree from the right-most node (which now is the "leftmost leaf node with the smallest heuristic value"). Having been expanded in this fashion, the search tree appears as in Figure 10.12.

At this point the algorithm seems to be on the right track. Because the heuristic value of this last node is only three, the **while** structure instructs us to continue pursuing this path, and the search focuses toward the goal, producing the search tree appearing in Figure 10.13. Comparing this with the tree in Figure 10.6 shows that, even with the temporary wrong turn taken early on by the new algorithm, the use of heuristic information has greatly decreased the size of the search tree and produced a much more efficient process.

After reaching the goal state, the **while** structure terminates, and we move on to traverse the tree from the goal node up to the root, pushing the productions encountered onto a stack as we go. The resultant stack appears as depicted earlier, in Figure 10.7.

Finally, we are instructed to execute these productions as they are popped from the stack. At this point, we would observe the puzzle-solving machine lower its finger and begin to move the tiles.

Questions/Exercises

1. What is the significance of production systems in artificial intelligence?

2. Draw a portion of the state graph for the eight-puzzle surrounding the node representing the following state:

4	1	3
	2	6
7	5	8

3. Using a breadth-first approach, draw the search tree that is constructed by a control system when solving the eight-puzzle from the following start state:

1	2	3
4	8	5
7	6	

4. Use pencil, paper, and the breadth-first approach to try to construct the search tree that is produced when solving the eight-puzzle from the following start state. (You do not have to finish.) What problems do you encounter?

4	3	
2	1	8
7	6	5

5. What analogy can be drawn between our heuristic system for solving the eight-puzzle and a mountain climber who attempts to reach the peak by considering only the local terrain and always proceeding in the direction of steepest ascent?

6. Using the heuristic presented in this section, apply the control-system algorithm of Figure 10.9 to the problem of solving the following eight-puzzle:

1	2	3
4		8
7	6	5

7. Refine our method of computing the heuristic value for a state of the eight-puzzle so that the search algorithm of Figure 10.9 does not make the wrong choice, as it did in the example in this section. Can you find an example in which your system still causes the search to go astray?

10.4 Artificial Neural Networks

With all the progress that has been made in artificial intelligence, many problems in the field continue to tax the abilities of computers based on the von Neumann architecture. Central processing units that execute sequences of instructions do not seem capable of perceiving and reasoning at levels comparable to those of the human mind. For this reason, many researchers are turning to machines with other architectures. One of these is the artificial neural network.

Basic Properties

As introduced in Chapter 2, artificial neural networks are constructed from many individual processors, which we will call *processing units* (or just *units* for short), in a manner that models networks of neurons in living biological systems. A biological neuron is a single cell with input tentacles called dendrites and an output tentacle called the axon (Figure 10.14). The signals transmitted via a cell's axon reflect whether the cell is in an inhibited or excited state. This state is determined by the combination of signals received

Figure 10.14

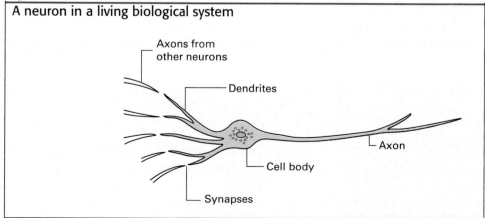

A neuron in a living biological system

Axons from other neurons

Dendrites

Axon

Cell body

Synapses

Figure 10.15

The activities within a processing unit

by the cell's dendrites. These dendrites pick up signals from the axons of other cells across small gaps known as synapses. Research suggests that the conductivity across a single synapse is controlled by the chemical composition of the synapse. That is, whether the particular input signal will have an exciting or inhibiting effect on the neuron is determined by the chemical composition of the synapse. Thus it is believed that a biological neural network learns by adjusting these chemical connections between neurons.

A processing unit in an artificial neural network is a simple device that mimics this basic understanding of the biological neuron. It produces an output of 1 or 0, depending on whether its effective input exceeds a given threshold value. This effective input is a weighted sum of the actual inputs, as represented in Figure 10.15. In this figure, the outputs of three processing units (denoted by v_1, v_2, and v_3) are used as inputs to another unit. The inputs to this fourth unit are associated with values called weights (denoted by w_1, w_2, and w_3). The receiving unit multiplies each of its input values by the weight associated with that particular input position and then adds these products to form the effective input ($v_1 w_1 + v_2 w_2 + v_3 w_3$). If this sum exceeds the processing unit's threshold value, the unit produces an output of 1; otherwise the unit produces a 0 as its output.

Following the lead of Figure 10.15, we adopt the convention of representing processing units as rectangles. At the input end of the unit, we place a smaller rectangle for each input, and in this rectangle we write the weight associated with that input. Finally, we write the unit's threshold value in the middle of the large rectangle. As an example, Figure 10.16 represents a processing unit with three inputs and a threshold value of 1.5. The first input is weighted by the value –2, the second is weighted by 3, and the third is weighted by –1. Therefore if the unit receives the inputs 1,1, and 0, its effective input is $(1)(-2) + (1)(3) + (0)(-1) = 1$, and thus its output is 0. But, if the unit receives 0, 1, and 1, its effective input is $(0)(-2) + (1)(3) + (1)(-1) = 2$, which exceeds the threshold value. The unit's output will thus be 1.

Figure 10.16

Representation of a processing unit

The fact that a weight can be positive or negative means that the corresponding input can have either an inhibiting or exciting effect on the receiving unit. (If the weight is negative, then a 1 at that input position reduces the weighted sum and thus tends to hold the effective input below the threshold value. In contrast, a positive weight causes the associated input to have an increasing effect on the weighted sum and thus increase the chances of that sum exceeding the threshold value.) Moreover, the actual size of the weight controls the degree to which the corresponding input is allowed to inhibit or excite the receiving unit. Consequently, by adjusting the values of the weights throughout an artificial neural network, we can program the network to respond to different inputs in a predetermined manner.

As an example, the simple network presented in Figure 10.17(a) is programmed to produce an output of 1 if its two inputs differ and an output of 0 otherwise. If,

Figure 10.17

A neural network with two different programs

Figure 10.18

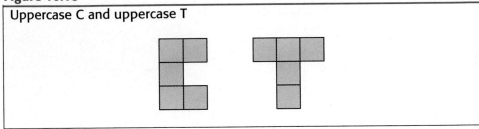

Uppercase C and uppercase T

however, we change the weights to those shown in Figure 10.17(b), we obtain a network that responds with a 1 if both of its inputs are 1s and with a 0 otherwise.

We should note that the network in Figure 10.17 is far more simplistic than an actual biological network. A human brain contains approximately 10^{11} neurons with about 10^4 synapses per neuron. Indeed, the dendrites of a biological neuron are so numerous that they appear more like a fibrous mesh than the individual tentacles represented in our figures.

A Specific Application

To appreciate the potential of artificial neural networks, let us consider the particular character recognition problem of distinguishing between the uppercase letters C and T, as represented in Figure 10.18. The problem is to identify either letter when it is placed in the field of vision, regardless of its orientation. All the patterns in Figure 10.19(a) should be identified as Cs, and all those in part (b) should be recognized as Ts.

We begin by assuming that the field of view consists of square pixels, each of which is the size of the squares from which the letters are constructed. Each of these

Figure 10.19

Various orientations of the letters C and T

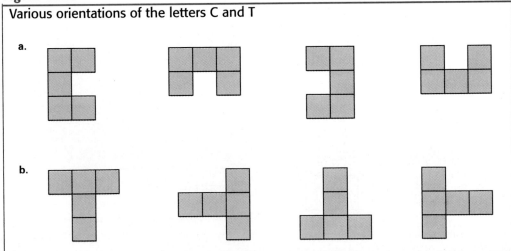

Figure 10.20

The structure of the character recognition system

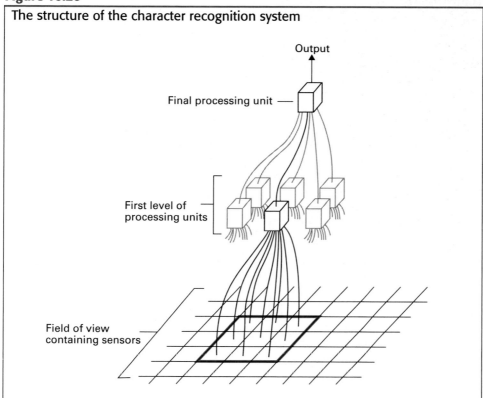

pixels is attached to a sensor that produces a 1 if that pixel is covered by the letter being viewed and produces a 0 otherwise. We then use the outputs from these sensors as the inputs to our artificial neural network.

The network contains two levels of processing units. The first level consists of many units—one for each three-by-three block of pixels in the field of view (see Figure 10.20). Each of these units has nine inputs, to which the sensors associated with that unit's three-by-three block are attached. (Note that the three-by-three blocks associated with the first-level processing units overlap. Thus each sensor provides input to nine of the processing units at the first level.)

The second level of our network consists of a single processing unit, with a separate input for each of the units in the first level. The processing unit at the second level has a threshold value of 0.5, and each of its inputs is associated with a weight of 1. Thus this unit produces an output of 1 if and only if at least one of its inputs is 1.

Each processing unit at the first level also has the threshold value of 0.5. Each input has a weight of –1, except for the input associated with the center pixel of that unit's three-by-three block, which has a weight of 2. Each of these units can therefore produce an output of 1 only if it receives a 1 from the sensor associated with the pixel in the center of the unit's three-by-three block.

Figure 10.21

The letter C in the field of view

Now, if the letter C is placed in the field of view (Figure 10.21), all the first-level processing units will produce an output of 0. This is because the only units whose center pixel is covered by the letter will also have at least two other pixels in their three-by-three blocks covered, and the signals received from these sensors will negate the effect of the center pixel. Consequently, if the letter in the field of view is C, all of the inputs to the second-level processing unit will be 0, which means that the output of the entire network will be 0.

In contrast, suppose that the letter in the field of view is T. Consider the three-by-three block whose center is the square covered by the bottom of the T's stem (Figure 10.22). The processing unit assigned to this square receives an effective input of 1 (2 from the center pixel and –1 from the other pixel covered by the stem). This exceeds the unit's threshold, so the unit sends an output of 1 to the upper-level unit. This, then, causes the upper-level unit to produce an output of 1.

In summary, we have an artificial neural network that distinguishes between the letters C and T, regardless of the letter's orientation in the field of view. If the letter is a C, the network produces a 0 as its output; if the letter is a T, the network produces a 1.

Of course, the ability to distinguish between just two letters is a far cry from the image-processing capabilities of the human mind. But the elegance of solutions such as these indicates that further research in the area is justified. Therefore, the field of artificial neural networks is an active area of research, with major efforts being placed on developing ways to design and program such networks. Typical goals relating to network design include determining how many processing units are required to solve certain problems and what patterns of connections between these units are most productive.

As for the subject of programming artificial neural networks, we have already seen that the task is that of assigning the proper weights to the various processing unit inputs throughout the system. This is normally done via a repetitive training process, in which sample inputs are applied to the network and then the weights are adjusted by small increments so that the actual output of the network approaches the desired output. As this process is repeated among the sample inputs, one hopes that the weights require less and less adjusting until the network begins to perform correctly over the entire range of sample data. What is needed is a strategy for adjusting these weights so that each new adjustment leads toward the overall goal rather than destroying the progress made on the previous samples.

Figure 10.22

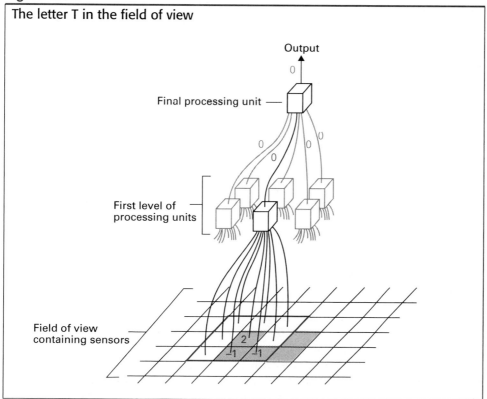

The letter T in the field of view

Small Scale to Large Scale

A recurring phenomenon in the development and testing of theories is the transition from small-scale experimentation to large-scale applications. Initial experimentation of a new theory often involves small, simple cases. If success is achieved, then the experimental environment is extended to more realistic, larger scale systems. Some theories are able to survive this transition; others are not. Sometimes success on the small scale is strong enough to encourage proponents of the theory to persist well after failures on the large scale have discouraged other researchers. In some cases, such persistence ultimately pays off; in others it represents wasted effort.

Such scenarios are readily observable in the field of artificial intelligence. One example is in the area of natural language processing, where early successes in limited settings led many to believe that general natural language understanding was just over the horizon. Unfortunately, extending success to the large scale has proved much more difficult, and victory is being achieved slowly as the result of significant effort. Another example is the subject of artificial neural networks, a topic that came on the scene with significant fanfare, then faded for several years when its large-scale capabilities came under question, and has now returned in a more subdued atmosphere. As indicated in the text, several subjects within the field of artificial intelligence, as well as computer science in general, are currently undergoing this transitional test.

Associative Memory

The human mind has the amazing capability to retrieve information that is associated with a current concern. When we experience certain smells, we readily recall memories of our childhood. The sound of a friend's voice may conjure an image of the person or perhaps memories of good times. Certain music generates thoughts of particular holiday seasons. These are examples of **associative memory**—the retrieval of information that is associated with, or relevant to, the information at hand.

To construct machines with associative memory has been a goal of research for many years. One approach is to apply techniques of artificial neural networks. For instance, consider a network consisting of many processing units that are interconnected to form a web with no inputs or outputs. (In some designs, called Hopfield networks, the output of each processing unit is connected as inputs to each of the other units, in other cases the output of a unit may be connected only to its immediate neighbors.) Each unit can be in its excited or inhibited state. If we represent an excited state by 1 and an inhibited state by 0, then the condition of the entire network can be envisioned as a configuration of 0s and 1s. Now suppose that the network is programmed in such a way that certain configurations of 0s and 1s are stable in the sense that when the network finds itself in one of these configurations, it will remain in that configuration. However, if the network is in a nonstable configuration, then the interaction of the processing units will cause the configuration to change—and continue changing until it wanders into a stable configuration.

If we start the network in a nonstable configuration that is close to a stable one, we would expect it to wander to that stable configuration. In a sense, when given a part of a stable configuration, the network is able to complete the configuration. Or, in other words, it is able to find the bit pattern that is associated with the partial pattern it is given. Thus if some of the bits are used to encode smells and others are used to encode childhood memories, then initializing the smell bits according to a certain stable configuration could cause the remaining bits to find their way to the associated childhood memory.

Let us consider the artificial neural network shown in Figure 10.23. Each circle in the figure represents a processing unit whose threshold value is recorded inside the circle. The lines connecting circles represent two-way connections between the corresponding units. That is, a line connecting two units indicates that the output of each unit is connected as an input to the other. Thus the output of the center unit is connected as an input to each of the units around the perimeter, and the output of each of the units around the perimeter is connected as an input to the center unit. Two connected units associate the same weight with each other's output. This common weight is recorded next to the line connecting the units. Thus the unit at the top of the diagram associates a weight of –1 with the input it receives from the center unit and a weight of 1 with the inputs it receives from its two neighbors on the perimeter. Likewise, the center unit associates a weight of –1 with each of the values it receives from the units around the perimeter.

The network operates in discrete steps in which all processing units respond to their inputs in a synchronized manner. To determine the next configuration of the network from its current configuration, we determine the effective inputs of each unit throughout the network and then allow all the units to respond to their inputs at the same time. The effect is that the entire network follows a coordinated sequence of compute effective inputs, respond to inputs, compute effective inputs, respond to inputs, etc.

Figure 10.23

An artificial neural network implementing an associative memory

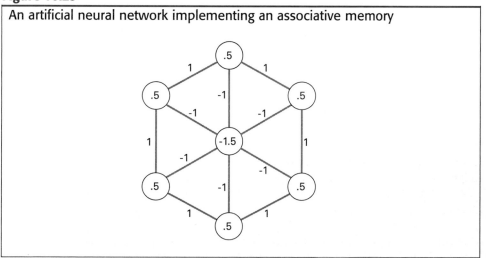

Consider the sequence of events that would occur if we initialized the network with its two rightmost units inhibited and the other units excited (Figure 10.24a). The two leftmost units would have effective inputs of 1, so they would remain excited. But, their neighbors on the perimeter would have effective inputs of 0, so they would become inhibited. Likewise, the center unit would have an effective input of –4, so it would become inhibited. Thus the entire network would shift to the configuration shown in Figure 10.24b in which only the two leftmost units are excited. Since the center unit would now be inhibited, the excited conditions of the leftmost units would cause the top and bottom units to become excited again. Meanwhile, the center unit would remain inhibited since it would have an effective input of –2. Thus the network would shift to the configuration in Figure 10.24c, which would then lead to the configuration in Figure 10.24d. (You may wish to confirm that a blinking phenomenon would occur if the network were initialized with only the upper four units excited. The top unit would remain excited while its two neighbors on the perimeter and the center unit would alternate between being excited and inhibited.)

Finally, observe that the network has two stable configurations: one in which the center unit is excited and the others are inhibited, and another configuration in which

Figure 10.24

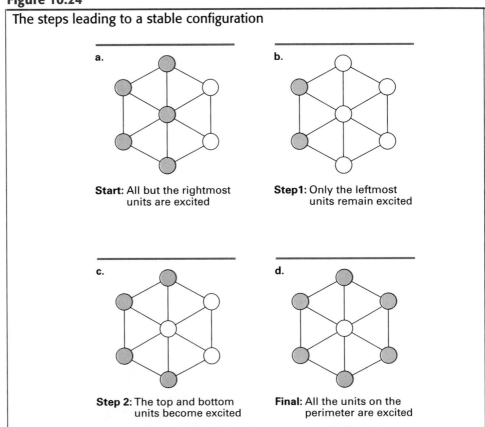

The steps leading to a stable configuration

a.

Start: All but the rightmost units are excited

b.

Step1: Only the leftmost units remain excited

c.

Step 2: The top and bottom units become excited

d.

Final: All the units on the perimeter are excited

the center unit is inhibited and the others are excited. If we initialize the network with the center unit excited and no more than two of the other units excited, the network will wander to the former stable configuration. If we initialize the network with at least four adjacent units on the perimeter in their excited states, the network will wander to the latter configuration. Thus we could say that the network associates the former stable configuration with initial patterns in which its center unit and fewer than three of its perimeter units are excited, and associates the latter stable configuration with initial patterns in which four or more of its perimeter units are excited. In short, the network represents an elementary associative memory.

Questions/Exercises

1. What is the output of the following processing unit when both its inputs are 1s? What about the input patterns 0, 0; 0, 1; and 1, 0?

2. Adjust the weights and threshold value of the following processing unit so that its output is 1 if and only if at least two of its inputs are 1s.

3. Design an artificial neural network that can detect which of the following two patterns is in its field of view.

4. Design an artificial neural network that can detect which of the following two patterns is in its field of view.

5. To which stable configuration will the network in Figure 10.23 wander if it is initialized with all its processing units inhibited?

10.5 Genetic Algorithms

The field of **genetic algorithms** is the research area that seeks to apply our understanding of natural evolution to the problem-solving task. The approach is to intermix the best performers within a collection of proposed solutions to obtain another generation of proposed solutions that represents improvements over the original collection. By repeating this process over and over, one hopes to simulate the evolutionary process and ultimately obtain feasible solutions to the problem at hand.

As an example, let us assume that you play poker with the same group of friends every Wednesday evening, and you want to develop a strategy that will maximize your winnings. An evolutionary approach to this problem would begin by identifying the various situations that may occur in a poker game and the potential responses to each. This, of course, would be a major undertaking since there would be many situations to be considered. Once this analysis was done, however, we could construct a poker-playing strategy by assigning a response to each situation. In turn, we could represent each strategy as a list of the form $S_1R_1, S_2R_2, \ldots, S_nR_n$, where each S is one of the potential situations and the following R is the response to be used in that situation. The representations for different strategies would contain the same sequence of situations, but these situations would be followed by different responses. To apply a given strategy, you would merely find the appropriate situation in the list and then perform the response that follows it.

The next step in our poker problem would be to select an initial collection of strategies and apply them during an evening of poker playing, recording the earnings

Behavior-Based Intelligence

Early work in artificial intelligence approached the subject in the context of explicitly writing programs to simulate intelligence. However, many argue today that human intelligence is not based on the execution of complex programs but instead by simple stimuli-response functions that have evolved over generations. This theory of "intelligence" is known as behavior-based intelligence because "intelligent" stimuli-response functions appear to be the result of behaviors that caused certain individuals to survive and reproduce while others did not.

Behavior-based intelligence seems to answer several questions in the artificial intelligence community such as why machines based on the von Neumann architecture easily outperform humans in computational skills but struggle to exhibit common sense. Thus behavior-based intelligence promises to be a major influence in artificial intelligence research. As described in the text, behavior-based techniques have been applied in the field of artificial neural networks to teach neurons to behave in desired ways, in the field of genetic algorithms to provide an alternative to the more traditional programming process, and in robotics to improve the performance of machines.

obtained under each strategy. Based on this analysis, we would then select the best of the initial strategies and group these selected strategies into pairs. From each of these pairs, we would produce two new strategies by first cutting the lists representing the two strategies in the pair and then attaching the head from each to the tail from the other (Figure 10.25). All these new strategies would form the collection of strategies to be tested the following week. Each week we would again select the best performing strategies and use them to produce yet another generation of strategies to be tested the following week. Thus, as the weeks go by, our process would simulate nature's evolutionary process in which the survivors of each generation reproduce to generate the next generation. In fact, we could even simulate mutations by arbitrarily changing a single response within a strategy at times.

Unfortunately, our poker example is somewhat unrealistic since it would not be possible to test a large generation of strategies in a single evening of poker. But if the process of playing test games could be automated, as is the case in many applications, the evolutionary approach would be feasible. This is the process proposed by research in genetic algorithms. First, one finds a way to represent potential solutions as strings of symbols. Then, a collection of potential solutions is generated and tested. The better examples from this collection are then crossed to form a new generation of potential solutions that are tested and used to form yet another generation. At times random mutations may be inserted during the crossing process.

The evolutionary approach has been applied in numerous settings with promising results. One of these settings has been designing configurations for artificial neural networks. Suppose, for example, we want to solve a problem by means of an artificial neural network that consists of a predetermined number of processing units. Before we begin training the network, we need to decide how the units should be connected. To this end, we agree to encode artificial neural network configurations as

Figure 10.25

Crossing two poker-playing strategies

a. Two strategies are cut in the same place

cut

SRSR ••• SR|SR ••• SR

SR'SR' ••• SR'|SR' ••• SR'

b. The tail of each strategy is attached to the head of the other, producing two new strategies

SRSR ••• SR –   – SR ••• SR

SR'SR' ••• SR'   SR' ••• SR'

strings of 0s and 1s in the following manner (Figure 10.26). Assuming that the number of processing units to be used in the network is n, we first label the processing units with the integers from 1 to n. We then build a square table with n rows and n columns. We place a 1 in the ith row and the jth column if the network being encoded has a connection from the output of the ith processing unit to the input of the jth unit. All other table entries are assigned the value 0. We then rewrite this table as a single string by writing the rows in the table one after the other.

Now, to find a good configuration for our particular problem, we select a variety of potential configurations and start the training process for each. After a short training period, we select those configurations that seem to be making the best progress, represent those configurations as strings of 0s and 1s, and cross these strings to obtain a new generation of potential configurations. In turn, this new generation would be partially trained and the best performers would be selected to produce still another generation. Such an approach has been successful in designing simple artificial neural networks.

Genetic algorithm techniques have also been applied to the task of program development, leading to a field known as **evolutionary programming.** The goal is to develop programs by allowing them to evolve rather than by explicitly writing

Figure 10.26

Coding the topology of an artificial neural network

a. The configuration of an artificial neural network

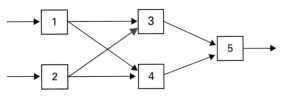

b. A table indicating how the units in the network are connected

	1	2	3	4	5
1	0	0	1	1	0
2	0	0	1	1	0
3	0	0	0	0	1
4	0	0	0	0	1
5	0	0	0	0	0

c. Encoded version of artificial neural network

00110001100000010000100000

them. An important step in this setting is to find ways in which parts of programs can be interchanged to produce meaningful new programs. The functional programming paradigm has proved useful in this context. Indeed, a program written in the functional paradigm consists of nested functions in which the output of one function is used as the input to another. Thus it is feasible that a function from one program could be exchanged with a function in another program without destroying the program's structure.

Following such reasoning, researchers have applied evolutionary programming techniques to the program development process using functional programming languages. The approach has been to start with a collection of programs that contain a rich variety of functions. The functions in this starting collection form the "gene pool" from which future generations of programs will be constructed. One then allows the evolutionary process to run for many generations, hoping that by producing each generation from the best performers in the previous generation, a solution to the target problem will ultimately evolve.

The field of evolutionary programming is still in its infancy. As yet, success has been obtained in relatively simple cases. For example, evolutionary techniques have been used to obtain programs that compute properties of simple geometric shapes, such as the area of a square or the circumference of a circle. A major problem is to identify the "best performers" out of a group of programs of which none seem to be anywhere close to the desired product. As is the case in other areas of genetic algorithms, whether the techniques being developed will be successfully up-scaled to solve significant, meaningful problems is still an open question. In any case, the field of genetic algorithms is representative of the creativity and imagination being applied in today's computer science research.

Questions/Exercises

1. Encode the configuration of the artificial neural network below using the system described in this section.

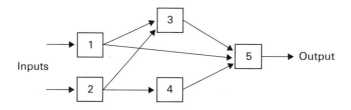

2. Select a problem that you feel would be suitable for the evolutionary approach and describe how potential solutions could be encoded as strings. Then, describe how these strings could be crossed to form future generations.

3. Give an argument to the effect that the functional programming paradigm is more compatible with evolutionary programming than the object-oriented paradigm.

10.6 Other Areas of Research

Let us now take a brief look at some other areas of research within the field of artificial intelligence.

Language Processing

We begin by considering the task of translating statements from one language to another. In Chapter 6 we learned the rudiments of the translation process (lexical analysis, parsing, and code generation) and how these steps were applied to the task of translating programs from high-level languages into low-level machine language. The ability to perform the translation gives the illusion that the machine actually understands the language being translated. (Recall from Section 6.1 the story told by Grace Hopper about managers who thought she was teaching computers to understand German.) In fact, as the early translators were being developed in the 1940s, many researchers believed that the ability to program computers to understand natural languages was only a few years away.

What these researchers failed to understand was the depth to which formal programming languages differ from natural languages such as English, German, and Latin. Programming languages are constructed from well-designed primitives so that each statement has only one grammatical structure and only one meaning. In contrast, a statement in a natural language can have multiple meanings depending on its context or even the manner in which it is communicated. Thus, to understand natural language, humans rely heavily on their acquired knowledge and associative memory abilities.

For example, the sentences

> Norman Rockwell painted people.

and

> Cinderella had a ball.

have multiple meanings that cannot be distinguished by parsing or translating each word independently. Instead, to understand these sentences requires the ability to comprehend the context in which the statement is made. In other instances the true meaning of a sentence is not the same as its literal translation. For example,

> Do you know what time it is?

often means "Please tell me what time it is," or if the speaker has been waiting for a long time, it may mean "You are very late."

To unravel the meaning of a statement in a natural language therefore requires several levels of analysis. The first of these is **syntactic analysis** whose major component is parsing. It is here that the subject of the sentence

> Mary gave John a birthday card.

is recognized as *Mary* while the subject of

> John got a birthday card from Mary.

is found to be *John*.

Another level of analysis is called **semantic analysis.** In contrast to the parsing process, which merely identifies the grammatical role of each word, semantic analysis is charged with the task of identifying the semantic role of each word in the statement. Semantic analysis seeks to identify such things as the action described, the agent of that action (which may or may not be the subject of the sentence), and the object of the action. It is through semantic analysis that the sentences "Mary gave John a birthday card" and "John got a birthday card from Mary" would be recognized as saying the same thing.

A third level of analysis is **contextual analysis.** It is at this level that the context of the sentence is brought into the understanding process. For example, it is easy to identify the grammatical role of each word in the sentence

The bat flew from his hand.

We can even perform semantic analysis by identifying the action involved as *flying,* the agent as *bat,* and so on. But it is not until we consider the context of the statement that the meaning of the statement becomes clear. In particular, it has a different meaning in the context of a baseball game than it does in the context of cave exploration. Moreover, it is at the contextual level that the true meaning of the question "Do you know what time it is?" would finally be revealed.

We should note that the various levels of analysis—syntactic, semantic, and contextual—are not necessarily independent. The subject of the sentence

Stampeding cattle can be dangerous.

is the noun *cattle* (modified by the adjective *stampeding*) if we envision the cattle stampeding on their own. But, the subject is the gerund *stampeding* (with object *cattle*) in the context of a troublemaker whose entertainment consists of starting stampedes. Thus the sentence has more than one grammatical structure—which one is correct depends on the meaning.

Another area of research in natural language processing concerns an entire document rather than individual sentences. Here the problems of concern fall into two categories: **information retrieval** and **information extraction.** Information retrieval refers to the task of identifying documents that relate to the topic at hand. An example is the problem faced by attorneys when trying to find all the case histories that relate to current litigation. Another example is the problem faced by users of the World Wide Web as they try to find the sites that relate to a particular topic.

Information extraction refers to the task of extracting information from documents so that it takes a form that is useful in other applications. This may mean identifying the answer to a specific question or recording the information in a form from which questions can be answered at a later date. One such form is known as a template. It is essentially a questionnaire in which specifics are recorded. For example, consider a system for reading a newspaper. The system may make use of a variety of templates, one for each type of article that may appear in a newspaper. If the system identifies an article as reporting on a burglary, it would proceed by trying to fill in the slots in the burglary template. This template would probably request such items as the address of the burglary, the time and date of the burglary, the items taken, and so on. In contrast, if the system identifies an article as reporting on a natural disaster, it would fill in the natural disaster template, which would lead the system toward identifying the type of disaster, amount of damage, and so on.

Another form in which information extractors record information is known as a **semantic net.** This is essentially a large linked data structure in which pointers are used to indicate associations among the data items. Figure 10.27 shows part of a semantic net in which the information obtained from the sentence

Mary hit John.

has been circled.

The task of developing computers that can understand natural language demonstrates how challenging research in artificial intelligence can become. As researchers solve some problems, additional problems surface.

Robotics

Robotics could be defined as the field within artificial intelligence aimed directly at building machines that behave intelligently. In effect, a robot is a physical incarnation

Figure 10.27

A semantic net

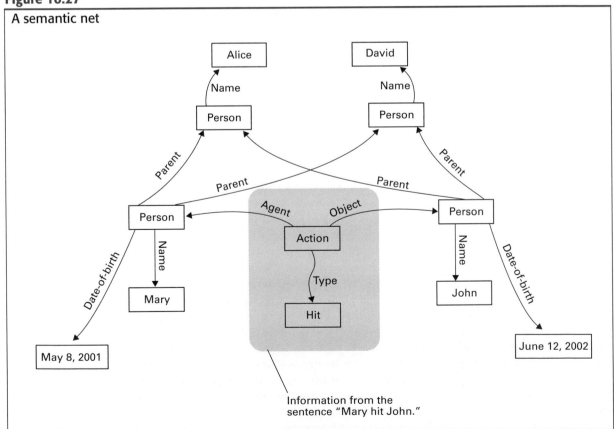

Information from the
sentence "Mary hit John."

of an agent, and therefore the subject of robotics encompasses research throughout the artificial intelligence spectrum. However, due to its association with physical equipment, robotics is often more narrowly identified with advances in mechanical and electrical engineering. Indeed, in the early days of robotics, the field was closely allied with the development of mechanical arms, elbows, wrists, and fingers. Research dealt not only with how such devices could be designed and manipulated but also with how knowledge of their location and orientation could be maintained and applied. (You are able to close your eyes and still touch your nose with your finger because your brain maintains a record of where your nose and finger are.) Other traditional fields of robotics focused on developing sensors and actuators to mimic biological input/output systems. An example is the subject of speech synthesis, which extends theories of how sentences are formed to include how devices can be built and controlled to produce the required sounds.

Today, research in robotics has broadened to embrace the less physical properties of robots. An example is found in the Robocup competition—an international competition of robot soccer teams—that serves as a forum for research toward developing a team of robots that can beat world-class human soccer teams by the year 2050. Here the emphasis is not just to build mobile robots that can "kick" a ball but to design a team of robots that cooperate with each other to obtain a common goal. Therefore, as much or more effort is extended to obtain collaboration than is extended to obtain motion.

Other researchers have focused on developing robots that learn to perform tasks. A traditional example is a vacuum cleaner that explores a house, learning the layout of rooms and furniture, and then develops its own plan for cleaning the house in the most efficient manner. Other examples include artificial pet dogs that learn to sit and roll over.

Another example of the breadth of research in robotics is the field known as evolutionary robotics in which theories of evolution are applied to develop robots with desired characteristics. Here we find the survival-of-the-fittest theory being used to develop devices that over multiple generations acquire their own means of balance or mobility. Much of the research in this area distinguishes between a robot's internal control system (largely software) and the physical structure of its body. For example, the control system for a swimming tadpole robot has been transferred to a similar robot with legs. Then evolutionary techniques were applied within the control system to obtain a robot that crawls. In other instances, evolutionary techniques have been applied to a robot's physical body to discover positions for sensors that are optimal for performing a particular task. More challenging research seeks ways to evolve control systems simultaneously with body structures.

To list all the impressive results from research in robotics would be an overwhelming task. There are multilegged devices that can walk up stairs, small machines that fly like insects, and smart weapons that direct themselves to their assigned targets. However, while relishing in these successes, we should note that the affection we feel for artificial pet dogs and the awesome power of smart weapons carries social and ethical questions that challenge society. Our future is what we make it.

Database Systems

The human mind is a marvelous device. How it stores its acquired knowledge and later identifies and extracts the particular items of information that are pertinent to the task at hand remains a mystery—a mystery that permeates many areas of artificial intelligence. How does the human mind recall the information needed to recognize images? How does the human mind apply the proper context when processing ambiguous statements in natural languages? How does the human mind store its knowledge of the real world so that it can reason about that knowledge?

Thus a fundamental problem of artificial intelligence is a database issue, and progress in both fields is applied in the other. Artificial intelligence techniques are applied to traditional database systems to provide better service, and database techniques are applied in artificial intelligence projects in an attempt to handle the massive amounts of real-world knowledge underlying the decision processes involved. In other cases research efforts in artificial intelligence and database systems attack the same problem from different perspectives.

One example is the problem of developing associative memory systems (associative database systems). We have already seen the need for such systems in the field of natural language processing where relevant real-world information must be applied to understand sentences according to their contexts, and we have discussed how artificial neural networks are being applied to the problem.

From the perspective of traditional database systems, the problem is to identify and retrieve information that is related to a topic rather than merely the information that is explicitly requested. Consider, for example, the problem of Web surfers trying to find information on the World Wide Web. The traditional approach is to require the surfer to identify key words and phrases that should appear in any relevant document. The system then searches through its database and retrieves those documents containing these words and phrases. Unfortunately, such a system is just a sieve based on syntax rather than semantics. It may overlook the most important documents because they deal with "cars" rather than with "automobiles." What the surfer would really like is a retrieval system with the intelligence to identify related (or associated) material rather than merely retrieving what was explicitly requested.

As another example, suppose we have a database consisting of the courses taught by the professors at a university along with the grades they awarded the students. Consider the following sequence of events: We ask the database for the number of A grades awarded by Professor Johnson last semester. The database replies, "none." We conclude that Professor Johnson was a rather demanding instructor and ask for the number of F grades awarded by Professor Johnson last semester. Again, the database replies, "none." We decide that Professor Johnson considers all students to be average except in extreme cases, so we ask for the number of C grades awarded by Professor Johnson last semester. The database again replies, "none." At this point we begin to get suspicious and ask whether Professor Johnson taught a course last semester. The database replies, "no." If only it had said so in the first place! We would like to have databases that retrieve the information we should have rather than the information for which we ask.

Recursion in Natural Language

Recursive structures involving sentences within sentences are common in English (as well as other languages), where the embedded sentence is called a clause. In fact, techniques for handling such structures were an early focus of research in computerized natural language processing systems. Sometimes these structures involve several layers of recursion, which blur the meaning of the sentence even though the overall structure is grammatically correct. For example, consider the sentence

> The man the horse that lost the race threw was not hurt.

This sentence involves three sentence structures—one within another. The outer sentence is

> The man was not hurt.

The next inner structure identifies the man as the one the horse threw. Within this structure is another sentence structure that identifies the horse as the one that lost the race. The following sentences involve slightly different recursive structures:

> The picture the man the woman who lives next door hired hung fell down.

> The new cook the chef who yells a lot hired but who could not sauté was fired.

Another topic pursued by both database and artificial intelligence research is the development of data storage and retrieval systems that can provide information that is implied by the stored data rather than merely respond with information that is explicitly stored. In this sense, progress in the field of data mining may someday prove useful to researchers in artificial intelligence. The goal is to develop databases that can reason about the information that is explicitly stored.

As a particular example, consider a database consisting of information about current world leaders. When asked if any such person is more than 10 feet tall, a traditional retrieval system would not be able to reply with the answer unless the height of each leader was actually stored in the database. On the other hand, an intelligent system could reply correctly without knowing each leader's height. The line of reasoning might proceed as follows: If there is a leader who is more than 10 feet tall, that would be significant and would be stored in the database. Therefore, since no leader is recorded as being that tall, there is no such leader.

This line of reasoning represents an important concept in database design—the distinction between closed-world databases and open-world databases. Loosely speaking, a **closed-world database** is one that is assumed to contain all true facts about the topic involved, whereas an open-world database may not. The ability to reject the hypothesis of a 10-foot world leader in the previous example was based on the closed-world assumption that if the fact is not recorded then it must be false. Likewise, a database containing subscribers to magazines might use the closed-world assumption to conclude that an individual does not subscribe to a particular magazine even though it does not contain a list of all the nonsubscribers.

Although the closed-world assumption appears innocent on the surface, its application can lead to subtle complications. Consider a database consisting of the single statement

Mickey is a mouse OR Donald is a duck.

From this statement alone we cannot conclude that Mickey is in fact a mouse. Thus the closed-world assumption forces us to conclude that the statement

Mickey is a mouse

is false. In a similar manner, the closed-world assumption forces us to conclude that the statement

Donald is a duck

is false. We see, then, that the closed-world assumption has led us to the contradictory conclusion that although at least one of the statements must be true, both are false. Understanding the limitations of such innocent-looking reasoning techniques is a goal of current research in fields of both artificial intelligence and database.

Expert Systems

An **expert system** is a software package designed to assist humans in situations in which an expert in a specific area is required. These systems are designed to simulate the cause-and-effect reasoning that human experts would follow if confronted with the same situations. Thus a medical expert system should propose the same procedure as a human medical expert who knows that a biopsy should be performed if an abnormality is noticed and an X ray shows the presence of mass in that location.

Expert systems are often organized as a collection of rules in the form of logic implications. For instance, the rule that an abnormality, confirmed by X rays, leads to the performance of a biopsy can be expressed as

(abnormality noticed and X ray shows presence of mass)
implies (perform biopsy)

Notice the similarity between the rules of an expert system and the productions of a production system. The first portion of the rule essentially states the preconditions for performing or concluding the statement found in the second portion. Indeed, many expert systems are essentially production systems, with the rules obtained from the human expert being the productions and the underlying reasoning based on these rules being simulated by the control system. In this context the collection of productions is often called the system's knowledge base, and the control system is sometimes referred to as an inference engine.

Do not be misled, however, into thinking that an expert system is merely a large version of the puzzle-solving system discussed earlier. Some expert systems are organized as collections of production systems that combine their efforts to solve problems. Examples include expert systems that are based on the **blackboard model** in which several problem-solving systems, called knowledge sources, share a common storage area called the blackboard. This blackboard contains the current state of the problem being solved and, since it is shared by all the knowledge sources, provides a medium through which the knowledge sources can contribute to the problem's solution. To coordinate the activities of the knowledge sources, a control module is provided that is given the task of activating the appropriate knowledge source at the appropriate time. In the terminology of the blackboard model, this control module is said to determine the "focus of attention" of the system.

Another distinction between an expert system and a simple production system is that an expert system is not necessarily charged with reaching a predetermined goal but is more likely to be charged with deriving well-founded advice. For example, suppose that an expert system is charged with the problem of diagnosing diseases. Ideally, one would like the systems to conclude with a definitive statement of the form "The disease is X," where in place of X the statement gives the name of the disease present. Unfortunately, such precision may not be possible. Instead, the best answer might be "The disease is most likely X" or perhaps "The disease is either X or Y. Perform the following test to determine which is more likely." Because of this ambiguity, the control system within an expert system may choose to follow several paths through the system's state graph and report on the results of each. In particular, if the production applied at some state is

> (rheumatoid factor present and patient has pain in joints)
>   implies (80% chance of rheumatoid arthritis)

then any further reasoning based on the fact that the disease is rheumatoid arthritis has the potential of being invalid.

As in other research areas, early applications of expert systems were limited to a few areas. Today, however, the number of areas in which expert systems find applications is extensive. One catalyst for this expansion was the realization that an expert system can be separated into its reasoning component and its knowledge component. By removing the knowledge base from an existing expert system, one is left with a system of reasoning routines, collectively known as an inference engine, that is likely to be applicable in other settings as well. New expert systems in other areas can therefore be constructed merely by attaching a new knowledge base to this already existing inference engine. Viewed in the context of production systems, the collection of productions make up a knowledge base whereas the control system is the inference engine. (Those who read the optional section on declarative programming in Chapter 6 will recognize the similarity between the structure of an expert system and that of a Prolog programming environment. The Prolog program is a knowledge base and the underlying resolution system is the inference engine. This similarity is a major reason for the popularity of Prolog in the field of artificial intelligence. Indeed, Prolog is an excellent language in which to develop expert systems.)

Questions/Exercises

1. Identify the ambiguities involved when translating the sentence "They are racing horses."

2. Compare the results of parsing the following two sentences. Then, explain how the sentences differ semantically.

   The farmer built the fence in the field.

   The farmer built the fence in the winter.

3. Based on the semantic net in Figure 10.27, what is the family relationship between Mary and John?

4. A database about magazine subscribers typically contains a list of subscribers to each magazine but does not contain a list of those who do not subscribe. How, then, does such a database determine that a person does not subscribe to a particular magazine?

5. What is the difference between a traditional database and a knowledge base for an expert system?

10.7 Considering the Consequences

Without a doubt, advances being made in artificial intelligence have the potential of benefiting humankind, and it is easy to become caught up in the enthusiasm generated by these potential benefits. However, there are also potential perils lurking in the future whose ramifications could be as devastating as their counterparts are beneficial. The distinction is often merely one's point of view or perhaps one's position in society—one person's gain may be another's loss. It is fitting then that we take a moment to look at advancing technology from alternative perspectives.

Some view the advancement of technology as a gift to humanity—a means of freeing humans from boring, mundane tasks and opening the door to more enjoyable lifestyles. But others see this same phenomenon as a curse that robs citizens of employment and channels wealth toward those with power. This, in fact, was a common message of the devoted humanitarian Mahatma Gandhi of India. He repeatedly argued that India would be better served by replacing large textile mills with spinning wheels placed in the homes of the peasants. In this way, he claimed, centralized mass production that employed only a few would be replaced by a distributed mass production system that would benefit multitudes.

History is full of revolutions with roots in the disproportionate distribution of wealth and privilege. If today's advancing technology is allowed to entrench such discrepancies, catastrophic consequences could result.

But the consequences of building increasingly intelligent machines is more subtle—more fundamental—than those dealing with power struggles between different segments of society. The issues strike at the very heart of humanity's self-image. In the nineteenth century, society was appalled by Charles Darwin's theory of evolution and the thought that humans may have evolved from lesser life forms. How then will society react if faced with the onslaught of machines whose mental capabilities challenge those of humans?

In the past, technology has developed slowly, allowing time for our self-image to be preserved by readjusting our concept of intelligence. Our ancient ancestors would have interpreted the mechanical devices of the nineteenth century as having supernatural intelligence, but today we do not credit these machines with any intelligence at all. But how will humanity react if machines truly challenge the intelligence of humans, or, more likely, if the capabilities of machines begin to advance faster than our ability to adapt?

We might get a clue to humanity's potential reaction to machines that challenge our intellect by considering society's response to IQ tests in the middle of the twentieth century. These tests were considered to identify a child's level of intelligence. Children in the United States were often classified by their performances on these tests and channeled into educational programs accordingly. In turn, educational opportunities were opened to those children who performed well on these tests, whereas children who performed poorly were directed toward remedial programs of study. In short, when given a scale on which to measure an individual's intelligence, society tended to disregard the capabilities of those who found themselves on the lower end of the scale. How then would society handle the situation if the "intellectual" capabilities of machines became compatible, or even appeared to be compatible, with those of humans? Would society discard those whose abilities were seen as "inferior" to those of machines? If so, what would be the consequences for those members of society? Should a person's dignity be subject to how he or she compares to a machine?

We have already begun to see the intellectual powers of humans challenged by machines in specific fields. Machines are now capable of beating experts in chess; computerized expert systems are capable of giving medical advice; and simple programs managing investment portfolios often outperform investment professionals. How do such systems affect the self-image of the individuals involved? How will an individual's self-esteem be affected as that individual is outperformed by machines in more and more areas?

Many argue that the intelligence possessed by machines will always be inherently different from that of humans since humans are biological and machines are not. Thus, they argue, machines will never reproduce a human's decision-making process. Machines may reach the same decisions as humans but those decisions would not be made on the same basis as those made by humans. To what extent, then, are there different kinds of intelligence, and would it be ethical for society to follow paths proposed by nonhuman intelligence?

In his book, *Computer Power and Human Reason,* Joseph Weizenbaum argues against the unchecked application of artificial intelligence as follows:

> Computers can make judicial decisions, computers can make psychiatric judgments. They can flip coins in much more sophisticated ways than can the most patient human being. The point is that they *ought* not be given such tasks. They may even be able to arrive at "correct" decisions in some cases—but always and necessarily on bases no human being should be willing to accept.

There have been many debates on "Computers and Mind." What I conclude here is that the relevant issues are neither technological nor even mathematical; they are ethical. They cannot be settled by asking questions beginning with "can." The limits of the applicability of computers are ultimately statable only in terms of oughts. What emerges as the most elementary insight is that, since we do not now have any ways of making computers wise, we ought not now to give computers tasks that demand wisdom.

You may argue that much of this section borders on science fiction rather than computer science. It was not too long ago, however, that many dismissed the question "What will happen if computers take over society?" with the same it-will-never-happen attitude. But in many respects, that day has now arrived. If a computerized database erroneously reports that you have a bad credit rating, a criminal record, or an overdrawn checking account, is it the computer's statement or your claim of innocence that will prevail? If a malfunctioning navigational system indicates that a fog-covered runway is in the wrong place, where will the aircraft land? If a machine is used to predict the public's reaction to various political decisions, which decision does a politician make? How many times has a clerk been unable to help you because "the computer is down"? Who (or what), then, is in charge? Have we not already surrendered society to machines?

Questions/Exercises

1. How much of today's population would survive if the machines developed over the last 100 years were removed? What about the last 50 years? What about 20 years? Where would the survivors be located?

2. To what extent is your life controlled by machines? Who controls the machines that affect your life?

3. Where do you get the information on which you base your daily decisions? What about your major decisions? What confidence do you have in the accuracy of that information? Why?

Chapter Review Problems

1. Sometimes the ability to answer a question depends as much on knowing the limits of knowledge as it does on the facts themselves. For example, suppose databases A and B both contain a complete list of employees who belong to the company's health insurance program, but only database A is aware that the list is complete.

What could database A conclude about a member who was not on its list that database B could not?

2. In the text we briefly discussed the problems of understanding natural languages as opposed to formal programming languages. As an example of the complexities involved in the case of natural languages, identify situations in which the

question "Do you know what time it is?" has different meanings.

3. As demonstrated by Problem 2, humans may use a question for a purpose other than asking. Another example is "Do you know that your tire is flat?" which is used to inform rather than to ask. Give examples of questions used to reassure, to warn, and to criticize.

4. Compare the roles of the prepositional phrases in the following two sentences (that differ by only one word):

   The pigpen was built by the barn.
   The pigpen was built by the farmer.

5. If a researcher uses computer models for studying the memorization capabilities and processes of the human mind, do the programs developed for the machine necessarily memorize to the best of the machine's abilities? Explain.

6. Give some examples of declarative knowledge. Give some examples of procedural knowledge.

*7. In the context of object-oriented programming, what parts of an object are used to store declarative knowledge? What parts are used to store procedural knowledge?

8. Which of the following activities do you expect to be performance oriented and which are simulation oriented?
   a. The design of a flight simulator
   b. The design of an automatic pilot system
   c. The design of a database dealing with library materials
   d. The design of a model of a nation's economy for testing theories
   e. The design of a program for monitoring a patient's vital signs

9. Identify a small set of geometric properties that can be used to distinguish between the symbols O, G, C, and Q.

10. Describe the similarities between the technique of identifying characteristics by comparing them to templates and the error-correcting codes discussed in Chapter 1.

11. Describe two interpretations of the following line drawing based on whether the "corner" marked A is convex or concave:

12. In the context of a production system, what is the difference between a state graph and a search tree?

13. Analyze the task of solving the Rubik's cube in terms of a production system. (What are the states, the productions, and so on?)

14. Analyze the task of investing in the stock market in terms of a production system. (What are the states, the productions, and so on?) What heuristic could be used to help the control system make decisions?

15. Analyze the task of playing a hole of golf in terms of a production system. (What are the states, the productions, and so on?) What heuristic could be used to help decide which production to apply?

16. In the text we mentioned that a production system is often used as a technique for drawing conclusions from known facts. The states of the system are the facts known to be true at each stage of the reasoning process, and the productions are the rules of logic for manipulating the known facts. Identify some rules of logic that allow the conclusion "John is tall" to be obtained from the facts that "John is a basketball player," "Basketball players are not short," and "John is either short or tall."

17. The tree below represents possible moves in a competitive game, showing that player X currently has a choice between move A and move B. Following the move of player X, player Y is allowed to select a move, and then player X is allowed to select the last move of the game. The leaf nodes of the tree are labeled W, L, or

T, depending on whether that ending represents a win, loss, or tie for player X. Should player X select move A or move B? Why? How does selecting a "production" in a competitive atmosphere differ from a one-person game such as the eight-puzzle?

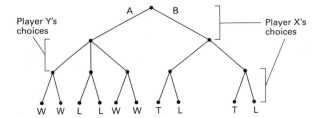

18. Analyze the game of checkers as a production system and describe a heuristic that could be used to determine which of two states is closer to the goal. How would the control system in this setting differ from that of a one-person game such as the eight-puzzle?

19. By considering the manipulation rules of algebra as productions, problems involving the simplification of algebraic expression can be solved in the context of a production system. Identify a set of algebraic productions that allow the equation $3/(2x + 1) = 2/(2x - 2)$ to be reduced to the form $x = 4$. What are some rules of thumb (that is, heuristic rules) used when performing such algebraic simplifications?

20. Draw the search tree that is generated by a breadth-first search in an attempt to solve the eight-puzzle from the following start state without using the assistance of any heuristic information.

	1	3
4	2	5
7	8	6

21. Draw the search tree that is generated by the algorithm of Figure 10.9 in an attempt to solve the eight-puzzle from the start state in Problem

18 if the number of tiles out of place is used as a heuristic.

22. Draw the search tree that is generated by the algorithm of Figure 10.9 in an attempt to solve the eight-puzzle from the following start state, assuming the heuristic used is the same as that developed in Section 10.3.

1	2	3
5	7	6
4		8

23. When solving the eight-puzzle, why would the number of tiles out of place not be as good a heuristic as the one used in Section 10.3?

24. What is the distinction between the technique of deciding which half of the list to consider when performing a binary search (Section 4.5) and deciding which branch to pursue when performing a heuristic search?

25. Note that if a state in the state graph of a production system has an extremely low heuristic value in comparison to the other states and if there is a production from that state to itself, the algorithm in Figure 10.9 can get caught in the loop of considering that state over and over again. Show that if the cost of executing any production in the system is at least one, then by computing the projected cost to be the sum of the heuristic value plus the cost of reaching the state along the path being traversed, this endless looping process will be avoided.

26. What heuristic do you use when searching for a route between two cities on a large road map?

27. List two properties that a heuristic should have if it is to be useful in a production system.

28. Suppose you have two buckets. One has a capacity of exactly 3 liters; the other has a capacity of 5 liters. You can pour water from one bucket to another, empty a bucket, or fill a bucket at any time. Your problem is to place exactly 4 liters of water in the 5-liter bucket.

Describe how this problem could be framed as a production system.

29. Suppose your job is to supervise the loading of two trucks, each of which can carry at most 14 tons. The cargo is a variety of crates whose total weight is 28 tons but whose individual weights vary from crate to crate. The weight of each crate is marked on its side. What heuristic would you use for dividing the crates between the two trucks?

30. Design an artificial neural network that can tell which of the following two patterns is in its field of view.

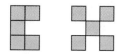

31. Design an artificial neural network that can tell which of the following two patterns is in its field of view.

32. Design an artificial neural network that can tell which of the following four patterns is in its field of view.

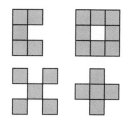

33. The following diagram represents an artificial neural network for an associative memory as discussed toward the end of Section 10.4. What pattern does it associate with any pattern in which only two units that are separated by a single unit are excited? What will happen if the network is initialized with all its units inhibited?

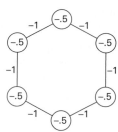

34. The following diagram represents an artificial neural network for an associative memory as discussed toward the end of Section 10.4. What stable configuration does it associate with any initial pattern in which at least three of the units on the perimeter are excited and the center unit is inhibited? What would happen if it were given an initial pattern in which only two opposing units on the perimeter were excited?

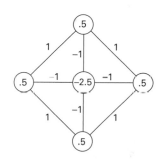

35. Design an artificial neural network for an associative memory (as discussed toward the end of Section 10.4) consisting of a rectangular array of processing units that tries to move toward stable patterns in which a single vertical column of units is excited.

36. How do the results of parsing the following two sentences differ? How do the results of semantic analysis differ?

Theodore rode the zebra.
The zebra was ridden by Theodore.

37. How do the results of parsing the following two sentences differ? How do the results of semantic analysis differ?

If X = 5 then add 1 to X else subtract 1 from X.
If X 5 then subtract 1 from X else add 1 to X.

38. Give an example in which the closed-world assumption leads to a contradiction.

39. Give two examples where the closed-world assumption is commonly used.

40. Adjust the weights and threshold values in the artificial neural network in Figure 10.17 so that its output is 1 when both inputs are the same (both 0 or both 1) and 0 when the inputs are different (one being 0 while the other is 1).

41. Draw a diagram similar to Figure 10.4 representing the process of simplifying the algebraic expression $7x + 3 = 3x - 5$ to the expression $x = -2$.

42. Expand your answer to the previous problem to show other paths that a control system might pursue when attempting to solve the problem.

43. Draw a diagram similar to Figure 10.4 representing the reasoning process involved when concluding that "Polly can fly" from the initial facts "Polly is a parrot," "A parrot is a bird," and "All birds can fly."

44. In contrast to the statement in the preceding problem, some birds, such as an ostrich or a robin with a broken wing, cannot fly. However, it would not seem reasonable to construct a deductive reasoning system in which all the exceptions to the statement "All birds can fly" are explicitly listed. How then do we as humans decide whether a particular bird can or cannot fly?

45. Explain how the semantics of the sentence "I read the new refrigerator warranty" depend on the context.

46. Describe how the problem of traveling from one city to another could be framed as a production system. What are the states? What are the productions?

47. Suppose you must perform three tasks, A, B, and C, that can be performed in any order (but not simultaneously). Describe how this problem can be framed as a production system and draw its state graph.

48. How does the state graph in the previous problem change if task C must be performed before task A?

49. Describe how a strategy for playing tic-tac-toe (naughts-and-crosses) could be developed using the genetic algorithm approach.

50. The method of crossing strategies described in Section 10.5 is known as single-point crossover. An alternative is two-point crossover in which the "middle" segments of two strategies are interchanged. Show that any strategy that can be constructed using one-point crossover can also be constructed using two-point crossover, and vice versa.

51. a. If the notation (i, j), where i and j are positive integers, is used to mean "if the entry in the ith position in the list is greater than the entry in the jth position, interchange the two entries," which of the following two sequences does a better job of sorting a list of length three?

(1, 3) (3, 2)

(1, 2) (2, 3) (1, 2)

b. Use this notational system to develop a genetic algorithm for developing a program that sorts lists of length ten.

52. Suppose each member in a group of robots is to be equipped with a pair of sensors. Each sensor can detect an object directly in front of it within a range of two meters. Each robot is shaped like a trash can and can move in any direction. Design a sequence of experiments to determine where the sensors should be placed to produce a robot that successfully pushes a basketball in a straight line. How does your sequence of experiments compare to an evolutionary system?

53. In the text we discussed how genetic algorithms cold be applied to populations represented by lists. Describe how they could be applied to populations represented by tree structures.

54. Changes in the context of a sentence can change the significance of the sentence as well as its meaning. In the context of Figure 10.27, how would the significance of the sentence "Mary hit John." change if the birth dates were in the 1960s? What if one were in the 1960s and the other in the 1990s?

55. Draw a semantic net representing the information in the following paragraph.

> Donna threw the ball to Jack, who hit it into center field. The center fielder tried to catch it, but it bounced off the wall instead.

Social Issues

The following questions are provided to help you understand some of the ethical/social/legal issues associated with the field of computing. The goal is not merely to answer these questions. You should also consider why you answered as you did and whether your justifications are consistent from one question to the next.

1. To what extent should researchers in nuclear power, genetic engineering, and artificial intelligence be held responsible for the way the results of their work are used? Is a scientist responsible for the knowledge revealed by his or her research? What if the resulting knowledge was an unexpected consequence?

2. How would you distinguish between intelligence and simulated intelligence? Do you believe there is a difference?

3. Suppose a computerized medical expert system gains a reputation within the medical community for giving sound advice. To what extent should a physician allow that system to alter his or her decisions regarding the treatment of patients? If the physician gives a treatment contrary to that proposed by the expert system and the system turns out to be right, is the physician guilty of malpractice? In general, if an expert system becomes well known within a field, to what degree could it hamper, rather than enhance, the ability of human experts when making their own judgments?

4. Many would argue that a computer's actions are merely consequences of how it was programmed, and thus a computer cannot possess free will. In turn, a computer should not be held responsible for its actions. Is a human's mind a computer? Are humans preprogrammed at birth? Are humans programmed by their environments? Are humans responsible for their actions?

5. Are there avenues that science should not pursue even though it may be capable of doing so? For instance, if it becomes possible to construct a machine with perception and reasoning skills comparable to those of humans, would the construction of such a machine be appropriate? What issues could the existence of such a machine raise? What are some of the issues being raised today by advancements in other scientific fields?

6. History abounds with instances in which the work of scientists and artists was affected by the political, religious, or other social influences of their times. In what ways are such issues affecting current scientific efforts? What about computer science in particular?

7. Many cultures today take at least some responsibility toward helping to retrain those whose jobs have been made redundant by advancing technology. What should/can society do as technology makes more and more of our capabilities redundant?

8. Suppose you receive a computer-generated bill for $0.00. What should you do? Suppose you do nothing and 30 days later you receive a second notice of $0.00 due in your account. What should you do? Suppose you do nothing and 30 days later you receive another notice of $0.00 due in your account along with a note stating that, unless the bill is paid promptly, legal action will be taken. Who is in charge?

9. Are there times when you associate personalities with your personal computer? Are there times when it seems vindictive or stubborn? Do you ever get mad at your computer? What is the difference between being mad *at* your computer and being mad *as a result of* your computer? Does your computer ever get mad at you? Do you have similar relationships with other objects such as cars, televisions, and ballpoint pens?

10. Based on your answers to Question 9, to what extent are humans willing to associate an entity's behavior with the presence of intelligence and awareness? To what extent should humans make such associations? Is it possible for an intelligent entity to reveal its intelligence in a means other than its behavior?

11. Many feel that the ability to pass the Turing test does not imply that a machine is intelligent. One argument is that intelligent behavior does not, in itself, imply intelligence. Yet the theory of evolution is based on the survival of the fittest, which is a behavior-based test. Does the theory of evolution imply that intelligent behavior is a predecessor to intelligence? Would the ability to pass the Turing test imply that machines were on their way to becoming intelligent?

12. Medical treatment has advanced to the point that numerous parts of the human body can now be replaced with artificial parts or parts from human donors. It is conceivable that this may someday include parts of the brain. What ethical problems would such capabilities raise? If a patient's neurons were replaced one at a time with artificial neurons, would the patient remain the same person? Would the patient ever notice a difference? Would the patient remain human?

Additional Reading

Banzhaf, W., P. Nordin, R. E. Deller, and F. D. Francone. *Genetic Programming: An Introduction.* San Francisco, CA: Morgan Kaufmann, 1998.

Lu, J. and J. Wu. *Multi-Agent Robotic Systems.* Boca Raton, FL: CRC Press, 2001.

Mitchell, M. *An Introduction to Genetic Algorithms.* Cambridge, MA: MIT Press, 1998.

Nilsson, N. *Artificial Intelligence: A New Synthesis.* San Francisco, CA: Morgan Kaufmann, 1998.

Nolfi, S. and D. Floreano. *Evolutionary Robotics.* Cambridge, MA: MIT Press, 2000.

Rumelhart, D. E. and J. L. McClelland. *Parallel Distributed Processing.* Cambridge, MA: MIT Press, 1986.

Russell, S. and P. Norvig. *Artificial Intelligence: A Modern Approach,* 2nd ed. Englewood Cliffs, NJ: Prentice-Hall, 2003.

Shapiro, L. G. and G. C. Stockman. *Computer Vision.* Englewood Cliffs, NJ: Prentice-Hall, 2001.

Weizenbaum, J. *Computer Power and Human Reason.* New York: W. H. Freeman, 1979.

Theory of Computation

In this chapter we consider questions regarding what computers can and cannot do. We will see how simple machines, known as Turing machines, are used to identify the boundary between problems that are solvable by machines and problems that are not. We will identify a particular problem, known as the halting problem, whose solution falls beyond the powers of algorithmic systems and therefore beyond the capabilities of today's as well as tomorrow's computers. Moreover, we will find that even among the machine-solvable problems, there are problems whose solutions are so complex that they are unsolvable from any practical point of view. We close by considering how knowledge in the field of complexity can be used to construct a public key encryption system.

Asterisks indicate suggestions for optional sections.

11.1 Functions and Their Computation

Our goal in this chapter is to investigate the capabilities of computers. We want to understand what machines can and cannot do and what features are required for machines to reach their full potential. We begin with the concept of computing functions.

A **function** in its mathematical sense is a correspondence between a collection of possible input values and a collection of output values so that each possible input is assigned a single output. An example is the function that converts measurements in yards into meters. With each measurement in yards, it assigns the value that would result if the same distance were measured in meters. Another example, which we could call the sort function, assigns each input list of numeric values to an output list whose entries are the same as those in the input list but are arranged in the order of increasing value. Still another example is the addition function whose inputs are pairs of values and whose outputs are values representing the sum of each input pair.

The process of determining the particular output value that a function assigns to a given input is called *computing the function*. The ability to compute functions is important because it is by means of computing functions that we are able to solve problems. To solve an addition problem we must compute the addition function; to sort a list we must compute the sort function. In turn, a fundamental task of computer science is to find techniques for computing the functions that lie beneath the problems we want to solve.

Consider, for example, a system in which a function's inputs and outputs can be predetermined and recorded in a table. Each time the output of the function is required, we merely look for the given input in the table where we find the required output. Thus the computation of the function is reduced to the process of searching the table. Such systems are convenient but limited in power because many functions cannot be represented completely in tabular form. An example is shown in Figure 11.1

Figure 11.1

An attempt to display the function that converts measurements in yards into meters

Yards (input)	Meters (output)
1	0.9144
2	1.8288
3	2.7432
4	3.6576
5	4.5720
.	.
.	.
.	.

where we have attempted to display the function that converts measurements in yards into equivalent measurements in meters. Since there is no limit to the list of possible input/output pairs, the table is destined to be incomplete.

A more powerful approach to computing functions is to follow directions provided by an algebraic formula rather than trying to display all possible input/output combinations in a table. We could, for example, use the algebraic formula

$$V = P(1 + r)^n$$

to describe how to compute the value of an investment of P after earning an annually compounded interest rate of r for n years.

But the expressive power of algebraic formulas has its limitations as well. There are functions whose input/output relationships are too complex to be described by algebraic manipulations. Examples include the trigonometric functions such as sine and cosine. If pressed to calculate the sine of 38 degrees, you might draw the appropriate triangle, measure its sides, and calculate the desired ratio—a process that cannot be expressed in terms of algebraic manipulations of the value 38. Your pocket calculator also struggles with the task of computing the sine of 38 degrees. In reality, it is forced to apply rather sophisticated mathematical techniques to obtain a very good approximation to the sine of 38 degrees, which it reports to you as the answer.

We see, then, that as we consider functions with increasing complexity, we are forced to apply more powerful techniques for computing them. Our question is whether we can always find a system for computing functions, regardless of their complexity. The answer is no. A striking result from mathematics is that there are functions that are so complex that there is no well-defined, step-by-step process for determining their outputs based on their input values. In turn, the computation of these functions lies beyond the abilities of any algorithmic system. These functions are said to be noncomputable, whereas the functions whose output values can be determined algorithmically from their input values are said to be **computable.**

The study of computable and noncomputable functions is an important undertaking in computer science. Since machines can only perform tasks described by algorithms, the study of computable functions is the study of the ultimate capabilities of machines. If we can identify capabilities that allow a machine to compute the entire set of computable functions and then build machines with these capabilities, we will be assured that the machines we build are as powerful as we can make them. Likewise, if we discover that the solution to a problem requires the computation of a noncomputable function, we can conclude that the solution to that problem lies beyond the capabilities of machines.

Questions/Exercises

1. Identify some functions that can be represented completely in tabular form.

2. Identify some functions whose outputs can be described as an algebraic expression involving their inputs.

3. Identify a function that cannot be described in terms of an algebraic formula. Is your function nonetheless computable?

4. Ancient Greek mathematicians used a straight-edge and compass to draw shapes. They developed techniques for finding the mid point on a straight line, constructing a right angle, and drawing an equal-lateral triangle. However, what were some "computations" that their "computational system" could not perform?

11.2 Turing Machines

In an effort to understand capabilities and limitations of machines, many researchers have proposed and studied various computational devices. One of these is the Turing machine that was proposed by Alan M. Turing in 1936 and is still used as a tool for studying the power of algorithmic processes today.

Turing Machine Fundamentals

A **Turing machine** consists of a control unit that can read and write symbols on a tape by means of a read/write head (Figure 11.2). The tape extends indefinitely at both ends and is divided into cells, each of which can contain any one of a finite set of symbols. This set is called the machine's alphabet.

At any time during a Turing machine's computation, the machine must be in one of a finite number of conditions, called states. A Turing machine's computation begins in a special state called the start state and ceases when the machine reaches another special state known as the halt state.

A Turing machine's computation consists of a sequence of steps that are executed by the machine's control unit. Each step consists of observing the symbol in the current tape cell (the one viewed by the read-write head), writing a symbol in that cell, possibly moving the read-write head one cell to the left or right, and then changing states. The exact action to be performed is determined by a program that tells the control unit what to do based on the machine's state and the contents of the current tape cell.

Figure 11.2

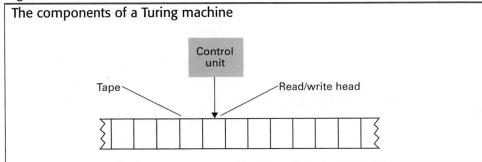

The components of a Turing machine

Control unit

Tape

Read/write head

Let us consider an example of a specific Turing machine. For this purpose, we represent the machine's tape as a horizontal strip divided into cells in which we can record symbols from the machine's alphabet. We indicate the current position of the machine's read/write head by placing a label under the current tape cell. The alphabet for our example consists of the symbols 0, 1, and *. The tape of our machine might appear as follows:

By interpreting a string of symbols on the tape as representing binary numbers separated by asterisks, we recognize that this particular tape contains the value 5. Our Turing machine is designed to increment such a value on the tape by 1. More precisely, it assumes that the starting position is at an asterisk marking the right end of a string of 0s and 1s, and it proceeds to alter the bit pattern to the left so that it represents the next larger integer.

The states for our machine are START, ADD, CARRY, OVERFLOW, RETURN, and HALT. The actions corresponding to each of these states and the content of the current cell are described in the table in Figure 11.3. We assume that the machine always begins in the START state.

Let us apply this machine to the tape pictured earlier that contains the value 5. Observe that when in the START state with the current cell containing * (as is our case), we are instructed by the table to rewrite the *, move the read/write head one cell to the left, and enter the ADD state. Having done this, the machine can be described as follows:

Figure 11.3

A Turing machine for incrementing a value				
Current state	Current cell content	Value to write	Direction to move	New state to enter
START	*	*	Left	ADD
ADD	0	1	Right	RETURN
ADD	1	0	Left	CARRY
ADD	*	*	Right	HALT
CARRY	0	1	Right	RETURN
CARRY	1	0	Left	CARRY
CARRY	*	1	Left	OVERFLOW
OVERFLOW	*	*	Right	RETURN
RETURN	0	0	Right	RETURN
RETURN	1	1	Right	RETURN
RETURN	*	*	No move	HALT

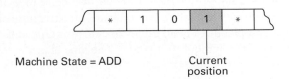

Machine State = ADD

Current
position

To proceed, we look at the table to see what to do when in the ADD state with the current cell containing 1. The table tells us to replace the 1 in the current cell with 0, move the read/write head one cell to the left, and enter the CARRY state. Thus the configuration of the machine becomes:

Machine State = CARRY

Current
position

We again refer to the table to see what to do next and find that when in the CARRY state with the current cell containing 0, we should replace the 0 with 1, move the read/write head one cell to the right, and enter the RETURN state. After doing this, the machine's configuration is as follows:

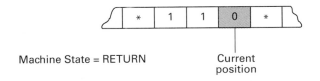

Machine State = RETURN

Current
position

From this situation, the table instructs us to proceed by replacing the 0 in the current cell with another 0, move the read/write head one cell to the right, and remain in the RETURN state. Consequently, we find our machine in the following condition:

Machine State = RETURN

Current
position

At this point, we see that the table instructs us to rewrite the asterisk in the current cell and HALT. The machine thus stops in the following configuration (the symbols on the tape now represent the value 6 as desired):

Machine State = HALT   Current position

The Church-Turing Thesis

The Turing machine in the preceding example can be used to compute the function known as the successor function, which assigns each nonnegative integer input value n to the output value $n + 1$. We need merely place the input value in its binary form on the machine's tape, run the machine until it halts, and then read the output value from the tape. A function that can be computed in this manner by a Turing machine is said to be **Turing computable.**

Turing's conjecture was that the Turing-computable functions were the same as the computable functions. In other words, he conjectured that the computational power of Turing machines encompasses that of any algorithmic system or, equivalently, that (in contrast to such approaches as tables and algebraic formulas) the Turing machine concept provides a context in which solutions to all the computable functions can be expressed. Today, this conjecture is often referred to as the **Church–Turing thesis,** in reference to the contributions made by both Alan Turing and Alonzo Church. Since Turing's initial work, much evidence has been collected to support this thesis, and today the Church–Turing thesis is widely accepted. That is, the computable functions and the Turing-computable functions are considered the same.

The Origins of Turing Machines

Alan Turing developed the concept of a Turing machine in the 1930s, well before technology was capable of providing the machines we know today. In fact, Turing's vision was that of a human performing computations with pencil and paper. Turing's goal was to provide a model by which the limits of "computational processes" could be studied. This was shortly after the publication in 1931 of Gödel's famous paper exposing the limitations of computational systems, and a major research effort was being directed toward understanding these limitations. In the same year that Turing presented his model (1936), Emil Post presented another model (now known as Post production systems) that has been shown to have the same capabilities as Turing's. As a testimony to the insights of these early researchers, their models of computational systems (such as Turing machines and Post production systems) still serve as valuable tools in computer science research.

The significance of this conjecture is that it gives insight to the capabilities and limitations of computing machinery. More precisely, it establishes the capabilities of Turing machines as a standard to which the powers of other computational systems can be compared. If a computational system is capable of computing all the Turing-computable functions, it is considered to be as powerful as any computational system can be.

Questions/Exercises

1. Apply the Turing machine described in this section (Figure 11.3), starting with the following initial status:

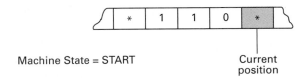

Machine State = START   Current position

2. Describe a Turing machine that replaces a string of 0s and 1s with a single 0.

3. Describe a Turing machine that decrements the value on the tape if it is greater than zero or leaves the value unaltered if it is zero.

4. Identify an everyday situation in which calculating takes place. How is that situation analogous to a Turing machine?

5. Describe a Turing machine that ultimately halts for some inputs but never halts for others.

11.3 Universal Programming Languages

In Chapter 6 we studied a variety of features found in high-level programming languages. In this section we apply our knowledge of computability to determine which of these features are actually necessary. We will find that most features in today's high-level languages merely enhance convenience rather than contribute to the fundamental power of the language.

Our approach is to describe a simple imperative programming language that is rich enough to allow us to express programs for computing all the Turing-computable functions (and thus all the computable functions). Hence, if a future programmer finds that a problem cannot be solved using this language, the reason will not be a fault of the language. Instead, it will be that there is no algorithm for solving the problem. A programming language with this property is called a **universal programming language.**

You may find it surprising that a universal language need not be complex. Indeed, the language we are about to present is quite simple. In turn, we will call it Bare Bones since it isolates the minimal set of requirements of a universal programming language.

The Bare Bones Language

Let us begin our presentation of Bare Bones by considering the declarative statements found in other programming languages. These statements allow programmers the luxury of thinking in terms of data structures and data types (such as arrays of numeric values and strings of alphabetic characters) even though the machine itself merely manipulates bit patterns without any knowledge of what the patterns represent. Before being presented to a machine for execution, a high-level instruction dealing with elaborate data types and structures must be translated into machine-level instructions that manipulate bit patterns to simulate the actions requested.

For convenience, we can interpret these patterns as numeric values represented in binary notation. Thus, all computations performed by a computer could be expressed as numeric computations involving nonnegative integers—it is all in the eye of the beholder. Moreover, programming languages could be simplified by requiring programmers to express algorithms in these terms (although this would place a larger burden on the programmer).

Since our goal in developing Bare Bones is to develop the simplest language possible, we will follow this lead. All variables in Bare Bones will be considered to represent bit patterns that, for convenience, we interpret as nonnegative integers in binary notation. Thus a variable currently assigned the pattern 10 will be said to contain the value two, whereas a variable assigned the pattern 101 will be said to contain five.

Using this convention, all variables in a Bare Bones program are of the same type so the language does not need declarative statements by which variable names and their associated properties are described. When using Bare Bones, a programmer can simply begin using a new variable name when it is needed, with the understanding that it refers to a bit pattern interpreted as a nonnegative integer.

Of course, a translator for our Bare Bones language must be able to distinguish variable names from the other terms. This is done by designing the syntax of Bare Bones so that the role of any term can be identified by syntax alone. For this purpose, we specify that variable names must begin with a letter from the English alphabet, which can be followed by any combination of letters and digits (0 through 9). Thus the strings XYZ, B747, abcdefghi, and X5Y can be used as variable names, whereas 2G5, %o, and x.y cannot.

Bare Bones contains three assignment statements and one control statement representing a loop. The language is a free format language, so each of these statements terminates with a semicolon, making it easy for a translator to separate statements that may appear on the same line. We, however, will adopt the policy of writing only one statement per line to enhance readability.

Each of the three assignment statements requests that the contents of the variable identified in the statement be modified. The first allows us to associate the value zero with a variable. Its syntax is

```
clear name;
```

where *name* can be any variable name.

The other assignment statements are essentially opposites of each other:

```
incr name;
```

and

```
decr name;
```

Again, *name* represents any variable name. The first of these statements causes the value associated with the identified variable to be incremented by one. Thus, if the variable Y were assigned the value five before the statement

```
incr Y;
```

is executed, then the value assigned to Y afterward would be six.

In contrast, the decr statement is used to decrement the value associated with the identified variable by one. An exception is when the variable is already associated with zero, in which case this statement leaves the value unaltered. Therefore, if the value associated with Y is five before the statement

```
decr Y;
```

is executed, the value four would be associated with Y afterward. However, if the value of Y had been zero before executing the statement, the value would remain zero after execution.

Bare Bones contains only one control structure represented by a while-end statement pair. The statement sequence

```
while name not 0 do;
   .
   .
   .
end;
```

(where *name* represents any variable name) causes any statement or statement sequence positioned between the while and end statements to be repeated as long as the value of the variable *name* is not zero. To be more precise, when a while-end structure is encountered during program execution, the value of the identified variable is first compared to zero. If it is zero, the structure is skipped, and execution continues with the statement following the end statement. If, however, the variable's value is not zero, the statement sequence within the while-end structure is executed, and control is returned to the while statement, whereupon the comparison is conducted again. Note that the burden of loop control is partially placed on the programmer, who must explicitly request that the variable's value be altered within the loop body to avoid an infinite loop. For instance, the sequence

```
incr X;
while X not 0 do;
   incr Z;
end;
```

results in an infinite process because once the while statement is reached, the value associated with X can never be zero, whereas the sequence

```
clear Z;
while X not 0 do;
   incr Z;
   decr X;
end;
```

ultimately terminates with the effect of transferring the value initially associated with X to the variable Z.

Observe that while and end statements must appear in pairs with the while statement appearing first. However, a while-end statement pair may appear within the instructions being repeated by another while-end pair. In such a case the pairing of while and end statements is accomplished by scanning the program in its written form from beginning to end while associating each end statement with the nearest preceding while statement not yet paired. Although not syntactically necessary, we often use indentation to enhance the readability of such structures.

As a closing example, the instruction sequence in Figure 11.4 results in the product of the values associated with X and Y being assigned to Z, although it has the side effect of destroying any nonzero value that may have been associated with X. (The while-end structure controlled by the variable W has the effect of restoring the original value of Y.)

Programming in Bare Bones

Keep in mind that our goal in presenting the language Bare Bones is to investigate what is possible, not what is practical. Bare Bones would prove to be awkward if used in an applied setting. On the other hand, we will soon see that this simple language fulfills our goal of providing a no-frills universal programming language. For now, we will merely demonstrate how Bare Bones can be used to express some elementary operations.

Figure 11.4

A Bare Bones program for computing X x Y

```
                clear Z;
                while X not 0 do;
                   clear W;
                   while Y not 0 do;
                      incr Z;
                      incr W;
                      decr Y;
                   end;
                   while W not 0 do;
                      incr Y;
                      decr W;
                   end;
                   decr X;
                end;
```

We first note that with a combination of the assignment statements, any value (any nonnegative integer) can be associated with a given variable. For example, the following sequence assigns the the value three to the variable X by first assigning it the value zero and then incrementing its value three times:

```
clear X;
incr X;
incr X;
incr X;
```

Another common activity in programs is to copy data from one location to another. In terms of Bare Bones, this means that we need to be able to assign the value of one variable to another variable. This can be accomplished by first clearing the destination and then incrementing it an appropriate number of times. In fact, we have already observed that the sequence

```
clear Z;
while X not 0 do;
   incr Z;
   decr X;
end;
```

transfers the value associated with X to Z. However, this sequence has the side effect of destroying the original value of X. To correct for this, we can introduce an auxiliary variable to which we first transfer the subject value from its initial location. We then use this auxiliary variable as the data source from which we restore the original variable while placing the subject value in the desired destination. In this manner, the movement of Today to Yesterday can be accomplished by the sequence shown in Figure 11.5.

We adopt the syntax

```
copy name1 to name2;
```

(where *name1* and *name2* represent variable names) as a shorthand notation for a statement structure of the form in Figure 11.5. Thus, although Bare Bones itself does

Figure 11.5

A Bare Bones implementation of the instruction "copy Today to Tomorrow"
| ```
clear Aux;
clear Tomorrow;
while Today not 0 do;
    incr Aux;
    decr Today;
end;
while Aux not 0 do;
    incr Today;
    incr Tomorrow;
    decr Aux;
end;
``` |
```

not have an explicit copy instruction, we often write programs as though it did, with the understanding that to convert such informal programs into real Bare Bones programs, we must replace the copy statements with their equivalent while-end structures using an auxiliary variable whose name does not clash with a name already used elsewhere in the program.

The Universality of Bare Bones

Let us now apply the Church-Turing thesis to confirm our claim that Bare Bones is a universal programming language. First, we observe that any program written in Bare Bones can be thought of as directing the computation of a function. The function's input consists of values assigned to variables prior to executing the program, and the function's output consists of the values of variables when the program terminates. To compute the function, we merely execute the program, starting with proper variable assignments, and then observe the variables' values when the program terminates.

Under these conditions the program

```
incr X;
```

directs the computation of the same function (the successor function) that is computed by the Turing machine example of Section 11.2. Indeed, it increases the value associated with X by one. Likewise, if we interpret the variables X and Y as inputs and the variable Z as the output, the program

```
copy Y to Z;
while X not 0 do;
  incr Z;
  decr X;
end;
```

directs the computation of the addition function.

Researchers have shown that the Bare Bones programming language can be used to express algorithms for computing all the Turing-computable functions. Combining this with the Church-Turing thesis implies that any computable function can be computed by a program written in Bare Bones. Thus Bare Bones is a universal programming language in the sense that, if an algorithm exists for solving a problem, then that problem can be solved by some Bare Bones program. In turn, Bare Bones could theoretically serve as a general-purpose programming language.

We say *theoretically* because such a language is certainly not as convenient as the high-level languages introduced in Chapter 6. However, each of those languages essentially contains the features of Bare Bones as its core. It is, in fact, this core that ensures the universality of each of those languages; all the other features in the various languages are included for convenience.

Although not practical in an application programming environment, languages such as Bare Bones find use within theoretical computer science. For example, in Appendix E we use Bare Bones as a tool to settle the question regarding the equivalence of iterative and recursive structures raised in Chapter 5. There we find that our suspicion of equivalence was, in fact, justified.

Questions/Exercises

1. Show that the statement `invert X;` (whose action is to convert the value of X to zero if its initial value is nonzero and to 1 if its initial value is zero) can be simulated by a Bare Bones program segment.

2. Show that even our simple Bare Bones language contains more statements than necessary by showing that the `clear` statement can be replaced with combinations of other statements in the language.

3. Show that the `if-then-else` structure can be simulated using Bare Bones. That is, write a program sequence in Bare Bones that simulates the action of the statement

    ```
    if X not 0 then S1 else S2;
    ```

    where S1 and S2 represent arbitrary statement sequences.

4. Show that each of the Bare Bones statements can be expressed in terms of the machine language of Appendix C. (Thus Bare Bones can be used as a programming language for such a machine.)

5. How can negative numbers be dealt with in Bare Bones?

6. Describe the function computed by the following Bare Bones program, assuming the function's input is represented by X and its output by Z:

    ```
    clear Z;
    while X not 0 do;
      incr Z;
      incr Z;
      decr X;
    end;
    ```

11.4 A Noncomputable Function

We now identify a function that is not Turing computable and so, by the Church-Turing thesis, is widely believed to be noncomputable in the general sense. Thus it is a function whose computation lies beyond the capabilities of today's computers.

The Halting Problem

The noncomputable function we are about to reveal is associated with a problem known as the **halting problem,** which (in an informal sense) is the problem of trying to predict in advance whether a program will terminate (or halt) if started under certain conditions. For example, consider the simple Bare Bones program

```
while X not 0 do;
  incr X;
end;
```

If we execute this program with the initial value of X being zero, the loop will not be executed and the program's execution will quickly terminate. However, if we execute the program with any other initial value of X, the loop will be executed forever, leading to a nonterminating process.

In this case, then, it is easy to conclude that the program's execution will halt only when it is started with X assigned the value zero. However, as we move to more complex examples, the task of predicting a program's behavior becomes more complicated. In fact, in some cases the task is impossible, as we shall see. But first we need to formalize our terminology and focus our thoughts more precisely.

Our example has shown that whether a program ultimately halts can depend on the initial values of its variables. Thus if we hope to predict whether a program's execution will halt, we must be precise in regard to these initial values. The choice we are about to make for these values may seem strange to you at first, but do not despair. Our goal is to take advantage of a technique called self-reference—the idea of an object referring to itself. This ploy has repeatedly led to amazing results in mathematics from such informal curiosities as the sentence "This statement is false" to the more serious paradox represented by the question "Does the set of all sets contain itself?" What we are about to do, then, is set the stage for a line of reasoning similar to "If it does, then it doesn't; but, if it doesn't, then it does."

In our case self-reference will be achieved by assigning the variables in a program an initial value that represents the program itself. To this end, observe that each Bare Bones program can be encoded as a single long bit pattern in a one-character-per-byte format using ASCII, which can then be interpreted as the binary representation for a (rather large) nonnegative integer. It is this integer value that we assign as the initial value for the variables in the program.

Let us consider what would happen if we did this in the case of the simple program

```
while X not 0 do;
  incr X;
end;
```

We want to know what would happen if we started this program with X assigned the integer value representing the program itself (Figure 11.6). In this case the answer is readily apparent. Since X would have a nonzero value, the program would become

Figure 11.6

Testing a program for self-termination

Encode the program as one long bit pattern using ASCII.

```
While X not 0 do;
  incr X;
end;
```

W h .... d ;

0111011101101000...0110010000111011

Assign this pattern to X and execute the program.

caught in the loop and never terminate. On the other hand, if we performed a similar experiment with the program

```
clear X;
while X not 0 do;
  incr X;
end;
```

the program would terminate since the variable X would have the value zero by the time the while-end structure is reached regardless of its initial value.

Let us, then, make the following definition: A Bare Bones program is **self-terminating** if executing the program with all its variables initialized to the program's own encoded representation leads to a terminating process. Informally, a program is self-terminating if its execution terminates when started with itself as its input. Here, then, is the self-reference that we promised.

Note that whether a program is self-terminating probably has nothing to do with the purpose for which the program was written. It is merely a property that each Bare Bones program either possesses or does not possess. That is, each Bare Bones program is either self-terminating or not.

We can now describe the halting problem in a precise manner. It is the problem of determining whether Bare Bones programs are or are not self-terminating. We are about to see that there is no algorithm for answering this question in general. That is, there is no single algorithm that, when given any Bare Bones program, is capable of determining whether that program is or is not self-terminating. Thus the solution to the halting problem lies beyond the capabilities of computers.

The fact that we have apparently solved the halting problem in our previous examples and now claim that the halting problem is unsolvable may sound contradictory, so let us pause for clarification. The observations we used in our examples were unique to those particular cases and would not be applicable in all situations. What the halting problem requests is a single, generic algorithm that can be applied to any Bare Bones program to determine whether it is self-terminating. Our ability to apply certain isolated insights to determine whether a particular program is self-terminating in no way implies the existence of a single, generic approach that can be applied in all cases. In short, we may be able to build a machine that can solve a particular halting problem, but we cannot build a single machine that we could use to solve any halting problem that arises.

The Unsolvability of the Halting Problem

We now want to show that solving the halting problem lies beyond the capabilities of machines. Our approach is to show that to solve the problem would require an algorithm for computing a noncomputable function. The inputs of the function in question are encoded versions of Bare Bones programs; its outputs are limited to the values 0 and 1. More precisely, we define the function so that the representation of a self-terminating program produces the output value 1 and the representation of a non–self-terminating program produces the output value 0. For the sake of conciseness, we will refer to this function as the *halting function*.

Our task is to show that the halting function is not computable. Our approach is the technique known as "proof by contradiction." In short, we prove that a statement is false by showing that it cannot be true. Let us, then, show that the statement "the halting function is computable" cannot be true. Our entire argument is summarized in Figure 11.7.

Figure 11.7

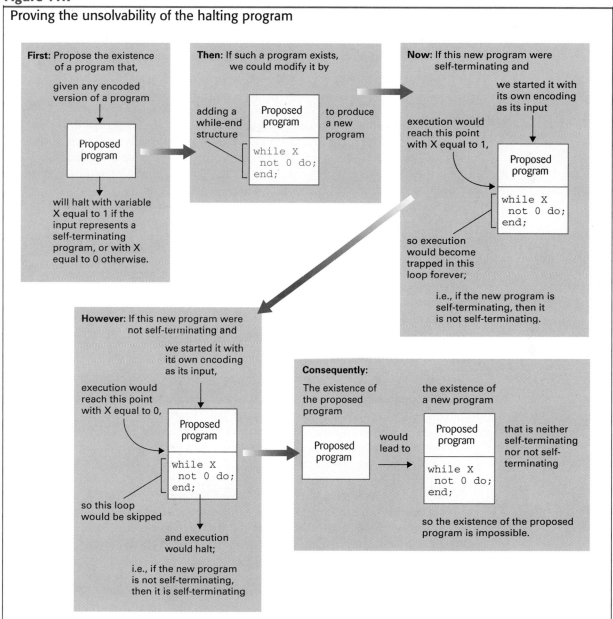

Proving the unsolvability of the halting program

Recursive Function Theory

Nothing tantalizes human nature more than to be told something cannot be done. Once researchers began to identify problems that are unsolvable in the sense that they have no algorithmic solutions, others began to study these problems to try to understand their complexity. Today, this field of research is a major part of the subject known as recursive function theory, and much has been learned about these super-difficult problems. Indeed, just as mathematicians have developed number systems that reveal "quantitative" levels beyond infinity, recursive function theorists have uncovered multiple levels of complexity within problems that exist well beyond the capabilities of algorithms.

If the halting function is computable, then (since Bare Bones is a universal programming language) there must be a Bare Bones program that computes it. In other words, there is a Bare Bones program that terminates with its output equal to 1 if its input is the encoded version of a self-terminating program and terminates with its output equal to 0 otherwise.

To apply this program we do not need to identify which variable is the input variable but instead merely to initialize all the program's variables to the encoded representation of the program to be tested. This is because a variable that is not an input variable is inherently a variable whose initial value does not affect the ultimate output value. We conclude that if the halting function is computable, then there is a Bare Bones program that terminates with its output equal to 1 if all its variables are initialized to the encoded version of a self-terminating program and terminates with its output equal to 0 otherwise.

Assuming that the program's output variable is named X (if it is not we could simply rename the variables), we could modify the program by attaching the statements

```
while X not 0 do;
end;
```

at its end, producing a new program. This new program must be either self-terminating or not. However, we are about to see that it can be neither.

In particular, if this new program were self-terminating and we ran it with its variables initialized to the program's own encoded representation, then when its execution reached the while statement that we added, the variable X would contain a 1. (To this point the new program is identical to the original program that produced a 1 if its input was the representation of a self-terminating program.) At this point, the program's execution would be caught forever in the while-end structure because we made no provisions for X to be decremented within the loop. But this contradicts our assumption that the new program is self-terminating. Therefore we must conclude that the new program is not self-terminating.

If, however, the new program were not self-terminating and we executed it with its variables initialized to the program's own encoded representation, it would reach the added while statement with X being assigned the value 0. (This occurs because the statements preceding the while statement constitute the original program that produces an output of 0 when its input represents a program that is not self-termi-nating.) In this case, the loop in the `while-end` structure would be avoided and the program would halt. But this is the property of a self-terminating program, so we are forced to conclude that the new program is self-terminating, just as we were forced to conclude earlier that it is not self-terminating.

In summary, we see that we have the impossible situation of a program that on the one hand must be either self-terminating or not and on the other hand can be nei-ther. Consequently, the assumption that led to this dilemma must be false.

We conclude that the halting function is not computable, and since the solution to the halting problem relies on the computation of that function we must conclude that solving the halting problem lies beyond the capabilities of any algorithmic sys-tem. Such problems are called **unsolvable problems.**

In closing, we should relate what we have just discussed to the ideas in Chapter 10. There, a major underlying question was whether the powers of computing machines include those required for intelligence itself. Recall that machines can solve only prob-lems with algorithmic solutions, and we have now found that there are problems with-out algorithmic solutions. The question, then, is whether the human mind embodies more than the execution of algorithmic processes. If it does not, then the limits we have identified here are also limits of human thought. Needless to say, this is a highly debat-able and sometimes emotional issue. If, for example, human minds are no more than programmed machines, then one would conclude that humans do not possess free will.

Questions/Exercises

1. Is the following Bare Bones program self-terminating? Explain your answer.
   ```
   incr X;
   decr Y;
   ```

2. Is the following Bare Bones program self-terminating? Explain your answer.
   ```
   copy X to Y;
   incr Y;
   incr Y;
   while X not 0 do;
     decr X;
     decr X;
     decr Y;
     decr Y;
   end;
   decr Y;
   while Y not 0 do;
   end;
   ```

3. What is wrong with the following scenario?

   In a certain community, everyone owns his or her own house. The house painter of the community claims to paint all those and only those houses that are not painted by their owners.

   (*Hint:* Who paints the house painter's house?)

11.5 Complexity of Problems

In Section 11.4 we investigated the solvability of problems. In this section we are interested in the question of whether a solvable problem has a practical solution. We will find that some problems that are theoretically solvable are so complex that they are unsolvable from a practical point of view.

Measuring a Problem's Complexity

We begin by returning to our study of algorithm efficiency that we started in Section 5.6. There we used big-theta notation to classify algorithms according to the time required to execute them. We found that the insertion sort algorithm is in the class $\Theta(n^2)$, the sequential search algorithm is in $\Theta(n)$, and the binary search algorithm is in $\Theta(\lg n)$. We now use this classification system to help us identify the complexity of problems. Our goal is to develop a classification system that tells us which problems are more complex than others and ultimately which problems are so complex that their solutions lie beyond practicality.

The reason that our present study is based on our knowledge of algorithm efficiency is that we wish to measure the complexity of a problem in terms of the complexity of its solutions. We consider a simple problem to be one that has a simple solution; a complex problem is one that does not have a simple solution. Note that the fact that a problem has a difficult solution does not necessarily mean that the problem itself is complex. After all, a problem has many solutions, one of which is bound to be complex. Thus to conclude that a problem itself is complex requires that we show that none of its solutions are simple.

In computer science, the problems of interest are those that are solvable by machines. The solutions to these problems are formulated as algorithms. Thus the complexity of a problem is determined by the properties of the algorithms that solve that problem. More precisely, the complexity of the simplest algorithm for solving a problem is considered to be the complexity of the problem itself.

But how do we measure the complexity of an algorithm? Unfortunately, the term *complexity* has different interpretations. One deals with the amount of decision making and branching involved in the algorithm. In this light, a complex algorithm would be one that involves a twisted, entwined set of directions. This interpretation might be compatible with the point of view of a software engineer who is interested in issues relating to algorithm discovery and representation, but it does not capture the concept of complexity from a machine's point of view. A machine does not really make decisions when selecting the next instruction for execution but merely follows its machine cycle over and over, each time executing the instruction that is indicated by the program counter. Consequently, a machine can execute a set of tangled instructions as easily as it can execute a list of instructions in a simple sequential order. This interpretation of complexity, therefore, tends to measure the difficulty encountered in an algorithm's representation rather than the complexity of the algorithm itself.

An interpretation that more accurately reflects the complexity of an algorithm from a machine's point of view is to measure the number of steps that must be performed when executing the algorithm. Note that this is not the same as the number of instructions appearing in the written program. A loop whose body consists of a single statement but whose control requests the body's execution 100 times is equivalent to 100 statements when executed. Such a routine is therefore considered more complex than a list of 50 individually written statements, even though the latter appears longer in written form. The point is that this meaning of *complexity* is ultimately concerned with the time it takes a machine to execute a solution and not with the size of the program representing the solution.

We therefore consider a problem to be complex if all its solutions require a lot of time. This definition of complexity is referred to as **time complexity.** We have already met the concept of time complexity indirectly through our study of algorithm efficiency in Section 5.6. After all, the study of an algorithm's efficiency is the study of the algorithm's time complexity—the two are merely inverses of each other. That is, "more efficient" equals "less complex." Thus, in terms of time complexity, the sequential search algorithm (that we found to be in $\Theta(n)$) is a more complex solution to the problem of searching a list than is the binary search algorithm (that we found to be in (Θlg n)).

Let us then apply our knowledge of the complexity of algorithms to obtain a means of identifying the complexity of problems. We define the (time) complexity of a problem to be $\Theta(f(n))$, where $f(n)$ is some mathematical expression in n, if there is an algorithm for solving the problem whose time complexity is in $\Theta(f(n))$ and no other algorithm for solving the problem has a lower time complexity. That is, the (time) complexity of a problem is defined to be the (time) complexity of its best solution. Unfortunately, finding the best solution to a problem and knowing that it is the best is often a difficult problem in itself. In such situations, a variation of big-theta notation called big O notation (pronounced "big oh notation") is used to represent what is known about a problem's complexity. More precisely, if $f(n)$ is a mathematical expression in n and if a problem can be solved by an algorithm in $\Theta(f(n))$, then we say that the problem is in $O(f(n))$ (pronounced "big oh of $f(n)$"). Thus, to say that a problem belongs to $O(f(n))$ means that it has a solution whose complexity is in $\Theta(f(n))$ but it could possibly have a better solution.

Our investigation of searching and sorting tells us that the problem of searching within a list of length n (when all we know is that the list has previously been sorted) is in $O(\lg n)$ since the binary search algorithm solves the problem. Moreover, researchers have shown that the searching problem is actually in $\Theta(\lg n)$ so the binary search represents an optimal solution for that problem. In contrast, we know that the problem of sorting a list of length n (when we know nothing about the original distribution of the values in it) is in $O(n^2)$ since the insertion sort algorithm solves the problem. The problem of sorting, however, is known to be in $\Theta(n \lg n)$, which tells us that the insertion sort algorithm is not an optimal solution (in the context of time complexity).

An example of a better solution to the sorting problem is the merge sort algorithm. Its approach is to merge small, sorted portions of the list to obtain larger sorted portions that can then be merged to obtain still larger sorted portions. Each merging process applies the merge algorithm that we encountered when discussing sequential

Figure 11.8

A procedure MergeLists for merging two lists

procedure MergeLists (InputListA, InputListB, OutputList)

if (both input lists are empty) **then** (Stop, with OutputList empty)
if (InputListA is empty)
  then (Declare it to be exhausted)
  else (Declare its first entry to be its current entry)
if (InputListB is empty)
  then (Declare it to be exhausted)
  else (Declare its first entry to be its current entry)
while (neither input list is exhausted) **do**
    (Put the "smaller" current entry in OutputList;
     if (that current entry is the last entry in its corresponding input list)
      then (Declare that input list to be exhausted)
      else (Declare the next entry in that input list to be the list's current entry)
)

Starting with the current entry in the input list that is not exhausted,
    copy the remaining entries to OutputList.

files (Figure 9.14). For convenience, we present it again in Figure 11.8, this time in the context of merging two lists. The complete (recursive) merge sort algorithm is presented as the procedure called MergeSort in Figure 11.9. When asked to sort a list, this procedure first checks to see if the list is shorter than two entries. If so, the procedure's task is complete. If not, the procedure divides the list into two pieces, asks other copies of the procedure MergeSort to sort these pieces, and then merges these sorted pieces together to obtain the final sorted version of the list.

To analyze the complexity of this algorithm, we first consider the number of comparisons between list entries that must be made when merging a list of length r with a list of length s. The merge process proceeds by repeatedly comparing an entry from one list with an entry from the other and placing the "smaller" of the two entries in the output list. Thus each time a comparison is made, the number of entries still to

Figure 11.9

The merge sort algorithm implemented as a procedure MergeSort

procedure MergeSort (List)

if (List has more than one entry)
  then (Apply the procedure MergeSort to sort the first half of List;
     Apply the procedure MergeSort to sort the second half of List;
     Apply the procedure MergeLists to merge the first and second
      halves of List to produce a sorted version of List
)

be considered is reduced by one. Since there are only $r + s$ entries to begin with, we conclude that the process of merging the two lists will involve no more than $r + s$ comparisons.

We now consider the entire merge sort algorithm. It attacks the task of sorting a list of length n in such a way that the initial sorting problem is reduced to two smaller problems, each of which is asked to sort a list of length approximately $n/2$. These two problems are in turn reduced to a total of four problems of sorting lists of length approximately $n/4$. This division process can be summarized by the tree structure in Figure 11.10, where each node of the tree represents a single problem in the recursive process and the branches below a node represent the smaller problems derived from the parent. Hence, we can find the total number of comparisons that occur in the entire sorting process by adding together the number of comparisons that occur at the nodes in the tree.

Let us first determine the number of comparisons made across each level of the tree. Observe that each node appearing across any level of the tree has the task of sorting a unique segment of the original list. This is accomplished by the merge process and therefore requires no more comparisons than there are entries in the list segment, as we have already argued. Hence, each level of the tree requires no more comparisons than the total number of entries in the list segments, and since the segments across a given level of the tree represent disjoint portions of the original list, this total is no greater than the length of the original list. Consequently, each level of the tree involves no more than n comparisons. (Of course the lowest level involves sorting lists of length one or less, which involves no comparisons at all.)

Now we determine the number of levels in the tree. For this, observe that the process of dividing problems into smaller problems continues until lists of length less than two are obtained. Thus the number of levels in the tree is determined by the number of times that, starting with the value n, we can repeatedly divide by two until the result is no larger than one, which is $\lg n$. More precisely, there are no more than

Figure 11.10

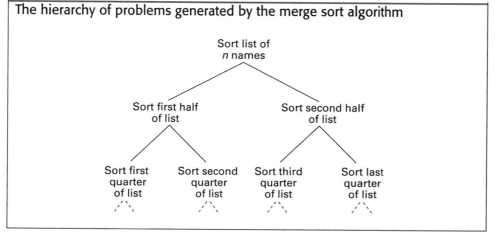

The hierarchy of problems generated by the merge sort algorithm

$\lceil \lg n \rceil$ levels of the tree that involve comparisons, where the notation $\lceil \lg n \rceil$ represents the value of $\lg n$ rounded up to the next integer.

Finally, the total number of comparisons made by the merge sort algorithm when sorting a list of length n is obtained by multiplying the number of comparisons made at each level of the tree by the number of levels in which comparisons are made. We conclude that this is no larger than $n \lceil \lg n \rceil$. Since the graph of $n \lceil \lg n \rceil$ has the same general shape as the graph of $n \lg n$, we conclude that the merge sort algorithm belongs to $O(n \lg n)$. Combining this with the fact that researchers tell us that the sorting problem has complexity $\Theta(n \lg n)$ implies that the merge sort algorithm represents an optimal solution to the sorting problem.

Polynomial Versus Nonpolynomial Problems

Suppose $f(n)$ and $g(n)$ are mathematical expressions. To say that $g(n)$ is bounded by $f(n)$ means that as we apply these expressions to larger and larger values of n, the value of $f(n)$ will ultimately become greater than that of $g(n)$ and remain greater than $g(n)$ for all larger values of n. In other words, $g(n)$ is bounded by $f(n)$ means that the graph of $f(n)$ will be above the graph of $g(n)$ for "large" values of n. For instance, the expression $\lg n$ is bounded by the expression n (Figure 11.11a), and $n \lg n$ is bounded by n^2 (Figure 11.11b).

We say that a problem is a **polynomial problem** if the problem is in $O(f(n))$, where the expression $f(n)$ is either a polynomial itself or bounded by a polynomial. The collection of all polynomial problems is represented by **P**. Note that our previous investigations tell us that the problems of searching a list and of sorting a list belong to P.

To say that a problem is a polynomial problem is a statement about the time required to solve the problem. We often say that a problem in P can be solved in polynomial time or that the problem has a polynomial time solution.

Identifying the problems that belong to P is of major importance in computer science because it is closely related to questions regarding whether problems have practical solutions. Indeed, problems that are outside the class P are characterized as

Figure 11.11

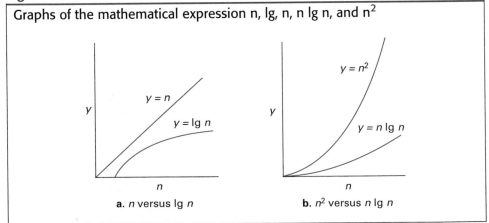

Graphs of the mathematical expression n, lg, n, n lg n, and n^2

a. *n* versus lg *n*

b. n^2 versus *n* lg *n*

Space Complexity

An alternative to measuring complexity in terms of time is to measure storage space requirements instead—resulting in a measure known as **space complexity.** That is, the space complexity of a problem is determined by the amount of storage space required to solve the problem. In the text we have seen that the time complexity of sorting a list with n entries is $O(n \lg n)$. The space complexity of the same problem is no more than $O(n + 1) = O(n)$. After all, sorting a list with n entries using the insertion sort requires space for the list itself plus space to store a single entry on a temporary basis. Thus, if we were asked to sort longer and longer lists, we would find that the time required for each task would increase more rapidly than the space required. This is in fact a common phenomenon. Since it takes time to use space, a problem's space complexity never grows more rapidly than its time complexity.

There are often tradeoffs made between time and space complexity. In some applications it may be advantageous to perform certain computations in advance and store the results in a table from which they can be retrieved quickly when needed. Such a "table lookup" technique decreases the time required to obtain a result once it is actually needed at the expense of the additional space required by the table. On the other hand, data compression is often used to reduce storage requirements at the expense of the additional time required to compress and decompress the data.

having extremely long execution times, even for inputs of moderate size. Consider, for example, a problem whose solution requires 2^n steps. The exponential expression 2^n is not bounded by any polynomial—if $f(n)$ is a polynomial, then as we increase the value of n, we will find that the values of 2^n will ultimately be larger than those of $f(n)$. This means that an algorithm with complexity $\Theta(2^n)$ will generally be less efficient, and thus require more time, than an algorithm with complexity $\Theta(f(n))$. An algorithm whose complexity is identified by an exponential expression is said to require exponential time.

As a particular example, consider the problem of listing all possible subcommittees that can be formed from a group of n people. Since there are $2^n - 1$ such subcommittees (we allow a subcommittee to consist of the entire group but do not consider the empty set to be a subcommittee), any algorithm that solves this problem must have at least $2^n - 1$ steps and thus a complexity at least that large. But, the expression $2^n - 1$, being an exponential expression, is not bounded by any polynomial. Hence any solution to this problem becomes enormously time-consuming as the size of the group from which the committees are selected increases.

In contrast to our subcommittee problem, whose complexity is large merely because of the size of its output, problems exist whose complexities are large even though their ultimate output is merely a simple yes or no answer. An example involves the ability to answer questions about the truth of statements involving the addition of real numbers. For instance, we can easily recognize that the answer to the question

"Is it true that there is a real number that when added to itself produces the value 6?" is yes, whereas the answer to "Is it true that there is a nonzero real number which when added to itself is 0?" is no. However, as such questions become more involved, our ability to answer them begins to fade. If we found ourselves faced with many such questions, we might be tempted to turn to a computer program for assistance. Unfortunately, the ability to answer these questions has been shown to require exponential time, so even a computer ultimately fails to produce answers in a timely manner as the questions become more involved.

The fact that the problems that are theoretically solvable but are not in P have such enormous time complexities leads us to conclude that these problems are essentially unsolvable from a practical point of view. Computer scientists call these problems **intractable.** In turn, the class P has come to represent an important boundary that distinguishes intractable problems from those that may have more practical solutions. Thus an understanding of the class P has become an important pursuit within computer science.

Deterministic Versus Nondeterministic

In many cases, there is a fine line between a deterministic and a nondeterministic "algorithm." However, the distinction is quite clear and significant. A deterministic algorithm does not rely on the creative capabilities of the mechanism executing the algorithm whereas a nondeterministic "algorithm" may. For instance, compare the instruction

> Go to the next intersection and turn either right or left.

and the instruction

> Go to the next intersection and turn right or left
> depending on what the person standing on the corner
> tells you to do.

In either case the action taken by the person following the directions is not determined prior to actually executing the instruction. However, the first instruction requires the person following the directions to make a decision based on his or her own judgment and is therefore nondeterministic. The second instruction makes no such requirements of the person following the directions—the person is told what to do at each stage. If several different people follow the first instruction, some may turn right, while others may turn left. If several people followed the second instruction and received the same information, they would all turn in the same direction. Herein lies an important distinction between deterministic and nondeterministic "algorithms." If a deterministic algorithm is executed repeatedly with the same input data, the same actions will be performed each time. However, a nondeterministic "algorithm" may produce different actions when repeated under identical conditions.

NP Problems

Let us now consider the **traveling salesman problem,** which involves a traveling salesman who must visit each of his clients in different cities without exceeding his travel budget. His problem, then, is to find a path (starting from his home, connecting the cities involved, and returning to his home) whose total length does not exceed his allowed mileage.

The traditional solution to this problem is to consider the potential paths in a systematic manner, comparing the length of each path to the mileage limit until either an acceptable path is found or all possibilities have been considered. This approach, however, does not produce a polynomial time solution. As the number of cities increases, the number of paths to be tested grows more rapidly than any polynomial. In turn, solving the traveling salesman problem in this manner is impractical for cases involving large numbers of cities.

We conclude that to solve the traveling salesman problem in a reasonable amount of time, we must find a faster algorithm. Our appetite is whetted by the observation that if a satisfactory path exists and we happen to select it first, our present algorithm terminates quickly. In particular, the following list of instructions can be executed quickly and has the potential of solving the problem:

```
Pick one of the possible paths, and compute its total distance.
If (this distance is not greater than the allowable mileage)
   then (declare a success)
   else (declare nothing)
```

However, this set of instructions is not an algorithm in the technical sense. Its first instruction is ambiguous in that it does not specify which path is to be selected nor does it specify how the decision is to be made. Instead it relies on the creativity of the mechanism executing the program to make the decision on its own. We say that such instructions are nondeterministic, and we call an "algorithm" containing such statements a **nondeterministic algorithm.**

Note that as the number of cities increases, the time required to execute the preceding nondeterministic algorithm grows relatively slowly. The process of selecting a path is merely that of producing a list of the cities, which can be done in a time proportional to the number of cities. Moreover, the time required to compute the total distance along the chosen path is also proportional to the number of cities to be visited, and the time required to compare this total to the mileage limit is independent of the number of cities. In turn, the time required to execute the nondeterministic algorithm is bounded by a polynomial. Thus it is possible to solve the traveling salesman problem by a nondeterministic algorithm in polynomial time.

Of course, our nondeterministic solution is not totally satisfactory. It relies on a lucky guess. But its existence is enough to suggest that perhaps there is a deterministic solution to the traveling salesman problem that runs in polynomial time. Whether or not this is true remains an open question. In fact, the traveling salesman problem is one of many problems that are known to have nondeterministic solutions that execute in polynomial time but for which no deterministic polynomial time solution has yet been found. The tantalizing efficiency of the nondeterministic solutions to these problems causes some to hope that efficient deterministic solutions will be found someday, yet most believe that these problems are just complex enough to escape the capabilities of efficient deterministic algorithms.

A problem that can be solved in polynomial time by a nondeterministic algorithm is called a **nondeterministic polynomial problem,** or an **NP problem** for short. It is customary to denote the class of NP problems by **NP.** Note that all the problems in P are also in NP, since any (deterministic) algorithm can have a nondeterministic instruction added to it without affecting its performance.

Whether all of the NP problems are also in P, however, is an open question, as demonstrated by the traveling salesman problem. This is perhaps the most widely known unsolved problem in computer science today. Its solution could have significant consequences. For example, in the next section we will learn that encryption systems have been designed whose integrity relies on the enormous time required to solve problems similar to the traveling salesman problem. If it turns out that efficient solutions to such problems exist, these encryption systems will be compromised.

Efforts to resolve the question of whether the class NP is, in fact, the same as the class P have led to the discovery of a class of problems within the class NP known as the **NP-complete problems.** These problems have the property that a polynomial time solution for any one of them would provide a polynomial time solution for all the other problems in NP as well. That is, if a (deterministic) algorithm can be found that solves one of the NP-complete problems in polynomial time, then that algorithm can be extended to solve any other problem in NP in polynomial time. In turn, the class NP would be the same as the class P. The traveling salesman problem is an example of an NP-complete problem.

In summary, we have found that problems can be classified as either solvable (having an algorithmic solution) or unsolvable (not having an algorithmic solution), as depicted in Figure 11.12. Moreover, within the class of solvable problems are two subclasses. One is the collection of polynomial problems that contains those problems with practical solutions. The second is the collection of nonpolynomial problems whose solutions are practical for only relatively small or carefully selected inputs. Finally, there are the mysterious NP problems that thus far have evaded precise classification.

Figure 11.12

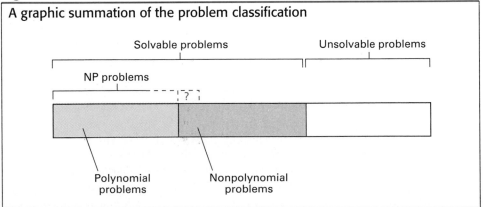

A graphic summation of the problem classification

Questions/Exercises

1. Suppose a problem can be solved by an algorithm in $\Theta(2^n)$. What can we conclude about the complexity of the problem?

2. Suppose a problem can be solved by an algorithm in $\Theta(n^2)$ as well as another algorithm in $\Theta(2^n)$. Will one algorithm always outperform the other?

3. List all of the subcommittees that can be formed from a committee consisting of the two members Alice and Bill. List all the subcommittees that can be formed from the committee consisting of Alice, Bill, and Carol. What about the subcommittees from Alice, Bill, Carol, and David?

4. Give an example of a polynomial problem. Give an example of a nonpolynomial problem. Give an example of an NP problem that as yet has not been shown to be a polynomial problem.

5. If the complexity of algorithm X is greater than that of algorithm Y, is algorithm X necessarily harder to understand than algorithm Y? Explain your answer.

11.6 Public Key Cryptography

In some cases the fact that a problem is difficult to solve has been turned into an asset rather than a liability. Of particular interest is the problem of finding the factors of a given integer—a problem for which an efficient solution has yet to be found, if one even exists. For example, armed with only paper and pencil, you may find the task of finding the factors of relatively small values such as 2,173 to be time consuming, and if the number involved was so large that its representation required several hundred digits, the task would be intractable even if modern technology were applied using the best factoring techniques currently known.

The failure to find an efficient way of determining the factors of large integers has long been a thorn in the side of many mathematicians, but in the field of cryptography it has been applied to produce a popular method of encrypting and decrypting

Safe Cracking

Combination locks, in which three numbers must be dialed in the correct order, require a would-be thief to solve a problem similar to that of the traveling-salesman problem within a reasonable amount of time. The fact that these locks have provided security for years demonstrates the intractability of such problems. Of course, a three number combination would not be satisfactory if different combinations could be tested and eliminated in microseconds, but since the number of possible combinations increases rapidly as the number of values in the combination increases, longer combination sequences can provide security in computer systems. This, in fact, is the underlying principle of passwords as well as many encryption systems.

messages. This method is known as the **RSA algorithm**—a name chosen to honor its inventors Ron Rivest, Adi Shamir, and Len Adleman. It is a means of encrypting messages using one set of values known as the encrypting keys and decrypting those messages using another set of values known as the decrypting keys. People who know the encrypting keys can encrypt messages, but they cannot decrypt messages. The only person who can decrypt messages is the one holding the decrypting keys. Thus the encrypting keys can be widely distributed without violating the security of the system.

Such cryptography systems are called **public key encryption** systems, a term that reflects the fact that the keys used to encrypt messages can be public knowledge without degrading the system's security. Indeed, the encrypting keys are often called the **public keys,** whereas the decrypting keys are called the **private keys** (Figure 11.13).

Modular Notation

To describe the RSA public key encryption system, it is convenient to use the notation $x \pmod{m}$, which is read "x modulo m" or usually just "x mod m," to represent the remainder obtained when the value x is divided by m. Thus 9 (mod 7) is 2 because $9 \div 7$ produces a remainder of 2. Similarly, 24 (mod 7) is 3 because $24 \div 7$ produces a remainder of 3, and 5 (mod 7) is 5 because $5 \div 7$ produces a remainder of 5. Note that $x \pmod{m}$ is x itself if x is an integer in the range 0 to $m - 1$.

Mathematics tells us that if p and q are prime numbers and m is an integer between 0 and pq then, for any positive integer k

$$1 = m^{k(p-1)(q-1)} \pmod{pq}$$

Figure 11.13

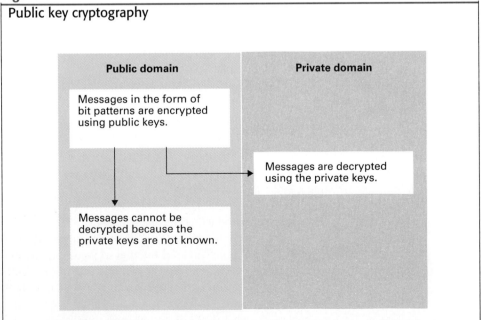

Public key cryptography

Public domain

Private domain

Messages in the form of bit patterns are encrypted using public keys.

Messages are decrypted using the private keys.

Messages cannot be decrypted because the private keys are not known.

Although we will not justify this claim here, it is advantageous to consider an example to clarify the statement. Suppose, then, that p and q are the prime numbers 3 and 5, respectively, and m is the integer 4. Then the statement claims that for any positive integer k, the value $m^{k(p-1)(q-1)}$ divided by 15 (the product of 3 and 5) will produce the remainder 1. In particular, if $k = 1$, then

$$m^{k(p-1)(q-1)} = 4^{1(3-1)(5-1)} = 4^8 = 65,536$$

which when divided by 15 produces the remainder 1 as claimed. Moreover, if $k = 2$, then

$$m^{k(p-1)(q-1)} = 4^{2(3-1)(5-1)} = 4^{16} = 4,294,967,296$$

which when divided by 15 again produces the remainder 1. Indeed, we would obtain the remainder 1 regardless of the positive integer chosen for k.

RSA Public Key Cryptography

We are now prepared to construct and analyze a public key encryption system based on the RSA algorithm. First we pick two distinct prime numbers p and q, whose product we will represent by n. Then we pick two other positive integers e and d such that $e \times d = k(p - 1)(q - 1) + 1$, for some positive integer k. We are calling these values e and d because they will be part of the encryption and decryption process, respectively. (The fact that values e and d can be chosen to satisfy the preceding equation is another fact from mathematics that we will not pursue here.)

Thus we have selected five values: p, q, n, e, and d. The values e and n are the encrypting keys. The values d and n are decrypting keys. The values p and q are only used for constructing the encryption system.

Let us consider a specific example for clarification. Suppose we choose 7 and 13 as the values for p and q. Then $n = 7 \times 13 = 91$. Moreover, the values 5 and 29 could be used for e and d because $5 \times 29 = 145 = 144 + 1 = 2(7 - 1)(13 - 1) + 1 = 2(p - 1)(q - 1) + 1$ as required. Thus, the encrypting keys are $n = 91$ and $e = 5$, and the decrypting keys are $n = 91$ and $d = 29$. We distribute the encrypting keys to anyone who may want to send us messages, but we keep the decrypting keys to ourselves.

We now consider how messages are encrypted. To this end, suppose a message is currently encoded as a bit pattern (perhaps using ASCII or Unicode) and the value of the pattern, when interpreted as a binary representation, is less than n. (If it is not less than n, we would chop the message into smaller segments and encrypt each segment individually.)

Let us assume that our message, when interpreted as a binary representation, represents the value m. Then, the encrypted version of the message is the binary representation of the value $c = m^e \pmod{n}$. That is, the encrypted message is the binary representation of the remainder obtained by dividing m^e by n.

In particular, if someone wanted to encrypt the message 10111 using the encrypting keys $n = 91$ and $e = 5$ as developed in the previous example, he or she would first recognize that 10111 is the binary representation for 23, then compute $23^e = 23^5 = 6,436,343$, and finally divide this value by $n = 91$ to obtain the remainder 4. The encrypted version of the message would therefore be 100, which is the binary representation of 4.

To decrypt a message that represents the value c in binary notation, we compute the value $c^d \pmod{n}$. That is, we compute the value c^d, divide the result by n, and retain the remainder. Indeed, this remainder will be the value m of the original message because

$$
\begin{aligned}
c^d \pmod{n} &= m^{e \times d} \pmod{n} \\
&= m^{k(p-1)(q-1)+1} \pmod{n} \\
&= m \times m^{k(p-1)(q-1)} \pmod{n} \\
&= m \pmod{n} \\
&= m
\end{aligned}
$$

Here we have used the facts that $m^{k(p-1)(q-1)} \pmod{n} = m^{k(p-1)(q-1)} \pmod{pq} = 1$ and that $m \pmod{n} = m$ (since $m < n$), as previously claimed.

Continuing with the preceding example, if we received the message 100, we would recognize this as the value 4, compute the value $4^d = 4^{29} = 288{,}230{,}376{,}151{,}711{,}744$, and divide this value by $n = 91$ to obtain the remainder 23, which produces the original message 10111 when expressed in binary notation.

In summary, an RSA public key encryption system is generated by selecting two prime integers, p and q, from which the values n, e, and d are generated. The values n and e are used to encrypt messages and are therefore the public keys. The values n and d are used to decrypt messages and are the private keys (Figure 11.14). The beauty of the system is that knowing how to encrypt messages does not allow one to decrypt messages. Thus the encrypting keys n and e can be widely distributed. Indeed, if your

Figure 11.14

Establishing a RSA public key encryption system

adversaries were to obtain these keys, they would still not be able to decrypt the messages they intercept. Only a person who knows the decrypting keys can decrypt messages.

The security of this system is based on the assumption that knowing the encrypting keys n and e does not allow one to compute the decrypting keys n and d. However, there are algorithms for doing exactly that! One approach would be to factor the value n to discover the values p and q, and then to determine d by finding a value k such that $k(p - 1)(q - 1) + 1$ is evenly divided by e (the quotient would then be d). On the other hand, the first step in this process can be time-consuming—especially if the values of p and q were chosen to be large. In fact, if p and q are so large that their binary representations require hundreds of digits, then the best known factoring algorithms would require years before the identities of p and q could be revealed from n. In turn, the content of an encrypted message would remain secure long after its significance had deteriorated.

To this date, no one has found an efficient way of decrypting messages based on RSA cryptography without knowing the decrypting keys, and thus public key encryption based on the RSA algorithm is widely used to obtain privacy when communicating over the Internet.

Questions/Exercises

1. Find the factors of 66,043. (Don't waste too much time on this one. The point is that it can be time-consuming.)
2. Using the public keys $n = 91$ and $e = 5$, encrypt the message 101.
3. Using the private keys $n = 91$ and $d = 29$, decrypt the message 10.
4. Find the appropriate value for the decrypting keys n and d in a RSA public key cryptography system based on the primes $p = 7$ and $q = 19$ and the encryption key $e = 5$.

Chapter Review Problems

1. Show how a structure of the form

   ```
   while X equals 0 do;
       .
       .
       .
   end;
   ```

   can be simulated with Bare Bones.

2. Write a Bare Bones program that places a 1 in the variable Z if the variable X is less than or equal to the variable Y and places a 0 in the variable Z otherwise.

3. Write a Bare Bones program that places the Xth power of 2 in the variable Z.

4. In each of the following cases write a program sequence in Bare Bones that performs the indicated activity:
   a. Assign 0 to Z if the value of X is even; otherwise assign 1 to Z.
   b. Calculate the sum of the integers from 0 to X.

5. Write a Bare Bones routine that divides the value of X by the value of Y. Disregard any remainder; that is, 1 divided by 2 produces 0, and 5 divided by 3 produces 1.

6. Describe the function computed by the following Bare Bones program, assuming the function's inputs are represented by X and Y and its output by Z:

```
copy X to Z;
copy Y to Aux;
while Aux not 0 do;
   decr Z;
   decr Aux;
end;
```

7. Describe the function computed by the following Bare Bones program, assuming the function's inputs are represented by X and Y and its output by Z:

```
clear Z;
copy X to AUX1;
copy Y to Aux2;
while Aux1 not 0 do;
   while Aux2 not 0 do;
      decr Z;
      decr Aux 2;
   end;
   decr Aux1;
end;
```

8. Write a Bare Bones program that computes the exclusive or of the variables X and Y, leaving the result in the variable Z. You may assume that X and Y start only with integer values of 0 and 1.

9. Show that if we allow instructions in a Bare Bones program to be labeled with integer values and replace the while loop structure with the conditional branch represented by the form

   if *name* not 0 goto label;

   where *name* is any variable and *label* is an integer value used elsewhere to label an instruction, then the new language will still be a universal programming language.

10. In this chapter we saw how the statement

    copy *name1* to *name2*;

    could be simulated in Bare Bones. Show how that statement could still be simulated if the while loop structure in Bare Bones were replaced withs a posttest loop expressed in the form

    repeat ... until (name equals 0)

11. Show that the Bare Bones language would remain a universal language if the while statement were replaced with a posttest loop expressed in the form

    repeat ... until (name equals 0)

12. Design a Turing machine that once started will use no more than a single cell on its tape but will never reach its halt state.

13. Design a Turing machine that places 0s in all the cells to the left of the current cell until it reaches a cell containing an asterisk.

14. Suppose a pattern of 0s and 1s on the tape of a Turing machine is delimited by asterisks at either end. Design a Turing machine that rotates this pattern one cell to the left, assuming that the machine starts with the current cell being the asterisk at the right end of the pattern.

15. Design a Turing machine that reverses the pattern of 0s and 1s that it finds between the current cell (which contains an asterisk) and the first asterisk to the left.

16. Summarize the Church-Turing thesis.

17. Is the following Bare Bones program self-terminating? Explain your answer.

```
copy X to Y;
incr Y;
incr Y;
while X not 0 do;
   decr X;
   decr X;
   decr Y;
   decr Y;
end;
decr Y;
while Y not 0 do;
   incr X;
   decr Y;
end;
while X not 0 do;
end;
```

18. Is the following Bare Bones program self-terminating? Explain your answer.

```
while X not 0 do;
end;
```

19. Is the following Bare Bones program self-terminating? Explain your answer.

```
while X not 0 do;
  decr X;
end;
```

20. Analyze the validity of the following pair of statements:

The next statement is true.
The previous statement is false.

21. Analyze the validity of the statement "The cook on a ship cooks for all those and only those who do not cook for themselves." (Who cooks for the cook?)

22. Suppose you were in a country where each person was either a truth teller or a liar. (A truth teller always tells the truth, a liar always lies.) What single question could you ask a person that would allow you to detect whether that person was a truth teller or a liar?

23. Summarize the significance of Turing machines in the field of theoretical computer science.

24. Summarize the significance of the halting problem in the field of theoretical computer science.

25. Suppose you needed to find out if anyone in a group of people had a birthday on a particular date. One approach would be to ask the members one at a time. If you took this approach, the occurrence of what event would tell you that there was such a person? What event would tell you that there was no such person? Now suppose that you wanted to find out if at least one of the positive integers has a particular property and you applied the same approach of systematically testing the integers one at a time. If, in fact, some integer has the property, how would you find out? If, however, no integer has the property, how would you find out? Is the task of testing to see if a conjecture is true necessarily symmetric with the task of testing to see if it is false?

26. Is the problem of searching through a list for a particular value a polynomial problem? Justify your answer.

27. Design an algorithm for deciding whether a given positive integer is prime. Is your solution efficient? Is your solution a polynomial or nonpolynomial one?

28. Is a polynomial solution to a problem always better than an exponential solution? Explain your answer.

29. Does the fact that a problem has a polynomial solution mean that it can always be solved in a practical amount of time? Explain your answer.

30. Charlie Programmer is given the problem of dividing a group (of an even number of people) into two disjoint subgroups of equal size so that the difference between the total ages of each subgroup is as large as possible. He proposes the solution of forming all possible subgroup pairs, computing the difference between the age totals of each pair, and selecting the pair with the largest difference. Mary Programmer, on the other hand, proposes that the original group first be sorted by age and then divided into two subgroups by forming one subgroup from the younger half of the sorted group and the other from the older half. What is the complexity of each of these solutions? Is the problem itself of polynomial, NP, or nonpolynomial complexity?

31. Why is the approach of generating all possible arrangements of a list and then picking the one with the desired arrangement not a satisfactory way to sort a list?

32. Suppose a lottery is based on correctly picking four integer values, each in the range from 1 to 50. Moreover, suppose that the jackpot grows so large that it becomes profitable to buy a separate lottery ticket for each possible combination. If it takes one second to buy a single ticket, how long would it take to buy one ticket for each combination? How would the time requirement change if the lottery required picking five numbers instead of four? What does this problem have to do with the material from this chapter?

33. Is the following algorithm deterministic? Explain your answer.

> **procedure mystery (Number)**
> **if** (Number > 5)
>   **then** (answer "yes")
>   **else** (pick a value less than 5 and
>   give this number as the answer)

34. Is the following algorithm deterministic? Explain your answer.

> **Drive straight ahead.**
> At the third intersection, ask the person standing
>   on the corner if you should turn right or left.
> Turn according to that person's directions.
> Drive two more blocks and stop there.

35. Identify the points of nondeterminism in the following algorithm:

> **Select three numbers between 1 and 100.**
> **if** (the sum of the selected numbers is greater
>   than 150)
>   **then** (answer "yes")
>   **else** (select one of the chosen numbers and
>   give that number as the answer)

36. Does the following algorithm have a polynomial or nonpolynomial time complexity? Explain your answer.

> **procedure mystery (ListOfNumbers)**
> Pick a collection of numbers from
>   ListOfNumbers.
> **if** (the numbers in that collection add to 125)
>   **then** (answer "yes")
>   **else** (do not give an answer)

37. Which of the following problems are in the class P?
  a. A problem with complexity n^2
  b. A problem with complexity $3n$
  c. A problem with complexity $n^2 + 2n$
  d. A problem with complexity $n!$

38. Summarize the distinction between stating that a problem is a polynomial problem and stating that it is a nondeterministic polynomial problem.

39. Give an example of a problem that is in both the class P and the class NP.

40. Suppose you are given two algorithms for solving the same problem. One algorithm has time complexity n4 and the other has time complexity 4n. For what size inputs is the former more efficient than the latter?

41. Suppose we were faced with solving the traveling salesman problem in a context involving 15 cities in which any two cities were connected by a unique road. How many different paths through the cities would there be? How long would it take to compute the length of all of these paths assuming that the length of a path can be computed in one microsecond?

42. How many comparisons between names are made if the merge sort algorithm (Figures 11.9 and 11.8) is applied to the list Alice, Bob, Carol, and David? How many are required if the list is Alice, Bob, Carol, David, and Elaine?

43. Give an example of a problem in each of the categories represented in Figure 11.12.

44. Design an algorithm for finding integer solutions for equations of the form $x^2 + y^2 = n$, where n is some given positive integer. Determine the time complexity of your algorithm.

45. Another problem that falls in the NP-complete category is the **knapsack problem,** which is the problem of finding which numbers from a list are the ones whose sum is a particular value. For example, the numbers 257, 388, and 782 are the entries in the list

  642 257 771 388 391 782 304

whose sum is 1427. Find the entries whose sum is 1723. What algorithm did you apply. What is the complexity of that algorithm?

46. Identify similarities between the traveling salesman problem and the knapsack problem (see Problem 45).

47. The following algorithm for sorting a list is called the bubble sort. How many comparisons between list entries does the bubble sort require when applied to a list of n entries?

procedure BubbleSort (List)
Counter 1;
while (Counter < number of entries in List) **do**
  [N the number of entries in List;
   while (N > 1) **do**
    (**if** (the Nth List entry is less than the
        entry preceding it)
      then (interchange the Nth entry
          with the preceding entry);
     N N 1
)
  ]

48. Use RSA public key encryption to encrypt the message 110 using the public keys $n = 91$ and $e = 5$.

49. Use RSA public key encryption to decrypt the message 111 using the private keys $n = 133$ and $d = 5$.

50. Suppose you know that the public keys to a public key encryption system based on the RSA algorithm are $n = 77$ and $e = 7$. What are the private keys? What allows you to solve this problem in a reasonable amount of time?

51. Find the factors of 107,531. How does this problem relate to this chapter?

52. What can be concluded if the positive integer n has no integer factors in the range from 2 to the square root of n? What does this tell you about the task of finding the factors of a positive integer?

Social Issues

The following questions are provided to help you understand some of the ethical/social/legal issues associated with the field of computing. The goal is not merely to answer these questions. You should also consider why you answered as you did and whether your justifications are consistent from one question to the next.

1. Suppose the best algorithm for solving a problem would require 100 years to execute. Would you consider the problem to be tractable? Why?

2. Should citizens have the right to encrypt messages in such a manner that precludes monitoring from government agencies? Does your answer provide for "proper" law enforcement? Who should decide what "proper" law enforcement is?

3. If the human mind is an algorithmic device, what consequences does Turing's thesis have in regard to humanity? To what extent do you believe that Turing machines encompass the computational abilities of the human mind?

4. We have seen that there are different computational models (finite tables, algebraic formulae, Turing machines, etc.) having different computational abilities. Are there differences in the computational capabilities of different organisms? Are there differences in the computational capabilities of different humans? If so, should humans with higher abilities be able to use those abilities to obtain higher lifestyles?

5. Today there are Web sites that provide road maps of most cities. These sites assist in finding particular addresses and provide zooming capabilities for viewing the layout of small neighborhoods. Starting with this reality, consider the following fictitious sequence. Suppose these map sites were enhanced with satellite photographs with

similar zooming capabilities. Suppose these zooming capabilities were increased to give a more detailed image of individual buildings and surrounding landscape. Suppose these images were enhanced to include real-time video. Suppose these video images were enhanced with infrared technology. At this point others could watch you inside your own home 24 hours a day. At what point in this progression were your privacy rights first violated? At what point in this progression do you think we moved beyond the capabilities of current spy-satellite technology? To what degree is this scenario fictitious?

6. Suppose a company develops and patents an encryption system. Should the national government of the company have the right to use the system as it sees fit in the name of national security? Should the national government of the company have the right to restrict the company's commercial use of the system in the name of national security? What if the company is a multinational organization?

7. Suppose you buy a product whose internal structure is encrypted. Do you have the right to decrypt the underlying structure? If so, do you have the right to use that information in a commercial manner? What about a noncommercial manner? What if the encryption was done using a secret encryption system, and you discover the secret. Do you have the right to share that secret?

8. Some years ago the philosopher John Dewey (1859–1952) introduced the term "responsible technology." Give some examples of what you would consider to be "responsible technology." Based on your examples, formulate your own definition of "responsible technology." Has society practiced "responsible technology" over the last 100 years? Should actions be taken to ensure that it does? If so, what actions? If not, why?

Additional Reading

Garey, M. R., and D. S. Johnson. *Computers and Intractability.* New York: W. H. Freeman, 1979.

Hamburger, H. and D. Richards. *Logic and Language Models for Computer Science.* Englewood Cliffs, NJ: Prentice-Hall, 2002.

Hofstadter, D. R. *Gödel, Escher, Bach: An Eternal Golden Braid.* St. Paul, MN: Vintage, 1980.

Hopcroft, J. E., R. Motwani, and J. D. Ullman. *Introduction to Automata Theory, Languages, and Computation,* 2nd ed. Boston: Addison-Wesley, 2001.

Lewis, H. R., and C. H. Papadimitriou. *Elements of the Theory of Computation,* 2nd ed. Englewood Cliffs, NJ: Prentice-Hall, 1998.

Sipser, M. *Introduction to the Theory of Computation.* Boston: PWS, 1996.

Smith, C. and E. Kimber. *Theory of Computing: A Gentle Introduction.* Englewood Cliffs, NJ: Prentice-Hall, 2001.

ASCII

The following is a partial listing of ASCII code, in which each bit pattern has been extended with a 0 on its left to produce the eight-bit pattern commonly used today.

Symbol	ASCII		Symbol	ASCII		Symbol	ASCII
line feed	00001010		>	00111110		^	01011110
carriage return	00001101		?	00111111		_	01011111
space	00100000		@	01000000		a	01100001
!	00100001		A	01000001		b	01100010
"	00100010		B	01000010		c	01100011
#	00100011		C	01000011		d	01100100
$	00100100		D	01000100		e	01100101
%	00100101		E	01000101		f	01100110
&	00100110		F	01000110		g	01100111
'	00100111		G	01000111		h	01101000
(	00101000		H	01001000		i	01101001
)	00101001		I	01001001		j	01101010
*	00101010		J	01001010		k	01101011
+	00101011		K	01001011		l	01101100
'	00101100		L	01001100		m	01101101
-	00101101		M	01001101		n	01101110
.	00101110		N	01001110		o	01101111
/	00101111		O	01001111		p	01110000
0	00110000		P	01010000		q	01110001
1	00110001		Q	01010001		r	01110010
2	00110010		R	01010010		s	01110011
3	00110011		S	01010011		t	01110100
4	00110100		T	01010100		u	01110101
5	00110101		U	01010101		v	01110110
6	00110110		V	01010110		w	01110111
7	00110111		W	01010111		x	01111000
8	00111000		X	01011000		y	01111001
9	00111001		Y	01011001		z	01111010
:	00111010		Z	01011010		{	01111011
;	00111011		[	01011011		}	01111101
<	00111100		\	01011100			
=	00111101		]	01011101			

Circuits to Manipulate
Two's Complement Representations

This appendix presents circuits for negating and adding values represented in two's complement notation. We begin with the circuit in Figure B.1 that converts a four-bit two's complement representation to the representation for the negative of that value. For example, given the two's complement representation of 3, the circuit produces the representation for −3. It does this by following the same algorithm as presented in the text. That is, it copies the pattern from right to left until a 1 has been copied and then complements each remaining bit as it is moved from the input to the output. Since one input of the rightmost XOR gate is fixed at 0, this gate will merely pass its other input to the output. However, this output is also passed to the left as one of the inputs to the next XOR gate. If this output is 1, the next XOR gate will complement its input bit as it passes to the output. Moreover, this 1 will also be passed to the left through the OR gate to affect the next gate as well. In this manner, the first 1 that is copied to the output will also be passed to the left, where it will cause all the remaining bits to be complemented as they are moved to the output.

Next, let us consider the process of adding two values represented in two's complement notation. In particular, when solving the problem

$$
\begin{array}{r}
0110 \\
+\ 1011 \\
\end{array}
$$

Figure B.1

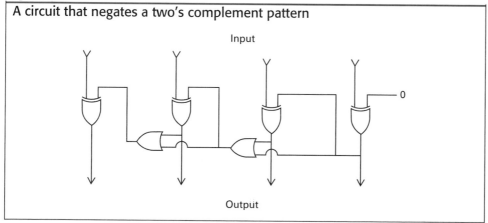

A circuit that negates a two's complement pattern

Input

0

Output

Figure B.2

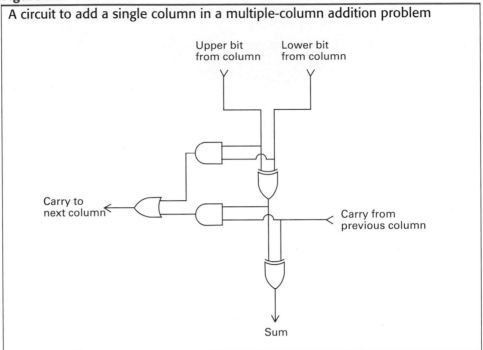

A circuit to add a single column in a multiple-column addition problem

we proceed from right to left in a column-by-column manner, executing the same algorithm for each column. Thus once we obtain a circuit for adding one column of such a problem, we can construct a circuit for adding many columns merely by repeating the single-column circuit.

The algorithm for adding a single column in a multiple-column addition problem is to add the two values in the current column, add that sum to any carry from the previous column, write the least significant bit of this sum in the answer, and transfer any carry to the next column. The circuit in Figure B.2 follows this same algorithm. The upper XOR gate determines the sum of the two input bits. The lower XOR gate adds this sum to the value carried from the previous column. The two AND gates together with the OR gate pass any carry to the left. In particular, a carry of 1 will be produced if the original two input bits in this column were 1 or if the sum of these bits and the carry were both 1.

Figure B.3 shows how copies of this single-column circuit can be used to produce a circuit that computes the sum of two values represented in a four-bit two's complement system. Each rectangle represents a copy of the single-column addition circuit. Note that the carry value given to the rightmost rectangle is always 0 because there is no carry from a previous column. In a similar manner, the carry produced from the leftmost rectangle is ignored.

The circuit in Figure B.3 is known as a *ripple adder* because the carry information must propagate, or ripple, from the rightmost to the leftmost column. Although simple in composition, such circuits are slower to perform their functions than more clever versions, such as the lookahead carry adder, which minimize this column-to-column propagation. Thus the circuit in Figure B.3, although sufficient for our purposes, is not the circuit that is used in today's machines.

Figure B.3

A circuit for adding two values in a two's complement notation using four copies of the circuit in Figure B.2

A Simple Machine Language

In this appendix we present a simple but representative machine language. We begin by explaining the architecture of the machine itself.

Machine Architecture

The machine has 16 general-purpose registers numbered 0 through F (in hexadecimal). Each register is one byte (eight bits) long. For identifying registers within instructions, each register is assigned the unique four-bit pattern that represents its register number. Thus register 0 is identified by 0000 (hexadecimal 0), and register 4 is identified by 0100 (hexadecimal 4).

There are 256 cells in the machine's main memory. Each cell is assigned a unique address consisting of an integer in the range of 0 to 255. An address can therefore be represented by a pattern of eight bits ranging from 00000000 to 11111111 (or a hexadecimal value in the range of 00 to FF).

Floating-point values are assumed to be stored in the eight-bit format discussed in Section 1.7 and summarized in Figure 1.26.

Machine Language

Each machine instruction is two bytes long. The first 4 bits provide the op-code; the last 12 bits make up the operand field. The table that follows lists the instructions in hexadecimal notation together with a short description of each. The letters R, S, and T are used in place of hexadecimal digits in those fields representing a register identifier that varies depending on the particular application of the instruction. The letters X and Y are used in lieu of hexadecimal digits in variable fields not representing a register..

Op-code	Operand	Description
1	RXY	LOAD the register R with the bit pattern found in the memory cell whose address is XY. *Example.* 14A3 would cause the contents of the memory cell located at address A3 to be placed in register 4.
2	RXY	LOAD the register R with the bit pattern XY. *Example:* 20A3 would cause the value A3 to be placed in register 0.
3	RXY	STORE the bit pattern found in register R in the memory cell whose address is XY.

Op-code	Operand	Description
		Example: 35B1 would cause the contents of register 5 to be placed in the memory cell whose address is B1.
4	0RS	MOVE the bit pattern found in register R to register S. *Example:* 40A4 would cause the contents of register A to be copied into register 4.
5	RST	ADD the bit patterns in registers S and T as though they were two's complement representations and leave the result in register R. *Example:* 5726 would cause the binary values in registers 2 and 6 to be added and the sum placed in register 7.
6	RST	ADD the bit patterns in registers S and T as though they represented values in floating-point notation and leave the floating-point result in register R. *Example:* 634E would cause the values in registers 4 and E to be added as floating-point values and the result to be placed in register 3.
7	RST	OR the bit patterns in registers S and T and place the result in register R. *Example:* 7CB4 would cause the result of ORing the contents of registers B and 4 to be placed in register C.
8	RST	AND the bit patterns in register S and T and place the result in register R. *Example:* 8045 would cause the result of ANDing the contents of registers 4 and 5 to be placed in register 0.
9	RST	EXCLUSIVE OR the bit patterns in registers S and T and place the result in register R. *Example:* 95F3 would cause the result of EXCLUSIVE ORing the contents of registers F and 3 to be placed in register 5.
A	R0X	ROTATE the bit pattern in register R one bit to the right X times. Each time place the bit that started at the low-order end at the high-order end. *Example:* A403 would cause the contents of register 4 to be rotated 3 bits to the right in a circular fashion.
B	RXY	JUMP to the instruction located in the memory cell at address XY if the bit pattern in register R is equal to the bit pattern in register number 0. Otherwise, continue with the normal sequence of execution. (The jump is implemented by copying XY into the program counter during the execute phase.) *Example:* B43C would first compare the contents of register 4 with the contents of register 0. If the two were equal, the pattern 3C would be placed in the program counter so that the next instruction executed would be the one located at that memory address. Otherwise, nothing would be done and program execution would continue in its normal sequence.
C	000	HALT execution. *Example:* C000 would cause program execution to stop.

High-Level Language Program Examples

This appendix presents sample programs in the languages Ada, C, C++, C#, FOR-TRAN, and Java. Each program receives a list of names typed at the keyboard, sorts the list using the insertion sort algorithm, and prints the sorted list on the monitor screen.

Ada

The language Ada, named after Augusta Ada Byron (1815–1851), who was an advocate of Charles Babbage and the daughter of poet Lord Byron, was developed at the initiative of the U.S. Department of Defense in an attempt to obtain a single, general-purpose language for all its software development needs. A major emphasis during Ada's design was to incorporate features for programming real-time computer systems used as a part of larger machines such as missile guidance systems, environmental control systems within buildings, and control systems in automobiles and small home appliances. Ada thus contains features for expressing activities in parallel processing environments as well as convenient techniques for handling special cases (called exceptions) that might arise in the application environment. Ada is an imperative language with many object-oriented characteristics and therefore represents a step in the evolution from imperative programming to modern object-oriented languages.

Figure D.1 presents a sample Ada program.

C

The language C was developed by Dennis Ritchie at Bell Laboratories in the early 1970s. Although originally designed as a language for developing system software, C has achieved popularity throughout the programming community and has been standardized by the American National Standards Institute.

C was originally envisioned as merely a step up from machine language. Consequently, its syntax is terse compared with other high-level languages that use complete English words to express some primitives that are represented by special symbols in C. This terseness allows for efficient representations of complex algorithms, which is a major reason for C's popularity. (Often a concise representation is more readable than a lengthy one.)

Figure D.2 presents a sample program in C.

Figure D.1

A sample Ada program

```
        --Program to manipulate a list
        with TEXT_IO;
        use TEXT_IO;
        procedure MAIN is
            subtype NAME_TYPE is STRING (1..8);
            LIST_LENGTH: constant := 10;
            NAMES: array (1..LIST_LENGTH) of NAME_TYPE;
            PIVOT: NAME_TYPE;
            HOLE: INTEGER;
        begin
        --First, get the names from the terminal.
            for K in 1..LIST_LENGTH loop
              GET(NAMES(K));
            end loop;
        --Sort the list (HOLE contains the location of the
        --              hole in the list from the time the
        --              pivot is removed until it is
        --              reinserted.)
            for N in 2..LIST_LENGTH loop
              PIVOT := NAMES(N);
              HOLE := N;
              for M in reverse 1..N - 1 loop
                if NAMES(M) > PIVOT
                    then NAMES(M + 1) := NAMES(M);
                    else exit;
                end if;
                HOLE := M;
              end loop;
              NAMES(HOLE) := PIVOT;
            end loop;
        --Now, print the sorted list.
            for K in 1..LIST_LENGTH loop
              NEW_LINE;
              PUT(NAMES(K));
            end loop;
        end MAIN;
```

C++

The language C++ was developed by Bjarne Stroustrup at Bell Laboratories as an enhanced version of the language C. The goal was to produce a language compatible with the object-oriented paradigm.

Figure D.3 presents an implementation of the insertion sort algorithm in C++. The last four statements in this program request that an object named namelist be established having "type" list and that this new object perform the operations getnames, sortnames, and printnames on itself. The preceding portion of the program defines the properties that any object of "type" list is to possess. In particular, any such object is to contain an internal array of characters called names and three oper-ations called `getnames`, `sortlist`, and `printnames`. Note that the definitions of these operations are the same as portions of the C language program in Figure D.2. The difference is that in the C++ program these operations are considered to be a part of an object's properties, whereas in the C program they are considered as units within the procedural part of the program.

C#

The language C# was developed by Microsoft to be a tool in the .NET Framework, which is a comprehensive system for developing application software for machines running Microsoft system software. As the example in Figure D.4 shows, a C# program looks much like a program in C++ or Java. Indeed, the reason Microsoft introduced C# as a different language was not that it is truly new in the language sense, but that, as a different language, Microsoft could customize specific features of the language without concern for standards that were already associated with other languages or for proprietary rights of other corporations. Thus the novelty of C# is in its role as a prominent language for developing software utilizing the .NET Framework. With

Figure D.2

A sample C program

```
/* Program to manipulate a list */

#include <stdio.h>
#include <string.h>

int main ()
{
  char names[10][9],pivot[9];
  int i,j;

/* get the names */
  for (i = 0; i < 10; ++i)
    scanf("%8s",names[i]);

/*sort the list */
  for (i = 1; i < 10; ++i)
  {
    strcpy(pivot,names[i]);
    j = i - 1;
    while ((j >= 0)&&(strcmp(pivot,names[j]) < 0))
      {strcpy(names[j+1],names[j]); --j;};
    strcpy(names[j+1], pivot);

  }

/*print the sorted list */
  for (i = 0; i < 10; ++i)
    printf ("%s\n",names[i]);
}
```

Figure D.3

A sample C++ program

```cpp
// Program to manipulate a list

#include <iostream.h>
#include <string.h>
#include <iomanip>
const int ListLength = 10;
// All list objects contain a list of names and three public
// methods called getnames, sortlist, and printnames.

class list
{private:
  char names[ListLength][9];

public:

void getnames()
{int i;
 for (i = 0; i < ListLength; ++i)
   cin >> std::setw(9) >> names[i];
}

void sortlist()
{int i,j;
  char pivot[9];
  for (i = 1; i < ListLength; ++i)
   {strcpy(pivot, names[i]);
    j = i - 1;
    while ((j >= 0) && (strcmp(pivot, names [j]) < 0))
      {strcpy(names[j+1], names[j]);
        --j;
      }
    strcpy(names[j+1], pivot);
   }
}

 void printnames()
 {int i;
  cout << endl;
  for (i = 0; i < ListLength; ++i)
   cout << names[i] << endl;
 }
};
// Establish an object called namelist and ask it to
// collect some names, sort them, and print the list.

int main()
{list namelist;
 namelist.getnames();
 namelist.sortlist();
 namelist.printnames();
}
```

Microsoft's backing, C# and the .NET Framework promise to be prominent players in the world of software development for years to come.

FORTRAN

FORTRAN is an acronym for FORmula TRANslator. This language was one of the first high-level languages developed (announced in 1957) and one of the first to gain wide acceptance within the computing community. Over the years its official description has undergone numerous extensions, meaning that today's FORTRAN language is much different from the original. Indeed, by studying the evolution of FORTRAN, one would witness the effects of research in programming language design. Although challenged by the newer object-oriented languages, FORTRAN continues to be a popular language within the scientific community. In particular, many numerical analysis and statistical packages are, and will probably continue to be, written in FORTRAN. Figure D.5 presents a sample program written in one of the earlier versions of FORTRAN.

Java

Java is an object-oriented language developed by Sun Microsystems in the early 1990s. Its designers borrowed heavily from C and C++. The excitement over Java is not due to the language itself, but because of the language's universal implementation and the vast number of predesigned templates that are available in the Java programming environment. The universal implementation means that a program written in Java can be executed efficiently over a wide range of machines; and the availability of templates means that complex software can be developed with relative ease. For example, templates such as applet and servlet streamline the development of software for the World Wide Web.

Figure D.6 presents a sample program in Java. Note the resemblance between Java and C++.

Figure D.4

A sample program in C#

```csharp
//  Program to manipulate a list

// All list objects contain a list of names and three public
// methods called GetNames, SortNames, and PrintNames.

class List {
  const int ListLength = 10;
  private String[] Names;

  List() {
    Names = new String[ListLength];
  }

  public void GetNames() {
    for(int i = 0; i < ListLength; i++)
      Names[i] = System.Console.ReadLine();
  }

  public void SortNames() {
    int j;
    String Pivot;
    for(int i = 1; i < ListLength; i++) {
      Pivot = Names[i];
      j = i - 1;
      while ((j>= 0) && String.Compare(Pivot, Names[j], true) < 0)) {
        Names[j+1] = Names[j];
        j--;
      }
    }
    Names[j+1] = Pivot;
  }

  public void PrintNames() {
    for(int i = 0; i < ListLength; i++)
      System.Console.WriteLine(Names[i]);
  }
}

//  Establish an object called NameList and ask it to
//  collect some names, sort them, ans print the results.

class Sort {
  public static void main() {
    List NameList = new List();
    NameList.GetNames();
    Namelist.SortNames();
    Namelist.PrintNames();
    Return 0;
  }
}
```

Figure D.5

A sample FORTRAN program

```
!     Program to manipulate a list
          INTEGER J,K
          CHARACTER(LEN=8) Pivot
          CHARACTER(LEN=8) DIMENSION(10) Names
!     First, get the names.
          READ(UNIT=5, FMT=100) (Names(K), K=1,10)
100       FORMAT(A8)
!         Now, sort the list.
OuterLoop: DO J=2,10
              Pivot = Names(J)
  InnerLoop: DO K=J-1, 1,-1
              IF (Names(K) .GT. Pivot) THEN
                      Names(K+1) = Names(K)
                  ELSE
                      EXIT InnerLoop
              ENDIF
              END DO InnerLoop
              Names (K+1) = Pivot
              END DO OuterLoop
!     Now, print the sorted list.
          WRITE(UNIT=6,FMT=400) (Names(K),K=1,10)
400       FORMAT ('',A8)
          END
```

Figure D.6

A sample Java program

```
// Program to manipulate a list

import java.io.*;

// All list objects contain a list of names and three public
// methods called getnames, sortnames, and printnames.

class list {
  final int ListLength = 10;
  private String[] names;
  public list() {
    names = new String[ListLength];
  }
  public void getnames() {
    int i;
    DataInput data = new DataInputStream(System.in);
    for (i=0; i < ListLength; i++)
      try {names[i] = data.readLine();}
        }
        catch(IOException e) {};
  }
  public void sortnames() {
    int i,j;
    String pivot;
    for (i=1; i < ListLength; i++) {
      pivot = names[i];
      j = i - 1;
      while ((j >= 0) && (pivot.compareTo(names[j]) < 0)) {
        names [j+1] = names[j];
        j--;
      }
      names[j+1] = pivot;
    }
  }
  public void printnames() {
    int i;
    for (i=0; i < ListLength; i++)
      System.out.println(names[i]);
  }
}

// Establish an object called namelist and ask it to
// collect some names, sort them, and print the results.
class sort {
  public static void main(String args[]){
    list namelist = new list();
    namelist.getnames();
    namelist.sortnames();
    namelist.printnames();
  }
}
```

APPENDIX

E

The Equivalence of Iterative and Recursive Structures

In this appendix, we use our Bare Bones language of Chapter 11 as a tool to answer the question posed in Chapter 4 regarding the relative power of iterative and recursive structures. Recall that Bare Bones contains only three assignment statements (`clear`, `incr`, and `decr`) and one control structure (constructed from a `while-end` statement pair). Moreover, this simple language has the same computing power as a Turing machine; thus, if we accept the Church-Turing thesis, we may conclude that any problem with an algorithmic solution has a solution expressible in Bare Bones.

The first step in the comparison of iterative and recursive structures is to replace the iterative structure of Bare Bones with a recursive structure. We do this by removing the `while` and `end` statements from the language and in their place providing the ability to divide a Bare Bones program into units along with the ability to call one of these units from another location in the program. More precisely, we propose that each program in the modified language consist of a number of syntactically disjoint program units. We suppose that each program must contain exactly one unit called `MAIN` having the syntactic structure of

```
MAIN: begin;
        .
        .
        .
      end;
```

(where the dots represent other Bare Bones statements) and perhaps other units (semantically subordinate to `MAIN`) that have the structure

```
unit: begin;
        .
        .
        .
      return;
```

(where *unit* represents the unit's name that has the same syntax as variable names). The semantics of this partitioned structure is that the program always begins execution at the beginning of the unit `MAIN` and halts when that unit's end statement is reached. Program units other than `MAIN` can be called as procedures by means of the conditional statement

```
if name not 0 perform unit;
```

(where *name* represents any variable name and *unit* represents any of the program unit names other than MAIN). Moreover, we allow the units other than MAIN to call themselves recursively.

With these added features, we can simulate the while-end structure found in the original Bare Bones. For example, a Bare Bones program of the form

```
while X not 0 do;
  S;
end;
```

(where *S* represents any sequence of Bare Bones statements) can be replaced by the unit structure

```
MAIN: begin;
          if X not 0 perform unitA;
      end;

unitA: begin;
          S;
          if X not 0 perform unitA;
       return;
```

Consequently, we may conclude that the modified language has all the capabilities of the original Bare Bones.

It can also be shown that any problem that can be solved using the modified language can be solved using Bare Bones. One method of doing this is to show how any algorithm expressed in the modified language could be written in the original Bare Bones. However, this involves an explicit description of how recursive structures can be simulated with the while-end structure of Bare Bones.

For our purpose, it is simpler to rely on the Church-Turing thesis as presented in Chapter 11. In particular, the Church-Turing thesis, combined with the fact that Bare Bones has the same power as Turing machines, dictates that no language can be more powerful than our original Bare Bones. Therefore, any problem solvable in our modified language can also be solved using Bare Bones.

We conclude that the power of the modified language is the same as that of the original Bare Bones. The only distinction between the two languages is that one provides an iterative control structure and the other provides recursion. Thus the two control structures are in fact equivalent in terms of computing power.

Answers to Questions/Exercises

Chapter 1

Section 1.1

1. One and only one of the upper two inputs must be 1, and the lowest input must be 1.

2. The 1 on the lower input is negated to 0 by the NOT gate, causing the output of the AND gate to become 0. Thus both inputs to the OR gate are 0 (remember that the upper input to the flip-flop is held at 0) so the output of the OR gate becomes 0. This means that the output of the AND gate will remain 0 after the lower input to the flip-flop returns to 0.

3. The output of the upper OR gate will become 1, causing the upper NOT gate to produce an output of 0. This will cause the lower OR gate to produce a 0, causing the lower NOT gate to produce a 1. This 1 is seen as the output of the flip-flop as well as being fed back to the upper OR gate, where it holds the output of that gate at 1, even after the flip-flop's input has returned to 0.

4. The flip-flop will be shielded from the circuit's input values when the clock is 0. The flip-flop will respond to the circuit's input values when the clock is 1.

5. a. The entire circuit is equivalent to a single XOR gate.
   b. This entire circuit is also equivalent to a single XOR gate.

6. a. 6AF2   b. E85517   c. 48

7. a. 0101111111011001011 1
   b. 0110000100001010
   c. 1010101111001101
   d. 0000000100000000

Section 1.2

1. In the first case, memory cell number 6 ends up containing the value 5. In the second case, it ends up with the value 8.

2. Step 1 erases the original value in cell number 3 when the new value is written there. Consequently, Step 2 does not place the original value from cell number 3 in cell number 2. The result is that both cells end up with the value that was originally in cell number 2. A correct procedure is the following:

Step 1. Move the contents of cell number 2 to cell number 1.
Step 2. Move the contents of cell number 3 to cell number 2.
Step 3. Move the contents of cell number 1 to cell number 3.

3. 32768 bits.

Section 1.3

1. Faster retrieval of data and higher transfer rates.

2. The point to remember here is that the slowness of mechanical motion compared with the speed of the internal functioning of the computer dictates that we minimize the number of times we must move the read/write heads. If we fill a complete surface before starting the next, we must move the read/write head each time we finish with a track. The number of moves therefore is approximately the same as the total number of tracks on the two surfaces. If, however, we alternate between surfaces by electronically switching between the read/write heads, we must move the read/write heads only after each cylinder has been filled.

3. In this application, a constant expansion and shrinking takes place within the data. If the information were stored on tape, this would result in an endless rewriting process to accommodate the upheaval taking place within the data. (One envisions the last block of the data yo-yoing back and forth as reservations earlier on the tape are made, dropped, or become outdated.) When using disk storage, however, each change affects only the portion of the data stored on the sector involved. Consequently, much less rewriting of data is required when updates are made.

4. Storage space is allocated in units of physical sectors (actually in units of groups of sectors in most cases). If the last physical sector is not full, additional text can be added without increasing the storage space allocated to the file. If the last physical sector is full, any addition to the document will require additional physical sectors to be allocated.

Section 1.4

1. Computer science.

2. The two patterns are the same, except that the sixth bit from the low-order end is always 0 for uppercase and 1 for lowercase.

3. a.

01010111	01101000	01100101	01110010
01100101	00100000	01100001	01110010
01100101	00100000	01111001	01101111
01110101	00111111		

b.

00100010	01001000	01101111	01110111
00111111	00100010	00100000	01000011
01101000	01100101	01110010	01111001
01101100	00100000	01100001	01110011
01101011	01100101	01100100	00101110

c.

00110010	00101011	00110011	00111101
00110101	00101110		

4.

5. a. 5   **b.** 9   **c.** 11   **d.** 6   **e.** 16   **f.** 18

6. a. 110   **b.** 1101   **c.** 1011   **d.** 10010   **e.** 11011   **f.** 100

7. In 24 bits, we can store three symbols using ASCII. Thus we can store values as large as 999. However, if we use the bits as binary digits, we can store values up to 16,777,215.

8. a. 15.15   **b.** 51.0.128   **c.** 10.160

9. As emphasized in the text, vector techniques are more conducive to changes in scale than images encoded as bit maps. For simple line drawings, they can also be more compact. On the other hand, vector techniques do not provide the same photographic quality that bit maps produce.

10. With a sample rate of 44,100 samples per second, one hour of stereo music would require 635,040,000 bytes of storage. Thus, it would just about fill a CD whose capacity is slightly more than 600MB.

Section 1.5

1. a. 42   **b.** 33   **c.** 23   **d.** 6   **e.** 31

2. a. 100000 **b.** 1000000   **c.** 1100000   **d.** 1111   **e.** 11011

3. a. $3\frac{1}{4}$ **b.** $5\frac{7}{8}$ **c.** $2\frac{1}{2}$ **d.** $6\frac{3}{8}$ **e.** $\frac{5}{8}$

4. a. 100.1   **b.** 10.11   **c.** 1.001   **d.** 0.0101   **e.** 101.101

5. a. 100111   **b.** 1011.110   **c.** 100000   **d.** 1000.00

Section 1.6

1. a. 3   **b.** 15   **c.** −4   **d.** −6   **e.** 0   **f.** −16

2. a. 00000110 **b.** 11111010   **c.** 11101111
d. 00001101 **e.** 11111111   **f.** 00000000

3. a. 11111111   **b.** 10101011   **c.** 00000100
d. 00000010   **e.** 00000000   **f.** 10000001

4. a. With 4 bits the largest value is 7 and the smallest is 8.
b. With 6 bits the largest value is 31 and the smallest is −32.
c. With 8 bits the largest value is 127 and the smallest is −128.

5. a. 0111 (5 + 2 = 7)   **b.** 0100 (3 + 1 = 4)   **c.** 1111 (5 + (−6) = −1)
d. 0001 (−2 + 3 = 1)   **e.** 1000 (−6 + (−2) = −8)

6. a. 0111   **b.** 1011 (overflow) **c.** 0100 (overflow)
d. 0001   **e.** 1000 (overflow)

7. a. 0110   **b.** 0011   **c.** 0100   **d.** 0010   **e.** 0001
     + 0001   + 1110   + 1010   + 0100   + 1011
       0111   0001   1110   0110   1100

8. No. Overflow occurs when an attempt is made to store a number that is too large for the system being used. When adding a positive value to a negative value, the result must be between the values being added. Thus, if the original values are small enough to be stored, the result is also.

9. a. 6 because 1110 → 14 – 8
  b. –1 because 0111 → 7 – 8
  c. 0 because 1000 → 8 – 8
  d. –6 because 0010 → 2 – 8
  e. –8 because 0000 → 0 – 8
  f. 1 because 1001 → 9 – 8

10. a. 1101 because 5 + 8 = 13 → 1101
  b. 0011 because –5 + 8 = 3 → 0011
  c. 1011 because 3 + 8 = 11 → 1011
  d. 1000 because 0 + 8 = 8 → 1000
  e. 1111 because 7 + 8 = 15 → 1111
  f. 0000 because –8 + 8 = 0 → 0000

11. No. The largest value that can be stored in excess eight notation is 7, represented by 1111. To represent a larger value, at least excess 16 (which uses patterns of 5 bits) must be used. Similarly, 6 cannot be represented in excess four notation. (The largest value that can be represented in excess four notation is 3.)

Section 1.7

1. a. $\frac{5}{8}$ b. $3\frac{1}{4}$ c. $\frac{9}{32}$ d. $-1\frac{1}{2}$ e. $(-\frac{11}{64})$

2. a. 01101011   b. 01111010 (truncation error)
  c. 01001100   d. 11101110   e. 11111000 (truncation error)

3. 01001001 ($\frac{9}{16}$) is larger than 00111101 ($\frac{13}{32}$). The following is a simple way of determining which of two patterns represents the larger value:

Case 1. If the sign bits are different, the larger is the one with 0 sign bit.

Case 2. If the sign bits are both 0, scan the remaining portions of the patterns from left to right until a bit position is found where the two patterns differ. The pattern containing the 1 in this position represents the larger value.

Case 3. If the sign bits are both 1, scan the remaining portions of the patterns from left to right until a bit position is found where the two patterns differ. The pattern containing the 0 in this position represents the larger value.

The simplicity of this comparison process is one of the reasons for representing the exponent in floating-point systems with an excess notation rather than with two's complement.

4. The largest value would be $7\frac{1}{2}$, which is represented by the pattern 01111111. As for the smallest positive value, you could argue that there are two "correct" answers. First, if you stick to the coding process described in the text, which requires the most significant bit of the mantissa to be 1 (called normalized form), the answer is $\frac{1}{32}$, which is represented by the pattern 00001000. However, most machines do not impose this restriction for values close to 0. For such a machine, the correct answer is $\frac{1}{256}$ represented by 00000001.

Section 1.8

1. In hexadecimal notation the message is B5E95EFA56.

2. Answers will vary. One possibility is bbabbbaaba (5, 5, b) (10, 7, a).

3. Color cartoons consist of blocks of solid color with sharp edges. Moreover, the number of colors involved is limited.

4. There would be 1,049,576 pixels, each requiring one byte to represent the pixel's color. The additional compression techniques involved in GIF would reduce this significantly, although their efficiency depends on the complexity of the image. Typically, simple images require no more than a few KB of storage when encoded using GIF. If JPEG's baseline standard were used, each two-by-two pixel block would require only six components. Assuming one byte per component, the 1024 by 1024 pixel image would require a maximum of 1.5MB, but again the additional compression techniques typically reduce such an image to under 100KB.

5. JPEG's baseline standard takes advantage of the fact that the human eye is not as sensitive to changes in color as it is to changes in brightness. Thus it reduces the number of bits used to represent color information without noticeable loss in image quality.

6. When encoding information, approximations are made. In the case of numeric data, these approximations are compounded when computations are performed, which can lead to erroneous results. Approximations are not as critical in the cases of images and sound because the encoded data are normally only stored, transferred, and reproduced. If, however, images or sound were repeatedly reproduced and then re-encoded, these approximations could compound and ultimately lead to worthless data.

Section 1.9

1. b, c, and e.

2. Yes. If an even number of errors occurs in one byte, the parity technique does not detect them.

3. In this case, errors occur in bytes a and d of Question 1. The answer to Question 2 remains the same.

4. a.
```
001010111    001101000    101100101
101110010    101100101    000100000
001100001    101110010    101100101
000100000    001111001    101101111
001110101    100111111
```

b. 100100010   101001000   101101111
   101110111   100111111   100100010
   000100000   001000011   001101000
   101100101   101110010   001111001
   101101100   000100000   001100001
   001110011   001101011   101100101
   001100100   100101110
c. 000110010   100101011   100110011
   000111101   100110101   100101110

5. a. BED   b. CAB   c. HEAD

6. One solution is the following:

A 0 0 0 0 0
B 1 1 1 0 0
C 0 1 1 1 1
D 1 0 0 1 1

Chapter 2

Section 2.1

1. On some machines this is a two-step process consisting of first reading the contents from the first cell into a register and then writing it from the register into the destination cell. On most machines, this is accomplished as one activity without using an intermediate register.

2. The value to be written, the address of the cell in which to write, and the command to write.

3. General-purpose registers are used to hold the data immediately applicable to the operation at hand; main memory is used to hold data that will be needed in the near future; and mass storage is used to hold data that will likely not be needed in the near future.

Section 2.2

1. The term *move* often carries the connotation of removing from one location and placing in another, thus leaving a hole behind. In most cases within a machine, this removal does not take place. Rather, the object being moved is most often copied (or cloned) into the new location.

2. A common technique, called relative addressing, is to state how far rather than where to jump. For example, an instruction might be to jump forward three instructions or jump backward two instructions. You should note, however, that such statements must be altered if additional instructions are later inserted between the origin and the destination of the jump.

3. This could be argued either way. The instruction is stated in the form of a conditional jump. However, because the condition that 0 be equal to 0 is always satisfied, the jump will always be made as if there were no condition stated at all. You will often find machines with such instructions in their repertoires because they provide an efficient design. For example, if a machine is designed to execute an instruction with a structure such as "If . . . jump to . . ." this instruction form can be used to express both conditional and unconditional jumps.

4. 156C = 0001010101101100
   166D = 0001011001101101
   5056 = 0101000001010110
   306E = 0011000001101110
   C000 = 1100000000000000

5. a. STORE the contents of register 6 in memory cell number 8A.
   b. JUMP to location DE if the contents of register A equals that of register 0.
   c. AND the contents of registers 3 and C, leaving the result in register 0.
   d. MOVE the contents of register F to register 4.

6. The instruction 15AB requires that the CPU query the memory circuitry for the contents of the memory cell at address AB. This value, when obtained from memory, is then placed in register 5. The instruction 25AB does not require such a request of memory. Rather, the value AB is placed in register 5.

7. a. 2356   b. A503 c. 80A5

Section 2.3

1. Hexadecimal 34

2. a. 0F   b. C3

3. a. 00   b. 01 c. four times

4. It halts. This is an example of what is often called self-modifying code. That is, the program modifies itself. Note that the first two instructions place hexadecimal C0 at memory location F8, and the next two instructions place 00 at location F9. Thus, by the time the machine reaches the instruction at F8, the halt instruction (C000) has been placed there.

Section 2.4

1. a. 00001011   b. 10000000   c. 00101101
   d. 11101011   e. 11101111   f. 11111111
   g. 11100000   h. 01101111   i. 11010010

2. 0011100 with the AND operation

3. 0011100 with the XOR operation

4. a. The final result is 0 if the string contained an even number of 1s. Otherwise it is 1.
   b. The result is the value of the parity bit for even parity.

5. The logical XOR operation mirrors addition except for the case where both operands are 1, in which case the XOR produces a 0, whereas the sum is 10. (Thus the XOR operation can be considered an addition operation with no carry.)

6. Use AND with the mask 11011111 to change lowercase to uppercase. Use OR with 00100000 to change uppercase to lowercase.

7. a. 01001101   b. 11100001 c. 11101111

8. a. 57   b. B8   c. 6F   d. 6A

9. 5

10. 00110110 in two's complement; 01011110 in floating-point. The point here is that the procedure used to add the values is different depending on the interpretation given the bit patterns.

11. One solution is as follows:

    12A7 (LOAD register 2 with the contents of memory cell A7.)
    2380 (LOAD register 3 with the value 80.)
    7023 (OR registers 2 and 3 leaving the result in register 0.)
    30A7 (STORE contents of register 0 in memory cell A7.)
    C000 (HALT.)

12. One solution is as follows:

    15E0 (LOAD register 5 with the contents of memory cell E0.)
    A502 (ROTATE 2 bits to the right the contents of register 5.)
    260F (LOAD register 6 with the value 0F.)
    8056 (AND registers 5 and 6, leaving the result in register 0.)
    30E1 (STORE the contents of register 0 in memory cell E1.)
    C000 (HALT.)

Section 2.5

1. a. 37B5
   b. One million times
   c. No. A typical page of text contains less than 4000 characters. Thus the ability to print five pages in a minute indicates a printing rate of no more than 20,000 characters per minute, which is much less than one million characters per second. (The point is that a computer can send characters to a printer much faster than the printer can print them; thus the printer needs a way of telling the computer to wait.)

2. The disk will make 50 revolutions in one second, meaning that 800 sectors will pass under the read/write head in a second. Since each sector contains 1024 bytes, bits will pass under the read/write head at approximately 6.5 Mbps. Thus communication between the controller and the disk drive will have to be at least this fast if the controller is going to keep up with the data being read from the disk.

3. A 300-page novel represented in ASCII consists of about 1MB or 8,000,000 bits. Thus approximately 139 seconds (or $2\frac{1}{3}$ minutes) would be required to transfer the entire novel at 57,600 bps.

Section 2.6

1. The pipe would contain the instructions B1B0 (being executed), 5002, and perhaps even B0AA. If the value in register 1 is equal to the value in register

0, the jump to location B0 is executed, and the effort already expended on the instructions in the pipe is wasted. On the other hand, no time is wasted because the effort expended on these instructions did not require extra time.

2. If no precautions are taken, the information at memory locations F8 and F9 is fetched as an instruction before the previous part of the program has had a chance to modify these cells.

3. a. The CPU that is trying to add 1 to the cell can first read the value in the cell. Following this the other CPU reads the cell's value. (Note that at this point both CPUs have retrieved the same value.) If the first CPU now finishes its addition and writes its result back in the cell before the second finishes its subtraction and writes its result, the final value in the cell reflects only the activity of the second CPU.

   b. The CPUs might read the data from the cell as before, but this time the second CPU might write its result before the first. Thus only the activity of the first CPU is reflected in the cell's final value.

Chapter 3

Section 3.1

1. A traditional example is the line of people waiting to buy tickets to an event. In this case there may be someone who tries to "break in line," which would violate the FIFO structure.

2. Options (b) and (c).

3. Real-time processing refers to coordinating the execution of a program with activities in the machine's environment. Interactive processing refers to a person's interaction with a program as it executes. Good real-time characteristics are needed for successful interactive processing.

4. Time-sharing is the technique by which multitasking is accomplished on a single-processor machine.

Section 3.2

1. *Shell:* Communicates with the machine's environment.
   File manager: Coordinates the use of the machine's mass storage.
   Device drivers: Handles communication with the machine's peripheral devices.
   Memory manager: Coordinates the use of the machine's main memory.
   Scheduler: Coordinates the processes in the system.
   Dispatcher: Controls the assignment of processes to CPU time.

2. The line is vague, and the distinction is often in the eye of the beholder. Roughly speaking, utility software performs basic, universal tasks, whereas application software performs tasks unique to the machine's application.

3. Virtual memory is the imaginary memory space whose apparent presence is created by the process of swapping data and programs back and forth between main memory and mass storage.

4. When the machine is turned on, the CPU begins executing the bootstrap, which resides in ROM. This bootstrap directs the CPU through the process of transferring the operating system from mass storage into the volatile area of main memory. When this transfer is complete, the bootstrap directs the CPU to jump to the operating system.

Section 3.3

1. A program is a set of directions. A process is the action of following those directions.

2. The CPU completes its current machine cycle, saves the state of the current process, and sets its program counter to a predetermined value (which is the location of the interrupt handler). Thus the next instruction executed will be the first instruction within the interrupt handler.

3. They could be given higher priorities so that they would be given preference by the dispatcher. Another option would be to give the higher-priority processes longer time slices.

4. If each process consumed its entire time slice, the machine could provide a complete quantum to almost 20 processes in one second. If processes did not consume their entire time slices, this value could be much higher, but then the time required to perform a context switch may become more significant (see Problem 5).

5. A total of 5000/5001 of the machine's time would be spent actually performing processes. However, when a process requests an I/O activity, its time slice is terminated while the controller performs the request. Thus if each process made such a request after only one microsecond of its quantum, the efficiency of the machine would drop to 1/2. That is, the machine would spend as much time performing context switches as it would executing processes.

Section 3.4

1. This system guarantees that the resource is not used by more than one process at a time; however, it dictates that the resource be allocated in a strictly alternating fashion. Once a process has used and relinquished the resource, it must wait for the other process to use the resource before the original process can access it again. This is true even if the first process needs the resource right away and the other process will not need it for some time.

2. If two cars enter opposite ends of the tunnel at the same time, they will not be aware of the other's presence. The process of entering and turning on the lights is another example of a critical region, or in this case we might call it a critical process. In this terminology, we could summarize the flaw by saying that cars at opposite ends of the tunnel could execute the critical process at the same time.

3. a. This guarantees that the nonshareable resource is not required and allocated on a partial basis; that is, a car is given the whole bridge or nothing at all.

b. This means that the nonshareable resource can be forcibly retrieved.

c. This makes the nonshareable resource shareable, which removes the competition.

4. A sequence of arrows that forms a closed loop in the directed graph. It is on this observation that techniques have been developed, allowing some operating systems to recognize the existence of deadlock and consequently to take appropriate corrective action.

Section 3.5

1. Names and dates are considered poor candidates because they are common choices and therefore represent easy targets for password guessers. The use of complete words is also considered poor because password guessers can easily write a program to try the words found in a dictionary. Moreover, passwords containing only characters are discouraged because they are formed from a limited character set.

2. Four is the number of different bit patterns that can be formed using two bits. If more privilege levels were required, the designers would need at least three bits to represent the different levels and would therefore probably choose to use a total of eight levels. In the same manner, the natural choice for fewer than four privilege levels would be two, which is the number of patterns that can be represented with one bit.

3. The process could alter the operating system program so that the dispatcher gave every time slice to that process.

Chapter 4

Section 4.1

1. An open network is one whose specifications and protocols are public, allowing different vendors to produce compatible products.

2. A router is a machine connecting two networks to form an internet. The term *gateway* is often used to refer to a router that connects a domain to the rest of an internet.

3. How about a mail order business and its clients, a bank teller and the bank's customers, or a pharmacist and his or her customers?

4. There are numerous protocols involved in traffic flow, verbal telephone communication, and etiquette.

Section 4.2

1. A network identifier identifies a domain, a host address identifies a machine within a domain. The two combined make up an IP address.

2. The complete Internet address of a host consists of the network identifier and the host address.

3. 3.4.5 represents the three-byte pattern 000000110000010000000101. The bit pattern 0001001100010000 would be represented as 19.16 in dotted decimal notation.

4. There could be several answers to this. One is that they both progress from the specific to the general. Internet addresses in mnemonic form begin with the name of a particular machine and progress to the name of the TLD. Postal addresses begin with the name of an individual and progress to increasingly larger regions such as city, state, and country. This order is reversed in IP addresses, which start with the bit pattern identifying the domain.

5. Name servers help translate mnemonic addresses into IP addresses. Mail servers send, receive, and store e-mail messages. FTP servers provide file transfer service.

Section 4.3

1. A URL is essentially the address of a document in the World Wide Web. A browser is a program that assists a user in accessing hypertext.

2. HTML is a particular markup language. XML is a standard for producing markup languages.

3. *Client side* and *server side* are adjectives used to identify whether an activity is performed at the client's computer of the server's computer.

Section 4.4

1. The link layer receives the message and hands it to the network layer. The network layer notes that the message is for another host, attaches another intermediate destination address to the message, and gives the message back to the link layer.

2. Unlike TCP, UDP is a connectionless protocol that does not confirm that the message was received at the destination.

3. Each message is assigned a hop count that determines the maximum number of times the message will be relayed.

4. Nothing really. A programmer at any host could modify the software at that host to keep such records. This is why sensitive data should be encrypted.

Section 4.5

1. The use of passwords protects data (and therefore information as well). The use of encryption protects information.

2. In the context of our study, the ECPA defines privacy rights involving electronic communication.

3. If compliance with a law is technically unfeasible, then that law will not (cannot) be obeyed. The requirements of the CALEA are technically, as well as financially, demanding-meaning that compliance with the law is problematic.

4. A domain's gateway is a router that merely forwards packets (parts of messages) as they pass through. Thus a firewall at the gateway cannot filter traffic by its content but merely by its address information.

Chapter 5

Section 5.1

1. A process is the activity of executing an algorithm. A program is a representation of an algorithm.

2. In the introductory chapter we cited algorithms for playing music, operating washing machines, constructing models, performing magic tricks, and the Euclidean algorithm. Many of the "algorithms" you meet in everyday life fail to be algorithms according to our formal definition. The example of the long-division algorithm was cited in the text. Another is the algorithm executed by a clock that continues to advance its hands and ring its chimes day after day.

3. The informal definition fails to require that the steps be ordered and unambiguous. It merely hints at the requirements that the steps be executable and lead to an end.

4. There are two points here. The first is that the instructions define a nonterminating process. In reality, however, the process will ultimately reach the state in which there are no coins in your pocket. In fact, this may be the starting state. At this point the problem is that of ambiguity. The algorithm, as represented, does not tell us what to do in this situation.

Section 5.2

1. One example is found in the composition of matter. At one level, the primitives are considered molecules, yet these particles are actually composites made up of atoms, which in turn are composed of electrons, protons, and neutrons. Today, we know that even these "primitives" are composites.

2. Once a procedure is correctly constructed, it can be used as a building block for larger program structures without reconsidering the procedure's internal composition.

3. X ← the larger input;
Y ← the smaller input;
while (Y not zero) do
 (Remainder ← remainder after dividing X by Y;
  X ← Y;
  Y ← Remainder);
GCD ← X

4. All other colors of light can be produced by combining red, blue, and green. Thus a television picture tube is designed to produce these three basic colors.

Section 5.3

1. a. if (n = 1 or n = 2)
       then (the answer is the list containing the single value n)

else (Divide n by 3, obtaining a quotient q and a remainder r.
   if (r = 0)
      then (the answer is the list containing q 3s)
   if (r = 1)
      then (the answer is the list containing (q – 1) 3s and two 2s;)
   if (r = 2)
      then (the answer is the list containing q 3s and one 2)

)

    b. The result would be the list containing 667 threes.

    c. You probably experimented with small input values until you began to see a pattern.

2. a. Yes. *Hint:* Place the first tile in the center so that it avoids the quadrant containing the hole while covering one square from each of the other quadrants. Each quadrant then represents a smaller version of the original problem.

    b. The board with a single hole contains $2^{2n}-1$ squares, and each tile covers exactly three squares.

    c. Parts (a) and (b) of this question provide an excellent example of how knowing a solution to one problem helps solve another. See Polya's fourth phase.

3. It says, "This is the correct answer."

Section 5.4

1. Change the test in the **while** statement to read "target value not equal to current entry and there remain entries to be considered."

2. Z ← 0;
X ← 1;
repeat (Z ← Z + X;
      X ← X + 1)
until (X = 6)

3. This has proven to be a problem with the C language. When the *do* and *while* key words are separated by several lines, readers of a program often stumble over the proper interpretation of a *while* clause. In particular, the *while* at the end of a *do* statement is often interpreted as the beginning of a *while* statement. Thus experience would say that it is better to use different key words to represent pretest and posttest loop structures.

4.

Cheryl	Alice	Alice
Gene	Cheryl	Brenda
Alice	Gene	Cheryl
Brenda	Brenda	Gene

5. It is a waste of time to insist on placing the pivot above an identical entry in the list. For instance, make the proposed change and then try the new program on a list in which all entries are the same.

6. procedure sort (List)
  N ← 1;
  while (N is less than the length of List) do
    (J ← N + 1;
    while (J is not greater than length of List) do
      (if (the entry in position J is less than the entry in position N)
        then (interchange the two entries)
      J ← J + 1)
  N ← N + 1)

7. The following is an inefficient solution. Can you make it more efficient?

procedure sort (List)
N the length of List;
while (N is greater than 1) do
  (J ← the length of List;
  while (J is greater than 1) do
    (if (the entry in position J is less than the entry in position J 1)
      then (interchange the two entries)
  J ← J − 1)
  N ← N − 1)

Section 5.5

1. The first name considered would be Henry, the next would be Larry, and the last would be Joe.

2. 8, 17

Section 5.6

1. If the machine can sort 100 names in one second, it can perform $\frac{1}{4}$ (10,000 − 100) comparisons in one second. This means that each comparison takes approximately 0.0004 second. Consequently, sorting 1000 names [which requires an average of $\frac{1}{4}$ (1,000,000 − 1000) comparisons] requires roughly 100 seconds or $1\frac{2}{3}$ minutes.

2. The binary search belongs to $\Theta(\lg n)$, the sequential search belongs to $\Theta(n)$, and the insertion sort belongs to $\Theta(n^2)$.

3. The class $\Theta(\lg n)$ is most efficient, followed by $\Theta(n)$, $\Theta(n^2)$, and $\Theta(n^3)$.

4. No. The answer is not correct, although it may sound right. The truth is that two of the three cards are the same on both sides. Thus the probability of picking such a card is two-thirds.

5. No. If the dividend is less than the divisor, such as in $\frac{3}{7}$, the answer given is 1, although it should be 0.

6. No. If the value of X is zero and the value of Y is nonzero, the answer given will not be correct.

7. Each time the test for termination is conducted, the statement "Sum = 1 + 2 + ... + I and I less than or equal to N" is true. Combining this with the termination condition "*I* greater than or equal to *N*" produces the desired conclusion "Sum = 1 + 2 + ... + *N*." Since *I* is initialized at zero and incremented by one each time through the loop, its value must ultimately reach that of *N.*

8. Unfortunately, no. Problems beyond the control of hardware and software design, such as mechanical malfunctions and electrical problems, can affect computations.

Chapter 6

Section 6.1

1. A program in a third-generation language is machine independent in the sense that its steps are not stated in terms of the machine's attributes such as registers and memory cell addresses. On the other hand, it is machine dependent in the sense that arithmetic overflow and truncation errors will still occur.

2. The major distinction is that an assembler translates each instruction in the source program into a single machine instruction, whereas a compiler often produces many machine-language instructions to obtain the equivalent of a single source program instruction.

3. The declarative paradigm is based on developing a description of the problem to be solved. The functional paradigm forces the programmer to describe the problem's solution in terms of solutions to smaller problems. The object-oriented paradigm places emphasis on describing the components in the problem's environment.

4. The third-generation languages allow the program to be expressed more in terms of the problem's environment and less in terms of computer gibberish than do the earlier-generation languages.

Section 6.2

1. Using a descriptive constant can improve the accessibility of the program.

2. A declarative statement describes terminology; an imperative statement describes steps in an algorithm.

3. Integer, real, character, and Boolean.

4. The if-then-else and while loop structures are very common.

5. All components of a homogeneous array have the same type.

Section 6.3

1. A local variable is accessible only within a program unit such as a procedure; a global variable is accessible program wide.

2. A function is a procedure that returns a value associated with the function's name.

3. Because that is what they are. I/O operations are actually calls to routines within the machine's operating system.

4. A formal parameter is an identifier within a procedure. It serves as a place-holder for the value, the actual parameter, that is passed to the procedure when the procedure is called.

5. A procedure is designed to perform an action, whereas a function is designed to produce a value. Thus the program is more readable if the name of a procedure rcflects the action it performs and the name of a function reflects the value it returns.

Section 6.4

1. *Lexical analysis:* the process of identifying tokens.
Parsing: the process of recognizing the grammatical structure of the program.
Code generation: the process of producing the instructions in the object program.

2. A symbol table is the record of information the parser has obtained from the program's declarative statements.

3.

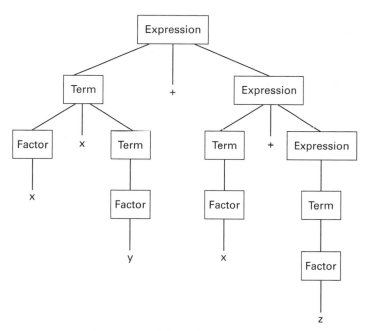

4. They are one or more instances of the substrings
forward backward cha cha cha
backward forward cha cha cha
swing right cha cha cha
swing left cha cha cha

Section 6.5

1. A class is the description of an object.

2. One would probably be `MeteorClass` from which the various meteors would be constructed. Within the class `LaserClass` one might find an instance variable named `AimDirection` indicating the direction in which the laser is aimed. This variable would probably be used by the `fire`, `turnRight`, and `turnLeft` methods.

3. The `Employee` class might contain features relating to an employee's name, address, years in service, etc. The `FullTimeEmployee` class might contain features relating to retirement benefits. The `PartTimeEmployee` class might contain features relating to hours worked per week, hourly wage, etc.

4. A constructor is a special method in a class that is executed when an instance of the class is created.

5. Some items in a class are designated as private to keep other program units from gaining direct access to those items. If an item is private, then the repercussions of modifying that item should be restricted to the interior of the class.

Section 6.6

1. The list would include techniques for initiating the execution of concurrent processes and techniques for implementing interprocess communication.

2. One is to place the burden on the processes, another is to place the burden on the data. The latter has the advantage of concentrating the task at a single point in the program.

Section 6.7

1. R, T, and V. For instance, we can show that R is a consequence by adding its negation to the collection and showing that resolution can lead to the empty statement, as shown here:

2. No. The collection is inconsistent, since resolution can lead to the empty statement, as shown here:

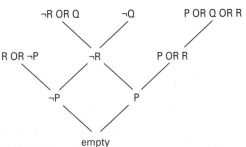

3. a. `thriftier(sue, carol)`
    `thriftier(sue, john)`
  b. `thriftier(sue, carol)`
    `thriftier(bill, carol)`
  c. `thriftier(carol, john)`
    `thriftier(bill, sue)`
    `thriftier(sue, carol)`
    `thriftier(bill, sue)`
    `thriftier(sue, john)`

4. `mother(X, Y) :- parent(X, Y), female(X).`
`father(X, Y) :- parent(X, Y), male(X).`

Chapter 7

Section 7.1

1. A long sequence of assignment statements is not as complex in the context of program design as a few nested if statements.

2. One approach is to intentionally place some errors in the software when it is designed. Then, after the software has supposedly been debugged, check to see how many of the original errors are still present. For example, if you intentionally place seven errors in the software and find that five have been removed after debugging, then you may conjecture that only $5/7$ of the total errors in the software have been removed.

3. How about the number of errors found after a fixed period of use? One problem here is that this value cannot be measured in advance.

4. One would be education. Humans were successfully teaching each other long before researchers began to try to understand how humans learn. Thus, education was dominated by practitioners and the techniques they had developed. Today, many would argue that the theoreticians have merely messed things up.

Section 7.2

1. System requirements are stated in terms of the application environment, whereas the specifications are stated in technical terms and identify how the requirements will be met.

2. The analysis phase concentrates on what the proposed system must accomplish. The design phase concentrates on how the system accomplishes its goals. The implementation phase concentrates on the actual construction of the system. The testing phase concentrates on making sure that the system does what it is intended to do.

3. The traditional waterfall approach dictates that the analysis, design, implementation, and testing phases be performed in a linear manner. The prototyping model allows for a more relaxed trial-and-error approach.

Section 7.3

1. The chapters of a novel build on one another, whereas the sections in an encyclopedia are largely independent. Hence a novel has more coupling between its chapters than an encyclopedia has between its sections. However, the sections within an encyclopedia probably have a higher level of cohesion than the chapters in a novel.

2. The accumulated score would be an example of data coupling. Other "couplings" that might exist would include fatigue, momentum, knowledge gained about an opponent's strategy, and perhaps self confidence. In many sports the cohesion of the units is increased by terminating the action and restarting the next unit from a fresh beginning. For example, in baseball each "at bat" starts without any base runners, even though the team may have finished the previous "at bat" with the bases loaded. In other cases the units are scored separately as in tennis where each set is won or lost without regard for the other sets.

3. This is a tough one. From one point of view, we could start by placing everything in a single module. This would result in little cohesion and no coupling at all. If we then begin to divide this single module into smaller ones, the result would be an increase in coupling. We might therefore conclude that increasing cohesion tends to increase coupling.

   On the other hand, suppose the problem at hand naturally divides into three very cohesive modules, which we will call A, B, and C. If our original design did not observe this natural division (for example, half of task A might be placed with half of task B, and so on), we would expect the cohesion to be low and the coupling high. In this case, redesigning the system by isolating tasks A, B, and C into separate modules would most likely decrease intermodule coupling as intramodule cohesion increases.

4. To add a personal touch, an object of type Catalogue could use the customer's name in its communication with the customer. For this, the Catalogue object would need to send a request to a Customer object to obtain the name of the customer.

Section 7.4

1. Simply trying to assemble the pieces would be a bottom-up approach. However, by looking at the puzzle box to see what the picture is supposed to look like adds a top-down component to your approach.

2. The client/server model would be one.

3. Design patterns lead to prefabricated building blocks from which large software systems can be constructed in a manner similar to the way in which complex devices are constructed from off-the-shelf components in other engineering disciplines.

4. A traditional programmer writes programs in terms of statements such as those introduced in Chapter 6. A component assembler builds programs by linking prefabricated blocks called components.

5. Traditional evolutionary prototyping is performed within the organization developing the software, whereas open-source development is not restricted to an organization. In the case of open-source development the person overseeing the development does not necessarily determine what enhancements will be reported, whereas in the case of traditional evolutionary prototyping the person managing the software development assigns personnel to specific enhancement tasks.

Section 7.5

1.

2.

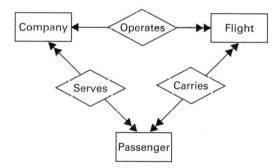

3. This question is one you should return to after you have read Chapter 7. Implementing a one-to-many relationship requires a structure such as a linked list by which all the related entities can be found, whereas a one-to-one relationship can be implemented by a single pointer from one entity to the related one.

Section 7.6

1. The purpose of testing software is to find errors. Therefore software engineers generally consider a test that does not reveal an error as a failure.

2. One would be to consider the amount of branching in the modules. For instance, a procedural module containing numerous loops and if-then-else statements would probably be more prone to errors than a module with a simple logical structure.

3. Boundary value analysis would suggest that you test the software on a list with 100 entries as well as a list with no entries. You might also perform a test with a list that is already in the correct order.

Section 7.7

1. In accompanying manuals, within the source program in the form of comments and well-written code, through interactive messages that the program itself writes at a terminal, through data dictionaries, and in the form of design documents such as structure charts, class diagrams, dataflow diagrams, and entity-relationship diagrams.

2. In both the development and modification phases. The point is that modifications must be documented as thoroughly as the original program. (It is also true that software is documented while in its use phase. For example, a user of the system might discover problems, which are then reported in the system user's manual. Moreover, books written on the use and design of popular software systems are common. These are sometimes written by people other than the original designers and after the software has been in use for some time and has gained popularity.)

3. Different people will have different opinions on this one. Some will argue that the program is the point of the whole project and thus is naturally the more important. Others will argue that a program is worth nothing if it is not documented, because if you cannot understand a program, you cannot use it or modify it. Moreover, with good documentation, the task of creating the program can be "easily" re-created.

Section 7.8

1. Courts have at times interpreted substantial similarity quite broadly, considering similarities far beyond those of the literal components of a program. The "nonliteral" components that have been considered include such things as program structure, design records, and the look and feel produced by the software.

2. Copyright and patent laws benefit society because they encourage creators of new products to make them available to the public. Trade secret laws benefit society because they allow a company to protect the steps in a product's development from competitors. Without such protection, companies would hesitate to make major investments in new products.

3. A disclaimer does not protect a company against negligence.

Chapter 8

Section 8.1

1. List: A listing of the members of a sports team.
   Stack: The stack of trays in a cafeteria.
   Queue: The line at a cafeteria.
   Tree: The organization chart of many governments.

2. The leaf (or terminal) nodes are D and C. B must be the root node because all the other nodes have parents.

3. If you were to write a program for playing a game of checkers, the data structure representing the checkerboard would probably be a static structure since the size of the board does not change during the game. However, if you were to write a program for playing a game of dominoes, the data structure representing the pattern of dominoes constructed on the table would probably be a dynamic structure since this pattern varies in size and cannot be predetermined.

4. A telephone directory is essentially a collection of pointers (telephone numbers) to people. The clues left at the scene of a crime are (perhaps encrypted) pointers to the perpetrator.

Section 8.2

1. 5 3 7 4 2 8 1 9 6

2. If R is the number of rows in the matrix, the formula is $R(J - 1) + (I - 1)$.

3. $(c \times i) + j$

4. The head pointer contains the NIL value.

5. Last ← the last name to be printed
Finished ← false
Current Pointer ← the head pointer;
while (Current Pointer not NIL and Finished = false) do
    (print the entry pointed to by Current Pointer,
    if (the name just printed = Last)
        then (Finished ← true)
    Current Pointer ← the value in the pointer
        cell in the entry pointed to by Current Pointer)

6. The stack pointer points to the cell immediately below the base of the stack.

7. Represent the stack as a one-dimensional array and the stack pointer as a variable of integer type. Then use this stack pointer to maintain a record of the position of the stack's top within the array rather than of the exact memory address.

8. Both empty and full conditions are indicated by the equal head and tail pointers. Thus additional information is required to distinguish between the two conditions.

9.

Section 8.3

1.

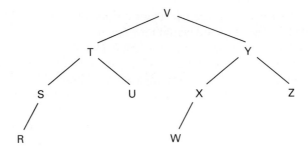

2. When searching for J:

When searching for P:

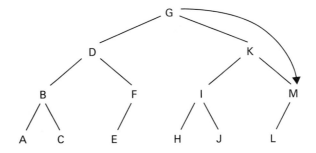

3.

<table>
<tr><td>

procedure PrintTree(Tree)

if (root pointer of Tree is not NIL)
    then (Apply the procedure PrintTree to the
           tree that appears as the left branch
           in Tree;
        Print root node of Tree;
        Apply the procedure PrintTree to the tree
           that appears as the right branch in Tree.)

</td><td>

procedure PrintTree(Tree)

if (root pointer of Tree is not NIL)
    then (Apply the procedure PrintTree to the
           tree that appears as the left branch
           in Tree;
        Print root node of Tree;
        Apply the procedure PrintTree to the tree
           that appears as the right branch in Tree.)

</td></tr>
</table>

Here, when K
is printed

4. At each node, each child pointer could be used to represent a unique letter in the alphabet. A word could be represented by a path down the tree along the sequence of pointers representing the spelling of the word. A node could be marked in a special way if it represented the end of a correctly spelled word.

Section 8.4

1. A type is a template; an instance of that type is an actual entity built from that template. As an analogy, dog is a type of animal, whereas Lassie and Rex are instances of that type.

2. A user-defined data type is a description of data organization, whereas an abstract data type includes operations for manipulating the data.

3. A point to be made here is that you have a choice between implementing the list as a contiguous list or a linked list. The choice you make will affect the structure of the procedures for inserting new entries, deleting old ones, and finding entries of interest. But, this choice should not be visible to a user of an instance of the abstract data type.

4. The abstract data type would at least contain a description of a data structure for storing the account balance and procedures for making a deposit and making a withdrawal via a check.

Section 8.5

1. Both abstract data types and classes are templates for constructing instances of a type. Classes, however, are more general in that they are associated with inheritance and may describe a collection of only procedures.

2. A class is a template from which objects are constructed.

3. The class might contain a circular queue along with procedures for adding entries, removing entries, testing to see if the queue is full, and testing to see if the queue is empty.

Section 8.6

1. a. A5   b. A5   c. A5

2. D50F, 2EFE, 5FFE

3. 2EA0, 2FB0, 2101, 20B4, D50E, E50F, 5EE1, 5FF1, DF14, B008, C000

4. When traversing a linked list in which each entry consists of two memory cells (a data cell followed by a pointer to the next entry), an instruction of the form DR0S could be used to retrieve the data and DR1S could be used to retrieve the pointer to the next entry. If the form DRTS were used, then the exact memory cell being referenced could be adjusted by modifying the value in register T.

Chapter 9

Section 9.1

1. The purchasing department would be interested in inventory records to place orders for more raw goods, whereas the accounting department would need the information to balance the books.

2. A database model provides an organizational perspective of a database that is more compatible with applications than the actual organization. Thus defining a database model is the first step toward allowing the database to be used as an abstract tool.

3. The application software translates the user's requests from the terminology of the application into terminology compatible with the database management system. The database management system in turn converts the requests into a form understood by the routines that actually manipulate the data in mass storage. These last routines perform the retrieval of data.

Section 9.2

1. a. G. Jerry Smith

b. Cheryl H. Clark

c. S26Z

2. One solution is

TEMP ← SELECT from JOB
                    where Dept = "PERSONNEL"
LIST ← PROJECT JobTitle from TEMP

In some systems this results in a list with a job title repeated, depending on how many times it occurred in the personnel department. That is, our list may contain numerous occurrences of the title secretary. It is more common, however, to design the PROJECT operation so that it removes duplicate tuples from the resulting relation.

3. One solution is

TEMP1 ← JOIN JOB and ASSIGNMENT
                    where JOB.JobId = ASSIGNMENT.JobId
TEMP2 ← SELECT from TEMP1
                    where TermDate = "*"
TEMP3 ← JOIN EMPLOYEE and TEMP2
                    where EMPLOYEE.EmplId = TEMP2.EmplId
RESULT ← PROJECT Name, Dept from TEMP3

4.
```
select JobTitle
   from JOB
   where Dept = "PERSONNEL"
```
```
select EMPLOYEE.Name, JOB.Dept
   from JOB, ASSIGNMENT, and EMPLOYEE
   where (Job.Job = ASSIGNMENT.JobId) and
       (ASSIGNMENT.EmplId = EMPLOYEE.EmplID)
       and (ASSIGNMENT.TermDate = "*")
```

5. The model itself does not provide data independence. This is a property of the data management system. Data independence is achieved by providing the data management system the ability to present a consistent relational organization to the application software even though the actual organization may change.

6. Through common attributes. For instance, the EMPLOYEE relation in this section is tied to the ASSIGNMENT relation via the attribute EmplId, and the ASSIGNMENT relation is tied to the JOB relation by the attribute JobId. Attributes used to connect relations like this are sometimes called connection attributes.

Section 9.3

1. There may be methods for assigning and retrieving the StartDate as well as the TermDate. Another method may be provided for reporting the total time in service.

2. One approach is to establish an object for each type of product in inventory. Each of these objects could maintain the total inventory of its product, the cost of the product, and links to the outstanding orders for the product.

3. As indicated at the beginning of this section, object-oriented databases appear to handle composite data types more easily than relational databases. Moreover, the fact that objects can contain methods that take an active role in answering questions promises to give object-oriented databases an advantage over relational databases whose relations merely hold the data.

Section 9.4

1. Once a transaction has reached its commit point, the database management system accepts the responsibility of seeing that the complete transaction is performed on the database. A transaction that has not reached its commit point does not have such assurance. If problems arise, it may have to be resubmitted.

2. One approach would be to stop interweaving transactions for an instant so that all current transactions can be completed in full. This would establish a point at which a future cascading rollback would terminate.

3. A balance of $100 would result if the transactions were executed one at a time. A balance of $200 would result if the first transaction were executed after the second transaction retrieved the original balance and before that second transaction stored its new balance. A balance of $300 would result if the second transaction were executed after the first retrieved the original balance and before the first transaction stored its new balance.

4. a. If no other transaction has exclusive access, the shared access will be granted.
   b. If another transaction already has some form of access, the database management system will normally make the new transaction wait, or it could roll back the other transactions and give access to the new transaction.

5. Deadlock would occur if each of two transactions acquired exclusive access to different items and then required access to the other.

6. The deadlock above could be removed by rolling back one of the transactions (using the log) and giving the other transaction access to the data item previously held by the first.

Section 9.5

1. You should be led through these stages:

2. The idea is to first divide the file to be stored into many separate files containing one record each. Next, group the one-record files into pairs, and apply the merge algorithm to each pair. This results in half as many files, each with two records. Furthermore, each of these two-record files is sorted. We can group them into pairs and again apply the merge algorithm to the pairs. Again we find ourselves with fewer but larger files, each of which is sorted. Continuing in this fashion, we are ultimately left with only one file that consists of all the original records but in sorted order. (If an odd number of files occurs at any stage of this process, we need merely to set the odd one aside and pair it with one of the larger files in the next stage.)

3. If the file is stored on tape or CD, its physical organization is most likely sequential. However, if the file is stored on magnetic disk, then it is most likely scattered over various sectors on the disk and the sequential nature of the file is a conceptual property that is supported by a pointer system or some form of a list in which the sectors on which the file is stored are recorded.

4. First find the target key in the file's index. There obtain the location of the target record. Then retrieve the record at that location.

5. A poorly chosen hash algorithm results in more clustering than normal and thus in more overflow. Since the overflow from each section of mass storage is organized as a linked list, searching through the overflow records is essentially searching a sequential file.

6. The section assignments are as follows:
   a. 0   b. 0   c. 3   d. 0   e. 3
   f. 3   g. 3   h. 3   i. 3   j. 0

   Thus all the records hash into buckets 0 and 3, leaving buckets 1, 2, 4, and 5 empty. The problem here is that the number of buckets being used (6) and the key values have the common factor of 3. (You might try rehashing these key values using 7 buckets and see what improvement you find.)

7. The point here is that we are essentially applying a hash algorithm to place the people in the group into one of 365 categories. The hash algorithm, of course, is the calculation of one's birthday. The amazing thing is that only 23 people are required before the probability is in favor of at least two of the birthdays being the same. In terms of a hashed file, this indicates that when hashing records into 365 available buckets of mass storage, clustering is likely to be present after only 23 records have been entered.

Section 9.6

1. Searching for patterns in dynamic data is problematic.

2. Class description—Identify characteristics of subscribers to a certain magazine. Class discrimination—Identify features that distinguish between subscribers of two magazines.

Cluster analysis—Identify magazines that tend to attract similar subscribers.
Association analysis—Identify links between subscribers to various magazines and different purchasing habits
Outlier analysis—Identify subscribers to a magazine who do not conform to the profile of normal subscribers.
Sequential pattern analysis—Identify trends in magazine subscription.

3. The data cube might allow sales data to be viewed as sales by month, sales by geographic region, sales by product class, etc.

4. Traditional database inquiries retrieve facts stored in the database. Data mining looks for patterns among the facts.

Section 9.7

1. The point here is to compare your answer to this question with that of the next. The two raise essentially the same question but in different contexts.

2. See previous problem.

3. You might receive announcements or advertisements for opportunities that you would not have otherwise received, but you might also become the subject of solicitation or the target of crime.

4. The point here is that a free press can alert the public to abuses or potential abuses and thus bring public opinion into play. In most of the cases cited in the text, it was a free press that initiated corrective action by alerting the public.

Chapter 10

Section 10.1

1. Those introduced in the chapter include reflex actions, actions based on real-world knowledge, goal seeking actions, learning, and perception.

2. Our purpose here is not to give a decisive answer to this issue but to use it to show how delicate the argument over the existence of intelligence really is.

3. Although most of us would probably say no, we would probably claim that if a human dispensed the same products in a similar atmosphere, awareness would be present even though we might not be able to explain the distinction.

4. There is not a right or wrong answer. Most would agree that the machine at least appears to be intelligent.

Section 10.2

1. In the remote control case, the system needs only to relay the picture, whereas to use the picture for maneuvering, the robot must be able to "understand" the meaning of the picture.

2. The possible interpretations for one section of the drawing do not match any of those of another section. To embed this insight into a program, you might isolate the interpretations allowable for various line junctions and then write a program that tries to find a set of compatible interpretations (one for each junction). In fact, if you stop and think about it, this is probably what your own senses did in trying to evaluate the drawing. Did you detect your eyes scanning back and forth between the two ends of the drawing as your senses tried to piece possible interpretations together? (If this subject interests you, you will want to read about the work of people such as D. A. Huffman, M. B. Clowes, and D. Waltz.)

3. There are four blocks in the stack but only three are visible. The point is that understanding this apparently simple concept requires a significant amount of "intelligence."

Section 10.3

1. Production systems provide a uniform approach to a variety of problems. That is, although apparently different in their original form, all problems reformulated into terms of production systems become the problem of finding a path through a state graph.

2.

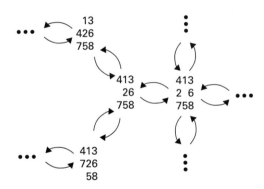

3. The tree is four moves deep. The upper portion appears as follows:

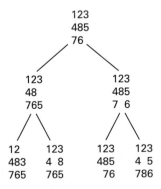

4. The task requires too much paper as well as too much time.

5. Our heuristic system for solving the eight-puzzle is based on an analysis of the immediate situation, just as is that of the mountain climber. This short-sightedness is what allowed our algorithm to proceed initially along the wrong path in the example of this section just as a mountain climber can be led into trouble by always plotting a course based only on the local terrain. (This analogy often causes heuristic systems based on local or immediate information to be called hill-climbing systems.)

6. The system rotates the 5, 6, and 8 tiles either clockwise or counterclockwise until the goal state is reached.

7. The problem here is that our heuristic scheme ignores the value of keeping the hole adjacent to the tiles that are out of place. If the hole is surrounded by tiles in their correct position, some of these tiles must be moved before those tiles still seeking their correct place can be moved. Thus it is incorrect to consider all those tiles surrounding the hole as actually being correct. To fix this flaw, we might first observe that a tile in its correct position but blocking the hole from incorrectly positioned tiles must be moved away from its correct position and later moved back. Thus each correctly positioned tile on a path between the hole and the nearest incorrectly positioned tile accounts for at least two moves in the remaining solution. We can therefore modify our projected cost calculation as follows:

First, calculate the projected cost as before. However, if the hole is totally isolated from the incorrectly positioned tiles, find a shortest path between the hole and an incorrectly positioned tile, multiply the number of tiles on this path by two, and add the resulting value to the previous projected cost.

With this system, the leaf nodes in Figure 10.10 have projected costs of 6, 6, and 4 (from left to right), and thus the correct branch is pursued initially.

Our new system is not foolproof. For example, consider the following configuration. The solution is to slide the 5 tile down, rotate the top two rows clockwise until those tiles are correct, move the 5 tile back up, and finally move the 8 tile to its correct position. However, our new heuristic system wants us to start by moving the 8 tile, because the state obtained by this initial move has a projected cost of only 6 compared with the other options that have costs of 8.

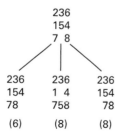

Section 10.4

1. All patterns produce an output of 0 except for the pattern 1, 0, which produces an output of 1.

2. Assign a weight of 1 to each input, and assign the unit a threshold value of 1.5.

3. Design a two-level network as described in the text. The lower-level units should assign each of their inputs the weight 1 and have a threshold of $7\frac{1}{2}$. Thus one of these units produces a 1 if the pattern in the field of view is the circle; otherwise, all the lower-level units produce an output of 0. In turn, if the upper-level unit assigns each of its inputs the weight 1 and has a threshold of $\frac{1}{2}$, then the entire network produces a 1 when the pattern is a circle and a 0 when the pattern is an X.

4. Design a two-level network as described in the text. Each lower-level unit should have a threshold of $2\frac{1}{2}$, assign the weight of 0 to the corner squares in its field of view, and assign the weight of 1 to the other squares. The only way one of these units can produce a 1 as its output is to have the C pattern in its field of view. In fact, if this is the pattern, two lower-level units produce an output of 1. Thus if the upper-level unit assigns each of its inputs the weight 1 and has a threshold of 1, then it produces an output of 1 when the pattern in the field of view is the C and an output of 0 when the pattern is the V.

5. The network will wander to the configuration in which the center processing unit is excited and all others are inhibited.

Section 10.5

1. 001010011000001000010000100000

2. How about the problem of developing a strategy for investing in the stock market?

3. The structure of a program based on the functional paradigm is that of functions within functions. That is, the structure is homogeneous at all levels. However, a program based on the object-oriented paradigm consists of objects that may contain methods as well as other objects. Thus the structure is not as homogeneous as that of a functional program. In turn, it is harder to mix the components of object-oriented programs to form new programs.

Section 10.6

1. Is the sentence describing what kind of horses they are, or is it telling what some people are doing?

2. The parsing process produces identical structures, but the semantic analysis recognizes that the prepositional phrase in the first sentence tells where the fence was built, whereas the phrase in the second sentence tells when the fence was built.

3. They are brother and sister.

4. It uses the closed-world assumption.

5. In many ways, the two are the same. However, traditional databases tend to contain only facts such as an employee's name, address, and so on, whereas knowledge bases tend to include rules such as "if raining, check rain gauge" that can be used to direct the reasoning process.

Section 10.7

1. There is no right or wrong answer.

2. There is no right or wrong answer.

3. There is no right or wrong answer.

Chapter 11

Section 11.1

1. How about the boolean operations AND, OR, and XOR. In fact, we used tables in Chapter 1 when introducing these functions.

2. The computation of a loan payment, the area of a circle, or a car's mileage.

3. Mathematicians call such functions transcendental functions. Examples include the logarithmic and trigonometric functions. These particular examples can still be computed but not by algebraic means. For example, the trigonometric functions can be calculated by actually drawing the triangle involved, measuring its sides, and only then turning to the algebraic operation of dividing.

4. One example is the problem of trisecting an angle. That is, they were unable to construct an angle that was one-third the size of a given angle. The point is that the Greek's straight-edge and compass computational system is another example of a system with limitations.

Section 11.2

1. The result is the following diagram:

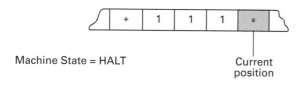

Machine State = HALT   Current position

2.

Current state	Cell content	Value to write	Direction to move	New state to enter
START	*	*	left	STATE 1
STATE 1	0	0	left	STATE 2
STATE 1	1	0	left	STATE 2
STATE 1	*	0	left	STATE 2
STATE 2	0	*	right	STATE 3
STATE 2	1	*	right	STATE 3
STATE 2	*	*	right	STATE 3
STATE 3	0	0	right	HALT
STATE 3	1	0	right	HALT

3.

Current state	Cell content	Value to write	Direction to move	New state to enter
START	*	*	left	SUBTRACT
SUBTRACT	0	1	left	BORROW
SUBTRACT	1	0	left	NO BORROW
BORROW	0	1	left	BORROW
BORROW	1	0	left	NO BORROW
BORROW	*	*	right	ZERO
NO BORROW	0	0	left	NO BORROW
NO BORROW	1	1	left	NO BORROW
NO BORROW	*	*	right	RETURN
ZERO	0	0	right	ZERO
ZERO	1	0	right	ZERO
ZERO	*	*	no move	HALT
RETURN	0	0	right	RETURN
RETURN	1	1	right	RETURN
RETURN	*	*	no move	HALT

4. The point here is that the concept of a Turing machine is supposed to capture the meaning of "to compute." That is, any time a situation occurs in which computing is taking place, the components and activities of a Turing machine should be present. For example, a person figuring income tax is doing a certain degree of computing. The computing machine is the person and the tape is represented by the paper on which values are recorded.

5. The machine described by the following table halts if started with an even input but never halts if started with an odd input:

Current state	Cell content	Value to write	Direction to move	New state to enter
START	*	*	left	STATE 1
STATE 1	0	0	right	HALT
STATE 1	1	1	no move	STATE 1
STATE 1	*	*	no move	STATE 1

Section 11.3

1.
```
clear AUX;
incr AUX;
while X not 0 do;
   clear X;
   clear AUX;
end;
while AUX not 0 do;
   incr X;
   clear AUX;
end;
```

2.
```
while X not 0 do;
   decr X;
end;
```

3.
```
copy X to AUX;
while AUX not 0 do;
   S1
   clear AUX;
end;
copy X to AUX;
invert AUX;  (See Question #1)
while AUX not 0 do;
   S2
   clear AUX;
end;
while X not 0 do;
   clear AUX;
   clear X;
end;
```

4. If we assume that X refers to the memory cell at address 40 and that each program segment starts at location 00, we have the following conversion table:

```
              Address    Contents
clear X;        00         20
                01         00
                02         30
                03         40
```

```
              Address    Contents
incr X;         00         11
                01         40
                02         20
                03         01
                04         50
                05         01
                06         30
                07         40
```

```
              Address    Contents
decr X;         00         20
                01         00
                02         23
                03         00
                04         11
                05         40
                06         22
                07         01
```

08	B1
09	10
0A	40
0B	03
0C	50
0D	02
0E	B1
0F	06
10	33
11	40

	Address	Contents
while X not	00	20
0 do;	01	00
.	02	11
.	03	40
.	04	B1
end;	05	WZ
	.	
	.	
	.	
	WX	B0
	WY	00

5. Just as in a real machine, negative numbers could be dealt with via a coding system. For example, the rightmost bit in each string can be used as a sign but with the remaining bits used to represent the magnitude of the value.

6. The function is multiplication by 2.

Section 11.4

1. Yes. In fact, this program halts regardless of the initial values of its variables, and therefore it must halt if its variables are initialized to the program's encoded representation.

2. The program halts only if the initial value of X ends in a 1. Since the ASCII representation of a semicolon is 00111011, the encoded version of the program must end in a 1. Therefore the program is self-terminating.

3. The point here is that the logic is the same as in our argument that the halting problem does not have an algorithmic solution. If the house painter paints his or her own house, then he or she does not and vice versa.

Section 11.5

1. We could conclude only that the problem has complexity $\Theta(2^n)$. If we could show that the "best algorithm" for solving the problem belongs to $\Theta(2^n)$, we could conclude that the problem belongs to $\Theta(2^n)$.

2. No. As a general rule, the algorithm in $\Theta(n^2)$ will outperform the one in $\Theta(2^n)$, but for small input values an exponential algorithm often outperforms

a polynomial algorithm. In fact, it is true that exponential algorithms are sometimes preferred as opposed to polynomial ones when the application involves only small inputs.

3. The point is that the number of subcommittees is growing exponentially, and from this point on, the job of listing all the possibilities becomes a laborious task.

4. Within the class of polynomial problems is the sorting problem, which can be solved by polynomial algorithms such as the insertion sort.

Within the class of nonpolynomial problems is the task of listing all the subcommittees that could be formed from a given parent committee.

Any polynomial problem is an NP problem. The Traveling Salesman problem is an example of an NP problem that has not been shown to be a polynomial problem.

5. No. Our use of the term *complexity* refers to the time required to execute an algorithm-not to how hard the algorithm may be to understand.

Section 11.6

1. $211 \times 313 = 66043$

2. The message 101 is the binary representation for 5. $5^e = 5^5 = 15625$. 15625 (mod 91) = 64, which is 1000000 in binary notation. Thus, 1000000 is the encrypted version of the message.

3. The message 10 is the binary representation for 2. $2^d = 2^{29} = 536870912$. 536870912 (mod 91) = 32, which is 100000 in binary notation. Thus, 100000 is the decrypted version of the message.

4. $n = p \times q = 7 \times 19 = 133$. To find d we need a positive integer value k such that $k(p - 1)(q - 1) + 1 = k(6 \times 18) + 1 = 108k + 1$ is evenly divisible by $e = 5$. The values $k = 1$ and $k = 2$ are not satisfactory, but $k = 3$ produces $108k + 1 = 325$, which is divisible by 5. The quotient 65 is the value of d.

INDEX

U.S. Department of Defense 503
User Datagram Protocol (UDP) 163
User-defined data type 342
User documentation 309
Utilitarianism 15
Utility software 114

V

Variable 236
Variable-length codes 57
Vector (image) 38
Verification (of software) 307
Virtual memory 118
Virus 165
Visual Basic 240
von Helmholtz, H. 184
von Neumann architecture 96, 101, 423
von Neumann bottleneck 96
von Neumann, John 76, 82

W

WAN. *See* Wide area network
Waiting (process) 121
Waltz, D. 542
Waterfall model 291
Weak AI 409
Web 147
Web page 147
Web server 148

Web site 147
Weight (in a processing unit) 424
Weighted sum 424
Weizenbaum, Joseph 408, 447
While control structure 179, 189, 191
Wide area network (WAN) 136
Window (in GUI) 116
Window manager 116
Windows (operating system) 110, 116, 240
Word processor 36
World War II 6
World Wide Web 11, 147
World Wide Web Consortium (W3C) 148
Worm 166
Worst-case analysis 208
Wound-wait protocol 382
Wozniak, Stephen 7
Wright brothers 82
Write operation 28

X

XML. *See* Extensible Markup Language
XOR. *See* Exclusive or

Z

Zip disk 30
Zip files 58
Ziv, Jacob 58